What's it all About?

Jerry's 20 Rules for Life is a faith-based book that offers practical advice and spiritual guidance on a range of everyday human trials. Here, Jerry shares the rules that he developed and honed to inform his decisions and guide his actions.

Based on his own experiences, Jerry's rules address situations we all encounter in our daily life. From taking on tasks that seem overwhelming, to making permanent and healthy changes in our lifestyle, these rules offer guidance and inspiration. Each rule is illuminated with real-life experiences, motivational quotes, and scriptural references.

While based on Christian theology, Jerry's Rules transcend any solitary religious belief and offer a wisdom and practicality that can be understood and appreciated regardless of personal conviction.

The book's tone is helpful and approachable, encouraging the reader to search for their own rules to guide their life.

JERRY'S 20 RULES FOR <u>MANAGING LIFE</u>

Copyright © 2019 by Gerald L. Penhollow
All rights reserved. No part of this book may be reproduced or transmitted in any form or by any means without written permission from the author.

"This material is neither made, provided, approved, nor endorsed by Intellectual Reserve, Inc, or The Church of Jesus Christ of Latter-day Saints. Any content or opinions expressed, implied, or included in or with the material are solely those of the owner and not those of Intellectual Reserve, Inc or The Church of Jesus Christ of Latter-day Saints."

The views and opinions expressed in this book are strictly those of the author. They do not necessarily reflect the opinion of any person, group, organization, or company that are quoted in this book. The author takes sole responsibility for the content of this book and illustrations used.

Cover-art illustration entitled *Portals Path* composed by Gerald L. Penhollow

A part of the cover-art representing a portal to an Earthly place is derived from an original oil painting entitled *Meadow Gate* by Oregon artist Carol Turner. Permission for use in the cover design is granted by the artist, having neither religious nor any other affiliation with the author, his experiences, beliefs, or views, they being uniquely his own.

A part of the cover-art representing a portal to Heaven's Gate is derived from an iStock.com picture, Stock photo ID:642310954, credited to: allanswart. The starfield used for the cover-art also comes from an iStock.com picture, Stock photo ID:178149253, credited to: kevron2001

Published in the United States by Gerald L. Penhollow.

Revision Five (Punctuation & Spelling Corrections – 26 Dec 2024)
PDF Printed in the United States by Gerald Penhollow, Dubuque, Iowa, U.S.A.

ISBN 978-1-734625-1-0

JERRY'S 20 RULES
FOR
MANAGING LIFE

Gerald L. Penhollow

To my wonderful wife Christine,
and
my children, and all my posterity,
and
my extended family,
and
my beautiful friends,
and
all my amazing readers,

I love and appreciate you all.

"We all have rules we live by to help us govern our lives. This book is my attempt to share a part of me with you."

Gerald L. Penhollow

WHAT'S INSIDE

What Was That Thought
Rule #0 'Write it Down Before You Forget It'
—{ i }—

Where Do You Want Me to Start
Rule #¼ 'The Introduction to the Rules'
—{ v }—

The No Rules, Rule
Rule #½ 'About the Author's Writing'
—{ xix }—

Try You Say? Do or Do Not
Rule #1 'Failure is Not an Option'
—{ 1 }—

I Thought You Did It?
Rule #2 'Don't Assume'
—{ 13 }—

He Punts
From the 35 Yard Line
Rule #3 'There are Fluid Goals & There are Solid Goals'
—{ 33 }—

Give Me 10 More
Rule #4 'Always Give 110 Percent'
—{ 55 }—

I Don't Know
Rule #5 'You Always Know Something'
—{ 73 }—

And He Shouts, "TIMBER!"
Rule #6 'You Cut Down a Forest One Tree at a Time'
—{ 93 }—

Listen to the Sound of Silence
Rule #7 'Need Help? Stop and Listen'
—{ 109 }—

What an Idiot
Rule #8 'Don't Catch Idiotitis'
—{ 135 }—

Guilty in the First Degree
Rule #9 'Don't Be Overly Judgmental of Yourself'
—{ 167 }—

I Feel a Change in The Air
Rule #10 'You Can't Change Other People, Only Yourself'
—{ 191 }—

The Blind Leading The Blind
Rule #11 'If You Can't Take Care of Yourself,
You Can't Take Care of Others'
—{ 217 }—

Adversity and the Blessings Therein
Rule #12 'No One Said It Was Going to be Easy'
—{ 247 }—

Smelling the Roses
Rule #13 'Focus on the Journey Not the Task'
—{ 263 }—

Now I Know My ABCs
Rule #14 'If You Want to Be an 'A' Student
Hang Out With the 'A' Students'
—{ 297 }—

Perfection
Rule #15 'What's Worth Doing is Worth Doing Right'
—{ 339 }—

To Be or Not To Be That is the Question
Rule #16 'Be Honest With Yourself'
—{ 393 }—

Are We Done Yet?
Rule #17 'Manage Your Procrastinations,
Or They Will Manage You'
—{ 429 }—

And The First Shall Be Last
Rule #18 'First Things First'
—{ 447 }—

Bend But Don't Break
Rule #19 'Preferences Bend, Principles Don't'
—{ 499 }—

Wait For It
Rule #20 'If Nothing Changes, Then Nothing Changes, and History Repeats Itself'
—{ 531 }—

What's That Rumbling Noise?
Rule #21 'Yesterday's Meal is Not Enough to Sustain Today's Needs'
—{ 567 }—

Who Are You?
The Greats Past & Present
—{ 593 }—

Where Can I Find It?
Index
—{ 625 }—

What Was That Thought

Rule #0 'Write it Down Before You Forget It'

Rule #0 'Write It Down Before You Forget It'

What Was That They Said?

Rule #0 is so true for me. There were times when I heard someone say something of profound interest that I wanted to share it with my wife. Sadly, I could not completely recall how they had worded it. Consequently, the depth of what they had said was not conveyed in my translation.

Rule #0 was born because of a need for a list of quick memory index triggers to help my recall. You see, as I get younger and younger every day, my forgetter continues to works better and better. Thus, the need for a tool (index list) to assist my memory recall.

After I have read a publication, there are times when I want to refer back to a central point contained within. In my attempt to find what I am looking for, if the hunt becomes too long, I get a lost and flustrated feeling. A feeling I don't particularly care to experience. You see, time is of great worth to me, as you will learn while reading this book.

To help cure that lost flustrating feeling that one may get, while on the hunt for that main point contained within, I created a memory index list. The list starts on the next page. I use the list myself, to trigger my brain into remembering the more profound wisdom and knowledge I have learned and recorded within this book.

Should you feel the need for a little assistance with your memory recall, then go ahead and copy the list on the next page. Keep it with you to study.

Rule #0: 'Write It Down Before You Forget It'

Jerry's List of Rules:

1. Failure is Not an Option
2. Don't Assume
3. There are Fluid Goals & There are Solid Goals
4. Always Give 110%
5. You Always Know Something
6. You Cut Down a Forest One Tree at a Time
7. Need Help? Stop and listen
8. Don't Catch Idiotitis
9. Don't Be Over Judgmental of Yourself
10. You Can't Change Other People, Only Yourself
11. If You Don't Take Care of Yourself, You Can't Take Care of Others
12. No One Said it Was Going to be Easy
13. Focus on the Journey Not the Task
14. If You Want to Be an 'A' Student, Hang Out With the 'A' Students
15. What is Worth Doing, is Worth Doing Right
16. Be Honest With Yourself
17. Manage Your Procrastinations, or They Will Manage You
18. First Things First
19. Preferences Bend, Principles Don't
20. If Nothing Changes, Nothing Changes and History Repeats Itself
21. Yesterday's Meal is Not Enough to Sustain Today's

Where Do You Want Me to Start

Rule #¼

'The Introduction to the Rules'

Rule #¼ 'The Introduction to the Rules'

Short & Sweet:

Jerry's Rules for Managing Life are just that. They are a set of rules that I use to manage my life. I use them as my teacher, my motivator, and my compass as I deal with the day-to-day issues of this life here on Earth.

I have a great many rules that I use in governing myself. The reason for so many rules is because of who I am today and who I want to be tomorrow. In this book, I only cover my top 20 rules I feel have had the most influence in governing my life. Perhaps, someday, if I live long enough, and God blesses me with the wisdom and skills to take less time than the ten years it took writing this book, I will write its sequel, 'Jerry's 20 More Rules for Managing Life, The Sequel'. And when I finish that, maybe there will time for another sequel 'Jerry's Lost 20 Rules for Managing Life Found'. Then I could call the series a trilogy. I am 63 years young today. Do you think I'll have a chance to make it happen? My answer: only if it is God's will to grant me that blessing.

In the Beginning:

Somewhere long, long, ago in the far, far, past there was a very, very, young boy (Me), watching TV. All young boys have their TV hero shows they can't miss. As a small boy, my first TV hero show was 'The Lone Ranger'. 'Hi-yo, Silver, away', was the Lone Range's cry at the beginning of the show and as he rode away at the end of the show. I'd run around the house straddling a broomstick shouting the Lone Ranger's words as I pretended to chase bad guys. The furniture became trees, bushes, and mountains to maneuver my broomstick horse around, and throw rugs became rivers to swim across, as the bad guys tried getting away.

As a young man, my favorite TV show was Star Trek with Captain James T. Kirk. As I watched each episode, I would listen for the catchy little phrases the actors would say. Like,

Captain Kirk saying, "Scotty, beam me up!", "I don't believe in the no-win scenario.", "Failure is not an option.", or Spock saying, "Captain, the odds are Twenty-seven Thousand Four Hundred and Fifty-two to One against us.".

As I went through the day, my mind would wait for the right opportunity to use one of these catchphrases. Like Mom shouting, "Jerry, dinner time!" I'd reply with, "Scotty, beam me up."

Sometimes, I'd use one of those catchy phrases in a humorous attempt to stall for a little more playtime. But, there were a few occasions when the words from my mouth just got me into trouble. Like at chore time when I was slacking off, Mom with a stern voice would shout, "Jerry, you had better get your butt into that kitchen and tackle those dishes." Being a bit of a smart-aleck, I thought to myself, why would I want to tackle the dishes? That could get them broken. I then made the mistake of replying with what I thought to be a creatively clever response, "Captain, the odds are 27,451.24 to 1 against us." Mom's response to my attempt at humor was swift. She walked over to where I was playing and brought her face to within inches of mine. Her expression showed me that she was in command of this ship. She bore her Captain's eyes deep into mine and responded, "Well, you had better start getting those odds more in your favor, or I assure you I can."

Thinking about what I had said, after the fact, I can see how my phrase of choice for portraying a little humor was probably not the best pick for the situation. It turned out not to be too funny for me then, but it is funny now.

Brain Washed:

I didn't realize it at the time, but listening to all those little catchphrases on TV is how my list of rules got its start.

There is a reason why TV shows, commercials, bill–boards, magazine ads, and companies in general, use catchphrases. They are memorable and command your attention.

Astronaut Neil Armstrong used this now-famous catchphrase to commemorate the NASA moon landing. "That's one small step for man, one giant leap for mankind." We will forever think of the first moon landing and remember Neil Armstrong's walk on the moon whenever we hear that phrase.

Actor Lenard Nimoy's character in Star Trek, Mr. Spock, has a famous one-word phrase that immortal–ized him to all his fans -- "Fascinating". Mr. Spock used that one-word phrase to describe almost everything and every situation.

Here are two of actor Clint Eastwood's immortal phrases: "Do you feel lucky, Punk? Well, do ya?" and "Go ahead; make my day."

Then there is actor Arnold Schwarzenegger's: "I'll be back."

The character Count Dracula's famous phrase: "Don't be afraid. All I want is to drink your blood." I used Count Dracula's phrase to scare the heck out of my little sisters. It is probably one of those catchphrases I shouldn't have remembered. It would have saved my lower backside (butt) from a few warmings if I hadn't.

The point I am trying to make with these catchphrases is that they are an easy way to brainwash our tiny little minds into remembering or recalling something: like an actor, a movie, a company, or a product.

The First, the Origin, Number One, Uno:

Failure is not an option was the first catchphrase I latched on to, to help better my life. The statements, 'I don't believe in the no-win scenario,' and 'Failure is not an option' were Captain Kirk's mottos that gave him courage as the Enterprise fought against impossible odds, according to Mr. Spock.

Failure is not an option became the first rule that I used as a motto to help me survive school. I had a learning disability in reading and writing that made passing school seem like one of Mr. Spock's impossible odds quotes. Armed with Rule #1

'Failure is not an Option', I was able to develop a set of tools that helped me work around my learning disabilities.

Back in my younger days, schools did not have programs to support learning disabled children. Nor did they have laptop computers. Even in my college years, the home computer did not exist. In my school days, learning disabilities or not, either you kept up, or you were left behind. Moreover, when you were left behind, you found that even your peers gave you no mercy.

I can't begin to tell you how much I love the freedom the computer has provided for my life. Without the aid of the computer, writing would be a lost art for me, and the chance to save my thoughts would be lost forever as well.

Be Fruitful and Multiply:

What seemed at first to be nothing more than a worthless little catchphrase, Rule #1 became a great and powerful tool that I still use in shaping my life today. *'Failure is not an Option'* would become my company's motto for 35 years.

Equipped with a brain that could hardly recall anything it read, I learned that I could easily remember catchphrases, which I now call rules.

In my grade school years, I dreaded history class. Because of my inability to recall names, dates, places, or events, I didn't do well on tests. With some index reasoning, I could recall events and their causes and effects. But as far as recalling to my mind a person's name to give them their historical credit, or the date an event happened, or where it took place was not happening. Thus, test day was a dread day for me.

I decided that this inability to recall information quickly needed a cool name. Therefore, after some heavy thinking, I decided to call it the 'Einstein Memory Factor'. The great theoretical physicist, Albert Einstein, had some of the same troubles in his general studies at school as I did (see, I am in great company). Einstein's comment to one of his teachers regarding this recall issue, I believe, was that he didn't want to clutter his mind remembering things he could look up. Whether this Einstein comment is true or not, it sounds good to me. So, I adopted it.

When I felt that life was about to bury me, and I needed encouragement, I would turn to those remembered TV catchphrases. I could always count on them to provide the needed wisdom, knowledge, and strength to give me a lift. And that is how my list of rules was born.

As I grew in life, so did my list of rules. Several of the rules I came up with myself, but for the most part, it was other people's great thinking that inspired my list of rules. I don't remember the names of all of these wise, helpful thinkers. I did tell you I have trouble remembering names.

The Written Word:

It was missionaries from my church, who came into my life and encouraged me to organize my rules into an orderly, prioritized written list. Later, other church missionaries challenged me to find scriptures and quotes to support my rules, eventually encouraging me to write a book for the world to read. Assuming the world wants to read them? Oops! I just broke Rule #2 *'Don't Assume'*.

The first two missionaries that challenged me to start sharing my list of rules were Elder Justin Jensen and Elder Austin Parker, serving in the Clearwater, Florida Ward at the time.

My wife and I had just come back to our Clearwater, Florida, home from our home in Dubuque, Iowa, when a friend in the church called and asked if I could help him repair his roof. My friend persuaded me to help by assuring me that all I would be doing was supervising the work. He promised that he would do all the hard work. I agreed to teach him and supervise. No sooner had we gotten started it became apparent that I, the one with 15 years roofing experience, would be the one doing 90% of the work, hard work.

Now, I had quit roofing for around 15 years by then. And I was now happily working at an executive job running my own computer company. Neither was I hardly the young man I was when I had done roofing for a living. I hate to admit it, but I had also put on several un-needed pounds.

Here I Come to Save the Day:

By the second day of roofing, the Florida rains were threatening us, and the heat had slowed my overweight body to a crawl. My wise friend quickly concluded that if he was to save his home from the rains, it was time to call in some additional help. Thus, on to the scene come Elder Jensen and Elder Parker.

Now that I had two strong, willing, healthy bodies, eager to work, and able to follow directions, I was able to once again go back to the training and supervising role.

While working with these two missionaries, we got to know each other. Each time I would share a life story, I would mention one of my rules. For example, when we were talking about eternal marriage, I shared the rule about *'Fluid Goals and Solid Goals'*. Each time I would mention one of my catchphrase rules, Elder Jensen would scramble to remove a small notebook and pen from his pocket and proceed to write down the quote. I wasn't sure I was comfortable with being quoted. I wasn't sure I wanted to be responsible for shaping these great young men's minds with a list of rules I had made up or collected from others. This was a list of rules I had gathered together to help me manage my life. I hadn't thought of my list of rules being of any value to anyone else.

You Want Me to Repeat What?

Soon Elder Jensen and Elder Parker were both stopping to pull out their pen and notebook. I had to remind the Elders that talking doesn't require stopping the hands from working, but writing does. We needed to worry more about getting the roof done than writing down my words on paper because the Florida rains can pop-up at any time. That got them to put away their pen and notebook and back to working on the roof. However, as soon as we took a rest break, their little notebooks were out, and they were asking me to repeat what I had shared earlier with them word for word.

Are you kidding me? Repeat word for word what I had said an hour ago? For sure, it was not going to happen with this brain of mine. Remember the 'Einstein Memory Factor'? Of course, I am not going to be able to repeat myself. Remember, I can't remember. Once something exits my mouth, regurgitating it from my brain a second time with the same precise wording rarely happens. No matter how poetic or noteworthy it is. That didn't stop the Elders. They would work on my brain, squeezing every little ounce of gray matter in that head of mine. They didn't stop getting me to think and think some more until they got what they wanted to be written down in that notebook of theirs.

Now, there is one fun, noteworthy little fact here I wish to share with you. Since my wife and I move back and forth from one state to another state, there are a lot of times that the missionaries don't realize we are active members of their church. Being the fun-loving, devilish person that I am, I enjoy playing a little mind game on the poor unknowing missionaries. Of course, it's all in good-spirited fun. So, while I am giving the missionaries my little nuggets of wisdom, my brain is also multi-tasking. It's working on the roof, sharing stories with the Elders, and working on ways to keep the Elders on their toes wondering if I am a member of their church or not. Or perhaps I am, but inactive. I know I am bad. What can I say? My wife tells me all the time that I am bad for teasing people. That may be something I need to repent of. Yet, it does give everyone a good laugh. I do enjoy doing things to bring humor into peoples' lives. Good wholesome laughter is something we all need. It can cure a lot of what troubles us.

Working and sharing with Elder Jensen and Elder Parker was the start of a wonderful relationship. My wife and I learned that their apartment was only four blocks away. Since they lived so close, we invited them over often. That opened the door for more fellowship and rule sharing opportunities.

Which, in turn, gave them more chances to whip out their pen and notebook to capture more of my quotes.

Now it's Time to Say Good-Bye to Another Missionary:

As things always change, so do the lives of the church missionaries, one missionary will transfer to a different ward in the mission district, and a new missionary will fill the vacancy. During our stay in Clearwater, we met Elder Kyler, Elder Anderson, Elder Peterson, Elder Garrett, Elder Richardson, Elder Lyons, and Elder Alohikea, to name a few.

My wife Chris and I soon became the one-spot-stop for the Elders' needs as they went about doing their missionary work. On many occasions, my wife served as a cook, tailor, and launderer. We enjoyed occasional dinners and breakfasts, with a few lunches thrown in, not to mention the stops at our home to get out of the Florida heat and to enjoy an ice-cold glass of water. My wife and I grew close to some missionaries and even closer to others. Caring for the missionaries, whichever state we were living in, has become a tradition.

We have become so close to the missionaries that we call each other family. The missionaries have bestowed upon my wife and me the honorary titles of Uncle Jerry and Aunt Chris, which we humbly and lovingly accept with gratitude.

I See the Light:

For some unknown reason, every one of the mis-sionaries that visited would manage somehow to get our conversation onto the subject of my rules. I would then have to explain anew the meaning of the rules and share the rules' stories with them. The Lord must have been watching this interaction I had going with the missionaries and my rules, and then decided that He needed to give me a little push to get me to take my list of rules to the next level.

It was the Clearwater, Florida missionaries that helped bring my rules out into the light to be shared with others. But, it was the Dubuque, Iowa missionaries that got me to sit down, organize, prioritize, and write the top 20 rules into a book format.

Elder Andrew Jackson, who served a part of his mission in the Dubuque Ward, was the biggest fan of my list of rules. He was having trouble organizing his mission and needed a little help with motivation. I am not sure why, but he was feeling lost.

My wife and I invited Elder Jackson and his companion Elder Pope, to eat dinner one night at our home. Once again, we shared information about our lives. I decided that since the missionaries in Florida loved my rules so much, I would share them with the Iowa church missionaries.

Elder Jackson's face lit up, his eyes opened wide, and his ears bent to catch every one of my rules. He couldn't write fast enough and still listen to everything I had to say. Elder Pope, on the other hand, enjoyed the discussion, but mostly he just listened attentively. Elder Jackson, however, acted as if he had just found the Holy Grail, an answer that he could use to manage all his major life issues. I couldn't blame Elder Jackson for his reaction. These life directing Rules I had developed over time, positively helped change and mold my life.

Shortly after that dinner, Elder Jackson pleaded with me to prioritize and write all my rules down and send them to him in an email. A couple of weeks later, as I was sharing stories and life experiences again with Elders Jackson and Pope, Elder Pope began to embrace the idea of writing the rules down. He then suggested that I should include scriptures and quotes to give the Rules more validity. Elder Jackson chimed in *"and add a few of your stories, for examples."*

Elder Pope's comment turned on two lightbulbs in my head. One lightbulb saying this is a great idea, and the other saying this will be months and months of work. Little did I know that instead of months, it would take years.

Elder Andrew Jackson and Elder James Pope both served their mission in the Dubuque, Iowa Ward for six months.

Each was transferred to a different location within the mission district at slightly different times. While we were together in the Dubuque Ward, both Elders continually encouraged me to put my rules in writing, so others might have a chance to read them. Both Elder Jackson and Elder Pope searched for scriptures they could apply to the rules. As I put pen to paper, or in my case fingers to computer keys, both of the Elders read my work and shared their comments to improve my writing.

My wife and I enjoyed the company and Godly spirit of Elder Andrew Jackson and Elder James Pope, two fine young men. I consider them both as sons and love them accordingly. As with the Florida missionaries, Chris and I also consider our Iowa missionaries as family members and still stay in close touch with them.

Lord Please Help:

The Lord always provides for my needs. As Elder Jackson and Elder Pope moved on in the mission field, and then eventually returning home, the Lord blessed us with new missionaries to help with the writing of this book. Each set of missionaries has shared a special talent that I needed to help push the work of this book forward to its completion. For example, Elder Jackson and Elder Pope were not super scriptorians. However, Elder Davila and Elder Hawkins were. They have been a great help at finding richly matched scriptures and famous quotes for my rules. There will continue to be, and have been, other talented missionaries that have assisted in the writing of this book. I feel this book is as much theirs as it is mine.

Closing Statement:

As I began to research scriptures and famous quotes to reinforce each of my rules, I found so many that I had a hard time choosing which ones to include and which ones to leave out. Therefore, I am going to dump a ton of scriptures and quotable quotes on you. There are two reasons for this; first, I find so many good ones it's hard not to include them all, and second, I want to include a wide variety because people relate to words, thoughts, and stories differently. Therefore, there are different quotes for different people.

You now know some of the story on how this book 'Jerry's Top 20 Rules for Managing Life' came to be. It is my hope that the information contained within these hours and hours, and years and years of writing will be a benefit to all who read it. Thank You.

Dedication

I dedicate this book to my family, which includes any LDS missionary that came into our home and blessed my life.

Rule #1/4 'Introduction to the Rules'

Special Thanks

I owe a great deal of thanks too many people for their help. But, out of that group, there are three special people I call my 'Fellow Teammates'. These three worked hard in the background to help me make this book the best read I could make it. They did not just work on one chapter. They worked on every chapter of this book. And not just once, but several times.

During the final drafting, these three special people spent months reading and rereading every chapter, helping me with ease of reading, clarity of understanding, and proper punctuation. I won't mention all the spelling errors they caught. Wait? I just did, LOL.

When I would get a chapter back, from one of these three, with their comments, there were times when I swear, I saw more red ink on the pages than black to read, LOL. No writer likes looking at a sea of red ink from their editors. My favorite love/hate comments from them on my writing were: 'I think this needs clarifying.', 'Be more specific.', 'This paragraph is clumsy, rewrite.' or 'You need to rethink and rewrite this last part.' The best comment I always enjoyed receiving was: 'You need to expound on this more.'. Expound on this? I thought that was what I had been doing for eight years. Eight years of writing! And now they want my brain to expound on this subject in a couple of weeks that took eight years to get out of my mind and onto paper the first time?

I didn't tell them, but my wife knew, that some of those editing comments depressed me to the point that I was ready to push the failure button and call it quits. I mean seriously, I thought I had sent them the best I had in me. Yet they believed there was more and better in me. When those depression times hit, my wife would give me a big hug, a little kiss as well when needed, and the encouraging words 'You can fix it. I know you have it within you, and it will be even better.'

Now that I have completed the book, I can truly say to them, 'Thanks for pushing my writing ability to that 110%' marker when I thought I had already reached that point but had not.'.

You, three special, people are **My Sister, Lauren Walker, and Melissa Meyer.** *And you hold a special place of thanks in my heart. You are and will be a loving part of my life forever. I know that you put your spirit of love into the creation of this book. To that, I am eternally thankful. You all deserve more thanks than I can put into words. Thanks for sharing your wonderful gifted talents with me in the writing of this book.*

The No Rules, Rule

Rule #½
'About the Author's Writing'

Rule #½ 'About the Author's Writing'

A Rule is Born:

Rule #¼ *'The Introduction to Rules'* explains the reasons I felt inspired to write this book. Then after writing Rule #¼, I decided I needed a chapter to explain why I write and to explain some of the unique nuances to my writing style. That is how this rule, Rule #½ came to be.

The God Question:

I don't claim to be a literary genius, not even close. With all the wonderful talents the good Lord has richly blessed me with, to which I give Him thanks, the ability to write a great masterpiece of literature is not one of them. That leaves me with a question I want to ask the Lord when I see him. Why is it that I am so inspired to write all the time when it is one of my least talented abilities?

Sure, as you read my writings, you may say that it is better than the average person's. However, you have no idea how many times I have to rewrite everything I write. I have rewritten this chapter eight times at this point. You would think that it would be perfect by now. Still, I am sure I can still find a few errors in this chapter. There is a point where I have to tell myself that I am not perfect, and perfection is a moving target. Therefore, in this case, if I don't define within reason what I want perfection to mean, I will never finish.

The Battle of Pen to Paper:

I try not to let a day go by without writing something. And I am not counting texting on my smartphone as writing. Even though I have been writing for over 50 years, it is still a bittersweet struggle for me. Most days, it takes me hours to write a single paragraph, and all day to write one page. Then after taking all day to write just one page, I bet you will find at least ten writing mistakes on that page, and that is after I have proofread the page 5 times. I can set the page down and not look at it or work on it for a week. Thinking to myself, 'I read it five times, and the page read well. It doesn't need any work. It is perfect.' I will then come back at the end of a week, read the page again, and say to myself .... Well, let me just say that what I would say about the writing wouldn't be good. Why? Because after reading it over again, I will find at least 20 mistakes on the page that I didn't see before. I swear, gremlins find my paper and screw with the writing when I am not looking. Tell me, God, please, why do I feel so inspired to write when it is a bittersweet struggle for me?

Why Do I Do It:

Why do I write? I am not sure God has ever given me the answer to the question of why He inspires me to write. Perhaps He did, and I am not listening, or perhaps His reasons are the same as mine.

Here is my conclusion. For one, though I may never reach perfection, I am a perfectionist, and my lack of good writing skills bugs me constantly. I have been told, and do believe, that the only way to get better at anything is to do it, and do it, and do it some more. My writings may never make it to the shelf of your public library, and I doubt greatly that I will ever (**warning:** use the word '*ever*' with caution, it is so permanent) receive any literary awards. But I have been told that if I keep writing, I will get better. Therefore, I will work on my writing skills, looking for that perfection until I can write no more.

Second, and the most important reason I write is for my children, grandchildren, great-grandchildren, and all my other posterity to come. How else are they going to get to know me? Some of my descendants with whom I have created memories will know a part of me. However, memories fade and distort with time. Then there will be great-grandchildren whom I will never meet. Can you think of a better way to share the undistorted lessons I have learned throughout my life than in a book of my own words? Is it not the duty of a father to teach their children, whether you are the father, the grandfather, or the great-grandfather? What better way can you teach your progenies than writing a book?

I write not for my benefit, but with a hope that somehow, through my writings, it will help me be a better father to my posterity now and after my death. It is for the legacy of my future generations that I write.

It is only through telling my stories personally that I have the best chance of sharing an undistorted view of my life. I don't do it for reasons of vanity or to be immortalized. As a father, I tell these stories to share the wisdom I have gleaned from my life experiences and share them through my viewpoint, even if it is only a tiny bit of wisdom. I do it in the hope that these stories will help make their path through life easier or at least a little better. Can you think of a better way to do that than through the writings of your own life stories?

It's All About Style:

You now know why I write. However, if you are going to attempt to read and understand my writing, you're going to need to know a little about how I write. I am not talking about whether I write with a pen, typewriter (that's old stuff), or on a computer (computer definitely). No, that is not what I am talking about. What I am talking about is writing style, format, sentence structure, and even spelling. In school, we were taught that based on what you were writing, i.e., book, essay, term paper, that there were different writing styles you should use. I remember the writing exercises and assignments all too well. Why, because I wasn't very good at adhering to any of them. Guess what? I still don't.

If, while you are reading, you look at my spelling or sentence structure, to try to figure out what writing style I used, give it up. Don't bother. Because, if you do, you'll find a few misspelled words, plus a few new words you won't find in the dictionary. You also may find some strange sentence structures that need to be re-written to read properly. But I can assure you that the writing style you will find is all mine.

Rule #1/2 'About the Author's Writing'

You see, my writing and my writing style is a reflection of me. The rules contained within the pages of this book are all about me. As you read, you may think from time to time that this book is pointing its wisdom at you, but it is not. If you wish to borrow some of my wisdom to help you in life, please feel free to help yourself. I don't mind sharing. I just don't want you to think that I am pointing the finger of knowledge directly at you. I can assure you that all of the rules and their wisdom are pointing their finger right at me. For wisdom is knowledge applied! And if you wish to apply this knowledge to your life, it may well become your wisdom.

I Did It My Way:

There are a few words in my vocabulary that to date are not found in any known published dictionary. I used a couple of my own words in the writing of this book. In college, I tried to get away with using a couple of my creative words in a short story I wrote for my English class. Upon review my sweet English teacher, Mrs. Vassel politely informed me of their improper use and honored me with a score of 80%. If not for my creative vocabulary, I would have received a 100%. I told her that I thought my newly created words showed imagination, creativity, and style. Her response was; if the word cannot be found in any existing published dictionary, then it is not a word that can be used. In fact, they are not words at all but are gibberish, and therefore my story contained gibberish. Thus, I should be happy that she gave the story the grade she did. I told her that they were in my dictionary. I then proceeded to rattle off the definition of the two new words I had used in the story. Well, that just got me a scowl from the teacher. To that non-verbal answer, I asked, "Where do new words come from? Somebody has to make them up?" Mrs. Vassel looked me sternly in the eyes and stated, "when a new word is required to describe something or is needed to give more clarity to the writing, the author will define the word and use it in a published paper or article. You are not an author, nor is this short story of yours being published. Therefore, your newly created vocabulary words, as I said, are only gibberish and carry no meaning. Be a little less creative on your next story, and your grade may improve."

Well, what do you think of that? I thought you went to school to learn creativity. I'll tell you what I think. It has been 40 years since I took Mrs. Vassel's English class, and since then, I have had a couple of my short stories and a few technical manuals published. Therefore, I am an author. Second, published or not, I have done and do a lot of writing, far more than most people. You know what? As I said earlier, writing is my least favorite thing to do. For me, writing takes a lot more time and thinking than the typical writer (what's typical?) Trying to write in the proper grammatical form makes my head hurt. Therefore, if I am going to do any sort of writing, I am going to do it my way. Including creating any new words I feel are appropriate.

Don't be afraid to be a little creative. You'll find that when you are doing things you don't enjoy doing, being a little creative can make to job a lot more fun.

Aren't You A Gem?

Throughout this book, just before a given paragraph, you may find a short heading in large bold print formatted similar to this, '**Why Do I Do This?**'. Do not mistake these as headings to the paragraphs that follow. They are not. They are a part of my writing style, and I call them 'Gem Tags.' I use the word '*Gem*' because they are a precious nugget of thought that came into my mind as I was writing, which reflects something about what I am writing. I use the word '*Tag*' because I use them to mark the place in my writing, where I had the thought.

A Gem Tag reflects something that is written within the given section. It reflects a thought that came to mind as I was writing the section. More times than not, they reflect something I found humorous or inspiring. The tag is there to give you deeper insight as to what I was thinking or trying to convey in my writing. Read the Gem Tag and then think about it as you read the paragraphs that follow.

Rule #1/2 'About the Author's Writing'

Each Gem Tag can have some type of influence on another gem tag. A group of Gem Tags may reflect the characteristics of the writing. For example, I may use a group of Gem Tags to promote a particular humoristic theme. It could reflect some part of a movie I was thinking about that I thought would humorously tie into the thoughts of my writing. They can also reflect any number of subjects that I feel tie in with the writing, and to each other; such as time, space, distance, life, or death. It could also reflect feelings or moods.

Each Gem Tag only reflects what is written within their section. A Gem Tag's section spans from its start point, where it was inserted in the writing, to the start point of the next Gem Tag. A Gem Tag can reflect any given meaning, emotion, or expression. As I said before, most of the time, I use the Gem Tags to express a little humor I derived from that section of writing. There are exceptions at times when I use Gem Tags to draw attention to a serious point I am attempting to convey. Though the Gem Tags may denote seriousness, there will typically be a bit of humor that can be derived from it as well. There are times, however, that I use the tags to get straight to the point. But for the most part, I use the tags just to be a little silly.

Gem Tags can be used as liberally as the writer wishes. This gives the writer the freedom to accent their writing as they choose. At the same time, it provides the reader a more in-depth understanding of what the writer was thinking at the time they wrote that section of text.

When I am asked to give any kind of talk, lecture, or speech, I will use Gem Tags frequently as markers. If I am giving a talk and I am running short of time, I'll use them to help me determine what material I can or can't skip. I will also use them to help me remember what mood or feeling I am trying to convey to my audience. As I write, I'll use them as a reminder of what is coming up next.

I used a lot of Gem Tags throughout this book. I hope that as you read, you will enjoy the challenge of figuring out each Gem Tag and why I used it.

What is in a Word:

For my enjoyment, I have included one of my non-word words' that Mrs. Vassel, my college English teacher, considered gibberish. The word is *'flustrate,' 'flustrated,'* or *'flustration.'*

Mrs. Vassel is correct. You will not find the word 'flustrate' or any variation of the word in any published dictionary. It is a word that I use quite often to describe my emotional state of being or the state of being I have put someone else in.

I will give you a little understanding of how a person can get into the state of being flustrated. The day after, I had completed all the corrections to the formatting and writing for the documenting of the word *'flustrate,'* the definition got erased. I wasn't sure I could rewrite the meaning as well as I had the first time. I searched all the possible computer files I could think of that may have contained even a partial copy. There were none. The definition was unrecoverable. I was going to have to start over from the beginning. I can tell you that I became very flustrated. I told the computer, (yes I talk to my computer) you flustrate me. I am so flustrated when writing this book. My flustration level couldn't get any higher, etc. How do you put someone else in a flustrated state? You erase their computer files.

Flustrate [*flŭs trāt*] (*flustrate, flustrated, flustration*)

> The word is a derivative of two words, *'frustrate'* and *'fluster',* whose definitions are combined to create a single word that describes both states of being existing simultaneously.

Rule #1/2 'About the Author's Writing'

Define:

Frustrate – **1.** To become disappointed, exasperated, or weary, because of thwarted goals or unsatisfied desires. **2.** To cause somebody to feel disappointed, exasperated, or weary because of thwarted goals or unsatisfied desires. **3.** A state of being where one feels disappointed, exasperated, or weary because of thwarted goals or unsatisfied desires.

Fluster - **1.** To become nervous or agitated, **2.** To cause somebody to become nervous or agitated, **3.** To be in a nervous or agitated state

Flustrate - **1.** To become disappointed, exasperated, or weary, and be nervous, or agitated at the same time because of thwarted goals or unsatisfied desires. **2.** To cause somebody to be disappointed, exasperated, or weary, and be nervous, or agitated at the same time because of thwarted goals or unsatisfied desires. **3.** To be in a disappointed, exasperated, or weary, and be in a nervous, or agitated state at the same time because of thwarted goals or unsatisfied desires.

Rule #1/2 'About the Author's Writing'

Usage:
1. You flustrate me with your constant nitpicking of my writing ability.
2. I am flustrated over all of this.
3. I'll flustrate him so much he won't know what to do.
4. I have so much flustration I can't think anymore.

There is another word I use that you will not find in a dictionary. That is the word 'Idiotitist'; you will find it defined in Rule #8 *'Don't Catch Idiotitist.'* It takes a whole chapter to explain this word. I hope you will enjoy reading Rule #8.

There Is Beauty All Around:

Writing is a form of art, and like the painter, we writers have our own unique brush strokes. What makes a painting by Picasso or Michelangelo, a great painting? Is it the artist, or is it the people who admire their art, or is it both? I say it is both.

You can write great literary works all day long. If no one admires the work, it may as well be placed in the dark. With no light on their work, how can its beauty shine? For that matter, how can there be beauty? As I see it, beauty is created in the admiring. Therefore, for the art to be a masterpiece, it requires an admirer.

Then there is the artist. Without the artist, there is no one to create the masterpiece. Without the masterpiece, there is nothing for the admirer to admire. Therefore, how can there be beauty without the artist and the admirer?

If your painting is loved by only one or your writings enjoyed by only a few, has not beauty been found within its work? To me, if it has been admired at all, then those that enjoyed its beauty have made it a masterpiece.

I have been told by some people, involved in the creating of this book that the part they have been involved with has helped them grow into better people. They stated that my writings had brought the beauty of their spirit to light. They called it enlightening.

Then there is my wife, who reads all my stories and says some have brought tears to her eyes. With others, I have tickled her to laughter. She swears to me that all are inspiring and have inspired her. If that is the case, then my stories have already been admired, and my wife has given me my literary prize in the form of hugs, kisses, and praises.

I Have It All:

What more could a writer ask for than I have already been given? My writing has been admired by those that are dearest to me. I have received the highest literary prize I could ask for. I am satisfied. This is my literary piece of art, my masterpiece, and the best legacy I can leave to my posterity.

Rule #1/2 'About the Author's Writing'

Try You Say? Do or Do Not

Rule #1
'Failure is Not an Option'

Rule #1 'Failure is Not an Option'

To The Point:

If you think you are going to fail, it increases the odds that you are going to fail. Don't go there. Stay focused on success; failure will take care of itself. This is the short of it.

Those who are successful know that the key to succeeding is in your mindset. And a successful mindset is one that does not believe in failure. That is why Rule #1 *'Failure is Not an Option'* is at the very top of my list of rules. I don't believe in failure. At the same time, I don't believe in setting one's self up for failure, either. The last sentence I just wrote is the heart of making Rule #1 successful. Therefore, I will repeat it. I don't believe in setting one's self up for failure, either.

Falling Short:

Yes, I agree, there are times when we all fall short of completing a goal we have set. You may then ask; how can I make the statement *'Failure is Not an Option'* when the chance of failure is out there? Well, I have an answer for those of you out there that say *'Failure IS an Option'*. You are correct; we all fall a little short at times in our lives. Jesus Christ and Heavenly Father both said we are imperfect beings, and all have or will sin. I can give you the scriptures to back this up.

> **(Bible New Testament: Romans 5:12)** [2]
> *12 Wherefore, as by one man sin entered into the world, and death by sin; and so death passed upon all men, for that all have sinned:*
>
> **(Bible New Testament: Romans 3:23)** [2]
> *For all have sinned, and come short of the glory of God;*

Rule #1 'Failure is Not an Option'

King Mosiah from the Book of Mormon said that man was less than the dust of the Earth he was made from:

> **(Book of Mormon: Mosiah 2:25-26)** [3]
> *25 And now I ask, can ye say aught of yourselves? I answer you, Nay. Ye cannot say that ye are even as much as the dust of the earth; yet ye were created of the dust of the earth; but behold, it belongeth to him who created you.*
>
> *26 And I, even I, whom ye call your king, am no better than ye yourselves are; for I am also of the dust.*

Some people, after reading these scriptures, fail to read and comprehend the rest of the scriptural teachings. They walk away saying, 'Why try? According to Mosiah, dirt is better than me.' I know for a fact that there are people that have said this. I have had to sit down with a few of them and explain the other half of the story. The fact is dirt is worthier than we are, and according to God's own words, we are made from the dust of the ground. The point that God is making is this; man is a sinner and will sin. Dirt, on the other hand, cannot sin. So, of course, dirt is more righteous than man is.

My point is that there are times in our lives that in the short-term we are going to fail. So what? That doesn't mean we need to be using any of our energy focusing on any form of failure. As soon as a part of us starts focusing in the direction of failure, we will start pulling ourselves towards that direction.

It is important to understand that focusing on failure breeds failure. This is why you need to keep your mind focused on 'Failure is Not an Option'. This rule is such a vital key to gaining success in life that I cannot stress its importance enough. Because it is so crucial to our success, I give it the status of Rule #1.

Hope for the Imperfect:

Although we all fall short, there is hope for us in all that we do. God is our Heavenly Father, and we are his spiritual children. We are his sons and daughters.

> **(Bible New Testament: 2 Corinthians 6:18)** [2]
> *18 And will be a Father unto you, and ye shall be my sons and daughters, saith the Lord Almighty.*
>
> **(Book of Mormon: Mosiah 5:7)** [3]
> *7 And now, because of the covenant which ye have made ye shall be called the children of Christ, his sons, and his daughters; for behold, this day he hath spiritually begotten you; for ye say that your hearts are changed through faith on his name; therefore, ye are born of him and have become his sons and his daughters.*

Like any loving father, Heavenly Father wants us to become perfect like Him. He wants us to be able to do the impossible. He has also given us the answer to how we can do that. It is through hope and faith in our Savior that we are able to do all things. We must have confidence that our faith will give us the strength and wisdom we will need. Jesus Christ, in his own words, tells us this:

> **(Bible New Testament: Matthew 17:20)** [2]
> *20 And Jesus said unto them, Because of your unbelief: for verily I say unto you, If ye have faith as a grain of mustard seed, ye shall say unto this mountain, Remove hence to yonder place; and it shall remove; and nothing shall be impossible unto you.*
>
> **(Bile New Testament: Luke 17:6)** [2]
> *6 And the Lord said, If ye had faith as a grain of mustard seed, ye might say unto this sycamine tree, Be thou plucked up by the root, and be thou planted in the sea; and it should obey you.*

(Book of Mormon: Moroni 7:33) 3
33 And Christ hath said: If ye will have faith in me ye shall have power to do whatsoever thing is expedient in me.

(Doctrine & Covenants 6:36) 4
36 Look unto me in every thought; doubt not, fear not.

David B Haight said this in a church conference talk, as he recalled a time when he was looking at a mustard seed in his hand:

(David B Haight, 2001 October General Conference, "Faith of Our Prophets") 6
Just imagine the analogy that the Savior was teaching the people. If you only had as much faith as that little tiny mustard seed—and I held it in my hand, and I could hardly see it—if you had that much faith you would say to the mountain, "Move hence," and it would move, if you had that much faith. "O ye of little faith," he told us.

You may not have the faith to move mountains today or tomorrow, but if you believe in the truth of the Lord's own words, you will move mountains someday. As you put your faith in Jesus Christ and believe in yourself that *'Failure is Not an Option'*, all things can come true.

Faith or Fear:

Faith and fear fight against one another. Fear is doubt, and doubt kills faith. Without faith, there is no hope. Without hope, you set yourself up for failure. Elder Kevin W. Pearson had this to say about faith and fear:

(Elder Kevin W. Pearson, 2009 April General Conference, "Faith in the Lord Jesus Christ") 7
Faith and fear cannot coexist. One gives way to the other. The simple fact is we all need to constantly build faith and overcome sources of destructive

disbelief. The Savior's teaching comparing faith to a grain of mustard seed recognizes this reality (see Matthew 13:31-32). Consider it this way: our net usable faith is what we have left to exercise after we subtract our sources of doubt and disbelief. You might ask yourself this question: "Is my own net faith positive or negative?" If your faith exceeds your doubt and disbelief, the answer is likely positive. If you allow doubt and disbelief to control you, the answer might be negative.

We do have a choice. We get what we focus on consistently. Because there is an opposition in all things, there are forces that erode our faith. Some are the result of Satan's direct influence. But for others, we have no one but ourselves to blame. These stem from personal tendencies, attitudes, and habits we can learn to change.

A person, who requested their name to be withheld from an article they wrote, found themselves divorced after a 27-year temple marriage. That person wrote these words about faith and fear.

(Name Withheld, 2010 September Ensign titled "Finding Hope after Divorce") 8
I learned many things during this excruciating time. The scriptures, prayer, my journal, and the temple became my primary links to daily strength. What changed my life, however, was learning to turn my fears over to the Lord. I learned that faith and fear cannot coexist in our minds. Fear inhibits faith and crowds our minds with worry so we cannot hear the Spirit. Fear needs to give way to faith in order for us to access the Lord's guidance and comfort. This was a huge realization for me. Worry consumes the present, crowding out all positive, inspired thought. Could I let go of the worry and turn my life over to the Lord? I knew I couldn't do it alone, but I also knew the Lord would help.

As this person points out, fear inhibits faith. Without faith, we cannot hear the Spirit of the Lord for guidance. Without the Lord's guidance, we cannot truly succeed in life.

The Question of Failure:

I would like to take a moment to point out something in regards to the article 'Finding Hope after Divorce' that you just read, and I will start by asking you a question. The person was married 27 years, a temple marriage, and is now divorced, did they fail? I am sure some of you were asking yourself that question. What is your opinion? Stop here and take a moment to ponder on my question before you read on.

My answer is: it depends on how you want to look at it. I will tell you how I look at it in the context of Rule #1 *'Failure is Not an Option'*, and I can give it to you with confidence even though the person tells us very little about their marriage. I say the person hasn't failed, not yet, and as far as I can tell by their article, they are on the right track to succeed.

Zig Ziglar, a famous American author, salesman, and motivational speaker, had this to say about failure: *"Failure is a detour, not a dead-end street."*

You see, here is where Rule #3 *'There are Fluid Goals and Solid Goals'* comes in to play. We will read more about this rule in its own chapter, but for now, in short, this is how it goes. I believe marriage, while here on Earth, to be a fluid goal. It is a Fluid Goal because it requires changes, or detours, as you go down the path to reach a solid goal. Why, because you can't control the people or events around you. You can only control you. Thus, solid goals are those goals you have control over. Therefore, Celestial Marriage (eternal marriage, one that is for time and eternity), a temple marriage, is a solid goal. I know that if I do all that I can and have faith in Jesus Christ and His atonement, I will have a Celestial Marriage in Heaven. It may not be to the person I currently share a temple marriage. Why? Because I don't control that person's will, they do. My current wife may change and decide that she doesn't want what I want. Therefore, my current wife is a fluid goal that will get me to my solid goal of a Celestial Marriage. Remember, if I do my part and have faith, Heavenly Father will do the rest.

If you don't quite understand Rule #3 yet, that is ok, you can read more about it later. For now, let me just say this; it is because of applying Rule #3 *'There are Fluid Goals and Solid Goals'* properly in our lives we find that we are not failing life as often as we think. In the case of the divorced person, it is not the end for him, he has learned a lot and is on the right path with the proper guidance.

I can tell you that I have been where that divorced person was. I am on my 2nd marriage going on 35 years. I thought the first marriage was the one for eternity, but things happened, and events tore us apart. I kept my faith in God, though at times, it was not easy, and now I have a far more wonderful match for an eternal mate. She is more than I could dream possible. Yet, like the first wife, my second wife also is a fluid goal. That does not mean I give this fluid goal any less worth, work, or commitment. Quite the contrary, fluid goals typically take more effort because you are not, nor should you try, to be in control of another's free agency.

The Wisdom of Man:

I know that my knowledge and wisdom in this mortal state in which I exist is significantly limited. If I measured it against God and His Son, Jesus Christ, my knowledge and wisdom would measure far smaller than any mustard seed in comparison. If my plan is not to fail, then why would I count on the wisdom of man and not on the Lord's wisdom to guide me?

The Spirit of Truth:

I bear you my testimony that I could not accomplish the many things I have done in my life today if it were not for my faith

Rule #1 'Failure is Not an Option'

in Christ, the Son of God, and, our Heavenly Father. It is through Him that I have learned that as long as I have His support and guidance, *'Failure is Not an Option'*.

I am not a man of great financial wealth or a man of position or great stature. What I am is a wonderfully happy man that knows the love of our Savior.

At one time in my life, I had lost the guiding Spirit of God, and without it, failure surrounded me. However, with hard work and earnest soul-searching, and the Lord's grace and mercy, I was able to tap back into that spiritual guidance. I can tell you from personal experience that I have seen, heard, and felt the difference of having the Lord's guiding Spirit with me versus not. With His guiding Spirit, *'Failure is Not an Option'*.

So, when I say *'Failure is not an option'*. I am telling myself this: that I believe that I have the faith and that I know that with our Savior's help, all things are possible.

I leave you with this last great quote from a Prophet of the Lord:

> **(Gordon B. Hinckley, 1983 October General Conference, "Live Up to Your Inheritance")** [9]
> *"You have not failed until you quit trying."*

Endnotes:

1 **King James Version of the Bible, The Old Testament of Our Lord and Saviour Jesus Christ.** Published by The Church of Jesus Christ of Latter-day Saints, Salt Lake City, Utah, USA. Copywrite 2013.

2 **King James Version of the Bible, The New Testament of Our Lord and Saviour Jesus Christ.** Published by The Church of Jesus Christ of Latter-day Saints, Salt Lake City, Utah, USA. Copywrite 2013.

3 **The Book of Mormon Another Testament of Jesus Christ.** Published by The Church of Jesus Christ of Latter-day Saints, Salt Lake City, Utah, USA. The first English edition published in Palmyra, New York, USA, in 1830. Copywrite 2013.

4 **The Doctrine and Covenants of The Church of Jesus Christ of Latter-Day Saints.** Containing Revelations Give to Joseph Smith, the Prophet. With some additions by his successors in the Presidency of the Church. Published by The Church of Jesus Christ of Latter-day Saints, Salt Lake City, Utah, USA. Copywrite 2013.

5 **The Pearl of Great Price.** A selection from the revelations, translations, and narrations of Joseph Smith, First Prophet, seer, and revelator to The Church of Jesus Christ of Latter-Day Saints. Published by The Church of Jesus Christ of Latter-day Saints, Salt Lake City, Utah, USA. Copywrite 2013.

6 **David B. Haight, 2001 October General Conference, "Faith of Our Prophets".** The 171st Semiannual General Conference of the Church of Jesus Christ of Latter-day Saints, October 6, 2001, Saturday afternoon session. Published in the Ensign magazine, Volume 31 Number 11, November 2001. An official magazine of the Church of Jesus Christ of Latter-day Saints, published by the Church of Jesus Christ of Latter-day Saints, 50 E. North Temple Street, Salt Lake City, UT, 84150-3220, USA. Also, retrieved Nov 26, 2019, from ChurchofJesusChrist.Org website: https://www.churchofjesuschrist.org/study/ensign/2001/11/faith-of-our-prophets?lang=eng

7 **Kevin W. Pearson, 2009 April General Conference, "Faith in the Lord Jesus Christ".** The 179th Annual General Conference of the Church of Jesus Christ of Latter-day Saints, April 4, 2009, Saturday afternoon session. Published in the Ensign magazine, Volume 39 Number 5 May 2009, page 40, paragraph 4. An official magazine of the Church of Jesus Christ of Latter-day Saints, published by the Church of Jesus Christ of Latter-day Saints, 50 E. North Temple Street, Salt Lake City, UT, 84150-3220, USA. Also, retrieved Nov 26, 2019, from ChurchofJesusChrist.Org website: https://www.churchofjesuschrist.org/study/ensign/2009/05/faith-in-the-lord-jesus-christ?lang=eng

Rule #1 'Failure is Not an Option'

8 **Name Withheld, 2010 September Ensign titled "Finding Hope after Divorce."** Published in the Ensign magazine Volume 40 Number 9, September 2010. An official magazine of the Church of Jesus Christ of Latter-day Saints, published by the Church of Jesus Christ of Latter-day Saints, 50 E. North Temple Street, Salt Lake City, UT, 84150-3220, USA. At the time of this article, the author wished his name to be withheld. Also, retrieved Nov 26, 2019, from ChurchofJesusChrist.Org website: https://www.churchofjesuschrist.org/study/ensign/2010/09/finding-hope-after-divorce.html?lang=eng#title1

9 **Gordon B. Hinckley, 1983 October General Conference, "Live Up to Your Inheritance".** The 153rd Semiannual General Conference of the Church of Jesus Christ of Latter-day Saints, October 1, 1983, Saturday Morning, General Women's Meeting. Published in the Ensign magazine, Volume 13 Number 11, November 1983. An official magazine of the Church of Jesus Christ of Latter-day Saints, published by the Church of Jesus Christ of Latter-day Saints, 50 E. North Temple Street, Salt Lake City, UT, 84150-3220, USA. Also, retrieved Nov 26,2019, from ChurchofJesusChrist.Org website: https://www.churchofjesuschrist.org/study/ensign/1983/11/live-up-to-your-inheritance?lang=eng

Rule #1 'Failure is Not an Option'

I Thought You Did It?

Rule #2
'Don't Assume'

Rule #2 'Don't Assume'

Cut to It:

Some people would say, the best way to get to the point on this rule is by breaking the word assume into three parts. Because the definition of this word is contained within the word itself. If you know what I am referring to, no explanation is needed. If not, don't worry about it. There are better ways to explain the word assume.

Quite simply put, to assume means you are making an uneducated or ill-informed decision.

The word assume is not a complex word to understand. Therefore, one would be led to believe that it is an easy word to avoid being accused of doing. For assuming lets unnecessary chance enter into your equation. And unnecessary chance is not something I believe anyone intentionally wants to be dealing with.

Anyone See Murphy?

The more you leave to chance or assumptions, the higher your probabilities are for failure. Have you heard of Murphy's Law? The law basically states that anything that can go wrong will go wrong if given a chance. The people most afflicted by Murphy's Law are those individuals that leave their decision making to acts of chance or base their decisions on assumptions.

The more you assume (violation of Rule #2 *'Don't Assume'*), the more likely you are to fail (violation of Rule #1 *'Failure is Not an Option'*). These two rules are twined together. The stronger you adhere to Rule #2, the greater the odds favor Rule #1 in succeeding.

Why Talk So Much?

Many of us would like to believe that cutting right to the point of a subject will give us all the tools and information we need to implement the concept into our lives. I am one of those that want to hear it straight up without all the fluff. I don't want to listen to someone repeat themselves over and over again.

I once worked for a district manager who, during our weekly conference call would repeat over and over again, the message she was trying to covey. In my opinion that half-hour meeting could have been finished in 10 minutes.

I 'got it' the first time. Or did I? In truth, we humans, for the most part, don't get it the first time. The 'say it once' method rarely works. We may hear the message the first time, but for some reason, we don't seem to be able to implement what was said or do what was asked of us. Hearing is not necessarily listening. The proof can be found in our religious life.

If we did implement or incorporate healthy behaviors or good habits into our life with perfect understanding the first time we heard them, then there would be no need for repetition or re-explanation. Right?

Let's take the case of Heavenly Father giving Moses the Ten Commandments. That should have been the end of God's teaching on the subject of the Ten Commandments. Therefore, we should be able to throw out all the supporting documentation on the subject contained within the Bible, and the Bible would then weigh half its current weight.

Think about it. If we all truly understood and practiced what we heard the first time, there would be no need to have things repeated. We wouldn't need to listen to talks in church on the same subjects over and over again. There would be no need for sermons and training that convey the same message only in different styles and wording. Can you imagine how happy that would make many of us? Do you realize how much faster we would gain wisdom and knowledge from the Lord? Can you conceive how much time that would free up for other things? Eliminating the sermon talks and retraining classes at church on Sunday would free up half a day of my life every week.

Could You Repeat That?

We as humans don't seem to learn well without being told the same thing over and over again in different words, styles, and formats. This is why, after having given you the sweet and simple understanding of Rule #2, I am going to continue writing on the subject. I will also be repeating myself. I do not apologize for this. As I said, I don't like hearing things more than once myself. Nevertheless, from my point of view, it seems that a lot of us really don't understand the importance of Rule #2 *'Don't Assume'* or we would be implementing it better into all aspects of our daily life.

For those of you that believe you practice the *'Don't* Assume' rule perfectly, feel free to stop reading here. I have given you the essence of Rule #2. For those of you that don't think you are perfect, I am going to keep on writing with the hope that somewhere within my writings, you, the reader, will find the spark that awakens and motivates you to a higher understanding of this rule. I pray a blessing upon you that you will gain the wisdom necessary to incorporate this vitally important rule into your life.

The Greatest Assumption Story:

There is one story in the Bible Old Testament that I believe to be one of the greatest examples God has given us for understanding the cause and effect of assuming. It is the story of King Balak and Balaam (a spiritual soothsayer or diviner) found in the book of Numbers 22:1-35. To gain a complete understanding of this story, I encourage you to read the whole chapter. It includes many pearls of wisdom that apply to our lives today just as well as they did thousands of years ago.

I will give you a short synopsis of what takes place in Numbers 22:1-35. Israel had just destroyed the Canaanites that fought against her. King Balak, the son of Zippor, saw this death and destruction and feared his people, the Moabites, would be next. So, King Balak requested that Balaam come and proclaim a curse on the Israelites. But, God told Balaam not

Rule #2 'Don't Assume'

to go. King Balak didn't like this answer and sent yet again princes, and men more honorable than they, with greater promises to Balaam if he came and cursed Israel.

The Lord had already told Balaam what he was to do. Yet Balaam comes back and again requests an answer to the same question—should he go to King Balak and curse Israel.

Now I need you to read and ponder Numbers 22:20-22 carefully, or you could get a little confused about what is going on. Keep in mind, as you read, that the Lord knows Balaam's heart and that in the future at another time, Balaam goes against the Lord. The Lord, at this point, is trying to give Balaam a chance to follow His instruction. Again, remember the Lord has told Balaam the first time not to go with the men to King Balak. The second time the Lord's answer to Balaam is more like a warning, He tells Balaam that if he chooses his own will over God's and goes with the men in the morning to see King Balak, that Balaam had better deliver God's message.

In the morning, Balaam gets on his devoted ass, an animal that had served him obediently for many years, and departed with the princes of Moab to see King Balak. God was very angry with Balaam for his choice. As a result, Balaam would either do as God had warned him or Balaam would die.

God sends an Angel to stand in Balaam's path to either get his attention to turn back or die if he tries to pass and continue on his journey. Three times Balaam tries to pass the Angel, and three times Balaam's Ass stops him. With each try, Balaam's animal tries harder, in the only way the ass knows how. The ass tried his best to get Balaam to see the Angel standing with a sword ready to smite his master. Each time Balaam's focus is only on his anger for his animal's disobedience. Balaam at first beats the ass for his stubborn disobedience, and on the third time, he threatens to kill the poor animal. It is clear at this point that Balaam is too focused on his anger towards his ass to see what is really going on. Finally, the Lord intervenes and opens Balaam's eyes to see the Angel.

I love this story. What a wealth of valuable information it contains. Balaam, because of his anger, was blinded to how threatening the situation was to his life. Do you see where Balaam's assumptions about the disobedience of his animal almost cost him his life? If Balaam had only taken a moment to ponder the situation that faced him, he could have easily put the pieces together, and thus his eyes would have been opened sooner. Instead, he let his anger cloud his mind. He should have asked himself, why is my animal, that has been so faithful to me, acting this way? Balaam knew the reactions of the ass were not normal. The ass had never before rebelled against his master. Then there is the fact that Balaam knew that the Lord was involved in what he was doing. Yet he did not think to ask God if there was a problem.

For our purpose, the point of Balaam's story is that assuming almost got him killed. Had he taken the time to do a little pondering and praying, Balaam could have saved himself and his faithful animal a lot of pain and hardship. It was only due to the mercy and love of God, and the ass, that Balaam was still alive.

Pump It Up:

When it comes to spiritual learning and gaining the truth therein, the scriptures and church leaders have told us how important it is not to leave things to assumption. They point out that the only way to gain the truth to any of the Lord's teaching is to do all that is within our power. Then, and only then will God help. If we did what the Prophets have told us, and retold us, we would leave very little room for assumptions in our lives.

> **(Bible New Testament: 1 Thessalonians 5:17-21)**[2]
> *17 Pray without ceasing.*
>
> *18 In every thing give thanks: for this is the will of God in Christ Jesus concerning you.*
>
> *19 Quench not the Spirit.*

20 Despise not prophesyings.

21 Prove all things; hold fast that which is good.

(Doctrine & Covenants 9:7-8)[4]
7 Behold, you have not understood; you have supposed that I would give it unto you, when you took no thought save it was to ask me.

8 But, behold, I say unto you, that you must study it out in your mind; then you must ask me if it be right, and if it is right I will cause that your bosom shall burn within you; therefore, you shall feel that it is right.

(Robert D. Hales, 2007 October General Conference, "Personal Revelation: The Teachings and Examples of the Prophets")[6]
I have learned that prayer provides a firm foundation for personal revelation. But more is required. While still a regional representative, I had the opportunity to learn from another Apostle, Elder Boyd K. Packer. We were assigned to reorganize a stake and began by kneeling in prayer together. After interviewing priesthood leaders and having prayer, Elder Packer suggested that we walk around the building together. As we walked, he demonstrated a vital principle of seeking personal revelation—the principle the Lord taught Oliver Cowdery: "Behold, ... you must study it out in your mind." (D&C 9:8.) We pondered our assignment, counseled together, and listened to the voice of the Spirit. When we went back, we prayed and studied further, and then we were prepared to receive revelation.

(Dieter F. Uchtdorf, 2011 April General Conference, "Waiting on the Road to Damascus")[7]
Our Father in Heaven expects us to study it out first and then pray for guidance...

The Work:

After reading these scriptures, do you think God has a problem with us making assumptions and not putting in the work to find out what the facts are?

There are too many times in our lives we make assumptions but still expect a specific outcome. How can we ensure success if we have not put in the true measure of work that is required to succeed?

Don't you believe that God has set the example of how we are to be living and working in our daily life? If you genuinely have that understanding, then you know that God expects us to put a full measure of work into any situation before we come to Him for help.

> **(Doctrine & Covenants 58:26)**[4]
> *26 For behold, it is not meet that I should command in all things; for he that is compelled in all things, the same is a slothful and not a wise servant; wherefore he receiveth no reward.*
>
> **(Doctrine & Covenants 107:100)**[4]
> *100 He that is slothful shall not be counted worthy to stand, and he that learns not his duty and shows himself not approved shall not be counted worthy to stand. Even so. Amen.*

When you don't put a full honest measure of work into a task, no matter what that task is, you leave gaps for assumptions, inviting chance or Murphy's Law to fill them in and creating opportunities for failure. The more gaps you let in, the less likely you are to succeed.

Stretch Yourself:

As I said before, we must always give 110 percent of ourselves and append to that our faith in Heavenly Father that He will fill in the assumption gaps. Giving 100 percent is not good enough, as you will read in Rule #4. Giving 100 percent means you have only applied what you know. You haven't stretched yourself. So, in order to learn and receive inspiration, you must stretch yourself.

Heavenly Father expects us to learn. That is why He sent us here. If we are not stretching ourselves, we are not learning. If we are not learning, Heavenly Father will not inspire us through the power of the Holy Ghost. Without inviting the inspiration of the Holy Ghost to add that extra 10%, we are inviting luck or Murphy's Law to fill in the gaps of assumption we cannot.

> **(Gospel Principles (Old), Chapter 2)[8]**
> *Even though we have forgotten, our Father in Heaven remembers who we were and what we did before we came here (see Discourses of Brigham Young, p. 50). He has chosen the time and place for each of us to be born so we can learn the lessons we personally need and do the most good with our individual talents and personalities.*
>
> **(Teachings of the Presidents of the Church: Joseph Smith, Chapter 18 "Beyond the Vail: Life in the Eternities")[9]**
> *Here, then, is eternal life—to know the only wise and true God; and you have got to learn how to be gods yourselves, and to be kings and priests to God, ... by going from one small degree to another, and from a small capacity to a great one; from grace to grace, from exaltation to exaltation, until you attain to the resurrection of the dead, and are able to dwell in everlasting burnings, and to sit in glory, as do those who sit enthroned in everlasting power. ...*

Assume Nothing:

I haven't said that we can never assume anything. That would be a statement that no one could fulfill. We don't know, nor can we know all there is to know about everything. We are not Gods... yet. Therefore, since we have not been endowed with infinite knowledge, there are things in our daily lives we must assume. But, I can tell you that the only time to assume is after you have applied Rule #4 'Always Give a 110 %' and you have used your faith in Heavenly Father to fill in any remaining assumption gaps.

Another thing to remember is that a well-educated guess is not an assumption.

Look It's So Small:

Many of us get so caught up in the big things we don't give enough detail to the small things. When in truth, and particularly in relationships, if we paid more attention to the little details, we wouldn't have so many big ones to deal with. It is the constant little assumptions we make, that act like painful tiny slivers under our fingernails, which erode the relationship. It is more often the small things that wear a relationship down than the big ones.

I would like to share a couple of examples of small assumptions from my relationship with my wife. Now, remember, I am writing this, so you are going to be reading about things that annoyed me. You can be assured that these stories do not negate from the hundreds of stories my wife could share about me annoying her.

Oh, Great and Powerful Oz:

There are many aspects of our lives that we assume too much where we should not. Religion is one of them, and relationships are another.

At this point, I would like to share a relationship story that happened to me. It's about husbands that assume too much

Rule #2 'Don't Assume'

and wives who feel their husbands must have become Gods because their husbands seem to think they know it all. Wives, I want you to know there is hope for us husbands.

Shortly after my wife and I were married, for some strange reason, my wife came to the assumption that I, the husband, knew everything. In fact, one day, I came down to the basement to put some dirty clothes in the laundry room. There, sitting on a shelf above the washing machine, was a plaque. The sign reads: 'When I married Mr. Right, I didn't know his first name was Always.' Now, if any of you men happen to find a similar plaque like this in your home, take heed and take the message to heart, seriously.

After reading the plaque, I was inspired with wisdom that I had better take my wife out to a nice dinner to set a mood that would allow us to have a gentle heart to heart talk about the plaque. During that talk, we pointed out a few of my minor flaws and minor lack of knowledge in some areas, and I did my best to assure her that there are things to which her wisdom and skills are far superior to mine. At the end of our talk, we both agreed that I did not have infinite knowledge of all things, nor had I reached Godhood... yet.

Now I am sure I used up every brownie point I had deposited in my wife's bank, and I may have even had to take out a loan of a few more before our conversation ended. In the end, my wife assured me the plaque would be put away unless, of course, it was needed again.

So, what does the story have to do with assuming? Well, of all the aspects of our lives, it is our relationships that are the most important. As I served as Elders Quorum President and in the Bishopric, I have had many opportunities to counsel couples. One of the most significant issues I found in their relationship was how much they each assumed they knew about the other, thus why should there be a need for real communication? Each person already knew what the other person was thinking, each of them already knew what the other person was going to say, so why did they need to listen to each other. Or why did they need to take just a polite second and ask their

Rule #2 'Don't Assume'

spouse about their thoughts or preferences when they think they already know the answer?

Instead of assuming, often wrongly, don't you think spending a little time gaining true knowledge and pondering it would better serve your relationship?

Now You See It and Now You Don't:

Removing plates from the dinner table: how could removing plates from the dinner table have anything to do with assuming, let alone cause an annoyance in a relationship? Well, let's see?

I tend to clean the food from my plate rather quickly and then sit back on my chair and talk, read, or do whatever for a while as I wait to see if my tummy tells my brain that it is no longer hungry and it's happily full.

My wife is a licensed childcare provider and had been for 20 years prior to our marriage. The children in her care were, for the most part, three years of age or under. Working with young children gave my wife an eye for looking at things from a distinct perspective; a perspective that I did not always fully appreciate.

From my wife's perspective, a child sitting at the table, not eating indicated to her that the child was done eating, and removing the plate from in front of them was a preventive measure. This action prevented the child from playing with the dishes, potentially breaking something and getting hurt, or at the very least, getting themselves in trouble.

As far as some wives are concerned, husbands are nothing more than a big child. As for myself, I have no idea where these wives get that idea. Do you?

Since I wasn't eating, and I wasn't putting more food on my plate, my wife assumed that I was done, and off she went with my plate to the sink. For a while, this became a ritual at mealtime. It didn't matter what meal it was: breakfast, lunch, or dinner. I had to keep one eye on the plate at all times, or it was gone faster than in the movie 'Gone in 60 Seconds'. I had a hard time making plate-watching a priority. At many a meal, if I wanted more to eat, I would have to get up and get a clean plate from the kitchen. My brain at the time could not comprehend the reasoning behind this ritual; of course, had I given it the proper attention, I would have understood what was happening.

There was one time during dinner that I had emptied my plate, and then I took a few minutes to converse with our dinner guest. As we were talking, my tummy sent a message to my brain, informing it that it wished to be provided a few more mashed potatoes. I do so love mashed potatoes. Therefore, as I was talking with our guest, keeping polite eye contact, of course, I scooped a large spoonful of mashed potatoes and dropped it on my plate. At least I thought I had. That is until I caught a glimpse of my missing plate just as the potatoes hit the table. You see, I assumed I had kept a well enough eye on my plate that it would still be on the table in front of me.

I am telling you; my wife was fast in those days. She developed this talent from caring for those little daycare children. As any well-trained mother knows, being faster than the child is a top priority, and my wife was good, very good.

Is it Alzheimer's?

This next story I call 'Is it Alzheimer's or just Losing My Mind?' My wife's daycare training did not stop at plates, nor did her personal exercises. She was diligent every day, whether there were daycare children in the home or not. My wife ensured she stayed in shape. If there is an item left out that wasn't in your hands being used, my wife will make sure that it was put away.

If I was out of sight for 10 seconds and she was near the item, it was gone when I got back. To top it off, where she would put the item was not necessarily where I would put it.

After 20 years of childcare, my wife's reaction to any item not being used or attended to is now a built-in autopilot response. Now we humans, when we are in autopilot response mode, don't always give the response much thought. The brain does not necessarily remember the details of the action. So, when I would return to get the item I needed, the item would be gone, and my wife would be as if nothing happened, and all was normal. I, on the other hand, would then spend a few minutes looking for the item, scratch my head a few times and then look a little more. After that, I would then ask the question, all husbands ask their wives, "Honey, did you see my whatever?" Now wives, what do you think the answer to that question is? "I haven't seen it, and I didn't touch it." Now husbands, what are you going to say to that? Nothing if you're smart. Well, every now and then, I wasn't too bright. To let the truth be known, I was not too smart much of the time.

So, What's the Point?

What is the point of these three stories concerning assumption? It is that with a little less assuming on both our part, and by applying some sincere pondering, and better communication from the both of us, we could have handled these small relationship-eroding issues much quicker and easier in our marriage.

Speaking for me, rather than allowing my first reaction of being annoyed to become my focus, I should have pondered the issues a little more deeply. Had I done a proper job of pondering the situation in my mind, for sure, I wouldn't have been contemplating ideas such as "my wife is out to make me think I am losing my mind," or at the least, "she is out to get me annoyed seriously."

Yes, gentlemen, contrary to belief, our companions are not out to annoy us. It is not some great conspiracy that the women are using to make men think we are losing our minds so that we will turn control of the world over to them. They already have control of us; we just don't know it. I am just trying to inject a little humor here to lighten the weight of this serious subject.

Instead of both my wife and I feeling upset and thinking either of us was out to annoy the other, we needed to eliminate the assumptions from the issues, ponder the situation more, and then communicate with each other better.

Today after almost 38 years of marriage, my wife and I can look back on how we foolishly handled these issues, and now we laugh together about them. Many of our past misunderstandings now make funny stories to share with our friends and guests. But the reason why we can laugh about them today is we finally took the proper course of action. We learned to ponder over the issues to find the solution and then properly communicate. This removes the assumptions and gains us understanding.

The Enemies of Assumption:

Knowledge, pondering, and faith in our Heavenly Father are the enemies of assumption. All three of these keys are needed to deal with assumptions in our lives. The most important or primary key to eliminating the assumption gaps from our lives is pondering. The more we ponder, the better. We do not give pondering it's proper due. To ponder means to think about (something) carefully before dealing with or concluding.

Wise Words:

We can have all the knowledge of a subject we want, but if you don't take the time to ponder how to use that knowledge, it is like trying to work with a tool without mastering how to use it. We can have all the faith that our Lord will be there to guide us, but unless we ponder over the issue, we cannot expect the spirit of the Holy Ghost to be there. How many times have we heard the words 'Search, Ponder, & Pray'?

We have been given faith through the spirit of the Holy Ghost, and we have been given the opportunity to gain knowledge. The Lord expects us to ponder over both of them and then pray to know how to use them in our daily lives. We can find examples of this throughout the scriptures.

> **(Doctrine and Covenants 30:3)**[4]
> 3 Wherefore, you are left to inquire for yourself at my hand, and ponder upon the things which you have received.

> **(Doctrine and Covenants 88:62)**[4]
> 62 And again, verily I say unto you, my friends, I leave these sayings with you to ponder in your hearts...

> **(Book of Mormon: 2 Nephi 32:8)**[3]
> 8 And now, my beloved brethren, I perceive that ye ponder still in your hearts; and it grieveth me that I must speak concerning this thing. For if ye would hearken unto the Spirit which teacheth a man to pray ye would know that ye must pray; for the evil spirit teacheth not a man to pray, but teacheth him that he must not pray.

In the Book of Mormon, 3 Nephi 17:2-3, we find what I think is a clearer and more direct scripture telling us what we need to do. In this scripture, the Nephites have just been given a wealth of knowledge from Jesus Christ. Jesus tells them to go home, ponder over it, and then pray to Heavenly Father for understanding.

> **(Book of Mormon: 3 Nephi 17:2-3)**[3]
> 2 I perceive that ye are weak, that ye cannot understand all my words which I am commanded of the Father to speak unto you at this time.
>
> 3 Therefore, go ye unto your homes, and ponder upon the things which I have said, and ask of the Father, in my name, that ye may understand, and prepare your minds for the morrow, and I come unto you again.

From the introduction to the Book of Mormon, the Prophets tell us this:

(Book of Mormon, Introduction)[3]
We invite all men everywhere to read the Book of Mormon, to ponder in their hearts the message it contains, and then to ask God, the Eternal Father, in the name of Christ if the book is true. Those who pursue this course and ask in faith will gain a testimony of its truth and divinity by the power of the Holy Ghost.

Elder Walter F. Gonzalez gave us this message from a church conference talk:

(Walter F. Gonzalez, 2007 October General Conference, "Today Is the Time")[11]
Eternal principles will take root in us as we take time not only to read the teachings of the prophets and the scriptures but also to ponder them in the spirit of prayer. Nephi, for example, took time to sit and ponder. By so doing, he was exposed to doctrinal pearls (see 1 Nephi 11:1). Take the time to do what the Lord has directed us to do: "Treasure these things up in your hearts, and let the solemnities of eternity rest upon your minds" (D&C 43:34). In a world that increasingly demands more of our time, it is essential that we take time to ponder in our homes, so that we may understand divine doctrine and its principles. As the Savior said, "Go ye unto your homes, and ponder upon these things ... that ye may understand, and prepare your minds for the morrow" (3 Nephi 17:3).

Final Words:

The scriptures and writings of the Prophets are given to us not only to be applied to our spiritual lives; they are also to be applied to every aspect of our daily lives. The three personal stories I shared with you about the dangers of assumptions in our relationships can and should be applied to all our dealings in life.

Rule #2 'Don't Assume'

We can't eliminate assuming completely from our lives. If we could, we would have no need for faith. But I do believe that in the fight to minimize assumptions, we all have a lot more work to do. We could all put more effort into pondering over issues before we react. This is one of the main keys to success with Rule #2.

The keys to minimizing assumptions are:

- Search for more knowledge
- Ponder over it
- Have faith in Heavenly Father and the power of the Holy Ghost
- Pray that you will gain the understanding that you need.

Do these things in your daily life, and I testify to you that you will be more successful in your dealings with our Heavenly Father, your family relationships, and your business.

Endnotes:

1 **King James Version of the Bible, The Old Testament of Our Lord and Saviour Jesus Christ.** Published by The Church of Jesus Christ of Latter-day Saints, Salt Lake City, Utah, USA. Copywrite 2013.

2 **King James Version of the Bible, The New Testament of Our Lord and Saviour Jesus Christ.** Published by The Church of Jesus Christ of Latter-day Saints, Salt Lake City, Utah, USA. Copywrite 2013.

3 **The Book of Mormon Another Testament of Jesus Christ.** Published by The Church of Jesus Christ of Latter-day Saints, Salt Lake City, Utah, USA. The first English edition published in Palmyra, New York, USA, in 1830. Copywrite 2013.

4 **The Doctrine and Covenants of The Church of Jesus Christ of Latter-Day Saints.** Containing Revelations Give to Joseph Smith, the Prophet. With some additions by his successors in the Presidency of the Church. Published by The Church of Jesus Christ of Latter-day Saints, Salt Lake City, Utah, USA. Copywrite 2013.

5 **The Pearl of Great Price.** A selection from the revelations, translations, and narrations of Joseph Smith, First Prophet, seer, and revelator to The Church of Jesus Christ of Latter-Day Saints. Published by The Church of Jesus Christ of Latter-day Saints, Salt Lake City, Utah, USA. Copywrite 2013.

6 **Robert D. Hales, 2007 October General Conference, "Personal Revelation: The Teachings and Examples of the Prophets".** The 177th Semiannual General Conference of the Church of Jesus Christ of Latter-day Saints, October 7, 2007, Sunday afternoon session. Published in the Ensign magazine, Volume 37 Number 11, November 2007, page-87 paragraph-4. An official magazine of the Church of Jesus Christ of Latter-day Saints, published by the Church of Jesus Christ of Latter-day Saints, 50 E. North Temple Street, Salt Lake City, UT, 84150-3220, USA. Also, retrieved Nov 26,2019, from ChurchofJesusChrist.Org website: https://www.churchofjesuschrist.org/study/ensign/2007/11/personal-revelation-the-teachings-and-examples-of-the-prophets.html?lang=eng#series_title1

7 **Dieter F. Uchtdorf, 2011 April General Conference, "Waiting on the Road to Damascus".** The 181st Annual General Conference of the Church of Jesus Christ of Latter-day Saints, April 2, 2011, Sunday morning session. Published in the Ensign magazine, Volume 41 Number 05, May 2011, page-75 paragraph-10. An official magazine of the Church of Jesus Christ of Latter-day Saints, published by the Church of Jesus Christ of Latter-day Saints, 50 E. North Temple Street, Salt Lake City, UT, 84150-3220, USA. Also, retrieved Nov 26, 2019, from ChurchofJesusChrist.Org website: https://www.churchofjesuschrist.org/study/ensign/2011/05/sunday-morning-session/waiting-on-the-road-to-damascus?lang=eng

8 **Gospel Principles (Old), Chapter 2** Published in the Gospel Principles Manual (old), Chapter 2. An official manual of the Church of Jesus Christ of Latter-day Saints. Published 1978 by the Church of Jesus Christ of Latter-day Saints, 50 E. North Temple Street, Salt Lake City, UT, 84150-3220, USA.

9 **Teachings of the Presidents of the Church: Joseph Smith, Chapter 18 "Beyond the Vail: Life in the Eternities".** Published in the Teachings of the Presidents of the Church: Joseph Smith, page-221, paragraph-5. An official manual of the Church of Jesus Christ of Latter-day Saints, published 2007 & 2011 by the Church of Jesus Christ of Latter-day Saints, 50 E. North Temple Street, Salt Lake City, UT, 84150-3220, USA. Also see, Teachings of the Presidents of the Church: Joseph Smith. (n.d.). Churchofjesuschrist.org. Retrieved February 17, 2019 from Churchofjesuschrist.org website: https://www.churchofjesuschrist.org/study/manual/teachings-joseph-smith/chapter-18?lang=eng.

11 **Walter F. Gonzalez, 2007 October General Conference, "Today Is the Time". ".** The 177th Semiannual General Conference of the Church of Jesus Christ of Latter-day Saints, October 6, 2007, Saturday Afternoon session. Published in the Ensign magazine, Volume 37 Number 11, November 2007, page-54 paragraph-5. An official magazine of the Church of Jesus Christ of Latter-day Saints, published by the Church of Jesus Christ of Latter-day Saints, 50 E. North Temple Street, Salt Lake City, UT, 84150-3220, USA. Also, retrieved Nov 26, 2019, from Ensign, ChurchofJesusChrist.Org website: https://www.churchofjesuschrist.org/study/ensign/2007/11/today-is-the-time?lang=eng

He Punts From the 35 Yard Line

Rule #3
'There are Fluid Goals & There are Solid Goals'

Rule #3 'There are Fluid Goals & There are Solid Goals'

Short & Sweet:

There are two types of goals we need to set in our lives, *fluid goals, and solid goals.* Understanding the differences between them is the key to better success.

Fluid goals are goals that you set, but yet you do not have control over all the elements. They contain conditions or elements beyond your control that must be met in order for the goal to succeed. If any of those other conditions happen to be under the control of other people, well, then you can, for sure, consider the goal to be a fluid goal.

Solid goals are goals you set and control nearly 100 percent of the elements. Thus, you are in 95 to 100 percent control of the outcome. I don't think you will find too many people that would complain about those kinds of odds for gaining success.

The Goalpost:

To say setting goals in our lives is important is an understatement. Goal setting is as vital to living a meaningful, fruitful life, as air and water are to sustaining life. Any successful person will tell you that without setting and completing goals, they could not have accomplished their dreams.

If you haven't bought into the fact that you need to set goals then it doesn't matter if you understand what a fluid goal and solid goal are. If, until now, you haven't believed in the value of goals setting, let me educate or inspire you on that first. I could direct you to hundreds of self-help authors and motivational books on this subject, in the hope that they would inspire your mind to the wisdom of goal setting. Instead, I am going to trust that you are not that far lost, and a few insightful words of wisdom will help you see the value of

Rule #3 'There are Fluid Goals & There are Solid Goals'

setting goals. Therefore, I have included a few (several) famous quotes to help stimulate your brain.

I know I am including a lot of quotes here, but you should have seen all the quotes I went through, reading for hours and hours. This is only a few compared to the many I read. I feel the ones I have chosen give enough variety of famous people so that there should be at least one quote you might relate to. Truth be told, I love all these quotes and I believe goal setting to be priceless.

Wisdom of the Ages:

(Elbert Hubbard)[6]
"Many people fail in life, not for lack of ability or brains or even courage but simply because they have never organized their energies around a goal."

(Dr. Norman Vincent Peale)[7]
"All successful people have a goal. No one can get anywhere unless he knows where he wants to go and what he wants to be or do!"

(Jim Rohn)[8]
"If you don't design your own life plan, chances are you'll fall into someone else's plan. And guess what they have planned for you? Not much."

(Franklin D. Roosevelt)[9]
"To reach a port, we must sail; Sail, not tie at anchor; Sail, not drift."

(Brian Tracy)[10]
"Goals allow you to control the direction of change in your favor."

(Earl Nightingale)[11]
"People with goals succeed because they know where they're going."

Rule #3 'There are Fluid Goals & There are Solid Goals'

(Zig Ziglar)[12]
"What you get by achieving your goals is not as important as what you become by achieving your goals."

(Jim Rohn)[13]
"I find it fascinating that most people plan their vacation with better care than they do their lives. Perhaps that is because escape is easier than change."

(Helen Keller)[14]
"It is for us to pray not for tasks equal to our powers, but for powers equal to our tasks, to go forward with a great desire forever beating at the door of our hearts as we travel toward our distant goal."

(James Allen)[15]
"Until input (thought) is linked to a goal (purpose) there can be no intelligent accomplishment."

(Thomas Fuller)[16]
"A good archer is known not by his arrows but by his aim."

(Robert A. Heinlein)[17]
"In the absence of clearly-defined goals, we become strangely loyal to performing daily trivia until ultimately we become enslaved by it."

(Gerald L. Penhollow)[18]
"Life is made up of hundreds of little Goals and a few big ones. There are Fluid Goals and Solid Goals, understanding the difference is the key to better success in our lives."

(Tony Robbins)[19]
"How am I going to live today in order to create the tomorrow I'm committed to?"

(Arnold H. Glasgow)[20]
"In life, as in football, you won't go far unless you know where the goalposts are."

Rule #3 'There are Fluid Goals & There are Solid Goals'

(Aristotle)[21]
"Man is a goal seeking animal. His life only has meaning if he is reaching out and striving for his goals."

(Kathy Seligman)[22]
"You can't hit a home run unless you step up to the plate. You can't catch a fish unless you put your line in the water. You can't reach your goals if you don't try."

(Catherine Pulsifer)[23]
"The unfortunate aspect about living life without your own goals is that you may very well reach a point in your life where you will wonder, 'what would have happened if I had only done..."

(Ralph Waldo Emerson)[24]
"The world makes way for the man who knows where he is going."

(Geoffrey F. Abert)[25]
"The most important thing about goals is having one."

(Denis Waitley)[26]
"The reason most people never reach their goals is that they don't define them, or ever seriously consider them as believable or achievable. Winners can tell you where they are going, what they plan to do along the way, and who will be sharing the adventure with them."

(Will Rogers)[27]
"Even if you're on the right track, you'll get run over if you just sit there."

(Edmund Hilary)[28]
"You don't have to be a fantastic hero to do certain things – to compete. You can be just an ordinary chap, sufficiently motivated to reach challenging goals."

Rule #3 'There are Fluid Goals & There are Solid Goals'

(Pablo Picasso)[29]
"Our goals can only be reached through a vehicle of a plan, in which we must fervently believe, and upon which we must vigorously act. There is no other route to success."

So Where Do I Put You?

Now that you have read all these beautiful, motivational quotes, I can tell you have bought into the importance of goal setting. A part of planning your goals is to know the type of goals you are dealing with and the category to place it.

In general, goals are categorized as long-term or shortterm. I'll add one more category to that, eternal goals. Whether the goal is short, long, or eternal, they are all a subset of either a fluid or a solid goal.

Placing your goals into the fluid or solid category is where many people fall short. Most people don't understand or recognize a fluid goal from a solid one. Most of the goals we have in life are fluid goals, yet people tend to handle them as if they are a solid goal. Thus, when they hit a bump in the road, they think it is a dead-end. When in truth, the fluid goal is just letting them know that they need to take a detour.

Glass of Water Please:

Let's see if I can clarify. As I said before, a fluid goal is a goal in which you do not control all the aspects. Many times, fluid goals require a little tweaking from the original goal. Most goals pretty much fall into the fluid goal category. Not all, but most.

Here are two examples of similar goals, one solid and the other fluid:

> Goal 1 Solid:
>> I will own my own house.

Rule #3 'There are Fluid Goals & There are Solid Goals'

Goal 2 Fluid:

I will own my own house in Honolulu, Hawaii, on Coconut Lane.

Why is goal 2 a fluid goal? Goal 2 has too many variables that are not under your control.

Now granted, since both these goals are for acquiring an item, there is a chance that you could accomplish either one. However, Goal 2 needs to be fluid. That is unless you like to gamble and think you can beat the odds of a 90% failure rate. This is not to say that you could not find that house on Coconut Lane to live in. And there is nothing wrong with setting high expectations.

If you set Goal 2 to a solid, precise expectation, however, you limit your options. Remember, also, as I said, many outside factors could stop Goal 2 from happening. Thus, as I pointed out already, you set yourself up for a high risk of failure. Yet, the concern should be more toward the fact that you limited your options.

When setting such a precise solid goal, there is another factor I want to point out. The one that I feel is most important. That is; what if the place you solidly set to live is not where God or life would prefer you to be? Thus, will you be truly happy? Please note that I said truly happy.

The God Factor:

In my life: God rules, then family, and then me. Let's take Goal 2 and say that work is requiring you to move to Honolulu, Hawaii. God knows that factor. But God prefers you to live elsewhere, other than Coconut Lane in Honolulu. By forcing Goal 2 to be solid, you'd miss out on who knows what? You may never know. You were not there; wherever there was that He preferred you to be. What happiness did you miss? Again, who knows? You weren't there.

This is not to say that God always cares exactly where you live. Then again, I can point to scriptures where, at times, God did.

Keep in mind that this goal-setting example is to be applied to all aspects of your life. Not just moving.

God is real, and we can choose to ignore that variable of life or not. The more we choose to ignore God in our planning, by making something a solid goal that would be best as a fluid goal, the more inflexible you must become to reach that goal. It is the nature of a solid goal to be inflexible. That is why it is called solid.

I repeat, God is a factor in all aspects of our goals. You can choose to ignore that factor of the equation all you want. That does not change it. It goes back to when people thought the Earth was flat and the Sun revolved around us. Think it all you want, it will not change the fact that the Earth is round, and we revolve around the Sun. You can ignore God in your goal planning all you want. That does not change the fact that He is a part of it.

You are My Destiny:

I am not one that believes life is predestined. However, I do believe there is a best path option set out for each individual. I like to call it the good, better, best path option. I could write another book on this topic alone.

What is the best path for your life? Only God knows the full picture and the best path to true happiness for you. Although He knows, you do not. You may think you do, then perhaps you know something I don't. I, on the other hand, don't remember my mother being handed a book or manual at my birth detailing, which options and paths are the best for my life. She sure didn't give it to me if she did. And I am pretty sure she would have. I also know for a fact that no manual came with my children, or I would have been more than happy to use it.

Please note, I did say a book or manual <u>detailing</u> my life. I did not say that we were left alone with no way of knowing which paths to choose. He did leave us books to guide us. They are just not as detailed as some of us would like. Making the best choices is a part of our learning (another book to write). Thus, I am sorry to say; your parents were not given a detailed manual written just for you. This is another good reason why learning how to set proper goals is important.

The Power of Will:

When you make goals solid based upon your will only, and God has additional plans for you which you did not include, you miss out on taking the best path. You may have chosen a good path. Maybe even the better path, but you may not have chosen the best. Thus, you will then miss out on some of the happiness God had planned for you.

Of course, how would you know the happiness, the learning, the experience you missed? Your fixed, inflexible goal never allowed you to experience the best. God tries to nudge you on to the best path, but He does not force you even though it would be for the best. No different than you would attempt to force your children. Unless, of course, it meant saving a life. Yet, even then, free will still has the choice.

When you feel your will knows the best path and you make a fluid goal solid, you must become inflexible to God's nudges to His will. The more you resist, the more God will gently attempt to persuade you to His best path for you. Of course, then you must become more inflexible and ridged to stay on your course.

Just like parents at some point, God stops nudging (but never stops loving) and allows you the path you have chosen to your inflexible solid goal. You may never know the blessings and happiness you missed by taking a more flexible path. When a moment is gone, it is gone. Time does not repeat; events may, and for some things, you may get a second chance, but time never turns back to allow reclaiming a moment in a different way.

Many never get a glimpse of what the best path would have brought to their life. As for me, God has given me the blessing to see the other possibilities and outcomes so that I may learn

Rule #3 'There are Fluid Goals & There are Solid Goals'

from my choices, that I may understand better when to make goals solid or fluid. I have learned that my will and my inflexibility came with a cost to obtain that goal. Whereas, I could have obtained that same goal by my being flexible enough to include God's will.

Your will or God's will? In the end, you have to ask yourself, was it worth the price? Always remember this, you may not be able to go back in time for a do-over, but you can learn from the past.

Trash It:

Let's think a little more about our Goal 2 house buying option. Do we throw Goal 2 out and don't even bother to make it? Well, that is what some people do because they only think in terms of solid, immoveable, obtainable goals. Me, I say, make the goal. There is nothing wrong with setting high expectations but stay flexible. Keep it fluid. Remember to take into account all the factors. You're not in control of all the elements in Goal 2. Staying rigid will break you when you are hit by the force of changes that are out of your control.

Always remember, Father in Heaven wants us happy. He wants us to reach our goals. He wants us to have the opportunity to fulfill our dreams. However, He also knows us better than we know our self. Therefore, He also knows the best path for obtaining that goal. God does love us and wants us happy in this temporal state of life.

The more flexible you are in your goal setting, the better the chance for success and happiness. I say, stay flexible with most of your goals. This does not mean there is no need for solid goal setting, not at all. There are parts of your life that need to be chiseled in stone.

> **(Bible New Testament: 1 Corinthians 2:9)[2]**
> *9 But as it is written, Eye hath not seen, nor ear heard, neither have entered into the heart of man, the things which God hath prepared for them that love him.*

Rule #3 'There are Fluid Goals & There are Solid Goals'

(Bible New Testament: Ephesians 2:4)[2]
4 But God, who is rich in mercy, for his great love wherewith he loved us,

(Book of Mormon: 2 Nephi 2:24-25)[3]
24 But behold, all things have been done in the wisdom of him who knoweth all things.
25 Adam fell that men might be; and men are, that they might have joy.

I Know You:

However, (yes, there is a, however) there are conditions God has set forth for our lives while here in mortality. God has plans and goals for us. In the Book of the Prophet Jeremiah, from the Bible Old Testament, God informs Jeremiah that he was foreordained to be a Prophet.

(Bible Old Testament: Jeremiah 1:5)[1]
5 Before I formed thee in the belly I knew thee; and before thou camest forth out of the womb I sanctified thee, and I ordained thee a prophet unto the nations.

In the Bible New Testament, Peter tells us how Christ was foreordained.

(Bible New Testament: 1 Peter 1:20)[2]
20 Who verily was foreordained before the foundation of the world,

Thomas S. Monson said this at a church General Conference Priesthood meeting:

(Thomas S. Monson, 2008 April General Conference, "Examples of Righteousness")[30]
"Every one of us has been foreordained for some work as [God's] chosen servant on whom he has seen fit to confer the priesthood and power to act in his name."

God has foreordained goals for all of us, but he has also given us all our free agency. We still have the freedom of choice while we learn and grow in this mortal state. We have the option to exercise that free agency at any time. And that includes not doing God's will. This is why the scripture tells us this:

> **(Doctrine & Covenants 121:34-37)[4]**
> *34 Behold, there are many called, but few are chosen. And why are they not chosen?*
>
> *35 Because their hearts are set so much upon the things of this world, and aspire to the honors of men, that they do not learn this one lesson—*
>
> *36 That the rights of the priesthood are inseparably connected with the powers of heaven, and that the powers of heaven cannot be controlled nor handled only upon the principles of righteousness.*
>
> *37 That they may be conferred upon us, it is true; but when we undertake to cover our sins, or to gratify our pride, our vain ambition, or to exercise control or dominion or compulsion upon the souls of the children of men, in any degree of unrighteousness, behold, the heavens withdraw themselves; the Spirit of the Lord is grieved; and when it is withdrawn, Amen to the priesthood or the authority of that man.*

Take that Side Street:

I keep most of my goals fluid that way, I can work them in with the will of Heavenly Father's foreordained destiny. I rarely know ahead of time what God's will is for me until I get there.

The more solid you try to make a fluid goal, the higher the chance for failure, and no one likes to fail. If you keep the goal fluid, what might have been a failure as a solid goal could turn out to be simply a sidestep or detour? You can think of it not as a failure but as the wise man Zig Ziglar did.

> **(Zig Ziglar)[31]**
> *"Failure is a detour, not a dead-end street."*

No one likes to hit a dead-end street, I sure don't. But I can handle detours. Remember Rule #1 'Failure is Not an Option'. I also know that if I handle the detours that are put in my path properly, and I have a righteous goal, God will bless me to accomplish it.

Depends How You Look at It:

In the two-goal examples I gave you, one could say that Goal 1, 'I will have a house of my own,' is a fluid goal, not a solid one. Here is the answer to that:

> **(Bible New Testament: John 14: 1-4)[2]**
> *1 Let not your heart be troubled: ye believe in God, believe also in me.*
>
> *2 In my Father's house are many mansions: if it were not so, I would have told you. I go to prepare a place for you.*
>
> *3 And if I go and prepare a place for you, I will come again, and receive you unto myself; that where I am, there ye may be also.*
>
> *4 And whither I go ye know, and the way ye know.*

Because of the Lord's Atonement, it is completely in my hands as to whether I make it to having a home in God's mansions. I didn't set a time as to when I would have a house or where it would be. If I don't have my own house here on Earth, I know that Jesus Christ's death and resurrection has promised me one with Him. This makes Goal 1 a solid goal.

I DO:

Here is another example of a fluid versus a solid goal from a marriage perspective. First, I need to establish that I, and those of my belief, believe that marriage can be for time and eternity. We call this type of marriage a 'Celestial Marriage' or 'Temple Marriage' because they are performed in a temple of the Lord by a person who has the Priesthood authority to bind couples for time and all eternity.

Rule #3 'There are Fluid Goals & There are Solid Goals'

(Bible New Testament: Matthew 16:19)[2]
19 And I will give unto thee the keys of the kingdom of heaven: and whatsoever thou shalt bind on earth shall be bound in heaven: and whatsoever thou shalt loose on earth shall be loosed in heaven.

(Bible New Testament: Matthew 18:18)[2]
18 Verily I say unto you, Whatsoever ye shall bind on earth shall be bound in heaven: and whatsoever ye shall loose on earth shall be loosed in heaven.

(Doctrine & Covenants 131:1-3)[4]
1 In the celestial glory there are three heavens or degrees;

2 And in order to obtain the highest, a man must enter into this order of the priesthood [meaning the new and everlasting covenant of marriage];

3 And if he does not, he cannot obtain it.

(Doctrine & Covenants 132:19)[4]
19 And again, verily I say unto you, if a man marry a wife by my word, which is my law, and by the new and everlasting covenant, and it is sealed unto them by the Holy Spirit of promise, by him who is anointed, unto whom I have appointed this power and the keys of this priesthood; and it shall be said unto them—Ye shall come forth in the first resurrection; and if it be after the first resurrection, in the next resurrection; and shall inherit thrones, kingdoms, principalities, and powers, dominions, all heights and depths—then shall it be written in the Lamb's Book of Life, that he shall commit no murder whereby to shed innocent blood, and if ye abide in my covenant, and commit no murder whereby to shed innocent blood, it shall be done unto them in all things whatsoever my servant hath put upon them, in time, and through all eternity; and shall be of full force when they are out of the world; and they shall pass by the angels, and the gods, which are set there, to their exaltation and glory in all things, as hath

been sealed upon their heads, which glory shall be a fulness and a continuation of the seeds forever and ever.

More Goals:

In this goal-setting scenario, Goal 3 is the solid goal which is: I will have a Celestial Marriage, and thus live in the Celestial Kingdom with my wife.

Goal 4 is a fluid goal, which is: I will have a Celestial Marriage with my current wife, Christine, and will live in the Celestial Kingdom with her.

Do you understand why Goal 3 is a solid, and Goal 4 is not? The solid goal is all in my control. As long as I follow the commandments as set out by Heavenly Father, He is bound to bless me with a Celestial Marriage. Heavenly Father cannot break the laws governing Celestial Marriage. If God did, He would cease to be God; for Heavenly Father, is bound to govern Himself by the same laws.

Goal 4 is fluid because I cannot control the will of my wife, Christine. She also has been endowed with free agency to choose her own goals and destiny.

Because my wife has her free agency, I cannot control at any given moment whether or not my wife is willing to be married to me for time and all eternity. For a Celestial marriage to work, both of the parties must be in sync. In the United States, unlike some countries, I cannot control whether or not my wife wishes to stay married to me till death do us part. Here in the United States, she could file for divorce at any time for any reason.

Red Light:

As a side note, I would like to throw in a warning to couples. There are times I have seen where a spouse will try to get their mate to do things their way by imposing unrighteous dominion over their mate. This would be considered an *been sealed upon their heads, which glory shall be a fulness and a continuation of the seeds forever and ever.*

More Goals:

In this goal-setting scenario, Goal 3 is the solid goal which is: I will have a Celestial Marriage, and thus live in the Celestial Kingdom with my wife.

Goal 4 is a fluid goal, which is: I will have a Celestial Marriage with my current wife, Christine, and will live in the Celestial Kingdom with her.

Do you understand why Goal 3 is a solid, and Goal 4 is not? The solid goal is all in my control. As long as I follow the commandments as set out by Heavenly Father, He is bound to bless me with a Celestial Marriage. Heavenly Father cannot break the laws governing Celestial Marriage. If God did, He would cease to be God; for Heavenly Father, is bound to govern Himself by the same laws.

Goal 4 is fluid because I cannot control the will of my wife, Christine. She also has been endowed with free agency to choose her own goals and destiny.

Because my wife has her free agency, I cannot control at any given moment whether or not my wife is willing to be married to me for time and all eternity. For a Celestial marriage to work, both of the parties must be in sync. In the United States, unlike some countries, I cannot control whether or not my wife wishes to stay married to me till death do us part. Here in the United States, she could file for divorce at any time for any reason.

Red Light:

As a side note, I would like to throw in a warning to couples. There are times I have seen where a spouse will try to get their mate to do things their way by imposing unrighteous dominion over their mate. This would be considered an

Rule #3 'There are Fluid Goals & There are Solid Goals'

(Bible New Testament: Matthew 16:19)[2]
19 And I will give unto thee the keys of the kingdom of heaven: and whatsoever thou shalt bind on earth shall be bound in heaven: and whatsoever thou shalt loose on earth shall be loosed in heaven.

(Bible New Testament: Matthew 18:18)[2]
18 Verily I say unto you, Whatsoever ye shall bind on earth shall be bound in heaven: and whatsoever ye shall loose on earth shall be loosed in heaven.

(Doctrine & Covenants 131:1-3)[4]
1 In the celestial glory there are three heavens or degrees;

2 And in order to obtain the highest, a man must enter into this order of the priesthood [meaning the new and everlasting covenant of marriage];

3 And if he does not, he cannot obtain it.

(Doctrine & Covenants 132:19)[4]
19 And again, verily I say unto you, if a man marry a wife by my word, which is my law, and by the new and everlasting covenant, and it is sealed unto them by the Holy Spirit of promise, by him who is anointed, unto whom I have appointed this power and the keys of this priesthood; and it shall be said unto them—Ye shall come forth in the first resurrection; and if it be after the first resurrection, in the next resurrection; and shall inherit thrones, kingdoms, principalities, and powers, dominions, all heights and depths—then shall it be written in the Lamb's Book of Life, that he shall commit no murder whereby to shed innocent blood, and if ye abide in my covenant, and commit no murder whereby to shed innocent blood, it shall be done unto them in all things whatsoever my servant hath put upon them, in time, and through all eternity; and shall be of full force when they are out of the world; and they shall pass by the angels, and the gods, which are set there, to their exaltation and glory in all things, as hath

attempt to supersede their mate's free agency. The Prophets tell you, and Heavenly Father tells you; give it up, stop. Free agency is a gift from God bestowed upon all. When a spouse imposes unrighteous dominion over their mate, the spouse is interfering with a blessing given to their mate by God. Repent or face the judgment of Heavenly Father. If you don't have a clear understanding of what God's definition of unrighteous dominion is, then it is time you find out. Your definition does not count; God's does.

Look a Rainbow:

On the brighter side, I will add this happy note regarding the current state of my marriage since I used it as an example. My wife and I have, at the time of this writing, been married for almost 38 years. That is not to say that we, like many couples, have not had our knockdown, dragged through the mud, hard times. As Christine and I work toward the goal of a Celestial Marriage, there have been a few detours. Most of the roadblocks we hit we placed in our own path. There were even times when our friends and family members were telling us to throw in the towel and end our marriage.

When my wife and I would first hit a roadblock, it did seem like a dead-end. We saw it as a failure at first. Like so many people, we allowed the blocked road to blind us. Not realizing that we had blinders on, we could not see a way around it. From our view, the marriage seemed to be at an end. However, after we allowed the initial shock of possible failure to calm, we each took an earnest inventory of ourselves, we fasted, and we prayed. That opened our eyes to a path around the roadblock. Heavenly Father never let us down. Some detours were long, rough roads, yet, as we chose to deal with the rough road we were traveling, He blessed us with a better understanding of each other. The marriage grew stronger and deeper. We learned that a good marriage requires a lot of effort to succeed. You cannot stop putting effort into your marriage when you hit a roadblock. That is the moment it requires the most effort to find a good detour.

Rule #3 'There are Fluid Goals & There are Solid Goals'

I knew I had an incredible woman when I married Chris. But I didn't realize how incredible until we hit what seemed to be dead ends in pursuit of our goal to be with each other in the Celestial Kingdom, and we took those detours.

It is Up to You:

Still, after 38 years of marriage, I can't say having Christine as my Celestial wife is a solid goal. The only way to make it a solid goal today, after 38 years of togetherness, is no different than it was yesterday, and that would be to take away her free agency. This is not an option because it introduces failure as soon as you do it. The answer to that has not changed in 38 years of marriage, either.

The taking of another person's free agency is not an option. I do not have the power to do so. I am not God. What I can do, and what I can control is to continue to develop all the Christ-like attributes possible to ensure the success of this celestial goal.

(Bible New Testament: 1 Peter 4:8)[2]
8 And above all things have fervent charity among yourselves: for charity shall cover the multitude of sins.

(Doctrine & Covenants 132:21-25)[4]
21 Verily, verily, I say unto you, except ye abide my law ye cannot attain to this glory.

22 For strait is the gate, and narrow the way that leadeth unto the exaltation and continuation of the lives, and few there be that find it, because ye receive me not in the world neither do ye know me.

23 But if ye receive me in the world, then shall ye know me, and shall receive your exaltation; that where I am ye shall be also.

24 This is eternal lives—to know the only wise and true God, and Jesus Christ, whom he hath sent. I am he. Receive ye, therefore, my law.

Rule #3 'There are Fluid Goals & There are Solid Goals'

25 Broad is the gate, and wide the way that leadeth to the deaths; and many there are that go in there at, because they receive me not, neither do they abide in my law.

(Doctrine & Covenants 4:5-7)[4]
5 And faith, hope, charity and love, with an eye single to the glory of God, qualify him for the work.

6 Remember faith, virtue, knowledge, temperance, patience, brotherly kindness, godliness, charity, humility, diligence.

7 Ask, and ye shall receive; knock, and it shall be opened unto you. Amen.

I pray Christine will continue choosing to endure with me in this mortal state. We pray together that as we both grow, we will understand the Lord's will for us. We also pray that each day, as we fight against the immoral ways of this world that constantly try to bombard us, His blessing will be upon us to guide us through the detours.

The Toolbox:

Prayer and scripture study are the tools the Lord has provided us to help us accomplish any goal we set, whether it is fluid or solid. The Lord doesn't care if your goal is one that is temporal or spiritual. Prayer and scripture study needs to be a vital part of success.

I testify to you that, had I not included my Father in Heaven's guidance as part of all my plans, there is not a goal or task I could have completed, whether it be work, home, my marriage, or my church duties.

I say this in the name of Jesus Christ. AMEN.

Rule #3 'There are Fluid Goals & There are Solid Goals'

Endnotes:

1 **King James Version of the Bible, The Old Testament of Our Lord and Saviour Jesus Christ.** Published by The Church of Jesus Christ of Latter-day Saints, Salt Lake City, Utah, USA. Copywrite 2013.

2 **King James Version of the Bible, The New Testament of Our Lord and Saviour Jesus Christ.** Published by The Church of Jesus Christ of Latter-day Saints, Salt Lake City, Utah, USA. Copywrite 2013.

3 **The Book of Mormon Another Testament of Jesus Christ.** Published by The Church of Jesus Christ of Latter-day Saints, Salt Lake City, Utah, USA. The first English edition published in Palmyra, New York, USA, in 1830. Copywrite 2013.

4 **The Doctrine and Covenants of The Church of Jesus Christ of Latter-Day Saints.** Containing Revelations Give to Joseph Smith, the Prophet. With some additions by his successors in the Presidency of the Church. Published by The Church of Jesus Christ of Latter-day Saints, Salt Lake City, Utah, USA. Copywrite 2013.

5 **The Pearl of Great Price.** A selection from the revelations, translations, and narrations of Joseph Smith, First Prophet, seer, and revelator to The Church of Jesus Christ of Latter-Day Saints. Published by The Church of Jesus Christ of Latter-day Saints, Salt Lake City, Utah, USA. Copywrite 2013.

6 **Elbert Hubbard, Goal Setting Quote.** Found on website https://the-happy-manager.com/tips/goal-setting-quotes/, and viewed on February 05, 2019. © 2007 - 2019 The Happy Manager | Web Design by Sutton Silver, The Happy Manager, is owned by Apex Leadership Ltd. Krystal Server.

7 **Dr. Norman Vincent Peale.** "Six Attitudes for Winners," Tyndale House Publishing (1989). Found on website https://www.azquotes.com/quote/1056776, and viewed on February 05, 2019.

8 **Jim Rohn.** Jim Rohn. (n.d.) BrainyQuote.com, BrainyMedia Inc, 2019. https://www.brainyquote.com/quotes/jim_rohn_165075, accessed February 5, 2019.

9 **Franklin Roosevelt.** Franklin D. Roosevelt Quotes. (n.d.). BrainyQuote.com. Retrieved February 5, 2019, from BrainyQuote.com Web site: https://www.brainyquote.com/quotes/franklin_d_roosevelt_143162.

10 **Brian Tracy.** Brian Tracy Quotes. (n.d.). BrainyQuote.com. Retrieved February 5, 2019, from BrainyQuote.com Web site: https://www.brainyquote.com/quotes/brian_tracy_386350.

11 **Earl Nightingale.** Earl Nightingale Quotes. (n.d.). BrainyQuote.com. Retrieved February 6, 2019, from BrainyQuote.com Web site: https://www.brainyquote.com/quotes/earl_nightingale_383343.

12 **Zig Ziglar.** Zig Ziglar Quotes. (n.d.). BrainyQuote.com. Retrieved February 6, 2019, from BrainyQuote.com Web site: https://www.brainyquote.com/quotes/zig_ziglar_120890.

Rule #3 'There are Fluid Goals & There are Solid Goals'

13. **Jim Rohn**. Jim Rohn. (n.d.). ThinkExist.com Quotations, Retrieved February 6, 2019, from ThinkExist.com Website http://thinkexist.com/quotation/i_find_it_fascinating_that_most_people_plan_their/289463.html.

14. **Helen Keller**. Helen Keller Quotes. (n.d.). BrainyQuote.com. Retrieved February 6, 2019, from BrainyQuote.com Web site: https://www.brainyquote.com/quotes/helen_keller_121474.

15. **James Allen**. Published in "As a man Thinketh" in 1903. Jamesallenlibrary.com. Retrieved February 6, 2019, from http://www.jamesallenlibrary.com/authors/james-allen/as-a-man-thinketh/thought-and-purpose.

16. **Thomas Fuller**. ThinkExist.com Quotations. Retrieved February 6, 2019, from ThinkExist.com Website http://thinkexist.com/quotation/a_good_archer_is_not_known_by_his_arrows_but_his/165512.html.

17. **Robert A. Heinlein**. Quotationspage.com, The Quotations Page, Quotation #2099 from Laura Moncur's Motivational Quotations. Retrieved February 6, 2019, from Quotationspage.com Website, http://www.quotationspage.com/quote/2099.html.

18. **Gerald L. Penhollow**. "Jerry's 20 Rules for Managing Life".

19. **Tony Robbins**. Tony Robbins Quotes. (n.d.). BrainyQuote.com. Retrieved February 6, 2019, from BrainyQuote.com Web site: https://www.brainyquote.com/quotes/tony_robbins_173237.

20. **Arnold H. Glasgow**. Arnold H. Glasgow Quotes. (n.d.). BrainyQuote.com. Retrieved February 6, 2019, from BrainyQuote.com Web site: https://www.brainyquote.com/quotes/arnold_h_glasow_150772

21. **Aristotle**. ThinkExist.com Quotations. Retrieved February 6, 2019, from ThinkExist.com Website http://thinkexist.com/quotation/man_is_a_goal_seeking_animal-his_life_only_has/297104.html.

22. **Kathy Seligman**. Lorenlung.wordpress.com "Devotions: Food for Body and Spirit" page, subtitle "Insirational Quotes". Retrieved February 6, 2019, from lorenlung.wordpress.com Website https://lorenlung.wordpress.com/inspirational-quotes/.

23. **Catherine Pulsifer**. Catherine Pulsifer (n.d.), Inspirational Quotes, inspirationalquotes4u.com, Retrieved February 6, 2019, from website: https://www.inspirationalquotes4u.com/pulsiferquotes/index.html.

24. **Ralph Waldo Emerson**. (n.d.). ThinkExist.com Quotations. Retrieved February 6, 2019, from ThinkExist.com Website http://thinkexist.com/quotation/the-world-makes-way-for-the-man-who-knows-where/535964.html.

25. **Geoffrey F. Abert**. (n.d.) ThinkExist.com Quotations. Retrieved February 6, 2019, from ThinkExist.com website: http://thinkexist.com/search/searchquotation.asp?search=The+most+important+thing+about+goals+is+having+one.

Rule #3 'There are Fluid Goals & There are Solid Goals'

26 **Denis Waitley**. (n.d.). ThinkExist.com Quotations. Retrieved February 6, 2019, from ThinkExist.com http://thinkexist.com/quotation/the_reason_most_people_never_reach_their_goals_is/13148.html.

27 **Will Rogers**. Will Rogers Quotes. (n.d.). BrainyQuote.com. Retrieved February 6, 2019, from BrainyQuote.com Website: https://www.brainyquote.com/quotes/will_rogers_104938.

28 **Edmund Hilary**. Edmund Hillary > Quotes > Quotable Quote (n.d). GoodReads.com. Retrieved November 26, 2019 https://www.goodreads.com/quotes/12605-you-don-t-have-to-be-a-hero-to-accomplish-great. Also, ThinkExist.com Quotations. Retrieved February 6, 2019, from ThinkExist.com http://thinkexist.com/quotation/you_don-t_have_to_be_a_fantastic_hero_to_do/340060.html.

29 **Pablo Picasso**. Pablo Picasso Quotes. (n.d.). BrainyQuote.com. Retrieved February 6, 2019, from BrainyQuote.com Website: https://www.brainyquote.com/quotes/pablo_picasso_120939.

30 **Thomas S. Monson, 2008 April General Conference, "Examples of Righteousness"**. The 178th Annual General Conference of the Church of Jesus Christ of Latter-day Saints, April 5, 2008, Saturday evening Priesthood session. Published in the Ensign magazine, Volume 38 Number 05, May 2008, page-66 paragraph-03. An official magazine of the Church of Jesus Christ of Latter-day Saints, published by the Church of Jesus Christ of Latter-day Saints, 50 E. North Temple Street, Salt Lake City, UT, 84150-3220, USA. Also, retrieved Nov 26, 2019, from Ensign, ChurchofJesusChrist.Org website: https://www.churchofjesuschrist.org/study/ensign/2008/05/examples-of-righteousness?lang=eng

31 **Zig Ziglar**. Zig Ziglar Quotes. (n.d.). BrainyQuote.com. Retrieved February 6, 2019, from BrainyQuote.com Web site: https://www.brainyquote.com/quotes/zig_ziglar_378594.

Rule #3 'There are Fluid Goals & There are Solid Goals'

Give Me 10 More

Rule #4
'Always Give 110 Percent'

Rule #4 'Always Give 110 Percent'

Simple Facts:

If at the end of the day you say; I have done all that I can do. I would ask you to ask yourself: Have I done more than I thought I could do? Have I grown just a little in any aspect of my life? Am I, in some way, a better person today than yesterday?

To grow and learn, it requires more from us than giving 100 percent. For, it is when we reach beyond our known abilities and tap into our unknown potential, that we exceed our current capabilities. To say I have given 100 percent is to say, "I have done what I know." In that same breath, you also said, "I have learned nothing new."

You give that extra 10 percent when you challenge yourself to contribute more than the requirements or exceed expectations. This is when you can say to yourself, "I have given 110 percent."

Do you challenge yourself to contribute more than the requirements or to exceed expectations? Or do you merely meet them?

Trash It:

Some people just don't get it when I tell them that to succeed, in any aspect of life, whether it is temporal or spiritual, you need to grow, and growth requires you to give 110 percent. They cannot grasp this giving of an extra 10 percent beyond the 100. They get stuck on this little fact that 100 percent is everything; therefore, there can be no more.

To those that cannot understand 'the giving 110% philosophy,' I say, you must also be the ones that believe that impossible means absolutely impossible. I call this type of person close-minded. Close-minded people also tend to be the same type of people that cannot think outside the box. They only see what's in the box. In their world, anything outside the box doesn't exist. What does not exist is, therefore impossible. To the closed-minded, anything over 100 percent cannot exist. Therefore, 110 percent cannot exist and is thus impossible.

I say what may be impossible today becomes possible tomorrow because of those individuals who stretch themselves beyond the 100 percent and give that extra 10 percent to do more and to learn more in order to have more than they had today.

There is a whole website that is all about how you can't give 110 percent. On this website, George Krueger and Mary-Lynn Foster pose a good argument on the theory of not being able to give more than 100 percent. I have included a part of the article for you to read. Some of you may agree with them. I do not.

> **(George Krueger & Mary-Lynn Foster, "Stop Giving 110 Percent to Be a Success")**[6]
> *"We hear people say this all the time – 'I gave 110 percent.'*
>
> *(It's funny – if you watch them closely, you'll see that, most of the time, most of the people who make this claim aren't even close. But that's not our point today.)*
>
> *This is a phrase we'd like to see just go away. It sets false expectations. You can't do it. You can't give 110 percent. It's physically impossible.*
>
> *If you believe you can, you're wrong. So stop trying.*
>
> *You're not a slacker if you don't give 110 percent. You won't come up short if you don't give 110 percent. Can you pour 8.8 ounces of liquid in a cup with an 8-ounce capacity? Of course not. By trying, you waste valuable energy and effort. Your capacity is 100 percent. That's the maximum, the most you can do.*
>
> *So, focus on giving 100 percent to everything you do. No more. No less."*

Rule #4 'Always Give 110 Percent'

Work

"Give 100 percent to your work. By the way, 100 percent still means going the extra mile, doing those things that most people don't do."

Punch a Hole in It:

Wow! What do you think of what George Krueger and Mary-Lynn Foster wrote? I'll start by repeating the last statement they made under the title 'Work'.

(George Krueger & Mary-Lynn Foster, "Stop Giving 110 Percent to Be a Success")[6]
"Give 100 percent to your work. By the way, 100 percent still means going the extra mile, doing those things that most people don't do."

Ok, they say to give 100 percent to your work. That is a good start. However, they didn't stop there, did they? George and Mary-Lynn go on to say, and I quote, "By the way, 100 percent still means going the extra mile...." My comment to that statement is, what do you think going the extra mile is? The 100 percent is doing what the job requirements are. The extra mile is 10 percent more; thus, you give 110 percent.

The Proof is In the Pudding:

Then there is the question George and Mary-Lynn ask you to think about: Can you pour 8.8 ounces of liquid in a cup with an 8-ounce capacity? My answer to the question is yes, I can pour 8.8 ounces into an 8-ounce capacity cup. They didn't say will the 8-ounce cup hold 8.8 ounces. Ok, you can say I gave a lame answer, but you cannot say I did not provide a factual answer.

Let's try to deal with the 8.8 ounces into an 8-ounce capacity cup this way. If I compress the 8.8 ounces of fluid into an 8-ounce pressurize container, I can get 8.8 ounces uncompressed into an 8-ounce container, and I have not broken the laws of physics as we know them today. You see,

Rule #4 'Always Give 110 Percent'

this is where I think beyond the boundaries, and that is the extra 10 percent.

Some may say that you cannot compress fluids. Well, you can. However, it requires a great deal of pressure to accomplish a little compression. For that reason, liquids and solids are sometimes referred to as being incompressible. With today's technology compressing fluid by 10% is possible; it may not be practical, but it is possible. Now, compressing carbon to create diamonds, which takes more pressure than compressing water to gain 10%, is practical and is performed every day.

Here is more proof that I can get a 110% into an 8-ounce capacity cup. Apple juice, that's right, let's use apple juice instead of water this time. Only this time I won't compress the juice, I will condense it. If I take and squeeze 100% apple juice right from a bag of fresh apples, I will have 100% apple juice. Agree? If I then boil out some of the water (which is a part of the apple juice that makes up its 100% juice), I then can condense the juice to a 110% concentrated juice. It is still apple juice. I then pour the concentrate into an 8-ounce cup. I now have a 110% apple juice in an 8-ounce container. To turn it back into only 100% apple juice, I reconstitute it.

Manufacturers have been using the concentrate method for years. Of course, the question with the manufactures directions to reconstitute is whether you are getting back your 100%, or is it a number other than 100%?

Can you beat the laws of physics? Well, no, but I don't believe we know all the laws, and I do believe the laws of physics bend. Let's look to the Bible for some help with this point of view.

> **(Bible New Testament: Mark 6:38-44)**[2]
> *38 He saith unto them, How many loaves have ye? go and see. And when they knew, they say, Five, and two fishes.*
>
> *39 And he commanded them to make all sit down by companies upon the green grass.*

Rule #4 'Always Give 110 Percent'

this is where I think beyond the boundaries, and that is the extra 10 percent.

Some may say that you cannot compress fluids. Well, you can. However, it requires a great deal of pressure to accomplish a little compression. For that reason, liquids and solids are sometimes referred to as being incompressible. With today's technology compressing fluid by 10% is possible; it may not be practical, but it is possible. Now, compressing carbon to create diamonds, which takes more pressure than compressing water to gain 10%, is practical and is performed every day.

Here is more proof that I can get a 110% into an 8-ounce capacity cup. Apple juice, that's right, let's use apple juice instead of water this time. Only this time I won't compress the juice, I will condense it. If I take and squeeze 100% apple juice right from a bag of fresh apples, I will have 100% apple juice. Agree? If I then boil out some of the water (which is a part of the apple juice that makes up its 100% juice), I then can condense the juice to a 110% concentrated juice. It is still apple juice. I then pour the concentrate into an 8-ounce cup. I now have a 110% apple juice in an 8-ounce container. To turn it back into only 100% apple juice, I reconstitute it.

Manufacturers have been using the concentrate method for years. Of course, the question with the manufactures directions to reconstitute is whether you are getting back your 100%, or is it a number other than 100%?

Can you beat the laws of physics? Well, no, but I don't believe we know all the laws, and I do believe the laws of physics bend. Let's look to the Bible for some help with this point of view.

(Bible New Testament: Mark 6:38-44)[2]
38 He saith unto them, How many loaves have ye? go and see. And when they knew, they say, Five, and two fishes.

39 And he commanded them to make all sit down by companies upon the green grass.

Work

"Give 100 percent to your work. By the way, 100 percent still means going the extra mile, doing those things that most people don't do."

Punch a Hole in It:

Wow! What do you think of what George Krueger and Mary-Lynn Foster wrote? I'll start by repeating the last statement they made under the title 'Work'.

> **(George Krueger & Mary-Lynn Foster, "Stop Giving 110 Percent to Be a Success")**[6]
> *"Give 100 percent to your work. By the way, 100 percent still means going the extra mile, doing those things that most people don't do."*

Ok, they say to give 100 percent to your work. That is a good start. However, they didn't stop there, did they? George and Mary-Lynn go on to say, and I quote, "By the way, 100 percent still means going the extra mile...." My comment to that statement is, what do you think going the extra mile is? The 100 percent is doing what the job requirements are. The extra mile is 10 percent more; thus, you give 110 percent.

The Proof is In the Pudding:

Then there is the question George and Mary-Lynn ask you to think about: Can you pour 8.8 ounces of liquid in a cup with an 8-ounce capacity? My answer to the question is yes, I can pour 8.8 ounces into an 8-ounce capacity cup. They didn't say will the 8-ounce cup hold 8.8 ounces. Ok, you can say I gave a lame answer, but you cannot say I did not provide a factual answer.

Let's try to deal with the 8.8 ounces into an 8-ounce capacity cup this way. If I compress the 8.8 ounces of fluid into an 8-ounce pressurize container, I can get 8.8 ounces uncompressed into an 8-ounce container, and I have not broken the laws of physics as we know them today. You see,

40 And they sat down in ranks, by hundreds, and by fifties.

41 And when he had taken the five loaves and the two fishes, he looked up to heaven, and blessed, and brake the loaves, and gave them to his disciples to set before them; and the two fishes divided he among them all.

42 And they did all eat, and were filled.

43 And they took up twelve baskets full of the fragments, and of the fishes.

44 And they that did eat of the loaves were about five thousand men.

(Bible New Testament: John 4:46)[2]
46 So Jesus came again into Cana of Galilee, where he made the water wine.

(Bible New Testament: John 2:3-11)[2]
3 And when they wanted wine, the mother of Jesus saith unto him, They have no wine.

4 Jesus saith unto her, Woman, what have I to do with thee? mine hour is not yet come.

5 His mother saith unto the servants, Whatsoever he saith unto you, do it.

6 And there were set there six waterpots of stone, after the manner of the purifying of the Jews, containing two or three firkins apiece.

7 Jesus saith unto them, Fill the waterpots with water. And they filled them up to the brim.

8 And he saith unto them, Draw out now, and bear unto the governor of the feast. And they bare it.

9 When the ruler of the feast had tasted the water that was made wine, and knew not whence it was: (but the servants which drew the water knew;) the governor of the feast called the bridegroom,

10 And saith unto him, Every man at the beginning doth set forth good wine; and when men have well drunk, then that which is worse: but thou hast kept the good wine until now.

11 This beginning of miracles did Jesus in Cana of Galilee, and manifested forth his glory; and his disciples believed on him.

Impossible You Say:

So, did Jesus break the laws of physics? Or does He just know more about them than we do? If you believe Jesus's story, that the fishes and the bread fed five thousand, then we can say the Apostles pulled more food out of the baskets than was put into them. Thus, can an 8-ounce container hold 8.8 ounces? Jesus Christ said, if we have the faith, we can perform all the miracles He did.

(Bible New Testament: Matthew 17:20)[2]
20 And Jesus said unto them, Because of your unbelief: for verily I say unto you, If ye have faith as a grain of mustard seed, ye shall say unto this mountain, Remove hence to yonder place; and it shall remove; and nothing shall be impossible unto you.

(Bible New Testament: Matthew 21:19-22)[2]
19 And when he saw a fig tree in the way, he came to it, and found nothing thereon, but leaves only, and said unto it, Let no fruit grow on thee henceforward for ever. And presently the fig tree withered away.

20 And when the disciples saw it, they marvelled, saying, How soon is the fig tree withered away!

21 Jesus answered and said unto them, Verily I say unto you, If ye have faith, and doubt not, ye shall not only do this which is done to the fig tree, but also if ye shall say unto this mountain, Be thou removed, and be thou cast into the sea; it shall be done.

Rule #4 'Always Give 110 Percent'

22 And all things, whatsoever ye shall ask in prayer, believing, ye shall receive.

Another Point of View:

Here is another group's way of looking at the 110 percent rule. We'll call them the '100 Percent Is Max' group. This group says humanity can never reach 110 percent because 100 percent is the max, the end, there is no more.

Based on this group's philosophy, if a person were to reach 100 percent they are at their full potential. The person can no longer learn anything new or do anything more. That's it; you are maxed out. No more to give, no more to gain.

I could be wrong, but I am going to make a bold statement and say, "mankind is always growing and learning." Therefore, based on the '100 Percent Is Max' group's philosophy, you can never give 100 percent of yourself. No matter how hard you try, you cannot. If you think you have reached that 100 percent mark, sorry, you would be wrong. Why? Well, using the '100 Percent Is Max' group's philosophy and adding in the truth of my statement that humanity is always learning and growing, you can never reach 100 percent.

Ouch! My head is hurting. Did you absorb all that?

I know that I am always growing and learning every day. So, for me, I find the 100 Percent Is Max group's philosophy, sad and depressing. To me, it is like saying, I can never reach my goal of 100 percent in this lifetime. No matter how hard I try. Therefore, I get zero motivation from this group's philosophy. Instead, it gives me the feeling of: Why try, I can't accomplish my goal anyway?

God said all shall be made perfect in Him. You cannot be perfect unless you are at 100%. Therefore, I can reach 100 percent and still continue to grow that 10 percent more. Because, in my faith, we believe that when we leave this mortal body and become perfected, learning continues.

(Bible New Testament: John 17:23)[2]

23 I in them, and thou in me, that they may be made perfect in one; and that the world may know that thou hast sent me, and hast loved them, as thou hast loved me.

(Doctrine & Covenant 76:69)[4]

69 These are they who are just men made perfect through Jesus the mediator of the new covenant, who wrought out this perfect atonement through the shedding of his own blood.

Your Choice:

If I have not given you a headache by now with all this thinking, let me try a little harder. As with everything you see, read, or observe in life, it comes down to a matter of viewpoint. So, how do we decide which view is for you? Is it the view: 100 percent is max? Or is it: we can do 110 percent? Or are they both the correct way to view life?

I am going to mix things up a bit and make it a little extra challenging. Let's see if you can tie all I am about to give you together. See if you can figure out how it fits in with the '100 Percent Is Max' group, or George Krueger and Mary-Lynn Foster arguments, vs my 110 percent philosophy. Try and keep up. If I lose you in my attempt to have a little fun while learning, I am sorry. Here I go.

How do we measure an inch? How do we determine how big an inch is? What color is red? How do we determine what the color of red is, or how red is red? When we are comparing things to be equal or not equal, must they be the same? Do we compare apples to apples, or can it be apples to oranges? Can an apple equal an orange?

Let's take the apples and oranges question first. Can an apple equal an orange? I say yes and no. It depends on how you are comparing them. If you are comparing them as fruit, then they are equal. Both belong to the fruit group. Both fruits also grow on trees. However, if you say an apple and orange are the same type of fruit, then you would be wrong. Can you tie this back to the '100 Percent Is Max group', or George Krueger and Mary-Lynn Foster arguments, vs my 110 percent philosophy?

Now let's take the color and inch questions and evaluate them together. What one person's eyes see may not be what another person sees. The distance of an inch can appear bigger to one than another. This is the same with color. Red can take on a different hue to two different people. So what color is red, and how red is red? These same sight color issues are found in animals and differ more between animal species than between human species. But I'll stick to humans, as I don't want to wind and twist your brain around too much by sidetracking too far out into left field. I am not trying intentionally to lose you. I am trying to give you something to think about as I make my point.

To get people to agree on what something is or is not when dealing with measurements or colors, we have to agree on a standard. Red is red based upon an industry standard that was agreed upon by a group. An inch is an inch because we all agree to use the same measuring stick. Therefore, the measuring stick we use must be perfectly cloned from the original.

If we are all using the same color standard, then we have agreed on what the color red will look like. Yet, when we view the color that we have determined to be red, it may look more vivid to one person than another. Then it does not matter how red the color red is. Or does it?

Because we all see colors differently, there are multiple groups that have determined what the color red will be. There is a Pantone color standard and a RAL color standard, for example. For each defined standard, if your eyes are good, you can see that the color red differs slightly. I prefer the Pantone color system.

Rule #4 'Always Give 110 Percent'

Let's get back to that cloned measuring stick. When measuring distance, we have the Imperial or United States customary system and the metric system. Which cloned stick standard are you using? Although I am required to use the Imperial or United States customary system more often, I prefer the metric system. I find the metric system more precise and simpler to use.

Which standard do you want to use as a part of governing your life? Is it George Krueger's and Mary-Lynn Foster's argument, the 100 Percent Is Max group, or is it my 110 Percent philosophy? How you want to manage your thinking and from what viewpoint you choose to view life will determine your choice. Any one of the options could get you to where you want to go in life. I like my choice of the color standard for red better. It's more vivid. I believe that the 110 percent philosophy is more precise, simpler, and more to the truth (vivid). And being more truthful, I believe, makes my choice, of 110 percent, right, and all the others wrong, (LOL). That is how I wish to view things. That is why I call this my book of rules. You don't agree with it? Don't, and write your own rules.

Define It for Me:

I think we can agree that everything is measured from a set standard or a base. Therefore, I thought it best that I defined my standard for Rule #4 *'Always Give 110 Percent'*:

> **Definition 1**: Giving what is required to complete the task is 100 percent. The additional 10 percent is given when you go the extra mile. Thus, you get 110 percent.

> **Definition 2**: Giving all you know at that point and time is, the 100 percent. Pushing forward in faith and reaching for what you don't know, while believing the knowledge will be given to you as you need it in order to succeed, that is the extra 10 percent. Thus, you get 110 percent.

The Main Point:

The whole point of Rule #4 *'Always Give 110 Percent'* is that it helps you and me stretch ourselves each day. By reaching for the unknown, having faith, trusting in the Father in Heaven that He will give us the tools that we need to give more than is simply required, you and I grow to be better than who we are today.

Rule #4 is a simple, easy way to remind me to stay focused, and it motivates me to work in the right direction in those times that I am tired and feel I can't go on. On many occasions, I feel I don't have the energy to continue. I would just prefer to be somewhere else than where I am. I wish the work would go away. My mind starts thinking of taking shortcuts or just doing the minimum required. This is where my belief in Rule #4 helps me to be a better person than I want to be at that moment. When I make it through a tough moment by giving 110 percent, afterward, I feel much better than if I had not given my best effort. Knowing that I did better than my best when I least wanted to work always makes for good motivational feelings.

If your brain can't handle the 110 percent concept, then, as I said, rewrite the rule. I am not here to dictate how you rule your life and the paths you take. But I am here to try and help you. I believe that I owe that to you, as in paying it forward. I believe the 110 percent philosophy is the best and the correct life governing option. I believe in the philosophy as I defined it. And I am pleased to share it with you for the purpose of helping you, be a better you.

I Believe:

The concept behind Rule #4 is to give you words of encouragement that will help you push beyond your comfort zone. It is in the 'My Rule Book' to help you and me to do our best always. It doesn't matter whether others notice that extra 10% we give or not. God is always watching and always knows.

Rule #4 'Always Give 110 Percent'

Whether God is watching, or not, does not matter. It is your mindset to the rule that matters.

I apply Rule #4 in my life, not because Father in Heaven is always watching me. I do it because it is the right thing to do. That is my mindset. It is who I want to be, and who I want to be, is a better me tomorrow than who I am today. I am sharing this rule with you to help you to be a better you.

Rule #4 will not work if you don't have the right mindset or you are not willing to put in the work. No matter what aspect of life, whether it is for temporal gain or spiritual uplifting, you must have a strong mindset when you are applying Rule #4. First, you must believe in the willpower of Rule #1 'Failure is Not an Option', and second, you must have a strong belief that you can do more than 100 percent.

Rule #4 *'Always Give 110 Percent'* is your greatest ally on the path to becoming better than you are today. It will pull you through when you hit that 100 percent wall and think you cannot make it any further.

A Few Words from The Famous:

There are many people, great and small, that have left us words of encouragement to help us see and go beyond who we are today. I am including a few (several, LOL) quotes from others that likewise want us to see our true worth. Please read them and enjoy them as I did.

> **(Henry Wadsworth Longfellow)[7]**
> *The heights by great men reached and kept,*
> *Were not attained by sudden flight,*
> *But they, while their companions slept,*
> *Were toiling upward in the night.*
>
> **(Joseph B. Wirthlin, 2008 October General Conference, "Come What May, and Love It")[8]**
> "One morning I remember pulling out a small card and threading it through my typewriter. Among the words that I typed for her were these: 'The simple

secret is this: put your trust in the Lord, do your best, then leave the rest to Him.'"

(Martin Luther King, Jr.)[9]
"If a man is called a streetsweeper, he should sweep streets even as Michelangelo painted, or Beethoven composed music, or Shakespeare wrote poetry. He should sweep streets so well that all the hosts of heaven and Earth will pause to say, Here lived a great streetsweeper who did his job well."

(Gordon B. Hinckley)[10]
"Mediocrity will never do. You are capable of something better."

(Denis M. Wagner III)[11]
"If someone tells you that you have potential it's because you haven't done anything yet, get busy."

(Joseph de Maistre)[12]
"There are no easy methods of learning difficult things; the method is to close your door, give out that you are not at home, and work."

(Antonio Porchia)[13]
"No one understands that you have given everything. You must give more."

(Author Unknown)[14]
"God gave us two ends - one to sit on and one to think with. Success depends on which one you use. Head you win, tail you lose."

(George Bernard Shaw)[15]
"When I was young, I observed that nine out of ten things I did were failures. So I did ten times more work."

(Swami Sivananda)[16]
"Put your heart, mind, and soul even to your smallest acts. This is the secret of success."

(Yogi Berra)[17]
"You give 100 percent in the first half of the game, and if that isn't enough in the second half you give what's left."

(Don Zimmer)[18]
"What you lack in talent can be made up with desire, hustle and giving 110 percent all the time."

(Bible New Testament: 1 Thessalonians 5:21)[2]
21 Prove all things; hold fast that which is good.

(Doctrine & Covenant 9:7-8)[4]
7 Behold, you have not understood; you have supposed that I would give it unto you, when you took no thought save it was tobask me.

8 But, behold, I say unto you, that you must study it out in your mind; then you must ask me if it be right, and if it is right I will cause that your bosom shall burn within you; therefore, you shall feel that it is right.

Closing Remarks:

My first four rules:

>Rule #1 *'Failure is Not an Option'*
>
>Rule #2 *'Don't Assume'*
>
>Rule #3 *'There are Fluid Goals and Solid Goals'*
>
>Rule #4 *'Always Gave 110 Percent'*

These rules are the heart of all the other 17 rules. These four rules form the base that is needed to succeed in implementing all the other 17 rules in this book. Study these four rules and see if you can understand why I placed them in the priority order that I have.

I look at Rule #4 as being the glue that binds all the other rules for living together. Rule #4 is the connecting link that holds the chain of rules together and keeps them all firmly in place in our hearts and minds. Rule #4 *'Always Give 110 Percent'* plays many roles and wears many hats. Rule #4 is the 'Implementer' for all the rules, and it is the 'Motivator' for implementing the rules. Rule #4 is also the 'Invoker' to our conscience, reminding us what we must do to grow, learn, and succeed beyond who we are today.

As children, our loving parents strive each day to help us to learn and grow while we are under their care. As you give 110% to your parents in their endeavor to help you grow, they will want to bless you even more. So, it is with Heavenly Father, for we are always under His care. If you give 110 percent to your heavenly parent, God, He too will bless your life.

I bear you this testimony that if you give God our Father in Heaven 110%, He will pour more blessings upon you beyond what you could ever imagine. I say this in the name of Jesus Christ. AMEN

Endnotes:

1 **King James Version of the Bible, The Old Testament of Our Lord and Saviour Jesus Christ.** Published by The Church of Jesus Christ of Latter-day Saints, Salt Lake City, Utah, USA. Copywrite 2013.

2 **King James Version of the Bible, The New Testament of Our Lord and Saviour Jesus Christ.** Published by The Church of Jesus Christ of Latter-day Saints, Salt Lake City, Utah, USA. Copywrite 2013.

3 **The Book of Mormon Another Testament of Jesus Christ.** Published by The Church of Jesus Christ of Latter-day Saints, Salt Lake City, Utah, USA. The first English edition published in Palmyra, New York, USA, in 1830. Copywrite 2013.

4 **The Doctrine and Covenants of The Church of Jesus Christ of Latter-Day Saints.** Containing Revelations Give to Joseph Smith, the Prophet. With some additions by his successors in the Presidency of the Church. Published by The Church of Jesus Christ of Latter-day Saints, Salt Lake City, Utah, USA. Copywrite 2013.

5 **The Pearl of Great Price.** A selection from the revelations, translations, and narrations of Joseph Smith, First Prophet, seer, and revelator to The Church of Jesus Christ of Latter-Day Saints. Published by The Church of Jesus Christ of Latter-day Saints, Salt Lake City, Utah, USA. Copywrite 2013.

6 **George Krueger & Mary-Lynn Foster.** (n.d.). Biggsuccess.com Blog "Stop Giving 110 Percent to Be a Success" June 20, 2012/in Personal Development /by George Krueger & Mary-Lynn Foster. Retrieved February 6, 2019, from Biggsuccess.com Web site: https://biggsuccess.com/2012/06/20/stop-giving-110-percent-to-be-a-success/.

7 **Henry Wadsworth Longfellow**, Henry Wadsworth Longfellow Quotes. (n.d.). BrainyQuote.com. Retrieved February 8, 2019, from BrainyQuote.com Web site: https://www.brainyquote.com/quotes/henry_wadsworth_longfello_129800.

8 **Joseph B. Wirthlin, 2008 October General Conference, "Come What May, and Love It."** The 178th Semiannual General Conference of the Church of Jesus Christ of Latter-day Saints, October 4, 2008, Saturday Afternoon Session. Published in the Ensign magazine, Volume 38 Number 11, November 2008, page-28, sub-titled 'Trust in the Father and the Son' paragraph-05. An official magazine of the Church of Jesus Christ of Latter-day Saints, published by the Church of Jesus Christ of Latter-day Saints, 50 E. North Temple Street, Salt Lake City, UT, 84150-3220, USA. Also, retrieved Nov 26, 2019, from Ensign, ChurchofJesusChrist.Org website: https://www.churchofjesuschrist.org/study/ensign/2008/11/come-what-may-and-love-it?lang=eng

9 **Martin Luther King, Jr.** Martin Luther King, Jr. Quotes. (n.d.). PassItOn.com. Retrieved February 7, 2019, from https://www.passiton.com/inspirational-quotes/3684-if-a-man-is-called-to-be-a-streetsweeper-he.

Rule #4 'Always Give 110 Percent'

10 **Gordon B. Hinckley**, (n.d.). January 5, 2017, Daily Quote: Mediocrity Will Never Do, www.Mormonchannel.org. Retrieved February 6, 2019, from https://www.mormonchannel.org/blog/post/daily-quote-mediocrity-will-never-do.

11 **Denis M. Wagner III.** He is the grandson of Gerald L. Penhollow. Denis contributed his personal quotes to support this book and helped in the editing.

12 **Joseph de Maistre**. (n.d.). Great Saying GreatSayings.net, Retrieved February 7, 2019, from GreatSayings.net https://www.greatsayings.net/joseph-de-maistre-sayings/there-is-no-easy-method-of-learning-difficult-things-the-method-is-to-close-the-613116.html.

13 **Antonio Porchia**. (n.d.). "Voices," 1943, translated from Spanish by W.S. Merwin) Wiki quote, en.wikiquote.org. Retrieved February 7, 2019, from https://en.wikiquote.org/wiki/Antonio_Porchia.

14 **Author Unknown**. (n.d.). FAMOUS QUOTES & QUOTATIONS, famous-quotes-and-quotations.com, Jim and Audri Lanford. Retrieved February 7, 2019, from http://www.famous-quotes-and-quotations.com/quote-on-success.html.

15 **George Bernard Shaw**. George Bernard Shaw Quotes. (n.d.). BrainyQuote.com. Retrieved February 7, 2019, from BrainyQuote.com Web site: https://www.brainyquote.com/quotes/george_bernard_shaw_161647.

16 **Swami Sivananda**. Swami Sivananda Quotes. (n.d.). BrainyQuote.com. Retrieved February 7, 2019, from BrainyQuote.com Web site: https://www.brainyquote.com/quotes/swami_sivananda_390760.

17 **Yogi Berra**. Yogi Berra > Quotes > Quotable Quotes. (n.d.). GoodReads.com. Retrieved February 7, 2019, from https://www.goodreads.com/quotes/261866-you-have-to-give-100-percent-in-the-first-half.

18 **Don Zimmer**. Don Zimmer Quotes. (n.d.). BrainyQuote.com. Retrieved February 8, 2019, from BrainyQuote.com Web site: https://www.brainyquote.com/quotes/don_zimmer_221729.

I Don't Know

Rule #5
'You Always Know Something'

Rule #5 'You Always Know Something'

In a Nut Shell:

How many times have we heard, a friend, a colleague, or a child say: 'I can't do that,' or 'I don't know how to do that,' or 'that's impossible'? Or additionally, 'I don't understand,' or 'I am not trained to do that job.' All of these are common responses when we are faced with new, unfamiliar, or daunting tasks.

But my favorite line comes from my children and grandchildren to that famous question we all ask whenever there is trouble, 'What happened'? Their unfailing response would be, 'I don't know?' Or even better, they would offer the silent shoulder-shrug indicating they were clueless. All parents love those kinds of answers from their children, don't they?

My kids could have been standing right in the middle of the action watching the event start to finish and still say, 'I don't know?' I hate to say it, but hearing that statement made me want to look inside their ears and see if I could see straight through their heads and out the other side. Or bend down and look them in the eyes and say, "Hello, anybody in there? You were standing right here, watching it all happen. You have got to know something?" Well, as you can see, I am showing a little of my poor parenting skills here, LOL, but all in fun.

Rule #5's statement means exactly what it says. It requires no explanation or interpretation. No matter the task or the situation, whether it is solving a small problem, or unraveling the mysteries of the universe, 'you always know something.' And that is where you start.

Focus on what you know, not what you don't know. Have faith that as you direct your attention to what you do know, other information will come into play to help you solve your problem or complete your task. There is always some fact, no matter how small, that you know about any given situation.

Rule #5 'You Always Know Something'

At first, that something you know may seem insignificant. It may be so insignificant that you don't even recognize what it is you do know. But your knowledge is vast and reliable, and that spark of information is there, tucked away in your brain. You can find it. Look for that one thing you do know, and as you discover that one thing, it will become two points of knowledge, then three, and so on. Always remember, what begins as a puzzle will become a complete picture.

It's Dark in Here:

When we are faced with an unknown or what seems to be an impossible task, fear is our biggest enemy. There is the fear of looking stupid, the fear of not knowing, the fear of failure, the fear of what will be, the fear of what will not be, ... etc. I placed Rule #5 in my top 20 rules to manage life because we humans tend to find more reasons to be afraid than reasons to be fearless.

I used to be afraid of taking on new things because I felt too stupid. Dealing with an unknown task has always been my biggest fear. Many times, I allowed fear to defeat me before I had even attempted to solve a problem. A fact I didn't know in my younger years is that most people walk around feeling unqualified for any given task.

Beauty & the Beast:

I would like to share with you a story from my teen years and an encounter with a very kind, young woman. Judy Zimmerman is her name. She opened my eyes to the wisdom of Rule #5 *'You Always Know Something'*.

One day in my high school science lab class, I was teamed up with a beautiful, young girl, who was a brilliant 'A' student, and who I also happened to have a crush on. In retrospect, I believe the teacher's reason for placing us together was because I was failing. At first, I didn't think this teacher was helping me at all. Now, not only was I fighting the fear of feeling stupid in this class, I also had to deal with my awkwardness with girls. I was never a ladies' man in high school. Around girls, particularly ones I thought were cute, I became tongue-tied and developed two left feet.

The chemistry teacher gave us a lab assignment that we were to work on as a team over the course of the week. On the first day of the assignment, all I could do was sit on my lab stool in complete silence. It took all my energy to fight my nervous fears each time this beautiful, charming young lady asked me to hand her something like a beaker or pass her any other object needed to complete the lab experiment.

As Judy worked on 'our' lab project, it seemed as if she knew exactly what she was doing with the experiment we were conducting. She appeared to possess pure confidence in all she did. Now, on the other hand, I just sat there trying not to look dumb, but that made me appear as dumb as I felt.

Judy tried her best to include me that first day. She looked at me with her cute smile and asked me questions in an attempt to include me in the experiment. She also did her best to make me feel more comfortable, but regardless of her attempts to help me, I just felt dumber and more nervous. I feared that if I tried talking to her that my brain would fog over, and I would become tongue-tied. As a result of the foggy brain and failing tongue, the only words that spewed from my mouth were half-intelligent statements that truly showed how little chemistry I understood.

I went home from school that first day feeling like the dumbest person on Earth. I was totally embarrassed by how I had handled myself in class with this young lady. I mean come on, guys dream of opportunities to work side by side with smart, beautiful people like Judy. And what did I do? I totally acted like a brainless amoeba. I had so badly wanted to impress her and had failed. Have you ever felt that way?

As I was lying in bed that night dreading the next day's class, I ran through ideas on how I could better approach the situation. A thought popped into my head, and a small voice said, 'just ask her.' 'Ask her what?' I thought to myself. 'Out on a date? I am not bold enough for that. What could I ask her without feeling stupid or foolish?' 'Just ask her,' the thought repeated.

Breaking the Ice:

The next day at school, I walked into the chemistry lab, and there she was, sitting at our station. Her shiny, long, dark hair was flowing down to her chest and across the back of her shoulders. She wore a beautiful smile, and her eyes glowed with warmth as she watched me walk to my seat. As I took my seat next to her, I, once again, became nervous. Then a moment of calmness came into my being, and a question appeared in my thoughts. I took a deep breath, and the words flowed clearly and calmly, with no nervous stutter. The dialog went something like this:

"How do you do it, Judy?" I asked.

"Do what?" she replied.

"Make chemistry class seem so easy. Like you know all the answers. I feel so stupid in this class. I don't know anything."

"I don't know the answers, or I wouldn't be taking this class," she replied. "But, I am not stupid either, nor are you. Everybody knows something, and that is where I start. Then I have trust in the teacher and allow the books to teach me the rest. If I look at the project as a whole, it becomes too much for my brain to handle. Or if I start thinking about what I don't know, I get really flustrated, and in that state of mind, I wouldn't have a clue what to do. So, I don't go there. I concentrate my mind on what I do know, not on what I don't know. This class scares me too. My parents expect me to get no less than an 'A' in all my classes. And I hate this class. It's like my hardest subject. I hate it, and if I think about it too much, I feel stupid."

Don't Look Fear in the Eye, Just Ignore Him:

Judy continued, "Don't look at the whole picture; in this case, meaning the project. It will swallow you up with all its unknowns, and overwhelm you. Particularly don't focus on the things that are your weak points. We all have weak points. Focus on what you do know. As I said, you're not stupid. You know more than you think you do, start there. You know what the lab equipment is used for, beakers, Bunsen burners, and so on, and you know how to read and write, or you wouldn't have gotten this far in school. Just take it one step at a time. Read the book, follow the examples, write down what you observe, and then we will talk about each other's results and write that up. It is simple if you keep it simple. I have no idea what we are going to find. That is the whole point of this chemistry project."

"I am terrible at writing reports," I said. "That is my biggest problem, and what I tend to focus on. My spelling sucks, and at the end of all of this, our grade is based upon our reports. Which is why I tend to focus on it. So, in the end, all the work on this project comes down to that dreaded, sucky, report I don't want to write. It hurts my head, thinking about all that writing. What I do like is playing with fires and chemicals. That's cool."

"See you do know something." She said, "Don't think about the writing. I'll help you get through the report. I love writing, but I don't care about playing with fire and chemicals. We'll make a great team."

I don't know if Judy honestly didn't like playing with fire and chemicals. I mean, come on, what teenager thinks that part of chemistry class is not cool? But, by Judy getting me to believe that she didn't like that part of the class, it gave me the courage to step up and lead the experiments. With the assurance of Judy's help to write the report, I was able to force the fears and doubts out of my mind. Chemistry lab started to become fun and easier. The idea that I did know something that could contribute to the project after all grew in my mind, and that became my focus. As my focus continued to grow stronger, the nervousness calmed, and my tongue became untied.

The Spell is Broken:

Now, despite all the beauty and the qualities that still enchanted me, the spell which bound my tongue, and made me a nervous wreck around Judy, was gone. Her wisdom taught me that I could do chemistry. Her kindness taught me that I could talk to a beautiful, sweet, smiling, young woman.

Her simple words of wisdom that day were another pivot point of my life, a pivot point that gave me a new confidence. I now had a new rule to help govern how I looked and handled my fears of inability. The words *'You Always Know Something'* would echo in my mind whenever I would start to focus on the fear of the unknown or my limited abilities.

Though I didn't realize it at the time, Judy was also teaching me Rule #6 *'You Cut Down a Forest One Tree at a Time'*. Rules #5 & 6 go hand and hand. Rule #5 *'You Always Know Something'* helps you find that first tree in the forest. Tackling that tree will give you the confidence and knowledge you will need to tackle the next tree; thus, we cut down the forest one tree at a time.

If it weren't for Judy, I would have more than likely gotten into trouble doing things teenage boys shouldn't do in chemistry class, like mixing the wrong chemicals just to see why the teacher didn't want us to do so. Or done something like my classmate, George, who once stuck a pair of long-handled tweezers into a lab bench electric outlet, and as a result, shut down the power for the whole right-wing of our school.

I never did ask Judy for a date, but I did walk her home after school a couple of times.

A Few That Shook the Hand of Fear:

The first thing in dealing with fear is to know you are not alone. Believe it or not, there is comfort in knowing that others have walked the same path as you. Many famous people know and live with fear in their lives each day. We also know these famous people overcame their fears and succeeded, or they wouldn't be famous. These famous people made it because they had, and applied, strict guiding rules. Guiding rules, no different than the ones written in this book. Their book of rules may be worded differently, but they still carry the same messages. I can assure you that their success is not because they are better people than we are. Yes, they may have talents we don't, but we also have abilities they don't. We all have our weak points, and we all have our strengths.

I am going to dump a ton of quotable quotes on you from other sources and famous people on the subject of fear. I do this for two reasons: one, I find so many good quotes it is hard not to include them all and two, I like to include a wide variety because people relate to inspirational words differently, therefore, different quotes for different people.

Here are a few quotable statements from famous people that have known and dealt with fear. Read them all and pick out the one that inspires you.

> **(Marvin J. Ashton, 1991 October General Conference, "Strengthen the Feeble Knees")[6]**
> *"Who among us has not experienced feeble knees or fear and uncertainty over the responsibilities we encounter in this mortal existence?"*
>
> **(Bible Old Testament: Job 4:14)[1]**
> *14 Fear came upon me, and trembling, which made all my bones to shake.*
>
> **(Henry Louis Mencken)[7]**
> *"The one permanent emotion of the inferior man is fear – fear of the unknown, the complex, the inexplicable. What he wants above everything else is safety."*
>
> **(Joan D. Vinge)[8]**
> *"Fear of the unknown is a terrible thing."*
>
> **(Betty Bender)[9]**
> *"Anything I've ever done that ultimately was worthwhile... initially scared me to death."*

(Michael Pritchard)[10]
"Fear is that little darkroom where negatives developed."

(Author Unknown)[11]
"Fear is faith that it won't work out."

(Dudley Nichols)[12]
"Fear is the highest fence."

(Samuel Butler)[13]
"Fear is static that prevents me from hearing myself."

(Khwāja Shams-ud-Dīn Muḥammad Ḥāfeẓ-e Shīrāzī, or "Hafiz")[14]
"Fear is the cheapest room in the house. I would like to see you living in better conditions."

(Sophie Tunnell)[15]
"Fear is a slinking cat I find beneath the lilacs of my mind."

(Lillian Russell)[16]
"We all have fear of the unknown what one does with that fear makes all the difference in the world."

(Ralph Waldo Emerson, Journals, 1833)[17]
"The wise man in the storm prays God, not for safety from danger, but for deliverance from fear."

You can see from the quotes you've just read that you're not alone in your fears. The only difference between the successful person and the unsuccessful person is that the successful person doesn't let the fear of failure, or the feeling of stupidity, stop them from achieving their goals.

Famous people apply Rule #5 and focus on what they know, not on what they don't know, in order to work past what they fear and move on to success.

Words of Encouragement:

Many people who have faced their fears try to leave behind words of encouragement in the hope of helping others through their fears and achieve success. That is one reason I am writing this book. I don't plan on getting rich and famous. No, I am writing this book for you with the hope that I can be like Judy Zimmerman or one of the other persons that inspired me to become the best me.

Most of the people that have inspired me to better heights don't have a clue what gift they have shared with me, and that is not important either. What is important is that I pass on what I have learned to any souls out in the world that are seeking direction and advice and do my best to inspire them. It is my hope that direction and inspiration will be found within the reading of these rules, I have dedicated a part of my life to write.

Here are some encouraging words from both famous people and scriptures that are meant to help you defeat fear, or at the very least, ignore it.

> **(Kevin W. Pearson, 2009 April General Conference, "Faith in the Lord Jesus Christ")**[18]
> *"Faith and fear cannot coexist. One gives way to the other. The simple fact is we all need to constantly build faith and overcome sources of destructive disbelief.*
>
> *Doubt is a negative emotion related to fear. It comes from a lack of confidence in one's self or abilities. It is inconsistent with our divine identity as children of God.*
>
> *Discouragement leads to distraction, a lack of focus. Distraction eliminates the very focus the eye of faith requires.*
>
> *Distraction leads to a lack of diligence, a reduced commitment to remain true and faithful and to carry on through despite hardship and disappointment.*

Rule #5 'You Always Know Something'

Disappointment is an inevitable part of life, but it need not lead to doubt, discouragement, distraction, or lack of diligence."

(David Joseph Schwartz)[19]
"Believe it can be done. When you believe something can be done, really believe, your mind will find the ways to do it. Believing a solution paves the way to solution."

(Pearl of Great Price: Moses 1:20)[5]
20 And it came to pass that Moses began to fear exceedingly; and as he began to fear, he saw the bitterness of hell. Nevertheless, calling upon God, he received strength, and he commanded, saying: Depart from me, Satan, for this one God only will I worship, which is the God of glory.

(Bible New Testament: 1 John 4:18)[2]
18 There is no fear in love; but perfect love casteth out fear: because fear hath torment. He that feareth is not made perfect in love.

(Book of Mormon: Moroni 8:16)[3]
16 …. Behold, I speak with boldness, having authority from God; and I fear not what man can do; for perfect love casteth out all fear.

(Babe Ruth)[20]
"Never let fear of striking out get in your way."

(Franklin D. Roosevelt)[21]
"The only thing we have to fear is fear itself."

(W. Clement Stone)[22]
"Thinking will not overcome fear but action will."

(Rabindranath Tagore)[23]
"You can't cross the sea merely by standing and staring at the water."

(Eleanor Roosevelt)[24]
"You must do the things you think you cannot do."

(Raymond Lindquist)[25]
"Courage is the power to let go of the familiar."

(J. K. Rowling "Harry Potter and The Chamber of Secrets")[26]
"It is our choices ... that show what we truly are, far more than our abilities."

(Eleanor Roosevelt, often quoted this Chinese proverb)[27]
"It is better to light one small candle than to curse the darkness."

(Mohandas Karamchand Gandhi)[28]
"The enemy is fear. We think it is hate; but, it is fear."

(Unknown)[29]
"Never be afraid to try something new. Remember, amateurs built the ark, professionals built the Titanic."

(John Wooden)[30]
"Don't let what you cannot do interfere with what you can do."

(Samuel Smiles)[31]
"Where there is a will there is a way."

(Publilius Syrus)[33]
"No one knows what he can do until he tries."

The Second Step:

We have learned that we share the same fear as others, and I have given you words of encouragement to read and inspire you. The second step in helping you implement Rule #5 is to understand that you are truly never alone in your fears; Heavenly Father is always with you. Put your trust in Him, that He will help you see what you do know, and believe that He can and will help you learn what you don't already know.

(Bible New Testament: 2 Timothy 1:7)[2]
7 For God hath not given us the spirit of fear; but of power, and of love, and of a sound mind.

(Bible Old Testament: Psalm 56:11)[1]
11 In God have I put my trust: I will not be afraid what man can do unto me.

(Bible Old Testament: Proverbs 29:25)[1]
25 The fear of man bringeth a snare: but whoso putteth his trust in the Lord shall be safe.

(Doctrine and Covenants: 68:6)[4]
6 Wherefore, be of good cheer, and do not fear, for I the Lord am with you, and will stand by you;

(James E. Faust, 1997 October General Conference, "Pioneers of the Future")[32]
"We must believe in God, the Eternal Father, and in His Son, Jesus Christ, and in the Holy Ghost. We must believe in the Atonement and the Resurrection of the Savior. We must believe in the words of the prophets, both ancient and modern. We should also believe in ourselves."

(Quentin L. Cook, 2007 October General Conference, "Live by Faith and Not by Fear")[34]
"We must live by faith and not by fear."

If you read my quotes above, then you read the Elder James E. Faust quote. That whole talk of his is filled with pearls of wisdom. In the next excerpt from that same talk, as you read it, you will see that he is teaching them to apply Rules #5 & 6 in their lives.

(James E. Faust, 1997 October General Conference, "Pioneers of the Future")[32]
"Action is inhibited by fear. You young men, along with the young sisters, are the future of the Church and, in some measure, of the world. You rightly have concerns about measuring up and finding your place in life. You more often recognize your inadequacies rather than your strengths.

Some of you may have concerns about leaving home and going into the unknown, such as the mission field. Some of you in your 20s and 30s are timid about taking on the responsibilities of marriage and family. You are properly concerned about your education--your training--to learn to use your minds and your hands. You must acquire a skill to be able to compete in today's world.

You have fears about being accepted. You worry about being popular in your age-group. It is natural to want to belong.

If you take each challenge one step at a time, with faith in every footstep, your strength and understanding will increase. You cannot foresee all of the turns and twists ahead. My counsel to you is to follow the direction of the Savior of the world: "Be not afraid, only believe." (Mark 5:36)

We can overcome all of our fears, not all at once, but one at a time. As we do so we will grow in confidence."

The Fear of Public Speaking:

I then read another section in that James E. Faust talk, and I had to laugh. I saw myself standing at the pulpit, at the request of the Stake President, giving a talk to the entire Florida, St Petersburg Stake Priesthood. Which is approximately 800 human bodies. I think we all can see ourselves in the position that this young man in Elder Faust's story was in. Anyone that has had to do any public speaking can relate to this story.

(James E. Faust, 1997 October General Conference, "Pioneers of the Future")[32]

"The following is the story of a young man who encountered a fear that each one of us has faced or will face at some time in our lives.

It was a hot July afternoon, and the chapel was filled for stake priesthood meeting. There was a young priest sitting on the stand in 'contained nervousness,' and after the hymn the stake president announced him as the next speaker.

He spread out his notes, and as he did so his quivering hands betrayed his fear. He began to speak, but soon his speech quickened to a gabble, his words wild and repetitive. Worse followed as he began to stammer and then stopped speaking altogether.

A heavy silence settled on the room. Who has not felt the terror of standing before an awesome audience? Everyone thought he would sit down, but no, he stayed on his feet, his head down. A few ominous seconds ticked by, and then he squared his shoulders and blurted out: 'Brethren, I ask for an interest in your faith and prayers, that I might have sureness of speech.'

Then he went back to where he had left off, speaking quietly but clearly. Soon his voice rose to its natural resonance, and he delivered his message to its full conclusion. It was not so much his message that thrilled those who were there. It was the image of that young man, unflinching even though he felt himself teetering on a precipice of fear, taking up the banner of courage and rallying himself for the cause of truth. (See Wayne B. Lynn, Lessons from Life (1987), 51-52)"

Short Summary:

Rule #5 *'You Always Know Something'* is a confidence-building rule. It is a rule to help you overcome your fear and get you started. Remember:

1.) Don't focus on what you don't know.

2.) Fact, you do know something.

3.) Use your faith and remember, you are never alone; God is with you.

Rule #5 'You Always Know Something'

4.) Invoke Rule #1 *'Failure is Not an Option'* to boost your willpower.

5.) Move forward with Rule #6 *'You Cut Down a Forest One Tree at a Time'*

Apply these five simple steps, and you can make it through anything. Rule #12 *'No One Said it Was Going to be Easy'* may apply to your situation as well. Nevertheless, you will succeed, and through the adversity, you will gain rich blessings. Above all, have faith in God and yourself.

Endnotes:

1 **King James Version of the Bible, The Old Testament of Our Lord and Saviour Jesus Christ.** Published by The Church of Jesus Christ of Latter-day Saints, Salt Lake City, Utah, USA. Copywrite 2013.

2 **King James Version of the Bible, The New Testament of Our Lord and Saviour Jesus Christ.** Published by The Church of Jesus Christ of Latter-day Saints, Salt Lake City, Utah, USA. Copywrite 2013.

3 **The Book of Mormon Another Testament of Jesus Christ.** Published by The Church of Jesus Christ of Latter-day Saints, Salt Lake City, Utah, USA. First English edition published in Palmyra, New York, USA, in 1830. Copywrite 2013.

4 **The Doctrine and Covenants of The Church of Jesus Christ of Latter-Day Saints.** Containing Revelations Give to Joseph Smith, the Prophet. With some additions by his successors in the Presidency of the Church. Published by The Church of Jesus Christ of Latter-day Saints, Salt Lake City, Utah, USA. Copywrite 2013.

5 **The Pearl of Great Price.** A selection from the revelations, translations, and narrations of Joseph Smith, First Prophet, seer, and revelator to The Church of Jesus Christ of Latter-Day Saints. Published by The Church of Jesus Christ of Latter-day Saints, Salt Lake City, Utah, USA. Copywrite 2013.

6 **Marvin J. Ashton, 1991 October General Conference, "Strengthen the Feeble Knees".** The 161st Semiannual General Conference of the Church of Jesus Christ of Latter-day Saints, October 6, 1991, Sunday Afternoon Session. Published in the Ensign magazine, Volume 21 Number 11, November 1991. An official magazine of the Church of Jesus Christ of Latter-day Saints, published by the Church of Jesus Christ of Latter-day Saints, 50 E. North Temple Street, Salt Lake City, UT, 84150-3220, USA. Also, retrieved Nov 26,2019, from Ensign, ChurchofJesusChrist.Org website: https://www.churchofjesuschrist.org/study/ensign/1991/11/strengthen-the-feeble-knees?lang=eng

7 **Henry Louis Mencken.** H. L. Mencken Quotes. (n.d.). BrainyQuote.com. Retrieved February 9, 2019, from BrainyQuote.com Web site: https://www.brainyquote.com/quotes/h_l_mencken_105112.

8 **Joan D. Vinge.** Joan D. Vinge Quotes. (n.d.). BrainyQuote.com. Retrieved February 9, 2019, from BrainyQuote.com Web site: https://www.brainyquote.com/quotes/joan_d_vinge_224852.

9 **Betty Bender.** "The Top 1%," Written by Dan Strutzel, Dale Carnegie & Associates. Published 2017 by Gildan Press an imprint of Gildan Media LLC. www.glidanmedia.com, ISBN 978-1-469-03714-1. Chapter 9 "Let Your Fears Polish You" page 3 of this chapter. ThinkExist.com Quotations. Retrieved February 6, 2019, from ThinkExist.com http://thinkexist.com/quotation/anything_i-ve_ever_done_that_ultimately_was/12911.html.

Rule #5 'You Always Know Something'

10. **Michael Pritchard**. (n.d.). ThinkExist.com Quotations. "Michael Pritchard quotes". ThinkExist.com Quotations Online 1 Jan. 2019. 9 Feb. 2019 http://thinkexist.com/quotes/michael_pritchard/.

11. **Author Unknown**. (n.d.). ThinkExist.com Quotations. ThinkExist.com Quotations Online 1 Jan. 2019. Retrieved 9 Feb. 2019 http://thinkexist.com/quotation/fear_is_faith_that_it_won-t_work_out/219151.htm

12. **Dudley Nichols**. (n.d.). ThinkExist.com Quotations. "Dudley Nichols quotes". ThinkExist.com Quotations Online 1 Jan. 2019. 9 Feb. 2019 http://thinkexist.com/quotes/dudley_nichols/.

13. **Samuel Butler**. (n.d.). ThinkExist.com Quotations. "Samuel Butler quotes". ThinkExist.com Quotations Online 1 Jan. 2019. 9 Feb. 2019 http://thinkexist.com/quotes/samuel_butler/.

14. **Khwāja Shams-ud-Dīn Muḥammad Ḥāfeẓ-e Shīrāzī**. (n.d.). goodreads.com "Quotable Quotes". Retrived February 09, 2019 from goodreads.com https://www.goodreads.com/quotes/68830-fear-is-the-cheapest-room-in-the-house-i-would.

15. **Sophie Tunnell**. (n.d.). ThinkExist.com Quotations. "Sophie Tunnell quotes". ThinkExist.com Quotations Online 1 Jan. 2019. 9 Feb. 2019 http://thinkexist.com/quotes/sophie_tunnell/.

16. **Lillian Russell**. Lillian Russell Quotes. (n.d.). BrainyQuote.com. Retrieved February 9, 2019, from BrainyQuote.com Web site: https://www.brainyquote.com/quotes/lillian_russell_197618.

17. **Ralph Waldo Emerson, Journals, 1833**. (n.d.). ThinkExist.com Quotations. Retrieved February 6, 2019, from ThinkExist.com http://thinkexist.com/quotation/the_wise_man_in_the_storm_prays_to_god-not_for/169365.html.

18. **Kevin W. Pearson, 2009 April General Conference, "Faith in the Lord Jesus Christ"**. The 179th Annual General Conference of the Church of Jesus Christ of Latter-day Saints, April 4, 2009, Saturday Afternoon Session. Published in the Ensign magazine, Volume 39 Number 05, May 2009 page 40 paragraph 4. An official magazine of the Church of Jesus Christ of Latter-day Saints, published by the Church of Jesus Christ of Latter-day Saints, 50 E. North Temple Street, Salt Lake City, UT, 84150-3220, USA. Also, retrieved Nov 26,2019, from Ensign, ChurchofJesusChrist.Org website: https://www.churchofjesuschrist.org/study/ensign/2009/05/faith-in-the-lord-jesus-christ?lang=eng

19. **David Joseph Schwartz**. David Joseph Schwartz Quotes. (n.d.). BrainyQuote.com. Retrieved February 9, 2019, from BrainyQuote.com Web site: https://www.brainyquote.com/quotes/david_joseph_schwartz_165752.

20. **Babe Ruth**. Babe Ruth Quotes. (n.d.). BrainyQuote.com. Retrieved February 9, 2019, from BrainyQuote.com Web site: https://www.brainyquote.com/quotes/babe_ruth_130004.

21. **Franklin D. Roosevelt**. Franklin D. Roosevelt Quotes. (n.d.). BrainyQuote.com. Retrieved February 9, 2019, from BrainyQuote.com Web site: https://www.brainyquote.com/quotes/franklin_d_roosevelt_109480.

Rule #5 'You Always Know Something'

22. **W. Clement Stone.** W. Clement Stone Quotes. (n.d.). BrainyQuote.com. Retrieved February 9, 2019, from BrainyQuote.com Web site: https://www.brainyquote.com/quotes/w_clement_stone_155728.

23. **Rabindranath Tagore.** Rabindranath Tagore Quotes. (n.d.). BrainyQuote.com. Retrieved February 9, 2019, from BrainyQuote.com Web site: https://www.brainyquote.com/quotes/rabindranath_tagore_383735.

24. **Eleanor Roosevelt.** Eleanor Roosevelt Quotes. (n.d.). BrainyQuote.com. Retrieved February 9, 2019, from BrainyQuote.com Web site: https://www.brainyquote.com/quotes/eleanor_roosevelt_100870.

25. **Raymond Lindquist.** (n.d.). ThinkExist.com Quotations. "Raymond Lindquist quotes". ThinkExist.com Quotations Online 1 Jan. 2019. 9 Feb. 2019 http://thinkexist.com/quotes/raymond_lindquist/.

26. **J. K. Rowling "Harry Potter and The Chamber of Secrets."** J. K. Rowling Quotes. (n.d.). BrainyQuote.com. Retrieved February 9, 2019, from BrainyQuote.com Web site: https://www.brainyquote.com/quotes/j_k_rowling_130071.

27. **Eleanor Roosevelt Quoting Chinese Proverb.** (n.d.). ThinkExist.com Quotations. "Eleanor Roosevelt quotes". ThinkExist.com Quotations Online 1 Jan. 2019. Retrieved February 9, 2019 from http://thinkexist.com/quotes/eleanor_roosevelt/.

28. **Mahatma Gandhi.** Mahatma Gandhi > Quotes > Quotable Quote. (n.d.). goodreads.com. Retrieved February 9, 2019 from https://www.goodreads.com/quotes/1214114-the-enemy-is-fear-we-think-it-is-hate-but.

29. **Unknown.** (n.d.). ThinkExist.com Quotations. "Similar quotes". Retrieved February 9, 2019, from BrainyQuote.com Web site: http://thinkexist.com/quotation/never_be_afraid_to_try_something_new-remember/12760.html.

30. **John Wooden.** John Wooden Quotes. (n.d.). BrainyQuote.com. Retrieved February 9, 2019, from BrainyQuote.com Web site: https://www.brainyquote.com/quotes/john_wooden_105700.

31. **Samuel Smiles.** Samuel Smiles. (n.d.). AZQuotes.com. Retrieved February 25, 2019, from AZQuotes.com Web site: https://www.azquotes.com/quote/802308. Also see, Samuel Smiles (2014). "Self-Help", p.156, Cambridge University Press.

32. **James E. Faust, 1997 October General Conference, "Pioneers of the Future".** The 167th Semiannual General Conference of the Church of Jesus Christ of Latter-day Saints, October 4, 1997, Saturday Priesthood Session. Published in the Ensign magazine, Volume 27 Number 11, November 1997. An official magazine of the Church of Jesus Christ of Latter-day Saints, published by the Church of Jesus Christ of Latter-day Saints, 50 E. North Temple Street, Salt Lake City, UT, 84150-3220, USA. Also, retrieved Nov 26,2019, from Ensign, ChurchofJesusChrist.Org website: https://www.churchofjesuschrist.org/study/ensign/1997/11/pioneers-of-the-future-be-not-afraid-only-believe?lang=eng

Rule #5 'You Always Know Something'

33 **Publilius Syrus**. Publilius Syrus Quotes. (n.d.). BrainyQuote.com. Retrieved February 9, 2019, from BrainyQuote.com Web site: https://www.brainyquote.com/quotes/publilius_syrus_140851.

34 **Quentin L. Cook, 2007 October General Conference, "Live by Faith and Not by Fear"**. The 177th Semiannual General Conference of the Church of Jesus Christ of Latter-day Saints, October 7, 2007, Sunday Morning Session. Published in the Ensign magazine, Volume 37 Number 11, November 2007 page 40 paragraph 4. An official magazine of the Church of Jesus Christ of Latter-day Saints, published by the Church of Jesus Christ of Latter-day Saints, 50 E. North Temple Street, Salt Lake City, UT, 84150-3220, USA. Also, retrieved Nov 26,2019, from Ensign, ChurchofJesusChrist.Org website: https://www.churchofjesuschrist.org/study/ensign/2007/11/live-by-faith-and-not-by-fear?lang=eng

And He Shouts, "TIMBER!"

Rule #6

'You Cut Down a Forest One Tree at a Time'

Rule #6 'You Cut Down a Forest One Tree at a Time'

Simply Put:

Rule #6 originates from the parable of a Farmer's need to clear a forest from his property in order to expand his cropland. If the Farmer, standing on his front porch, contemplating the expansive task, focused on all the trees, he might never start, due to the overwhelming amount of work before him. Instead, a wise Farmer picks out one tree and focuses all his efforts to remove it, chopping, sawing, clearing the branches, and hauling away the wood. He then focuses on the next tree until it is cut down and completely cleared from his land. One tree, one small task; cut it down, haul it away, and pull the stump. The wise Farmer does not focus on tackling the forest to expand his planting ground. Instead, he focuses on cutting down one tree at a time.

'You Cut Down a Forest One Tree at a Time' is a metaphor we can apply to the tasks we deal with in our daily lives. Simply stated, the Forest represents a complete task that you have been assigned, or a main goal that you have set for yourself. The Trees represent the little subtasks or steps that it will take to finish the task or achieve the overall objective. I could restate Rule #6 as *'Focus on Doing the Task One Step at a Time'*. However, I prefer the metaphor of the forest and trees. Nature always brings me closer to God and allows me to feel His love a little more.

We are a Team:

Rule #5 *'You Always Know Something'* and Rule #6 *'You Cut Down a Forest One Tree at a Time'* work in tandem. Rule #5 is the kick-starter, and Rule #6 is the mover. Rule #5 kick starts you into action by convincing you that you are endowed with the needed knowledge, and Rule #6 moves you from the beginning of the project/task to the completion, one step at a time. Thus, the two rules work in tandem to help prevent you

Rule #6 'You Cut Down a Forest One Tree at a Time'

from being swallowed up by the fear that the task is more than you can handle.

Just Lazy:

Some of us don't accomplish our goals or successfully complete short-term projects, let alone long-term endeavors because, well, let's face it; all humans in some form or another have a naturally lazy tendency. I did say all humans, did I not? The last time I checked, I belong to the human race, so I too am infected with naturally lazy tendencies. You wouldn't believe that of me if you met me, as you can hardly catch me sitting idle. I have learned how to fight against those lazy demons. My wife says when I die, she is going to have my gravestone carved with the motto, 'I can still outwork you.' Just because I am seen as a hard worker, does not mean that I don't have this same naturally lazy demon running around in my head. As I said, I have learned how to catch my demon, when he gets out, and stuff him back in his cage. Rule #6 is one of the rules that help me overcome my impulse to be idle.

Many people in the world have a hard time overcoming this naturally lazy tendency. Teenagers are possessed with this demon so badly at times it prevents them from picking up their dirty clothes off the bedroom floor and putting them in the hamper. Or even worse, they fail to maintain the general housekeeping of their room. The naturally lazy demon can be tough to defeat.

Procrastination is another tough demon that tempts us, and he has many demon friends: fear, low self-esteem, ignorance, perfection, etc. Out of all of procrastination's demonic friends, rumor has it, that lazy is his best friend. Whenever procrastination is in town, naturally lazy is tagging right along. Some say their friendship is so close, you can't separate them.

The bigger the task is, the harder the job will look, and thus the more likely Mr. Lazy and Mr. Procrastinator will pay you a visit. I know them well (LOL).

Rule #6 'You Cut Down a Forest One Tree at a Time'

Fear not, there is a way to control those two demons. Rule #6 is one weapon against them. By mentally breaking up any job into several smaller tasks, it creates the impression that less work is required and makes the job mentally more manageable.

Those who procrastinate, and we all do at times, should study Rule #17 *'Manage Your Procrastinations or They Will Manage You'*, then come back and apply Rule #5 and Rule #6 to your task.

So Big:

Some of us humans have learned to overcome our natural lazy tendencies. However, we still don't always do what needs to be done because, when we look at the task as a whole, it seems too big. It scares us to death. We don't believe that we have the ability within ourselves to complete the task. The task is so big, and we are so little.

Even when we break the forest down to one tree, that one tree can look too big to handle. Although we know we have some knowledge to apply to the task at hand when we stop and survey the whole project, the fear of what we don't know can be so overwhelming we feel incapable of handling it. Yet if you apply Rule #5, you will find the knowledge needed that puts the ax in your hands. No matter how big that tree looks, it will come down one chop at a time. Then you move to the next tree, find the knowledge within you, and cut it down.

For those of us that allow fear to swallow us up, you need to study and grasp the concept of Rule #5 very clearly. Have faith in yourself and God. If you can't have faith in yourself at first, then start with our Heavenly Father. He is always there for us to lean on. God could do the work for us, but then we would miss out on what we could learn by taking the journey. But that is a different chapter, Rule #13 *'Focus on the Journey Not the Task'*. Have faith in God, for He is bound to help.

(Doctrine & Covenants 82:10)[4]
10 I, the Lord, am bound when ye do what I say;

Rule #6 'You Cut Down a Forest One Tree at a Time'

> **(Bible Old Testament: Isaiah 41:17)**[1]
> *17 When the poor and needy seek water, and there is none, and their tongue faileth for thirst, I the Lord will hear them, I the God of Israel will not forsake them.*

You Want Me To Build What:

Perhaps the three greatest examples of tasks so big they seemed impossible are the three stories from scripture: Noah, Jared, and Nephi, who all were asked to build boats. These boats were not just some small little vessels, no we are talking big ocean fairing boats. These boats would have to withstand the harshest storms of the seas.

Noah was asked of God to build an Ark 450 feet long, by 75 feet wide, by 45 feet tall, with three floors in it and lots of rooms. These measurements are based on a general agreement that a cubit equals 18 inches.

> **(Bible Old Testament: Genesis 6:14-16)**[1]
> *14 ¶ Make thee an ark of gopher wood; rooms shalt thou make in the ark, and shalt pitch it within and without with pitch.*
>
> *15 And this is the fashion which thou shalt make it of: The length of the ark shall be three hundred cubits, the breadth of it fifty cubits, and the height of it thirty cubits.*
>
> *16 A window shalt thou make to the ark, and in a cubit shalt thou finish it above; and the door of the ark shalt thou set in the side thereof; with lower, second, and third stories shalt thou make it.*

Let's take a step back and look at the bigger picture of Noah's boat-building assignment. His goal was not just to build a boat, it was also to restore all flesh to the Earth after God destroyed it. How would you react if God handed you a task of that magnitude? I would feel very overwhelmed.

Rule #6 'You Cut Down a Forest One Tree at a Time'

(Bible Old Testament: Genesis 6:5-8, 13, 17-22)[1]

5 ¶ And God saw that the wickedness of man was great in the earth, and that every imagination of the thoughts of his heart was only evil continually.

6 And it repented the Lord that he had made man on the earth, and it grieved him at his heart.

7 And the Lord said, I will destroy man whom I have created from the face of the earth; both man, and beast, and the creeping thing, and the fowls of the air; for it repenteth me that I have made them.

8 But Noah found grace in the eyes of the Lord.

13 And God said unto Noah, The end of all flesh is come before me; for the earth is filled with violence through them; and, behold, I will destroy them with the earth.

17 And, behold, I, even I, do bring a flood of waters upon the earth, to destroy all flesh, wherein is the breath of life, from under heaven; and every thing that is in the earth shall die.

18 But with thee will I establish my covenant; and thou shalt come into the ark, thou, and thy sons, and thy wife, and thy sons' wives with thee.

19 And of every living thing of all flesh, two of every sort shalt thou bring into the ark, to keep them alive with thee; they shall be male and female.

20 Of fowls after their kind, and of cattle after their kind, of every creeping thing of the earth after his kind, two of every sort shall come unto thee, to keep them alive.

21 And take thou unto thee of all food that is eaten, and thou shalt gather it to thee; and it shall be for food for thee, and for them.

22 Thus did Noah; according to all that God commanded him, so did he.

Rule #6 'You Cut Down a Forest One Tree at a Time'

Unlike Noah and Nephi, who only had to rescue their small families, Jared had a whole tribe of people to carry across the ocean. Granted, Noah also had the animals to deal with, but I think people can be more of a pain. Jared not only had to build one barge for God, oh no, not just one, he had to create eight barges.

> **(Book of Mormon: Ether 2:16-17)[3]**
> *16 And the Lord said: Go to work and build, after the manner of barges which ye have hitherto built. And it came to pass that the brother of Jared did go to work, and also his brethren, and built barges after the manner which they had built, according to the instructions of the Lord. And they were small, and they were light upon the water, even like unto the lightness of a fowl upon the water.*
>
> *17 And they were built after a manner that they were exceedingly tight, even that they would hold water like unto a dish; and the bottom thereof was tight like unto a dish; and the sides thereof were tight like unto a dish; and the ends thereof were peaked; and the top thereof was tight like unto a dish; and the length thereof was the length of a tree; and the door thereof, when it was shut, was tight like unto a dish.*

Now building a barge is a little different than building a ship. Barges are designed to carry grain or materials and are sealed so that no air, water, or light can seep in to ruin the cargo. Barges are not meant to transport people or livestock. It's impossible for a living person to survive for months in an airtight vessel without light. Although Jared had built many barges, these new barges had features that had to be redesigned. Jared was skilled in boat building, but this new task from God presented huge complications. How would Jared allow for light or fresh air to enter a sealed boat?

> **(Book of Mormon: Ether 2:19-23)[3]**
> *19 And behold, O Lord, in them there is no light; whither shall we steer? And also we shall perish, for*

Rule #6 'You Cut Down a Forest One Tree at a Time'

in them we cannot breathe, save it is the air which is in them; therefore we shall perish.

20 And the Lord said unto the brother of Jared: Behold, thou shalt make a hole in the top, and also in the bottom; and when thou shalt suffer for air thou shalt unstop the hole and receive air. And if it be so that the water come in upon thee, behold, ye shall stop the hole, that ye may not perish in the flood.

21 And it came to pass that the brother of Jared did so, according as the Lord had commanded.

22 And he cried again unto the Lord saying: O Lord, behold I have done even as thou hast commanded me; and I have prepared the vessels for my people, and behold there is no light in them. Behold, O Lord, wilt thou suffer that we shall cross this great water in darkness?

23 And the Lord said unto the brother of Jared: What will ye that I should do that ye may have light in your vessels? For behold, ye cannot have windows, for they will be dashed in pieces; neither shall ye take fire with you, for ye shall not go by the light of fire.

(Book of Mormon: Ether 3:3-6)[3]
3 Behold, O Lord, thou hast smitten us because of our iniquity, and hast driven us forth, and for these many years we have been in the wilderness; nevertheless, thou hast been merciful unto us. O Lord, look upon me in pity, and turn away thine anger from this thy people, and suffer not that they shall go forth across this raging deep in darkness; but behold these things which I have molten out of the rock.

4 And I know, O Lord, that thou hast all power, and can do whatsoever thou wilt for the benefit of man; therefore touch these stones, O Lord, with thy finger, and prepare them that they may shine forth in darkness; and they shall shine forth unto us in the

Rule #6 'You Cut Down a Forest One Tree at a Time'

vessels which we have prepared, that we may have light while we shall cross the sea.

5 Behold, O Lord, thou canst do this. We know that thou art able to show forth great power, which looks small unto the understanding of men.

6 And it came to pass that when the brother of Jared had said these words, behold, the Lord stretched forth his hand and touched the stones one by one with his finger. And the veil was taken from off the eyes of the brother of Jared, and he saw the finger of the Lord; and it was as the finger of a man, like unto flesh and blood; and the brother of Jared fell down before the Lord, for he was struck with fear.

The last boatbuilder we will talk about is Nephi. God commanded Nephi to build a large boat, to sail across uncharted waters, for an unknown distance, to reach a promised land he had never seen before. Noah had his sons to help. Jared had all the Jaredites to help. Nephi had only two unwilling brothers and they hated him. Nephi had never built a boat in his life, and his brothers were eager to point out the folly in Nephi's plan.

(Book of Mormon: 1 Nephi 17:17-20)[3]
17 And when my brethren saw that I was about to build a ship, they began to murmur against me, saying: Our brother is a fool, for he thinketh that he can build a ship; yea, and he also thinketh that he can cross these great waters.

18 And thus my brethren did complain against me, and were desirous that they might not labor, for they did not believe that I could build a ship; neither would they believe that I was instructed of the Lord.

19 And now it came to pass that I, Nephi, was exceedingly sorrowful because of the hardness of their hearts; and now when they saw that I began to be sorrowful they were glad in their hearts, insomuch that they did rejoice over me, saying: We

> knew that ye could not construct a ship, for we knew that ye were lacking in judgment; wherefore, thou canst not accomplish so great a work.
>
> 20 And thou art like unto our father, led away by the foolish imaginations of his heart; yea, he hath led us out of the land of Jerusalem, and we have wandered in the wilderness for these many years; and our women have toiled, being big with child; and they have borne children in the wilderness and suffered all things, save it were death; and it would have been better that they had died before they came out of Jerusalem than to have suffered these afflictions.

Let My People Go:

My final example of a great hero from the Bible, who was given a seemingly impossible task, is Moses, chosen by God to free his people from Egyptian rule. What a task to be given! The Lord asked -- and Moses did it.

I hate to admit it, but there has been a time or two where the Lord, through my church, has asked me to do a simple task and I complained. One pitiful example—when finally, after working 45 days straight, I was granted a day off. Well, the Lord had other plans for me. He asked me to give up this precious day off to assist a family that needed my help. I complained about it to the Lord, and I complained to myself. I complained about having to give up just one day of my life to serve others. Who do you think was asked to do the more laborious task, Moses or me? Poor Moses, of course.

I know I complained about a little thing. Nonetheless, to make myself feel better about it, I can say that even Moses, who had already seen God do a lot of great miracles, complained and that kindled God's anger. Why? Because Moses thought part of the task the Lord had given him was too hard. You see, Moses wasn't eloquent at speech and he needed to convince the Pharaoh to let God's people go. Instead of having faith in God's judgment, Moses whined about how unqualified he was.

Rule #6 'You Cut Down a Forest One Tree at a Time'

How many of us have complained about our tasks? Did I just mention I had?

> **(Bible Old Testament: Exodus 4:10-16)**[1]
>
> 10 ¶ And Moses said unto the Lord, O my Lord, I am not eloquent, neither heretofore, nor since thou hast spoken unto thy servant: but I am slow of speech, and of a slow tongue.
>
> 11 And the Lord said unto him, Who hath made man's mouth? or who maketh the dumb, or deaf, or the seeing, or the blind? have not I the Lord?
>
> 12 Now therefore go, and I will be with thy mouth, and teach thee what thou shalt say.
>
> 13 And he said, O my Lord, send, I pray thee, by the hand of him whom thou wilt send.
>
> 14 And the anger of the Lord was kindled against Moses, and he said, Is not Aaron the Levite thy brother? I know that he can speak well. And also, behold, he cometh forth to meet thee: and when he seeth thee, he will be glad in his heart.
>
> 15 And thou shalt speak unto him, and put words in his mouth: and I will be with thy mouth, and with his mouth, and will teach you what ye shall do.
>
> 16 And he shall be thy spokesman unto the people: and he shall be, even he shall be to thee instead of a mouth, and thou shalt be to him instead of God.

Do You See It:

All four men, Noah, Jared, Nephi, and Moses, were given tasks of so great a size it would humble any man, yet they completed the task. Read and study the stories of what they had to deal with. It was a lot more than just building a ship or walking a few people out of a country to another land. Yet each one of these men accepted the task and handled it one-step at a time.

There is one other thing I am sure you found while reading their stories; at least I hope you did. Just because God chose them for a mission, this did not mean they couldn't ask for help. Help was always available, either from other people or from God Himself.

God has promised us the same blessings as He did Moses and the others. These blessings do not just apply to the tasks God gives us; they apply to every task we do in our daily lives. God is our Father and loves us no differently than a father should love his son. I believe in that love and count on His love every day of my life.

There is no task so big that we can't handle it. Just cut down that forest one tree at a time. And remember, no one said you had to do it alone.

Encouragement From Others:

I use the forest and tree as my example to motivate me. My wife doesn't particularly care for my choice of words, but we all have different ways of saying the same thing. That is the beauty of speech and the written word. There are many ways to say the same thing. Here are a few passages of scripture and famous quotes from others.

> ### (Book of Mormon: Alma 37:6-7)[3]
> *6 Now ye may suppose that this is foolishness in me; but behold I say unto you, that by small and simple things are great things brought to pass; and small means in many instances doth confound the wise.*
>
> *7 And the Lord God doth work by means to bring about his great and eternal purposes; and by very small means the Lord doth confound the wise and bringeth about the salvation of many souls.*
>
> ### (Doctrine & Covenants 64:33)[4]
> *33 Wherefore, be not weary in well-doing, for ye are laying the foundation of a great work. And out of small things proceedeth that which is great.*

(Lao Tzu)[6]
"The journey of a 1000 miles begins with 1 step."

(Chinese Proverb)[7]
"To get through the hardest journey we need take only one step at a time, but we must keep on stepping."

(Unknown)[8]
"Learn to focus on the task at hand, take it one step at a time, life is too expensive a gadget to be operated on trial and error."

(Indian Proverb)[9]
"When we take one step toward God, he takes seven steps towards us."

(Martin Luther King, Jr.)[10]
"Take the first step in faith. You don't have to see the whole staircase, just take the first step."

Final Words:

I have given you a few scriptural references of men who lived thousands of years ago who were given extraordinary tasks to accomplish. But there are stories of people achieving the impossible in more current history. People such as Abraham Lincoln, who, against the odds, ended slavery by working to pass the 13th Amendment to the Constitution even though it cost him his life. Mahatma Gandhi liberated India from British oppression, and Nelson Mandela helped end apartheid rule in South Africa.

Although Lincoln ended slavery, it wasn't until people such as Martin Luther King, Jr. and Rosa Parks stood up to inequality and led the battle in the civil rights movement that real freedom started to become a reality for African-Americans. The people I have named are well-known individuals, and so are their tasks. Rosa Parks worked as a poor seamstress. Abe Lincoln grew up a simple Midwest boy, and Nelson Mandela spent 27 years of his life in prison. Martin Luther King, Jr.

began his career as a pastor of a small church, and while living his vocation, lost his life. Moses was not of noble birth, but a humble Israelite at birth. These people are well-known individuals today, and so are their world-changing tasks. I don't mention them solely for their exceptional accomplishments, but to point out that they were simple people equal to you and me.

These people completed great tasks, yet as I said before, they accomplished them by cutting down the forest one tree at a time, seeking the help of others, and above all, having faith in God. You also can handle any task you are given if you apply this principle.

If fear of the unknown has a grip on you and is stopping you from getting started, then apply Rule #5 *'You Always Know Something'*. If procrastination is your enemy, then apply Rule #17 *'Manage Your Procrastinations or They Will Manage You'*. Then grab your chainsaw or ax, if that is all you have, and get started. God is always with you.

Rule #6 'You Cut Down a Forest One Tree at a Time'

Endnotes:

1 **King James Version of the Bible, The Old Testament of Our Lord and Saviour Jesus Christ.** Published by The Church of Jesus Christ of Latter-day Saints, Salt Lake City, Utah, USA. Copywrite 2013.

2 **King James Version of the Bible, The New Testament of Our Lord and Saviour Jesus Christ.** Published by The Church of Jesus Christ of Latter-day Saints, Salt Lake City, Utah, USA. Copywrite 2013.

3 **The Book of Mormon Another Testament of Jesus Christ.** Published by The Church of Jesus Christ of Latter-day Saints, Salt Lake City, Utah, USA. The first English edition published in Palmyra, New York, USA, in 1830. Copywrite 2013.

4 **The Doctrine and Covenants of The Church of Jesus Christ of Latter-Day Saints.** Containing Revelations Give to Joseph Smith, the Prophet. With some additions by his successors in the Presidency of the Church. Published by The Church of Jesus Christ of Latter-day Saints, Salt Lake City, Utah, USA. Copywrite 2013.

5 **The Pearl of Great Price.** A selection from the revelations, translations, and narrations of Joseph Smith, First Prophet, seer, and revelator to The Church of Jesus Christ of Latter-Day Saints. Published by The Church of Jesus Christ of Latter-day Saints, Salt Lake City, Utah, USA. Copywrite 2013.

6 **Lao Tzu.** Lao Tzu Quotes. (n.d.). BrainyQuote.com. Retrieved February 10, 2019, from BrainyQuote.com Web site: https://www.brainyquote.com/quotes/lao_tzu_137141.

7 **Chinese Proverb.** *Chinese Proverbs. (n.d.). QuotesWave.com. Retrieved February 10, 2019, from QuotesWave.com. Website: http://www.quoteswave.com/picture-quotes/83274. Source: wellnessinspo* Posted on February 13, 2013 via self-harm-support, from http://cuttingsupport.tumblr.com/post/ 39019462925/as-long-as-we-keep-stepping-we-will-be-a-little.

8 **Unknown.** Unknown Quotes. (n.d) searchquotes.com. *Retrieved February 10, 2019, from* searchquotes.com website: www.searchquotes.com/quotation/Learn_to_focus_on_the_task_at_hand%2C_take_it_one_step_at_a_time%2C_life_is_too_expensive_a_gadget_to_be/350699/. The author is unknown and there is no other information than that given at this time.

9 **Indian Proverb.** (n.d.). ThinkExist.com Quotations. "Indian Proverb quotes". ThinkExist.com Quotations Online 1 Jan. 2019. 10 Feb. 2019 http://thinkexist.com/quotes/indian_proverb/2.html. The author is unknown and there is no other information than that given at this time.

10 **Martin Luther King, Jr.** (n.d.). ThinkExist.com Quotations. "Martin Luther King, Jr. quotes". ThinkExist.com Quotations Online 1 Jan. 2019. 10 Feb. 2019 http://thinkexist.com/quotes/martin_luther_king,_jr./.

Rule #6 'You Cut Down a Forest One Tree at a Time'

Listen to the Sound of Silence

Rule #7

'Need Help? Stop and Listen'

Rule #7 'Need Help? Stop and Listen'

In a Nutshell:

Listening is one of the most important aspects of gaining understanding. Yet, most of us truly don't grasp the concept of its full benefits. The art of listening takes more practice than playing the piano or mastering the violin.

When we learn the true art of listening, we gain access to a wealth of knowledge that can help us in solving our most complex issues. The trouble is most of us are not masters at listening, we are amateurs. Thus, when we need help or strive for understanding, we find ourselves lost searching high and low, unable to find the answers we seek. Yet, in most cases, the answer has been given to us many times.

If we have been given the answer, why is it we don't have it? I mean, we asked, and you say it was given, so where is it? Well, it went right past us. Even though we were physically present when the answer was announced, illustrated, or explained, we missed it. Why? Because we weren't paying attention and thus didn't hear the answer.

Hearing is not listening. They are two different words completely. It takes more than your ears hearing a sound to qualify as listening.

> **(Andre Gide)**[6]
> *"Everything has been said before, but since nobody listens we have to keep going back and beginning all over again."*

In a nutshell, there is no simple answer to the question, 'how does one listen properly'. I can't pack all the information needed into a simple, direct sentence to fit in a nutshell. Understanding how to be a good listener relies on several factors besides just hearing someone talk. There are no simple shortcuts to developing and applying good listening skills. It takes a lot of study and practice.

Knowledge is Everything, "NOT":

Knowing how to listen does not instantly make us good listeners, but it is a good solid start. Listening, as with anything else you want to be good at, takes practice. Lots of practice. Listening takes much more practice than other skills do. I am still practicing.

I would like to be able to say that because I am armed with some knowledge on the subject that I'm a good listener. I am not. That is why 'Rule #7 *'Looking for Help? Stop and Listen'* is on my list. It is on my list to remind me that I need to be a better listener and that if I don't practice, I will not get better.

Faster than a Speeding Bullet:

We take one of our most fundamental God-given senses, listening, and assume (here is where Rule #2 comes in) that we understand how to use it properly to communicate with others. It is a scientific fact that hearing is one of the slowest senses to register in the brain. Sight, smell, and touch are registered and deciphered by the brain far quicker. The brain has to slow down the other senses, like a time warp, to synchronize them to the sounds we hear.

Peter Michael Senge (born 1947) is an American scientist and director of the Center for Organizational Learning at the MIT Sloan School of Management. He gives us these inspiring words on listening:

> **(Peter Senge)**[7]
> *"To listen fully means to pay close attention to what is being said beneath the words. You listen not only to the 'music,' but to the essence of the person speaking. You listen not only for what someone knows, but for what he or she is. Ears operate at the speed of sound, which is far slower than the speed of light the eyes take in. Generative listening is the art of developing deeper silences in yourself, so you can slow our mind's hearing to your ears' natural speed, and hear beneath the words to their meaning."*

Alms, Alms, Alms:

Learning to use all our senses as we listen is not a simple task. There are many religious groups, as well as others, like some professions in the medical field, who spend their entire lives training themselves to be better listeners. Many of these groups use different forms of meditation as a means of clearing their minds so they may better connect to their surroundings and/or receive spiritual insight. Some of these groups will practice the art of listening for hours a day, and others an entire lifetime.

It is a very small percentage of people that take the time in their lives to practice the art of listening. How much time do you spend training yourself to listen? Most people don't even spend 10 minutes a week.

Other than my parents yelling at me to pay attention every now and then when I was younger, and perhaps a few times as I became older, I don't recall having been given any formal training in the art of listening. I do remember being put in the corner of a room for not listening, with the hope that it would teach me to listen better. I also remember being yelled at for not being quiet, but I don't know if that was for being too noisy or to teach me how to listen?

How much quality training do we as parents give our children? My guess is that as parents, when our children are born, we check to see that they have two good ears, and then we make funny noises at them in an attempt to get a giggly laughter response, thus verifying the child's ability to hear. Thus, we have determined that the child knows how to properly listen, as well. Then as they grow, how much training do our children receive in the art of listening? Hearing is not listening, is it?

What about adults? Do we continue our education in listening?

Learning the Art of Not Listening:

To better understand the art of listening, let's first define a few qualities that are not conducive to good listening. Many of us make some common mistakes that liken the listening experience to looking at the Grand Canyon on a foggy day. I found an article by Dr. Larry K. Langlois, a Family and Marriage Counselor, that addresses a few of these mistakes. Dr. Langlois writes about listening so well already, I saw no reason to rewrite it in my own words. Read what he has to say about bad listening habits, and see if you are guilty of any.

> **(Dr. Larry K. Langlois, Family and Marriage Counselor)**[8]
>
> ***Some confuse listening with discussing:***
> "*Listening is a one-way process; it involves hearing and understanding a message that another person is conveying. Discussing, on the other hand, is a two-way interchange of ideas. While discussion involves listening skills, the art of listening is important in its own right and must sometimes be used alone.*
>
> *Effective listening requires full attention, rather than the rapid switching between listening and talking that is involved in discussion. This rapid switching can preclude the more intensive, careful listening that allows a person to reveal more details.*
>
> ***Some confuse listening with problem-solving:***
> *To listen is to understand, not to propose solutions. Helping to find solutions might be a next step, but it is not part of the listening process. In fact, it may even interfere with helpful listening.*
>
> *When we as listeners have already made up our minds about something, we may block out messages that do not fit our expectations. Disappointment, anxiety, fear, or other negative emotions can also block out even the clearest messages. Instead of projecting our feelings onto what someone is telling us, we need to concentrate on hearing the speaker's feelings.*

Learning the Art of Not Listening:

To better understand the art of listening, let's first define a few qualities that are not conducive to good listening. Many of us make some common mistakes that liken the listening experience to looking at the Grand Canyon on a foggy day. I found an article by Dr. Larry K. Langlois, a Family and Marriage Counselor, that addresses a few of these mistakes. Dr. Langlois writes about listening so well already, I saw no reason to rewrite it in my own words. Read what he has to say about bad listening habits, and see if you are guilty of any.

> **(Dr. Larry K. Langlois, Family and Marriage Counselor)**[8]
> ***Some confuse listening with discussing:***
> *"Listening is a one-way process; it involves hearing and understanding a message that another person is conveying. Discussing, on the other hand, is a two-way interchange of ideas. While discussion involves listening skills, the art of listening is important in its own right and must sometimes be used alone.*
>
> *Effective listening requires full attention, rather than the rapid switching between listening and talking that is involved in discussion. This rapid switching can preclude the more intensive, careful listening that allows a person to reveal more details.*
>
> ***Some confuse listening with problem-solving:***
> *To listen is to understand, not to propose solutions. Helping to find solutions might be a next step, but it is not part of the listening process. In fact, it may even interfere with helpful listening.*
>
> *When we as listeners have already made up our minds about something, we may block out messages that do not fit our expectations. Disappointment, anxiety, fear, or other negative emotions can also block out even the clearest messages. Instead of projecting our feelings onto what someone is telling us, we need to concentrate on hearing the speaker's feelings.*

Rule #7 'Need Help? Stop and Listen'

Alms, Alms, Alms:

Learning to use all our senses as we listen is not a simple task. There are many religious groups, as well as others, like some professions in the medical field, who spend their entire lives training themselves to be better listeners. Many of these groups use different forms of meditation as a means of clearing their minds so they may better connect to their surroundings and/or receive spiritual insight. Some of these groups will practice the art of listening for hours a day, and others an entire lifetime.

It is a very small percentage of people that take the time in their lives to practice the art of listening. How much time do you spend training yourself to listen? Most people don't even spend 10 minutes a week.

Other than my parents yelling at me to pay attention every now and then when I was younger, and perhaps a few times as I became older, I don't recall having been given any formal training in the art of listening. I do remember being put in the corner of a room for not listening, with the hope that it would teach me to listen better. I also remember being yelled at for not being quiet, but I don't know if that was for being too noisy or to teach me how to listen?

How much quality training do we as parents give our children? My guess is that as parents, when our children are born, we check to see that they have two good ears, and then we make funny noises at them in an attempt to get a giggly laughter response, thus verifying the child's ability to hear. Thus, we have determined that the child knows how to properly listen, as well. Then as they grow, how much training do our children receive in the art of listening? Hearing is not listening, is it?

What about adults? Do we continue our education in listening?

> ***Being judgmental:*** *The fastest way to stop a person from talking, especially about painful and difficult subjects, is to criticize them*
>
> ***Indulging the need to correct errors:*** *When people are expressing strong feelings, they often exaggerate or overstate the facts—sometimes in anger and with accusations. As we listen, we need to concentrate on hearing the message, rather than on correcting the facts.*
>
> ***Blocking:*** *It's easy to misunderstand a message when we really don't want to hear it. No matter how clearly it is stated, we can reject, reinterpret, or fail to comprehend an unpleasant message. When we as listeners have already made up our minds about something, we may block out messages that do not fit our expectations."*

Focus, Focus, Come on Stay Focused:

As much as we humans like to think that we are great at multi-tasking, when it comes to listening, we cannot be properly tuned in to the words of inspiration, guidance, or instruction, whether from God, a professional instructor, or a friend, when the mind or any other part of the body is busy doing something else. The mind and body must be focused on hearing what is being said to us to gain true understanding. I find this quote from M. Scott Peck to ring true:

> **(Morgan Scott Peck)**[9]
> *"You cannot truly listen to anyone and do anything else at the same time."*

Do you want a good understanding of what the 'lack of focus' is? Who better to study than young children listening to a lecture? Studies show that the focus span of a three-year-old child is 5 minutes or less. A ten-year-old attention span is about 10 minutes tops. Sadly, for many adults, it is about the same. Ouch! Did I say that? Did you hear that?

Rule #7 'Need Help? Stop and Listen'

We cannot hear answers to our cries for help if we lack good listening skills. One of the more important skills in good listening is proper focus. Please note that I said proper focus.

True focus in any type of communication is the first step to being a good listener. Calming your mind and focusing your attention on the circumstances around you will help you manage your world, allow you to block out unwanted distractions, and concentrate your attention on listening. Good focus requires you to be aware of all your senses: sight, smell, touch, taste, and hearing, as well as your body movements. Any unexpected environmental input can distract you while you are listening and thus cause you to miss a vital piece of information. Focusing starts with focusing on yourself, your whole being, then you will be able to hear the information you need for better communication, heal-their relationships, and improved job performance.

Giving your full attention to a person or a task, particularly in this day and age, is not easy. Today it is standard to multi-task almost everything you do. However, it is counter-productive to multi-task while listening. Multi-tasking is the enemy of a good listener. Why? Because good listening in itself requires a tremendous amount of multi-tasking that will keep the best human brain busy.

When I talk about eliminating distractions while listening, I don't mean you must remain idle while having a casual conversation. Doing dishes, cooking dinner, working in the garden, or driving the car are all fine to do during a casual conversation; but are not fine when having an important conversation.

As I have said, there are many ways outwardly we show that we are not totally focused on the speaker. Some examples are: playing with something in your hands, chewing gum, eating, working, or moving around the room. All of these actions require a part of our brain and attention and keep us from being totally focused.

Rule #7 'Need Help? Stop and Listen'

There is a scripture in the 'Book of Mormon' that expresses a good example of a people not hearing because they are not focused:

> **(Book of Mormon: 3 Nephi 11: 3-4)[3]**
> *3 And it came to pass that while they were thus conversing one with another, they heard a voice as if it came out of heaven; and they cast their eyes round about, for they understood not the voice which they heard; and it was not a harsh voice, neither was it a loud voice; nevertheless, and notwithstanding it being a small voice it did pierce them that did hear to the center, insomuch that there was no part of their frame that it did not cause to quake; yea, it did pierce them to the very soul, and did cause their hearts to burn.*
>
> *4 And it came to pass that again they heard the voice, and they understood it not.*

It was not until verses 5-6 that the people did hear and understand:

> **(Book of Mormon: 3 Nephi 11: 5-7)[3]**
> *5 And again the third time they did hear the voice, and did open their ears to hear it; and their eyes were towards the sound thereof; and they did look steadfastly towards heaven, from whence the sound came.*
>
> *6 And behold, the third time they did understand the voice which they heard; and it said to them:*
>
> *7 Behold my Beloved Son, in whom I am well pleased, in whom I have glorified my name—hear ye him.*

And why did the people hear and understand? Verse 5 tells us the answer: '... *did open their ears to hear it; and their eyes were towards the sound thereof; and they did look steadfastly towards heaven, from whence the sound came ...*' (3 Nephi 11: 5). As the verse tells us, the people finally gave the voice their full attention. They opened their ears, looked steadfast into the heavens, and they were focused.

Formulating a reply in your mind while listening is the biggest violation of 'don't multi-task and try to listen' that I can think of, yet many people do it. Let me reiterate; rather than listening to the information a person is trying to communicate; most listeners focus on formulating a reply. When you are focused more on yourself than on the information you need to be receiving, you fail at listening.

Albert Guinon, a French playwright, wrote many inspirational quotes. I find this quote to fit here quite well.

> **(Albert Guinon)**[10]
> *"There are people who, instead of listening to what is being said to them, are already listening to what they are going to say themselves."*

Then there is a scripture from the New Testament that I feel applies very well to the point I am trying to make:

> **(Bible New Testament: James 1:19)**[2]
> *19 Wherefore, my beloved brethren, let every man be swift to hear, slow to speak, ...*

When in *James 1:19* he says *'slow to speak'* I believe this applies to your thoughts as well.

Stephen R. Covey, a famous speaker, and motivational author, puts it into perspective very well in this famous quote:

> **(Stephen R. Covey, "7 Habits of Highly Effective People")**[11]
> *"Seek first to understand, then to be understood."*

> **(Oliver Wendell Holmes, Sr.)**[12]
> *"It is the province of knowledge to speak. And it is the privilege of wisdom to listen."*

In my opinion, the second biggest violation of multi-tasking while listening is this: you think you know what the other person is going to say before they say it. Because you assume you know what the person is going to say, your thoughts begin to wander. Thus, you allow your mind to multi-task rather than focusing on listening.

Please let what you are about to read soak into your brain. That is, before you make any conclusions, you must first collect all the information you can to gain understanding. To assume you know what someone is going to say while you are listening breaks Rule #2 *'Don't Assume'*, and breaking Rule #2 will more than likely lead to breaking Rule #1 *'Failure Is Not An Option'*.

Anything that distracts you from hearing all the information brings you closer to failure, the failure of true understanding, and without the complete message, you will fail to get the help you need for yourself or others.

Here is another good quote that I think is worth mentioning at this point:

> **(Kenneth A. Wells)**[13]
> *"A good listener tries to understand what the other person is saying. In the end he may disagree sharply, but because he disagrees, he wants to know exactly what it is he is disagreeing with."*

Hey! Can You Hear Me?

Listening is not just a matter of hearing sounds and interpreting their meaning. There is a second part of listening, and that is observing body language and the emotions they convey. Often it does not require sound at all. Ask any deaf person. They may not hear sounds, but they understand the art of listening to the world around them better than most people. Being deaf is a handicap to listening, but hearing is only a small factor in practicing proper listening skills. A UCLA research study has shown that only 7% of communication is based on the actual words we say. As for the rest, 38% comes from tone of voice, and the remaining 55% comes from body language. I will add another vital key

Rule #7 'Need Help? Stop and Listen'

to the UCLA research study, I feel they left out, and that is above all, we must learn to listen with our spirit and our heart.

> **(Dr. Larry K. Langlois)**[14]
> ***Learn to read nonverbal messages:*** *"Only about 30 percent of our communication is verbal; the rest is nonverbal. In other words, most of the messages we convey to others are communicated by facial expression, body language, voice inflections, positioning, and other nonverbal means. Even a simple phrase like 'What do you think of that!' can express disgust, anger, humor, surprise, or interest by the way it is said."*
>
> *"The Lord urges us to 'be still and know that I am God' (D&C 101:16). This suggests that we cannot understand God or hear whatever message he might have for us if we are unwilling to be still and listen. By implication, we cannot understand anyone else or hear what they have to say unless we are willing to set aside our own concerns, postpone trying to convey messages, be still, and listen."*

However, by using good listening skills, which means tuning in to more than a person's words, I could understand the concern they were trying to articulate.

I have been in many counseling sessions listening to what a person was verbally expressing, yet their words really weren't conveying a clear meaning of their thoughts, concerns, or problem. However, by using good listening skills, which means tuning in to more than a person's words, I could understand the concern they were trying to articulate. Many of us have a hard time putting into words the message we want to convey to another; that is why listening to words alone does not make for a good listener. If that were the case, we would all be great communicators and writers; think about it.

Rule #7 'Need Help? Stop and Listen'

What Am I Listening For?

The third part of listening is to understand what information it is that you need to hear. This is another vital key to successful listening. Are you listening to what you want to hear, or are you listening to what you need to hear? When you seek answers to questions, often the answers you receive are not the answers you expected, nor are they the answers you may have thought you needed. As you implement the first part of listening, which is to focus, be careful you do not focus on what you think the answer should be, or there is a very good chance that you will miss hearing the true answer or fail to gain the knowledge you are seeking. Listening does not require understanding, but understanding requires listening.

The fourth part of listening is harmony. As a conductor directs an orchestra through a symphony, so must all the information flowing into your head from all your senses be guided and directed to its place in the brain to be stored and deciphered. Additionally, you cannot let one instrument play so loud it drowns out the others, nor so softly that it doesn't register in the brain. No instrument gets center stage, but each an important part to play.

Timing is everything when it comes to having good harmony. As you listen, a lot is going on. Many different pieces and types of information must be sorted through. As your brain processes and conducts this orchestra of information, you are in the same span of time analyzing it to find the understanding you seek. This is not an easy task.

Handling, managing, conducting, whatever word you want to use, they all describe the organizational process of listening. Listening is a complex art. One missed gesture, emotion, or word can change what you take away from the experience. Missing or adding a simple word, such as 'not' changes the whole meaning. Miss a simple word, and you miss what you needed to hear to learn what you needed to learn. Miss the emotion in how a statement is spoken and you miss the intent of what was said. Miss a body movement, a hand gesture, or head tilt, and you miss understanding the depth of what is being conveyed.

Translating It All With Wisdom:

Part five of listening and the final part of this complex puzzle is wisdom. It is wisdom that gives us the final key, the last puzzle piece that completes the picture of proper communication. The wisdom to know what to listen to and what not to listen to. The wisdom to comprehend the non-verbal aspects like body language, emotions, and history. The wisdom to know when to speak and when not to speak. The wisdom to know the words that needed to be spoken but were not spoken. Finally, the wisdom to take in all this information and take away the understanding you need.

There are many different kinds of wisdom required to become a Master Listener. That list is endless, and I know for sure that my mind does not contain enough wisdom or knowledge to cover that list. Nor do I think that while I am in this temporal (physical) Earthly state of being that my brain could contain the knowledge and wisdom needed to become a true Master Listener. That being said, I plan to use all my God-given talents while in this existence to train myself to become a Master Listener.

We all have been given gifts, talents, and limitations. It is a part of Heavenly Father's plan for us while we live in this mortal state. We have to deal with the fact that we all have limitations. These same limitations prevent us from becoming Master Listeners, but that does not mean we cannot become good listeners. Though our abilities are sometimes limited, it does not mean that we cannot improve. Denying or ignoring your limitations will hinder your ability to become a good listener.

You need to understand that your limitations are not a curse but a blessing. Limitations are given to us to learn faith, and with faith, we are granted access to the wisdom and knowledge of the true Master Listener, the power of the Holy Ghost, and our savior Jesus Christ.

Rule #7 'Need Help? Stop and Listen'

When you exercise your faith in the Savior, He will grant access to His endless wisdom and knowledge, and thus make up for your limitations. Heavenly Father has provided us the Master Listener, and He has promised that all who ask Him in faith will be blessed with what they need. Here are a few scriptures to back up my statement:

(Bible New Testament: James 1:5-8)[2]

5 If any of you lack wisdom, let him ask of God, that giveth to all men liberally, and upbraideth not; and it shall be given him.

6 But let him ask in faith, nothing wavering. For he that wavereth is like a wave of the sea driven with the wind and tossed.

7 For let not that man think that he shall receive any thing of the Lord.

8 A double minded man is unstable in all his ways.

(Bible New Testament: Matthew 7:7-8)[2] or (Book of Mormon: 3 Nephi 14:7-8)[3]

7 Ask, and it shall be given you; seek, and ye shall find; knock, and it shall be opened unto you:

8 For every one that asketh receiveth; and he that seeketh findeth; and to him that knocketh it shall be opened.

(Bible New Testament: Luke 11:9-13)[2]

9 And I say unto you, Ask, and it shall be given you; seek, and ye shall find; knock, and it shall be opened unto you.

10 For every one that asketh receiveth; and he that seeketh findeth; and to him that knocketh it shall be opened.

11 If a son shall ask bread of any of you that is a father, will he give him a stone? or if he ask a fish, will he for a fish give him a serpent?

12 Or if he shall ask an egg, will he offer him a scorpion?

13 If ye then, being evil, know how to give good gifts unto your children: how much more shall your heavenly Father give the Holy Spirit to them that ask him?

(Bible Old Testament: Job 32:7-11)[1]

7 I said, Days should speak, and multitude of years should teach wisdom.

8 But there is a spirit in man: and the inspiration of the Almighty giveth them understanding.

9 Great men are not always wise: neither do the aged understand judgment.

10 Therefore I said, Hearken to me; I also will shew mine opinion.

11 Behold, I waited for your words; I gave ear to your reasons, whilst ye searched out what to say.

(Bible New Testament: 1 Corinthians 2:12-14)[2]

12 Now we have received, not the spirit of the world, but the spirit which is of God; that we might know the things that are freely given to us of God.

13 Which things also we speak, not in the words which man's wisdom teacheth, but which the Holy Ghost teacheth; comparing spiritual things with spiritual.

14 But the natural man receiveth not the things of the Spirit of God: for they are foolishness unto him: neither can he know them, because they are spiritually discerned.

(Doctrine & Covenants 88:63-66)[4]

63 Draw near unto me and I will draw near unto you; seek me diligently and ye shall find me; ask, and ye shall receive; knock, and it shall be opened unto you.

64 Whatsoever ye ask the Father in my name it shall be given unto you, that is expedient for you;

> 65 And if ye ask anything that is not expedient for you, it shall turn unto your condemnation.
>
> 66 Behold, that which you hear is as the voice of one crying in the wilderness—in the wilderness, because you cannot see him—my voice, because my voice is Spirit; my Spirit is truth; truth abideth and hath no end; and if it be in you it shall abound.

I also would like to share with you the words of Elder Russell M. Nelson to support my statement on limitations and faith:

> **(Russell M. Nelson, 1991 April General Conference, " Listen to Learn")**[15]
>
> *"To all of God's children, either able to hear or deaf to mortal sound, He offers this reward: 'Incline your ear, and come unto me: hear, and your soul shall live.' (Isa. 55:3.)*
>
> *Your soul will be blessed as you learn to listen, then listen to learn from children, parents, partners, neighbors, and Church leaders, all of which will heighten capacity to hear counsel from on high.*
>
> *Carefully listen to learn from the Lord through the still small voice—the Holy Spirit—which leads to truth.*
>
> *Listen to learn by studying scriptures that record His holy mind and will.*
>
> *Listen to learn in prayer, for He will answer the humble who truly seek Him.*
>
> *The wise listen to learn from the Lord. I testify of Him and certify that as we 'hearken and ... hear the voice of the Lord,' we will be blessed, 'for the hour of his coming is nigh' (D&C 133:16–17), in the name of Jesus Christ, amen."*

The Bad Speaker:

Here is another example of limitations and faith called 'The Bad Speaker'. The story comes from a talk that John A. Green

Rule #7 'Need Help? Stop and Listen'

gave at the April 1981 church General Conference about a man having a difficult time giving a talk at church. The talk was so broken up and misspoken that it made it very hard to listen to the speaker. It would have been easier for John to close off his mind and ignore the message. John was thinking along those lines when the thought came to him that perhaps he needed to learn to listen better. He did, which lead to an answer to a gospel question he had had on his mind for ten years. The following are John's closing remarks:

(John A. Green, 1981 April Ensign, "A Lesson from My Conscience: Learning to Listen in Church")[16]

"I am now convinced that he taught me by the Spirit. But I am equally convinced that I would not have benefited from his talk had I not made an effort to listen by the Spirit. Above and beyond receiving the answer to the question that had bothered me for ten years, I learned that the call to listen is every bit as important as the call to speak or teach. Jesus himself taught in his native Nazareth; but hearing they heard not, and it profited them nothing.

That experience taught me something about my limitations. It taught me that I personally need to make a continual effort to listen spiritually in my meetings and classes. I believe this takes preparation on my part, just as it takes preparation on the part of the speakers and teachers.

I believe there are great things in store if I can develop the ability to listen by the Spirit. And I believe that by listening in that way, I can personally contribute to the spirit of any meeting or class I attend."

Here is yet another excerpt by David McConkie, about learning to listen to gain understanding from the Holy Ghost:

> **(David M. McConkie, 2011 February Ensign, "A Lesson from My Conscience: Learning to Hear and Understand the Spirit")**[17]
> "To learn the Spirit of God, we must learn to listen with our hearts. President Boyd K. Packer, President of the Quorum of the Twelve Apostles, said: 'The Spirit is a still, small voice—a voice that is felt rather than heard. It is a spiritual voice that comes into the mind as a thought put into your heart.'
>
> Learning to hear and understand the Spirit takes considerable effort. But the Lord has promised that the faithful will 'receive revelation upon revelation, knowledge upon knowledge, that [they may] know the mysteries and peaceable things—that which bringeth joy, that which bringeth life eternal' (D&C 42:61)."

Direct And To The Point:

President Brigham Young is a man after my own heart. I love how Brigham's words put it right straight out there for you. He just tells you like it is as he does here in this quote I have included:

> **(Brigham Young) 'Teachings of Presidents of the Church: Brigham Young' (1997), 68, 4)**[18]
> "If you want the mind and will of God ... , get it, it is just as much your privilege as of any other member of the Church and Kingdom of God. It is your privilege and duty to live so that you know when the word of the Lord is spoken to you and when the mind of the Lord is revealed to you. I say it is your duty to live so as to know and understand all these things."

I met President Spencer W. Kimball and conversed with him for over an hour. What a blessing the memories of that conversation was and still is to me. He was an inspirational man who understood what it takes to receive answers from Father in Heaven. In a talk at a Church General Conference,

Rule #7 'Need Help? Stop and Listen'

he reminded us about a very important point to remember when asking for God's help in prayer.

> **(Spencer W. Kimball, 1979 October General Conference, "We Need a Listening Ear")[19]**
> *"It would not hurt us, either, if we paused at the end of our prayers to do some intense listening-even for a moment or two-always praying, as the Savior did, 'not my will, but thine, be done, (Luke 22:42)."*

I loved the wisdom of Benjamin Franklin when he said:

> **(Benjamin Franklin, John Bartlett, comp., Familiar Quotations, Boston: Little, Brown and Company, 1968, p. 422)[20]**
> *"Work as if you were to live a hundred years, pray as if you were to die tomorrow."*

President Harold B. Lee gives us these words to ponder, along with a few words from Isaiah.

> **(Harold B Lee, 1972 April General Conference, "A Time of Decision")[21]**
> *"What a wonderful feeling of security can come in a crisis to one who has learned to pray and has cultivated listening ears so that he can 'call, and the Lord shall answer'; when he can cry and the Lord shall say, 'Here I am.' (Bible Old Testament; Isaiah 58:9)."*

I enjoyed this talk by Paul H. Dunn that I have included. I tried to find a way to cut out small sections of his talk to put into my writing, but I felt I couldn't without ruining some of the best parts. I believe all of what Paul had to say applies to listening. I hope you enjoy reading this insert from Paul H. Dunn's talk as much as I did.

> **(Paul H. Dunn, 1971 October General Conference, "What Is a Teacher")[22]**
> *"We have been taught well in this great conference, my brothers and sisters, and I have been thinking a great deal about teaching and great teachers. Last*

evening, Elder Marion D. Hanks brought to our attention the situation concerning his departed cousin, a Brother [Ivan] Frame, who had a deep impact on humanity. He mentioned that one of the great tributes paid at his funeral was that every boy should have a Brother Frame in his life.

I have thought about that, and I thank God repeatedly for such an individual in my life. He was a 78-year-old man who was assigned to be a priests adviser to six of us who were in our struggling teens and challenged with the future. His name was Charles B. Stewart. His son is here today as president of the great Tabernacle Choir.

I don't know what you thought about a 78-year-old man when you were 16, but some of us questioned the wisdom of our bishop, for we thought he had literally brought Moses back.

I remember the first day I reported to my class in that rickety old upper room of the Hollywood Ward. There was that kind, gentle man to greet me. He took me by the hand as he had the other boys and said, 'You're Harold Dunn's son, aren't you?'

I said, 'Yes, sir.'

He talked a little bit about me, my family, and showed a great personal interest. And then he said, 'Paul, one of the requirements for being a member of this class is to think a new thought every day.' He said, 'Do you have one this morning?'

Well now, I hadn't had a new thought in years, and he could see my plight, and he said, 'All right, I will teach you one. Listen carefully. 'Attention is the mother of memory.' Now can you repeat it back?' And I tried and finally gave it back to him. He permitted me to enter.

We had a wonderful class. It ended; as I went to leave he said, 'I forgot to tell you-before you go home you've got to give me another new idea.' I thought, I *won't go home. I didn't have one, and so he said, 'Now listen very carefully and I will teach you one that you'll always remember.' He said, 'Oh, what a tangled web we weave, When first we practise to deceive.' I've never forgotten it.*

Another week passed, and we went through a similar experience. I still didn't have a new thought. He said, 'Listen very carefully. 'There's an odd little voice ever speaking within that prompts us to duty and warns us from sin. And what is most strange, it makes itself heard, though it gives not a sound and says never a word.' And I've never forgotten that one.

I started to go home and found he wouldn't let me go until I cited another. When I couldn't he said, 'Listen carefully. There was a wise old owl who sat in an oak, and the longer he sat the less he spoke. The less he spoke, the more he heard. Oh, Paul, why can't you be like that wise old bird?'"

The Sum of All Things:

I think out of all the quotes and scripture I have included in this rule, I find that it is the simplest statements that tend to make the most significant impact. I don't think that Jesus Christ could have said it any simpler than he did in this scripture:

(Bible New Testament: Matthew 11:15)[2]
15 He that hath ears to hear, let him hear.

And for those that may need things spelled-out for clarity, I will close with this final writing from Herbert G. Lingren.

Herbert G. Lingren[23]
I speak because I know my needs,
I speak with hesitation because I know not yours,
My words come from my life's experiences.
Your understanding comes from yours.
Because of this, what I say,
And what you hear, may not be the same.
So, if you will listen carefully,
Not only with your ears,
But with your eyes and with your heart,
Maybe somehow, we can communicate.
(I added the following)
If we use the spirit of God, the Holy Ghost to guide,
Our communications will give us understanding,
And our feelings will not hide.

If you learn to stop and calm your mind long enough, you will find that a solution will come to you. I bear you my testimony of this in the name of Jesus Christ. AMEN

Rule #7 'Need Help? Stop and Listen'

Endnotes:

1 **King James Version of the Bible, The Old Testament of Our Lord and Saviour Jesus Christ.** Published by The Church of Jesus Christ of Latter-day Saints, Salt Lake City, Utah, USA. Copywrite 2013.

2 **King James Version of the Bible, The New Testament of Our Lord and Saviour Jesus Christ.** Published by The Church of Jesus Christ of Latter-day Saints, Salt Lake City, Utah, USA. Copywrite 2013.

3 **The Book of Mormon Another Testament of Jesus Christ.** Published by The Church of Jesus Christ of Latter-day Saints, Salt Lake City, Utah, USA. The first English edition published in Palmyra, New York, USA, in 1830. Copywrite 2013.

4 **The Doctrine and Covenants of The Church of Jesus Christ of Latter-Day Saints.** Containing Revelations Give to Joseph Smith, the Prophet. With some additions by his successors in the Presidency of the Church. Published by The Church of Jesus Christ of Latter-day Saints, Salt Lake City, Utah, USA. Copywrite 2013.

5 **The Pearl of Great Price.** A selection from the revelations, translations, and narrations of Joseph Smith, First Prophet, seer, and revelator to The Church of Jesus Christ of Latter-Day Saints. Published by The Church of Jesus Christ of Latter-day Saints, Salt Lake City, Utah, USA. Copywrite 2013.

6 **Andre Gide.** Andre Gide Quotes. (n.d.). BrainyQuote.com. Retrieved February 10, 2019, from BrainyQuote.com Web site: https://www.brainyquote.com/quotes/andre_gide_105039.

7 **Peter Senge.** Peter Senge. (n.d.). AZQuotes.com. Retrieved February 10, 2019, from AZQuotes.com Web site: https://www.azquotes.com/quote/669977.

8 **Dr. Larry K. Langlois.** Larry Kent Langlois. (n.d.). healthprovidersdata.com. Retrieved February 10, 2019 from healthprovidersdata.com (Health Providers Data) website: https://healthprovidersdata.com/hipaa/codes/NPI-1972720506-dr-larry-kent-langlois-phd.

9 **Morgan Scott Peck.** M. Scott Peck Quotes. (n.d.). BrainyQuote.com. Retrieved February 10, 2019, from BrainyQuote.com Web site: https://www.brainyquote.com/quotes/m_scott_peck_140346.

10 **Albert Guinon.** *Albert Guinon Quotes.* (n.d.). *Quotes.net.* Retrieved February 10, 2019, from https://www.quotes.net/quote/20374. Albert Guinon (1863-1923) was a French playwright.

11 **Stephen R. Covey,** "7 Habits of Highly Effective People". Stephen Covey Quotes. (n.d.). BrainyQuote.com. Retrieved February 10, 2019, from BrainyQuote.com Web site: https://www.brainyquote.com/quotes/stephen_covey_636491.

Rule #7 'Need Help? Stop and Listen'

12. **Oliver Wendell Holmes, Sr.** Oliver Wendell Holmes, Sr. Quotes. (n.d.). BrainyQuote.com. Retrieved February 10, 2019, from BrainyQuote.com Web site: https://www.brainyquote.com/quotes/oliver_wendell_holmes_sr_385593.

13. **Kenneth A. Wells**, *'Guide to Good Leadership'* ThinkExist.com Quotations. "Kenneth A. Wells quotes". (n.d.). ThinkExist.com Quotations Online 1 Jan. 2019. 10 Feb. 2019 http://en.thinkexist.com/quotes/kenneth_a._wells/. The author is unknown and there is no other information than that given at this time.

14. **Dr. Larry K. Langlois.** Larry Kent Langlois. (n.d.). healthprovidersdata.com. Retrieved February 10, 2019 from healthprovidersdata.com (Health Providers Data) website: https://healthprovidersdata.com/hipaa/codes/NPI-1972720506-dr-larry-kent-langlois-phd.

15. **Russell M. Nelson, 1991 April General Conference, " Listen to Learn".** The 161st Annual General Conference of the Church of Jesus Christ of Latter-day Saints, April 6, 1991, Saturday Afternoon Session. Published in the Ensign magazine, Volume 21 Number 05, May 1991. An official magazine of the Church of Jesus Christ of Latter-day Saints, published by the Church of Jesus Christ of Latter-day Saints, 50 E. North Temple Street, Salt Lake City, UT, 84150-3220, USA. Also, retrieved Nov 26,2019, from Ensign, ChurchofJesusChrist.Org website: https://www.churchofjesuschrist.org/study/ensign/1991/05/listen-to-learn?lang=eng

16. **John A. Green, 1981 April Ensign, "A Lesson from My Conscience: Learning to Listen in Church".** Published in the Ensign magazine, Volume 11 Number 04, April 1981. An official magazine of the Church of Jesus Christ of Latter-day Saints, published by the Church of Jesus Christ of Latter-day Saints, 50 E. North Temple Street, Salt Lake City, UT, 84150-3220, USA. Also, retrieved Nov 26,2019, from Ensign, ChurchofJesusChrist.Org website: https://www.churchofjesuschrist.org/study/ensign/1981/04/a-lesson-from-my-conscience-learning-to-listen-in-church?lang=eng

17. **David M. McConkie, 2011 February Ensign, "Learning to Hear and Understand the Spirit".** Published in the Ensign magazine, Volume 41 Number 02, Page 41 Paragraph 8, February 2011. An official magazine of the Church of Jesus Christ of Latter-day Saints, published by the Church of Jesus Christ of Latter-day Saints, 50 E. North Temple Street, Salt Lake City, UT, 84150-3220, USA. Also, retrieved Nov 26,2019, from Ensign, ChurchofJesusChrist.Org website: https://www.churchofjesuschrist.org/study/ensign/2011/02/learning-to-hear-and-understand-the-spirit.html?lang=eng#title1

Rule #7 'Need Help? Stop and Listen'

18. **Brigham Young, "Teachings of Presidents of the Church: Brigham Young,"** Published in the Teachings of the Presidents of the Church: Brigham Young, "The Influence of the Holy Ghost" page-68 paragraph-4. An official manual of the Church of Jesus Christ of Latter-day Saints, published 1997 by the Church of Jesus Christ of Latter-day Saints, 50 E. North Temple Street, Salt Lake City, UT, 84150-3220, USA. Also, retrieved Nov 26,2019, from ChurchofJesusChrist.Org website:
https://www.churchofjesuschrist.org/study/manual/teachings-brigham-young/chapter-10?lang=eng

19. **Spencer W. Kimball 1979 October General Conference, "We Need a Listening Ear".** The 149th Semiannual General Conference of the Church of Jesus Christ of Latter-day Saints, October 6, 1979, Saturday Morning Session. Published in the Ensign magazine, Volume 9 Number 11, November 1979. An official magazine of the Church of Jesus Christ of Latter-day Saints, published by the Church of Jesus Christ of Latter-day Saints, 50 E. North Temple Street, Salt Lake City, UT, 84150-3220, USA. Also, retrieved Nov 26,2019, from Ensign, ChurchofJesusChrist.Org website:
https://www.churchofjesuschrist.org/study/ensign/1979/11/we-need-a-listening-ear?lang=eng

20. **Benjamin Franklin** From John Bartlett, comp., Familiar Quotations, Boston: Little, Brown and Company, 1968, p. 422), and also from Benjamin Franklin Quotes. (n.d.). BrainyQuote.com. Retrieved February 10, 2019, from BrainyQuote.com Web site:
https://www.brainyquote.com/quotes/benjamin_franklin_165454.

21. **Harold B Lee, 1972 April General Conference, "A Time of Decision".** The 142nd Annual General Conference of the Church of Jesus Christ of Latter-day Saints, April 9, 1972, Sunday Morning Session. Published in the Ensign magazine, Volume 2 Number 7, July 1972. An official magazine of the Church of Jesus Christ of Latter-day Saints, published by the Church of Jesus Christ of Latter-day Saints, 50 E. North Temple Street, Salt Lake City, UT, 84150-3220, USA. Also, retrieved February 10, 2019 from churchofjesuschrist.org website:
https://www.churchofjesuschrist.org/general-conference/1972/04/a-time-of-decision?lang=eng.

22. **Paul H. Dunn, 1971 October General Conference, "What Is a Teacher".** The 141st Semiannual General Conference of the Church of Jesus Christ of Latter-day Saints, October 3, 1971, Sunday Morning Session. Published in the Ensign magazine, Volume 1 Number 12, December 1971. An official magazine of the Church of Jesus Christ of Latter-day Saints, published by the Church of Jesus Christ of Latter-day Saints, 50 E. North Temple Street, Salt Lake City, UT, 84150-3220, USA. General Conference October 1971 'What is a Teacher?'. Retrieved February 10, 2019 from churchofjesuschrist.org website:
https://www.churchofjesuschrist.org/study/ensign/1971/12/what-is-a-teacher?lang=eng.

Rule #7 'Need Help? Stop and Listen'

23 Herbert G. Lingren, "The Poem". Lingren, Herbert G., "G92-1092 Listening--With Your Heart As Well As Your Ears" (1992). *Historical Materials from University of Nebraska-Lincoln Extension.* 552. Retrieved January 28, 2019 from digitalcommons.unl.edu website: http://digitalcommons.unl.edu/extensionhist/552.

Also found in an article, https://www.bicmagazine.com/listening-an-essential-skill/, by Dr. Shirley A. White, Career Strategist, Success Images May 1, 2014, 5:00 AM. There is no other information on the author than that given at this time.

What an Idiot

Rule #8
'Don't Catch Idiotitis'

Rule #8 'Don't Catch Idiotitis'

Straight & to the Point:

I can't get any straighter to the point of explaining Rule #8 *'Don't Catch Idiotitis'* than this; don't be judgmental, not of others and not of yourself.

Is There a Doctor In The House?

"Idiotitis" is a word I created to describe what I consider to be a person's mental state in which the person has become over judgmental. In this state, a person tends to think the people around him are idiots but fails to include himself. A person with Idiotitis neglects to realize that we all have imperfections that we strive to improve. Instead of working to perfect his or her own flaws, this person spends their time passing judgment on other people and their mistakes. A person infected with Idiotitis refuses to acknowledge the fact that by their own standards, they are just as big an idiot as the rest of the human race.

> **(Bible New Testament: Matthew 7:3-4)**[2]
> *3 And why beholdest thou the mote that is in thy brother's eye, but considerest not the beam that is in thine own eye?*
>
> *4 Or how wilt thou say to thy brother, Let me pull out the mote out of thine eye; and, behold, a beam is in thine own eye?*

Idiotitis is a mental disease that can blacken the purest of souls. It is a disease that one can easily catch and then spend the rest of their days trying to cure. It clings to the cells of your spirit and corrupts your thoughts into forms of self-righteousness.

Idiotitis can be self-inflicted in many ways and for different reasons. Some catch Idiotitis when they allow the negative pressures of life get them down. As a result, the person becomes judgmental against what they feel is the world's injustice to them.

Others inflict Idiotitis upon themselves when they feel that their own intellect, knowledge, and wisdom is superior to others. In their superiority, they look down on other people. Again, this is a form of casting judgment. To the people that have this form of Idiotitis, the Lord gives you this message:

> **(Book of Mormon: Jacob 2:13-14)**[3]
> *13 And the hand of providence hath smiled upon you most pleasingly, that you have obtained many riches; and because some of you have obtained more abundantly than that of your brethren ye are lifted up in the pride of your hearts, and wear stiff necks and high heads because of the costliness of your apparel, and persecute your brethren because ye suppose that ye are better than they.*
>
> *14 And now, my brethren, do ye suppose that God justifieth you in this thing? Behold, I say unto you, Nay. But he condemneth you, and if ye persist in these things his judgments must speedily come unto you.*

Another form of Idiotitis where one person passes judgment on another person to make himself feel equal. This typically happens when a person thinks that he/she has been unrightfully judged. Thereby they become judgmental towards others. People with this type of Idiotitis start judging others to try and counter-act the harsh judgment they feel was sentenced upon them. I call this form of Idiotitis 'taking it out on others.'

> **(Bible New Testament: Matthew 7:1-2)**[2]
> *1 Judge not, that ye be not judged.*
>
> *2 For with what judgment ye judge, ye shall be judged: and with what measure ye mete, it shall be measured to you again.*

The Scriptures Overflow:

I counted at least 20 scriptures alone that warn us of the consequences of judging others. That doesn't include all the Church of Jesus Christ of Latter-day Saints conference talks that I, in my religion, consider scripture. Nor am I including the writings of many other religious groups. Additionally, we can include hundreds of quotes by famous people that have shared their wisdom on the subject. I am sure by the time I counted all the sources offering advice on judgment, there would be millions of documents.

I just quoted Matthew 7:1-2, which I feel is the best scriptural warning on casting judgment upon others. I won't include all the scriptures, but I thought perhaps a few more would help enlighten your mind and spirit.

> **(Bible New Testament: Matthew 23: 25-26)[2]**
> *25 Woe unto you, scribes and Pharisees, hypocrites! for ye make clean the outside of the cup and of the platter, but within they are full of extortion and excess.*
>
> *26 Thou blind Pharisee, cleanse first that which is within the cup and platter, that the outside of them may be clean also.*
>
> **(Bible New Testament: 1 Corinthians 13: 4-5)[2]**
> *4 Charity suffereth long, and is kind; charity envieth not; charity vaunteth not itself, is not puffed up,*
>
> *5 Doth not behave itself unseemly, seeketh not her own, is not easily provoked, thinketh no evil;*
>
> **(Bible Old Testament: Ecclesiastes 7: 9)[1]**
> *9 Be not hasty in thy spirit to be angry: for anger resteth in the bosom of fools.*
>
> **(Bible Old Testament: Proverbs 14: 29)[1]**
> *29 He that is slow to wrath is of great understanding: but he that is hasty of spirit exalteth folly.*

(Bible Old Testament: Proverbs 13: 10)[1]

10 Only by pride cometh contention: but with the well advised is wisdom.

(Bible Old Testament: Proverbs 28: 25)[1]

25 He that is of a proud heart stirreth up strife: but he that putteth his trust in the Lord shall be made fat.

(Bible New Testament: 1 Thessalonians 5: 14-15)[2]

14 Now we exhort you, brethren, warn them that are unruly, comfort the feebleminded, support the weak, be patient toward all men.

15 See that none render evil for evil unto any man; but ever follow that which is good, both among yourselves, and to all men.

(Bible New Testament: James 4: 11-12)[2]

11 Speak not evil one of another, brethren. He that speaketh evil of his brother, and judgeth his brother, speaketh evil of the law, and judgeth the law: but if thou judge the law, thou art not a doer of the law, but a judge.

12 There is one lawgiver, who is able to save and to destroy: who art thou that judgest another?

(Bible New Testament: Romans 2:1-3)[2]

1 Therefore thou art inexcusable, O man, whosoever thou art that judgest: for wherein thou judgest another, thou condemnest thyself; for thou that judgest doest the same things.

2 But we are sure that the judgment of God is according to truth against them which commit such things.

3 And thinkest thou this, O man, that judgest them which do such things, and doest the same, that thou shalt escape the judgment of God?

(Bible New Testament: John 8:7)[2]

7 So when they continued asking him, he lifted up himself, and said unto them, He that is without sin among you, let him first cast a stone at her.

(Bible New Testament: Titus 3:2-6)[2]

2 To speak evil of no man, to be no brawlers, but gentle, shewing all meekness unto all men.

3 For we ourselves also were sometimes foolish, disobedient, deceived, serving divers lusts and pleasures, living in malice and envy, hateful, and hating one another.

4 But after that the kindness and love of God our Saviour toward man appeared,

5 Not by works of righteousness which we have done, but according to his mercy he saved us, by the washing of regeneration, and renewing of the Holy Ghost;

6 Which he shed on us abundantly through Jesus Christ our Saviour;

(Bible New Testament: Luke 18:10-14)[2]

10 Two men went up into the temple to pray; the one a Pharisee, and the other a publican.

11 The Pharisee stood and prayed thus with himself, God, I thank thee, that I am not as other men are, extortioners, unjust, adulterers, or even as this publican.

12 I fast twice in the week, I give tithes of all that I possess.

13 And the publican, standing afar off, would not lift up so much as his eyes unto heaven, but smote upon his breast, saying, God be merciful to me a sinner.

14 I tell you, this man went down to his house justified rather than the other: for every one that exalteth himself shall be abased; and he that humbleth himself shall be exalted.

President Wilford Woodruff says one of the Keys of the mysteries of the Kingdom and an eternal principle is not condemning others.

> **(History of the Church, 3:385; from a discourse given by Joseph Smith on July 2, 1839, in Montrose, Iowa; reported by Wilford Woodruff and Willard Richards.)[6]**
> *"I will give you one of the Keys of the mysteries of the Kingdom. It is an eternal principle, that has existed with God from all eternity: That man who rises up to condemn others, finding fault with the Church, saying that they are out of the way, while he himself is righteous, then know assuredly, that that man is in the high road to apostasy; and if he does not repent, will apostatize, as God lives."*

I Had A Dream:

Let's address for a moment two of the most important Idiotitis issues which allow Satan into our heart, and bring misery upon others and ourselves: racism and stereotyping. Anytime we categorize humans into dissimilar groups, we are either classifying them by race or stereotyping them.

Racism, in any form, should not be tolerated. Why do we allow cultural differences to separate us? Why do we allow the color of a person's skin to determine how we treat them? What does it matter whether a person is black, white, yellow, or red? By the way, I have never seen a black man yet to this very day. Nor have I seen a white man or red man. I have seen some very dark brown people, and some reddish-skinned people, and some with a tint of yellow to their skin. But, have you ever indeed seen a solid black or pure snow-white race of people? Nor have I seen any one race or country that does not share many of the same issues in their culture.

I can pick out ten people that have very little in common other than being classified as a part of the white race, right here in the USA without going to another country, and socially they will accept each other because they have their race in common. Then again, I can pick out ten people here in the USA, that have a lot in common but are of a different race or culture, and they won't get along socially only due to their race or cultural difference.

Not all people are racist, and the world is doing better at breaking down that barrier. Yet despite all the progress the human race has made, racism is still one of the biggest causes of Idiotitis. I can't wait until we find intelligent life on other planets. I pray that by then, we Earthlings will have eliminated racism.

White or Black, What is The Difference:

How do we stop racism from infecting us with Idiotitis? I enjoyed and agreed with actor Morgan Freeman's solution to this issue. I believe his statement applies to all forms of racism. In an interview with Mike Wallace on a TV show called '60 Minutes' Morgan Freeman had this to say about racism;

> **(Morgan Freeman "60 Minutes TV show interview with Mike Wallace")**[7]
> *Mike Wallace asked Morgan Freeman, "So how are we going to get rid of racism?" Morgan Freeman answers, "Stop talking about it. I'm going to stop calling you a Whiteman; And then I ask you to stop calling me a Blackman. I know you as Mike Wallace and you know me as Morgan Freeman."*

I agree with Morgan Freeman's statement. We just need to stop talking about racism and start treating each other as we would treat ourselves. Our Father in Heaven put it this way.

> **(Bible Old Testament: 1 Samuel 16:7)**[1]
> *7 But the Lord said unto Samuel, Look not on his countenance, or on the height of his stature; because I have refused him: for the Lord seeth not as man seeth; for man looketh on the outward appearance, but the Lord looketh on the heart*

Rule #8 'Don't Catch Idiotitis'

(Book of Mormon: Jacob 2:21)₃
21 Do ye not suppose that such things are abominable unto him who created all flesh? And the one being is as precious in his sight as the other. And all flesh is of the dust; and for the selfsame end hath he created them, that they should keep his commandments and glorify him forever.

It saddens me that my dad was a racist. He was always making racial statements. Like the statement, "All black people should be shipped back to Africa." I would reply, "I am sorry Dad, but not all black people come from Africa." Or he would make a statement expressing the point that he believed that all black people are slow and lazy. And for that reason, he would never have a black man work for him. My reply to these types of statements would be something like, "Really, Dad? Then how come, Jesse Owens, a black man, is considered perhaps the greatest and most famous athlete in track and field history? Jesse set three world records, and was a four-time Olympic gold medalist." My Dad would never answer me when I would reply with these types of statements to debunk his reasoning.

Stereotyping, Is That like Typing on Dual Typewriters?

Stereotyping categorizes individuals or groups according to an oversimplified standardized image or idea. I would like to share with you a personal example of unrighteous stereotyping and racism all in one. During my internship as a Hearing Aid Practitioner, there was a fellow worker that stereotyped all people from India. He stated that he would not perform hearing tests on people from India because even if they had serious hearing loss, they were all too cheap to buy hearing aids, and it was a waste of his time. This Hearing Aid Practitioner was assigned as my teacher and mentor. Though he had a lot of good qualities, it is sad to say that this was not one of them. My teacher had a bad case of Idiotitis due to his stereotyping of people. He did teach me a lesson from his poor example, though, and that was that I should treat everyone as equals.

Stereotyping is the second biggest cause of Idiotitis. When you stereotype people, you are passing unrighteous judgment. Here are a few judgment calls people make about others that I consider unrighteous stereotyping:

> Fat people are fat due to their own faults. They are lazy and eat too much.
>
> When driving, beware of teenage girls. They don't pay attention when driving because they are too busy texting on their phones.
>
> Beware of teenage boys. They like to drive too fast and don't pay attention because they are too busy watching the good-looking girl in the other car while she is texting.

The Biggest Idiot of All:

Then we have the smaller cases of Idiotitis. Yet, as small as they are, they still turn on the negative attitude that darkens the soul with unrighteous judgments.

The trouble with the smaller cases of Idiotitis is that most people don't realize they have Idiotitis, until one day, the mirror catches up with them, and they see this big beam sticking out of their eye.

I would like to share with you a personal story of me catching a small case of Idiotitis. Some co-workers and I decided to go out for lunch to a restaurant down the road from where we worked. It was a typical August day in Clearwater, Florida, there was lots of sunshine with the temperature and humidity hovering around 98 degrees. The day was so humid you could take a shower using the water hanging in the air. And there was no option for protecting your car from the sweltering heat in the company parking lot as there was no shade to be found. Nor could you leave your car windows cracked open to help cool the car because of Florida's unpredictable torrential rains. As a result, parking the car in the company parking lot quickly turned the car into an easy bake oven. Believe it or not, it has been proven that in Florida, you can fry an egg in a skillet sitting on your car's dashboard.

As we opened my car doors to get in, we all paused for a moment to allow the pent-up heat to escape. As the hot air bellowed out of the car to join the rest of the warm Florida air, I felt its searing heat, and more sweat began to run down my face. Welcome to another hot, sunny Florida day, I thought to myself.

After letting the car cool for a moment, all five of us squeezed into the hot, steamy car and drove down the road to the restaurant. Once there, the plan was to enjoy the cool air conditioning of the establishment as we played a few games of pool and ate our lunch. When I got to the restaurant parking lot, my hope was to park the car facing south under a couple of trees I knew were at that end of the parking lot. Thus, shading the car and saving us from having to jump back into another easy bake oven as we drove back to work. As I pulled into the parking lot, I saw those beautiful shade trees and those four nicely shaded parking spots. The only shaded parking spots in the whole lot. But there was one problem; there was a beautiful sparkling metallic red Chevy Corvette parked lengthwise across all four parking spots.

No, the driver couldn't take up just one spot as any decent driver would do. He had to have all four. This left everyone else, including me, parked out under Florida's beautiful, hot, sunny sky. Does anyone want to guess what I was thinking? Well, needless to say, I became infected with Idiotitis instantly.

As a result of this infection, my attitude all during lunch was one of annoyance. My thoughts were constantly occupied by this idiot's car, taking up all four shaded spots. I wondered if this inconsiderate driver was there in that same air-cooled restaurant enjoying lunch and sucking down a cold drink.

things like: What a jerk? This person is an idiot! Where did they get their license out of a Cracker Jack box?

How Do We Get Control of This?

To stop Idiotitis from infecting us, we as human beings must end all forms of unrighteous judgment, both big and small, but to do that, we must give due diligence to the effort if we are going to succeed. It is the day by day, hour by hour, minute by minute, issues that we must monitor within ourselves.

Idiotitis is a disease more contagious than chicken pox or measles and more common than the common cold. It is an epidemic that is sweeping the world. It is a mental disease that if the CDC (Centers for Disease Control and Prevention) were monitoring, they would find the number of people infected would far exceed those of any other illness the world has ever known.

Yet, as widespread as Idiotitis is and as easy as it can be caught, it can just as easily be cured and completely wiped out. The cure for Idiotitis is readily available and easily obtained. It doesn't cost a penny, nor does it require a trip to the drug store to pick up a prescription. There is no human-made antibiotic that can cure Idiotitis. We all have the cure for this mental disease within us. Many can learn to cure themselves. For others with more severe cases, it may require the help of someone else, which may include professional advice. The cure for Idiotitis is a simple one, but sometimes challenging to implement. Oh, the cure itself is simple enough, but we humans tend to complicate things.

What is the cure for Idiotitis? It is love, as in love one another. No matter in what form you apply it, the primary ingredient for curing Idiotitis is love for one another.

I Have A Good Feeling Coming On.

Patience, kindness, long-suffering, charity, and service: these are the attributes that bring forth love for one another, which is the cure for Idiotitis. Each of us has the ability to nurture these qualities within ourselves and others.

As I said, there is no monetary cost. What it does take is a constant effort on our part to cultivate the positive attributes I just mentioned. That is the only way we can stamp out, or at least keep Idiotitis in remission. The more we strengthen the qualities of patience, kindness, long-suffering, charity, in combination with service for our fellow man, the more love for others grows within us. Carlos H. Amado stated it this way:

> **(Carlos H. Amado, 2008 April General Conference, "Service, a Divine Quality")[8]**
> *"Kindness, love, patience, understanding, and unity will increase as we serve, while intolerance, jealousy, envy, greed, and selfishness decrease or disappear. The more we give of ourselves, the more our capacity to serve, understand, and love will grow".*
>
> *"Those who serve will always seek to please God and live in harmony with Him. They will be full of peace; they will have a cheerful countenance and a spirit of kindness."*
>
> *"Those who serve will strive to ennoble, build, and lift their fellowmen; therefore, they will find the good in others, and they will not find reason or have time to become offended. They develop the virtue of praying for those who criticize. They don't expect recognition or reward. They possess the love of Christ."*

Just Sing, Sing A Song:

We are bombarded with people and situations that can infect us with Idiotitis many times a day. Regardless of our efforts, it is easy to slip backward and allow Idiotitis to fester again. This is why we must build a shield around us and constantly fortify ourselves with a positive attitude.

One way of fortifying ourselves is through music. There are many kinds of music that can help. Some people find reinforcement through classical music. For me, it is a good Gospel hymn. Here is a hymn I picked to help me.

(LDS Hymn Book: Hymn 228 'You Can Make the Pathway Bright')[9]

1 You can make the pathway bright, Fill the soul with heaven's light, If there's sunshine in your heart; Turning darkness into day, As the shadows fly away, If there's sunshine in your heart today. If there's sunshine in your heart, You can send a shining ray That will turn the night today; And your cares will all depart, If there's sunshine in your heart today.

2 You can speak the gentle word To the heart with anger stirred, If there's sunshine in your heart; Tho it seems a little thing, It will heaven's blessings bring, If there's sunshine in your heart today. If there's sunshine in your heart, You can send a shining ray That will turn the night today; And your cares will all depart, If there's sunshine in your heart today.

3 You can do a kindly deed To your neighbor in his need, If there's sunshine in your heart; And his burden you will share As you lift his load of care, If there's sunshine in your heart today. If there's sunshine in your heart, You can send a shining ray That will turn the night today; And your cares will all depart, If there's sunshine in your heart today.

4 You can live a happy life In this world of toil and strife, If there's sunshine in your heart; And your soul will glow with love From the perfect Light above, If there's sunshine in your heart today. If there's sunshine in your heart, You can send a shining ray That will turn the night today; And your cares will all depart, If there's sunshine in your heart today.

And The Words Lifted Me:

When the temptation to judge becomes a real challenge, I have a few scriptures that help to remind me of the true person I want to be.

(Bible New Testament: 1 Corinthians 13:1-8)[2]
1 Though I speak with the tongues of men and of angels, and have not charity, I am become as sounding brass, or a tinkling cymbal.

2 And though I have the gift of prophecy, and understand all mysteries, and all knowledge; and though I have all faith, so that I could remove mountains, and have not charity, I am nothing.

3 And though I bestow all my goods to feed the poor, and though I give my body to be burned, and have not charity, it profiteth me nothing.

4 Charity suffereth long, and is kind; charity envieth not; charity vaunteth not itself, is not puffed up,

5 Doth not behave itself unseemly, seeketh not her own, is not easily provoked, thinketh no evil;

6 Rejoiceth not in iniquity, but rejoiceth in the truth;

7 Beareth all things, believeth all things, hopeth all things, endureth all things.

8 Charity never faileth: but whether there be prophecies, they shall fail; whether there be tongues, they shall cease; whether there be knowledge, it shall vanish away.

(Bible New Testament: Romans 12:16-19)[2]
16 Be of the same mind one toward another. Mind not high things, but condescend to men of low estate. Be not wise in your own conceits.

17 Recompense to no man evil for evil. Provide things honest in the sight of all men.

18 If it be possible, as much as lieth in you, live peaceably with all men.

19 Dearly beloved, avenge not yourselves, but rather give place unto wrath: for it is written, Vengeance is mine; I will repay, saith the Lord.

(Bible Old Testament: 1 Samuel 16:7)[1]

7 But the Lord said unto Samuel, Look not on his countenance, or on the height of his stature; because I have refused him: for the Lord seeth not as man seeth; for man looketh on the outward appearance, but the Lord looketh on the heart

A Few Words From Others:

As I say in all my rules, I know I include an overabundance of quotes and scriptures. I do this because I want to ensure that there is something for everyone. I may have overdone myself a little bit this time with all the quotes I am about to hit you with. But I couldn't resist. They are all so good. Before I conclude with my final story, I would like to share with you several wise quotes from people you may have heard of.

(Jesse Jackson)[10]

"Never look down on anybody unless you're helping them up."

(Mahatma Gandhi)[11]

"Before the throne of the Almighty, man will be judged not by his acts but by his intentions. For God alone reads our hearts."

(Paul Valéry)[12]

"Our judgements judge us, and nothing reveals us, exposes our weaknesses, more ingeniously than the attitude of pronouncing upon our fellows."

(Shannon L. Alder)[13]

"I am tired of people saying that poor character is the only reason people do wrong things. Actually, circumstances cause people to act a certain way. It's from those circumstances that a person's attitude is affected followed by weakening of character. Not the reverse. If we had no faults of our own, we should *not take so much pleasure in noticing those in others and judging their lives as either black or white, good or bad. We all live our lives in shades of gray."*

(Steve Maraboli, "Unapologetically You: Reflections on Life and the Human Experience")[14]

"When you're too religious, you tend to point your finger to judge instead of extending your hand to help."

(Shannon L. Alder)[15]

"Often those that criticize others reveal what he himself lacks."

(Earl Nightingale)[16]

"When you judge others, you do not define them, you define yourself."

(Paulo Coelho)[17]

"We can never judge the lives of others, because each person knows only their own pain and renunciation. It's one thing to feel that you are on the right path, but it's another to think that yours is the only path."

(Mother Teresa)[18]

"When we judge others we leave no room to love them."

(H. Jackson Brown, Jr.)[19]

"Let the refining and improving of your own life keep you so busy that you have little time to criticize others."

(Unknown)[20]

Rule #8 'Don't Catch Idiotitis'

(Billy Connolly)[21]
"Before you judge a man, walk a mile in his shoes. After that, who cares? He's a mile away and you've got his shoes."

(Wayne Dyer)[22]
"When you judge another, you do not define them, you define yourself."

(Sydney J. Harris)[23]
"We evaluate others with a Godlike justice, but we want them to evaluate us with a Godlike compassion."

(Jean-Jacques Rousseau)[24]
"Do not judge, and you will never be mistaken."

(Chinese proverb)[25]
"One moment of patience may ward off great disaster. One moment of impatience may ruin a whole life."

(Woodrow M. Kroll)[26]
"Quite honestly, most people are quick to "write someone off." But our God is a God of the second chance. Learn from One who is patient with you, and you'll learn to be patient with others."

(Jerry Bridges)[27]
"Every day God patiently bears with us, and every day we are tempted to become impatient with our friends, neighbors, and loved ones. And our faults and failures before God are so much more serious than the petty actions of others that tend to irritate us! God calls us to graciously bear with the weaknesses of others, tolerating them and forgiving them even as He has forgiven us."

(Richard Cecil)[28]
"God's way of answering the Christian's prayer for more patience, experience, hope and love often is to put him into the furnace of affliction."

Rule #8 'Don't Catch Idiotitis'

(Henry Wadsworth Longfellow)[29]
"All things come round to him who will but wait."

(Unknown) [30]
"If you are tempted to lose patience with your fellowman; stop and think how patient God has been with you."

Sigmund Freud:

Some Psychologists believe in constructive negative venting. They say that negative venting is a positive way of letting your anger out. They believe that there is no problem with negative venting as long as you don't harm others or yourself. That it is a constructive way of getting your emotions out of your system and under control.

A few examples of negative venting are:

> 1: Going to an isolated place, scream and shout until you can't or don't feel like shouting anymore.
>
> 2: Throwing things that are non-destructive in a safe room until you burn that negative energy up.
>
> 3: Just find a safe way to let all that negative energy out.

To express what is bothering you is fine. To express it negatively is not. It is my opinion that negativity begets negativity, and thus creates more negativity, and negative feelings are not of God but are tools of Satan.

Anger is a form of unrighteous judgment. Unrighteous judgment is negative energy. It is my opinion that energy in any form must be managed and controlled. Allowing any type of energy to run wild is not what I would call you managing it. It is instead managing you. I do not consider negative venting proper managing or control.

On top of that, adding negative energy to negative energy is just adding fuel to the fire that heats up the pot. The way to control anger is not by releasing control, which only builds more anger. The better way to control anger is to add positivity to your life. Positivity will counterbalance the anger and allow you to manage it better. When you find yourself getting angry, find a way to refuel the positive energy within you.

You'll Do It My Way:

I would like to conclude with one final, personal story. This story is a bit long, but please take the time to read it through to the end. I believe you will find value in the reading.

Let me give you a little background, I am currently working as a Hearing Aid Practitioner. My office (or practice) is in a Sam's Club retail warehouse located in the wonderful river town of Dubuque, Iowa. Please note I don't work for Sam's Club. I work for the company that makes the hearing aids that Sam's Club sells. At the time this story takes place, I had only been working for the company for three months.

Let me recap for you part of the day's events. My District Manager (DM) came into town to evaluate my performance and to ask me to commit to some goals she had set for me. Most of the time, she was at the office, we didn't see eye to eye on much of anything. Ever have one of those days with a manager?

When it came time to sit down, with the DM, to discuss the evaluation, the conversation did not go well. I felt like all the goals and expectations were being dictated to me but in an asking way. And in my opinion, they were unreasonable. They were goals I felt no one could meet. To top it off, these goals were being set by a DM that had never had a Hearing Aid Practitioner license or worked on my side of the fence. She knew about numbers (Bean Counters I call them) but she knew nothing about how to do the work I perform.

It wasn't until the end of our conversation that the DM, now frustrated with me for refusing to sign the paper to commit to her goals and expectations, asked me for my reasons. I calmly and politely informed her that those were her goals, not mine, and by signing the paper, it would make them my goals. I

Rule #8 'Don't Catch Idiotitis'

stated that I was not going to commit to meeting goals that I believed were impossible to meet. I told her that my word is my bond. I don't give my commitment or my word to things I don't feel I can accomplish. I explained to the DM that I did believe in setting goals, so long as there was a good possibility of reaching them. I told the DM that there were too many factors out of my control to meet her goals. Therefore, they were her goals for me not my goals for me. I went on to say that I would give her my word, or sign a paper that stated that I would do everything I could to help her meet her goals. But I made it clear that I was not going to sign or agree to do something I believed I could not do. She responded that if I changed my attitude, and thought more positively, I could meet her goals. She then added that everyone else had signed the form; therefore, she saw no reason why I wouldn't.

My next comments may not have been the best way to respond, but I felt the DM was now attempting to badger me into signing this form. I replied that I can believe that I will grow wings and fly all day long, that does not mean it is going to happen - no matter how positive my attitude is. Moreover, as far as signing those papers, as my mother would say, just because all the others jump off the bridge doesn't make it the right choice, nor does it mean I have to. The DM walked away, and I thought that was the end of it. But an hour later after doing other DM work, she returned, ready to come at me again.

To help you understand the next part of our conversation, I need to explain one of the goals the DM wanted me to commit to. She expected me to more than double the number of hearing tests I performed each day. She wanted me to complete four hearing tests a day and to guarantee to meet that number. Remember, this number is coming from a person that has never performed a hearing test. The issues here are that performing a lousy hearing test, which includes doing all the tests but at a minimal level of service possible and still keep your license to practice, takes about 1 hour. A good hearing test, which includes educating the client, takes at least 2 hours. I only do my best. Well, 4 hours times 2 hours

Rule #8 'Don't Catch Idiotitis'

equal 8 hours. That can be done in an 8-hour workday, right? No, it cannot because you also have to handle 6 to 10 service appointments each day. A service appointment plus paperwork is 30 to 45 minutes. To add to my defense, there was not then, nor is there now, any Hearing Aid Practitioner within the company that can average four hearing tests a day every day. I hope you can see where I was coming from.

I informed the DM once again that the only way to meet the numbers she was asking me to commit to would be to do half a hearing test, which is a violation of my license. And then there is the fact that I could not guarantee four people a day would want to be tested unless I went out into the store and hogtied people and dragged them into the testing booth. Then the store could deal with the lawsuits. Looking back, as true as it may be, it was not the best comment to make.

Despite my reply, she persisted. She was relentless and insisted I commit to her goals and sign the papers accordingly. I could not believe this, DM! I took a long inward breath to help calm myself. I needed guidance from Heavenly Father before I said another word. I mentally paused to say a quick prayer. After I finished, I calmly looked the DM straight in the eye with a sincere face and stated that if not committing to her numbers was that big of an issue, she could fire me, or I would resign, whichever she preferred. All I was going to commit to was what I felt was under my control. I would come to work each day, put in an honest day's work, and I would give my best to help the business succeed by fulfilling the company motto 'Helping People Hear Better.' I told her I believed in the company motto, and I believed that what I do and how I do it improves people's lives.

What this DM failed to understand was that giving my word is my commitment, and not living up to a promise would violate one of my core moral beliefs. Violating my beliefs was one bridge I was not jumping off, no matter how many others did.

I want to take a moment before finishing this story to say that I am not advocating that people threaten their boss with quitting. While dealing with the DM during that day, part of my thoughts was in prayer with Heavenly Father asking for inspiration on how to handle the situation. I also knew that I would have my wife's support. And if I did quit or get fired, in the short term, I still had the means to meet my financial obligations. All those factors helped me make the decision to hold fast to my beliefs and make the statement to the DM that I did.

Also, I felt that what was being asked of me was no small matter. As I stated, I felt it would violate one of my core moral beliefs, that giving my word is a promise and a bond, no different than keeping one of God's eternal laws. Neither is there a difference when you break one of God's laws than when you violate a promise. There is a price to pay, a price that I believed was too high.

As you can tell, I was having a very challenging day. Though I was calm on the outside, inside, I was a pot of hot, boiling nerves. The DM sorted through the paperwork in her hand, pulled out the middle page, and set it on the chair in front of her. She then packed up her stuff, including the copies of the unsigned documents, handed me the middle copy, and in a very direct, stern voice made one final statement before walking to the exit, "This is your quarterly assessment and goals report, read it and make improvement where required."

When the DM left that day, I wasn't sure that I was going to have my job much longer. By the end of my workday, I was drained and not in a real positive mood. The thought of losing my job didn't bother me. I felt right in what I had said and was willing to accept the outcome. I felt safe in my faith and belief in God's support. Dealing with all the negative input of the day got to me. The negativity and flustration were eating at me, and I had a hard time pushing it out of my thoughts.

Needless to say, by the end of the DM's visit, I had allowed the day's events to turn my thoughts negative. Mentally, I criticized the DM for all the things we disagreed about. There were many, so many I completely ignored any of the DM's positive comments.

Criticism, which is another form of passing unrighteous judgment, had now allowed Idiotitis to creep into my mind. And I do mean literally. One of my thoughts was, "This woman is an idiot. She is nothing more than a bean counter who cares more about counting the beans than she cares about people." I think I would call that a judgmental statement, don't you?

And You Thought That Was the End to the Day?

Sadly, the day was not done with me yet. While things were heating up between the DM and me in the store, things outside were more than cooling off. As I looked outside through the big automated doors, I saw 3 inches of freshly fallen snow on the ground. It was freezing cold outside, the winds were gusting up to 25 mph, and snow was still falling. This was not helping my negative mood. As much as I wanted to, I couldn't go home yet. I still had work to do, and I had some in-store shopping to do as well. I grabbed the closest shopping cart and ran around the store as quickly as I could, gathering what I needed, and then checked out. Now I was really, really ready to go home. In fact, I had been ready to go home as soon as the DM left. I was well overdue for getting out of the office and out of Sam's Club, and to the peace and quiet of home.

As I went out the exit, the wind whipped at my face, and ice-cold snow blew down my neck, sending a nice, stimulating chill through my body. Not fun! Fighting the cold, snowy weather was tough enough. Then add to that the fact that all employees are required to park at the far end of the parking lot. And guess what? None of the parking lot between the store and my car had been plowed, making the trip to the car even slower and colder. As I pushed my cart, the slushy snow continually jammed up the wheels. It was only by brute force that kept the cart moving forward.

By the time I got to my car and unloaded the cart, my hands and face were half-frozen, and my legs and arms were beaten

Rule #8 'Don't Catch Idiotitis'

up from forcing the shopping cart across the snow-covered parking lot. The only thing left was to push the cart to the closest outside cart stall, and then head back to the car and enjoy my awesome heated seat.

Now, knowing that at the end of the day, there is a chance I might be pushing a shopping cart to my car, I always park next to a cart return stall. And also, in preparation for the day that dementia may set in, whenever possible, I always park in the same spot. So, in just a few short steps, I could responsibly relieve myself of the cart. Then I would be out of there and call the day done.

As I pushed the empty cart to the front of my car and towards the cart stall, I saw Tim, the afternoon-until-closing Cart Attendant. His job is to ensure there are always carts available for customers. So, Tim spends most of his time outside running around the parking lot gathering up carts and returning them to a waiting area just inside the store by the entry doors.

Tim's a young, skinny man in his early twenties. He could hardly weigh over 125 pounds. When he was a child, he had gotten seriously ill. I'm not sure what the illness was, but it left Tim partially paralyzed on his right side. His right arm and hand are barely useable, and he limps on his right leg. Yet, with only one good arm and leg, Tim managed to drag long trains of carts back into the store every day.

Today was no different for Tim, with the exception of the weather. He had to fight the 25-mph wind, the blowing snow, and the unplowed parking lot his entire shift. As I stood there holding on to my cart with 10 minutes of shopping time left before the store closed, Tim was busily gathering up the few remaining carts in the lot. I stood there for a moment and watched as Tim struggled to get his train of carts to the door while the wind and snow continued to hit me directly in the face. Tim amazed me, I had had a hard fight with just one cart, and here he was maneuvering a train of them. Tim had gathered up most of the remaining carts, only two or three

Rule #8 'Don't Catch Idiotitis'

remained close to the front of the store. That is with one exception, which was my cart that was out here in the boonies.

Now, I could have easily just left the cart there for Tim. After all, it was his job. Besides, I had other problems to deal with, such as getting out of the cold and getting rid of my nagging, negative attitude. Then the lights came on in my brain, and inspiration was granted access, and it was telling me what I needed to do. It was telling me that I needed to do something positive to counteract my negativity. Perhaps, like doing something nice for someone. My hands were gripping my positive solution: the cart.

With my face to the wind, I decided to finish the job and freeze the other half of me. I began pushing the cart as hard and fast as I could back towards the store. You would think that with each chilling step I took away from those heated car seats that my attitude would have become more annoyed at the world. But it was quite the opposite. With each step I took, I grew warmer inside, and a smile spread across my face.

Partway there, Tim greeted me with his own smile, grinning from ear to ear, and a compliment. He thanked me twice and told me how I had really helped him out, that he was chilled to the bone, and not looking forward to going all the way out there to get that last cart. He said he even thought about leaving it, but knew it might cost him his job or, at the least, he would get a good chewing out.

I thanked Tim for his words of kindness and assured him that pushing the cart back had helped me more than it had helped him. I then grabbed Tim's hand, shook it with a firm grip, and thanked him for all his hard work. I am not sure if Tim understood why I was thanking him. He thanked me one more time, and I thanked him again, and then I headed back to the car with a warmer heart and a clearer brain.

Negative begets negative, positive negates negative. Remember that. By helping others and bringing smiles to their faces, you can't help but get a warm, loving heart, and that warm, loving heart will pump the warm, loving blood right into your brain and push the negative out. I don't know of anyone who does a true act of kindness that isn't rewarded with love right back. It is called losing yourself in service to others.

When our judgment day comes, we will be judged for our thoughts as well as our actions. And with that statement, I end this writing with a scripture worth repeating.

> **(Bible New Testament: Matthew 7:1-2)[2]**
> *1 Judge not, that ye be not judged.*
>
> *2 For with what judgment ye judge, ye shall be judged: and with what measure ye mete, it shall be measured to you again.*

Rule #8 'Don't Catch Idiotitis'

Endnotes:

1 **King James Version of the Bible, The Old Testament of Our Lord and Saviour Jesus Christ.** Published by The Church of Jesus Christ of Latter-day Saints, Salt Lake City, Utah, USA. Copywrite 2013.

2 **King James Version of the Bible, The New Testament of Our Lord and Saviour Jesus Christ.** Published by The Church of Jesus Christ of Latter-day Saints, Salt Lake City, Utah, USA. Copywrite 2013.

3 **The Book of Mormon Another Testament of Jesus Christ.** Published by The Church of Jesus Christ of Latter-day Saints, Salt Lake City, Utah, USA. The first English edition published in Palmyra, New York, USA, in 1830. Copywrite 2013.

4 **The Doctrine and Covenants of The Church of Jesus Christ of Latter-Day Saints.** Containing Revelations Give to Joseph Smith, the Prophet. With some additions by his successors in the Presidency of the Church. Published by The Church of Jesus Christ of Latter-day Saints, Salt Lake City, Utah, USA. Copywrite 2013.

5 **The Pearl of Great Price.** A selection from the revelations, translations, and narrations of Joseph Smith, First Prophet, seer, and revelator to The Church of Jesus Christ of Latter-Day Saints. Published by The Church of Jesus Christ of Latter-day Saints, Salt Lake City, Utah, USA. Copywrite 2013.

6 **Joseph Smith, Jr..** History of the Church, 3:385; from a discourse given by Joseph Smith on July 2, 1839, in Montrose, Iowa; reported by Wilford Woodruff and Willard Richards. The Church of Jesus Christ of Latter-day Saints, Salt Lake City, Utah. Also, see "Teachings of Presidents of the Church: Joseph Smith" Published in the Teachings of the Presidents of the Church: Joseph Smith, "Beware the Bitter Fruits of Apostasy" Chapter-27 page-318 paragraph-01. An official manual of the Church of Jesus Christ of Latter-day Saints published 2007 by the Church of Jesus Christ of Latter-day Saints, 50 E. North Temple Street, Salt Lake City, UT, 84150-3220, USA.

7 **Morgan Freeman,** "60 Minutes TV show interview with Mike Wallace" Aired, June 14, 2006 11:40 AM EDT, on '60 Minutes Entertainment' CBS News. Retrieved February 11, 2019, from CBSNEWS.COM website: https://www.cbsnews.com/video/freeman-on-black-history/ .

8 **Carlos H. Amado, 2008 April General Conference, "Service, a Divine Quality"** The 178th Annual General Conference of the Church of Jesus Christ of Latter-day Saints, April 5, 2008, Saturday Afternoon Session. Published in the Ensign magazine, Volume 38 Number 5, May 2008 Page-36 Paragraph-6. An official magazine of the Church of Jesus Christ of Latter-day Saints, published by the Church of Jesus Christ of Latter-day Saints, 50 E. North Temple Street, Salt Lake City, UT, 84150-3220, USA. Also, retrieved Nov 26,2019, from Ensign, ChurchofJesusChrist.Org website: https://www.churchofjesuschrist.org/study/ensign/2008/05/service-a-divine-quality?lang=eng

Rule #8 'Don't Catch Idiotitis'

9 **Song "You Can Make the Pathway Bright,"** Hymns of the Church of Jesus Christ of Latter-day Saints page: 228. Text by: Helen Silcott Dungan, ca. 1899. An official Hymn Book of the Church of Jesus Christ of Latter-day Saints published 1985 by the Church of Jesus Christ of Latter-day Saints, 50 E. North Temple Street, Salt Lake City, UT, 84150-3220, USA.

10 **Jesse Jackson**. ThinkExist.com Quotations. "Jesse Jackson quotes." (n.d.). ThinkExist.com Quotations Online 1 Jan. 2019. 11 Feb. 2019 http://thinkexist.com/quotes/jesse_jackson/.

11 **Mahatma Gandhi**. Mahatma Gandhi Quotes. (n.d.). BrainyQuote.com. Retrieved February 12, 2019, from BrainyQuote.com Web site: https://www.brainyquote.com/quotes/mahatma_gandhi_160866.

12 **Paul Valéry**. Paul Valery. (n.d.). AZQuotes.com. Retrieved February 12, 2019, from AZQuotes.com Web site: https://www.azquotes.com/quote/300786.

13 **Shannon L. Alder**. Shannon L. Alder Quotes (n.d.). goodreads.com. Retrieved February 11, 2019, from godreads.com website: https://www.goodreads.com/author/quotes/1391130.Shannon_L_Alder.

14 **Steve Maraboli, "Unapologetically You: Reflections on Life and the Human Experience."** Steve Maraboli Quotes. (n.d.). goodreads.com. Retrieved February 11, 2019, from godreads.com website: https://www.goodreads.com/work/quotes/25086973-unapologetically-you-reflections-on-life-and-the-human-experience?page=2.

15 **Shannon Alder**. Shannon L. Alder Quotes. (n.d.). goodreads.com. Retrieved February 11, 2019, from godreads.com website: https://www.goodreads.com/author/quotes/1391130.Shannon_L_Alder.

16 **Earl Nightingale**. Earl Nightingale Quotes. (n.d.). goodreads.com. Retrieved February 11, 2019, from godreads.com website: https://www.goodreads.com/author/quotes/140743.Earl_Nightingale.

17 **Paulo Coelho**. ThinkExist.com Quotations. Paulo Coelho quotes. (n.d.). ThinkExist.com Quotations Online 1 Jan. 2019. 11 Feb. 2019 http://thinkexist.com/quotes/paulo_coelho/.

18 **Mother Teresa**. Mother Teresa. (n.d.). AZQuotes.com. Retrieved February 12, 2019, from AZQuotes.com Web site: https://www.azquotes.com/quote/661944.

19 **H. Jackson Brown, Jr.**. H. Jackson Brown, Jr.. (n.d.). AZQuotes.com. Retrieved February 12, 2019, from AZQuotes.com Web site: https://www.azquotes.com/quote/38130.

20 **Unknown**. Pot Calling The Kettle Black Quotes. (n.d.). QuotesGram.com Retrieved February 12, 2019, from QuotesGram.com website: https://quotesgram.com/pot-calling-the-kettle-black-quotes/. The author is unknown and there is no other information than that given at this time.

21 **Billy Connolly**. Billy Connolly. (n.d.). AZQuotes.com. Retrieved February 12, 2019, from AZQuotes.com Web site: https://www.azquotes.com/quote/583248.

Rule #8 'Don't Catch Idiotitis'

22 **Wayne Dyer**. Wayne Dyer. (n.d.). AZQuotes.com. Retrieved February 12, 2019, from AZQuotes.com Web site: https://www.azquotes.com/quote/84131.

23 **Sydney J. Harris**. Sydney J. Harris. (n.d.). AZQuotes.com. Retrieved February 12, 2019, from AZQuotes.com Web site: https://www.azquotes.com/quote/556433.

24 **Jean-Jacques Rousseau**. Jean-Jacques Rousseau. (n.d.). AZQuotes.com. Retrieved February 12, 2019, from AZQuotes.com Web site: https://www.azquotes.com/quote/546861.

25 **Chinese proverb**. Chinese proverb Quotation (n.d.), SearchQuotes.com. Retrieved February 12, 2019, from SearchQuotes.com website: http://www.searchquotes.com/quotation/One_moment_of_patience_may_ward_off_great_disaster._One_moment_of_impatience_may_ruin_a_whole_life./655968/. The author is unknown and there is no other information than that given at this time.

26 **Woodrow M. Kroll**. Woodrow M. Kroll. (n.d.). AZQuotes.com. Retrieved February 12, 2019, from AZQuotes.com Web site: https://www.azquotes.com/quote/780457.

27 **Jerry Bridges**. Jerry Bridges. (n.d.). AZQuotes.com. Retrieved February 12, 2019, from AZQuotes.com Web site: https://www.azquotes.com/quote/787425.

28 **Richard Cecil**. Richard Cecil. (n.d.). AZQuotes.com. Retrieved February 12, 2019, from AZQuotes.com Web site: https://www.azquotes.com/quote/51609.

29 **Henry Wadsworth Longfellow**. Henry Wadsworth Longfellow Quotes. (n.d.). BrainyQuote.com. Retrieved February 12, 2019, from BrainyQuote.com Web site: https://www.brainyquote.com/quotes/henry_wadsworth_longfello_141012.

30 **Unknown**. Source Unknown Quotes. (n.d.). allauthor.com. Retrieved February 12, 2019, from allauthor.com Web site: https://allauthor.com/quote/71284/. The author is unknown, and there is no other information than that given at this time.

Guilty in the First Degree

Rule #9
'Don't Be Overly Judgmental of Yourself'

Guilty in the First Degree

Rule #9
'Don't Be Overly Judgmental of Yourself'

Rule #8 'Don't Catch Idiotitis'

22. **Wayne Dyer**. Wayne Dyer. (n.d.). AZQuotes.com. Retrieved February 12, 2019, from AZQuotes.com Web site: https://www.azquotes.com/quote/84131.

23. **Sydney J. Harris**. Sydney J. Harris. (n.d.). AZQuotes.com. Retrieved February 12, 2019, from AZQuotes.com Web site: https://www.azquotes.com/quote/556433.

24. **Jean-Jacques Rousseau**. Jean-Jacques Rousseau. (n.d.). AZQuotes.com. Retrieved February 12, 2019, from AZQuotes.com Web site: https://www.azquotes.com/quote/546861.

25. **Chinese proverb**. Chinese proverb Quotation (n.d.), SearchQuotes.com. Retrieved February 12, 2019, from SearchQuotes.com website: http://www.searchquotes.com/quotation/One_moment_of_patience_may_ward_off_great_disaster._One_moment_of_impatience_may_ruin_a_whole_life./655968/. The author is unknown and there is no other information than that given at this time.

26. **Woodrow M. Kroll**. Woodrow M. Kroll. (n.d.). AZQuotes.com. Retrieved February 12, 2019, from AZQuotes.com Web site: https://www.azquotes.com/quote/780457.

27. **Jerry Bridges**. Jerry Bridges. (n.d.). AZQuotes.com. Retrieved February 12, 2019, from AZQuotes.com Web site: https://www.azquotes.com/quote/787425.

28. **Richard Cecil**. Richard Cecil. (n.d.). AZQuotes.com. Retrieved February 12, 2019, from AZQuotes.com Web site: https://www.azquotes.com/quote/51609.

29. **Henry Wadsworth Longfellow**. Henry Wadsworth Longfellow Quotes. (n.d.). BrainyQuote.com. Retrieved February 12, 2019, from BrainyQuote.com Web site: https://www.brainyquote.com/quotes/henry_wadsworth_longfello_141012.

30. **Unknown**. Source Unknown Quotes. (n.d.). allauthor.com. Retrieved February 12, 2019, from allauthor.com Web site: https://allauthor.com/quote/71284/. The author is unknown, and there is no other information than that given at this time.

Rule #9 'Don't Be Overly Judgmental of Yourself'

The Simple Facts:

Rule #9 is an extension of Rule #8 *'Don't Catch Idiotitis'*. The difference being is that in this rule, I am only talking about casting unrighteous judgment upon yourself. It is one thing to evaluate your mistakes and correct them. It is a totally different thing to beat yourself up over your mistakes.

I have a terrible bad habit of rehashing the foolish mistakes I have made in my life. Not because I'm trying to learn from them, but only to remind myself of how stupid I was. That is why I had to make an appendage to Rule #8; thus, Rule #9 was born.

Once you have repented and have made restitution for your mistake, that is the end of it. Period. This is easier said than done for me and probably for most of us.

If you believe that Jesus Christ is our Savior and died for our sins, then once you have forsaken your sin and have made restitution to the point that is humanly possible, then God's grace and Jesus Christ's sacrifice satisfy the rest.

> **(Book of Mormon: 2 Nephi 25:23)**[3]
> *23 For we labor diligently to write, to persuade our children, and also our brethren, to believe in Christ, and to be reconciled to God; for we know that it is by grace that we are saved, after all we can do.*
>
> **(Book of Mormon: 2 Nephi 2:6-8)**[3]
> *6 Wherefore, redemption cometh in and through the Holy Messiah; for he is full of grace and truth.*
>
> *7 Behold, he offereth himself a sacrifice for sin, to answer the ends of the law, unto all those who have a broken heart and a contrite spirit; and unto none else can the ends of the law be answered.*

8 Wherefore, how great the importance to make these things known unto the inhabitants of the earth, that they may know that there is no flesh that can dwell in the presence of God, save it be through the merits, and mercy, and grace of the Holy Messiah, who layeth down his life according to the flesh, and taketh it again by the power of the Spirit, that he may bring to pass the resurrection of the dead, being the first that should rise.

(Book of Mormon: Alma 7:11-13)[3]
11 And he shall go forth, suffering pains and afflictions and temptations of every kind; and this that the word might be fulfilled which saith he will take upon him the pains and the sicknesses of his people.

12 And he will take upon him death, that he may loose the bands of death which bind his people; and he will take upon him their infirmities, that his bowels may be filled with mercy, according to the flesh, that he may know according to the flesh how to succor his people according to their infirmities.

13 Now the Spirit knoweth all things; nevertheless the Son of God suffereth according to the flesh that he might take upon him the sins of his people, that he might blot out their transgressions according to the power of his deliverance; and now behold, this is the testimony which is in me.

(Book of Mormon: Mosiah 3:17)[3]
17 And moreover, I say unto you, that there shall be no other name given nor any other way nor means whereby salvation can come unto the children of men, only in and through the name of Christ, the Lord Omnipotent.

(Bible New Testament: Luke 5:20)[2]
20 And when he saw their faith, he said unto him, Man, thy sins are forgiven thee.

Rule #9 'Don't Be Overly Judgmental of Yourself'

What is Good for the Goose is Good for the Gander:

All the quotes and scriptures I used in Rule #8 *'Don't Catch Idiotitis'* apply to Rule #9. I could just copy all the quotes and scriptures from Rule #8 and reprint them here, but that would make this writing overly long. Instead, I strongly recommend you read Rule #8 before reading Rule #9.

Also, all of the guidance given in Rule #8 needs to be thoroughly understood to implement Rule #9 successfully. Why? You may ask. For this reason: how you treat other people, in this case, is no different from how you need to treat yourself. So, I hope you have already read Rule #8. If not, stop here and go read it!

It is All About Me:

The philosophy behind Rule #9 hinges on the belief that Jesus Christ died to save us from our sins, opening the door for us to return to live once again with Heavenly Father.

> **(Book of Mormon: Alma 12:33-35)**[3]
> *33 But God did call on men, in the name of his Son, (this being the plan of redemption which was laid) saying: If ye will repent, and harden not your hearts, then will I have mercy upon you, through mine Only Begotten Son;*
>
> *34 Therefore, whosoever repenteth, and hardeneth not his heart, he shall have claim on mercy through mine Only Begotten Son, unto a remission of his sins; and these shall enter into my rest.*
>
> *35 And whosoever will harden his heart and will do iniquity, behold, I swear in my wrath that he shall not enter into my rest.*
>
> **(Book of Mormon: Alma 34:14-16)**[3]
> *14 And behold, this is the whole meaning of the law, every whit pointing to that great and last sacrifice;*

> *and that great and last sacrifice will be the Son of God, yea, infinite and eternal.*
>
> *15 And thus he shall bring salvation to all those who shall believe on his name; this being the intent of this last sacrifice, to bring about the bowels of mercy, which overpowereth justice, and bringeth about means unto men that they may have faith unto repentance.*
>
> *16 And thus mercy can satisfy the demands of justice, and encircles them in the arms of safety, while he that exercises no faith unto repentance is exposed to the whole law of the demands of justice; therefore only unto him that has faith unto repentance is brought about the great and eternal plan of redemption.*

You can disagree with my statement about Jesus Christ's Atonement. However, you must keep in mind that this rule, as with all my other rules, was written to help me govern my life. Yet it is my hope that through sharing what I believe to be inspired thoughts that this rule, along with all my other rules in this book, will open your mind and enlighten your soul.

Wash, Rinse, and Repeat:

When it came to accepting forgiveness for my sins, Rule #9 was one of the hardest of the rules to implement. Forgiving others, even at my hardest time, was easier than forgiving myself. To really, truly grasp Rule #9 and then explain, in this chapter, how to apply its forgiving philosophy, I had to repeatedly study and review its guiding principles. I read book after book, listened to sermons, and more sermons. I listened to lecture after lecture, all on the subject of forgiveness. Yet, I still found it hard to forgive myself. So, I started writing down what I had learned. Then I wrote it again, and again. I wrote to myself on how I could apply Rule #9 to me. Each version, I wrote, came from looking back at different aspects in my life where forgiveness was missing yet needed. With each variation I wrote, I found myself growing in understanding. I could feel the inspiration of the Holy Ghost giving me the wisdom I needed for clarity of understanding. I wrote at least 15 stories of the what, how, and why I needed Rule #9. Within those writings, I found my answer. I also found that they all contained a similar pattern of wisdom.

It is All About Balance:

As we grow and learn, there are some mistakes that we make in life that we cannot totally correct on our own. Some things once broken, just cannot be repaired, replaced, or substituted.

This creates a dilemma between two spiritual laws that govern our morals. They are justice and mercy. These two eternal laws have somewhat of a yin & yang relationship, wherein we need them both, and they need each other to maintain our spiritual balance. Yet in their attempt to balance our spiritual wellbeing, they cannot. Why? Because they both take from the other. Justice takes away from mercy and mercy from justice. Therein lies the dilemma. Both justice and mercy are needed. Yet on their own, one would consume the other and cause a spiritual imbalance. An imbalance that based upon eternal spiritual laws cannot exist. You cannot have a north pole of a magnet without having a south pole. Without a south pole, everything would be north; therefore, there would be no north. You cannot have forward movement, without a backward movement, because everything is relative upon the opposite.

There must be a giver and a taker to have balance. In the case of the laws of justice and mercy, there is not a giver and taker. They are both takers. To gain spiritual balance, these laws require a third spiritual law. And that is the law of sacrifice.

You can take Jesus Christ out of the equation for Rule #8 and Rule #9 if you want, but as for me, I cannot. Why? Because both rules 8 & 9 require the laws of justice and mercy. And to maintain their balance requires the law of sacrifice. I believe

Jesus Christ fulfills the law of sacrifice. In fact, He is the sacrifice.

Play It Again, Sam:

Let us go over this again another way. Justice cannot be robbed, and though mercy may be extended from the injured party to the perpetrator, the mercy that is offered may not be enough to 'right the wrong.' And justice must still be satisfied, or the scale becomes unbalanced.

> **(D. Todd Christofferson, 2014 October General Conference, "FREE Forever, to Act for Themselves")6**
> *"But as a consequence of being perfectly just, there are some things God cannot do. He cannot be arbitrary in saving some and banishing others. He 'cannot look upon sin with the least degree of allowance.' He cannot allow mercy to rob justice."*
>
> **(Book of Mormon: Alma 42:25)3**
> *25 What, do ye suppose that mercy can rob justice? I say unto you, Nay; not one whit. If so, God would cease to be God.*

Justice requires accountability (an obligation or willingness to accept responsibility or to account for one's actions). To escape accountability, the sinner looks for mercy from the injured party. This is particularly true when accountability comes at a high price for the sinner.

Without justice or accountability, the injured party from whom mercy is being asked must take the loss. If mercy is always extended from the injured party without retribution from the offending party, there is no accountability. Without accountability, there is no need for justice, and without justice, there is no need for mercy. Likewise, if justice is always served, there is no mercy. Without mercy, we leave no room for forgiveness for the errors and mistakes that we make as we go down the road of life.

Rule #9 'Don't Be Overly Judgmental of Yourself'

There is no perfect human that has lived or lives on Earth but Jesus Christ. All fall short of perfection, and sinning is therefore inevitable. Thus, the need for mercy. Without mercy, justice would condemn us all as sinners and chain us all to hell.

Hell being a constant torment of your soul and you being your own tormentor. For any righteously moral person, there are those moral emotional feelings such as regret, remorse, guilt, shame, unworthiness, depression, and the list goes on. Without mercy, these emotions consume you with a never-ending fire burning your soul. I believe I have felt them all, with greater sadness and pain than my soul can or could bear alone. Without the mercy of forgiveness, I believe that my emotional torment would never end as Helaman points out:

> **(Book of Mormon: Helaman 12:25-26)[3]**
> 25 And I would that all men might be saved. But we read that in the great and last day there are some who shall be cast out, yea, who shall be cast off from the presence of the Lord;
>
> 26 Yea, who shall be consigned to a state of endless misery, fulfilling the words which say: They that have done good shall have everlasting life; and they that have done evil shall have everlasting damnation. And thus it is. Amen.

We must have both justice and mercy, and neither can be greater than the other, or one will rule over the other. If the scale of justice and mercy is not kept balanced, in either direction, there is an injustice. Injustice creates chaos. I don't believe in chaos, nor do I believe that the God I know and believe in does either.

> **(Bible New Testament: 1 Corinthians 14:33)[2]**
> 33 For God is not the author of confusion, but of peace, as in all churches of the saints.

Therefore, justice and mercy must balance. Yet, as I said before, they cannot balance themselves. That requires a third element to be added. And that's the law of sacrifice. Our

Father in Heaven provided the sacrifice to balance the scale of justice and mercy. A sacrifice that you can freely partake of to end the torment of your soul. A blessed sacrifice to help you stop being your own tormentor. God gave us His only begotten Son, for the law of sacrifice. Through the acceptance of the Atonement of His Son, Jesus Christ, you can and will find the mercy you need and yet satisfy the demands that justice requires. Thereby gaining balance to your soul, that will give you the peace, love, and harmony we all seek.

> **(Book of Mormon: Alma 34:8-10)**[3]
> *8 And now, behold, I will testify unto you of myself that these things are true. Behold, I say unto you, that I do know that Christ shall come among the children of men, to take upon him the transgressions of his people, and that he shall atone for the sins of the world; for the Lord God hath spoken it.*
>
> *9 For it is expedient that an atonement should be made; for according to the great plan of the Eternal God there must be an atonement made, or else all mankind must unavoidably perish; yea, all are hardened; yea, all are fallen and are lost, and must perish except it be through the atonement which it is expedient should be made.*
>
> *10 For it is expedient that there should be a great and last sacrifice; yea, not a sacrifice of man, neither of beast, neither of any manner of fowl; for it shall not be a human sacrifice; but it must be an infinite and eternal sacrifice.*
>
> **(Book of Mormon: Mosiah 15:8-9)**[3]
> *8 And thus God breaketh the bands of death, having gained the victory over death; giving the Son power to make intercession for the children of men—*
>
> *9 Having ascended into heaven, having the bowels of mercy; being filled with compassion towards the children of men; standing betwixt them and justice; having broken the bands of death, taken upon himself their iniquity and their transgressions,*

having redeemed them, and satisfied the demands of justice.

(Book of Mormon: Enos 1:2-6)[3]

2 And I will tell you of the wrestle which I had before God, before I received a remission of my sins.

3 Behold, I went to hunt beasts in the forests; and the words which I had often heard my father speak concerning eternal life, and the joy of the saints, sunk deep into my heart.

4 And my soul hungered; and I kneeled down before my Maker, and I cried unto him in mighty prayer and supplication for mine own soul; and all the day long did I cry unto him; yea, and when the night came I did still raise my voice high that it reached the heavens.

5 And there came a voice unto me, saying: Enos, thy sins are forgiven thee, and thou shalt be blessed.

6 And I, Enos, knew that God could not lie; wherefore, my guilt was swept away.

(Book of Mormon: 2 Nephi 9:26)[3]

26 For the atonement satisfieth the demands of his justice upon all those who have not the law given to them, that they are delivered from that awful monster, death and hell, and the devil, and the lake of fire and brimstone, which is endless torment; and they are restored to that God who gave them breath, which is the Holy One of Israel.

Walking the Tightrope:

I believe in a balance to all things.

(Book of Mormon: 2 Nephi 2:11)[3]

11 For it must needs be, that there is an opposition in all things. If not so, my first-born in the wilderness, righteousness could not be brought to pass.

Rule #9 'Don't Be Overly Judgmental of Yourself'

> **(Book of Mormon: 2 Nephi 2:15)**[3]
> *15 And to bring about his eternal purposes in the end of man, after he had created our first parents, and the beasts of the field and the fowls of the air, and in fine, all things which are created, it must needs be that there was an opposition; even the forbidden fruit in opposition to the tree of life; the one being sweet and the other bitter.*

For every action, there is a reaction. Why? Because there are both temporal and spiritual laws that exist to govern all things. These laws are eternal and have existed since the beginning of time. God himself adheres to the laws. If He did not, He would cease to be God. Therefore, if God could break the rules without a reaction or consequence, then we could break the rules without consequence. Then why would we need rules at all? Can you imagine what state the universe would be in without laws and consequences? I don't believe we or the universe could exist without laws governing us.

> **(Book of Mormon: Alma 42:21-22)**[3]
> *21 And if there was no law given, if men sinned what could justice do, or mercy either, for they would have no claim upon the creature?*
>
> *22 But there is a law given, and a punishment affixed, and a repentance granted; which repentance, mercy claimeth; otherwise, justice claimeth the creature and executeth the law, and the law inflicteth the punishment; if not so, the works of justice would be destroyed, and God would cease to be God.*

Some people that believe the universe, they play in, needs balance, but don't believe in the existence of God or the need for the Atonement of Jesus Christ. They believe that the laws governing the universe balance themselves. Well to them I say this: the corner of the universe you play in is a speck of God's back yard that He plays in, and where do you think all the laws for governing the universe came from?

Rule #9 'Don't Be Overly Judgmental of Yourself'

It is All About Mediation:

Since I am not a Steven Hawking or Albert Einstein, let's size things back down and move on from dealing with the laws governing the universe, which do affect us, to just dealing with the moral and spiritual laws that govern us under Rule #9.

If there must be a balance to all things (and as I stated before and I believe there is) then when things cannot be balanced with repentance and retribution there must be mediation; a way to compensate for the difference so that justice can be satisfied and mercy can be rendered. Then balance can be achieved.

> **(Bible New Testament: Acts 13:38-39)[2]**
> *38 ¶ Be it known unto you therefore, men and brethren, that through this man is preached unto you the forgiveness of sins:*
>
> *39 And by him all that believe are justified from all things, from which ye could not be justified by the law of Moses.*

This mediator must be someone with capabilities far beyond those of a mortal man. This person must be someone that has an understanding of all the laws of the physical and spiritual universe and the means by which to apply them in a way that does not violate the laws themselves. Someone that has the strength, power, wisdom, and knowledge that I know I do not possess.

> **(Bible New Testament: Luke 7:48-50)[2]**
> *48 And he said unto her, Thy sins are forgiven.*
>
> *49 And they that sat at meat with him began to say within themselves, Who is this that forgiveth sins also?*
>
> *50 And he said to the woman, Thy faith hath saved thee; go in peace.*

Rule #9 'Don't Be Overly Judgmental of Yourself'

(Book of Mormon: 2 Nephi 2:25-28)[3]

25 Adam fell that men might be; and men are, that they might have joy.

26 And the Messiah cometh in the fulness of time, that he may redeem the children of men from the fall. And because that they are redeemed from the fall they have become free forever, knowing good from evil; to act for themselves and not to be acted upon, save it be by the punishment of the law at the great and last day, according to the commandments which God hath given.

27 Wherefore, men are free according to the flesh; and all things are given them which are expedient unto man. And they are free to choose liberty and eternal life, through the great Mediator of all men, or to choose captivity and death, according to the captivity and power of the devil; for he seeketh that all men might be miserable like unto himself.

28 And now, my sons, I would that ye should look to the great Mediator, and hearken unto his great commandments; and be faithful unto his words, and choose eternal life, according to the will of his Holy Spirit;

It is my belief that Father in Heaven (a Supreme Being if you wish) chose his first-born Son for the task of being our mediator, and bestowed upon Him all the powers and blessings to fulfill that calling.

(Book of Mormon: Alma 13:5-7)[3]

5 Or in fine, in the first place they were on the same standing with their brethren; thus this holy calling being prepared from the foundation of the world for such as would not harden their hearts, being in and through the atonement of the Only Begotten Son, who was prepared—

Rule #9 'Don't Be Overly Judgmental of Yourself'

(Book of Mormon: 2 Nephi 2:25-28)[3]

25 Adam fell that men might be; and men are, that they might have joy.

26 And the Messiah cometh in the fulness of time, that he may redeem the children of men from the fall. And because that they are redeemed from the fall they have become free forever, knowing good from evil; to act for themselves and not to be acted upon, save it be by the punishment of the law at the great and last day, according to the commandments which God hath given.

27 Wherefore, men are free according to the flesh; and all things are given them which are expedient unto man. And they are free to choose liberty and eternal life, through the great Mediator of all men, or to choose captivity and death, according to the captivity and power of the devil; for he seeketh that all men might be miserable like unto himself.

28 And now, my sons, I would that ye should look to the great Mediator, and hearken unto his great commandments; and be faithful unto his words, and choose eternal life, according to the will of his Holy Spirit;

It is my belief that Father in Heaven (a Supreme Being if you wish) chose his first-born Son for the task of being our mediator, and bestowed upon Him all the powers and blessings to fulfill that calling.

(Book of Mormon: Alma 13:5-7)[3]

5 Or in fine, in the first place they were on the same standing with their brethren; thus this holy calling being prepared from the foundation of the world for such as would not harden their hearts, being in and through the atonement of the Only Begotten Son, who was prepared—

It is All About Mediation:

Since I am not a Steven Hawking or Albert Einstein, let's size things back down and move on from dealing with the laws governing the universe, which do affect us, to just dealing with the moral and spiritual laws that govern us under Rule #9.

If there must be a balance to all things (and as I stated before and I believe there is) then when things cannot be balanced with repentance and retribution there must be mediation; a way to compensate for the difference so that justice can be satisfied and mercy can be rendered. Then balance can be achieved.

> **(Bible New Testament: Acts 13:38-39)**[2]
> *38 ¶ Be it known unto you therefore, men and brethren, that through this man is preached unto you the forgiveness of sins:*
>
> *39 And by him all that believe are justified from all things, from which ye could not be justified by the law of Moses.*

This mediator must be someone with capabilities far beyond those of a mortal man. This person must be someone that has an understanding of all the laws of the physical and spiritual universe and the means by which to apply them in a way that does not violate the laws themselves. Someone that has the strength, power, wisdom, and knowledge that I know I do not possess.

> **(Bible New Testament: Luke 7:48-50)**[2]
> *48 And he said unto her, Thy sins are forgiven.*
>
> *49 And they that sat at meat with him began to say within themselves, Who is this that forgiveth sins also?*
>
> *50 And he said to the woman, Thy faith hath saved thee; go in peace.*

6 And thus being called by this holy calling, and ordained unto the high priesthood of the holy order of God, to teach his commandments unto the children of men, that they also might enter into his rest—

7 This high priesthood being after the order of his Son, which order was from the foundation of the world; or in other words, being without beginning of days or end of years, being prepared from eternity to all eternity, according to his foreknowledge of all things—

(Book of Mormon: Alma 42:15)[3]
15 And now, the plan of mercy could not be brought about except an atonement should be made; therefore God himself atoneth for the sins of the world, to bring about the plan of mercy, to appease the demands of justice, that God might be a perfect, just God, and a merciful God also.

Jesus Christ provides a means for us to be given mercy and at the same time for justice to be served. He accomplished this through His atoning sacrifice, a sacrifice which neither you nor I could do for ourselves. This is vitally important to understand. When you genuinely comprehend the atoning sacrifice of Jesus Christ, you will realize why unrightfully passing judgment upon yourself (better known as beating yourself up) is fruitless.

We can never pay the full price for some of the mistakes we have made in our lives, that is what Christ's atoning sacrifice is about. He is our mediator. All we have to do is accept His gift, and by accepting His gift, our lives become balanced again.

(Book of Mormon: Alma 34:8-10)[3]
8 And now, behold, I will testify unto you of myself that these things are true. Behold, I say unto you, that I do know that Christ shall come among the children of men, to take upon him the transgressions of his people, and that he shall atone for the sins of the world; for the Lord God hath spoken it.

9 For it is expedient that an atonement should be made; for according to the great plan of the Eternal God there must be an atonement made, or else all mankind must unavoidably perish; yea, all are hardened; yea, all are fallen and are lost, and must perish except it be through the atonement which it is expedient should be made.

10 For it is expedient that there should be a great and last sacrifice; yea, not a sacrifice of man, neither of beast, neither of any manner of fowl; for it shall not be a human sacrifice; but it must be an infinite and eternal sacrifice.

(Book of Mormon: 2 Nephi 2:27-28)[3]
27 Wherefore, men are free according to the flesh; and all things are given them which are expedient unto man. And they are free to choose liberty and eternal life, through the great Mediator of all men, or to choose captivity and death, according to the captivity and power of the devil; for he seeketh that all men might be miserable like unto himself.

28 And now, my sons, I would that ye should look to the great Mediator, and hearken unto his great commandments; and be faithful unto his words, and choose eternal life, according to the will of his Holy Spirit;

(Book of Mormon: Moroni 10:32-33)[3]
32 Yea, come unto Christ, and be perfected in him, and deny yourselves of all ungodliness; and if ye shall deny yourselves of all ungodliness, and love God with all your might, mind and strength, then is his grace sufficient for you, that by his grace ye may be perfect in Christ; and if by the grace of God ye are perfect in Christ, ye can in nowise deny the power of God.

33 And again, if ye by the grace of God are perfect in Christ, and deny not his power, then are ye sanctified in Christ by the grace of God, through the shedding of

Rule #9 'Don't Be Overly Judgmental of Yourself'

> *the blood of Christ, which is in the covenant of the Father unto the remission of your sins, that ye become holy, without spot.*

I do not fully understand how Christ was able to atone for our sins, the powers it took, what governing laws were needed, or how they were applied. All we are told in the scriptures is that when Christ prayed in the Garden of Gethsemane for our sins, the pain was great. So great that Christ bled from every pore. Even with all the powers and blessings that Father in Heaven had bestowed upon Him, He knew the burden He was accepting and the pain He would have to bear. Yet He accepted it. Jesus Christ knew that, even for Himself, the atonement would be hard. It was so hard that He asked Heavenly Father if that bitter cup He was to drink from could be removed. Yet still, He qualified His request with an appendage. That if there were no other way, He would do His Father's will.

(Bible New Testament: 1 John 1:7)[2]
7 But if we walk in the light, as he is in the light, we have fellowship one with another, and the blood of Jesus Christ his Son cleanseth us from all sin.

(Book of Mormon: 3 Nephi 27:13)[3]
13 Behold I have given unto you my gospel, and this is the gospel which I have given unto you—that I came into the world to do the will of my Father, because my Father sent me.

(Doctrine & Covenants: 19:16-19)[4]
16 For behold, I, God, have suffered these things for all, that they might not suffer if they would repent;

17 But if they would not repent they must suffer even as I;

18 Which suffering caused myself, even God, the greatest of all, to tremble because of pain, and to bleed at every pore, and to suffer both body and spirit—and would that I might not drink the bitter cup, and shrink—

19 Nevertheless, glory be to the Father, and I partook and finished my preparations unto the children of men.

(Book of Mormon: 3 Nephi 1:14)[3]
14 Behold, I come unto my own, to fulfil all things which I have made known unto the children of men from the foundation of the world, and to do the will, both of the Father and of the Son...

It is All About Ownership:

I would like to share with you an issue I had in dealing with a mistake I made. It was one of those mistakes that no matter what I did as restitution, I could not put things back to the way they were. Keep in mind that the mistake I made is not the story here. We all make mistakes in our lives. Whether they are the same as mine or different from mine is not important. The important fact is that full restitution on our own was and is not possible. That is the key point to look at.

Here is a little background to help you understand where my mind was set before I truly understood Christ's Atonement. When I was very, very, young it seemed I got blamed for everything, whether I did it or not. The discipline my father handed out as judgment was extreme. It would be considered severe child abuse in this day and age.

At that time of my life, it did not seem to matter to my father whether I was guilty or innocent. If the issue at hand seemed to point in my direction, I was the one receiving the punishment...punishment I would not wish to be used on any child. Yet, comparing my life to some of my friends and others, my dad's punishments were mild. I may have come out with cuts and bruises, but I never had any of my bones broken. I have seen and have read stories of children receiving far worse than I did. Thus, I count myself blessed.

Now, you would think that as a kid, if I was going to get punished for a mistake, whether I did it or not that I would have learned to try and lie my way out of the situation to escape the punishment. I mean, after all, if I lied, there was a good chance the story I made up would be good enough to escape my father's wrath. I did not choose the path of a liar. Instead, I listened to a small voice I heard within me. As I listened to that still small voice, it gave me comfort. It assured me that I had a far greater worth within me and that no unjust punishment could take that from me unless I allowed it. That was my honor and my integrity.

Because of my father's unjust punishments, as a young child, I made a promise to God and myself. That promise was to always own up to any mistake I made so that no other person would suffer for something I had done.

Well, as honorable as my vow was always to own responsibility for my actions, that vow was getting in the way when it came to Christ atoning for my sins.

I would lay all the guilt and punishment for my error upon myself. I wasn't going to share it with anyone. In my mind, I believed I was protecting others from bearing my mistake and my burden. After all, it was my mistake, my fault, and my responsibility to deal with whatever outcome was handed to me.

The problem with this way of thinking is that there are times when you make a mistake that no matter what you do, you can't fix it. No restitution or punishment can ever satisfy the mistake. As a result, you find yourself in a never-ending loop of punishment that consists of constantly beating yourself up as you try to atone for your error. Why are you caught in this endless loop of punishment? It is because neither you nor any other human can do enough to correct for some mistakes.

(Book of Mormon: Mosiah; 14:4-6)[3]
4 Surely he has borne our griefs, and carried our sorrows; yet we did esteem him stricken, smitten of God, and afflicted.

5 But he was wounded for our transgressions, he was bruised for our iniquities; the chastisement of

Rule #9 'Don't Be Overly Judgmental of Yourself'

> *our peace was upon him; and with his stripes we are healed.*
>
> *6 All we, like sheep, have gone astray; we have turned every one to his own way; and the Lord hath laid on him the iniquities of us all.*
>
> **(Bible New Testament: Luke 22:42-44)**[2]
> *42 Saying, Father, if thou be willing, remove this cup from me: nevertheless not my will, but thine, be done.*
>
> *43 And there appeared an angel unto him from heaven, strengthening him.*
>
> *44 And being in an agony he prayed more earnestly: and his sweat was as it were great drops of blood falling down to the ground.*

But the truth is that someone a long time ago already made up for my errors. Thus, for me to continue punishing myself is, number one, fruitless and two, forsakes the atoning gift given to me by Jesus Christ. By not accepting His atonement, I was taking the honor from Him and the love that He desired for me: a gift that He had freely given to me.

To carry this thought farther, it also says that I don't need Christ's Atonement to get back into heaven. Rejecting Christ's Atonement also disrespects God, our Father in Heaven. A Father who gave His only begotten Son to save us, a Father who had to stand by and watch as His Son carried all the pain of our sins.

When Christ atoned for our mistakes to balance the books, it was not only for those people that were willing to accept His gift. Nor does He suffer only at the time we decide to let Him take a burden from us. In the garden, when Christ suffered for our sins, just prior to His death, He suffered for everyone's sins all at one time. When I say everyone, I mean those that had already died, those who were and are living, and for those who are not yet born.

(Book of Mormon: 1 Nephi 11:33)[3]
33 And I, Nephi, saw that he was lifted up upon the cross and slain for the sins of the world.

(Bible New Testament: Colossians 1:14)[2]
14 In whom we have redemption through his blood, even the forgiveness of sins:

Whether a person accepts Christ's Atonement or not is up to the individual person. Accepting or not accepting Christ's Atonement changes nothing as far as how much Christ suffered for all of us. His suffering is done, and all that Heavenly Father asks of you and me is that we acknowledge and accept His Son's gift. No strings attached; we all receive Christ's atoning gift freely upon acceptance.

(Bible New Testament: 1 John 1:7)[2]
7 But if we walk in the light, as he is in the light, we have fellowship one with another, and the blood of Jesus Christ his Son cleanseth us from all sin.

(Bible New Testament: Hebrews 8:12)[2]
12 For I will be merciful to their unrighteousness, and their sins and their iniquities will I remember no more.

(Book of Mormon: 2 Nephi 31:17 & 20)[3]
17 Wherefore, do the things which I have told you I have seen that your Lord and your Redeemer should do; for, for this cause have they been shown unto me, that ye might know the gate by which ye should enter. For the gate by which ye should enter is repentance and baptism by water; and then cometh a remission of your sins by fire and by the Holy Ghost.

20 Wherefore, ye must press forward with a steadfastness in Christ, having a perfect brightness of hope, and a love of God and of all men. Wherefore, if ye shall press forward, feasting upon the word of Christ, and endure to the end, behold, thus saith the Father: Ye shall have eternal life.

Rule #9 'Don't Be Overly Judgmental of Yourself'

I have to take ownership of my mistakes, repent, and make restitution as much as possible, but beating myself up endlessly over my mistakes is not required. This statement applies not just to me but to everyone. I give you the following scripture to support my statement.

> **(Book of Mormon: Mosiah 4:6-8)**[3]
> *6 I say unto you, if ye have come to a knowledge of the goodness of God, and his matchless power, and his wisdom, and his patience, and his long-suffering towards the children of men; and also, the atonement which has been prepared from the foundation of the world, that thereby salvation might come to him that should put his trust in the Lord, and should be diligent in keeping his commandments, and continue in the faith even unto the end of his life, I mean the life of the mortal body—*
>
> *7 I say, that this is the man who receiveth salvation, through the atonement which was prepared from the foundation of the world for all mankind, which ever were since the fall of Adam, or who are, or who ever shall be, even unto the end of the world.*
>
> *8 And this is the means whereby salvation cometh. And there is none other salvation save this which hath been spoken of; neither are there any conditions whereby man can be saved except the conditions which I have told you.*

There is only one way you can balance the books, and that is to come to an actual understanding of Jesus Christ's atoning sacrifice and accept it.

> **(Bible New Testament: Acts 5:31)**[2]
> *31 Him hath God exalted with his right hand to be a Prince and a Saviour, for to give repentance to Israel, and forgiveness of sins*

(Preach My Gospel: *A Guide to Missionary Service*, Lesson 2: The Plan of Salvation)[7]
As we rely on the Atonement of Jesus Christ, He can help us endure our trials, sicknesses, and pain. We can be filled with joy, peace, and consolation. All that is unfair about life can be made right through the Atonement of Jesus Christ.

A Little Bit of Gratitude Goes a Long Way:

I would like to take a moment to thank two of our young Sister missionaries, Sister Madison Schrader, and Sister Hailey Romero for their help in writing Rule #9. These sisters and other young men and women volunteer to be called to dedicate two years of their life between high school and college to serve a full-time mission. They do this at their own expense. They go wherever the Church says the Lord has called them. They do it to share the Lord's redeeming message that life is eternal, and our mistakes in this life can be forgiven through the atoning blood of Jesus Christ.

These young missionaries are serving throughout the world. They search for those who are ready to accept Christ in their life. They do it so that others may regain balance back in their life by accepting the atoning sacrifice of Jesus Christ and thus find great peace and happiness in this temporal state on earth. They do it so that others can find their way to a peaceful and eternal life with their family. They do it so that others may once again live with God, our Heavenly Father, who governs over all beings in righteousness.

Remember, no unclean thing can enter the Celestial Kingdom of Heaven, and only through the atoning blood of God's Son can justice and mercy wash our slate clean and purify us.

I leave you my testimony of the truthfulness of the gospel of Jesus Christ and God's endless love for us. It is my prayer that the reading of Rules #8 & #9 will provide you with a greater understanding of God's mercy and justice.   AMEN

Rule #9 'Don't Be Overly Judgmental of Yourself'

Endnotes:

1 **King James Version of the Bible, The Old Testament of Our Lord and Saviour Jesus Christ.** Published by The Church of Jesus Christ of Latter-day Saints, Salt Lake City, Utah, USA. Copywrite 2013.

2 **King James Version of the Bible, The New Testament of Our Lord and Saviour Jesus Christ.** Published by The Church of Jesus Christ of Latter-day Saints, Salt Lake City, Utah, USA. Copywrite 2013.

3 **The Book of Mormon Another Testament of Jesus Christ.** Published by The Church of Jesus Christ of Latter-day Saints, Salt Lake City, Utah, USA. The first English edition published in Palmyra, New York, USA, in 1830. Copywrite 2013.

4 **The Doctrine and Covenants of The Church of Jesus Christ of Latter-Day Saints.** Containing Revelations Give to Joseph Smith, the Prophet. With some additions by his successors in the Presidency of the Church. Published by The Church of Jesus Christ of Latter-day Saints, Salt Lake City, Utah, USA. Copywrite 2013.

5 **The Pearl of Great Price.** A selection from the revelations, translations, and narrations of Joseph Smith, First Prophet, seer, and revelator to The Church of Jesus Christ of Latter-Day Saints. Published by The Church of Jesus Christ of Latter-day Saints, Salt Lake City, Utah, USA. Copywrite 2013.

6 **D. Todd Christofferson**, 2014 October General Conference, "Free Forever, to Act for Themselves." The 184th Semiannual General Conference of the Church of Jesus Christ of Latter-day Saints, October 4, 2014, Saturday Morning Session. Published in the Ensign magazine, Volume 44 Number 11, November 2014, page-16. An official magazine of the Church of Jesus Christ of Latter-day Saints, published by the Church of Jesus Christ of Latter-day Saints, 50 E. North Temple Street, Salt Lake City, UT, 84150-3220, USA. Also, see The Church of Jesus Christ of Latter-day Saints, Churchofjesuschrist.org. Retrieved February 12, 2019, from Churchofjesuschrist.org website:
https://www.churchofjesuschrist.org/study/ensign/2014/11/saturday-morning-session/free-forever-to-act-for-themselves?lang=eng.

7 **Preach My Gospel:** *A Guide to Missionary Service.* "Lesson 2: The Plan of Salvation," *Preach My Gospel: A Guide to Missionary Service* Version: 2/18, Page-52 Paragraph-3, Published by The Church of Jesus Christ of Latter-day Saints, 16229 000, Printed in the United States of America. Also, see The Church of Jesus Christ of Latter-day Saints, Churchofjesuschrist.org. Retrieved February 12, 2019, from Churchofjesuschrist.org website:
https://www.churchofjesuschrist.org/manual/preach-my-gospel-a-guide-to-missionary-service/lesson-2-the-plan-of-salvation?lang=eng.

Rule #9 'Don't Be Overly Judgmental of Yourself'

I Feel a Change in The Air

Rule #10
'You Can't Change Other People, Only Yourself'

Rule #10 'You Can't Change Other People, Only Yourself'

The Simple Facts:

Can we change other people? Good question, don't you think? A lot of people are convinced they can. Well, the truth is, you can't.

What you can do is set a good or bad example for others to follow. You may even be a good persuader who can influence the outcome of other's decisions. Satan sure is a good persuader (according to the Bible in Genesis 3:1-6), look what he did to Eve. Did Satan make Eve go against God's commandment? The answer is no, Satan did not. What Satan did do was persuade Eve to go against God's commandment. But Eve still had to make a choice.

Here is the bare fact: we as humans do our own choosing. Whether you feel you were persuaded or not, you are accountable for every choice you make. Though Satan sorely tempted Eve, Eve was still held responsible for her decision.

We all are endowed with a power called 'free agency.' This power is the freedom to make our own choices. Therefore, you cannot change other people. You can only change yourself.

While you can't change another person, you can influence how he or she thinks, acts, or responds, and you can influence how they impact others. But in the end, when choices are made, it is through the act of free agency. That is why the responsibility for all actions rest upon the individual performing the action and not anyone else.

The Person of My Mind:

It is one thing to see potential in a person and then do what you can to help that person develop that potential, but it is wrong to think that you can change a person into who or what you think they ought to be.

Rule #10 'You Can't Change Other People, Only Yourself'

When a person is not able or willing to see the same potential within themselves as you do, they will not change. Only when they see the need to change will they, and only then because they want to, not because you want them to.

The most tragic example of thinking you can change a person into who you think that person should be is when it involves an intimate relationship.

How many times have you known someone that becomes involved in a relationship, not based on who their potential mate is at that moment, but instead based on who they think the person can be in the future? They feel confident that they are qualified to change their companion, and so they go into the relationship believing the person will transform into the image of the person they see in their mind. I have seen the story many times where person 1 bases their relationship with person 2 on some magical guarantee that person 1 has the power to change person 2. Yet person 2 is completely happy being who they are and thinks that person 1 is basing their relationship on the fact of who person 2 is today.

As a father, mother, bishop, or close friend, it is heartbreaking to watch a relationship that is based on fantasy or wishful thinking rather than reality. Any relationship that starts on a foundation where one person thinks they are going to change the basic, fundamental lifestyle of the other person is a relationship whose destiny is far more likely to fail than to succeed.

I Changed My Mind:

I would like to share with you a story, based upon actual events, of another type of relationship change that can happen between couples in a marriage. This story is about a friend of mine who I'll call Karen.

Some very serious issues developed in Karen's marriage. Although the issues existed from the beginning, the problems they would cause would not be realized until several years into her marriage.

Rule #10 'You Can't Change Other People, Only Yourself'

At the beginning of Karen's marriage, she and her husband had many things in common. For several years they were very happy with their relationship. They were a happy young couple that shared many of the same friends who had a similar lifestyle. They all liked to party, drink alcohol, and smoke marijuana. Karen and her husband lived what they called a carefree, fun life.

The relationship was solid, and life was good. That is until somewhere down the road of life, Karen decided that there needed to be a change in their lifestyle. For Karen, the need for change started when she came to realize how their lifestyle would affect their children. Upon this realization, she took a hard look at how they were living and decided what changes needed to be made. But her husband did not agree.

Growing up, Karen had a religious background, and now, with the changes she wanted to make in her life, she thought it was time to set things right with God. She started cleaning up her act, no more heavy social parties, no alcoholic drinks, and no smoking which included marijuana. Her lifestyle changes also included returning to church on Sunday. This act, in turn, leads Karen to get involved in church activities.

Karen learned that in her renewed religious life and with her lifestyle changes, she was much happier; that is all except with her marriage. Soon Karen found herself having strong arguments with her husband over his unwillingness to change. Eventually, Karen gave up on arguing with her husband. But then the arguments were replaced by a darkened silence between them.

This couple's once-close relationship now became distant and cold. My friend, Karen, became bitter because her husband could not see the need to change, neither for the betterment of their children nor for his own personal growth. The husband couldn't or didn't understand why his wife wanted to destroy what had been a mutually happy relationship. As far as he was concerned, he wasn't what was destroying the marriage; he hadn't changed. He was still the same man she had married.

For years, Karen never let up on her husband. She was on his case all the time, telling him how he needed to shape up and see beyond his childish ways. Another effect of Karen's lifestyle change was that she decided they needed better friends, and so she stopped going to parties with her husband and socializing with their old party friends. She now called her old party friends, delinquent children.

Karen surrounded herself with new friends that shared her new values and guess what; her husband didn't much care for her new friends and their "goody-two-shoes values" as he called it. This put another rift in their already strained marriage.

It was bad enough that the couple hardly spoke to each other, but now there was very little socializing as well. Thus, Karen stopped being a good wife, and the husband stopped being a good husband.

This couple went from having a lot in common at the beginning of their marriage to having very little in common other than their children.

Luke, Use the Force:

Karen was still convinced that she could salvage their marriage by remolding her husband into a partner that would fit into her newfound lifestyle. She was determined to make it happen even if it took a baseball bat slammed over his head.

Karen was convinced that her new lifestyle was best for her husband and their children. She believed that her husband needed to change. When attempts to remold her husband continued to fail, Karen started to feel hopeless and lost in their marriage. Hence, she decided it was time to call in the professionals. No question about it, her mind was made up. They were going to a marriage counselor. Do you think the husband agreed to marriage counseling? No, not even a little.

Well, Karen was firmly set on the two of them getting marriage counseling and was not going to budge. The husband, on the other hand, was not budging either and was firmly refusing to go.

To resolve this issue, Karen pulled out a bigger baseball bat and took a swing. What was the bigger baseball bat she used on her husband? It was to threaten him with divorce and take him for every penny he had if he didn't go to counseling. Well, that threat worked. Karen won that battle. Her husband reluctantly went to counseling as an unwilling participant.

As you can guess, the counseling didn't succeed in fixing the main issues in their marriage. It wasn't a total loss, though, because it did at least get the two of them to start talking to each other again, and that was seriously needed for the children's sake.

The counseling helped a little in a few other areas as well. One big issue Karen continued to have with her husband was smoking marijuana. She wanted him to quit altogether. Well, the husband refused to give up his weed habit. But he did agree to a compromise, he would stop smoking it in the house. At that moment, Karen felt that was a compromise she could live with. It was a start, at least. However, she lost hope when she learned that his compromise was to move his weed smoking from the house to their garage. This wasn't as big of a step forward in their relationship as she had thought it would be. But it was progress, even if it was a half a baby step.

The Dark Side:

Just as Karen's hopes that their marriage still had a chance, that their relationship might improve, it instead took a turn for the worse and moved to a new realm of bad. Now it was the children bringing problems into the marriage. You see, the children picked up on their father's current lifestyle and their mother's former lifestyle, and started smoking marijuana. From there, they rapidly graduated to hard-core drugs. This was a completely new reality for Karen to deal with.

The husband had known about the children smoking marijuana and hadn't shared that information with his wife.

Rule #10 'You Can't Change Other People, Only Yourself'

He didn't see it as an issue. It was just marijuana. On the same hand, he didn't recognize how short the fall is from marijuana to hard-core drugs. His only defense when his wife discovered the seriousness of their children's drug abuse was that he didn't know what the kids had been doing or he would have done something. Karen was furious. She blamed her husband for their children's drug addiction.

Both parents tried to stop the children's drug usage but had little to no success. The husband, however, refused to acknowledge any connection to his marijuana usage and the children's drug habit.

It didn't take long before their children found their way to new sleeping quarters with a smaller bed in a smaller room called jail. Seeing her children in jail brought Karen to the final boiling point with her marriage. She now had one child in jail and another on probation. Karen was ready to throw in the towel, get a divorce, and rid herself of her worthless mate, along with all the pain he had caused in her and her children's lives. She placed all the blame for all their problems on her husband for not opening his eyes and changing. She planned to make him pay and pay big time. She would hire the best lawyer money could buy and take her husband to the cleaners. In fact, she wasn't going to use a spin washer on him. She was going for the old fashion hand-cranked wringer washer. She wanted to turn that wringer lever ever so slowly as she wrung every penny out of him. And then she was going to run him through that wringer again just to make sure she got every drop.

Bonds of Friendship:

Karen and I had known each other for a long time. We went to school together, and along with some other mutual friends, we shared a lot of great times through High School.

Karen, our mutual friends, and I had an unusually hard life growing up, which bonded us into a very close family-like friendship. Though we felt we could not trust the world around us, we always took comfort in knowing that we could

Rule #10 'You Can't Change Other People, Only Yourself'

always trust and depend on each other. The bonds of our loyal friendship created a connection so strong that it glued us together as one. Even though we had our differences in how we viewed the world, our differences didn't seem to matter. We shared a strong common bond in that we each came from severely dysfunctional families. Each of our families was dysfunctional in a different way and for various reasons; which in turn meant we had diverse personalities and unique issues to deal with. Yet, our bond helped us look past our differences. We somehow learned to love each other for who we were. Now I am not saying we didn't step on each other's toes from time to time. In any close relationship or friendship, stepping on one another's toes is always bound to happen. But the bond of our friendship always held us together.

As a group, we looked out for and cared for each other. When any of us felt lost, afraid, and alone, we always knew we had a place where we could find safety and comfort.

There were times when it wasn't safe for a friend in our group to stay at their own home, and thus for a night or so, they became one of our homeless. To help, we would try to find a way for that friend to stay at one of our homes until it was safe for them to return to their own. It wasn't hard finding a place to hang out during the day. But when night came, there were times when bringing them to one of our homes to sleepover wasn't an option. When this happened, we felt our parents had tied our hands, forcing us to the only option we knew we had left. And that was to go against our parent's rule of not leaving the house after bedtime.

Generally, one or two of us would sneak out of the house any way we could, without getting caught, and go to where our homeless friend was waiting and keep them company through the night. Then, just before dawn, we would sneak back into our bed; praying all the time that during the night, our absence had not been discovered. We took the risk despite the consequences we knew there would be if we had been caught. We all believed that no matter the price we might pay, helping our friend was worth it. Why? Because more times than not, we felt that our little group of friends were more like family than our parents.

Friendship Has No Boundaries, or Agree to Disagree:

If one of us got in trouble, it didn't matter what kind of problem it was, we were all there to help. Even if the trouble was an action or behavior, we disapproved of. We might have expressed our disapproval and disappointment in each other, but we didn't condemn each other. Instead, any criticism or reprimand we offered was done out of our love for each other. No matter what, we stood together, whether it was beside our friends or in front of them, whatever it took to help or protect them. I can tell you that there were a few times I stepped up and took the hit for a friend, and I knew that if the circumstances were reversed, they would do the same for me.

Our friendship was so strong, our bond so deep that perhaps only war buddies sharing a foxhole on a battlefield might truly understand our devotion to each other. Like my older brother, Dave, he understood what it meant to be bonded in friendship. Dave served our country in the US Army through three tours of duty on the battlefields of Vietnam. Dave had to be able to trust and depend on his foxhole buddies as if his life depended on it because it did. This was the same strength of the bond between my friends and me.

The One:

Within any close group of friends, there always seems to be one person that everyone else brings their troubles to in search of comfort and answers. Despite all my personal trials growing up, I was the oldest in the group and the one that seemed to have the most level head on his shoulders *(please note I said seemed)*; therefore, I was the one that others came to for counsel and comfort.

Unbreakable Bond:

Time can't be stopped, and soon all the members of our group were grown-up and moving on to different places and taking different paths in life. Despite the different paths and distance that came between us, our bonds of friendship still hold strong to this day. I could be in trouble now today at my old age, all I'd have to do is send a call for help to any member of our small group, and there is no doubt in my mind that they would come and give of themselves to assist in any way they could; even if that person happened to be an ex-wife (I prefer the term, "former wife"). Guess what? One of them is my former wife, who lives two doors up the street from me. She is still one of my best friends and is also best friends with my current wife of 38 years.

Continuing Karen's Story:

My path in life had moved me away from what I call my hometown. Karen, on the other hand, never left. After I left town, we didn't stay as closely in touch. We knew bits and pieces of what was happening in each other's lives, but that was about it. In my later years, life called me back to my hometown to care for my aging parents. After I had moved back, Karen and I once again shared closer communication and kept each other abreast of the happenings in our lives.

All things in life have a reason, and my being the counselor for our little group during our high school years lead me to other callings and positions. I have served as a group counselor, a financial counselor, and a marriage counselor. Karen knew this about me, so when she heard that I was back in town, she came to me to talk about her marriage troubles and to seek my advice.

Hang Him She Says:

By the time Karen contacted me, she was already tying the noose around her husband's neck to hang him. Our conversation went something like this.

Rule #10 'You Can't Change Other People, Only Yourself'

She asked me if I thought there was any way I could help her to get her husband to see that he needed to change his ways. I told her that I didn't know. I wasn't talking with her husband that I was talking to her. I reminded her that her husband resented the closeness our little friend group shared, and I really didn't think he would be willing to talk with me. Then I asked her, "Is there any way I can convince you to change you?"

Karen replied, "What does that mean?"

I said, "Well, for one, you can start by not trying to force your husband to change. Stop beating him up verbally. Then you can also start being a good wife again."

At first, Karen took offense to my statement and started to justify all of her actions to date. I sat there with a sincere caring expression and listened to everything she had to say. Then when she tired of talking, I asked her, "Do you hear the condemning anger in your speech?"

Looking Back:

I told her, "Look back to when we were kids hanging out together. We looked after one another, even though we had our differences. Some of you smoked marijuana, or pot as we called it. Some of our friends drank alcohol, and some did drugs back then. Others used sex as an escape. For me, I never agreed with the pot-smoking, drugs, or alcohol drinking. Remember, I had an alcoholic mother and an abusive father. I used to voice my disagreements and concerns over your choices of escape, but I never tried to force you to change. Instead, it was the opposite of our little group. We always supported each other. Look at how strong our relationship is still today. Despite the different paths each of our lives has taken, the different lifestyle or beliefs we have, our differences don't matter, we still have a strong, trusting bond. To this day, I feel I can trust you with my life. Can you not say the same?"

"Yes, I can," she answered, "That is why I am here."

Rule #10 'You Can't Change Other People, Only Yourself'

I asked, "Why, do you think that is? Think about it. Therein lies your answer. You and your husband, despite your now differences in lifestyle, still share a powerful common bond, your children. Even if you divorce him, you'll not be rid of your husband. The children belong to both of you, not just you. And you'll have to deal with him on that issue. You want to think back to when your mother wasn't there for you. Try thinking back to the fights my divorced parents had over us. You were there."

"Think about it, you are the one who changed your lifestyle in this marriage of yours, not your husband."

"So, what are you saying? That I should change back to who I was? I thought you for one would be pleased with my new choice of lifestyle?"

"I am," I said in a cheerfully raised voice, "I am very happy with how you have turned yourself around, and I am not saying to go backward. I think this is who you have always been in your heart. I saw this person in you the first time we met. We survived a lot growing up, and we (meaning our little group) made some unwise choices because of all the stress and dysfunction in our homes. I thought I had a hard life with hard choices to make. One of those hard choices was deciding to live with an alcoholic mom and the consequences of living under those conditions compared to the alternative--the wonderful life of living with an abusive dad. But you, some of the choices you were forced to make, you made far greater sacrifices than any of us."

"Let's talk about your first child before you met your husband. You had a hard choice to make, and you felt forced into the decision you made. It was an incredibly hard choice, and either way, you went, meant sacrificing a part of yourself forever. You didn't have any real support. Your whole family was against you, and the young man that should have been there to support you wasn't. We were there for you, but in this case, the trouble you were in, pregnancy, was way beyond anything we could help with. Look, here is the point I am trying to make. Back then, you weren't making good choices and got yourself into a tough situation. Because you were pregnant, unmarried, and not of legal age, people were forcing their choices on you and giving you ultimatums. How did it feel being forced to listen to all the negative comments? They attacked you for who you were as a person and your lifestyle choices. Did it make you feel like changing your ways, or did you feel more like digging in? When you reluctantly chose their way, how did that affect your relationship with your family?"

Which Way Do I Go?

"When you allow the world to push you in the direction you don't want to go, you pretend to become someone you are not. You never really changed because it wasn't ever really your choice to change. It does not matter if a proposed change is good for you or not. If your mind is set to a mode of feeling forced, it goes negative. If you stay in a forced changed condition long enough, you begin to feel stuck in a pretend world. Soon it seems impossible to get back to the person you really feel you are. I know you, and you have been in this mode before. Don't you feel a bit like this now?"

I continued. "You may want to take a look at how you are handling your new lifestyle changes with respect to how you are dealing with the people around you. Like your husband and some of your old friends."

Then I reminded her, "You can't change other people; you can only change yourself. When you force another person's will to your way by using what they feel are unreasonable ultimatums, well, the effects in the long term are usually not good. Generally, when people change under forced conditions, the change is short-lived, and they will end up converting back to who they were before."

Common Ground:

"Karen, you and I are of different religious sects. Yet, I think we can agree that we both believe in Jesus Christ. Let's take a look at what the scriptures tell us and see if we can come to an

Rule #10 'You Can't Change Other People, Only Yourself'

and got yourself into a tough situation. Because you were pregnant, unmarried, and not of legal age, people were forcing their choices on you and giving you ultimatums. How did it feel being forced to listen to all the negative comments? They attacked you for who you were as a person and your lifestyle choices. Did it make you feel like changing your ways, or did you feel more like digging in? When you reluctantly chose their way, how did that affect your relationship with your family?"

Which Way Do I Go?

"When you allow the world to push you in the direction you don't want to go, you pretend to become someone you are not. You never really changed because it wasn't ever really your choice to change. It does not matter if a proposed change is good for you or not. If your mind is set to a mode of feeling forced, it goes negative. If you stay in a forced changed condition long enough, you begin to feel stuck in a pretend world. Soon it seems impossible to get back to the person you really feel you are. I know you, and you have been in this mode before. Don't you feel a bit like this now?"

I continued. "You may want to take a look at how you are handling your new lifestyle changes with respect to how you are dealing with the people around you. Like your husband and some of your old friends."

Then I reminded her, "You can't change other people; you can only change yourself. When you force another person's will to your way by using what they feel are unreasonable ultimatums, well, the effects in the long term are usually not good. Generally, when people change under forced conditions, the change is short-lived, and they will end up converting back to who they were before."

Common Ground:

"Karen, you and I are of different religious sects. Yet, I think we can agree that we both believe in Jesus Christ. Let's take a look at what the scriptures tell us and see if we can come to an

Rule #10 'You Can't Change Other People, Only Yourself'

I asked, "Why, do you think that is? Think about it. Therein lies your answer. You and your husband, despite your now differences in lifestyle, still share a powerful common bond, your children. Even if you divorce him, you'll not be rid of your husband. The children belong to both of you, not just you. And you'll have to deal with him on that issue. You want to think back to when your mother wasn't there for you. Try thinking back to the fights my divorced parents had over us. You were there."

"Think about it, you are the one who changed your lifestyle in this marriage of yours, not your husband."

"So, what are you saying? That I should change back to who I was? I thought you for one would be pleased with my new choice of lifestyle?"

"I am," I said in a cheerfully raised voice, "I am very happy with how you have turned yourself around, and I am not saying to go backward. I think this is who you have always been in your heart. I saw this person in you the first time we met. We survived a lot growing up, and we (meaning our little group) made some unwise choices because of all the stress and dysfunction in our homes. I thought I had a hard life with hard choices to make. One of those hard choices was deciding to live with an alcoholic mom and the consequences of living under those conditions compared to the alternative--the wonderful life of living with an abusive dad. But you, some of the choices you were forced to make, you made far greater sacrifices than any of us."

"Let's talk about your first child before you met your husband. You had a hard choice to make, and you felt forced into the decision you made. It was an incredibly hard choice, and either way, you went, meant sacrificing a part of yourself forever. You didn't have any real support. Your whole family was against you, and the young man that should have been there to support you wasn't. We were there for you, but in this case, the trouble you were in, pregnancy, was way beyond anything we could help with. Look, here is the point I am trying to make. Back then, you weren't making good choices understanding of how Christ would have you handle your marriage situation."

"There were strong social barriers among the Jews at the time of Christ, much like you with your husband and some of your old friends. The Savior mingled freely among the publicans and sinners, which was far different from the Pharisees, who believed sinners should not be guests in their houses."

> **(Bible New Testament: Matthew 9:10-13)**[2]
> *10 ¶ And it came to pass, as Jesus sat at meat in the house, behold, many publicans and sinners came and sat down with him and his disciples.*
>
> *11 And when the Pharisees saw it, they said unto his disciples, Why eateth your Master with publicans and sinners?*
>
> *12 But when Jesus heard that, he said unto them, They that be whole need not a physician, but they that are sick.*
>
> *13 But go ye and learn what that meaneth, I will have mercy, and not sacrifice: for I am not come to call the righteous, but sinners to repentance.*

"The Pharisees treated sinners poorly and condemned them, and Christ rebuked their unkindliness saying."

> **(Bible New Testament: Matthew 9:12)**[2]
> *9 They that be whole need not a physician, but they that are sick.*

"Jesus's enemies complained that He mingled and ate with sinners, but Jesus justified His ways. He taught more clearly the purpose of God's love toward sinners and the joy celebrated in heaven over even one sinner that repents. The Savior asked them:"

> **(Bible New Testament: Matthew 18:12-14)**[2]
> *12 "How think ye? If a man have an hundred sheep, and one of them be gone astray, doth he not leave the ninety and nine, and goeth into the mountains, and seeketh that which is gone astray?*

Rule #10 'You Can't Change Other People, Only Yourself'

13 "And if so be that he find it, verily I say unto you, he rejoiceth more of that sheep, than of the ninety and nine which went not astray.

14 "Even so it is not the will of your Father which is in heaven, that one of these little ones should perish."

"Then there is the scripture of the adulteress. You talk about doing something unlawful or unrighteous; the act of adultery in old Jewish law was considered equal to the crime of murder. Only two witnesses had to testify that you were an adulteress, and you would be judged guilty. In the story, you are about to read, not only were there two witnesses, but the woman was also caught in the very act of committing adultery and taken straight to Jesus to hear His judgment. The Jewish law in this matter was unmistakable. If a woman was found guilty, she was to be taken into the street in public and stoned to death. "

(Bible New Testament: John 8:4-11)[2]

4 They say unto him, Master, this woman was taken in adultery, in the very act.

5 Now Moses in the law commanded us, that such should be stoned: but what sayest thou?

6 This they said, tempting him, that they might have to accuse him. But Jesus stooped down, and with his finger wrote on the ground, as though he heard them not.

7 So when they continued asking him, he lifted up himself, and said unto them, He that is without sin among you, let him first cast a stone at her.

8 And again he stooped down, and wrote on the ground.

9 And they which heard it, being convicted by their own conscience, went out one by one, beginning at the eldest, even unto the last: and Jesus was left alone, and the woman standing in the midst.

> *10 When Jesus had lifted up himself, and saw none but the woman, he said unto her, Woman, where are those thine accusers? hath no man condemned thee?*
>
> *11 She said, No man, Lord. And Jesus said unto her, Neither do I condemn thee: go, and sin no more.*

"Jesus did not dispute the Jewish law nor its punishment. What He pointed out to the crowd was that they, too, were sinners, just as guilty as the woman was. If they were to punish her, they would have to punish themselves. How about you, Karen? Are your hands clean from sin? Yet by your actions, you condemn your husband and your old friends."

"Jesus was kind and forgiving to the adulteress. Keep in mind, that even though Jesus did not condemn her, He did not condone her adulteress behavior either. In John 8:11, He commands her to go and sin no more."

"I am not saying that you should condone your husband's wrongful conduct. Wrong is wrong, and we don't condone or support wrong conduct, but we do not condemn the person either. Judgment is not ours said the Lord."

"Notice that the scriptures do not say whether or not the woman committed adultery ever again. Why? Because that wasn't the point. The lesson is that we are not to judge. Only God knows all the facts that lead the woman to commit adultery, much like you, and I know the reasons for the paths we have chosen that lead to the mistakes we have made."

"Here is a question for you: If God allows us our free agency to choose, and does not force us to change, by His example, should we not do the same for the people in our lives?"

"Let's talk about the story of the prodigal son in Luke 15:11-32. Talk about a guy who liked to party and live a carefree life; that was the prodigal son. Do you think the father was happy with his son's conduct? I think not."

"When the prodigal son decided he was ready to leave his father's farm, he asked his father for his share of the inheritance. Think about it, the father was not even dead yet.

The father could have cursed his son, not given him a dime, or could have used the inheritance as a tool to persuade the son to change his ways. Yet, he didn't. Instead, the father gave the prodigal son the inheritance AND a blessing. After the son left, the father prayed for his son's safe return. The father didn't give up on his son, and he did not try to force his son to change either.

"I'll end my use of Bible scriptures on you with one of my favorite quotes from the Lord himself."

> **(Bible New Testament: Matthew 7:3-4)**[2]
> *3 And why beholdest thou the mote that is in thy brother's eye, but considerest not the beam that is in thine own eye?*
>
> *4 Or how wilt thou say to thy brother, Let me pull out the mote out of thine eye; and, behold, a beam is in thine own eye?*

Who Is Better?

"You may have found more enlightenment from your religion than your husband has at this point in his life. But I can point out ten people that have more enlightenment than you or I do, and I can point out others that are even more enlightened than those first 10. The point is no one in this mortal state is not a sinner. That is why the scriptures tell us that we are not to pass judgment upon other people or try to force anyone to change."

Karen, feeling flustrated, replies, "So what are you telling me? That I am stuck in this hellish life, and there is no escape?"

"Not at all," I laughed. "As I told you, you do not have to put up with bad behavior. That includes your husband's. You do not condone it or condemn it. If you do either, you make his problem yours. What you do is keep his problem his and allow him to decide what he is going to do about it."

Simple Yet Hard:

Karen, feeling even more flustrated, replied, "I understand what you are saying, but what I am not understanding is how I do that."

"Well, the answer is a simple one, but due to human nature and our emotional makeup, it is not so easy to implement. As I suggested before, go home and be the best Christian wife you can be. Set a good example of what your newfound lifestyle is all about. Do I need to read you the scripture on loving your enemy, forgiving those that despise you, having the pure love of Christ? Greet your husband with a smile and put away the baseball bat. Help him to understand why you have chosen the lifestyle you have by living your example. Do this, and your husband will have one of two responses; he will either come to see the same light as you and want to change, or he will despise who you have become and want to divorce you. Either way, he chooses, you will have given him the option to decide how to solve his own problem."

Karen went home and did what I had suggested. Eleven months later, I received a phone call from her. Now, I wish I could tell you that she called to tell me her husband had changed, and they are doing well. And that their marriage was wonderful. But that is not how the conversation went. Instead, she informed me that her husband had decided he wanted a divorce. His reason, as Karen stated it, was that she was too much of a 'goody-two-shoes' and he couldn't deal with it anymore.

The divorce could have been a messy one, but because Karen did all she could to love her husband and be a good wife, the only failing the husband could claim against her was that she was too good. He couldn't handle it. Karen realized that she was the one who had changed the relationship in the marriage and could not condemn her husband for that. Thus, instead of a contentious divorce, it was an equitable one, and the two of them were able to maintain a friendship. Instead of fighting one another during the divorce, they focused on how they could better help their children.

The Relationship:

There are times in any relationship, whether it is, marriage, family, or friends, that change comes to one person and not the other, and differences develop. Differences in relationships are not necessarily a bad thing. In many cases, it is the differences in talents, personalities, experiences, and beliefs that help make people stronger together than they would be apart.

There are times when differences develop within the relationship that hinder a couple; however, that does not mean the relationship needs to end. A loss of any relationship leaves a sad scar on our life. I do not condone a break up of any relationship, particularly a marriage. Differences can be worked out. All mistakes in any relationship can be mended and forgiven to save the relationship. However, there are times when people choose themselves over the needs of the relationship and refuse to compromise. Likewise, some principles should not be compromised. Only when all options have been tried, and there are righteous principles at stake, do I see a reason for a relationship to end.

All About You:

I know the story I just shared with you is a bit lengthy, but I believe that the story points out an essential principle of Rule #10 *'You Can't Change Others, Only Yourself'*; that is you can't change another person, even if the change is for their betterment. What you can do is evaluate yourself and your environment to see what changes you can make directly or indirectly to better your relationship with others.

Though Karen had made internal changes to improve herself, there were also external changes that she needed to make to improve her relationship with her husband.

Another thing about the story I would like to point out is that because Karen and I are both Christians, I used only Bible stories to help strengthen any point I was trying to make. To this, I say, whether you are a Christian or not, the supporting principles being taught by the selected Bible stories still hold true for anyone with virtuous values.

Words of the Greats:

We have come to that time in the writing of this rule that I share with you a few choice quotes that my friends and I found on the subject of change. It is my hope that you will find one or two quotes that will stick with you so that you may recall them to mind when needed.

(Ernest Hemingway)[6]
"There is nothing noble in being superior to your fellow man; true nobility is being superior to your former self."

(George Bernard Shaw)[7]
"Progress is impossible without change; and those who cannot change their minds cannot change anything."

(Clive Staples Lewis)[8]
"A proud man is always looking down on things and people; and of course, as long as you are looking down, you cannot see something that is above you."

(Ralph Waldo Emerson)[9]
"Make the most of yourself....for that is all there is of you."

(William Faulkner)[10]
"Always dream and shout higher than you know you can do. Do not bother just to be better than your contemporaries or predecessors. Try to be better than yourself."

(Albert Einstein)[11]
"Once we accept your limits, we go beyond them."

(Madonna Louise Ciccone)[12]
"No matter who you are, no matter what you did, no matter where you've come from, you can always change; become a better version of yourself."

(Jim Rohn) [13]
"Formal education will make you a living: self-education will make you a fortune."

(Confucius) [14]
"When you see a good person, think of becoming like her/him. When you see someone not so good reflect on your own weak points."

(Stephen Richards) [15]
"Minds are like flowers, they only open when the time is right."

(Mahatma Gandhi) [16]
"You must be the change that you wish to see in the world."

(John F. Kennedy) [17]
"Change is the law of life. And those who look only back to the past or present are certain to miss the future."

(Viktor E. Frankl) [18]
"When we are no longer able to change a situation – we are challenged to change ourselves."

(Jim Rohn) [19]
"You must take personal responsibility. You cannot change the circumstances, the seasons, or the wind, but you can change yourself. That is something you have charge of."

(Barack Obama) [20]
"Change will not come if we wait for some other person or some other time. We are the ones we've been waiting for. We are the change we seek."

(Leo Tolstoy) [21]
"Everyone thinks of changing the world, but no one thinks of changing himself."

Rule #10 'You Can't Change Other People, Only Yourself'

(Bible New Testament: Romans 14:5)[2]
5 One man esteemeth one day above another: another esteemeth every day alike. Let every man be fully persuaded in his own mind.

(Bible Old Testament: Proverbs 15:31-32)[1]
31 The ear that heareth the reproof of life abideth among the wise.

32 He that refuseth instruction despiseth his own soul: but he that heareth reproof getteth understanding.

(Book of Mormon: 2 Nephi 2:16)[3]
16 Wherefore, the Lord God gave unto man that he should act for himself. Wherefore, man could not act for himself save it should be that he was enticed by the one or the other.

(Book of Mormon: 2 Nephi 10:23)[3]
23 Therefore, cheer up your hearts, and remember that ye are free to act for yourselves—to choose the way of everlasting death or the way of eternal life.

(Book of Mormon: Helaman 14:30)[3]
30 And now remember, remember, my brethren, that whosoever perisheth, perisheth unto himself; and whosoever doeth iniquity, doeth it unto himself; for behold, ye are free; ye are permitted to act for yourselves; for behold, God hath given unto you a knowledge and he hath made you free.

(Doctrine & Covenants: 37:4)[4]
4 Behold, here is wisdom, and let every man choose for himself until I come. Even so. Amen.

(Doctrine & Covenants: 101:78)[4]
78 That every man may act in doctrine and principle pertaining to futurity, according to the moral agency which I have given unto him, that every man may be accountable for his own sins in the day of judgment.

> **(Doctrine & Covenants: 58:28)**[4]
> *28 For the power is in them, wherein they are agents unto themselves. And inasmuch as men do good they shall in nowise lose their reward.*

Closing Statement:

We all have been equally blessed with the power of free agency that allows us to choose the path we wish to follow in life. Life is all about changes and deciding how we, as individuals, will deal with it. That is the beauty of having free agency. As an adult, it is our choice, not anyone else's, that determines which path or lifestyle we wish to live. The rights of one's choice need to be protected so long as their choice does not conflict with the rights of others.

I close this writing by giving thanks to God for inspiring me to write my thoughts for others to read and ask the Lord that my book will inspire you, the reader, to live a better life.

In closing, I have one final quote I feel sums up the principles behind Rule #10. I leave it with you to read from Ezra Taft Benson.

> **(Ezra Taft Benson, 1985 October General Conference, 'Born of God')**[22]
> *"The Lord works from the inside out. The world works from the outside in. The world would take people out of the slums. Christ would take the slums out of people, and then they would take themselves out of the slums.*
> *The world would mold men by changing their environment. Christ changes men, who then change their environment. The world would shape human behavior, but with Christ you can change human nature."*

Rule #10 'You Can't Change Other People, Only Yourself'

Endnotes:

1 **King James Version of the Bible, The Old Testament of Our Lord and Saviour Jesus Christ.** Published by The Church of Jesus Christ of Latter-day Saints, Salt Lake City, Utah, USA. Copywrite 2013.

2 **King James Version of the Bible, The New Testament of Our Lord and Saviour Jesus Christ.** Published by The Church of Jesus Christ of Latter-day Saints, Salt Lake City, Utah, USA. Copywrite 2013.

3 **The Book of Mormon Another Testament of Jesus Christ.** Published by The Church of Jesus Christ of Latter-day Saints, Salt Lake City, Utah, USA. The first English edition published in Palmyra, New York, USA, in 1830. Copywrite 2013.

4 **The Doctrine and Covenants of The Church of Jesus Christ of Latter-Day Saints.** Containing Revelations Give to Joseph Smith, the Prophet. With some additions by his successors in the Presidency of the Church. Published by The Church of Jesus Christ of Latter-day Saints, Salt Lake City, Utah, USA. Copywrite 2013.

5 **The Pearl of Great Price.** A selection from the revelations, translations, and narrations of Joseph Smith, First Prophet, seer, and revelator to The Church of Jesus Christ of Latter-Day Saints. Published by The Church of Jesus Christ of Latter-day Saints, Salt Lake City, Utah, USA. Copywrite 2013.

6 **Ernest Hemingway.** Ernest Hemingway. (n.d.). AZQuotes.com. Retrieved February 12, 2019, from AZQuotes.com Web site: https://www.azquotes.com/quote/1186695.

7 **George Bernard Shaw.** George Bernard Shaw. (n.d.). AZQuotes.com. Retrieved February 12, 2019, from AZQuotes.com Web site: https://www.azquotes.com/quote/268354.

8 **C. S. Lewis.** C. S. Lewis. (n.d.). AZQuotes.com. Retrieved February 12, 2019, from AZQuotes.com Web site: https://www.azquotes.com/quote/346268.

9 **Ralph Waldo Emerson** Ralph Waldo Emerson. (n.d.). AZQuotes.com. Retrieved February 12, 2019, from AZQuotes.com Web site: https://www.azquotes.com/quote/89307.

10 **William Faulkner.** William Faulkner. (n.d.). AZQuotes.com. Retrieved February 12, 2019, from AZQuotes.com Web site: https://www.azquotes.com/quote/766331.

11 **Albert Einstein.** Albert Einstein. (n.d.). AZQuotes.com. Retrieved February 12, 2019, from AZQuotes.com Web site: https://www.azquotes.com/quote/87358.

12 **Madonna Louise Ciccone.** Madonna Ciccone. (n.d.). AZQuotes.com. Retrieved February 12, 2019, from AZQuotes.com Web site: https://www.azquotes.com/quote/371364.

13 **Jim Rohn.** Jim Rohn. (n.d.). AZQuotes.com. Retrieved February 12, 2019, from AZQuotes.com Web site: https://www.azquotes.com/quote/1294059.

Rule #10 'You Can't Change Other People, Only Yourself'

14 **Confucius**. Confucius. (n.d.). AZQuotes.com. Retrieved February 12, 2019, from AZQuotes.com Web site: https://www.azquotes.com/quote/367642.

15 **Stephen Richards**. Stephen Richards Quotes. (n.d.). goodreads.com. Retrieved February 12, 2019, from goodreads.com website: https://www.goodreads.com/quotes/516448-minds-are-like-flowers-they-only-open-when-the-time.

16 **Mahatma Gandhi**. Mahatma Gandhi. (n.d.). AZQuotes.com. Retrieved February 12, 2019, from AZQuotes.com Web site: https://www.azquotes.com/quote/1416953.

17 **John F. Kennedy**. John F. Kennedy. (n.d.). AZQuotes.com. Retrieved February 12, 2019, from AZQuotes.com Web site: https://www.azquotes.com/quote/156159.

18 **Viktor E. Frankl**. Viktor E. Frankl. (n.d.). AZQuotes.com. Retrieved February 12, 2019, from AZQuotes.com Web site: https://www.azquotes.com/quote/101844.

19 **Jim Rohn**. Jim Rohn. (n.d.). AZQuotes.com. Retrieved February 12, 2019, from AZQuotes.com Web site: https://www.azquotes.com/quote/249560.

20 **Barack Obama**. Barack Obama. (n.d.). AZQuotes.com. Retrieved February 12, 2019, from AZQuotes.com Web site: https://www.azquotes.com/quote/218564.

21 **Leo Tolstoy**. Leo Tolstoy. (n.d.). AZQuotes.com. Retrieved February 12, 2019, from AZQuotes.com Web site: https://www.azquotes.com/quote/295490.

22 **Ezra Taft Benson, 1985 October General Conference, "Born of God"**. The 155th Semiannual General Conference of the Church of Jesus Christ of Latter-day Saints, October 5, 1985, Saturday Morning Session. Published in the Ensign magazine, Page 6, Volume 15 Number 11, November 1985. An official magazine of the Church of Jesus Christ of Latter-day Saints, published by the Church of Jesus Christ of Latter-day Saints, 50 E. North Temple Street, Salt Lake City, UT, 84150-3220, USA. Also, retrieved Nov 26,2019, from Ensign, ChurchofJesusChrist.Org website: https://www.churchofjesuschrist.org/study/ensign/1985/11/born-of-god?lang=eng

Rule #10 'You Can't Change Other People, Only Yourself'

The Blind Leading The Blind

Rule #11

'If You Can't Take Care of Yourself, You Can't Take Care of Others'

Rule #11 'If You Can't Take Care of Yourself, You Can't Take Care of Others'

Warning:

Rule #11 *'If You Can't Take Care of Yourself, You Can't Take Care of Others'* has been rated 'A' for 'Attitude and 'S' for Strong Opinion' by the Author. A person with an opposing opinion of that of the Author may find the subject matter contained within this writing too irritating to read. The Author's opinion may or may not be the opinion of any agency, private or public, and the government will not confirm or deny any collaboration with the Author. Though reading, in general, has not been found to be hazardous to your health, the reading of Rule #11, has been known to cause mild to moderate irritation, anger, frustration, and mild headaches. Should the reader experience a higher than normal flustration rate, high blood pressure can occur, which may cause a light break out of hives on the face, or if holding this book, a mild rash on the hands. In a few rare cases, repeated vomiting was reported. If you start to notice any of these symptoms, stop reading immediately, and chill out for a while. It may be necessary to lie down and take a short nap to recover from your condition. If, as you continue to read, the symptoms persist, find someone or something to make you laugh. Laughter can cure most any emotional upset this material may cause. If you are allergic to laughter, you are beyond this Author's help and may need to seek professional advice.

Please note that this Author does not have a degree in psychology, nor is he a licensed psychologist. Although, he is a licensed HAM. Therefore, any advice taken from this author is at your own discretion. The author dissolves himself of any legal action from the reader for not adhering to this warning. If you do choose to continue reading Rule #11 it is at your own risk, and you assume all responsibility for your reactions.

Dealing With Myself:

The warning above is mainly meant to be taken humorously, but within that humor, there is a bit of truth. I do have an overly strong opinion on Rule #11, and because of that, I have the need to remind myself to lighten up and try to see things from a different point of view. Rule #11 is one of those rules you can carry too far, or not far enough.

I created Rule #11 to help me deal with my strong opinions and attitudes. You say, what attitude? Well, here is an example: In certain situations, it is very easy for me to become overly judgmental of how things should be done, versus how they are being done. I call it the 'My Way is Best' attitude, which does not always take into account the fact that being right does not make it right; think about that one.

Snap, Crackle, Pop:

There is always more than one way to accomplish a task or goal. How I get the task done is more important to me than the task itself. It is the planning and implementation of the plan that requires greater skill. If all you had to do to complete a task is to snap your fingers, then all you would learn is how to be a great finger snapper.

More Powerful Than a Locomotive, Able to Leap Tall Buildings in a Single Bound – Up, Up and Away:

With my planning methodology, my way of thinking is this: I am the straight-line kind of a guy. This means, take the quickest path, the least amount of time, the least chance for error, that will give the best results: Not better, but best. With this train of thought, I don't always take into account whether or not my way is the harder road to take. That's because I am Superman's cousin, and taking the harder path doesn't bother me, lol. Of course, now that I am getting a little older, these days, I feel like someone is washing my clothes in kryptonite. This means taking the harder road is a lot harder than my body would like. I am now starting to believe that perhaps I need to add this factor into my thinking.

Which brings me to my point. We all can't accomplish a task or goal the same way. We all have different limitations. That does not mean that when the task is completed, it won't be the best it can be. Using my planning methodology and the 'My Way is Best' attitude, I am right. Why? Because I believe that the path I take is the most efficient and direct way. And because I am Superman's cousin, I can do it whether it is the hard road or not. But not everyone is Superman's cousin, and they may have to take the longer, less efficient route. Wherefore I am right but wrong. If you take on the 'My Way is Best' attitude as I had (Note: Had), you will most likely find yourself working on the project alone a lot. Of course, the upside is you can do it your way and be right, lol.

Three Blind Mice:

I have the same strong opinions and attitudes when, from my viewpoint, it looks like it is the blind leading the blind or the uneducated teaching the uneducated. I tend to get overly critical. This is when I have to remind myself to invoke Rule #7 *'Focus On The Journey Not The Task'* and Rule #8 *'Don't Catch Idiotitis'*.

Rule #11 helps me to put things into a proper perspective. I call it humbling myself. On some subjects, we all have strong opinions and ideas, but that does not make us the expert we may think we are. Nor does it give us a license to dictate to others how things ought to be done. As I said, "There are many ways to accomplish a goal or meet most challenges in life." To which some of us will take the short route, and others will take the long way. The key is that we get where we need to go. Whatever the route you choose, there is a lesson to be taught along the way.

The task is the goal. Yet the task is not as important as how we accomplish our goal and what we learn along the way. It is in the taking of the journey, and the route we choose in pursuing our goal that helps us with our growth here on Earth as well as in Heaven.

My most significant trouble in dealing with Rule #11 is not the rule, for the rule is solid and true. No, my trouble is not with the rule. It is with the people that either do not understand the rule or they just simply do not believe that the rule applies to them. There are so many so-called experts in the world that want to teach you how to tie your shoes, yet they do not have the first clue on how to properly tie their own.

How Do I Say It?

As I was coming up with the defining statement for Rule #11, I must have thought of at least a dozen or more ways to phrase it. Here are just a few statements I discussed with my wife and friends:

> 'The Blind Leading the Blind'
> 'You Need to Learn Before You Can Teach'
> 'If you Cannot Help Yourself'
> 'How Do You Expect to Help Others?'
> 'Following the Blind'
> 'Do What I Say Not What I do'
> 'Teach By Example'
> 'You Can't Give Others What You Don't Have'

All of these statements pretty much describe Rule #11 *'If You Can't Take Care of Yourself, You Can't Take Care of Others'* in one way or another. But I had to pick the one that I felt best described my thoughts in one simple statement.

Where is Your License?

So, who is qualified to teach? Do you have to have a license or a degree to be qualified to help or educate another person? Well, that depends on the type of help or education needed to complete the task. I think I would rather have a well-educated and experienced surgeon operating on me, rather than your average neighbor that just bought a new set of stainless-steel

Rule #11 'If You Can't Take Care of Yourself, You Can't Take Care of Others'

kitchen knives and wants to try them out on you, no matter how sharp his new knives might be. Yet, there is a vast difference between allowing the neighbor to perform major surgery and permitting the neighbor to put a Band-Aid on a cut.

The question to ask is not, does the person hold a license or degree, but ought to be how qualified are they? I have sought help from a lot of licensed/degreed people that have left me wondering just how qualified they really were and questioning how they ever got their license/degree in the first place. Have you ever been left wondering how a person ever earned their degree?

Qualifications come in many ways and don't always result in a license or a degree as proof. Noah wasn't a licensed boat builder. Nor do I think he ever had any boat-building experience. Yet the Lord felt Noah was the one qualified to build His Ark.

> **(Bible Old Testament: Genesis 6:13-14)**[1]
> *13 And God said unto Noah, The end of all flesh is come before me; for the earth is filled with violence through them; and, behold, I will destroy them with the earth.*
>
> *14 Make thee an ark of gopher wood; rooms shalt thou make in the ark, and shalt pitch it within and without with pitch.*

Nephi likewise was not a master boat builder when the Lord called on him to build a ship to bring his family across the ocean.

> **(Book of Mormon: 1 Nephi 17:8)**[3]
> *8 And it came to pass that the Lord spake unto me (Nephi), saying: Thou shalt construct a ship, after the manner which I shall show thee, that I may carry thy people across these waters.*

Rule #11 'If You Can't Take Care of Yourself, You Can't Take Care of Others'

The brother of Jared, another non-experienced boat builder, was asked by the Lord to build a string of barges to bring the Jaredites across the Ocean.

> **(Book of Mormon: Ether 2:6, 16-17)**[3]
>
> *6 And it came to pass that they did travel in the wilderness, and did build barges, in which they did cross many waters, being directed continually by the hand of the Lord....*
>
> *16 And the Lord said: Go to work and build, after the manner of barges which ye have hitherto built. And it came to pass that the brother of Jared did go to work, and also his brethren, and built barges after the manner which they had built, according to the instructions of the Lord. And they were small, and they were light upon the water, even like unto the lightness of a fowl upon the water.*
>
> *17 And they were built after a manner that they were exceedingly tight, even that they would hold water like unto a dish; and the bottom thereof was tight like unto a dish; and the sides thereof were tight like unto a dish; and the ends thereof were peaked; and the top thereof was tight like unto a dish; and the length thereof was the length of a tree; and the door thereof, when it was shut, was tight like unto a dish.*

These men were called upon to build boats and not simple boats. These boats had to endure the harshest conditions, survive raging storms and tidal waves while they crossed the ocean. None of these men were master boat builders. Yet they built incredible boats. How did they accomplish this complex assignment? They successfully completed the task because they had a qualified teacher, God. God knew these were the men because He knew they were teachable.

A teachable man can do anything if given the right teacher.

I am not a licensed electrician, carpenter, or plumber, yet I have done both simple and complex work in all these fields of construction with as good as, if not better than, professional

Rule #11 'If You Can't Take Care of Yourself, You Can't Take Care of Others'

results, according to my wife and the few friends I have helped. I have built three new master bathrooms, one for my family, and two for friends. I converted my basement into a man cave. I replaced a 75-year-old steep, narrow staircase leading to the basement laundry room with a beautiful oak staircase (which licensed pros said could not be done). And I have entirely rewired four houses.

That is only a few of the non-licensed tasks I have completed. I have also replaced or repaired more roofs for people than I care to remember. Note: I dislike roofing. (I would use the word hate, but my wife does not like that word.) Even though I dislike roofing, I was an unlicensed pro at it, and whenever a poor widow or low-income family in the church needed help, I was the one the bishop would call.

Supporting Tidbits:

You can become a professional in a field without getting a license. So, how did I become a professional at construction work? At the age of 14, I started working with my dad in construction, with that training, I gained a lot of knowledge about roofing. To add to that experience, after I had spent 6 ½ years in the United States Air Force, stationed in the cold state of Wyoming, I moved to the state of Florida to warm up. There in the warm Florida sunshine, I found that there was a lot of construction work for a 24-year-old hardworking man. Thus, the first Florida job I took to support myself was that of a roofer and a hot tar roofer at that.

Hot tar roofing in the Florida summer is one of the hottest, most miserable jobs you can do. But the best thing I learned from that experience was that I needed to get my butt in college to better my education and so that I could quit roofing forever.

Yes, those three years of roofing in Florida changed the direction of my life forever. From that moment on, I decided I wasn't going to support myself for the rest of my life doing any kind of construction work. Thus, no license required.

Rule #11 'If You Can't Take Care of Yourself, You Can't Take Care of Others'

Although I am not licensed in the field of construction field, that isn't to say I wasn't trained. One of my greatest teachers in construction was my father. Even though he was not well educated or licensed, he was a master builder. At the age of five, I watched my father build our first home, one concrete block at a time. My father would work all day in a hot steel foundry, and then come home and work until dark, mixing mortar and laying concrete blocks.

We lived in a possible floodplain of the Mississippi River. For that reason, my father put extra care into constructing our home. During the flood of 1965, most of the houses and buildings in our neighborhood suffered major damage, but our home didn't because of his skillful craftsmanship. Most of the houses around us had to be torn down, yet our home remained intact with very little damage. At the peak of the flood, there were over 8 feet of water on the ground floor, and the water was within inches of reaching the second floor. Once the waters receded, over a foot of mud covered the ground floor. My dad had sealed the wood paneling on the walls so well with wood oil that only about 2 inches of the paneling and the baseboards had to be refinished. It cost our neighbors thousands of dollars to repair their homes. It cost my Dad less than a couple of hundred dollars and a little hard work to repair ours.

Watching my dad build that house taught me the meaning of what a hard day's work really meant. In my mind's eye, I can still see those days as clearly as if it were today.

My dad taught me that it is not a license that qualifies a person, and to be truly educated, it takes far more than having great teachers. The wisdom I learned from him is that true education and knowledge comes from the hard work you put into training yourself.

Where's the Attitude?

As I said to you at the beginning of this rule, I have a big attitude I need to control when it comes to Rule #11. At times, when dealing with issues associated with Rule #11, a flustrated attitude comes over me like in the TV show 'The Hulk,' when David Banner turns into the big, green giant. In David Banner's case, as with mine, it is triggered by anger. My anger, in this case, happens when I observe the uneducated teaching the uneducated. It is like watching the blind lead the blind as they march their way toward the edge of an unseen cliff, and I can't do anything to stop it. I see this happen nearly every day of my life, and I find it very challenging to stand by and watch. These people are not educated enough to take care of themselves, yet they believe they are wise enough to teach others.

> **(Bible New Testament: Matthew 15:14)[2]**
> *14 Let them alone: they be blind leaders of the blind. And if the blind lead the blind, both shall fall into the ditch.*

There is another part of this mindset that adds to my attitude. That is dealing with people that have the 'do what I say and not what I do' mentality. This type of person really bugs me. My mom had this issue of the 'do what I say and not what I do.' So, I believe that my attitude, when confronted with this type of thinking, stems from my life experiences with her. Mom, I love you, but the truth is the truth.

Then there are the receivers that drink up all this uneducated advice and believe it to be heaven-sent. These are the people that are looking for a quick, easy way to solve their problem. They are not willing to take the time to learn, nor are they willing to pay the price to resolve their issues correctly. When I say pay the price, you can take that literally. The person is not willing to pay a professional for help or the cost of educating themselves. Thus, they go to the uneducated or inexperienced for advice or answers. Why, because in the short term, it is a cheap and easy way to fix their problem. But sooner or later, they will find that they got what they were willing to pay for. They wind up no better off in the end than when they started. Of course, when that happens, they blame the failure on the uneducated person they relied on and not on their own lack of willingness to put forth the required effort or the needed investment to accomplish their goals.

Let's talk about the uneducated person that gives the unqualified advice. What is his or her motive? In most cases, they genuinely want to help.

Plus, there are good warm-hearted feelings one gets when they think they are helping other people. Yet, when the help they offer is of no value, the feelings are short-lived because, in the end, both sides lose. Why? Because typically, when the advice fails to deliver a good result, the person in need will blame the well-intended advisor for the undesirable outcome. Often neither parties learn a lesson from the experience.

Then we have what I call the 'overly charged ego educator' situation. In this case, the educator's ego drives him to give advice on subjects he is unfamiliar with. Why? Because the power of the educator's ego wants to show the uneducated person that he, the educator, is smarter than he really is. A wise educator would admit to the uneducated person that they don't know the answer. The 'I don't know' statement would show far more knowledge and wisdom on the educator's part.

In situations where you are dealing with an overly charged ego educator, the outcome tends to be that both parties lose. Why, because when failure does happen, and the odds are significantly against success for reasons already stated, the educator will blame the failure on the uneducated person for not properly implementing his so-called good advice. From the viewpoint of the uneducated person, he will end up thinking that his educator is less educated than his educator pretends he is. Also, due to the educator's poor advice, a trust will be broken, and the uneducated person will no longer value any of that particular educator's advice. The sad thing is that neither side tends to learn anything positive from the experience. Do you see the positive lesson that can be learned in this scenario? If I have to point it out, then I suggest re-reading.

Rule #11 'If You Can't Take Care of Yourself, You Can't Take Care of Others'

I Have the Answer to Everything:

Similar to the overly charged ego educator, there are degreed or licensed people who think that just because they are seasoned professionals in one line of work, it gives them instant knowledge of other types of work. This type of person is not driven by their ego. Instead, this type of person believes that because they are a degreed/licensed expert in one area that that qualifies them as experts in fields they were never trained in. I have degrees and licenses, yet those licenses don't state that I can answer or solve every issue I might come across.

We need to remember that when helping ourselves or others, that knowing when you don't have the answer is critical and that knowing where to get the answer is crucial.

Storytime:

I want to share with you a few true stories of people who couldn't help themselves out of their own troubling situations, yet they believe they were qualified to help others in similar troubles.

Boyfriend Girlfriend Troubles:

The first story involves a 28-year-old divorced woman with two children who dropped out of high school after two years. Since her divorce, she has not been able to stay in a proper stable relationship. From time to time she comes to visit and to have dinner with my wife and me. At one of these dinner gatherings, I casually asked her how life was going for her and the children. The conversation started with small talk about her children, but then quickly changed. She was eager to tell us all about the troubles she was having with her new boyfriend and didn't know what to do.

Then, our dinner guest, immediately after telling us about her boyfriend troubles, proceeds to tell us about her girlfriend, who is having marital issues. She tells us that she is counseling her friend and has offered advice on how her friend

Rule #11 'If You Can't Take Care of Yourself, You Can't Take Care of Others'

can save her marriage. After listening to her talk about her boyfriend and friend's marital issues, I can tell you that both women had similar problems that could have been resolved with similar solutions. I know because I have been trained in relationship counseling. This story is a true example of the blind leading the blind.

Not only is this young woman uneducated in relationship counseling, but she also can't see that if she had the experience of solving her boyfriend issues, she might have half a chance of helping her girlfriend solve her issue.

Free Room and Board:

In another instance, I have stood by and listened as one parent gave strong counsel to another parent on how to raise her child. Yet, the parent giving the counsel has one child serving time in a federal prison for using drugs, and two others serving time in juvenile detention. Is there something wrong with this picture?

Who's Got the Money:

Here is a true story and an excellent example of the financial blind leading the blind. A couple in their 50s is having financial troubles, and adding to their burden, both of their grown children, a son and a daughter in their late 30s, have been living at home for the last four years. The daughter, we will call Mary, is divorced with two children living with her. The son, we'll call Bob, has a wife that lives with him.

Mary has a drug, alcohol, and cigarette habit. Bob has at least two bad habits. He drinks beer like water, and is a chain cigarette smoker. Neither Mary, Bob, or Bob's wife work.

On the plus side, neither Mary, Bob, nor Bob's wife has any major health issues that would keep them from working. Yet Mary and Bob's parents are supporting them all financially. Oh! And where do you think the money comes from to support Bob and Mary's bad habits? Thanks, Mom and Dad.

Rule #11 'If You Can't Take Care of Yourself, You Can't Take Care of Others'

To support their grown children, the parents stopped paying the mortgage on the house, and the utilities. To add to the parent's financial troubles, some questionable tax deductions were taken over the years, and the IRS is now demanding payment.

My wife is very close to Bob and Mary's parents, and the mother frequently seeks out my wife for help and guidance, which in turn means my wife comes to me for advice. I shared with my wife one of my favorite metaphors. I told her that if she really wanted to help Bob and Mary's parents, then she needed to teach them to stop focusing on the smoke and figure out how to put out the fire.

The smoke and fire metaphor symbolize one of the biggest obstacles many people encounter when coping with their problems. They get so caught up in dealing with the effects (the smoke) caused by the real issue (the fire) that they are blinded from even seeing the real issue (the fire). If they would deal with putting out the fire (the real issue), then the smoke (the effects) would permanently be resolved.

In the case of Bob and Mary's parents, if the parents would first learn to handle their own financial issues (the fire), they, in turn, could adequately teach their children how to manage their economic issues (the smoke). This story is one of my favorite examples of Rule #11 *'You Can't help Others if You Can't help Yourself'*. So many times, I see people financially helping others when they can't handle their own finances. Once again, you can see the results of 'the blind leading the blind.'

(Bible New Testament: Luke 6:39)[2]
39 And he spake a parable unto them, Can the blind lead the blind? shall they not both fall into the ditch?

(Cammi Pham)[6]
"Helping people when you don't have the skills or time will do more harm than good.

Offering help when you can't do a good job will do more harm than good. It's like teaching a blind person how to paint. You make people miss the opportunities to find better help. Your kindness can hurt people too, in some instances. One of the easiest ways to destroy a relationship is by offering help that you can't deliver."

Row, Row, Row, Your Boat:

Here is a story told by a Sunday school teacher, Grant Bourgeous. He both understood and applied the principles of Rule #11. Had he not, it may have cost him his life and the lives of others.

Grant's story is about one of his Boy Scout adventure trips and a valuable lesson he learned while on that trip. At the time of his story, Grant was a Boy Scout leader. He and several other leaders decided to take a group of young Boy Scouts canoeing down a small river. While the scouts were sleeping, a light early morning rain had moved in. Due to the rain, the leaders decided that they needed to get an earlier start to ensure a safe trip to their next stopping point down the river. Normally this small river flowed slowly, and when the scouts started out that day, the river still seemed fine. Grant and another leader decided they would stay at the end of the pack to help any canoers that lagged behind. What the two leaders didn't know was that farther back upstream, the storm was raging, and drenching rains were flooding the area. Halfway through the boy's track to their next stop, the canoeing started to get rough. The river was raising 4, then 5, and then to 6 feet over normal. It was time to get out of the river completely. But, the banks on both sides of the river at that point were too high and steep to pull the canoes out.

Grant was getting worried that the situation was becoming unmanageable. The boys in the lead had canoed around a sharp bend in the river out of Grant's sight. That worried Grant, as it should, for, the river current had now gone from mild to insanely wild. Then, in only a few short minutes, more of the boys disappeared from Grant's sight, and his fears became reality. As he approached that same sharp bend in the

Rule #11 'If You Can't Take Care of Yourself, You Can't Take Care of Others'

river, Grant could hear the sounds of screams coming from ahead. His view of the boys was still blocked, so he had no idea what the situation was. The closer Grant came to rounding the bend, the louder and more hysterical the screams sounded. Frantically and as fast as Grant could, he dug his paddle into the water over and over again. His arms were throbbing and aching with pain. He could feel his hands starting to stiffen and cramp from gripping the paddle so tightly. Finally, he had maneuvered his canoe to the other side of the bend and had a full view of the boys. At first sight, terror struck him. The boys were in serious trouble.

A large tree had fallen across the major portion of the river. Several groups of boys had taken the bend too narrowly to maneuver around it. One canoe was caught in the tree and sticking almost straight up into the air. The boys were out of the canoes and in the water, clinging to the branches of the tree. The force of the swift river was pushing the boys hard against the tree and threatened to pull them under.

Grant and his canoeing partner tried to safely wedge their canoe between the riverbank and the tree, but as the canoe hit the bank, the current slammed into the canoe, throwing it sideways into the tree and flipping it over. Grant and his canoeing partner were thrown into the swiftly moving river and began struggling for their lives. Grant quickly reached out and, with one hand, got a tight grip on one of the branches. Grant clung to the branch and tried to maneuver to a more secure position. He couldn't get his feet to touch the river bottom. All he had for help were his arms, and they were exhausted from the paddling. The river current tried it's best to pull Grant's body under the tree, but Grant was still winning that battle.

As a leader, Grant was more worried about the boys than himself. He fought the river current to get a look at the boys. Quickly he counted them, and they were all still hanging on but struggling to keep their heads above water. Grant could feel he was losing strength fast. His right arm, the only arm he could get wrapped around a lifesaving branch, was

Rule #11 'If You Can't Take Care of Yourself, You Can't Take Care of Others'

weakening its grip. Grant knew there wasn't much time, and the river would have him. He needed to decide what he was going to do and do it fast.

Grant assessed the whole of the situation. The boys were maybe 8 to 10 feet away from him in deeper water. The bank, on the other hand, was less than 5 feet away. He was thinking. 'Should I try to pull myself to the boys or head for the bank and safer ground?' Grant knew that every foot farther out into the river, the current would be stronger and more dangerous. What if he did reach the boys? There was a good chance that if he did reach the boys, his strength would be spent. Grant thought that if he struggled to get to the boys from his current position that there was only a slight chance of saving them, and a good chance that they all might drown. At this point, Grant knew he could barely help himself, let alone another. In his mind, there was only one right answer to all their troubles.

As any good leader should, Grant knows that he can't help others if he can't help himself. Grant's canoeing partner was in the water with him but closer to the bank. Grant motioned to him that they were to go for the bank and not the boys.

Once he and his partner got closer to the bank, they were able to touch bottom and get a solid foothold. Grant then pushed himself on top of the tree trunk and pulled his partner up with him. After taking a moment to catch his breath and gather a little more strength, Grant and his partner started to shimmy their way down the tree out into the river to save the boys.

Grant's partner stopped halfway between the boys and the bank to set up a rescue chain. Grant made his way to the boys, and one by one started helping them out of the river and onto the tree. Each boy then made his way to the end of the tree and up the riverbank to safe ground.

The other boys that had made it safely around the fallen tree, and had found a place to pull in downriver. They then made their way on land back to the fallen tree. All the scouts and leaders were together again and safe.

Rule #11 'If You Can't Take Care of Yourself, You Can't Take Care of Others'

Grant's canoeing story is a good example of how to apply Rule #11 properly. If Grant had not saved himself first, there was a very good chance that they all could have died.

Can you see the similarities between Bob and Mary's parent's story of financial troubles and Grant's canoeing adventure? Bob and Mary's parents were drowning in financial debt due to poor management. Had they saved themselves first, they would have been in a better position to help their children. But instead, they all drowned.

A Family Affair:

I would like to share with you one more true story with a little different twist. Another friend of mine, I will call Sara, is having trouble with her siblings.

For Sara, if there wasn't one thing pulling the bonds of family love apart, there was another. There seemed to be more dysfunction among her siblings than function. Good loving relationships and communication between some of the siblings hung by a thread, while contact with other siblings at least for the moment, appeared to be totally lost.

Sara has a deep emotional need for family unity; a feeling she missed out on in her childhood years. Because of this, Sara has an emotional emptiness with her siblings. To compensate for the emptiness, Sara feels a great responsibility, drive, and desire to pull the family back together again. She has taken on this goal with all its challenges to mend every wound between siblings.

The noble cause of restoring family bonds is a worthy quest. But it is also a quest that can cause more destruction in relationships than it bonds a family together. In Sara's case, she tends to try to own the responsibility for all the issues between her siblings. Whether it is her trouble or not, she makes it her issue. In Sara's quest to resolve the family issues that were not her own, she became flustrated to the point of depression.

Rule #11 'If You Can't Take Care of Yourself, You Can't Take Care of Others'

Sara didn't realize it, but her depression really extended from her own negative emotional family wounds of childhood. It was these emotions, hidden deep within her subconsciousness, that was the real catalyst for the sibling quest and its need for family harmony. Again, I say, "It was not, nor is it a bad quest." But before Sara started this journey, she should have taken the time to learn how to attend to her own negative emotions relating to her family. But Sara had not. As a result, these emotions became the controlling factor in her decision process and the cause of poor decision making throughout her quest. This widened the gap even greater between all the siblings and deepened Sara's depression. This is the only outcome one could predict. How could there be any other? Sara hadn't taken the time to learn what was needed to manage her own issue on the subject, yet she was attempting to fix her siblings' exact same issues.

The quest weighted so heavy on Sara's mind she couldn't get her brain to turn off enough at night to allow her to sleep. Now, Sara's sleep deprivation damaged her health and added another health issue to deal with.

Though Sara herself can't see it, her quest for sibling peace is taking a much deeper toll on her emotionally than any gains she is receiving from it. It has consumed most of her thoughts to the point of obsession. It has consumed her so much that it is almost impossible to have a normal conversation with her that does not include a discussion regarding her siblings and the loss of connection between them.

Sara's sibling quest has now started to place a strain on the family bonds between her, her husband, and her children. Sara is well on her way for setting the stage for her family play called 'Separating Families,' starring her own immediate family, which does not include Sara's siblings. Sara may soon find that this play she is writing will soon mirror the issues she is having with her siblings.

Again, I say that Sara's quest for sibling peace and unity is a noble and worthy cause. It is not the quest that is the issue. Rather it is Sara's management of the quest and its

Rule #11 'If You Can't Take Care of Yourself, You Can't Take Care of Others'

accompanying trials that are the issues. For one, she has allowed the quest to consume too much of her time. Second, she is taking on 'monkeys' --issues that are not her's to own. Third, she has allowed the sibling troubles to seep into her immediate family. So now the quest and its fallout have infected and strains the bonds of closeness and unity she shares with her husband and kids.

While on the journey of Sara's 'Family Unity Quest,' she has neglected or violated several rules I have written in this book and a few I have not. Like God's law of man's free agency to choose their own path. Then there is the rule of the road to learning, and that is, we all must travel our own road. Another cannot travel the road for us, nor can we travel the road for them.

> **(Book of Mormon: Helaman 14:30)[3]**
> *30 And now remember, remember, my brethren, that whosoever perisheth, perisheth unto himself; and whosoever doeth iniquity, doeth it unto himself; for behold, ye are free; ye are permitted to act for yourselves; for behold, God hath given unto you a knowledge and he hath made you free.*
>
> **(Doctrine & Covenants 101:78)[4]**
> *78 That every man may act in doctrine and principle pertaining to futurity, according to the moral agency which I have given unto him, that every man may be accountable for his own sins in the day of judgment.*

I can recite several rules from this book Sara has broken. But I will leave that to you, the reader, to test your skills at understanding this book of rules. I will share this one rule with you to help jump start your thinking process. Sara needs to gain a better understanding of Rule #13 *'Focus on the Journey, Not the Task'*. Though completing the task is essential, it is far more important how we make the journey. Each of us, though we may have the same task, can have different journeys we must take to get there. If another person shortens our route while completing a task, we may lose out on valuable opportunities to learn, and we may end up having

Rule #11 'If You Can't Take Care of Yourself, You Can't Take Care of Others'

to take the same trip all over again due to not learning the lesson or skills we needed to on the first trip.

Another metaphor that I have heard, and if Sara applied to her life, it would help her, is 'Who Owns the Monkey?' In this case, the word monkey refers to the problem. If Sara stopped playing with other people's barrels of monkeys, she would have more time to deal with her own barrel of monkeys and have a lot less emotional upset to process and manage. Then perhaps she would start sleeping better at night, which would lead to better health and clearer thinking.

Sara's story, as with the other stories I have shared with you, show a similar pattern. That is: trying to solve an issue in another person's life, has caused serious issues in the helper's own immediate family and personal life.

(The Teachings of Ezra Taft Benson: Chapter 19-Page 244)[7]

"Only the wholesome have the capacity to lift and encourage one another to greater service, to greater achievement, to greater strength."

(Bible The New Testament: Luke 6:40-44)[2]

40 The disciple is not above his master: but every one that is perfect shall be as his master.

41 And why beholdest thou the mote that is in thy brother's eye, but perceivest not the beam that is in thine own eye?

42 Either how canst thou say to thy brother, Brother, let me pull out the mote that is in thine eye, when thou thyself beholdest not the beam that is in thine own eye? Thou hypocrite, cast out first the beam out of thine own eye, and then shalt thou see clearly to pull out the mote that is in thy brother's eye.

43 For a good tree bringeth not forth corrupt fruit; neither doth a corrupt tree bring forth good fruit.

Rule #11 'If You Can't Take Care of Yourself, You Can't Take Care of Others'

44 For every tree is known by his own fruit. For of thorns men do not gather figs, nor of a bramble bush gather they grapes.

Moving On:

I could go on and on with more of these true-life experiences, but I think you get my drift.

Let's talk about some social and governance issues which advocate the blind leading the blind factor. This should be fun.

The Uneducated System:

One of these social/government issues is in our public-school system. We wonder why our education system is having trouble educating our children and grandchildren. Well, for one, we don't pay the wages needed to hire highly educated individuals to train our children. At the same time, how can we expect our educators to teach our children when parents don't instill proper discipline and moral values in their children?

Once upon a time in one state where I lived, the school system needed help so badly due to budget cuts that they asked for volunteers as teaching assistants. There was no requirement other than a willingness to work, a quick background check, and leaving a set of your fingerprints at the police station.

As an incentive to volunteer, the person could then use the volunteer hours they earned to receive food subsidies from other agencies to help feed their family. Overall the program was not a bad idea for helping the poor help themselves. But when you take a closer look at how the program was implemented, many of these untrained volunteer assistants were being used to actually do the share of the work that should be left to a trained qualified teacher. Do you see anything wrong with that picture?

Rule #11 'If You Can't Take Care of Yourself, You Can't Take Care of Others'

The Government's Contribution:

Another contributing factor is how our government works to keep costs down. To help provide work for the poor, many government jobs are set aside for only poor people. These jobs help the needy help themselves so that they may become more self-sustaining, reduce the burden on government funds, and keep them busy (idle hands cause more trouble than working hands). Now, I don't have any issues with doing what we can to provide good jobs. Work is vital to a well-balanced, healthy life and equally important to a well-balanced, healthy society.

It is the positions, these unqualified people fill within the government structure that concerns me. That includes our public schools in some states. In many of our government positions you can find a non-degreed assistant actually doing the work for which a degree is required. The government claims they can do this to cut costs because the assistant is supervised by a person that is qualified and has a degree. Hmm! Do you see a downhill problem with this?

The Well-educated:

Another contributing factor to the failing quality of teaching in our society falls on the well-educated. Our society needs more of our well-educated people giving back their time and talent to educate others.

It is sad that in our society, things are geared more towards a money and demand system; the higher the demand, the greater the value. That factor causes a catch-22. With our current system, to get better-qualified teachers, we need to attract them by offering them an equal or better wage than they could get elsewhere. After all, they are highly educated, and therefore there is a higher demand for their service, thus a higher value. If we increase the teacher's wages to attract better-qualified teachers, then the schools will have to recover that cost by raising the cost of tuition. Raising the cost of tuition will decrease the number of eligible students who can afford the cost to attend.

Rule #11 'If You Can't Take Care of Yourself, You Can't Take Care of Others'

If we raise the student's or student's family wages to compensate for the tuition increase, then the overall cost of goods will have to increase to cover the student's/student's family wage increase. By the time you make all the cost adjustments, the initial teacher's salary increase is meaningless.

A solution to this catch-22 is to implement a different variable into the mix. That variable is to get people who are the well-educated to freely give back their time and talent to help the less fortunate. I am happy to say that there are those in our society that do freely give back, but sadly there are not enough.

Space the Final Frontier:

This makes me think of a Star Trek movie 'First Contact' and a general statement that was made in one scene. The Starship Enterprise had traveled back in time, and in this scene, Capt. Picard is explaining to a woman from that period of time how life differs in the future. Picard tells the woman that in the future, money is not the driving force that runs the economy; that mankind strives to work for the betterment of mankind than for his own material gains. That sounds nice, doesn't it?

Try You Say? Do or Do it:

In the end, Rule #11 comes down to you and me as individuals. Each of us must strive to do our best by giving 110%, Rule #3, every day. As we do this, we must have an I'll do it attitude and not an I will try attitude. We need to seek first to educate ourselves before we try to educate others. Then set a good example by implementing and doing in our life what we are preaching to others.

I like the way this woman learned the lesson of helping herself first, which in turn also sets an example for others to follow and why. Here is her quotable quote:

> **(Nozomi Morgan)**[8]
> *"Before you assist others, always put your oxygen mask on first.*

Rule #11 'If You Can't Take Care of Yourself, You Can't Take Care of Others'

But, I've learned from my experiences that helping others is almost impossible to achieve if you are going through turbulence in your life or career.

If your current situation is unstable, how can you possibly help others?

Your job, first and foremost, is to help yourself and take care of your own needs. That's why the flight attendants encourage you to secure your oxygen mask first. If you don't, you and the person you want to help could both go down.

Put your oxygen mask on first."

Educating ourselves is only the beginning, once we have become learned, as I stated earlier, we need to give back to others freely. It is by teaching others we learn to truly master and hone our own knowledge and skills.

We also need to understand who we are to help first, second, and then third. First, we must help ourselves, then our immediate family, then the extended family, and then others.

(George P. Lee, 1982 October General Conference, 'Behold My Beloved Son, in Whom I Am Well Pleased')[9]
"The Lord Jesus wants us to build the necessary character, righteousness, industry, and godliness into our lives first. Then we are to do the same for others."

(Marvin J. Ashton, 1981 October General Conference, 'Give with Wisdom That They May Receive with Dignity')[10]
"Charity should start in our own homes. Too many of us extend charity to others when it is often most needed within the family circle."

Rule #11 'If You Can't Take Care of Yourself, You Can't Take Care of Others'

The Sum of All:

In closing, I leave you a final word or two from those individuals that I feel have far more wisdom than I. Famous quotes from famous people on Rule #11.

(Simplereminds.com)[11]
"Putting yourself first doesn't mean you don't care about others. It means you're smart enough to know you can't help other if you don't help yourself first."

(Arvind Devallia)[12]
"You need to help yourself before you help the world"

(Lori Deschene)[13]
"And when you make the effort to help yourself, you can better help other people—and the world."

(Bible The New Testament: Luke 22:32)[2]
32 But I have prayed for thee, that thy faith fail not: and when thou art converted, strengthen thy brethren.

(Bible The New Testament: 1 Timothy 4:15-16)[2]
15 Meditate upon these things; give thyself wholly to them; that thy profiting may appear to all.

16 Take heed unto thyself, and unto the doctrine; continue in them: for in doing this thou shalt both save thyself, and them that hear thee.

Rule #11 'If You Can't Take Care of Yourself, You Can't Take Care of Others'

Of all the quotes and words, I have used in this chapter, a simple statement by Marion G. Romney best sums up my thoughts on Rule #11 *'If You Can't Take Care of Yourself, You Can't Take Care of Others'*.

> **(Marion G. Romney, 1982 October General Conference, Welfare Session, "The Celestial Nature of Self-reliance")**[14]
> *"How can we give if there is nothing there? Food for the hungry cannot come from empty shelves. Money to assist the needy cannot come from an empty purse. Support and understanding cannot come from the emotionally starved. Teaching cannot come from the unlearned. And most important of all, spiritual guidance cannot come from the spiritually weak."*

Rule #11 'If You Can't Take Care of Yourself, You Can't Take Care of Others'

Endnotes:

1. **King James Version of the Bible, The Old Testament of Our Lord and Saviour Jesus Christ.** Published by The Church of Jesus Christ of Latter-day Saints, Salt Lake City, Utah, USA. Copywrite 2013.

2. **King James Version of the Bible, The New Testament of Our Lord and Saviour Jesus Christ.** Published by The Church of Jesus Christ of Latter-day Saints, Salt Lake City, Utah, USA. Copywrite 2013.

3. **The Book of Mormon Another Testament of Jesus Christ.** Published by The Church of Jesus Christ of Latter-day Saints, Salt Lake City, Utah, USA. The first English edition published in Palmyra, New York, USA, in 1830. Copywrite 2013.

4. **The Doctrine and Covenants of The Church of Jesus Christ of Latter-Day Saints.** Containing Revelations Give to Joseph Smith, the Prophet. With some additions by his successors in the Presidency of the Church. Published by The Church of Jesus Christ of Latter-day Saints, Salt Lake City, Utah, USA. Copywrite 2013.

5. **The Pearl of Great Price.** A selection from the revelations, translations, and narrations of Joseph Smith, First Prophet, seer, and revelator to The Church of Jesus Christ of Latter-Day Saints. Published by The Church of Jesus Christ of Latter-day Saints, Salt Lake City, Utah, USA. Copywrite 2013.

6. **Cammi Pham**. Cammi Pham Quotes, Cammiphan.com. Retrieved February 13, 2019, from cammipham.com website: http://www.cammipham.com/helping/.

7. **The Teachings of the Presidents of the Church: Ezra Taft Benson** Published in the Teachings of the Presidents of the Church: Ezra Taft Benson, Chapter 19, page-244, paragraph-5. An official manual of the Church of Jesus Christ of Latter-day Saints published 2014 by the Church of Jesus Christ of Latter-day Saints, 50 E. North Temple Street, Salt Lake City, UT, 84150-3220, USA. Also, retrieved Nov 26,2019, from, ChurchofJesusChrist.Org website: https://www.churchofjesuschrist.org/study/manual/teachings-of-presidents-of-the-church-ezra-taft-benson/chapter-19-leadership?lang=eng

8. **Nozomi Morgan**. Nozomi Morgan Quotes, huffingtonpost.com. Retrieved February 13, 2019, from huffingtonpost.com website: https://www.huffingtonpost.com/nozomi-morgan/before-you-help-others-yo_b_8267004.html.

9. **George P. Lee, 1982 October General Conference, "Behold My Beloved Son, in Whom I Am Well Pleased"** The 152nd Semiannual General Conference of the Church of Jesus Christ of Latter-day Saints, October 3, 1982, Sunday Afternoon Session. Published in the Ensign magazine, Volume 12 Number 11, November 1982. An official magazine of the Church of Jesus Christ of Latter-day Saints, published by the Church of Jesus Christ of Latter-day Saints, 50 E. North Temple Street, Salt Lake City, UT, 84150-3220, USA. Also, retrieved Nov 26,2019, from, ChurchofJesusChrist.Org website: https://www.churchofjesuschrist.org/study/ensign/1982/11/behold-my-beloved-son-in-whom-i-am-well-pleased?lang=eng

Rule #11 'If You Can't Take Care of Yourself, You Can't Take Care of Others'

10 **Marvin J. Ashton, 1981 October General Conference, "Give with Wisdom That They May Receive with Dignity"** The 151st Semiannual General Conference of the Church of Jesus Christ of Latter-day Saints, October 3, 1981, Welfare Session. Published in the Ensign magazine, Volume 11 Number 11, November 1981. An official magazine of the Church of Jesus Christ of Latter-day Saints, published by the Church of Jesus Christ of Latter-day Saints, 50 E. North Temple Street, Salt Lake City, UT, 84150-3220, USA. Also, retrieved Nov 26,2019, from Ensign, ChurchofJesusChrist.Org website: https://www.churchofjesuschrist.org/study/ensign/1981/11/give-with-wisdom-that-they-may-receive-with-dignity?lang=eng

11 **Simplereminders.com**. - Simplereminders.com. (n.d.). gomcgil.com. Retrieved February 24, 2019, from gomcgil.com Web site: https://gomcgill.com/putting-yourself-first-doesnt-mean-you-dont-care-about-others-it-means/. The author is unknown, or we are unsure who the original author is. There is no other information than that given at this time.

12 **Arvind Devalia**. Arvind Devalia Quotes. (n.d.). arvinddevalia.com. Retrieved February 13, 2019, from arvinddevalia.com website: https://www.arvinddevalia.com.

13 **Lori Deschene**. Tiny Buddha Quotes. (n.d.). TinyBuddha.com. Retrieved March 10, 2010, from TinyBuddha.com website: https://tinybuddha.com/wisdom-quotes/.

14 **Marion G. Romney, 1982 October General Conference, Welfare Session, "The Celestial Nature of Self-reliance"**. - The 152nd Semiannual General Conference of the Church of Jesus Christ of Latter-day Saints, October 2, 1982, Welfare Session. Published in the Ensign magazine, Volume 12 Number 11, November 1982. An official magazine of the Church of Jesus Christ of Latter-day Saints, published by the Church of Jesus Christ of Latter-day Saints, 50 E. North Temple Street, Salt Lake City, UT, 84150-3220, USA. Also, retrieved Nov 26,2019, from Ensign, ChurchofJesusChrist.Org website: https://www.churchofjesuschrist.org/study/ensign/1982/11/the-celestial-nature-of-self-reliance?lang=eng.

Rule #11 'If You Can't Take Care of Yourself, You Can't Take Care of Others'

Adversity and the Blessings Therein

Rule #12

'No One Said It Was Going to be Easy'

Rule #12 'No One Said It Was Going to be Easy'

Give it to Me Straight:

Now you would think that Rule #12 *'No One Said It Was Going to be Easy'* is all about telling yourself or others to quit whining. Or perhaps you may phrase it like this, 'Suck it up,' 'Get over it,' or 'Move on with your life.' But that is not the case. In truth, Rule #12 *'No One Said It Was Going to be Easy'* is all about blessings, from where they emanate, the timing of their arrival, why they are granted, and how we recognize them.

To understand my interpretation of Rule #12, you need to know how I look at blessings. You need to recognize the three 'Ws' of blessings. They are Where, When, and Why.

I wrote a book titled 'Where Blessings Come From.' It is from a collection of stories I have written about my childhood. A friend of mine proofread the book as I was writing it, and while doing so, he found it challenging to correlate the title of the book with the contents of the story. He couldn't see where blessings had anything to do with the tragedies of my life that I had detailed in the book. He said the parts of the book he had proofed to-date read more like a drama than an inspirational story. I promised him that before he finished proofreading my book that the reason for the title would be apparent. I also promised him that for those who are blind to the story's true meaning, I would write a more direct explanation at the end.

For the direct answer to the question of how my life tragedies were the subject of a book titled, 'Where Blessings Come From,' I decided to write an epilogue to clarify how my life tragedies were blessings. In the epilogue, I shared my testimony of what I believe to be true regarding blessings and from where, when, and why they come to us. To support the book and my testimony, I added a few doctrinal scriptures for corroboration. The answer I gave was simple.

Rule #12 'No One Said It Was Going to be Easy'

From where do all blessings come? They come from God. When do blessings come to us? When we do things, God has asked us to do. Why do we receive blessings? The answer to the why is because God is our Heavenly Father, and He loves us.

What troubled my friend was how the book's title related to the story in that he couldn't comprehend how adversities in life are blessings from God and fall under the same guidelines as other, more positively perceived blessings.

I hope that as you read this rule, you will come to the same understanding that I have. *'No One Said It Was Going to be Easy'* is really all about being blessed.

Give it to Me Not So Straight:

God's blessings come in all sizes and shapes to fit every circumstance of our life. Whether the blessing is in the form of another person's help or God himself turns up in a more direct way to aid us, a blessing may be revealed in a simple little moment or in a great event.

To those people that God sends to us to bless our lives, we should give gratitude for their willingness to serve and help their fellow beings. But first and foremost, always remember, it is God we need to give thanks to for watching over us and sending the blessing our way.

It is my testimony and belief that all blessings come from God, through His Son, Jesus Christ, and the Holy Ghost. With the Holy Spirit guiding you, you need only to look carefully, and you will find the blessings in all your adversities, oppositions, joys, happiness, and service to others.

Blessings come from each moment of life, a gift that God has given us. Life, itself, is a great blessing. The day we were born into this mortal state is the greatest blessing of all. And each day of life thereafter is an extension of that great blessing. Can you think of any other circumstance that could have granted us the experiences and knowledge we needed to progress? I cannot. Being given the opportunity to live in this mortal state is the greatest gift God ever has given us. The giving of His Son is second, only because had we not come to live in this Earthly state, we would not have needed His Son's sacrifice.

Challenges:

Be grateful for each day of life and the challenges they present. God has given us the opportunity for challenges in our life to prove us capable, to provide us with strength, to give us wisdom and knowledge, to help us become better people, and to have an equal chance to become more like him. These are just a few of the great blessings God our Heavenly Father has blessed us with.

Blessings are received through life's challenges. Look for the blessings in your adversities, and you will find them. Two great Prophets of old left us these writings to testify to us that mortal life is a blessing from God to be cherished.

> **(The Pearl of Great Price: Moses 5:10)**[5]
> *10 And in that day Adam blessed God and was filled, and began to prophesy concerning all the families of the earth, saying: Blessed be the name of God, for because of my transgression my eyes are opened, and in this life I shall have joy, and again in the flesh I shall see God.*
>
> **(Book of Mormon: 2 Nephi 2:25)**[3]
> *25 Adam fell that men might be; and men are, that they might have joy.*

God is no respecter of persons. Thus, He gives His blessings to all individuals liberally regardless of stature. In all things, God treats us equally fair and just. Are we not his children? Do we not treat all our children fairly and justly? Let us hope that is true, I do so pray.

I believe God does treat us all equally. That does not mean that we all receive the same blessings. Yet, I believe we are all given the blessings we need. Through a Prophet of the Lord, Joseph Smith, we have been given a book called the Doctrine and Covenants (D&C). In the D&C 78:17 we read in Jesus Christ's own words;

Rule #12 'No One Said It Was Going to be Easy'

> **(Doctrine and Covenant 78:17)**[4]
> *17 "Verily, verily, I say unto you, ye are little children, and ye have not as yet understood how great blessings the Father hath in his own hands and prepared for you."*

The Law:

God, from the beginning, has set the laws in motion that govern all things heavenly and earthly. He, Himself, also adheres to those laws, or He would cease to be God. There are laws that govern why the Sun will rise each morning and set each night. So are there heavenly laws that govern blessings. We can read this in Doctrine and Covenant 130:20-21 and 132:5.

> **(Doctrine and Covenant 130:20-21)**[4]
> *20 There is a law, irrevocably decreed in heaven before the foundations of this world, upon which all blessings are predicated.*
>
> *21 And when we obtain any blessing from God, it is by obedience to that law upon which it is predicated.*
>
> **(Doctrine and Covenant 132:5)**[4]
> *5 For all who will have a blessing at my hands shall abide the law, which was appointed for that blessing, and the conditions thereof, as were instituted from before the foundation of the world.*

Life & Family:

If you have read some of the stories I have written about my life and family, you may be asking, what about Mom being crippled for the rest of her life or any other person being crippled, for that matter, is a blessing? What kind of blessing can you interpret from that? What about the family being torn apart and scattered in multiple directions? Where are or what are the blessings extracted from that? They may seem hidden or difficult to understand, but they do exist. I know because I have been part of or lived through these adversities and received the blessings they offered.

Rule #12 'No One Said It Was Going to be Easy'

Because of the life circumstances that my whole family has endured, I have been blessed with a sure knowledge of God's love for me. I have been stretched to the boundaries of my limits. Yet I rebounded from them wiser, with greater understanding, wisdom, compassion, and love. Through our family's adversities, I have better learned to forgive others as well as myself for shortcomings.

> **(Bible Old Testament: Isaiah 30:20)**[1]
> *20 And though the Lord give you the bread of adversity, and the water of affliction, yet shall not thy teachers be removed into a corner any more, but thine eyes shall see thy teachers:*
>
> **(Alistair MacLeod)**[6]
> *No one has ever said that life is to be easy. Only that it is to be lived.*

The Burden of the Load:

It is through my greatest adversities and oppositions that I have received my greatest blessings. I have to admit that there were times in my life when I wondered if I was being exempted from God's blessings. I also had times when I thought that for sure, the burdens I carried would far exceed my abilities to endure them.

During one of those hard times, I searched the Bible to see if I could find a passage from God that would tell me that my adversities would never exceed my abilities. I found this in the New Testament, 1 Corinthians.

> **(Bible New Testament: 1 Corinthians 10:13)**[2]
> *13 There hath no temptation taken you but such as is common to man: but God is faithful, who will not suffer you to be tempted above that ye are able; but will with the temptation also make a way to escape, that ye may be able to bear it.*

The above passage of scripture says you will not be tempted beyond that which you can bear. The scripture does not, however, include the ability to endure all adversity or opposition.

Many people confuse temptation with adversity. Though some temptations may contain adversity, they are not the same. Temptation is a question of choice. Adversity does not always give you a choice. This leaves me to wonder how far God will allow adversity to press upon us. I looked again at the biblical prophets for that answer and asked myself this question; How far did the adversary push God's Prophets? The answer to that question is, for some Prophets, it was to their death.

Triumphal Ending:

There is a promise in the scriptures that He gives us to balance out our adversities or afflictions. The promise is that if we endure our affliction, we will be blessed and will triumph in the end.

> **(Doctrine and Covenants 121:6-10)**[4]
> *6 Remember thy suffering saints, O our God; and thy servants will rejoice in thy name forever.*
>
> *7 My son, peace be unto thy soul; thine adversity and thine afflictions shall be but a small moment;*
>
> *8 And then, if thou endure it well, God shall exalt thee on high; thou shalt triumph over all thy foes.*
>
> *9 Thy friends do stand by thee, and they shall hail thee again with warm hearts and friendly hands.*
>
> *10 Thou art not yet as Job; thy friends do not contend against thee, neither charge thee with transgression, as they did Job.*

I am Here:

God, our Heavenly Father, has promised that He and His blessings will always be available to us. Although, at times, we may feel that we are facing life alone, I bear you my testimony with an assurance that you are not. That is unless you are choosing to do so.

Look at your adversities and afflictions and search for the positive, and you will find it within them. Reach for it. Grab hold of it. Believe you can find it, and you will. The positive is there I assure you. Find that positive, and you'll find the blessings God has given you.

Lessons Learned:

Life's oppositions, adversities, and afflictions have left me with many stories of lessons learned, and blessings gained. It is my wish to share those stories and my testimony with you. I don't write my stories with the hope of being a great published author. I don't write to be a great anything. I write them with a hope that perhaps you will get a chance to read one, and as you do, it will bless and enrich your life. If I bless but one person's life, with my writings, that, in turn, will bless me ten-fold.

It is my hope that God will help me use my life's oppositions, adversities, and afflictions to lighten the burdens that others may be carrying while they deal with issues in their life. Therein rests the joy of my labors and why I have written down a few of my childhood stories, along with my testimony and this book of rules.

> **(Matthew Henry)**[7]
> *Extraordinary afflictions are not always the punishment of extraordinary sins, but sometimes the trial of extraordinary graces."*
>
> **(John Adams)**[8]
> *The furnace of affliction produces refinement in states as well as individuals. And the new Governments we are assuming in every part will require a purification from our vices, and an augmentation of our virtues, or there will be no blessings.*

Patience is a Virtue:

I am a convert to the Church of Jesus Christ of Latter-day Saints; some call us Mormons. Mormon is not the name members of this church preferred to be referred to as. The more appropriate way to addresses us is as a member of the Church of Jesus Christ of Latter-day Saints.

I converted to the church at the age of twenty-three while serving in the United States Armed Forces. I started reading the Old and New Testament Bible when I was very young. In fact, even before I could read, my mother would read out loud to us some of the Bible stories. I wish that at the time while I was growing up that I had known of the additional scriptures in the Book of Mormon and the Doctrine and Covenants. I think now that perhaps those scriptures in the Book of Mormon would have helped me to better understand the reason for the adversities I experienced in my youth. In those days, many times, I questioned God's purpose for giving me life, and for the life I was living.

> **(Book of Mormon: Alma 34:40-41)**[3]
> *40 And now my beloved brethren, I would exhort you to have patience, and that ye bear with all manner of afflictions; that ye do not revile against those who do cast you out because of your exceeding poverty, lest ye become sinners like unto them;*
>
> *41 But that ye have patience, and bear with those afflictions, with a firm hope that ye shall one day rest from all your afflictions.*

No Limits:

We have and will be given all the blessings we will ever need during this mortal state here on Earth. The blessings are there. They are in life's trials and tribulations. They are in our pain, our joy, our suffering, and our celebration. Sometimes the blessing stands out as clear, as a bright, sunny day, and sometimes it is more elusive as if it stands behind a light fog. Then again, that fog can be substantial, making it harder to see the blessing within. No matter the circumstance, a blessing will be a part of it. They are and will always be there, every second of our lives.

It is we who hold the key to recognizing a blessing. And we will see the blessing the moment we as individuals realize that in some part of whatever adversity we are facing, there is a positive experience. When we, in our hearts and minds, reach out and find the positive, no matter how small that positive maybe seem to be, it is in that moment that our eyes will be opened and we will see what it is that we have been blessed with.

No matter how much negativity a circumstance may press upon you, there is always a positive to be found. Those positives are your blessings. Finding a positive or blessing is not always an easy task. Sometimes it seems almost impossible. Almost I say, but never truly impossible.

We need to start by having faith and hope as we earnestly search for the positive in our afflictions or adversities. Then and only then will the power of the Holy Ghost help us find it. Through the Holy Ghost, our hearts and eyes will be open to witness the blessings. The Holy Ghost will help us gain a positive understanding of a difficult situation. As we nurture the positive, it will grow. With that, compassion grows as well. As compassion grows, it becomes easier and easier to see how we were or are being blessed.

From my heart, I tell you this: without blessings, we wouldn't make it through any of life's lessons, hard or easy. The blessing in our lives saves us in all circumstances. Life isn't meant to be easy or hard. It is intended to teach, and the blessings of life are there to help sustain us.

I Don't See It:

For some of life's troubles, it may take years before you are willing to see your blessings. Anger, despair, depression, hopelessness, and fear are the internal enemies that blind us and bind us. Don't feed them. I testify to you that they are hungry and easily fed. Seek for the positive and the Holy

Ghost will free your eyes and loosen the knot that binds your heart. You will then triumph over these internal enemies, and the blessings of God will be revealed.

Am I Glowing Yet?

Through the pressures of life, and the blessings that have kept me from being crushed to a powder, I've become a diamond in the rough in my old age. I'm now being placed against the polishing wheel. Slowly I'm being ground down and polished by the diamond-powdered sandpaper. Sometimes I feel like I'm still being sanded with the coarse grade or perhaps the medium. The sandpaper of my life certainly doesn't feel like the nice smooth extra-fine grade stuff yet. Perhaps with a little more time in this life and a lot more blessings, I'll get brilliant enough to shine before God and return home to live in His presence.

You may find the coal analogy humorous. I can assure you, however, that I am quite serious. I am sure God knew that when he sent me to Earth, I'd be a tough piece of coal to change. So, to give me an equal chance, God gave me the blessings of a few more challenging opportunities. My life experience has included a lot of opposition sprinkled heavily with adversity, for extra sparkle. Those challenging opportunities and adversities, in turn, have and continue to transform me, so that I may become one of his brilliant diamonds.

Final Wisdom:

As I look back on my life, I find that there has always been positive in every adverse situation I have ever been in. I leave you my testimony of God's love for us and the blessings He gives us, to which we hold the key to opening our eyes and hearts.

I'll end this writing with one fairly lengthy section of scripture contained in the Book of Mormon. I hope this section of scripture will help you find the clarity that I have found in understanding God's blessings. For me, it answers why there are trials of adversity in our lives and why life's path is filled with opposition.

> **(Book of Mormon: 2 Nephi 2:10-29)**[3]
>
> 10 And because of the intercession for all, all men come unto God; wherefore, they stand in the presence of him, to be judged of him according to the truth and holiness which is in him. Wherefore, the ends of the law which the Holy One hath given, unto the inflicting of the punishment which is affixed, which punishment that is affixed is in opposition to that of the happiness which is affixed, to answer the ends of the atonement—
>
> 11 For it must needs be, that there is an opposition in all things. If not so, my first-born in the wilderness, righteousness could not be brought to pass, neither wickedness, neither holiness nor misery, neither good nor bad. Wherefore, all things must needs be a compound in one; wherefore, if it should be one body it must needs remain as dead, having no life neither death, nor corruption nor incorruption, happiness nor misery, neither sense nor insensibility.
>
> 12 Wherefore, it must needs have been created for a thing of naught; wherefore there would have been no purpose in the end of its creation. Wherefore, this thing must needs destroy the wisdom of God and his eternal purposes, and also the power, and the mercy, and the justice of God.
>
> 13 And if ye shall say there is no law, ye shall also say there is no sin. If ye shall say there is no sin, ye shall also say there is no righteousness. And if there be no righteousness there be no happiness. And if there be no righteousness nor happiness there be no punishment nor misery. And if these things are not there is no God. And if there is no God we are not, neither the earth; for there could have been no creation of things, neither to act nor to be acted upon; wherefore, all things must have vanished away.
>
> 14 And now, my sons, I speak unto you these things for your profit and learning; for there is a God, and he hath created all things, both the heavens and the earth, and all things that in them are, both things to act and things to be acted upon.

Rule #12 'No One Said It Was Going to be Easy'

15 And to bring about his eternal purposes in the end of man, after he had created our first parents, and the beasts of the field and the fowls of the air, and in fine, all things which are created, it must needs be that there was an opposition; even the forbidden fruit in opposition to the tree of life; the one being sweet and the other bitter.

16 Wherefore, the Lord God gave unto man that he should act for himself. Wherefore, man could not act for himself save it should be that he was enticed by the one or the other.

17 And I, Lehi, according to the things which I have read, must needs suppose that an angel of God, according to that which is written, had fallen from heaven; wherefore, he became a devil, having sought that which was evil before God.

18 And because he had fallen from heaven, and had become miserable forever, he sought also the misery of all mankind. Wherefore, he said unto Eve, yea, even that old serpent, who is the devil, who is the father of all lies, wherefore he said: Partake of the forbidden fruit, and ye shall not die, but ye shall be as God, knowing good and evil.

19 And after Adam and Eve had partaken of the forbidden fruit they were driven out of the garden of Eden, to till the earth.

20 And they have brought forth children; yea, even the family of all the earth.

21 And the days of the children of men were prolonged, according to the will of God, that they might repent while in the flesh; wherefore, their state became a state of probation, and their time was lengthened, according to the commandments which the Lord God gave unto the children of men. For he gave commandment that all men must repent; for he showed unto all men that they were lost, because of the transgression of their parents.

22 And now, behold, if Adam had not transgressed he would not have fallen, but he would have remained in the garden of Eden. And all things which were created must have remained in the same state in which they were after they were created; and they must have remained forever, and had no end.

23 And they would have had no children; wherefore they would have remained in a state of innocence, having no joy, for they knew no misery; doing no good, for they knew no sin.

24 But behold, all things have been done in the wisdom of him who knoweth all things.

25 Adam fell that men might be; and men are, that they might have joy.

26 And the Messiah cometh in the fullness of time, that he may redeem the children of men from the fall. And because that they are redeemed from the fall they have become free forever, knowing good from evil; to act for themselves and not to be acted upon, save it be by the punishment of the law at the great and last day, according to the commandments which God hath given.

27 Wherefore, men are free according to the flesh; and all things are given them which are expedient unto man. And they are free to choose liberty and eternal life, through the great Mediator of all men, or to choose captivity and death, according to the captivity and power of the devil; for he seeketh that all men might be miserable like unto himself.

28 And now, my sons, I would that ye should look to the great Mediator, and hearken unto his great commandments; and be faithful unto his words, and choose eternal life, according to the will of his Holy Spirit;

29 And not choose eternal death, according to the will of the flesh and the evil which is therein, which giveth the spirit of the devil power to captivate, to bring you down to hell, that he may reign over you in his own kingdom.

I leave you this writing and testimony,

In the name of Jesus Christ,

AMEN.

Rule #12 'No One Said It Was Going to be Easy'

Endnotes:

1 **King James Version of the Bible, The Old Testament of Our Lord and Saviour Jesus Christ.** Published by The Church of Jesus Christ of Latter-day Saints, Salt Lake City, Utah, USA. Copywrite 2013.

2 **King James Version of the Bible, The New Testament of Our Lord and Saviour Jesus Christ.** Published by The Church of Jesus Christ of Latter-day Saints, Salt Lake City, Utah, USA. Copywrite 2013.

3 **The Book of Mormon Another Testament of Jesus Christ.** Published by The Church of Jesus Christ of Latter-day Saints, Salt Lake City, Utah, USA. The first English edition published in Palmyra, New York, USA, in 1830. Copywrite 2013.

4 **The Doctrine and Covenants of The Church of Jesus Christ of Latter-Day Saints.** Containing Revelations Give to Joseph Smith, the Prophet. With some additions by his successors in the Presidency of the Church. Published by The Church of Jesus Christ of Latter-day Saints, Salt Lake City, Utah, USA. Copywrite 2013.

5 **The Pearl of Great Price.** A selection from the revelations, translations, and narrations of Joseph Smith, First Prophet, seer, and revelator to The Church of Jesus Christ of Latter-Day Saints. Published by The Church of Jesus Christ of Latter-day Saints, Salt Lake City, Utah, USA. Copywrite 2013.

6 **Alistair MacLeod** Alistair MacLeod. (n.d.). AZQuotes.com. Retrieved November 29, 2019, from AZQuotes.com Web site: https://www.azquotes.com/quote/401567. Also, see Alistair MacLeod (2010). "The Lost Salt Gift of Blood," p.150, New Canadian Library

7 **Matthew Herny.** Matthew Henry. (n.d.). AZQuotes.com. Retrieved November 29, 2019, from AZQuotes.com Web site: https://www.azquotes.com/quote/130100. Also, see Matthew Henry (2016). "Book of Job - Complete Bible Commentary Verse by Verse," p.188, Editora Dracaena

8 **John Adams.** John Adams. (n.d.). AZQuotes.com. Retrieved November 29, 2019, from AZQuotes.com Web site: https://www.azquotes.com/quote/1309363. Also, see John Adams, Charles Francis Adams (1854). "The Works of John Adams, Second President of the United States: With a Life of the Author, Notes and Illustrations," p.418

Rule #12 'No One Said It Was Going to be Easy'

Smelling the Roses

Rule #13

'Focus on the Journey Not the Task'

Rule #13 'Focus on the Journey Not the Task'

Give Me the Short Version:

'Focus on the Journey Not the Task' means precisely that. The journeys we take in life, the daily tasks we are challenged to complete, teach us the lessons we are here to learn and provide us with the life experiences we are here to enjoy. Whether the task is work-related or it is a task of enjoyment, if we don't take time to pay attention to the journey, we miss out on many rich learning opportunities connected with that task. It is the journey, not the task, that is the most important part of self-development. As we take the journey, we gain an understanding of who we are, the potential we have within us, and with faith, we will become the person God wants us to be.

Enjoying the Task:

The task may be something as simple as taking a bicycle ride. It doesn't matter whether the ride you take is for a little exercise or if the purpose is for enjoying time with your companion, the events that take place during the journey teach you about life and yourself. The journey is what molds you, not the task. Elder Dieter Uchtdorf told this story about riding his bicycle with his wife, Harriet:

> **(Dieter F. Uchtdorf, 2012 October General Conference, "Of Regrets and Resolutions")**[6]
> *My wife, Harriet, and I love riding our bicycles. It is wonderful to get out and enjoy the beauties of nature. We have certain routes we like to bike, but we don't pay too much attention to how far we go or how fast we travel in comparison with other riders.*
>
> *However, occasionally I think we should be a bit more competitive. I even think we could get a better time or ride at a higher speed if only we pushed ourselves a little more. And then sometimes I even*

Rule #13 'Focus on the Journey, Not the Task'

make the big mistake of mentioning this idea to my wonderful wife.

Her typical reaction to my suggestions of this nature is always very kind, very clear, and very direct. She smiles and says, "Dieter, it's not a race; it's a journey. Enjoy the moment."

How right she is!

Sometimes in life we become so focused on the finish line that we fail to find joy in the journey.

Summarizing:

I feel that the last sentence in Elder Dieter Uchtdorf's story sums up his story well and is worth repeating. *"Sometimes in life we become so focused on the finish line that we fail to find joy in the journey."*

As I pondered over Elder Uchtdorf's last sentence, it reformed in my mind with a few simple changes. As I rewrote his statement in my mind, I felt it gave the sentence a more profound and vibrant meaning. If I may, I would like to share those changes with you. I will start by taking out the words *finish line* and replace it with one word--*task*. Then after the word *joy*, add the word *knowledge or wisdom*. The sentence would now read, *"Sometimes in life, we become so focused on the task that we fail to find joy, knowledge, or wisdom in the journey."*

Of course, if I change just one word in what Elder Dieter Uchtdorf said, the statement becomes my words and not the words of a church Apostle. You can see that by doing the small changes in the sentence, the meaning of the statement becomes stronger. These are the thoughts and interpretations of his statement that came to my mind as I pondered and prayed over what Elder Uchtdorf had said. I think you will agree with me that both statements share the same concept. Ponder His story yourself and gain your own understanding.

Rule #13 'Focus on the Journey, Not the Task'

Don't Sweat the Little Things:

Gaining a clear understanding of Rule #13 *'Focus on the Journey Not the Task'* can help provide us with a clearer understanding of what the purpose of our life is. As we apply the principles of Rule #13 to our lives, we can gain much more wisdom and knowledge from the experiences. I am going to provide you with a few stories to help illustrate my point. First, I'll show how Rule #13 can be a tremendous help for those who have issues with micromanaging.

Have you ever heard the saying, *'Don't sweat the little things'*? We all are familiar with a person, perhaps it is even you, who has a need to control every aspect of every detail of how a job is done. I myself have micromanagement issues, which is why I point this out.

When we micromanage, we tend to take away free agency from those around us. First, this is not a good way to win friends or influence people. Second, this is not a productive way to manage. Third, you rob other people of the life experiences they would have had had they taken the journey on their own.

I am not saying that we should not have rules and procedures to follow. Without them, we would be living in chaos. There is a big difference between managing and micromanaging.

I use my own personal stories to illustrate a point in many of my writings. This time I will use a story about my daughter. You see, the apple really doesn't fall too far from the tree, like father, like daughter. As many fathers do, I have had to watch helplessly, several times, as my poor daughter struggled with problems in her life impaired by some of the personality traits, she inherited from me. It appears she did get a few of her father's genes, and micromanaging is one of them.

A Mother's Love:

At the time of this story, my daughter, Jennifer, had five young girls still living at home. The oldest daughter's name is

Rule #13 'Focus on the Journey, Not the Task'

Kyelynn, age 15. Then there is Olivia 13; Lindsey 8, Meghan 6, and Elizabeth 3. Helping four young girls to manage their lives, and caring for a 3-year old that seems to get attacked by about every germ the other four children bring home from school, can test any mother's managing abilities.

I recently spent two weeks with my lovely daughter and her family in California, where my son-in-law, Denis, was, at the time, enrolled in a military training school for the Army. Anyone who has ever gone to college and carried a full load of courses knows the work does not stop at the end of the last class. Every night there is a ton of homework to be completed in preparation for the next day's classes.

When I was in college, coming home after a hard day at school, the last thing on my mind would have been sharing a meal with my family, followed by a full evening of excitement. All I ever wanted to do was to take a short nap in the hope of rejuvenating my mind and body so that I would have the energy to prepare for the next day.

But the situation was different for my son-in-law. His girls overly love him. Every evening (while I was there) the moment the girls heard his truck driving down the long driveway towards the house, they all started screaming, "Daddy's home! Daddy's home!" as loud as they could. Poor Denis, tired from the day and loaded down with homework for the evening, still kept a smile on his face as he walked through the door. His girls all ran to him, wanting to be the first to share stories from their day or trying to get their father to play with them for a little while. Denis, with a loving smile, could only give each of his daughters a few moments of much-needed attention, then he had to go to his desk and get back to his studies. His young daughters reluctantly gave up the fight for their father's attention and went back to playing wildly and somewhat noisily around the house. I think the girls stayed loud and rambunctious in an attempt to distract their father, to convince him to give up his studies, and join them in their play.

Rule #13 'Focus on the Journey, Not the Task'

Due to Denis's overloaded work schedule, the responsibilities of handling and running the home were left to his wife, my daughter Jennifer. I was amazed by Jennifer as I watched her start every day at 5:30 am, even though many a night she did not get to bed until well after 11 pm. During waking hours, 95 percent of her time was spent caring for the family's needs.

Impressively, Jennifer was very organized at getting the tasks done around the home. There were times however that the stress of daily life, plus having a share of her father's gene pool, brought out the over-organizer in her, better known as micromanaging. Thus, Jennifer becomes a micromanager.

The more tasks there are, the less time there is, and the less time there is, the more important it seems to organize. The desire to organize then is driven to the point that she begins micromanaging. Thus, Jennifer, the micromanager, emerges.

There is a difference between the organizer and the micromanager. The philosophy of the micromanager is that the more tasks you have to manage, the tighter control you need to exercise over each task. The micromanager believes that all tasks, down to the tiniest detail, need to be organized under one single controller, and she/he is that controller. The micromanager's way of think is that by implementing this philosophy, all tasks should be (note I said should be) done more efficiently. Thus, achieving the desired outcome--that each task should require (note the word should again) less time to complete.

The micromanager believes that with this philosophy, they can shrink the time required for each daily task so that each chore will fit into the daily-allotted time slot. I think it's a great philosophy. If it were not for one minor catch. You see, for micromanagement to work, the manager must be able to control all of the factors involved as they live and carry on in their daily life. Good luck!

My daughter believes that if she super micromanages all of those 'have-to' tasks required in raising her five young girls, she can fit all of the chores into her 5:30 am to 11:00 pm day.

Rule #13 'Focus on the Journey, Not the Task'

Piece of cake! No sweat! Right? There is no unpredictability in the daily life of raising children. Correct?

At this stage of Jennifer's life, time is a precious commodity. She never seems to be able to find enough of it, and her stress is only compounded by the scarcity of support she receives from her husband due to his military work and school requirements. Jennifer's situation is virtually impossible to micromanage. It's a difficult state for any mother raising children minus half a husband. There is no question that excellent organizational skills serve an important role in time management. Jennifer, however, does not choose the Organizer's hat to help her manage her life, she instead slaps on her micromanager cap and gets to work. She decides that my wonderful, sweet grandchildren need a more centrally controlled, organized life. There is no need to ask the girls for their input because Micromanager Jennifer feels she knows precisely how to organize their lives better. After all, they are just children, and she is the mom.

Let's take a look at one example. My daughter laid out a well-organized, detailed plan for the kids to keep their bedrooms clean and their clothes and closets tidy and well-ordered. In Jennifer's plan, there was a place for everything, and everything should be kept in its place, right? Socks paired and properly matched. Undergarments nicely folded. Pajamas separated by style. One-piece pajamas with legs in one stack, nightgowns in another stack, and two-piece pajamas properly paired in a different stack. T-Shirts and blouses both separated and stacked. Place the long sleeves in one pile and short sleeves in another pile. The girls were directed to separate jeans and dress pants as they do the other clothes. When possible, clothes were to be hung on hangers in color-coordinated outfits. Then the outfits would be hung in the closet and organized by style and color. Shoes should be paired appropriately and laid out on the closet floor in order and arranged according to style. All the clothes that could not be hung in the closet were to be acceptably folded, coordinated by color in stacks, and placed in the appropriately labeled dresser drawer or closet shelf.

Rule #13 'Focus on the Journey, Not the Task'

Then for the final touch to Jennifer's organizational plan-- dirty and clean clothes should never be mixed. I can understand that. Absolutely no dirty clothes should ever be found on the bed or bedroom floor. All dirty clothes should be delivered directly to the laundry room as soon as is reasonably possible.

Hmmm! As soon as possible within reason. That's a dangerously open-ended statement to make to a young child or teenager. But what else could Jennifer say; that the clothes must be delivered to the laundry room immediately? If she said that and the girls took her words literally, there might be naked kids running through the house as they deliver their dirty clothes to the laundry room. No, it was better to leave the statement with some flexibility as to how the dirty clothes rule was to be carried out.

It seems like a well-thought-out, detailed plan. Don't you think? Can you imagine walking into your children's room and seeing the clothes in the closet and dresser drawers in perfect, color-coordinated order? You have just solved your children's issues of not being able to find their clothes, especially at 5:30 am when their poor little eyes can scarcely focus, let alone pick out a color-coordinated outfit and the corresponding shoes for the day.

While I was there, Jennifer spent an entire day frantically organizing one of the children's rooms. She did it to show them how she expected them to organize their clothes and keep their room clean and tidy. Note, Jennifer did not implement her detailed plan for organizing the girls' rooms. Jennifer dictated the organizational plan and expected the girls to implement it. Jennifer will be the micromanager that enforces the plan's organizational rules.

The plan should (that word should again) work, right? If followed, it would save time and keep the children's rooms clean. I mean, Jennifer offered examples and demonstrated to the girls how to manage their laundry per her instructions. She taught them how to fold the clothes so they would fit in the drawer and not need to be stored on the floor or tossed on

Rule #13 'Focus on the Journey, Not the Task'

the bed. She even demonstrated how to properly put clothes on a hanger. How many of you mothers reading this think that this is a great plan? It is a great plan. But, is it a plan that can be easily implemented by children whose ages range from 3 years to 15 years old? Jennifer said that each child, including the 3-year-old, was responsible for her own area of the room. I know, because out of concern, I questioned her about it. I was there. I stood by as she presented the plan to the girls.

So, the question is: how do you help a micromanager see the flaw in a beautifully laid-out process? You see, the main issue in getting them to see a flaw in their process is that most of the time, there is no direct flaw. In fact, micromanagers come up with some of the best and most efficient methods. No matter how sound a process may be on paper, in implementation, it can be a disaster. On paper, a plan doesn't always take in to account all the human factors.

A parent may come up with a great process that perfectly details each step to success for any number of chores. Yet when children are involved, the implementation of any micromanaged plan doesn't go too smoothly. Children are not predictable and difficult to manage; thus, even with the best process, the results are not totally reliable.

As parents, we cannot go to our drafting boards or computers and map out a plan with all the details to micromanage every aspect of our children's lives. Even with all the wisdom of age that has been endowed upon us parents, this is an impossible task. Give it up before you start. Do you think you can take your plan, present it to your children, and expect them to have your same knowledge and wisdom to understand the value of the plan? And then implement it with perfection? Our children have not yet taken the journey in life, their eyes are not yet open to the lessons and the wisdom that our eyes have been opened to.

Children are not robots. As parents, we cannot merely reprogram them with a new and better process. Despite the fact that children come from the same gene pool, their

Rule #13 'Focus on the Journey, Not the Task'

emotions, understanding, attitudes, and physical and mental abilities all vary with each child. Additionally, they haven't yet traveled the road we have and lack the life experience we have to understand the how and why of our well-intended advice.

The journeys our children take as they fulfill the tasks in their daily life stimulates their growth in knowledge and deepens their understanding of who they are as an individual, who they want to become, and who they will become. All of the experiences that happen along the way are more important to our children and grandchildren's development than any singular task.

By micromanaging a child's life, we rob them of that journey. Each journey they take, every task they work to complete, imparts in them the understanding they need to gain the wisdom (the why) behind the knowledge (how-to).

Children don't need to be micromanaged. They do, however, need boundaries and limits. They haven't taken many life journeys yet; therefore, children don't understand where the dangers lay along the journey's path. We, as parents, have ventured down the journey's path, and have learned from the journeys we have walked (I pray). That is why it is our responsibility as parents to offer guidance, the needed rules, and loving discipline to help them manage their boundaries. We, as parents, do this to help protect our children from the harm they may encounter or from the harm we may have encountered as we took the journey before them. As our children are encouraged to stretch their abilities and talents, they need to be given the responsibility to manage the task their way while living within the boundaries parents and God has set for them, or they will not learn the much-needed lessons the journey provides.

When you give your children responsibility, you are also giving them accountability. You cannot hold a child accountable if they are not given the responsibility that goes with it.

Rule #13 'Focus on the Journey, Not the Task'

When parents micromanage, a large portion of the child's responsibility is taken away. But yet many micromanaging parents continue to hold the child accountable. Accountability and responsibility go hand-in-hand. Without responsibility, there can be no accountability; likewise, they are also proportional. The more responsibility, the more accountability. This is how Heavenly Father teaches us.

If we eliminate the responsibility and the accountability from the task, we take away the journey, and without the journey, as humans, we become stagnant and cease to grow.

Let's get back to my daughter and her plan to micromanage her children's laundry. Jennifer had spent hours going through all the kid's clothes and shoes reorganizing, matching, and color coordinating outfits. Then she sat the girls down, and with great care and words of wisdom, she explained her methods and the reasons for the new process. For emphasis, she presented them with a visual example of her organizational skills and her hard day's work. She showed them a beautifully organized closet and drawers. And as she did, she pointed out all the details that went into organizing them.

The girls had now been taught, and they had now been shown. So now they know what to do and how to do it, right?

It didn't take long for my daughter's process to fall apart. The children's room became an unbelievable mess. Clean clothes were found in every corner of the room. There was hardly a spot on the floor you could walk on without stepping on clothes. Clothes were on the desk, on the bed, and under the bed.

You can imagine the contention that developed between my granddaughters and their mother. I don't have to explain it, do I? I understood it well. I was there. But I think you can draw your own picture of the scene that took place.

Jennifer was furious. All of that hard work, all of the cleaning and organizing she had done, was destroyed in just a few days. The kids were upset and angry. They felt they had no rights,

Rule #13 'Focus on the Journey, Not the Task'

no power to manage their own clothes the way they wanted. The kids felt the process was forced upon them. And even though Jennifer had done a beautiful job selling her plan, they had not bought into it. How could they? As kids, they didn't have the wisdom to understand the beauty of their mother's plan.

At the moment, this was not a happy house. Jennifer waited for Denis to come home and then went to him for support. Denis calmly listened and patiently waited for Jennifer to finish her explaining and complaining about the children's attitude towards her organizational plans. This took a while.

I was in the living room listening as Jennifer spoke to Denis in the bedroom. It wasn't hard to hear every word my daughter said. It wasn't as if I were eaves-dropping, she was making her words quite loud and clear.

Once Jennifer had voiced her opinion on the subject, she calmed down. Denis then suggested to my daughter that perhaps her micromanagement plan may put too much of a challenge on the girls. That she may want to rethink her plan, look at the situation from a different perspective. Perhaps she should give the girls broader boundaries and more freedom on how they manage the responsibility of their room and clothes.

I wasn't sure my daughter was buying into what her husband was trying to tell her. So, like a good father, I asked if I could be invited into their conversation and share my two-cents worth of advice for them to think on. Of course, my two-cents fell in line with what my son-in-law had suggested. I just explained it to Jennifer in a different way.

It came down to this. My daughter had tasks she expected the girls to do. Those tasks were: clothes were not to be found on the floor, including the closet floor, and for the girls to find their own clothes in the morning and get dressed quickly.

Jennifer became so focused on ensuring the girls accomplished the tasks that she wanted them to complete that she felt she had to micromanage the task. By doing this,

Rule #13 'Focus on the Journey, Not the Task'

Jennifer bypassed the journey the girls needed to take. A journey that would give them a better understanding of the need to organize their possessions and their individual space by themselves. Each girl needed to handle the task based upon her current knowledge. Plus, a little extra knowledge would be provided by the boundaries the parents set for the task.

Boundaries are what the children need to understand why organizational skills are required. Examples of some boundary setting could be: Finding their own clothes for school in the morning and still getting appropriately dress on time. Have an inspection time set to when the girl's rooms must be clean and tidy. Give a laundry time as to when the dirty clothes must be in the laundry room. Once the boundaries are set, leave the girls to determine how they organize things to live within those boundaries. That is not to say they can't ask for advice.

The hope is that the experience the girls have by taking the journey on their own leads them to personal growth. And it will provide them with wisdom and knowledge, along with a better understanding of how to apply organizational skills in their life. This process is far better than merely following directions like a robot that has no choice in its programming. Thus, my reason for Rule #13 *'Focus on the Journey Not the Task'*.

As I said before, sometimes, micromanaging is required. Like in my military Air Force days when I worked on the Minuteman Nuclear Missile Systems. When working with nuclear weapons, I can see a reason to micromanage every aspect of the job. I certainly wouldn't want to be responsible for blowing up a nuclear bomb in my neighbor's backyard. In the Air Force, we had a clear step-by-step process for everything we did. And if, for some reason, there wasn't a process in place to cover a task, a committee was formed to create a new procedure and thoroughly test it before anyone was allowed to start the task. Yes, I can see why

Rule #13 'Focus on the Journey, Not the Task'

micromanaging is required when dealing with nuclear weapons.

However, when it comes to dealing with people and relationships, even though they may seem to be as volatile as a nuclear bomb, micromanagement is not the preferred method of interaction.

When dealing with people, we need more leadership and less management as this quote points out:

> **(Peter Ferdinand Drunker)**[7]
> *Management is doing things right; leadership is doing the right things.*

Another Tale:

Rule #13 '*Focus on the Journey Not the Task'* applies to a wide area of our lives. I'd like to share a story about a boy who learned to drive a big John Deere tractor and disk a 250-acre cornfield at the age of 8. Have you looked at the size of an average 8-year-old boy lately?

A Little Explaining:

For those of you who are not farmers or have no knowledge of what disking a field is, I'll give you a short explanation. A big tractor pulls a wide, heavy piece of equipment called a disk-harrow, disk for short. A disk-harrow is a farm implement used to till and break up the soil on a patch of land where crops are to be planted. The disk-harrow can contain up too several rows of 24-inch razor-sharp smooth steel disks. Each full row can contain 20 or more of these 24-inch disks, giving the implement lots of slicing power.

In my day, we plowed the fields and then disked them. First, you plowed. The plow's job is to dig down deep into the earth and overturn the soil. This process buries the prior year's crop residue deep below the growing line where it decomposes and becomes next year's fertilizer. At the same time, last year's crop residue, which is now fertilizer, is brought to the top and allowed to oxygenate. Oxygenating the soil is an essential part of the crop growing process.

The process of plowing leaves the dirt in huge chunks. The disk-harrow is then used to break up the chunky soil and spread it out. This process prepares the field for planting and allows for better oxygenation of the ground.

Today in 2019, farmers don't plow; they only disk the fields. And some farmers don't even disk. They just plant.

Telling the Story:

Now let's get back to the story. I was excited and thrilled at the opportunity to drive one of my Uncle Johnny's big green John Deere tractors. Yet at the same time, fear ran through my body. I was intimidated by the tractor's massive steel frame and overall size.

I climbed up the side of the tractor to the seat using whatever safe handhold I could grab ahold of. And I do mean climb. Standing on the ground, the tractor seat was more than 6 feet over the top of my head. Once I was in the seat, I had to sit there in silence and listen to a safety lecture from Uncle Jonny. He warned me that my failure to pay attention could easily get me killed. One wrong move, and I could get knocked off the tractor and sliced to pieces by the sharp edges of the disk.

You see, back then, once you engaged the clutch, the transmission kept the tractor wheels moving; no hand or foot required. You had a throttle level that governed the speed of the tractor, not a foot pedal. Tractors back in my time didn't have nice comfy air-conditioned cabs or power steering. Nor did they have any safety switch under the seat that stopped the tractor when the rider wasn't sitting down properly. A safety switch under the seat wouldn't have done me any good anyway. For one, I didn't weigh enough to activate a switch, and two, I had to stand just, so I was able to reach all the pedals and controls. In fact, my uncle had to wire a wooden block to one of the pedals so I could reach it with my foot.

Rule #13 'Focus on the Journey, Not the Task'

After the safety lecture packed with warnings, Uncle Johnny went over what all the controls and pedals were used for. As he talked, I assured him I understood how to use everything. My uncle again recited his warning. Only this time, his words were a lot sterner, and I could see in his face how serious he was about the danger of driving the tractor and how important it was that I pay attention. Then he added a few more instructions with details to clarify what might happen as I disked the field.

Uncle Johnny warned me that if I hit a large, hard clump of dried dirt with the front wheels, it would cause the steering wheel to jerk, and my scrawny body would easily be thrown off the tractor. Then I'd either be crushed under the tractor's monstrous back wheels, or be sliced up by the freshly sharpened disk, or both. Either way, my life would be over in less than a few seconds. He further informed me that the tractor would happily continue disking the ground without me and not stop until it had traveled through the fence, across the ditch, and into the Maquoketa River. He then said that he would take no particular pleasure in bringing the tragic news of my death to my mother. Nor did he wish to pull a perfectly good tractor out of the river. The last words of instructions, he shouted loud and clear at me over the roar of the tractor engine, "keep your head on straight and pay attention."

To Uncle Johnny, the task at hand was a simple one. Take the tractor and run the disk over all those large clumps of dirt and have that 250-acre field done before sunset. To me, my uncle's task was merely a great, fun, scary adventure. At least that is how I looked at it when I first started.

The journey I took going through that adventure taught me many valuable pearls of wisdom. It gave me a better appreciation of my uncle's work, and it proved to me that an 8-year-old kid can handle a dangerous task if he stays focused and keeps his head on straight.

I could write for hours about that tractor adventure and the lessons I learned. Like the fear I felt in my chest the first time, the tractor was moving a little too fast, and I had to remember

Rule #13 'Focus on the Journey, Not the Task'

how to change the speed. Or the first time the front wheels hit a large clump of dried dirt, the tractor's steering wheel jerked sharply and almost threw me to the ground, just as my uncle had warned.

When I hit that clump of dirt, I thought I was going to be known, in that small Iowa farm community, as the first 8-year-old boy to have died of a heart attack from driving a tractor.

By the middle of the day, my arms ached so from the strain of keeping the tractor on a straight and steady course each time the front wheels tried to veer as they hit a large clump of hard dirt. Or from the strain of forcing the wheels to turn and head back in the direction the tractor had just come each time I reached one end of the field or the other. Back and forth. Back and forth. I drove that tractor. My arms ache now today just from thinking about it. I pictured myself never fishing or playing baseball again. I had visions of my brothers and sister having to feed me and pulling more pranks on me than they already do. That wasn't the picture I had in my mind when I started that journey. Back then, I was thinking more on the lines of building the arms of the cartoon character 'Popeye the Sailor Man'. But instead, they were feeling more as 'Whimpey the Wiener Man.'

After 4 1/2 hours of driving and disking, the fear of managing that huge, big boy tractor was gone as well. I had that green beast well conquered, so the fun was over, and from that point on, it was just hard painful work. And by the end of that 10-hour job, the heat of the day and the pain that ran through my body drained all the adventure the journey may have had out of me.

You Ask, You Get:

A couple of lessons from the journey of the tractor:

One: I learned the meaning of the words, commitment, and responsibility.

Rule #13 'Focus on the Journey, Not the Task'

Since the beginning of that spring, I had begged my mom and uncle to let me help disk the fields. Not because I wanted to be a big helper around the farm. No, it was because I wanted that first-time adventure. That feeling you get from doing something new, you believe, is going to be exciting. So, exciting, you don't consider the fear and the pain portion of the job at the time you ask for permission.

I played a wildcard to get my uncle to allow me to do the disking. I asked Uncle Johnny how old he was when he first drove the tractor and worked in the fields? I knew how old he was before I asked – 8 years old, just like me. I had heard most of his hard work and labor stories repeated on several occasions. I told my uncle that if he was old enough at eight years old, then I was old enough, and that convinced him. He, in turn, convinced my mother.

That was a big decision on my Uncle Johnny's part. It meant that he was taking on the responsibility and supervision of my well-being. He only did it because I had given him my word that I was capable and responsible enough to do the job. When you tell Uncle Johnny you are capable and willing to take on a serious responsibility, he holds you to your word. That day I learned the hard lesson of precisely what those words meant.

Two: I also gained a clearer understanding of the phrase *'be careful what you wish for.'*

I had been dreaming of driving tractors since the first time I saw one working in a field, as I rode in a car with my father down a country road. I don't mean I just wanted to drive a tractor, I wanted to do what I saw that Farmer doing. Pulling those big, shiny implements that dug up the dirt and threw clouds of dust into the air. It looked so cool.

I can tell you that after a day of eating the dry dust kicked up by the disk, suffering ten long hours as the heat of the sun beat down on me out in that field, and dealing with the aches and pains in my arms and legs over the next few days, I was not sure the excitement of that adventure was worth it.

I will never forget the events of that day. From then until now, images of that journey still come into my head. I ponder over the thoughts and pictures I see with my mind's eye. There are innumerable lessons I learned from the experience of the journey I took that day to complete that task. I have shared only a couple with you. I wish I could share them all, but that is for another book.

(Helen Keller)[8]
It is for us to pray not for tasks equal to our powers, but for powers equal to the tasks, to go forward with great desire forever beating at the door of our hearts as we travel toward our distant goal.

(Joseph B. Wirthlin, 1990 October General Conference, "The Straight and Narrow Way")[9]
I know that each of us has much to do. Sometimes we feel overwhelmed by the tasks we face. But if we keep our priorities in order, we can accomplish all that we should. We can endure to the end regardless of temptations, problems, and challenges.

The Why:

The point of telling this story is to give you a different perspective on why Rule #13 *'Focus on the Journey Not the Task'* is so imperative in our lives. If I had totally focused only on performing the task in a timely manner, and never had taken the time or thought to ponder over the wealth of treasure the journey had provided me, I would have missed so much. The journey I took that day helped mold and prepared me for the rest of life's journey.

The Smith:

Joseph Smith, a Prophet chosen by our Heavenly Father, so, says the Church of Jesus Christ of Latter-day Saints. To which I am a member, and believe Joseph is a chosen Prophet.

Joseph Smith, like so many of the Lord's Prophets, had to take the journey to gain the knowledge and wisdom he needed to fulfill his task. His task was to determine which Church was the right one to join.

As part of that journey, Joseph attended different churches to gain understanding. He also studied the Bible, which imparted in him some of God's knowledge. These two parts of his journey guided him as he sought an answer from God and prepared him for the answer he would receive from Heavenly Father and His Son.

Joseph Smith left behind his testimony of that journey, as an example for us. I am including a large portion of his testimony below. You may have read or heard of Joseph Smith's story before. I am asking you to read it. As you read, focus on the journey Joseph Smith took to complete his task. Look for the understanding of how the journey was the key to Joseph gaining the answer he sought. If he had not taken that journey, I don't believe Joseph Smith would have found the answer to his question. It's a question that anyone who believes in God has asked themselves at one time or another. The question: Which church is the true church of God? Or is any church the true church of God?

> **(Pearl of Great Price: Joseph Smith-History 1:5-24)[5]**
> *5 Some time in the second year after our removal to Manchester, there was in the place where we lived an unusual excitement on the subject of religion. It commenced with the Methodists, but soon became general among all the sects in that region of country. Indeed, the whole district of country seemed affected by it, and great multitudes united themselves to the different religious parties, which created no small*

Rule #13 'Focus on the Journey, Not the Task'

stir and division amongst the people, some crying, "Lo, here!" and others, "Lo, there!" Some were contending for the Methodist faith, some for the Presbyterian, and some for the Baptist.

6 For, notwithstanding the great love which the converts to these different faiths expressed at the time of their conversion, and the great zeal manifested by the respective clergy, who were active in getting up and promoting this extraordinary scene of religious feeling, in order to have everybody converted, as they were pleased to call it, let them join what sect they pleased; yet when the converts began to file off, some to one party and some to another, it was seen that the seemingly good feelings of both the priests and the converts were more pretended than real; for a scene of great confusion and bad feeling ensued—priest contending against priest, and convert against convert; so that all their good feelings one for another, if they ever had any, were entirely lost in a strife of words and a contest about opinions.

7 I was at this time in my fifteenth year. My father's family was proselyted to the Presbyterian faith, and four of them joined that church, namely, my mother, Lucy; my brothers Hyrum and Samuel Harrison; and my sister Sophronia.

8 During this time of great excitement my mind was called up to serious reflection and great uneasiness; but though my feelings were deep and often poignant, still I kept myself aloof from all these parties, though I attended their several meetings as often as occasion would permit. In process of time my mind became somewhat partial to the Methodist sect, and I felt some desire to be united with them; but so great were the confusion and strife among the different denominations, that it was impossible for a person young as I was, and so unacquainted with men and things, to come to any certain conclusion who was right and who was wrong.

9 My mind at times was greatly excited, the cry and tumult were so great and incessant. The Presbyterians were most decided against the Baptists and Methodists, and used all the powers of both reason and sophistry to prove their errors, or, at least, to make the people think they were in error. On the other hand, the Baptists and Methodists in their turn were equally zealous in endeavoring to establish their own tenets and disprove all others.

10 In the midst of this war of words and tumult of opinions, I often said to myself: What is to be done? Who of all these parties are right; or, are they all wrong together? If any one of them be right, which is it, and how shall I know it?

11 While I was laboring under the extreme difficulties caused by the contests of these parties of religionists, I was one day reading the Epistle of James, first chapter and fifth verse, which reads: If any of you lack wisdom, let him ask of God, that giveth to all men liberally, and upbraideth not; and it shall be given him.

12 Never did any passage of scripture come with more power to the heart of man than this did at this time to mine. It seemed to enter with great force into every feeling of my heart. I reflected on it again and again, knowing that if any person needed wisdom from God, I did; for how to act I did not know, and unless I could get more wisdom than I then had, I would never know; for the teachers of religion of the different sects understood the same passages of scripture so differently as to destroy all confidence in settling the question by an appeal to the Bible.

13 At length I came to the conclusion that I must either remain in darkness and confusion, or else I must do as James directs, that is, ask of God. I at length came to the determination to "ask of God,"

Rule #13 'Focus on the Journey, Not the Task'

concluding that if he gave wisdom to them that lacked wisdom, and would give liberally, and not upbraid, I might venture.

14 So, in accordance with this, my determination to ask of God, I retired to the woods to make the attempt. It was on the morning of a beautiful, clear day, early in the spring of eighteen hundred and twenty. It was the first time in my life that I had made such an attempt, for amidst all my anxieties I had never as yet made the attempt to pray vocally.

15 After I had retired to the place where I had previously designed to go, having looked around me, and finding myself alone, I kneeled down and began to offer up the desires of my heart to God. I had scarcely done so, when immediately I was seized upon by some power which entirely overcame me, and had such an astonishing influence over me as to bind my tongue so that I could not speak. Thick darkness gathered around me, and it seemed to me for a time as if I were doomed to sudden destruction.

16 But, exerting all my powers to call upon God to deliver me out of the power of this enemy which had seized upon me, and at the very moment when I was ready to sink into despair and abandon myself to destruction—not to an imaginary ruin, but to the power of some actual being from the unseen world, who had such marvelous power as I had never before felt in any being—just at this moment of great alarm, I saw a pillar of light exactly over my head, above the brightness of the sun, which descended gradually until it fell upon me.

17 It no sooner appeared than I found myself delivered from the enemy which held me bound. When the light rested upon me I saw two Personages, whose brightness and glory defy all description, standing above me in the air. One of them spake unto me, calling me by name and said, pointing to the other—This is My Beloved Son. Hear Him!

Rule #13 'Focus on the Journey, Not the Task'

18 My object in going to inquire of the Lord was to know which of all the sects was right, that I might know which to join. No sooner, therefore, did I get possession of myself, so as to be able to speak, than I asked the Personages who stood above me in the light, which of all the sects was right (for at this time it had never entered into my heart that all were wrong)—and which I should join.

19 I was answered that I must join none of them, for they were all wrong; and the Personage who addressed me said that all their creeds were an abomination in his sight; that those professors were all corrupt; that: "they draw near to me with their lips, but their hearts are far from me, they teach for doctrines the commandments of men, having a form of godliness, but they deny the power thereof."

20 He again forbade me to join with any of them; and many other things did he say unto me, which I cannot write at this time. When I came to myself again, I found myself lying on my back, looking up into heaven. When the light had departed, I had no strength; but soon recovering in some degree, I went home. And as I leaned up to the fireplace, mother inquired what the matter was. I replied, "Never mind, all is well—I am well enough off." I then said to my mother, "I have learned for myself that Presbyterianism is not true." It seems as though the adversary was aware, at a very early period of my life, that I was destined to prove a disturber and an annoyer of his kingdom; else why should the powers of darkness combine against me? Why the opposition and persecution that arose against me, almost in my infancy?

21 Some few days after I had this vision, I happened to be in company with one of the Methodist preachers, who was very active in the before mentioned religious excitement; and, conversing with him on the subject of religion, I took occasion to give him an account of the vision which I had had. I was greatly surprised at his behavior; he treated my communication not only lightly, but with great contempt, saying it was all of the devil, that there were no such things as visions or revelations in these days; that all such things had ceased with the apostles, and that there would never be any more of them.

22 I soon found, however, that my telling the story had excited a great deal of prejudice against me among professors of religion, and was the cause of great persecution, which continued to increase; and though I was an obscure boy, only between fourteen and fifteen years of age, and my circumstances in life such as to make a boy of no consequence in the world, yet men of high standing would take notice sufficient to excite the public mind against me, and create a bitter persecution; and this was common among all the sects—all united to persecute me.

23 It caused me serious reflection then, and often has since, how very strange it was that an obscure boy, of a little over fourteen years of age, and one, too, who was doomed to the necessity of obtaining a scanty maintenance by his daily labor, should be thought a character of sufficient importance to attract the attention of the great ones of the most popular sects of the day, and in a manner to create in them a spirit of the most bitter persecution and reviling. But strange or not, so it was, and it was often the cause of great sorrow to myself.

24 However, it was nevertheless a fact that I had beheld a vision. I have thought since, that I felt much like Paul, when he made his defense before King Agrippa, and related the account of the vision he had when he saw a light, and heard a voice; but still there were but few who believed him; some said he was dishonest, others said he was mad; and he was ridiculed and reviled. But all this did not destroy the

> *reality of his vision. He had seen a vision, he knew he had, and all the persecution under heaven could not make it otherwise; and though they should persecute him unto death, yet he knew, and would know to his latest breath, that he had both seen a light and heard a voice speaking unto him, and all the world could not make him think or believe otherwise.*

God could have picked anyone, but He chose Joseph Smith, a fourteen-year-old boy. Why not a scholarly man? A man educated and well versed in the Scriptures? Why did He pick Moses for all those tasks God required of him? (You can read Moses's story on how God had chosen him in the Bible Old Testament the Book of Exodus).

I believe God could have picked anyone to do His work. However, I also believe that no matter who God chose, the person would have had to take a journey similar to Joseph Smith's or Moses', which prepared them to do God's will.

Missionary Moments:

My last example of Rule #13 has to do with missionary work. As we share our beliefs of the Gospel with our friends, we cannot expect those who hear about our faith or listen to stories about our spiritual life to gain an instant understanding of our testimony.

The task: Learning a gospel principle and gaining a testimony can only be accomplished by taking the journey. To get a solid testimony our friends must focus on the journey, not the task, because it is somewhere within the journey that the task (learning a gospel principle) is accomplished As our friends take that journey, with faith, God will bless them with the gift of the Holy Ghost, which will testify to them of the truthfulness of the gospel principles contained within their journey. We can help them with that journey. As Heavenly Father called Moses and Joseph Smith, we as members of God's Church have been called to help our friends on their journeys back to Heavenly Father's presence.

Rule #13 'Focus on the Journey, Not the Task'

I am going share with you how we can impart our religious beliefs to our friends; thereby, helping them take that spiritual journey to gain the truthfulness of God our Heavenly Father, His son Jesus Christ, and the Holy Ghost.

Whether you are a member of my church or not, if you are a Christian, these steps I am outlining to bring others closer to God still apply. Here are my thoughts for a good way we all can do missionary work.

1.) Setting a good Christian example not only in all our church meetings but in all aspects of our lives, in our homes, at work, school, shopping, and times of recreation, particularly in times of fun. We notice people more, and you will be noticed more when you are enjoying yourself. Why, because we all love to share in a little joy and laughter. It bonds us closer together as friends.

2.) Inviting your friends into your home and to church activities so they can experience your working knowledge of the gospel, and your testimony in action. This doesn't require anything special of you. Be yourself, an excellent example of a servant of the Lord. This is what your friends need to see. Share it with them.

3.) Share a simple testimony of the gospel with your friends. What is a simple testimony? It can be as simple as this: No, thank you, we don't drink coffee. We have been warned that coffee is not suitable for us, and if we abstain from it, the Lord will bless us. You can easily find a conversation where you can share your marriage is different because you were married in the temple of the Lord for time and all eternity. There is always an opportunity to share a simple testimony of your belief in the power of one member of the Godhead, whether it's about God, Jesus Christ, or the Holy Ghost.

4.) Teaching your friends how we pray. If you think this requires you to give a formal lesson on prayer, it does not. When my wife and I go out to eat, we still pray over the food, thanking God that we are blessed enough to be able to still afford the luxury of dining out when so many cannot, and we ask Father in Heaven to bless the food. As we pray, we always use the proper method of prayer. And we do this whether we are eating at a fast-food restaurant, like our favorite, Hardee's, or a formal dinner place. With no pressure, we ask our friends if they would care to join us as we bless the food. I cannot think of a person that has turned us down yet in my 63 years of life.

5.) Pray to Heavenly Father to know when the time is right to invite your friends to meet the missionaries in a casual setting, like a nice dinner in your home. Trust that the missionaries are guided by the Spirit of God. They are not there to pressure your friends into taking the gospel discussions to meet some quota. The missionaries have no quotas. A set of missionaries that are correctly doing the Lord's work are very much in tune with the Holy Ghost and Heavenly Father's plan to help your friends see the light of His gospel. Again, I say trust the missionaries. They have only love in their hearts for you and your friends. We have had the same friends over to our home with the missionaries there many times before the missionaries felt it was time to ask our friends if they would be interested to hear the gospel discussions. You know what? A lot of our friends politely said no. But, guess what: we are still friends.

6.) If your friends feel inspired to take the discussions, let the missionaries do the teaching. That is what the missionaries have been called and given the authority, to do. Our job as members is to share our testimony and be there to support our friends. Supporting our friends is what friends are for.

Rule #13 'Focus on the Journey, Not the Task'

7.) Continue to work with your friends every day, and each day find a way to share some part of your testimony of the gospel.

8.) The journey doesn't stop at baptism. Whether it's your friend that was baptized or a new member with whom you're not well acquainted with, get acquainted with them, and give them that fellowship, love, and support that they will need; those are things that all of us need.

This is also accomplished by doing simple things:

- Greet new members at church each Sunday with a simple greeting.
- Ask new members with sincerity a few simple personal questions; such as how is your spouse or children, how was your week, anything exciting at work? If you can't find the sincerity you need to do this, then I suggest you ask God for some sincerity. You may not like His solution, but I can assure you it will be better than answering Him before the judgment seat why you didn't.
- Find something you have in common with the new member you can share in.
- Remember, they may have become unpopular with their old friends. This could be a time of isolation for the new member as they adjust. In either case, they are going to need casual friends as well as strong, new friends.
- See if there are simple projects you can work on together with the new member; whether it is a project of theirs or one of yours.

These are just a few of the many things we can do to help new members continue their journey.

I have shared with you some sound advice on how we can help our friends through their journey to finding God. I haven't offered any new suggestions that the Leaders of my Church haven't already shared. I could quote you 20 or more pages of scriptures and talks from the Church Leaders, with respect to member missionary work. By putting their suggestions into my own words, I hope that I am able to share with you the way I see we can fulfill God's commandment. Heavenly Father has commanded us to help our friends focus on their journey back to Him. He has also given us a promise and a blessing to go forward with that commandment.

> **(Doctrine & Covenants 18:13-18)**[4]
> *13 And how great is his joy in the soul that repenteth!*
>
> *14 Wherefore, you are called to cry repentance unto this people.*
>
> *15 And if it so be that you should labor all your days in crying repentance unto this people, and bring, save it be one soul unto me, how great shall be your joy with him in the kingdom of my Father!*
>
> *16 And now, if your joy will be great with one soul that you have brought unto me into the kingdom of my Father, how great will be your joy if you should bring many souls unto me!*
>
> *17 Behold, you have my gospel before you, and my rock, and my salvation.*
>
> *18 Ask the Father in my name, in faith believing that you shall receive, and you shall have the Holy Ghost, which manifesteth all things which are expedient unto the children of men.*

This is my testimony to you of how Rule #13 *'Focus on the Journey Not the Task'* can be applied to missionary work.

Way too Long, Finish Up:

In this write-up, I have shown you how Rule #13 pertains to our lives, and how we can apply its philosophy. I believe that by the proper application of Rule #13 to our daily lives, our eyes will be fully opened to see and enjoy experiences we

Rule #13 'Focus on the Journey, Not the Task'

might have otherwise missed. And we will gain greater wisdom and knowledge than we would have with our eyes half-closed. I testify to you that the philosophy of Rule #13 will mold you into a better person, and your life will be richly blessed for it. *'Focus on the Journey Not the Task'*.

I say this in the name of Jesus Christ.

AMEN

Rule #13 'Focus on the Journey, Not the Task'

Endnotes:

1 **King James Version of the Bible, The Old Testament of Our Lord and Saviour Jesus Christ.** Published by The Church of Jesus Christ of Latter-day Saints, Salt Lake City, Utah, USA. Copywrite 2013.

2 **King James Version of the Bible, The New Testament of Our Lord and Saviour Jesus Christ.** Published by The Church of Jesus Christ of Latter-day Saints, Salt Lake City, Utah, USA. Copywrite 2013.

3 **The Book of Mormon Another Testament of Jesus Christ.** Published by The Church of Jesus Christ of Latter-day Saints, Salt Lake City, Utah, USA. The first English edition published in Palmyra, New York, USA, in 1830. Copywrite 2013.

4 **The Doctrine and Covenants of The Church of Jesus Christ of Latter-Day Saints.** Containing Revelations Give to Joseph Smith, the Prophet. With some additions by his successors in the Presidency of the Church. Published by The Church of Jesus Christ of Latter-day Saints, Salt Lake City, Utah, USA. Copywrite 2013.

5 **The Pearl of Great Price.** A selection from the revelations, translations, and narrations of Joseph Smith, First Prophet, seer, and revelator to The Church of Jesus Christ of Latter-Day Saints. Published by The Church of Jesus Christ of Latter-day Saints, Salt Lake City, Utah, USA. Copywrite 2013.

6 **President Dieter F. Uchtdorf, 2012 October General Conference, "Of Regrets and Resolutions."** The 182nd Semiannual General Conference of the Church of Jesus Christ of Latter-day Saints, October 6, 2012, Saturday Morning Session. Published in the Ensign magazine, Volume 42 Number 11, Page 23 Paragraph 14, November 2012. An official magazine of the Church of Jesus Christ of Latter-day Saints, published by the Church of Jesus Christ of Latter-day Saints, 50 E. North Temple Street, Salt Lake City, UT, 84150-3220, USA. Retrieved February 10, 2019, from churchofjesuschrist.org website: https://www.churchofjesuschrist.org/study/ensign/2012/11/saturday-morning-session/of-regrets-and-resolutions?lang=eng

7 **Peter Ferdinand Drunker.** Peter Drucker. (n.d.). AZQuotes.com. Retrieved February 20, 2019, from AZQuotes.com Web site: https://www.azquotes.com/quote/81878. Also see, "Seven Habits of Highly Effective People" by Stephen R. Covey, (p. 101), 1989.

8 **Helen Keller.** Helen Keller Quotes. (n.d.). BrainyQuote.com. Retrieved November 29, 2019, from BrainyQuote.com Web site: https://www.brainyquote.com/quotes/helen_keller_114884

9 **Joseph B. Wirthlin, 1990 October General Conference, "The Straight and Narrow Way."** The 160th Semiannual General Conference of the Church of Jesus Christ of Latter-day Saints, October 7, 1990, Sunday Morning Session. Published in the Ensign magazine, Volume 20 Number 11, November 1990. An official magazine of the Church of Jesus Christ of Latter-day Saints, published by the Church of Jesus Christ of Latter-day Saints, 50 E. North Temple Street, Salt Lake City, UT, 84150-3220, USA. Retrieve February 10, 2019, from churchofjesuschrist.org website: https://www.churchofjesuschrist.org/study/ensign/1990/11/the-straight-and-narrow-way?lang=eng.

Rule #13 'Focus on the Journey, Not the Task'

Now I Know My ABCs

Rule #14
'If You Want to Be an 'A' Student Hang Out With the 'A' Students'

Rule #14
'If You Want to Be an 'A' Student Hang Out With the 'A' Students'

The Beginning is The End:

Rule #14 *'If You Want to Be an 'A' Student Hang Out With the 'A' Students'* is total inspiration from Heaven and literally changed my life. Either God or one of His guiding Angels that watches over me whispered this rule into my ear. There are times in my life when I have to be hit directly on the head in order to wake up the brain so that I can truly understand a principle that is right in front of me. But seriously, in this case, literally and truthfully, I heard this rule whispered to me within my mind. Not just once, but three times.

The fundamentals of this rule are simple. If you want to be the best, at whatever you set out to accomplish, you need the best tools you can get your hands on. In addition to the best tools, you also need to surround yourself with people that:

1.) are seeking the same goal

2.) have the skills to learn

3.) have a motivated attitude that pushes them to the top of the class.

In other words, they are the 'A' students in whatever it is you are seeking to learn.

The Big Bang Theory or The God Principle:

The principles that form the fundamental truths that support Rule #14 have existed from the beginning of the beginning, no matter wherever your theory of where the beginning is.

The ability to recognize Rule #14 and to implement its principle in your life is different for each of us. Sadly, some people never learn how to tap into the potentials of this rule. Yet Rule #14, whether we understand it or not, influences

Rule #14 'If You Want to Be an 'A' Student Hang Out With the 'A' Students'

each and every one of us each day. It is a rule that you either learn to manage directly, or else indirectly, it will manage you.

As I became aware of Rule #14, the idea that I could employ this philosophy to the betterment of my life and subsequently understanding that the power of the guiding principle could bestow limitless blessings upon me was mind-blowing. It was as great of an awakening to me as learning how to make fire was to the caveman. Rule #14 lit the fires of my mind and opened the door to learning that allowed the knowledge of the universe to flow in and stay in. It is one of the most wonderful gifts of wisdom God has given me as a blessing.

Learning the Hard Way:

I want to share with you the story of how the light of Rule #14 came to me and how it has vanquished the dark fog in my mind that created a barrier that hindered my ability to learn. To do that, I need you to step back in time with me so I can give you a little history about my life and my joys of pain (No, just pain) in learning.

In my younger school years, grades 1 through 10, becoming a wise, educated man, seemed an impossible task. My brain gave the impression it was going to resist every effort the teachers or I made on it to gather more knowledge. During those years, most of my school grades were Cs and Ds, based on a grading system where an A is the best and F the worst. I am not sure I ever made more than a single A. And if I made a B, I can tell you it was time for a happy dance and a celebration. Anytime I earned a B, it filled me with a little hope that learning was a possibility. It also meant one less whipping.

My Dad had a rule, bringing home any grade less than a C+ merited an automatic lashing with a leather belt to the butt. You see, my Dad's theory was that a good butt lashing would motivate me to work harder and thus inspire my brain to function harder. How well do you think that worked? What my dad never comprehended was that my brain was already working at maximum capacity. And what my brain really

Rule #14 'If You Want to Be an 'A' Student Hang Out With the 'A' Students'

needed was to be trained on how to work smarter, not harder. Dad never caught on to the 'work smarter, not harder' concept. Nor did I until high school was well behind me.

As you can surmise, I got my butt whipped just about every report card day. There was nothing I could do about it. Fortunately, in the 4th grade, my Mom took care of the problem. She divorced my father, and after that, I didn't see much of him. But by that time, I was already ten years old, and I was pretty well convinced that there was little or nothing I could do to improve in school or change my learning disability.

As a young kid, I felt that somehow or in some way, I had been cheated out of a few desperately needed brain cells. I came up with a theory on how it happened too. My theory was that either my older brother, born just before me or my younger sister, born just after me, were each given an additional portion of brains that were supposed to be reserved for me. Why did I think this? Well, neither my older brother nor my younger sister ever had any trouble making good grades in school. Learning was easy for them, but not for me. Therefore, either my old brother got a share of the brains intended for me, or when I was born, I left some behind, and my younger sister thought they were hers, or worst case both. My theory seems silly and far-fetched now, but as a kid, I was desperate for an explanation. Regardless of my hard work, the low grades and the whippings persisted. I grew up truly feeling that I had been shorted a few brain cells and believing school and I was not meant to get along.

Towards the end of my sophomore year, I dropped out of school. Financial issues at home required me to get a full-time job. And even though Dad's lashings didn't help improve my performance in the education department, they did condition me to have a good work ethic. Unfortunately, without a formal education, I only qualified for jobs that paid minimum wage.

A minimum wage was not cutting it. The only logical solution for me was to get my GED and then join the military, which meant I had to go back to school. School, a word that fills me

Rule #14 'If You Want to Be an 'A' Student Hang Out With the 'A' Students'

with dread. I thought for sure I wouldn't be able to handle the informal school setting offered in preparation for the GED any better than I did traditional high school. Instead, I found that the teachers at the learning center were different than other teachers I had encountered. They all did an exceptional job of preparing me for the GED test. Their help enabled me to pass my GED test in 6 months. Because of my hard-working attitude, one teacher, in particular, took a liking to me and gave me a lot of one-on-one training. She was as an Angel sent from God. It seems like God is always sending Angels to help me in life.

My wife is one of those Angels too.

To the Left, To the Left, To the Left Right Left:

As soon as I had my GED in hand, I was at the military recruiter's office signing up to join the Air Force. After months of military boot camp and basic training, I found myself back in school. That's right, that dreaded word *school* again. I studied and trained to work on nuclear weapons for 18 months.

I joined the Air Force because my GED math scores were just high enough for the Air Force to place me in a job in the field of electronics. My recruiter found me a position in the Minuteman III Missile System program. At the time, it was the military's top nuclear intercontinental ballistic missile weapon system.

The first few weeks of school were nerve-racking. If I failed any section of the 18-month course, I could be transferred to a job of peeling potatoes or worse, discharged. Neither of those alternatives sounded good to me. No, I did not want to peel potatoes for a living. That did not sound appealing at all. Being discharged was not on my list of preferred options, either. I needed the financial security the Air Force offered. That was the whole reason I signed up to serve my country for 5 ½ years.

Rule #14 'If You Want to Be an 'A' Student Hang Out With the 'A' Students'

After a couple weeks of classes, I settled in and accepted the fact that I was back in school, and I needed to make it work. Acceptance and commitment were the first steps I took to calm my fears. Once my fear was under control, military school seemed to get easier, and I started earning those coveted B letter grades, the ones that had always eluded me until now. At the time, I didn't reflect on why the military school was so much easier than grade school. So many other things in life were stressing me out that I was just glad the worry of school had eased. It felt so good receiving B's. Seeing them on my evaluation sheet was a morale boost. It changed my attitude toward my learning ability, and it gave me some much-needed self-confidence.

You're Getting Warmer:

After my commitment to the military was up, I returned to civilian life. Sadly, however, my military training left me with a skill set that didn't transfer to many jobs in the civilian market. Let's face it, there are not many civilian jobs dealing with nuclear weapons in the USA. I suppose I could have applied for an overseas terrorist job. LOL. No, I don't think so. So, since a career as high paying terrorist wasn't an option, I once again found myself working in jobs that paid little better than minimum wage.

After spending five cold years in Wyoming working for the military, I decided it was time to live in a much warmer climate, like Florida. Why Florida, and not some other warm state, like Hawaii? Hawaii was just a little too far from my home state of Iowa and my family. And did I mention that I knew a good-looking young woman that lived in Florida? She enticed me with the lure of her companionship, the promise of a good job, warm weather, and the beautiful white sandy beaches of the Gulf of Mexico to relax on. She also mentioned that if I wished to further my education that Florida had a lot of great education centers that offered electronic and computer degrees.

**Rule #14 'If You Want to Be an 'A' Student
Hang Out With the 'A' Students'**

Other than the going back to school part, she presented an offer that was hard for a young, single man like me to turn down. Particularly since no other warm state in the union was willing to match the offer or presented better options.

I moved to Florida, and for the first few years, I lived and worked in a motel, as well as other jobs in construction to make a living. It wasn't a great life, and it certainly wasn't the attractive life the young woman had presented to me, but I was surviving. As for the beautiful young woman? Well, let's just say that beauty only goes so far, and several months after I arrived, the relationship ended.

I See the Light:

I remember clearly the events of the day that inspiration struck, and Rule #14 lit up my mind. It was July, and there was a record-breaking heatwave moving through the state. That summer, I was working as a Hot Tar Roofer. The Florida sun was sizzling hot, doing its level best to bake my brains and body. Truthfully, I drank at least 5 gallons of water. While it sounds comical, overhydration is no laughing matter, nor is it healthy for the body. But neither is heat exhaustion, and it was either stay hydrated or die of heatstroke.

A Little Background Please:

Replacing a roof at any time of the year is a risky business. Because at some point in the replacement progress, your entire house is exposed to the outside elements. In Florida, this is more prevalent during the summer months due to the tropical rains that occur.

These tropical storms are both a curse and a blessing. You ask, "Why"? Well, most Northerners don't truly know what a summer rain is. But if you have ever lived in Florida, you would have the wisdom of understanding, that you thank God for the rain that cooled the air and ground, which in-turn blesses you with the much-needed relief from the heat. Of course, once the sun returns, this blessing becomes a curse as the persistent heat turns the fresh rainwater into steam, making the humidity rise to an even more unbearable level than before and creating an effect where walking outdoors feels more like walking into a very, hot indoor sauna.

For the roofing companies, heat and humidity are not an issue; those are the workers' problems to deal with. For the company, the tropical storms pose a different problem. One of these big babies can sneak up and drench you and the house you are working on, making it wetter, soggier, and more disgusting than any child's sopping-wet diaper you have ever changed.

A tropical rainstorm is not a little bit of rain. It's a storm that pops up with minimal warning and drops anywhere from three to five inches of rain in an hour's time. Do you have any idea how much damage an exposed house takes after being pounded for an hour by torrential rain? Let's not say an hour. Let's make it 15 to 20 minutes. Imagine dumping a five-gallon bucket of water over your head. How long did it take, and how wet do you get? That's what you'd experience if you were standing outside in one of these storms.

If your mind didn't comprehend the humorous analogy between being drenched by a tropical storm and a soaked diaper, and your face at the moment had this confused blank stare that states I don't get it, then you haven't changed enough diapers in your lifetime. Wait till you're a great grandfather and have five grown children, who gave birth to your eighteen grandchildren, who then gave birth to your eight great-grandchildren. You'll laugh then.

I assure you a sopping wet diaper can be drier than an exposed house that just got drenched by a tropical storm.

The ceiling falls to the floor, and on its way down covers everything in its path. It then mixes with the carpet. Everything at the ground level is floating in two to three inches of water. The drywall that hung on the wall is now bulging and decaying and can no longer support the family pictures and paintings. Every part of what was once a beautiful house

Rule #14 'If You Want to Be an 'A' Student Hang Out With the 'A' Students'

interior is now adding color and flavor to the carpet-drywall mix brewing on the floor.

The picture in your mind can be about as nasty as your imagination can make it. And the smell? After the house sits for a few days while the insurance adjuster assesses the damage, the aroma is pretty close to that of a refrigerator or freezer full of food left unplugged for days. Oh, wait! The refrigerator and freezer have been left unplugged for days because the electricity had to be turned off for protection. We can't be mixing water and electricity.

The damage caused by a house exposed to just one of these storms can put a roofing company out of business. I can assure you that the customer doesn't blame the weatherman for a lousy forecast if his house gets damage. He holds the roofing company responsible. The weatherman may have predicted a sunny day, but that's not his problem if mother nature does not comply. If roofers could sue the weather forecasters for an incorrect forecast, the roofing companies would be rich. For this reason, roofing companies, if legally state licensed (in Florida, many are not) have to carry liability insurance with a high dollar coverage and the premium is costly. Collect a claim against that policy, and the cost skyrockets.

A house receiving the amount of damage I described is very rare, but it does happen. I personally know of two cases. Neither of which were with the roofing company I worked for. Jack, the company owner, was a very cautious man, a born Floridian that I believe knew how to read and predict the weather better than any forecaster.

Oh! Did I mention that the bay area where I lived in is the lightning capital of the world? The weather determines if and when the roofing company makes a dollar and your employees are able to work. As a roofer, whether I work or not determines if I eat and pay the bills that week. So, if the conditions for rain are low, making the chance high for a bright, sunny, day the roofer works, no matter how hot the day is. There were no safety agencies such as OSHA to ensure

Rule #14 'If You Want to Be an 'A' Student Hang Out With the 'A' Students'

employee safety back when I was a roofer. Heatstroke and second-degree sunburns were just a part of the risk. And yes, from time to time, roofers do get hit by lightning.

The heat and lightning are dangerous to deal with, but if as you work, you play it smart; they're beatable. There are other dangers involved in hot tar roofing more likely to happen that I worried about. These are just as dangerous and can cause just as much pain. The heat of the work may drain the energy from your body, leaving you to feel like a limp wet overcooked noodle at the end of the day. But, the hot boiling tar itself can and has fried a person to death. It's not the way I would want to die. There was (note the word was) a guy I had worked with several seasons and grew to be friends with. Due to a work disagreement with the foreman, he quit and went to work for another roofing company. On the second week at his new job, he tripped on a piece of work equipment and fell off the one-story flat roof into an opened tar kettle. He lived long enough to jump out of the kettle and then died a few minutes later. The hot tar cooled and incased 60% of the lower and upper left side of his body.

The workers that were there at the time of the incident say it happened because he was unacquainted with the team's work habits and didn't see the piece of equipment placed on the roof by a fellow worker. The equipment? A shovel that had been laid by the ladder to be taken off the roof by the next worker going down.

I was told by his girlfriend that an autopsy found traces of alcohol in my friend's bloodstream, and the insurance company was trying to blame the accident on the consumption of alcohol mixed with the heat of the day in an attempt not to pay. I don't drink alcohol, but a lot of the roofing guys did during lunch. And with some, it did end up being a little too much. I knew my friend well and had eaten enough lunches with him to know that he would never risk his life or job by working drunk. I also knew a lot of other workers that had been fired for that very reason. All of this is sad but true.

Rule #14 'If You Want to Be an 'A' Student Hang Out With the 'A' Students'

Now the odds of falling into a hot tar kettle are slim. That still leaves a lot of other ways of getting severely burned by molten tar. Such as, while you are rolling out the tar paper, the hot tar mopper hits your hand, leg, or foot with a mop full of tar. I experienced all three burns in small degrees.

Because you are standing on a freshly hot tarred roof, some of the guys wore lightweight tennis shoes to help keep their feet cool. And to help cool the rest of their body, some were dumb enough to only wear long-legged shorts and tank top tee-shirts. Not me. I wore heavy leather ankle boots and thick denim jeans. No, tank top for me, but I did wear a short-sleeve tee-shirt, and opened a buttoned short-sleeve shirt.

Wearing gloves is another suggested safety guideline, but rarely followed. It is hard to handle and maneuver the tar paper, rolling it out to cover freshly laid hot tar while wearing gloves. The tar paper roll has to be rolled out flat and straight down the length of the roof to ensure proper coverage and thickness, without any kinks that could later turn into cracks and cause a potential for leaks. Many times, I have picked up a partial roll of tar paper to start a new run, and as I did, I found myself shaking hands with a blob of uncooled tar that clung to the edge of the roll. You want to talk about being hot-handed? LOL. Ever shake hands with a hot piece of tar? It was during those moments I thought very strongly about getting my gloves, but I was too tired, hot, burned, and sore to climb down the ladder to get them from the truck. It just seemed like a long journey in the heat that included another painful trip up and down a tar splattered, rickety ladder to get those gloves. And then I'd be pulling them on and off all thru the day anyway. Besides, the other guys rarely wore theirs, and being in my early twenties, I didn't want to look like a wimp next to my fellow employees. These are construction workers' people! Capiche?

Long-sleeve shirts, thick denim jeans, heavy leather boots, and leather gloves were the recommended wear, but not enforced. Remember! No safety laws back then. Whatever your employer enforced was the rule. How long do you think

Rule #14 'If You Want to Be an 'A' Student Hang Out With the 'A' Students'

you would last dressed to those standards standing under the sun, 98 degrees cool with 90% humidity?

Most of the time, I ran the hot tar kettle and carried the hot molten tar in a five-gallon tin bucket up to the roof. The tar is used to seal the new tar paper to the roof, and to do so, its temperature needs to be an average of 450 to 550 degrees. To compensate for cooling while carrying it from the kettle to the roof the tar while in the kettle needs to stay at around 650 degrees.

So, my biggest fear wasn't getting hit by a hot mop or burned by hot tar on the end of a roll. My biggest horror was water getting anywhere near the boiling tar. You see, water and hot tar don't mix well. It is like mixing hot oil and water. Not a good combo and very explosive. Your own sweat is a source of water. So, you have to be careful around the hot tar kettle. When even a drop of your sweat hits the hot tar, it can cause the boiling tar to explode into an eruption like a solar flare. If you're not fast enough to move out of its way, tiny pieces of hot tar will then splatter on to your body. When you are carrying a 5-gallon bucket of this stuff, you wipe the sweat from your face and arms before you start. Then you pray that you make it to your destination before another drop forms and falls from your body and into the bucket. There is no place to run when you are the one carrying the bucket. You can't put the bucket down to wipe the fresh sweat from your arm. The heat of the bucket will burn the customer's grass, and that will come out of your pocket. Nor can you drop the bucket before the sweat hits the tar and explodes. If you are climbing the ladder when that sweat hits, you grit your teeth and just keep climbing. There is no escaping the pain that will follow. And if you think that splatter of tar is going to miss you, well don't. Tar has a mind of its own and will hunt for any piece of bare skin it can find to land on.

I don't care how small the burn area is, when you are getting burned at 450 to 650 degrees, it doesn't feel good. If you think a 200 degrees variance makes much difference, it doesn't. It is the same pain level at either temperature. The hotter it is means it digs into your skin a little deeper. This is the point where no matter how hot a day it is, you rethink your decision not to wear that long sleeve shirt, and you promise yourself you will wear one tomorrow. But you don't.

Side note, I always wore heavy leather gloves while working around the kettle and carrying the bucket. So, I wasn't completely stupid.

The End of Days:

Back to my epiphany. I had labored hard all that day. Multiple splatters of hot tar had burned and blistered their way deep into my skin. The skin and tar had now become one, and the only way to remove the tar was to peel it off and take the skin with it. As I stretched out in a tub of warm water, attempting to soak the grime out of my pores and ease the pain in my body. I looked at all the tar burn scars that dotted my arms and part of my chest. As I peeled off another piece of tar attached to the blistered skin from my arm, I said to myself out loud, "This will leave another scar." The stinging pain awakened my tired mind. I once again reflected on the fact that this was not the career I had hoped for. Nor was it the way I planned to support myself for the rest of my life.

Then that dreaded idea of going back to school blossomed in my mind. The thought was strong. I wondered why? I knew the answer but didn't want to admit it. Education was the only permanent solution to my situation.

While I lay in the tub, the thought, 'I need to go back to school' grew stronger and stronger. I kept fighting it, telling myself I wasn't cut out of good solid school stock. My brain just didn't function well in a classroom. The harder I pushed back on thoughts of returning to school, the more intense the need to go back became. School was winning.

Slowly I started letting a little of the positive aspects of going back to school warm my soul. Perhaps I could build on the electronic training had I received in the military. But just as quickly the darkness of failure crept back into my mind and

Rule #14 'If You Want to Be an 'A' Student Hang Out With the 'A' Students'

defeated any positive notions of school, I pondered. My mind flooded with images of report cards filled with pitiful grades. I could hear the crack of my father's lashings across my backside, and the pain of those memories followed.

Visions of returning to school weren't giving up the fight, and the idea continued to haunt me. The fear of failure, however, had won more ground, and despair was attempting to set in. I needed to break the school curse.

There was only one important option that I had not tried yet, and I needed to do. I bowed my head forward, folded my arms tight to my body, closed my eyes, and uttered a prayer to my Father in Heaven. I told Him that if I did find a way to go back to school, I needed Him to help me. I needed to understand how I was going to make it with my limited brainpower. I told Him that I needed something more than just me because just me was not going to cut it.

An answer came to me as a thought sounding in my mind. I heard it clearer than someone talking to me just a few feet away. Yet I knew the voice was in my head, and it sounded similar to my own. It said, "If you want to be an 'A' student, you need to hang out with the 'A' students." I answered the voice back with my thoughts vocally and loudly and said, "What?" Then I heard the voice repeat the same message. I answered back only a little stronger, "Say what? Are you crazy? Why would an 'A' student want to hang out with a pea brain like me?" Then I heard it a third time in a fading voice, "If you want to be an 'A' student, you need to hang out with the 'A' students." Then there was silence, and I was left to ponder on the inspiration I had just been given.

I repeated the inspired message to myself out loud, as I tried to grasp the full meaning of what was being conveyed to me. As I heard the words ring in my ears, I felt the warmth of their wisdom fill me. No, the warmth was not due to the fact that I was soaking in a hot bath. It was like a warm, calming hug to my soul.

Rule #14 'If You Want to Be an 'A' Student Hang Out With the 'A' Students'

Judy, Judy, Judy:

I slid down, deep into the waters of the tub, and meditated on the meaning of what I had heard. I repeated the message again, out loud. As I did a memory popped into my head. I was in high school chemistry, and a young woman named Judy Zimmerman had offered to team up with me for a lab project.

My normal lab partner was a friend that lived at the end of the block from me, George O'Rourke. Trumpet George, I called him. Why? Because George was learning to play the trumpet with the school band. Every day George had to carry his trumpet as he walked to and from school. Whenever George walked home with me, he complained about how heavy his trumpet was until I volunteered to relieve him of the burden.

George was also Mister Popular, and he liked being a class clown. He worked harder to get a laugh out of his classmates than he did on his school assignments. George's personality and behavior made chemistry class a blast, literally, and since I was usually his lab partner, I was guilty of joining in the fun.

Just to give you an idea of our shenanigans, during one chemistry class, George and I knocked out the electrical power to the school's whole west wing for two hours, and no, I am not going to tell you how we did it.

Judy and George had only one thing in common. George was a handsome young man, and Judy was extremely cute. That is where their similarities stopped. Judy never tried to do anything to draw attention to herself, where George tried to be at the center of everything, all eyes on him.

I had known Judy since 5th grade. We weren't close friends but friendly enough that we would sit and talk from time to time. In class, I was continually glancing in Judy's direction to see what she was up to. To be truthful, it was mainly because she was so cute, and my heart had a little crush on her. Every time I would look her way, Judy was listening to the teacher's lecture, reading her chemistry book, or working

Rule #14 'If You Want to Be an 'A' Student Hang Out With the 'A' Students'

on class experiments. Judy seemed to always be focused on her schoolwork. She was an 'A' student in all her classes.

As I sat in the tub filtering through my memories, I focused on one moment in particular with Judy. The chemistry teacher had the class switch up lab partners for a new experiment that would take a couple of weeks to complete. If you ask me, I think the teacher did that because the class was becoming unruly, and he wanted to separate a few of the troublemakers--like George and me.

Side note: Looking back, I was disappointed in myself. In high school, I felt deeply isolated and lonely, so sometimes, I went along with the crowd in an attempt to feel liked and included. Sometimes that meant acting like George. Instead, I should have been the stronger Alpha male and set a good example, too often, I was weak and allowed myself to be pulled in with the crowd, participating in their performance. The problem was, it wasn't the direction my heart and soul really wanted to go.

This is an important point because my heart and soul really wanted to be headed in the direction I saw Judy going.

Returning to the story.

During the partner change up, Judy came over and asked me if I wanted to team up with her. I was in shock but was able to squeak out a 'yes.'

That lab project is one of the few times in the history of my schooling that I got an A. Well, an A-, but that is still in the 'A' category. Judy showed me how to write the reports and helped me organize my notes. She also corrected my grammar and spelling, that alone made Judy a Heavenly Angel in my estimation. I couldn't thank her enough for all her help. Halfway through that lab project, I asked Judy if she would continue to be my partner after that assignment was complete. No, I wasn't asking her to marry me; although I probably thought about it. I was asking her to be my lab partner, not a life partner.

Rule #14 'If You Want to Be an 'A' Student Hang Out With the 'A' Students'

I told her that I really needed her help. She said she couldn't. It wouldn't be fair to her current lab partner, who at the moment was stuck working with George. If Judy agreed to be my partner, her friend would have to work with George for the remainder of the year. I couldn't say much in response since I had allowed George to convince me to team up at the being of the semester.

Since Judy couldn't switch lab partners, I did the next best thing I could think of and asked her if I could walk her home from school. I offered to carry her books or just keep her company. Sadly, she shot down that proposal, as well. Judy thanked me for the offer and said she would if she could, but her father had strict rules against socializing with boys--no exceptions, period. She went on to point out that her regular lab partner was a girl, chosen on purpose because of her father's strictness. She said it had taken a lot of courage to ask me to be her partner for this project. She had been afraid she would get in trouble with her father, but figured if he did become upset, she could blame it on the teacher.

Toward the end of our conversation, Judy brushed her hair back with her hands, revealing her full face. She had an incredible pair of lips, forming a sweet, gentle smile. Her cheeks were flushed, and her glistening brown eyes were looking directly into mine. In a smooth, soft voice, she said something that surprised me. Her voice simply said that she had enjoyed partnering with me. It wasn't much, but that look on her face and in her eyes was expressing more. The compliment left me speechless with my heart skipping beats for a moment. Had Judy just told me something important, or did my cupid miss a hint? In that silent moment, as I gazed at her face, I wanted to burn a picture in my mind of this beautiful girl and protect it for time and eternity. I thought deeply of asking her if she'd be my girl, but something within me said just take the moment and the compliment, breathe it in and be happy with that. That thought woke me from her trance and calmed my emotions down from a bonfire to warm burning coals. Very warm burning coals. I returned Judy's compliment by telling her that hanging out with her had made me a better student. She let out a little giggling sound and smiled as she backed away, keeping her eyes glued to mine. Then she slipped around the corner and disappeared. I stood there watching her leave and wanting to follow. And that was the end of that.

Judy was an 'A' student, and during those two weeks, I studied with her; I was and felt like an 'A' student too. Other than a few shorter conversations when our paths would cross, nothing ever happened between Judy and me. Not even one date. I did sneak in one walk. I mean, what should you do when you run into a lady walking in the same direction? You do the gentlemanly thing, walk home with her and carry her books, right?

Rub a Dub Dub Me in a Tub:

Still soaking in the warm bathtub, I continued to ponder the good memories and feelings of those moments with Judy. As I reflected on them, I felt peace and joy rush into me, and the pain from the tar burns on my arms faded away. The joy of that short journey I had retaken with Judy was so powerful that it made it easy to forget about the stinging in my skin and the scars on my body. It had been a significant moment in my life with another one of God's angels.

And the Rocket's Red Glare:

As the thoughts of Judy faded back from where they came, another memory popped into my head. This one was about my schooling experience while in the military. I was envisioning in my mind's eye my military friends and me in our classroom working on one of our assignments together. I remembered how the learning environment there seemed much easier and more comfortable.

I'll never forget our Training Instructor's opening remarks on the first day of class. To paraphrase his words:

> This is not a class of individuals. We are a team, and one-quarter of your grade is based on your

Rule #14 'If You Want to Be an 'A' Student Hang Out With the 'A' Students'

ability to function as a team. Failing a quarter of your grade gets you washed out of my part of the course and perhaps the program. Therefore, if your teammate is failing or falling behind, then you need to consider it as if you, personally, are failing or falling behind. At some point in your training, you will be performing hands-on training, and you will be working on a dummy Minuteman III missile in mockup Minuteman III missile silos. It will be important that your team works as one. You will be troubleshooting and repairing a dummy Minuteman III missile. You will handle all the equipment as if it is real, and some of the equipment is. The Minutemen III missile is the most powerful nuclear weapon in the military's arsenal. Nuclear weapons and the equipment you will be working on are not toys. You cannot just say 'Oops!' if one of your team members makes a mistake. Saying 'Oh Shit!' will be a far, far, understatement to what the consequences could be. Because in real life with real nuclear weapons, you would all be dead. Work together and help each other to be your best. I want everyone in this class to receive nothing less than 100% at the end of this course. This is your class, and you will be the best. You all are starting this next part of your 18-month training course together, and at the end of the next 12-months, I want to see you all together graduating as one. Boys and girls welcome to the real start of your new military career. When you have successfully finished, you will be men and women, ready to help keep our country safe.

As I remembered his speech, I came to understand why learning in the military was easier than when I was in grade school. My team members were there to support me in areas where I was weak. I was better and faster at learning with hands-on training than with other training styles. In fact, in a

Rule #14 'If You Want to Be an 'A' Student Hang Out With the 'A' Students'

hands-on environment, I learned faster than my teammates. Many times, I taught them.

Grasping the mechanics of things is easier for me than it is for most people. Show me how to do something one time, and I usually get it. Yet when it came to reading comprehension, I was terrible. My writing skills... well, forget it. Grammar and spelling are at the bottom of my skills list. Thank God, I now have a computer and word processing to help me overcome these weaknesses, or you would not be reading this book. Even with the aid of the computer and the blessing it has brought to my life, I still rely on my wonderful grandson, my sister, and others to proofread all my writings. I find that I still need to work as a member of a team to be successful.

Individually, the people I trained with in my military course were not 'A' student quality, but when we worked together, we formed an 'A' student team. Our team graduated with the highest combined score of any other class that trained before us. This awarded us the option of serving at our 'first base of choice'. That meant I could choose where I wanted to live and work. I would be transferred to the base of my choosing after training was complete. And because of the nature of the missile job I was to perform, I would, more than likely, stay there for the remainder of my military career.

My brain started to get well heated by the inspirational power of Rule #14, on the other hand, my bathtub water was getting cold. I stepped out of the tub with a mission. Empowered with this new ruling principle, it was time to take action and work out how I was going to implement it for the betterment of my life.

The End is the Beginning:

And that my friends is how I was inspirationally given Rule #14. What I haven't told you is how it came to be a new ruling principle in my life.

You have to have faith before you can gain a testimony. The next part of the story is how I used my faith to gain knowledge of the truthfulness of the guiding principles empowered in Rule #14. It is one thing to understand that a rule exists, but it is another to have an actual knowledge of the power of the rule when you choose to adhere to it. The only way to gain this knowledge is by implementing the rule successfully. That can only be done when you take hold of the Rule and implement it with the appended faith that the Lord will guide your path to success. Poor implementation of any Rule will be a failure, and the only testimony you get from failure is the power of a failed Rule.

Without God's guidance, you are setting yourself up for failure. You need his guidance to succeed. He is the Master Teacher, the number one 'A' student in all things. Why would you not want Him as a part of your team? Just because I now had this new Rule in my head did not mean I had the knowledge and wisdom of how to implement it.

There were still a thousand unanswered questions of how, what, or where associated with going back to school. I mean, you don't just say, "Ok, I am going back to school," and then you walk out the door with a backpack. Basic questions had to be answered: What kind of education should I be going for? Then, what school should I go to? What will the cost be? Where will the money come from? How do I manage work and school at the same time? How do I get the other 'A' students to hang out and study with this pea-size-brain student? And a pea brain student is precisely how I classified myself at that time.

As we seek the answers to our questions, we can only be guided through the many obstacles and detours that lie in our path to success by hearing God's guidance, conveyed to us through the powerful influences of the Holy Ghost. It always comes back to faith before knowledge.

Finding the Power Within:

Rule #14 is about faith, implementation, and going to college. *College*, I dreaded that word more than the word *school*. This

Rule #14 'If You Want to Be an 'A' Student Hang Out With the 'A' Students'

brings instant fear to mind, and that is why I needed to exercise faith in God's inspiration.

Since I loved my job in the military working on the electronic equipment and computers that supported the missiles, the career choice was easy. I decided to study something to do with electronics. Finding the school was a lot harder.

In my day, there was no internet, no web surfing for information. I am not sure the word personal computer (PC) existed yet either. I needed a school that was nearby, close enough that I could commute back and forth from work or home (motel at the time). I called a technical college in Tampa, which was about an hour's drive. After talking to them, I decided to turn them down. However, for some reason, the college really wanted me. A college recruiter came to my motel to convince me that I would be a good fit. She explained that part of my military training would qualify me to test out of some of the basic electronic classes, which would, in turn, reduce the cost for my degree.

The idea of cutting costs intrigued me, and this was the only college in the area that had offered me credit for my military schooling. The offer was tempting, and I was ready to accept it when an echo of the words for Rule #14 whispered quietly in my mind. I felt inspired to turn down the offer to test out of any classes.

So, I declined her offer to test out and countered by asking if she could provide me with a list of students in my classes that were 'A' students in high school. The recruiter looked at me, puzzled for a few moments, and then she replied, saying she thought she could work something out.

Then we talked about the cost and financing, an area I knew nothing about other than I was poor enough to apply for welfare, but self-reliant enough not to. The recruiter assured me that with $100, my GI bill's re-education benefits, and a small student loan, I could cover the costs for all my school needs. But the deal was based on whether I could keep my grades up. She also informed me that I didn't have to start paying back my student loans until six months after I had completed my schooling and that their college had a 90% job placement average in my chosen field of study. That would be, of course, if I graduated with a 3.0-grade average or higher. I signed the papers. The college was picked. The next thing I had to do was figure out how I was going assemble my team of 'A' students.

Breaking Barriers or Splitting the Atom:

On the first day of classes, I stopped by the recruiter's office to see if she had my list ready, and sure enough, a woman of her word, she did. She handed me a list of names that she felt were the best people to start a study group with.

> **(Book of Mormon: Moroni 7:5)**[3]
> *5 For I remember the word of God which saith by their works ye shall know them; for if their works be good, then they are good also.*
>
> **(Book of Mormon: 3 Nephi 14:16-18)**[3]
> *16 Ye shall know them by their fruits. Do men gather grapes of thorns, or figs of thistles?*
>
> *17 Even so every good tree bringeth forth good fruit; but a corrupt tree bringeth forth evil fruit.*
>
> *18 A good tree cannot bring forth evil fruit, neither a corrupt tree bring forth good fruit.*

Now I needed to figure out how I was going to get a group of 'A' students to let a pea-brain like me join their group. I thought for sure this was going to be the hardest part. I mean, these guys cluster together like iron filings to a magnet. They seem to be able to pick each other out of a crowd, and then they magically group together. You could have a football stadium filled with people and then start with all the brainy nerds sprinkled about the stadium. If you mark them with some sort of tracker, you will find that within minutes, the brainy nerds would start clustering into a group. I can see myself monitoring little pinpoints of light on a tracking device coming together into a giant glowing ball. Once the group

Rule #14 'If You Want to Be an 'A' Student Hang Out With the 'A' Students'

cluster is formed, there is no penetrating it. All the non 'A' student people just bounce off the barrier that forms around them. Somehow, I had to penetrate that barrier. The key to penetrating the barrier was one's IQ. The stronger the IQ, the easier it is to join a cluster. I wasn't giving myself much hope with the energy of my IQ.

I had been praying to Heavenly Father for help on how to penetrate one of these brainy nerd clusters weeks before school started. God inspired me with a plan. One of the reasons I did not opt to test out of any classes was that I needed a few easy courses. By already knowing most of the course material it gave me a better chance at acing the weekly tests. This, in turn, would make me look like an 'A' student. I hoped that this would draw the brainy cluster to me.

I had several other assets that played to my advantage. For one, the military had already trained me on just about every piece of electronic equipment that we used during our school labs. Most of the students in my class had never seen, let alone worked with an Oscilloscope, Frequency Meter, or a Multimeter used for reading volts, ohms, and amps.

Then there was the social aspect of the brainy cluster barrier that I would need to break through as well. I had one up on them in that area too. I mean think about it, I served in the US Air Force working on nuclear missiles during the Vietnam War. Because of my particular job classification, the military awarded me the Vietnam Active Wartime Duty ribbon. Having this ribbon stated that I served my country in an active wartime environment. This allowed me the opportunity to share my 'war' stories. The fact that I worked on doomsday weapons made my service more intriguing. Working on nuclear weapons during wartimes makes for very cool conversations, especially in a group of potential electronic engineering nerds.

Another factor in my favor was my age. I was 24, classified as the old man in the class. All the other students were 20 or under. Also, most of them still lived at home. I, on the other hand, lived in a not so luxurious, but moderately 'cool' motel

Rule #14 'If You Want to Be an 'A' Student Hang Out With the 'A' Students'

suite with a heated swimming pool frequented by lots of out of town girls on vacation looking for fun.

Ready, Set, Go:

I was scared but ready to put my plan into action. The first two weeks of school were the hardest. Either I got my 'A' team together by the end of the second week, or I would not be able to make it happen. I needed to get an 'A' on every quiz and test. If the teacher asked a question and I answered it, I needed to respond with a solid fact, no mistakes, and deliver my reply with confidence. Correctly answering all the questions was vital to the plan's success. It would directly point me out to the 'A' students as one of their kind.

Although I had already learned a lot of the course material in military school and these classes were easier, I want to make it clear that school was still not easy for me. I continued to have issues with reading and comprehension, and my course work required a lot of reading. Grammar and spelling were also a challenge. I had my work cut out for me. I studied until well past midnight every night. During the day, if I had any free time, I spent it reading and re-reading. Every time I walked into the classroom, I walked in with an air that this class was a piece of cake. When in truth, I was scared out of my mind that I would not be able to pull this off.

During week two, just before the weekly test, one of the 'A' students on my list, Luis, came to me with a question. To say Luis was gifted at learning is an understatement.

Luis could have been anything he wanted to be, but felt that an electronic engineering degree was the right choice for him. But Luis's father, you see, was a brilliant surgeon and was pushing Luis to join him in the medical field. Because his father was paying his tuition plus his room and board, Luis could only attend a school his father approved of. Luis' love of engineering persisted, and in the end, his father agreed to allow him to go for the Electronic engineering degree. As Luis pointed out to me, his father had only relented because many of the classes during the first four years were the same for either degree. The only difference was 15 credit hours, which equated to one semester heavily loaded with classes. Additionally, Luis promised his dad that after he earned his Electronic engineering degree that he would consider continuing his education in the medical field

I share this story about Luis to help you comprehend how smart he was compared to me, and how nervous I became when this highly intelligent guy approached me with a question.

I had to look and talk with the confidence of a man that knew the answer to any question Luis might ask. Luis was pulling a group together, and I had not migrated to him, so he was coming to me to check me out. Luis was the key I needed for breaking into the brainy cluster he was creating. I knew that his questions were his way of inviting me into the group.

By the end of our conversation, I had broken the barrier, and I was now a part of the group. Luis, Brian, and I quickly became good friends and agreed to add three more brainiacs to our cluster, which would round it out nicely.

Splitting the Second Atom:

It was time to put part two of my plan into action, or I was going to sink fast. I had been inspired by a way to reduce all the reading and writing that the classwork demanded, and the plan required group participation.

I couldn't think of a better setting for introducing part 2 of my plan than to invite the newly formed 'A' Team to my place for a little pool party. To sweeten the deal, I offered to supply all pizzas and drinks (soda) they could consume. Now, I am not sure if it was the food that motived them to come to the party or the comment, I made about the young ladies who enjoyed taking an evening swim in the motel pool. Either way, the whole group showed up. There was a lot of pizza eating that day by all, including a few of the poolside young ladies.

Rule #14 'If You Want to Be an 'A' Student Hang Out With the 'A' Students'

Keep the Motor Running:

Just before the end of what had been a tremendous fun-filled evening, I presented my plan to the group. "Guys," I said, "I have an idea how to make school more fun and a lot easier. The fun part is that we all come over to my place to do our group studying. Then I have this idea that if we all agree to, will reduce our study time. There are six of us. We all have to do the same reading and lecture note-taking. Basically, there are 24 chapters of reading. Let's each take four chapters. When it is time for your chapter, you will supply the summary notes and a short lecture for the group. That way, we can all greatly reduce our reading time and thus have more free time. We can do the same with the lecture notes. Why should all of us take notes each day when we can reduce it to once a week. Each of us takes a day and provides copies for the rest of us. I'll start by taking Friday for my lecture note day. I work here at the Motel on Friday nights so I don't go out on Fridays. This gives you guys a chance for an earlier start on the weekend. However, since I am taking the hit for losing Friday to studying for you guys, I would like the option of taking the later chapters for reading."

Now the truth is I wanted Friday because it gave me until Monday to have all the notes nicely written in a formal handout style. It gave me time to make the notes or lab reports look neat and organized. As I called it, an "'A' student look." The same went for the reading assignments. I am a very slow reader and writer, and I needed all the time I could get to prepare to teach the others.

Everyone in the group accepted my inspired plan, and the implementation worked great all through college. School was so much easier and fun. Our group bonded well, so well, that 5 of the 6 of us stayed friends through our entire college years. We all took the same classes every semester. After graduating, Brian and I both went to work for the same company. Brian and I have stayed in contact for 43 years and counting.

Rule #14 'If You Want to Be an 'A' Student Hang Out With the 'A' Students'

Luis' father convinced him to continue with his schooling to become a doctor. I haven't heard from Luis or any of the others from our 'A' team since college.

Did you just ask me how well I did in school using God's inspired plan? What was my grade point average at graduation? With a lot of hard work and inspiration, I graduated with a grade point average of 3.97, with 4.0 being the highest possible average.

Still Keeping the Motor Running:

It has been 43 years since I received my engineering degree, and now compared to then, the education system has changed a lot. Most college classes are taken at home on your computer over the internet. There is very little sitting in a classroom staring at a teacher. That makes putting an 'A' student support team together almost impossible. Still, it can be done. It just takes a little different approach. I know because at the age of 58, due to my financial situation, I needed to return to the workplace after a brief experience with retirement that was shorter than I would have preferred.

Not only did I have to give up my early retirement, I also found myself in a position where going back into the workforce required a career change. A career change that required more education. More education equals more schooling.

This time I was going to do like Luis and go into the medical field. But I was not going for a degree in medicine. No, at my age, I decided to do something a little easier on the brain. I became a state-licensed Hearing Aid Specialist or Practitioner.

If you think becoming a licensed Hearing Aid Specialist is easy, think again. You have to know and identify all the medical conditions of the ear. You have to study, learn, and know all the 100s of parts of the ear that make up the ability to hear and what their function is. Then add in all the state laws and ethics governing Hearing Aids. And that is just the tip of the iceberg.

Rule #14 'If You Want to Be an 'A' Student Hang Out With the 'A' Students'

Are You Listening?

I tell you once again that I have not been blessed with a highly intelligent brain. I do, however, know how to listen to inspiration from my Father in Heaven. There was a great mathematician from India named Srinivasa Ramanujan, who had been invited to Trinity College at Cambridge, England, to be mentored by another renowned math professor G. H. Hardy. Ramanujan came up with many brilliant new math formulas, yet he had a difficult time writing the required proofs. One day, Professor Hardy asked Ramanujan how he came to think up these equations and how he knew they were correct without doing the proofs. Ramanujan told Professor Hardy that if he told him he would not believe him. Sometime later on, Ramanujan ended up in the hospital close to death. Professor Hardy, with more sincerity and heart, asked him again to explain the secret to his ability. Ramanujan tells him, "God writes it on my tongue, and I listen and quickly write it down before it goes away."

If you want to know how to apply Rule #14, it requires you to listen and hear inspiration from above. Finding an 'A' student to help you on your journey is one thing, finding the right 'A' student is another--that requires inspiration.

The Same but Different:

This time as I studied for my new career, the Lord introduced me to a different type of an 'A' student team. Team member number one was the Godhead: Heavenly Father, Jesus Christ, and the Holy Ghost, who all work as one. Team member number two was my computer. The computer gave me the means to deal with my reading and writing issues. Team member number three was the internet, which provided me with cliff notes and lots of sample practice tests to study from. Team member number four was my iPad with apps that played an essential part in my studies.

With the help of God putting me in the right place at the right time, I was able to gain access to team member number five;

Rule #14 'If You Want to Be an 'A' Student Hang Out With the 'A' Students'

the doctor that wrote one of the primary textbooks used for the class.

Team member number six was my previous computer skills. Because of my computer skills and the Lord's inspiration, I converted all nine textbooks to an electronic PDF file that allowed me to quickly and easily search the reading material for answers.

Team member number four, my iPad, helped me with my inability to read and speak the Latin medical words I needed to learn via an app I downloaded.

Let's identify my 'A' student team for this scenario. My team members: 1st the God Head, 2nd personal computer applications, 3rd the internet, 4th my iPad apps, 5th the doctor that wrote the primary textbook, and 6th my previous computer skills.

How well did my 'A' teamwork? Well, by listening to the inspirational promptings of the Holy Ghost, a blessing given to me by my Father in Heaven, and a lot of long hours studying and applying Rule #4 *'Always Give 110%'*, I completed the 2-year study course in 9 months and passed the state license exam on the first try.

It is important to note that less than 20% of the applicants pass the state exam the first time, and only 60% pass the second time. I don't point this out to boast or brag about my intellect, quite the opposite. I contribute 100% of my success to my 'A' student team; without which leaves me a 0% chance of passing on my own. Without them, I would have failed. I added an additional 10% to the team to make the Rule #4 quota of a 110%.

All Aspects of Life:

The use of the 'A' student rule applies to more than just our formal education. It applies to all aspects of our life. How well you apply the 'A' student rule will determine your success in the workplace, your theological growth, your social life, and

Rule #14 'If You Want to Be an 'A' Student Hang Out With the 'A' Students'

overall it will help define who you are and who you can become.

> **(Brian Tracy)[6]**
> *Your choice of people to associate with, both personally and business-wise, is one of the most important choices you make. If you associate with turkeys, you will never fly with the eagles.*
>
> **(Donny Osmond)[7]**
> *Always surround yourself with people who are better than you. If you're hanging around bad people, they're going to start bringing you down . . . But, if you surround yourself with good people, they're going to be pulling you up.*

How It Indirectly Manages Us:

Either you manage how Rule #14 is implemented in your life, or the world around you will manage it for you. In one instance, you have control of your destiny. In the other, life controls you, and if that happens, you'll become a wave tossed by the direction of the wind.

The higher the quality of the people you place in your life to help influence and mentor your growth, the better your chances are of becoming the person you want to be.

The scriptures are full of warnings of who we need to associate within our lives and the effects our associations have on the paths we take in life.

> **(Book of Mormon: Moroni 7:11)[3]**
> *11 For behold, a bitter fountain cannot bring forth good water; neither can a good fountain bring forth bitter water; wherefore, a man being a servant of the devil cannot follow Christ; and if he follow Christ he cannot be a servant of the devil.*
>
> **(Book of Mormon: Alma 17:2)[3]**
> *2 Now these sons of Mosiah were with Alma at the time the angel first appeared unto him; therefore*

Rule #14 'If You Want to Be an 'A' Student Hang Out With the 'A' Students'

Alma did rejoice exceedingly to see his brethren; and what added more to his joy, they were still his brethren in the Lord; yea, and they had waxed strong in the knowledge of the truth; for they were men of a sound understanding and they had searched the scriptures diligently, that they might know the word of God.

(Bible New Testament: 2 Thessalonians 3:6)[2]
6 Now we command you, brethren, in the name of our Lord Jesus Christ, that ye withdraw yourselves from every brother that walketh disorderly, and not after the tradition which he received of us.

(Bible New Testament: 2 Corinthians 6:17)[2]
17 Wherefore come out from among them, and be ye separate, saith the Lord, and touch not the unclean thing; and I will receive you.

(Bible Old Testament: Proverbs 13:20)[1]
20 He that walketh with wise men shall be wise: but a companion of fools shall be destroyed.

(Bible Old Testament: Proverbs 14:18)[1]
18 The simple inherit folly: but the prudent are crowned with knowledge.

(Bible Old Testament: Proverbs 22:22-25)[1]
22 Rob not the poor, because he is poor: neither oppress the afflicted in the gate:

23 For the Lord will plead their cause, and spoil the soul of those that spoiled them.

24 Make no friendship with an angry man; and with a furious man thou shalt not go:

25 Lest thou learn his ways, and get a snare to thy soul.

(Bible Old Testament: Proverbs 29:24)[1]
24 Whoso is partner with a thief hateth his own soul: he heareth cursing, and bewrayeth it not.

Rule #14 'If You Want to Be an 'A' Student Hang Out With the 'A' Students'

(Bible New Testament: 1 Corinthians 5:9-11)[2]

9 I wrote unto you in an epistle not to company with fornicators:

10 Yet not altogether with the fornicators of this world, or with the covetous, or extortioners, or with idolaters; for then must ye needs go out of the world.

11 But now I have written unto you not to keep company, if any man that is called a brother be a fornicator, or covetous, or an idolater, or a railer, or a drunkard, or an extortioner; with such an one no not to eat.

(Bible New Testament: 2 Corinthians 6:14)[2]

14 Be ye not unequally yoked together with unbelievers: for what fellowship hath righteousness with unrighteousness? and what communion hath light with darkness?

(Mark Twain)[8]

Keep away from people who try to belittle your ambitions. Small people always do that, but the really great make you feel that you, too, can become great.

(Marcus Geduld)[9]

You get smarter by being challenged. It's not necessarily the case that being around dumb people makes you dumb. What's true is that you get dumber by being around people who don't challenge you, unless you're challenged in some other ways

(David B. Haight)[10]

To develop good thoughts and acts, we must live and associate with good people.

(Warren Buffett)[11]

"It's better to hang out with people better than you. Pick out associates whose behavior is better than yours and you'll drift in that direction."

I could continue writing about how the 'A' student rule applies to all aspects of our life, but I think you have heard enough

Rule #14 'If You Want to Be an 'A' Student Hang Out With the 'A' Students'

from me. It is time to hear from other people. I am going to start my list of quotes with one that has a little humor and truth from Jay Leno.

> **(Jay Leno)**[12]
> *Well, it looks like John Boehner will be the new Speaker of the House. He is the son of a bartender, one of 12 children. He grew up in a two room home with just one bathroom, worked his way through school, became the first person in his family to graduate from college. And, sadly, fell in with the wrong crowd and wound up in Congress.*

Now to the More Serious Side:

It is my hope that a few of these great quotes will convey the inspiration I am trying to give you.

> **(Sarah Dessen)**[13]
> *The choices you make now, the people you surround yourself with, they all have the potential to affect your life, even who you are, forever.*

> **(John Wooden)**[14]
> *Whatever you do in life, surround yourself with smart people who'll argue with you.*

> **(Reba McEntire)**[15]
> *It's very important to surround yourself with people you can learn from.*

> **(Russell Simmons)**[16]
> *Surround yourself with people who are smarter than you.*

> **(Albert Einstein)**[17]
> *Intelligence is not the ability to store information, but to know where to find it.*

> **(Albert Einstein)**[18]
> *Everybody is a genius. But if you judge a fish by its ability to climb a tree, it will live its whole life believing that it is stupid.*

Rule #14 'If You Want to Be an 'A' Student Hang Out With the 'A' Students'

(Joe Lo Truglio)[19]
You surround yourself with amazing, grade-A talent, and you're going to have to lift your game. You kind of thrive just by being around such people.

(Henry Ford)[20]
"I am not the smartest, but I surround myself with competent people."

The End is The Beginning:

The greatest 'A' student and teacher in my life has been, and always will be, my Lord and Savior Jesus Christ. I can think of no greater 'A' student and teacher than Christ. He is the best example to study with, listen to, and follow.

I plan to be the best that I can be in this life. Therefore, I need to learn from the best, so I read and study Christ's teaching and inspiring words each day. Then I work on applying them to my daily life in all that I do.

Though I am not perfect, through Jesus Christ, I can be made perfect. By listening to the Holy Ghost, a gift and power that has been given me and is available to all through obedience to the Lord's teachings, you can gain the truth and knowledge of all things. My life has been blessed beyond measure by this principle. It has blessed me with the ability to overcome personal trials in my life that otherwise would have been impossible to overcome. In my working career, there are many things that I have accomplished that I know I could not have done without my 'A' student team. I know that the reason I receive the wisdom and knowledge I need to succeed each day is because I hang out with the greatest 'A' student team of all, Heavenly Father, His Son Jesus Christ, my Lord and Savior, and the Holy Ghost. AMEN

Spiritual 'A' Student, True Disciple of God:

As I pondered over the last few paragraphs I wrote, a thought came to my mind that challenged me to define what I thought the qualities of a Spiritual 'A' Student, a true disciple of the

Rule #14 'If You Want to Be an 'A' Student Hang Out With the 'A' Students'

Lord, are. And I wondered if I could adequately answer the prompting's request? I closed my eyes and prayed for a few minutes for guidance and then searched through my research papers and found a piece of paper with scriptures and notes Elder Anthony Covington had given me. From that, I was inspired to write the following;

A spiritual 'A' student learns from the Master and then teaches others.

> **(Bible New Testament: John 13:12-17)[2]**
> *12 So after he had washed their feet, and had taken his garments, and was set down again, he said unto them, Know ye what I have done to you?*
>
> *13 Ye call me Master and Lord: and ye say well; for so I am.*
>
> *14 If I then, your Lord and Master, have washed your feet; ye also ought to wash one another's feet.*
>
> *15 For I have given you an example, that ye should do as I have done to you.*
>
> *16 Verily, verily, I say unto you, The servant is not greater than his lord; neither he that is sent greater than he that sent him.*
>
> *17 If ye know these things, happy are ye if ye do them.*

A spiritual 'A' student Cares for others and helps even when it is inconvenient.

> **(Bible New Testament: Matthew 1:18-20)[2]**
> *18 Now the birth of Jesus Christ was on this wise: When as his mother Mary was espoused to Joseph, before they came together, she was found with child of the Holy Ghost.*
>
> *19 Then Joseph her husband, being a just man, and not willing to make her a publick example, was minded to put her away privily.*
>
> *20 But while he thought on these things, behold, the angel of the Lord appeared unto him in a dream,*

Rule #14 'If You Want to Be an 'A' Student Hang Out With the 'A' Students'

saying, Joseph, thou son of David, fear not to take unto thee Mary thy wife: for that which is conceived in her is of the Holy Ghost.

A spiritual 'A' student sets an example for others to follow.

(Book of Mormon: 3 Nephi 18:16)[3]
16 And as I have prayed among you even so shall ye pray in my church, among my people who do repent and are baptized in my name. Behold I am the light; I have set an example for you.

A spiritual 'A' student labors freely to lay out the plan of success for others to follow:

(Bible Old Testament: Proverbs 4:18)[1]
18 But the path of the just is as the shining light, that shineth more and more unto the perfect day.

Above all else, a spiritual 'A' student must possess charity:

(Book of Mormon: Moroni 7:44-47)[3]
44 If so, his faith and hope is vain, for none is acceptable before God, save the meek and lowly in heart; and if a man be meek and lowly in heart, and confesses by the power of the Holy Ghost that Jesus is the Christ, he must needs have charity; for if he have not charity he is nothing; wherefore he must needs have charity.

45 And charity suffereth long, and is kind, and envieth not, and is not puffed up, seeketh not her own, is not easily provoked, thinketh no evil, and rejoiceth not in iniquity but rejoiceth in the truth, beareth all things, believeth all things, hopeth all things, endureth all things.

46 Wherefore, my beloved brethren, if ye have not charity, ye are nothing, for charity never faileth. Wherefore, cleave unto charity, which is the greatest of all, for all things must fail—

Rule #14 'If You Want to Be an 'A' Student Hang Out With the 'A' Students'

47 But charity is the pure love of Christ, and it endureth forever; and whoso is found possessed of it at the last day, it shall be well with him.

(Bible New Testament: 1 Corinthians 13:2-13)[2]
2 And though I have the gift of prophecy, and understand all mysteries, and all knowledge; and though I have all faith, so that I could remove mountains, and have not charity, I am nothing.

3 And though I bestow all my goods to feed the poor, and though I give my body to be burned, and have not charity, it profiteth me nothing.

4 Charity suffereth long, and is kind; charity envieth not; charity vaunteth not itself, is not puffed up,

5 Doth not behave itself unseemly, seeketh not her own, is not easily provoked, thinketh no evil;

6 Rejoiceth not in iniquity, but rejoiceth in the truth;

7 Beareth all things, believeth all things, hopeth all things, endureth all things.

8 Charity never faileth: but whether there be prophecies, they shall fail; whether there be tongues, they shall cease; whether there be knowledge, it shall vanish away.

9 For we know in part, and we prophesy in part.

10 But when that which is perfect is come, then that which is in part shall be done away.

11 When I was a child, I spake as a child, I understood as a child, I thought as a child: but when I became a man, I put away childish things.

12 For now we see through a glass, darkly; but then face to face: now I know in part; but then shall I know even as also I am known.

13 And now abideth faith, hope, charity, these three; but the greatest of these is charity.

In Closing:

Before I close, I want to take a moment once again to thank a few people that have supported me while writing this rule, and then I'll finish this rule by giving you a few of my favorite scriptures to ponder over.

Many thanks go to Elder Brandon Hansen, Elder Aaron Capell, Elder Calvin Cook, and Elder Zackery Ewell. Of course, as always great love and thanks to my wife Christine, my grandson Denis Wagner III, my sister Rebecca, and the others involved.

> **(Book of Mormon: Moroni 10: 32)**[3]
> *32 Yea, come unto Christ, and be perfected in him, and deny yourselves of all ungodliness; and if ye shall deny yourselves of all ungodliness, and love God with all your might, mind and strength, then is his grace sufficient for you, that by his grace ye may be perfect in Christ; and if by the grace of God ye are perfect in Christ, ye can in nowise deny the power of God.*
>
> **(Book of Mormon: 1 Nephi 17:3)**[3]
> *3 And thus we see that the commandments of God must be fulfilled. And if it so be that the children of men keep the commandments of God he doth nourish them, and strengthen them, and provide means whereby they can accomplish the thing which he has commanded them; wherefore, he did provide means for us while we did sojourn in the wilderness.*
>
> **(Book of Mormon: 2 Nephi 2:15-16)**[3]
> *15 ... it must needs be that there was an opposition; even the forbidden fruit in opposition to the tree of life; the one being sweet and the other bitter.*
>
> *16 Wherefore, the Lord God gave unto man that he should act for himself. Wherefore, man could not act for himself save it should be that he was enticed by the one or the other.*

Rule #14 'If You Want to Be an 'A' Student Hang Out With the 'A' Students'

(Bible New Testament: 1 John 3:22)[2]
22 And whatsoever we ask, we receive of him, because we keep his commandments, and do those things that are pleasing in his sight.

(Bible New Testament: 1 John 3:24)[2]
24 And he that keepeth his commandments dwelleth in him, and he in him. And hereby we know that he abideth in us, by the Spirit which he hath given us.

Rule #14 'If You Want to Be an 'A' Student Hang Out With the 'A' Students'

Endnotes:

1 **King James Version of the Bible, The Old Testament of Our Lord and Saviour Jesus Christ.** Published by The Church of Jesus Christ of Latter-day Saints, Salt Lake City, Utah, USA. Copywrite 2013.

2 **King James Version of the Bible, The New Testament of Our Lord and Saviour Jesus Christ.** Published by The Church of Jesus Christ of Latter-day Saints, Salt Lake City, Utah, USA. Copywrite 2013.

3 **The Book of Mormon Another Testament of Jesus Christ.** Published by The Church of Jesus Christ of Latter-day Saints, Salt Lake City, Utah, USA. The first English edition published in Palmyra, New York, USA, in 1830. Copywrite 2013.

4 **The Doctrine and Covenants of The Church of Jesus Christ of Latter-Day Saints.** Containing Revelations Give to Joseph Smith, the Prophet. With some additions by his successors in the Presidency of the Church. Published by The Church of Jesus Christ of Latter-day Saints, Salt Lake City, Utah, USA. Copywrite 2013.

5 **The Pearl of Great Price.** A selection from the revelations, translations, and narrations of Joseph Smith, First Prophet, seer, and revelator to The Church of Jesus Christ of Latter-Day Saints. Published by The Church of Jesus Christ of Latter-day Saints, Salt Lake City, Utah, USA. Copywrite 2013.

6 **Brain Tracy**. Brian Tracy. (n.d.). AZQuotes.com. Retrieved February 13, 2019, from AZQuotes.com Web site: https://www.azquotes.com/quote/534354.

7 **Donny Osmond**. Donny Osmond. (n.d.). AZQuotes.com. Retrieved February 13, 2019, from AZQuotes.com Web site: https://www.azquotes.com/quote/843272.

8 **Mark Twain**. Mark Twain. (n.d.). AZQuotes.com. Retrieved February 13, 2019, from AZQuotes.com Web site: https://www.azquotes.com/quote/344135.

9 **Marcus Geduld**. Marcus Geduld Quote. (n.d.). quora.com. Retrieved February 13, 2019, From quora.com website: https://www.quora.com/If-hanging-out-with-smart-people-makes-you-smarter-does-hanging-out-with-dumb-people-make-you-dumber-If-so-how-might-this-affect-dumb-people-Both-their-feelings-self-esteem-and-their-intelligence-over-time.

10 **David B. Haight,** David B. Haight. (n.d.). AZQuotes.com. Retrieved November 23, 2019, from AZQuotes.com Web site: https://www.azquotes.com/quote/920452

11 **Warren Buffett**. Warren Buffett. (n.d.). AZQuotes.com. Retrieved February 13, 2019, from AZQuotes.com Web site: https://www.azquotes.com/quote/40637.

12 **Jay Leno**. Jay Leno. (n.d.). AZQuotes.com. Retrieved February 13, 2019, from AZQuotes.com Web site: https://www.azquotes.com/quote/1177145.

Rule #14 'If You Want to Be an 'A' Student Hang Out With the 'A' Students'

13 **Sarah Dessen**. Sarah Dessen. (n.d.). AZQuotes.com. Retrieved February 13, 2019, from AZQuotes.com Web site: https://www.azquotes.com/quote/456454.

14 **John Wooden**. John Wooden. (n.d.). AZQuotes.com. Retrieved February 13, 2019, from AZQuotes.com Web site: https://www.azquotes.com/quote/320229.

15 **Reba McEntire**. Reba McEntire. (n.d.). AZQuotes.com. Retrieved February 13, 2019, from AZQuotes.com Web site: https://www.azquotes.com/quote/193476.

16 **Russell Simmons**. Russell Simmons. (n.d.). AZQuotes.com. Retrieved February 13, 2019, from AZQuotes.com Web site: https://www.azquotes.com/quote/272325.

17 **Albert Einstein**. Albert Einstein. (n.d.). AZQuotes.com. Retrieved February 13, 2019, from AZQuotes.com Web site: https://www.azquotes.com/quote/400720.

18 **Albert Einstein**. Albert Einstein. (n.d.). AZQuotes.com. Retrieved February 13, 2019, from AZQuotes.com Web site: https://www.azquotes.com/quote/369274.

19 **Joe Lo Truglio**. Joe Lo Truglio. (n.d.). AZQuotes.com. Retrieved February 13, 2019, from AZQuotes.com Web site: https://www.azquotes.com/quote/1020981.

20 **Henry Ford**. Henry Ford (n.d.). DailyFT, ft.lk. Retrieved February 13, 2019, From ft.lk Web site: http://www.ft.lk/columns/surround-yourself-with-the-best-people-you-can-find/4-69735.

Perfection

Rule #15
'What's Worth Doing is Worth Doing Right'

Rule #15 'What's Worth Doing is Worth Doing Right'

Why I Do It:

'What's worth doing is worth doing right'. A simple statement filled with solid, truthful meaning. Rule #15 is a strong, motivating statement that fills you with purpose and strength. In my mind's eye, I can envision and hear a leader of a group encouraging the team by shouting, "If we are committed to doing this, then let's do it and do it right." I can hear the people cheering back with pride and determination in their hearts.

When you look back at work, you have done or a goal you have accomplished, and you know you did your best, and it shows, doesn't it give you a sense of wellbeing? It may have taken you several tries. It may have been the hardest thing you have ever done. But when you finished the work was done right. And your heart is filled with peace and goodwill. You experience a joy that fills you with renewed strength and vitality. My spirit grows stronger each time I look back at work I have done, and I know inside I did my best and then some.

I don't think you could find a man or woman in all of history that would disagree with the integrity and value of doing things right. That being the case, you would think implementing Rule #15 in all we do in daily life would be a given. I mean, it is a simple, easy to live by rule. Right?

Defining the quantity and quality of Rule #15 can be problematic. What is good enough for one person is not good enough for another. Some people's standards are too low, yet on the other hand, other people's standards are too high. There are extremes in both directions. That is part of the reason our world is filled with rules, regulations, and standards. Yet all of those guidelines are continually in a state of flux.

Rule #15 is not as straightforward as it seems. There are many facets to implementing Rule #15. Which makes the straightforward statement *'What's Worth Doing is Worth Doing Right'* more complicated to implement than one would think. That is why I will be inundating you with so many true-to-life stories.

I hope that by sharing with you these different perspectives, it will open your eyes, and thus you'll gain the insight needed to manage this rule. I use the prism-effect to illustrate how people looking at the same job often have different perspectives not only about how the work should be done, but also what will define success and completion. Perhaps one of these stories will give you a view that enlightens you, and provides you with the needed wisdom to manage Rule #15.

Noah and the Ark:

Of course, another reason for all the stories in this chapter is the fact that Rule #15 'pushes my buttons.' What do I mean by that? Well, on many topics, I have strong opinions. For those topics, I have to build a floodgate in my mind to prevent these strong opinions from freely flowing out of my mouth in a negative manner. Otherwise, my thoughts come out so strong they overwhelm and flood the world with more negativity than positivity, and defeat my intent to use my voice to enlighten others.

When it comes to Rule #15, I have a very strong opinion. At this point in my life, I am sure that I need to build a pair of stronger floodgates than I have. And also make those gates a little harder and slower to open when they do. As it is now when giving (pushing the button) my opinion on this rule, the floodgates swing wide open, and every little opinion wants out all at once. That being said, I will do my best to control the flow of my knowledge that is about to come your way.

Holding Back the Flood:

So, is there a happy medium? Can we bring a solid understanding to *'What's Worth Doing is Worth Doing Right'*? The answer is yes, we can. It is all a matter of perspective. We need to evaluate the expectations of a given

Rule #15 'What's Worth Doing is Worth Doing Right'

job to adjust our perspective. Then we need to ensure that our perception of a job well done matches the expectations set forth by all the parties involved.

Setting proper expectations is the first step to a successful outcome. The second step is to meet those expectations. The third step, but not a required step, is to exceed those expectations by a fair margin. By doing step three, you ensure that the job will meet expectations with a cherry added to the top. People always enjoy getting a little more than they expected. And I have also found that a borderline job can leave room for a person to question if the quality of the work meets their expectations. The cherry leaves no room for that. By using this formula, you have a far better chance of a successful outcome. I use this formula not only in the work I do for others but also in the work I do for myself.

Without proper expectations, you are setting yourself up for failure, and failure is a violation of Rule #1 *'Failure is Not an Option'*. Along with violating Rule #1, you may also find yourself violating Rule #8 *'Don't Catch Idiotitis'*.

How does Rule #8 play into the expectation's aspect of Rule #15? It's simple. You can catch Idiotitis when you don't have a proper understanding of the expectations for a given task, and later you rethink your work and believe you could have done better. Later in this chapter, I will explain the effect of Rule #8 on Rule #15.

Setting up proper expectations is the key to success. Viewing a task is like looking through a prism, a slight change in the angle of the prism creates a different view. When multiple people must work together, everyone involved in a project must look through the prism at the same angle. If they don't, they will all have a different view of the task, the requirements and will thus have different expectations of what needs to be done to achieve a successful outcome. No matter how slight the difference is from one person's perspective to another's, that distinction can change the outcome.

Rule #15 'What's Worth Doing is Worth Doing Right'

Let's start by asking this question: In a work environment where you provide a service who sets the expectations? Do you set them, or does the customer? One would hope that the customer's expectations and yours are the same. The sad reality is that in too many cases, the customer's expectations and yours are not the same. This generally happens because of assumptions being made by the parties involved, which is a violation of Rule #2 *'Don't Assume'*. Breaking Rule #2 will automatically increase the possibility of failure, which in turn breaks Rule #1 *'Failure is Not an Option'*.

Doing Everything Right, But Wrong:

Here is a story from my past that points out very clearly that doing everything right can yield the wrong results when expectations are not fully understood. I titled this story 'The Unsatisfied Satisfied Client.'

Before my first retirement, I owned a successful computer company. We developed a process that not only maintained a higher computer server and workstation reliability rate but could also do it cheaper. We did this by adhering to a strict maintenance schedule, which included reimaging systems and replacing equipment before it failed. We proved that by being proactive versus retroactive, we could maintain a higher than average system uptime and keep the client's overall operating cost down significantly. All of our clients were more than pleased with our services. That is all but one.

This particular customer really had nothing to complain about. His dissatisfaction with our work was a result of looking through that prism at a different angle. Changing the angle generates a change in one's perspective, and that changes how the expectations are set.

When I was informed that one of our Florida clients was not happy with our services, and wanted to cancel their contract, I was shocked. No client had ever quit us to date, and they would be the first. I couldn't understand how this client could be so upset with the service his company had received. Before he contracted with our company, all of his computers and software were only running at an average of 75% uptime. With us, the client's uptime was at 96%, with a cost savings of 30%.

This client was one of our smaller customers, and if we lost his account, it would hardly put a dent in our overall profits. But disregarding a small client was not how our company or I did business. All of our clients were equally important, whether they were big or small.

To gain a clearer understanding of the client's dissatisfaction, I sent our salesman to meet with the client in person. The salesman reported back that the client felt he was overpaying for what he was receiving based on our services. Mark, our salesman, tried but could not get the client to see otherwise. The client requested the cost for our services to be cut in half, or our contractual agreement voided.

Now the client was not paying any more or any less than any of our other clients. And in fact, his production uptime was better than most of our other clients. His overall cost for service was also down by 30% compared to what he paid prior to contracting with us. I was having a tough time grasping the fact that this client was complaining about the cost.

To see if I could salvage the client relationship, I decided to visit him. I wanted to see if I could see the situation from his perspective. Then perhaps I could figure out a way to make the client happy again. From that meeting, I found that the client's issue was a direct result of how he viewed the value of our services. It was all about perspective and perception.

For years this customer had become accustomed to seeing the support technicians running around the office fixing computers during business hours. By physically seeing them, he was able to see what he was paying for. He wanted us to provide a support technician on-site at no additional charge so he could see his money at work. It didn't matter that an on-site technician wasn't needed. The client was unable to reconcile the cost of our services without being able to see where his money was going physically.

But, you see, with our computer services you would have rarely seen our technicians. Most of the work was done in the background before any computer or system failure, thus preventing most failures from occurring. Our maintenance times were scheduled for off-hours, limiting interruptions to our client's workers. Workers rarely experienced any failure, or more importantly, as in this case, ever saw us in the office. Our technicians only showed up in those moments of sudden and rare failures, that required immediate onsite attention.

Our support process was in direct conflict with the customer's expectations. The way we worked kept our cost down and the system uptime high. No matter how many times I showed him how our process worked and the numbers behind the costs, I could not get the client to understand the benefits we provided his company. He wanted that extra body on site but was not willing to pay for it. Our margins on the client's contract were not high enough to cover the cost of hiring an onsite full-time support technician. We loved happy clients, so I did the next best thing and allowed the client to break his contract without penalty. We also helped the client find a young full-time tech that could be onsite during working hours. We, my company, were only happy when the client was happy, so we both came away from the deal satisfied.

On a side note, two years later, that client returned to ask for our services, but at the time, we didn't have the resources to take on another client. Not stretching yourself too thin is another life lesson that needs a 'Rule.'

I Can See Clearly Now:

As the story shows, our company was doing everything that was agreed upon in the client's contract; thus, there appears to be no violation of Rule #15. Yet, the client believed he was not getting a fair value to cost. The value was there and then some but hidden from the client's sight. The failure of Rule #15, in this case, was the client's perception of how he saw value versus how the contract was being enforced. This was a client that needed to see the work happening around him physically, or he was utterly blind to it. This is where the difference in human nature needs to be taken into account, or the prism effect (point of view) will get in the way of properly implementing Rule #15.

Making Two Points Out of One:

Here is another example of the prism effect and Rule #15. I include this illustration because it addresses a pitfall I see happening in our society. And if not addressed, will play a significant role in the fall of humanity. I am not talking about the atom or hydrogen bomb. It has to do with family, family unity, and how we give credit where credit is due to each other to keep the bonds of the family together. Failure in the family unit will be humankind's biggest undoing, and Rule #15 is right in the middle of it. The prism effect plays a major role in understanding the application of Rule #15 in the family unit. Let's look at how Rule #15 and the prism effect work in a relationship where one spouse's work is that of a fulltime domestic homemaker and the other spouse is employed outside the home in a corporate environment. In this example, I'll share a personal story about my relationship with my wife. Personality is everything, I say that with a smile. Pay close attention as you read.

These days my employment requires me to work full-time outside of the home, and my wife's full-time duty, as agreed upon, is to handle the care of our home. There are many things that my wife does every day that I, off in my own busy little world, fail to value properly or acknowledge the quality of the work she has done and the contribution she has made.

Determining the value of the work, acknowledging how well the task was done, and recognizing that proper value through gratitude and affirmation was given, is what Rule #15 is all about.

Though I understand the principles of Rule #15, in my relationship with my wife, I sometimes become short-sighted in its implementation. You see, as in my story of the unsatisfied client, I don't always see the hard work my wife puts into her housekeeping duties. Thus, I sometimes fail to appreciate the full worth of the essential jobs she does.

My wife works hard all day managing a long list of chores, and because I am away from home, I rarely see the work being done. On a day-to-day basis, it is hard to notice what work has been done because there is very little change in the house to notice. Everything is in its place, the house is clean and tidy, dishes are washed, and laundry is done. In fact, if you think about it, it's the lack of any significant change that marks her skills and makes what she does for our home and family the great value it is. I can assure you, that if she weren't diligent in managing the household chores, in a short time, the house would be a messy disaster, and the lack of implementing Rule #15 would be easily noticed.

My wife works diligently to implement Rule #15 *'What's Worth Doing is Worth Doing Right'* in all that she does in her domestic housewife roll. She is like a magician, hustling around the house when no one is looking doing the chores that assure our home is clean and orderly. For example, every morning, as I am getting dressed, I put my hand into the sock drawer, and 99% of the time, just like magic, there is a clean pair of socks ready to pull out and put on. Compare that to my unsatisfied Client's computer up time of 96%. Her rate of success is better than I did for my clients.

Finding clean tee shirts, socks, and underwear in the dresser drawers is a value that is physically easy to see. Thus, making it easier for me to note that I need to praise (properly value) her for doing excellent quality work. And I do mean work. If you think getting clothes clean to their best is just a matter of sticking them in the washing machine, throwing in a little soap, and then turning the machine on. Then you need to take a few lessons from my wife on what clean really is.

Toe to Toe:

There is no one I know that can keep whites as white as my wife does. I sometimes wonder if the brilliant white socks I pull fresh from my dresser drawer aren't a brand-new pair

Rule #15 'What's Worth Doing is Worth Doing Right'

instead of the aged, dirt-stained socks I threw in the laundry just days before. But upon close inspection, I discover that annoying little hole my big toe loves to drill in the tip of the sock, proving that, in fact, they are those same formerly dirt-stained socks.

There is no question in my mind that when it comes to Rule #15 and my wife doing the laundry, it is done right. Doing the laundry is a task where the work may go unseen, but the results can be easily noticed, making it easy to give the task value.

Are You Blind?

Many other household chores my wife excels at are not as easily seen. As I said before, greatness is not always easily observed in the work that we do. As it was the case with my unsatisfied Client, so it is with me. From time to time, I become blind to the work being done around me. In one way or another, we are all very guilty of failing to value the work of other people or taking for granted someone else's contribution. You can't truly appreciate the quality of how someone has applied Rule #15 *'What's Worth Doing is Worth Doing Right'* when you don't know all of the facts.

Back to the Wife:

Due to my domestic chore blindness, there have been more times than I care to count when I have failed to give my wife the credit she deserved and note the value of her time and effort for a completed household task. In addition to this failing, I tend to point out tasks that have not been completed. For anyone married, I don't have to point out that it is not a good way to win your wife's favor or keep your marriage on the path to happily ever after.

By *only* pointing out the tasks that are not done, in my wife's mind, I have also devalued any work she had completed, which in-turn devalues her method of implementing Rule #15. Failing to respect and value the work and contribution of a spouse in any marriage, whatever their job may be, does not build a stronger, better family unit. And the fall of the family unit will greatly contribute to the fall of humanity. For if we cannot show proper care and respect for our spouse, how do we expect to know how to show it to others?

Where Were You?

I wasn't home all day. I have no idea what may have transpired, what extra housework may have needed immediate attention, causing a delay in the completion of my wife's other duties. Sometimes I tended to forget that there are only so many hours in a day, and what I can accomplish in a day's time does not always equate to what another person is capable of doing. These factors, as well as others, need to be calculated into the implementation of *'What's Worth Doing is Worth Doing Right'*.

When you come home and see uncompleted tasks or perhaps not completed in a way that you would expect, it does not necessarily translate to a failure of Rule #15. Or, if you think a job was not done correctly because a band-aid was used to fix a problem in need of a permanent solution, you may need to rethink your judgment. Sometimes applying a band-aid as a temporary solution is the right decision for the present moment.

Look There is a Crack:

Getting back to this idea of selective blindness, of only seeing certain things and ignoring others, we need to examine the why. We cannot start the correction process without discovering the reason why we limit our focus and judgment. At least I can't. In my search for harmony in my relationship and my need to manage this partial blindness, here is what I found. It is my perfectionist nature to examine everything around me. I pass over those items that are well cared for and maintained at a high level, but focus in on all the flaws I see. By focusing on the flaws, looking around, and seeing only work that still needs to be done or identifying some job, that,

Rule #15 'What's Worth Doing is Worth Doing Right'

in my opinion, hasn't been done to my standard, dismisses and diminishes all the work that has been done and done well.

My brain is always busy working on something. Even in my sleep, I have active, busy working dreams. I have resolved many issues while sleeping. My waking hours are worse. My perfectionist's brain is always scanning my surroundings. It processes all that it sees and determines if corrections are needed. If not, my mind determines that to give it any more thought is a waste and stamps it as clutter to be thrown out or at best archived in a deep dark hole in the back of my brain.

Things that don't need correcting are then, for the most part, ignored. My mind is already far too busy working on all the imperfections that it feels needs fixing. Please note: All tasks not done are considered imperfections needing correction. And since *'Failure is Not an Option'* is Rule #1, disposing of any unfinished task to make room for new tasks is not an option. I can delay a task for another task, but all tasks must be completed to perfection. Thus, my mind stays busy inventorying and analyzing all uncompleted tasks. What part of the task is not completed? What are the possible processes I could employ to complete the task? And until the task is complete, I am resolved, and my brain is engaged to find solutions to any tasks that have no easy or apparent fixes. Since my mind is kept so busy managing tasks that I believe need correcting, there is little or no time given to those jobs that have been done and done well. So, in a blink, something deemed complete or correct is blocked out of my mind and goes completely unnoticed. This point is key to understanding why I am blind to or ignore the completed task.

However, when I come across some new, great piece of work or talent that deserves to be admired, my mind takes a moment to stop and enjoy it, to analyze it. This falls under Rule #14 *'If You Want to Be an A Student Hang out With the A Students'*. Analyzing 'A' quality work is like seeing all the answers to a test, and all you have to do is study and memorize the answers to replicate the work. That method of study and analysis has been a vital component in my learning habits.

Rule #15 'What's Worth Doing is Worth Doing Right'

Seeing how things are done right is how I learn to do it right. It is the mundane everyday tasks that my mind gives no thought to unless something needs to be fixed.

My flaw-finding habit comes across as a type of criticism when directed at someone else's work. Particularly since, due to the way my mind works, I fail to give credit for things that are done right. My suggestions for improvement are not intended as criticism. From my point of view, the glass is half full, not half empty. Almost anything can be improved upon. Yet the minute I point out how I think something could be better, my words are taken as criticism.

Wanting to improve something does not make it broken or worthless. That includes people. I always want to fix, make better, or improve things. This process towards perfectionism is, in part, how I learn to better myself. I continuously look for ways to improve my own work as well as that of other people. Still, in my old age, I have not learned to stop myself from seeking flaws. But life's experiences have taught me that when it comes to other people's work, I need to cage those flaw-finding thoughts in my head and not let them escape out of my mouth. And even when I am asked for my opinion, I must still assess my words before I speak. I tend to be blunt, and while that is an excellent attribute for getting directly to a point, I find it can be a hindrance when offering sensitive feedback. Thus, thoughtful consideration is required before speaking.

Tis I:

This flaw-finding characteristic is a core part of me. Over time it has been well-honed. I've had a variety of jobs, and no matter the profession, the tasks I've been given have entailed the use of my talent to find defects and fix or prevent them, sooner than later.

Earlier in this book, I mentioned my career in the military playing with nuclear weapons, and discussed my computer company and the many banking computer systems we maintained. Now, as a Hearing Aid Practitioner, I have saved

Rule #15 'What's Worth Doing is Worth Doing Right'

lives by diagnosing life-threatening conditions that other practitioners, including doctors, have failed to recognize. My ability to quickly assess flaws or possible flaws has been highly valued in these careers. There is no room for error when targeting a nuclear missile, or counting the correct number of zeros in front of the decimal for an accurate bank balance?

This ability to find flaws has blessed me in a way that has helped me excel in my careers and save lives. While this flaw-finding is a positive attribute in the working world, it can easily become fault-finding and turn negative in relationships.

This talent of mine can quickly turn from a blessing to a curse. It has gotten me into a lot of unhappy situations in my younger years and still does from time to time. Thankfully in my old age, I have learned that great care must be taken in 'the when and how' to implement this gift. Finding flaws while applying Rule #15 can turn into unrighteous judgment. Being right does not necessarily translate into being righteous. *'What's Worth Doing is Worth Doing Right'* cannot be equally applied to all situations, trying to do so could find you crossing the line into the realm of unrighteous judgment instead of just evaluating good quality workmanship. If you don't comprehend this philosophy, then I recommend reading or rereading Rule #8 'Don't Catch Idiotitis' and perhaps Rules #9 & 10 as well.

My wife loves my perfectionist personality when I apply that attitude to **my** tasks. She doesn't appreciate it when it spills into her tasks, nor should she. I wish I could tell you that this never happens. But if that were the case, I wouldn't be writing about this as a guiding principle to Rule #15. It is this part of the guiding principle to Rule #15 I have to work on the hardest. The prism effect with respect to Rule 15# is an everyday demon to my perfectionist blessing that I continuously fight in my relationships. Pay close attention to how you implement Rule #15 in your relationships. If you don't, well, let's just say you may not have a relationship to worry about. The ones closest to you tend to be the ones that

Rule #15 'What's Worth Doing is Worth Doing Right'

are overlooked the most. We just naturally expect things to be done the way we think is right, and that can be a big mistake.

The Changing of One's Mind:

In my younger years, I didn't understand how to deal with my perfectionist nature as well as I do now. Thus, when it emerged, and that was often, life became a serious challenge. Not only was it an issue when dealing with others, it was double trouble when it came to dealing with myself.

Rule #15, combined with a perfectionist attitude, can really get in the way of success and happiness. For me, it meant always finding flaws in everything I did. The consequence was that nothing I ever did was done right. As a kid, I knew this because my father was there to point out every flaw I didn't see. Just one flaw in my work and he would find it, and then ensure that flaw was well pointed out. From his constant criticism, I learned that it only took one flaw to make me feel that a task was incomplete. If I could just fix that one flaw, the job would be done. Not a chance. My father could always find another flaw. Therefore, all my work remained imperfect and incomplete. It is like saying I'll be there tomorrow. But you can't. For tomorrow never comes. For tomorrow is always the next day forever.

This attitude, this constant pull toward an unachievable perfection, is a core part of my makeup. For me to be able to tag a job as finished, I have to find a way for my thought process to handle these real or perceived never-ending flaws. I have to find that one perspective that will satisfy my mind and enable it to call a job complete and well done.

The amount of thought power required to force this perspective change varies greatly depending upon the type of task. Take this book for instance. It takes me a great deal of thought power to accept the fact that what I have written is at the point where I can call it finished. And any errors that may remain are not important enough to subtract from its overall quality.

I Can See That a Mile Away:

This next story is an example of how I used that forced different perspective to convince myself that a task was completed to the point that I could consider the job done well and done right. Now before I start the story, I want to point out that the flaws that could be seen did not affect the quality of the work, and that if a very picky, hypercritical person were looking for the flaws, they'd still have a hard time finding them.

The Great Wall of China:

In the backyard next to the side of my house, I had to build a retaining wall. I constructed this new wall out of the same stackable 55-pound blocks I had used for the retaining wall in the front yard.

Once the new retaining wall was complete, and I mentally classified it as finished, I was able to step back and admire it. It was indeed a work of art. Done to perfection. Each block stacked perfectly. To ensure that the wall was perfectly level, I did not use the average carpenter's four-foot bubble level. No sir! I used a four-foot bubble level with an additional digital read-out and built that wall to a .01-degree tolerance level from zero in all measurable directions.

The new wall's soft sandy tan color stood out, looking clean and fresh. It had that new look to it, with that clean, rich earthy concrete block smell. From where I stood, viewing my new wall, I spotted something out of the far corner of my left-eye that quickly drew my attention to an issue. That beautiful new wall dwarfed in size to the front wall, but yet still had the ability to ruin the beauty of the old wall—at least in my estimation. I stepped back to get a better view of both walls.

Exposure to the weather over the years had not been friendly to the older retaining wall. Age had allowed black mold to set up homesteading squatter's rights. As I walked closer to the wall, I didn't get that earthy concrete smell. No, what I

Rule #15 'What's Worth Doing is Worth Doing Right'

experienced was a strong, pungent musty smell filling my nostrils.

My genius brain quickly came up with a fix to this imperfection distracting from my, close-to-flawless-as-a-man-can-get, new creation. Truthfully, it wasn't all that hard to figure out. I simply needed to get out the high-powered pressure washer and blast those wall squatters back to where they belonged. Which for the moment was anywhere besides my wall.

Remove Those Intruders:

Well, my plan didn't play out as simply and quickly as I had imagined it would. I had set a timer of 30 minutes to wash the wall. If I added a couple of snooze alarms, maybe it would take an hour at best for this poor old man to get the job done.

Finding and digging out the pressure washer from the storage shed took the better part of 20 minutes. Then the gasoline engine that runs the unit had collected a few cobwebs as it had been fast asleep for the last two years. This made starting the engine more challenging than I cared to tolerate. I pulled on that starter rope so many times my right arm was nearly spent. I thought even if I did get it started, I wouldn't have any muscle power in that right arm to spare for pressure-washing. Then I still had to hook up the 100-foot water hose to the water source and drag it out to the wall where the attack on those black moldy squatters was about to take place.

One thing was clear in my mind, and that was, that this was one fight where they were going to be the losers, and I was going to be the winner. That thought kept me going as the snooze alarms had already gone off, and my tired body urged me to take a break. That max hour I had given myself for the whole task was used up before the actual power washing had even begun. Well, I'd just have to steal time from another job and sacrifice a little more sleep to solve that issue. And that is how it went.

Rule #15 'What's Worth Doing is Worth Doing Right'

I was about to begin pressure washing when I noticed another menacing issue. I had not totally ignored it, but at the same time, had not thoroughly thought through how I was going to handle it. You see, I had planted some Green Mound Juniper evergreen shrubs along the top of the wall to keep children from playing on it and falling off. Over the last 15 years, these plants, as predicted, have grown over the wall adding an attractive dark green accent to the sandy tan color. The beauty of using this ground covering shrub as a wall accent is that it does not attach itself to the wall, it just hangs over.

The shrubs stay hardy even in the harshest Iowa weather and grows very low to the ground. Thus, they remain green and don't block our view through the bay window that overlooks the wall. Their tiny needle leaves are very sharp and prickly, which makes it a natural deterrent and keeps children from playing to near to the wall. And if you'd like to test it, just grab the shrub with your bare hand. You will also find that your hand had just been punctured by a hundred tiny little ever so sharp swords. You may also find a few teeny drops of blood in your palm. Yes, it's yours, the plant doesn't bleed red.

Even though you may hear some minor crying due to the pricks, the children get as a warning. This protective barrier the shrub makes is an excellent feature for preventing major injuries the little ones might otherwise receive. Yet as awesome as this protective feature is, one may come to disagree with its greatness when the time comes for cleaning the wall underneath it.

To tackle the handling of the shrub's branches, I found the most durable pair of waterproof gloves I could wear and still manage to use the pressure-washer.

Wall cleaning finally began and then took even more time than I expected. The mold had a grip on the wall and had locked itself deep within the blocks. To get enough pressure to force the mold's eviction, I had to be close enough with the cleaning wand that I could only remove a max-width of a two-inch strip on each pass. Then there was the fact that I couldn't pressure wash the wall through the shrubs. No sir. Each shrub branch had to be lifted to clean the wall under them. Ever try managing a high-powered pressure washer with one arm (the one that started the engine), and raise a 5 to 10-pound branch with the other that wants to eat you as you moved it out of the way? It was painfully slow going, and I do mean bloody painful. But hey, six hours later, all those squatters were gone. At least I believed I had evicted them all. That is until I examined the wall more closely...after it had dried.

The Fight Continues, Only It's Not the Same Fight:

There were a few squatters hidden and tucked deep behind the shrubs in the small cracks, still clinging to the wall for their lives. By the time I had found the intruders hide-a-way, I had already cleaned up the mess and stored all the tools. The water hose was neatly rolled and put back where it belonged. My work clothes, which had gotten soaking wet during the cleaning process, were now in the laundry. And now I was neat, clean, and dry. I truly wanted to leave those unseen squatters to their peace. But then comes along that perfectionist attitude of mine wanting to have a talk. I don't think I need to tell you what it was saying to me. And at that moment it was winning.

It was time I needed to force myself to look at this issue with a different perspective. Either I was going to be marking this job as an incomplete, imperfect task, or I needed a new inspired view. To do that, I needed a day or two to think and pray.

As I got home from work the next day and climbed out of the car, there was that freshly cleaned (minus a couple of unseen squatters) wall looking back at me. As soon as the wall saw me, it started talking to me, "I am as imperfect as you, and I am here to remind you of that. And, in my imperfection, I will help you become perfect. Leave my small hidden imperfections as a reminder to you of your own imperfections that you cannot clean away. When you see me each day, use me as a reminder. That only through Christ, can you be made perfect. And without him, your imperfections will remain, and you'll be the incomplete task. Don't worry about me. For my imperfections are well hidden. No one will know they are there but you. I'll need another good cleaning soon enough, as will you. But, as for now, we are both clean enough. So, let's count this task well done and done right."

Steady There Steady:

I hope that you are gaining a better understanding of how to interpret the weight of *'What's Worth Doing is Worth Doing Right'*. Beware of the prism effect with Rule 15#. As I said, it is something I have to deal with daily. The way I implement this rule is of vital importance to the stability of the type of person I want to be.

I added this story to point out the concerns caused by the prism effects with Rule 15#. The how and when of viewing and evaluating the quality of a task is critically important to consider and is often overlooked. Please note, I did not say rarely, I said often. Therefore, reflect and consider carefully how you use Rule #15 in your life.

In My Opinion:

When employing Rule #15 *'What's Worth Doing is Worth Doing Right,'* we must beware of becoming the partisan viewer. Judgment from a non-participant leads to breaking Rule #8 *'Don't Catch Idiotitis'*. Any job or task should be subject only to the expectations of the participants. But everyone has an opinion and often enough some sideline partisan viewer sitting in the bleachers looks through the prism and has a completely different perspective of how the work should be done and what a successful outcome looks like.

The partisan viewer passes judgment on the quality of other people's work based upon partisan's expectations. From his point of view, he concludes that the quality of the workmanship is low, and the work must have been done by an

Rule #15 'What's Worth Doing is Worth Doing Right'

idiot. He comes to this conclusion because he compares the work to his own quality or standards.

In truth, the partisan viewer's opinion as to whether the work was done right or not is irrelevant. The work was not being done for him or by him.

If the parties involved in the work are satisfied with the quality, then the work was done right.

How many times have you watched from the sidelines and judged another person's work to be inferior? Yet you are not a part of the project, nor do you know or understand what the expectations are? Negatively judging other people's work when you don't have a proper understanding of what the expectations are is another form of Idiotitis. Thus, in support of Rule #15, we invoke Rule #8 *'Don't Catch Idiotitis'*.

Please remind yourself: If you don't know all the facts and it is not your project, then nine times out of ten, it is best to keep negative opinions to yourself, or you may find yourself catching a case of foot-in-mouth disease.

Greetings from the Greeter:

This true-to-life story demonstrates the prism effect, and its impact on the interaction of Rule #8 *'Don't Catch Idiotitis'* and Rule #15 *'What's Worth Doing is Worth Doing Right'*.

Sam's Club has a smartphone app called 'Scan & Go.' With this app, you can scan all your items and pay for them using your cell phone. Once you have completed your shopping with the 'Scan & Go' app, it will display a barcode that must be scanned by the Sam's Club door greeter as the customer exits the store. The purpose of the door greeter is to validate that the customer has properly scanned the correct number of items with the Scan & Go app. After the door greeter has confirmed the count, he uses a handheld unit to send a purchase approval to the customer's Scan & Go app. Once this action is complete, the customer may exit the store.

Rule #15 'What's Worth Doing is Worth Doing Right'

idiot. He comes to this conclusion because he compares the work to his own quality or standards.

In truth, the partisan viewer's opinion as to whether the work was done right or not is irrelevant. The work was not being done for him or by him.

If the parties involved in the work are satisfied with the quality, then the work was done right.

How many times have you watched from the sidelines and judged another person's work to be inferior? Yet you are not a part of the project, nor do you know or understand what the expectations are? Negatively judging other people's work when you don't have a proper understanding of what the expectations are is another form of Idiotitis. Thus, in support of Rule #15, we invoke Rule #8 *'Don't Catch Idiotitis'*.

Please remind yourself: If you don't know all the facts and it is not your project, then nine times out of ten, it is best to keep negative opinions to yourself, or you may find yourself catching a case of foot-in-mouth disease.

Greetings from the Greeter:

This true-to-life story demonstrates the prism effect, and its impact on the interaction of Rule #8 *'Don't Catch Idiotitis'* and Rule #15 *'What's Worth Doing is Worth Doing Right'*.

Sam's Club has a smartphone app called 'Scan & Go.' With this app, you can scan all your items and pay for them using your cell phone. Once you have completed your shopping with the 'Scan & Go' app, it will display a barcode that must be scanned by the Sam's Club door greeter as the customer exits the store. The purpose of the door greeter is to validate that the customer has properly scanned the correct number of items with the Scan & Go app. After the door greeter has confirmed the count, he uses a handheld unit to send a purchase approval to the customer's Scan & Go app. Once this action is complete, the customer may exit the store.

Rule #15 'What's Worth Doing is Worth Doing Right'

me as a reminder. That only through Christ, can you be made perfect. And without him, your imperfections will remain, and you'll be the incomplete task. Don't worry about me. For my imperfections are well hidden. No one will know they are there but you. I'll need another good cleaning soon enough, as will you. But, as for now, we are both clean enough. So, let's count this task well done and done right."

Steady There Steady:

I hope that you are gaining a better understanding of how to interpret the weight of *'What's Worth Doing is Worth Doing Right'*. Beware of the prism effect with Rule 15#. As I said, it is something I have to deal with daily. The way I implement this rule is of vital importance to the stability of the type of person I want to be.

I added this story to point out the concerns caused by the prism effects with Rule 15#. The how and when of viewing and evaluating the quality of a task is critically important to consider and is often overlooked. Please note, I did not say rarely, I said often. Therefore, reflect and consider carefully how you use Rule #15 in your life.

In My Opinion:

When employing Rule #15 *'What's Worth Doing is Worth Doing Right,'* we must beware of becoming the partisan viewer. Judgment from a non-participant leads to breaking Rule #8 *'Don't Catch Idiotitis'*. Any job or task should be subject only to the expectations of the participants. But everyone has an opinion and often enough some sideline partisan viewer sitting in the bleachers looks through the prism and has a completely different perspective of how the work should be done and what a successful outcome looks like.

The partisan viewer passes judgment on the quality of other people's work based upon partisan's expectations. From his point of view, he concludes that the quality of the workmanship is low, and the work must have been done by an

Rule #15 'What's Worth Doing is Worth Doing Right'

When a customer doesn't use the Sam's Club Scan & Go app, but instead checks out using a self-checkout station or goes through a line with a cashier, he is given a paper receipt that must be shown to the door greeter before exiting the store. Here again, just prior to exiting the store, it is the door greeter's duty to validate the number and type of items the customer has purchased and matched them against the paper receipt. This final check is done to help prevent human error (and shoplifting).

The process sounds simple enough for a door greeter to perform, right? Perhaps that is true for some greeters, but not as easy for others. When the store is busy, getting through the exit can be a little slow. Customers and their shopping carts can get backed up even with the best greeter. The most significant trouble for the door greeter is in the timing of the customer flow exiting the store. It is like an unpredictable wave. Sometimes the wave of customers is small, and sometimes the wave is big. And then there are times when a tsunami hits the exit door, and you never know what earthquake may have caused it.

Sam's Club does its part in contributing to the welfare of the community by hiring people with disabilities through Goodwill and other organizations. Want to guess what one of the jobs they can be assigned is? You are a good guesser. You got it, door greeter.

At the Sam's Club location where my Hearing Aid Center is, I know of at least three people with disabilities who are door greeters. They check receipts and shopping carts as customers exit the store.

One greeter, in particular only has the use of his right arm. For him, using the handheld scanning unit to approve the customer's Scan & Go purchase can be a little challenging. But he manages it. Another one of the door greeters is almost deaf in one ear and is completely deaf in the other. Having a conversation with this greeter can be difficult when the noise level in the store is high. A third greeter does not have the use of his legs and is wheelchair-bound. The same accident that

Rule #15 'What's Worth Doing is Worth Doing Right'

damaged his legs also injured his brain, and now his thinking is sometimes a little slow. From time to time, he has to refocus, and it takes his mind a moment to catch up with the rest of his body. It's a short cognitive delay, but a bit longer than what is classified as normal. (What is normal? I am not normal.) The wheelchair restriction makes it more difficult to see and count all the items in the customer's cart. But he does it.

You can imagine that from time to time, partly due to customer issues and partly due to the door greeter's disabilities, traffic jams at the store exit will happen. Thus, you may be stuck in the exit line a few extra minutes as you try to leave the store with the items you have purchased.

Can you guess what I am leading to with this story? You got it. You're good. You must be a psychic? This one is all about judgment and expectations. The question is, whose expectations? You can guess some of the comments I hear from customers stuck in that exit jam. Or the comments impatient customers make when they have to wait a few extra moments for a disabled greeter to check their receipt as they head out the door?

Concerning *'What's Worth Doing is Worth Doing Right'*, what are the expectations we are dealing with in this story? Here we have a group of people that have physical obstacles and limitations they have to deal with every hour of their life. Despite this, they are giving their best to contribute to society and their own welfare. These are people that do the job right, and yes, that may require a little patience and compassion from the people they are serving.

I can tell you that I know these three people in this story. They are kind-hearted, they are determined to care for themselves, and they struggle every day at work with their disabilities. My heart goes out to them.

I personally have heard far too many negative comments about the quality of the work these greeters perform. Yet I've never heard management complaining about any of them not showing up for their shift. In fact, if called to come in to make up for someone else not showing up, they do. In my opinion, their job sucks and is one that I would not wish to perform. They have to stand on solid concrete 6 to 8 hours a day. And in the winter, they are right next to the door as it opens a thousand times a day, blasting them with frigid, cold air. They only get two 15-minute breaks and a 30-minute lunch break from that exit/entrance door in an 8-hour period. If their shift is only 6 hours, then they don't even get the 30-minute lunch break.

Would you prefer to take away more of their dignity by putting them all on welfare and at the same time raise our taxes, or should we all show more patience and compassion? When the negative comments sound, who is the one that has the Idiotitis?

To get our prism aligned so that we are all looking through it from the same viewpoint as we apply Rule #15, in this case, requires perhaps a little more compassion and charity in our hearts. Consideration for other's infirmities, seen or unseen, requires us to step back a moment and put ourselves in the other's shoes for a while and view their life from that perspective and not ours. This is the best method I know to use when learning to improve compassion and charity towards others.

Beauty is in the Eye of the Beholder:

I have one last Rule #15 and the prism effect story I would like to share with you before I flip to another side of Rule #15. This story is all about heart and shows that perspective is everything when it comes to applying Rule #15 in your life. This is a personal story that Gordon B. Hinckley shared in a church General Conference meeting. The story so inspired my heart that I felt it would be a shame not to share it with you. As you read, I hope that the story will encourage you to reconsider your perspective and how you look at another person's work.

Rule #15 'What's Worth Doing is Worth Doing Right'

(Gordon B. Hinckley, 1993 October General Conference, "Bring Up a Child in the Way He Should Go.")[6]

A few days ago there came to my office a man from Las Vegas, Nevada. His wife and married daughter were with him. When we had accomplished the purpose of his visit, the younger woman asked if I would accept something from her thirteen-year-old daughter. She unwrapped a painting of two butterflies around a flowering shrub.

The mother explained that her daughter had been struck by a car in a terrible accident when she was four years of age. Her body was badly broken. She was left paralyzed from the shoulders down, a quadriplegic without the use of arms or legs. She had painted this picture holding a brush between her teeth and moving her head.

As I listened to that story, the painting grew in beauty and value before my eyes. It became more than a portrayal of butterflies. It represented remarkable courage in the face of blinding adversity; tenacious practice in holding and moving the brush; pleading prayers for help; faith—the faith of a child, nurtured by loving parents, that she could create beauty notwithstanding her handicap.

Some might say that this is not a masterpiece. Without knowledge of its origin, that could be the judgment. But what is the test of art? Is it not the inspiration which comes from looking at it?

I will hang this small painting in my study so that during occasional hours of struggle there will come into my mind the picture of a beautiful little girl, robbed of the use of her feet and hands, gripping the handle of a paintbrush in her teeth to create a thing of beauty. Thank you, Krystal, for what you have done for me.

Rule #15 'What's Worth Doing is Worth Doing Right'

It is amazing and captivating that changing your view ever so slightly as you look through the prism changes everything, even though the prism is the same. The old adage 'One man's garbage is another man's treasure' can be applied to so many aspects of our life. Perspective, perspective, remember it.

Pushing My Lazy Daisy Button:

Time for that flip-side of Rule #15 I mentioned. When I first completed the writing of this rule and was ready to tuck it neatly into the book where it would live, it was politely pointed out to me that there were some concerns about this next section of Rule #15 coming up. It was feared that I might have flipped to the dark side. Meaning my writing began to read more negative than positive, more condemning than teaching. To them, the section seemed to express more of my flustrations and venting than that of educating and uplifting my readers to better heights.

After a moment of review and a long pause for consideration, I determine their viewpoint was entirely valid, and a rewrite was required to reflect a more positive stance. So, I pulled out the contents of this section as it was written. About 18 pages worth and months of work.

I liked what I had written. It was good stuff, and some of it was pretty funny reading. I couldn't just delete it from my computer. Therefore, I printed off a copy and archived that version of Rule #15 away in my vault, where 20 years from now, just perhaps, one of my great-grandchildren will discover it. Hopefully, they'll blow off the dust, and read it. From that, they will learn that I had a magic button that could set me off on a rampage. As they read, they'll hear me in their mind venting and blowing off steam about a subject related to Rule #15 that pushes my aggravation button. The magic word is 'laziness.'

Laziness, that would be the flip-side of Rule #15 we still need to cover. Failure to apply *'What's Worth Doing is Worth Doing Right'* due to laziness is a shame. *(Note: Being pulled by the dark side. "Jerry, use the force." During one of my* rewrites, my sweet, positive thinking wife requested I soften my last statement on laziness, and the few not so kind words that I wanted to use with the word **shame**. And I did. May the force be with you; that would be my wife.)

(Doctrine & Covenants 107:100)[4]
100 He that is slothful shall not be counted worthy to stand, and he that learns not his duty and shows himself not approved shall not be counted worthy to stand. Even so. Amen.

(Bible, Old Testament: Proverbs 18:9)[1]
9 He also that is slothful in his work is brother to him that is a great waster.

(Sterling W. Sill)[7]
"The greatest opportunity of our lives is to wake ourselves up and get going. There is so much to be done and so little time to do it. We should impress ourselves with the seriousness of slothfulness."

(Henry B. Eyring)[8]
"We are to learn our duty from the Lord, and then we are to act in all diligence, never being lazy or slothful. The pattern is simple but not easy to follow. We are so easily distracted."

(Jules Renard)[9]
"Laziness is nothing more than the habit of resting before you get tired."

I am the extreme opposite of lazy. I am a workaholic. An addict to work. I am not totally sure why? The closest I can come to understand the whys of my working habits is that I enjoy the great feeling of happiness I get from seeing what my work has accomplished. Then there are issues with my learning disabilities. To overcome them, I have had to work three times harder than most people to complete the same task. I can also say without a doubt that the largest part of the credit for my working attitude goes to my parents.

There is no question in my mind that my parents had a lot to do with my work habits. As I evaluate the attributes of all 8 of my brothers and sisters. The one trait we all have in common is being hard workers. From as far back as my memories can take me, my parents taught us that responsibility and accountability are learned through hard work. At the age of four, my chores were, putting away the dishes, bring the cows in for milking morning and night, and collecting the freshly laid eggs from the chickens in the coop. Oh! And putting away the dishes did not mean only the ones I could reach. Those places I couldn't reach meant climbing up on a chair and then on to the countertop if required. It was my responsibility to get the job done. Whatever that took without breaking a dish. Thus, responsibility meets accountability.

To be classified as not being lazy does not mean you have to carry your work habits to the extreme, as I do. I am not a good example to follow when it comes to how much work is too much work. I set a goal to meet in a task for that day, and I don't stop until I achieve it. And if I do reach it and feel I have a little extra energy and time, I continue pushing forward to see how much farther I can go. If I can force my eyes open, between five-second naps, and my heart is still beating, and the blood is still pumping, and if I am still able to stand, then I can work and usually do.

Not everyone has the same norm when it comes to working versus needing rest and relaxation. There are typical standards for work based upon the jobs that we are all judged by. However, the judgment of others is not as important as to how you view your own work habits. Are you being lazy? Could you give more? Only you and God can be the real judge of that. You know if you pushed yourself to that 110 percent mark (Rule #3) or not.

How do you cure laziness? I can give you three cures to start with. Sometimes it takes all three and then some. I'll talk about the *'and then some'* in a bit. Here are the three I give the most credit to:

> In the number one spot-- **Parents**
> Parents play a crucial role in their children's work habits. Note the word *'habit.'* Good or bad habits are,

Rule #15 'What's Worth Doing is Worth Doing Right'

for the most part, learned. I believe that a part of our gene pool also plays a small roll in habits, but proper education can overcome a bad gene. Parents, not schools or friends, are the first defense against learning second-rate work habits. Parents are accountable for their children's education and work habits. And it starts at a very, very, young age. Having a child pick up their own toys, or helping mommy pick things up at the age of one, is not considered child abuse. It is called education.

My wife ran a daycare for 25 years. Caring for children whose ages ran from newborn to three. The parents were always impressed at how my wife could get their one-year-old to do the things they did for her. And do it most of the time happily.

The earlier you learn good habits, the stronger they become as you grow. Learn a bad habit at a young age; the harder it is to break. This is why parents take the number one spot.

If you want (I do), to throw God into this, even he says parents are accountable for their child's upbringing. Look it up. I did, here are a few comments.

(Bible, Old Testament: Isaiah 54:13) [1]
13 And all thy children shall be *taught of the Lord; and great* shall be *the peace of thy children.*

(Bible, Old Testament: Proverbs 22:6) [1]
6 Train up a child in the way he should go: and when he is old, he will not depart from it.

(Bible, Old Testament: Deuteronomy 6:6-7) [1]
6 And these words, which I command thee this day, shall be in thine heart:

7 And thou shalt teach them diligently unto thy children, and shalt talk of them when thou sittest in thine house, and when thou walkest by the way, and when thou liest down, and when thou risest up.

Rule #15 'What's Worth Doing is Worth Doing Right'

(Bible, Old Testament: Exodus 34:7)[1]
7 Keeping mercy for thousands, forgiving iniquity and transgression and sin, and that will by no means clear the guilty; visiting the iniquity of the fathers upon the children, and upon the children's children, unto the third and to the fourth generation.

(Bible, New Testament: 1 Timothy 5:8)[2]
8 But if any provide not for his own, and specially for those of his own house, he hath denied the faith, and is worse than an infidel.

(Book of Mormon: Mosiah 4: 14-15)[3]
14 And ye will not suffer your children that they go hungry, or naked; neither will ye suffer that they transgress the laws of God, and fight and quarrel one with another, and serve the devil, who is the master of sin, or who is the evil spirit which hath been spoken of by our fathers, he being an enemy to all righteousness.

15 But ye will teach them to walk in the ways of truth and soberness; ye will teach them to love one another, and to serve one another.

(Doctrine and Covenants 93:40)[4]
40 But I have commanded you to bring up your children in light and truth.

(Doctrine and Covenants 68: 25 & 28)[4]
25 And again, inasmuch as parents have children in Zion, or in any of her stakes which are organized, that teach them not to understand the doctrine of repentance, faith in Christ the Son of the living God, and of baptism and the gift of the Holy Ghost by the laying on of the hands, when eight years old, the sin be upon the heads of the parents.

28 And they shall also teach their children to pray, and to walk uprightly before the Lord.

Rule #15 'What's Worth Doing is Worth Doing Right'

In the number two spot -- **Necessity**.

Necessity means it is a requirement. Meaning you can't get there without it. Simple as that. I consider necessity more of a dictator, not a self-motivator. You need it, and the only way to get it is to do something about it. That something will require some type of work. You may not understand the value of work, but you do know to get there, in this case, requires it. So, you do what you have to do. If there is a need and it requires work, then you can't be lazy. For work and laziness are opposites.

Necessity is not the cure for laziness I prefer, nor do I believe it is the one I want as my primary motivator. Yet, there are times, in all our lives, that necessity dictates our choice to do it, and do it right when we usually wouldn't.

In the number three spot -- **Motivation**.

Necessity is a type of motivator. But in this case, I am referring to the types of motivations that entice not dictate. I am looking for those incentives that give you the motivation to do the work and do it right out of your own self-desire. Necessity deals in needs. The motivators I am talking about deal in wants. Even if what you want is a need, you do it because your own desire was heightened by a positive motivation that gave you the extra nudge to do it.

Though it may be about the same task and for the same outcome, motivators can be different for each one of us.

Motivation is a good cure for laziness, and though it is still not the best reason for getting up and doing the work, it is a good source for helping. The hard part about motivators is finding the right one that works for you and your circumstance.

It would be great if, in your heart, your only motive for doing the work was because it is the right thing to do. No other strings attached. This is the best reason for doing anything.

Rule #15 'What's Worth Doing is Worth Doing Right'

You Take the High Road I'll Take the Low Road:

Taking shortcuts. There is a plethora of reasons for choosing a shortcut. However, in my book of rules rarely does taking a shortcut equate to a job done right, and generally gives room for error.

A shortcut modifies a set of rules for a procedure. Whether it is making a trip shorter by cutting through the forest, or removing a couple of steps when assembling an atom bomb, a shortcut introduces risk, which introduces error, which introduces failure.

I am not saying that improving a process is a bad thing. Removing unnecessary steps that waste time is great. Anyone that knows me, knows that anytime time or energy can be saved and still maintain or even better the task, I support it. Coming up with a better process without sacrificing the end results is fantastic. These types of changes must be tested and proven before implemented. Doing better leads us to do our best.

Shortcuts do not fall into the category of proven safe. A shortcut is called a shortcut because it has risk. Known and unknown risk. If the path were safe, we'd all take it. A shortcut may work once or twice. I'll even give it three times. That does not, however, make it any safer to do the next time.

In my life, I have found, anytime a shortcut was taken, more times than not, it turned out not to be a shortcut at all.

Time and inconvenience are the two biggest instigators that seduce people into taking shortcuts that risk *'What's Worth Doing is Worth Doing Right'* to fail.

I Don't Want To:

Another reason we may choose to take a shortcut is a dislike for an action that is a requirement to ensure the task is done right. Those dislikes may be small or big. In either case, they seduce us into taking a shortcut. This next story is all about a

Rule #15 'What's Worth Doing is Worth Doing Right'

trivial dislike that forced a decision to make a minor shortcut that carried enormous consequences.

Time... a Precious Commodity:

A computer technician I used to supervise once crashed a bank's marketing computer system. The error could have cost our company millions of dollars in penalties. Fortunately, although not a minor loss, it only cost our company four days of extra work and a forfeit of the income for the work we were initially scheduled to perform. I won't talk about the time we lost. It won't do any good because we can't get that back, can we?

What caused the bank's computer system to fail? It was a processual error that occurred while upgrading the computer system's secondary operating system. Thankfully we had identified the flaw within the upgrade in our lab before we had tried to apply it to any of our clients. The error could have destroyed all data on the client's computer system and force a system shutdown by corrupting the operating system software as well. We were able to create a simple procedural fix to prevent the error from happening. Our computer technician that was sent to the client's site knew of the problem and the exact procedure to follow to avoid it. Thus, not only did the computer technician know of the issue, management had directly instructed him, before going to the bank, to use the fix.

Now, the chance that this particular error would occur was very low. However, the fix was simple and worked 100% of the time. Therefore Rule #1 *'Failure is Not an Option'* is kept in balance, and the work would not only have been done right, but it also would have been done right the first time.

All that the corrected procedure required was that the computer technician performed the system upgrade using 15 decompressed data disks instead of 3 compressed data disks. We also found that in some cases upgrading the system using the 15 decompressed disks was faster than allowing the

Rule #15 'What's Worth Doing is Worth Doing Right'

system to perform the decompression of the 3 data disks during the install.

The computer technician ignored the instructions he was given. For him, it was inconvenient to carry 15 data disks onto the plane. In those days, a data disk could not be processed through the airport security screening system for fear of erasing all the data on the disk. Thus, they had to be removed from whatever carry on they were stored in and hand-inspected by security. Three disks were a little annoying. Fifteen disks, well therein lays the dislike. Since the odds were in technician's favor that the error would not occur.... Let's take the shortcut. But the error did occur, and he was utterly unprepared. He spent four additional days resolving the issue, causing extreme inconvenience to the bank, his employer, himself, and his family.

I said I wouldn't, but I am going to talk a little about the lost time factor? I know this technician to be a very family orientated person. He is one who enjoys spending as much time with his family as he can. In his career choice, working overtime happens a lot. So, I know getting free time to spend with his family is as valuable to him as it is to me. Those are days and moments with his family he can never get back.

Then there is the additional production time lost by the bank and its employees needing access to the system's database. New tasks kept coming in and piling up. Which required overtime on their part to catch up once the system was back up. And if the bank had invoked the penalty clause in their contract, our technician could have been fired, and a hefty monetary penalty placed upon our company.

All this happened because he didn't apply Rule #15 to the task, and instead, he applied a simple shortcut that worked most of the time to satisfy a dislike. Hmmm! A shortcut that worked most of the time. Want to calculate the cost-saving on a shortcut that worked most of the time in this case? Even something that seems so little, when intentionally ignored, can lead to catastrophic consequences.

Rule #15 'What's Worth Doing is Worth Doing Right'

The Shorter, the Better:

At times many of us intentionally ignore doing the little things when working on completing a bigger task. Perhaps it is because we feel it will save us time, or it will cost less in the short term. Or you take the shortcut because you just don't like doing that part of the task. So, in the spirit of convenience, we choose to take a shortcut. By doing so, we skip (what we think are) unnecessary steps, but those steps might be crucial in the long term. Please remember this.

Cover or Not to Cover?

This next true story is far less dramatic. And in exchange for permission to tell it, I promised not to use the person's name.

In a land far, far away, lives a princess and her wonderful husband, the prince (that's me). This princess is very dear and close to my heart, some days more than others. Not a day goes by that I don't give thanks to the Lord for her. I know with surety that I would find it hard to live without this princess, and I fear for the day that I might have to.

The princess is an excellent housekeeper. Yet she, like other princesses, has her lazy moments (not that I would say that). She has a bad habit of not properly covering leftover food. Now I call that more than being a little lazy (I for sure didn't say that).

We all know what happens when you leave the lid off certain foods. Leave the cover off the onion container and see what happens. The smell of onion penetrates every other uncovered food in the refrigerator. Not to mention how bad the onion stinks all by itself. It takes forever to get that stinky smell out of the fridge.

All leftover meals, desserts, meats, and veggies, once left uncovered dry out, are no longer fit to eat and have to be thrown out. Of course, the princess claims in her defense that this food is not wasted. When the food is no longer fit to eat, she places it outside to do her part to feed God's creatures. I

Rule #15 'What's Worth Doing is Worth Doing Right'

have attempted to point out to her that even in the wilds of the state & national parks, the rangers warn against the feeding of wild animals. And for several good reasons. The main one being is that in the long run, it is not beneficial for the animal's health and wellbeing. How far do you think this statement got me with the princess? Far less than an inch.

The princess's failure to cover the leftovers has become a bad habit and happens far more often than I would like. Actually, it drives me crazy.

When I was growing up, there were times when the only thing at our house to eat was a lard sandwich. Seeing food unnecessarily wasted reminds me of those days of want and hunger. And then when I think about the starving children all over the world, it is difficult for me to stand by and see food wasted or go to wild animals, particularly when it takes minimal effort to resolve the issue.

Why does she skip the lid? Well, she has admitted that she has a mild case of pure laziness when it comes to covers. She doesn't want to take the time to hunt down the proper cover for the container. But would you like to guess who organizes the cupboards where the covers are stored? I have confronted her on this subject several times because I can't find where she puts the covers either. Instead, I use the Press'n Seal wrapping paper to cover the leftovers before putting them in the refrigerator. Her response to my solution is:

 1.) It costs money, and she doesn't like wasting the plastic wrap when a lid is available. (Hmmm! Ok! Then use the cover!)

 2.) It's a struggle to get the Press & Seal wrapping paper out of the box.

 3.) The cutting edge on the box used to cut the wrapping paper is a pain in the b___.

There has been a time or two when the princess has attempted to cover the leftovers with the Press'n Seal, and the results were more than comical. But at the time, not to the royal

Rule #15 'What's Worth Doing is Worth Doing Right'

princess. You see, the princess tends to have more than a little trouble using the cutting edge on the box. Once upon a time when the princess struggled to get her royal subject, the cutting edge, to do its part of the work, she pulled down so hard on the wrapping paper that the roll of Press'n Seal was flung out of the box and across the room. By the time aerodynamics had determined that Press'n Seal really can't fly, 3 yards of tacky wrapping paper had unraveled off the roll and laid sprawled on the floor. The look on the princess's face was priceless. But not so priceless that pictures were allowed to be taken of the event.

I have to admit that the quality of the cutting edge on the Press'n Seal box could be a lot better. I struggle with it, as well. In fact, the issue has driven me from time to time to a state of wanting to throw the Press'n Seal box out along with the leftovers. Therefore, I really have no counter-argument. I understand the princess's dilemma. Yet, it is what it is.

As for the princess's concerns over the cost of the Press'n Seal, I do have a rebuttal. First, the cost of wasted food far outweighs the cost of the Press'n Seal wrapping paper needed to preserve the food for future consumption. Second, there's no reason to save the food if it won't be edible in the future—Rule #15 *'What's Worth Doing is Worth Doing Right'*. Either store the food properly or throw it away.

Failing to cover food before placing it in the refrigerator is a very minor issue compared with the overall importance of the marriage relationship. The prince is a very understanding person, and he assures you that, while bothersome, this issue does not affect his relationship with the princess. The small amount of money lost because of food spoilage is affordable at this time in our life. As a wise person once said:

(Gerald L. Penhollow)
"Choose wisely the battles you intend to win, for some are better lost. For at times, a loss can give a greater gain than winning."

Rule #15 'What's Worth Doing is Worth Doing Right'

There is a 'however' to this story. When you look at the bigger picture, the princess is missing a powerful and valuable point. From a personal perspective, the failure to apply Rule #15 will lead you to create bad habits. And in the future, those bad habits could cost you far more than a little food.

I personally am trying to replace as many bad habits as I can with good habits. So, I skip hunting in that cupboard jungle for the lids and go straight for the Press'n Seal wrapping paper every time. Despite the battle with the box's cutting edge, the one size fits all is my solution.

I have tried for years to get the fair princess to look through that prism from my angle. She is getting closer. There is hope. In fact, she is even closer now that I asked her to proofread this chapter, LOL.

The Third Choice:

There are always options for resolving bad habits that tend to prevent a person from adhering to Rule #15. Let's take another look at the princess's issue with the covering of the food. The princess's food covering issue extends beyond leftovers. When opening plastic bags of frozen food instead of properly resealing the bag after being cut open, she will just grab the bag around the opening and give the bag a few good twists. This makes the bag opening appear to be sealed, and more than likely is for the moment. Then the remaining bag of frozen food is placed back in the freezer. Sooner or later, due to temperature changes, the bag's sealing twist unravels and exposes the food to freezer burn.

Making Amends:

During the process of writing the princess's story, the prince and the princess discussed the issue of the uncovered food to see if a solution could be found. And we did, or the prince did. Because he loves having a happy princess. A store had a huge clearance sale on various sizes of Ziploc freezer bags. The prices of the bags were less than a penny per bag. This resolved the cost issue. And the lid is right there. Zip and it is sealed and locked. However, despite the fight with the Press'n Seal cutting edge, it still has its place in sealing the food as well. Somethings like sealing the exposed part of a large cut watermelon just can't be done well with a Ziploc bag. I agreed with the princess to take on as much of the struggles with the Press'n Seal as reasonable. Thereby giving relief to most of the princess's heated battles. A cool solution for the food and prince & princess, who lived happily ever after.

We all have minor issues in our lives to deal with that affect the implementation of Rule #15. I, for sure, have mine. Despite the minor issues my princess is dealing with, she is still the fairest princess in the land, and she is mine.

The Moral to the Story:

By setting good habits in all that you do, you set yourself on the road for having a good strong moral character for the times when you are seriously tested. You must always remember that it is usually the small things you neglect that grow into big things. So please cover the food.

> ### (Book of Mormon: Alma 37:46)[3]
> *46 O my son, do not let us be slothful because of the easiness of the way; for so was it with our fathers; for so was it prepared for them, that if they would look they might live; even so it is with us. The way is prepared, and if we will look we may live forever.*
>
> ### (Carl B. Cook, 2011 October General Conference, "It Is Better to Look Up")[10]
> *Why is it a challenge to consistently look up in our lives? Perhaps we lack the faith that such a simple act can solve our problems. For example, when the children of Israel were bitten by poisonous serpents, Moses was commanded to raise up a brass serpent on a pole. The brass serpent represented Christ. Those who looked up at the serpent, as admonished by the prophet, were healed. (See Numbers 21:8-9.) But many others failed to look up, and they perished. (See 1 Nephi 17:41.)*

Alma agreed that the reason the Israelites did not look to the serpent was that they did not believe doing so would heal them. Alma's words are relevant to us today:

"O my brethren, if ye could be healed by merely casting about your eyes that ye might be healed, would ye not behold quickly, or would ye rather harden your hearts in unbelief, and be slothful ... ?

"If so, wo shall come upon you; but if not so, then cast about your eyes and begin to believe in the Son of God, that he will come to redeem his people, and that he shall suffer and die to atone for [our] sins; and that he shall rise again from the dead." (Alma 33:21-22; see also verses 19-20.)

(Bible, Old Testament: Numbers 21:6-9)[1]

6 And the Lord sent fiery serpents among the people, and they bit the people; and much people of Israel died.

7 ¶ Therefore the people came to Moses, and said, We have sinned, for we have spoken against the Lord, and against thee; pray unto the Lord, that he take away the serpents from us. And Moses prayed for the people.

8 And the Lord said unto Moses, Make thee a fiery serpent, and set it upon a pole: and it shall come to pass, that every one that is bitten, when he looketh upon it, shall live.

9 And Moses made a serpent of brass, and put it upon a pole, and it came to pass, that if a serpent had bitten any man, when he beheld the serpent of brass, he lived.

(Bible, Old Testament: 2 Kings 5:9-15)[1]

9 So Naaman came with his horses and with his chariot, and stood at the door of the house of Elisha.

Rule #15 'What's Worth Doing is Worth Doing Right'

10 And Elisha sent a messenger unto him, saying, Go and wash in Jordan seven times, and thy flesh shall come again to thee, and thou shalt be clean.

11 But Naaman was wroth, and went away, and said, Behold, I thought, He will surely come out to me, and stand, and call on the name of the Lord his God, and strike his hand over the place, and recover the leper.

12 Are not Abana and Pharpar, rivers of Damascus, better than all the waters of Israel? may I not wash in them, and be clean? So he turned and went away in a rage.

13 And his servants came near, and spake unto him, and said, My father, if the prophet had bid thee do some great thing, wouldest thou not have done it? how much rather then, when he saith to thee, Wash, and be clean?

14 Then went he down, and dipped himself seven times in Jordan, according to the saying of the man of God: and his flesh came again like unto the flesh of a little child, and he was clean.

15 ¶ And he returned to the man of God, he and all his company, and came, and stood before him: and he said, Behold, now I know that there is no God in all the earth, but in Israel:

Time, Mind Fuel to Think About:

Time is something we should all have on our minds. For there never seems to be enough of it to go around. At least not in my life. I have more things I want to accomplish and enjoy than I am sure I have God-given days to live.

When you have the ability to apply *"What's Worth Doing is Worth Doing Right'* the first time, and you don't, you lose time. And time is the most precious commodity you can lose. Once time has passed, it cannot be replayed or replaced.

Rule #15 'What's Worth Doing is Worth Doing Right'

Time is so important we give it a value measured in nanoseconds, seconds, minutes, hours, days, weeks, months, years, decades, etc. Money is of importance and is given a value, measured in pennies, nickels, dimes, quarters, dollars, etc. Yet unlike money, time can never be recreated. You cannot create more time to make the day last longer. You cannot put time in a bank to be saved for use later when more is needed. Neither can used time be replaced. You cannot shorten your day by extracting and disposing time from it. You can waste time, however. You can waste all the time you think you can afford. In our universe time is a constant that is constantly moving forward. You can only use what time you have been allotted at the moment it is allotted. Think about this the next time you don't feel like taking the time to do things right the first time. Because anything else will cost you more time, which you have no way of reclaiming. Once a second is gone, it is gone.

Inspirational Moment:

The greatest example of a person that understood *'What's Worth Doing is Worth Doing Right'* is our Lord and Savior, Jesus Christ. He followed through and did the right thing to save all of us. In the end, He was willing to suffer and bleed because it was the right thing to do, and He was the only one who could do it. In the end, He gave up His Earthly life for us.

Parents, you are our first defense to a better future. The rise of the next generation falls to you. With that comes all the responsibility and its accompanying accountability. Instilling in your children the proper guiding principles of Rule #15 falls mainly to you.

Parents, to adequately implement Rule #15 *'What's Worth Doing is Worth Doing Right,'* you need the supporting wisdom of all the other rules that are written in this book. For all the other rules have a cause & effect on this rule. Please read and absorb:

Rule #15 'What's Worth Doing is Worth Doing Right'

(Spencer W. Kimball, 1979 April General Conference, "Fortify Your Homes Against Evil")[11]

"Parents should not leave the training of children to others. There seems to be a growing tendency to shift this responsibility from the home to outside influences such as the school and the church, and of greater concern, to various child-care agencies and institutions. Important as these outward influences may be, they never can adequately take the place of the influence of the mother and the father. Constant training, constant vigilance, companionship, and being watchmen of our own children are necessary in order to keep our homes intact and to bless our children in the Lord's own way."

"The Doctrine and Covenants makes it very clear. It is the responsibility of the parents to teach their children. All other agencies are secondary. If parents do not teach their children —their children —they will be held responsible."

(L. Tom Perry, 1983 April General Conference, "Train Up a Child")[12]

"Today, I would like you to pause, ponder, and think of the value of an immortal soul, especially the ones entrusted to you as parents. Where are your priorities? Have you committed yourself to give the sufficient time necessary to train your children?"

It is the proper implementation of Rule #15 that will bring us to that better tomorrow. Parents without your proper teaching of Rule #15 to your children, humanity will be lost.

This is why I have included so many true-life stories and why it is one of the longest chapters in the book. Rule #15 is vitally important to me, and I hope now it is to you as well.

(Bible, Old Testament: Deuteronomy 6:2-9)[1]

2 That thou mightest fear the Lord thy God, to keep all his statutes and his commandments, which I command thee, thou, and thy son, and thy son's son,

Rule #15 'What's Worth Doing is Worth Doing Right'

all the days of thy life; and that thy days may be prolonged.

3 ¶ Hear therefore, O Israel, and observe to do it; that it may be well with thee, and that ye may increase mightily, as the Lord God of thy fathers hath promised thee, in the land that floweth with milk and honey.

4 Hear, O Israel: The Lord our God is one Lord:

5 And thou shalt love the Lord thy God with all thine heart, and with all thy soul, and with all thy might.

6 And these words, which I command thee this day, shall be in thine heart:

7 And thou shalt teach them diligently unto thy children, and shalt talk of them when thou sittest in thine house, and when thou walkest by the way, and when thou liest down, and when thou risest up.

8 And thou shalt bind them for a sign upon thine hand, and they shall be as frontlets between thine eyes.

9 And thou shalt write them upon the posts of thy house, and on thy gates.

Honoring the Support Team:

It is time to give thanks to those who helped put this rule together. There was a lot of help needed to iron out my writing imperfection. I will start with my poor wife, who once again sat and listened to me read this chapter over and over again to find the flaws and correct them. She is, as always, a sweety pie.

Then there is Elder Tristin Anderson. I want to thank him for hunting down several particular points of scriptures I wanted to include. Thank You, Elder Anderson.

There is also a new member that has been added to my writing team, and that is my sister Rebecca. I want to thank her for all the hours she spent on Rule #15, finding the 23 pages of

Rule #15 'What's Worth Doing is Worth Doing Right'

quotes that she thought would go nicely with this rule. I thought I was a little crazy and going a little overboard by including the many famous quotes I put in the book. My sister's quote finding has all the rest of us on the writing team beat. Her reason for all the quotes she says is that she wanted to do the job right.

Relax; no, I didn't include all 23 of my sister's pages. Although the size of this chapter may look as if I did. I only allowed her to include her 10 best quotes. Rebecca said it was harder for her to narrow it down to only 10 than it was for her to find the 23 pages of quotes. Rebecca's 10 favorite quotes contribution are the last ten famous people quotes at the end of this chapter. She did a great job.

I know Rule #15 is not the last rule in this book. But it is the rule I saved for last to write. In writing this book, I don't know how I could have accomplished all that I have without the support of my friends and family. Everyone that has contributed to this project is an incredible person with super inspirational powers. It is with deep love and hugs that I give thanks to you all. I know I could not have completed this book without the support of every one of you. Thank You!

Parting Quotes to Fill Your Mind:

As always, I leave you with a couple of good quotes. Well, maybe more than a couple. Perhaps a few; no, definitely more than a few. I would say its several quotes, but I think it's a lot more than that as well. Anyhow, here they are starting with scriptural passages first, then on to the word of famous people. My sister, Rebecca, my support staff, and I hope that as you read each quote, you find the wisdom contained within.

(Book of Mormon: 3 Nephi 27:8)[3]
8 And how be it my church save it be called in my name? For if a church be called in Moses' name then it be Moses' church; or if it be called in the name of a man then it be the church of a man; but if it be called in my name then it is my church, if it so be that they are built upon my gospel.

Rule #15 'What's Worth Doing is Worth Doing Right'

(Bible, New Testament: Luke 9:62)[2]
62 And Jesus said unto him, No man, having put his hand to the plough, and looking back, is fit for the kingdom of God.

(Bible, New Testament: Matthew 6:33)[2]
33 But seek ye first the kingdom of God, and his righteousness; and all these things shall be added unto you.

(Bible, New Testament: Matthew 25:14-29)[2]
14 ¶ For the kingdom of heaven is as a man travelling into a far country, who called his own servants, and delivered unto them his goods.

15 And unto one he gave five talents, to another two, and to another one; to every man according to his several ability; and straightway took his journey.

16 Then he that had received the five talents went and traded with the same, and made them other five talents.

17 And likewise he that had received two, he also gained other two.

18 But he that had received one went and digged in the earth, and hid his lord's money.

19 After a long time the lord of those servants cometh, and reckoneth with them.

20 And so he that had received five talents came and brought other five talents, saying, Lord, thou deliveredst unto me five talents: behold, I have gained beside them five talents more.

21 His lord said unto him, Well done, thou good and faithful servant: thou hast been faithful over a few things, I will make thee ruler over many things: enter thou into the joy of thy lord.

22 He also that had received two talents came and said, Lord, thou deliveredst unto me two talents: behold, I have gained two other talents beside them.

23 His lord said unto him, Well done, good and faithful servant; thou hast been faithful over a few things, I will make thee ruler over many things: enter thou into the joy of thy lord.

24 Then he which had received the one talent came and said, Lord, I knew thee that thou art an hard man, reaping where thou hast not sown, and gathering where thou hast not strawed:

25 And I was afraid, and went and hid thy talent in the earth: lo, there thou hast that is thine.

26 His lord answered and said unto him, Thou wicked and slothful servant, thou knewest that I reap where I sowed not, and gather where I have not strawed:

27 Thou oughtest therefore to have put my money to the exchangers, and then at my coming I should have received mine own with usury.

28 Take therefore the talent from him, and give it unto him which hath ten talents.

29 For unto every one that hath shall be given, and he shall have abundance: but from him that hath not shall be taken away even that which he hath.

(Bible, New Testament: 1 Peter 5:2-3)[2]
2 Feed the flock of God which is among you, taking the oversight thereof, not by constraint, but willingly; not for filthy lucre, but of a ready mind;

3 Neither as being lords over God's heritage, but being ensamples to the flock.

(Bible, New Testament: 1 Peter 5:8)[2]
8 Be sober, be vigilant; because your adversary the devil, as a roaring lion, walketh about, seeking whom he may devour:

Rule #15 'What's Worth Doing is Worth Doing Right'

(Bible, New Testament: 1 Thessalonians 5:21-22)[2]

21 Prove all things; hold fast that which is good.

22 Abstain from all appearance of evil

(Bible, New Testament: James 1:22)[2]
22 But be ye doers of the word, and not hearers only, deceiving your own selves.

(Bible, Old Testament: Proverbs 10:4)[1]
4 He becometh poor that dealeth with a slack hand: but the hand of the diligent maketh rich.

(Bible, Old Testament: Proverbs 4:26)[1]
26 Ponder the path of thy feet, and let all thy ways be established.

(Book of Mormon: 1 Nephi 3:7)[3]
7 And it came to pass that I, Nephi, said unto my father: I will go and do the things which the Lord hath commanded, for I know that the Lord giveth no commandments unto the children of men, save he shall prepare a way for them that they may accomplish the thing which he commandeth them.

(Book of Mormon: 1 Nephi 3:14-15)[3]
14 But Laman fled out of his presence, and told the things which Laban had done, unto us. And we began to be exceedingly sorrowful, and my brethren were about to return unto my father in the wilderness.

15 But behold I said unto them that: As the Lord liveth, and as we live, we will not go down unto our father in the wilderness until we have accomplished the thing which the Lord hath commanded us.

16 Wherefore, let us be faithful in keeping the commandments of the Lord;

(Book of Mormon: 2 Nephi 10: 23)[3]
23 Therefore, cheer up your hearts, and remember that ye are free to act for yourselves—to choose the way of everlasting death or the way of eternal life.

Rule #15 'What's Worth Doing is Worth Doing Right'

(Book of Mormon: Moroni 10: 32)[3]
32 Yea, come unto Christ, and be perfected in him, and deny yourselves of all ungodliness; and if ye shall deny yourselves of all ungodliness, and love God with all your might, mind and strength, then is his grace sufficient for you, that by his grace ye may be perfect in Christ; and if by the grace of God ye are perfect in Christ, ye can in nowise deny the power of God.

(Stephen Covey)[13]
Doing more things faster is no substitute for doing the right things.

(Philip Stanhope, 4th Earl of Chesterfield)[14]
Whatever is worth doing at all is worth doing well.

(Hunter S. Thompson)[15]
"Anything worth doing, is worth doing right."

(Og Mandino)[16]
Always do your best. What you plant now, you will harvest later.

(Duke Ellington)[17]
A problem is a chance for you to do your best.

(David Cameron)[18]
I believe that in life, you have to give things your best shot, do your best. You have to focus on what needs to be done, do the right thing, not the popular thing.

(Mike Farrell)[19]
If you try to do your best there is no failure

(St. Francis of Assisi)[20]
"Start by doing what's necessary; then do what's possible; and suddenly you are doing the impossible."

(Laura Ingalls Wilder)[21]
Every job is good if you do your best and work hard. A man who works hard stinks only to the ones that have nothing to do but smell.

Rule #15 'What's Worth Doing is Worth Doing Right'

(Arthur C. Clarke)[22]
"The limits of the possible can only be defined by going beyond them into the impossible."

(G.M. Trevelyan)[23]
"Never tell a young person that anything cannot be done. God may have been waiting centuries for someone ignorant enough of the impossible to do that very thing."

Rule #15 'What's Worth Doing is Worth Doing Right'

Endnotes:

1 **King James Version of the Bible, The Old Testament of Our Lord and Saviour Jesus Christ.** Published by The Church of Jesus Christ of Latter-day Saints, Salt Lake City, Utah, USA. Copywrite 2013.

2 **King James Version of the Bible, The New Testament of Our Lord and Saviour Jesus Christ.** Published by The Church of Jesus Christ of Latter-day Saints, Salt Lake City, Utah, USA. Copywrite 2013.

3 **The Book of Mormon Another Testament of Jesus Christ.** Published by The Church of Jesus Christ of Latter-day Saints, Salt Lake City, Utah, USA. The first English edition published in Palmyra, New York, USA, in 1830. Copywrite 2013.

4 **The Doctrine and Covenants of The Church of Jesus Christ of Latter-Day Saints.** Containing Revelations Give to Joseph Smith, the Prophet. With some additions by his successors in the Presidency of the Church. Published by The Church of Jesus Christ of Latter-day Saints, Salt Lake City, Utah, USA. Copywrite 2013.

5 **The Pearl of Great Price.** A selection from the revelations, translations, and narrations of Joseph Smith, First Prophet, seer, and revelator to The Church of Jesus Christ of Latter-Day Saints. Published by The Church of Jesus Christ of Latter-day Saints, Salt Lake City, Utah, USA. Copywrite 2013.

6 **Gordon B. Hinckley, 1993 October General Conference, "Bring Up a Child in the Way He Should Go."** The 163rd Semiannual General Conference of the Church of Jesus Christ of Latter-day Saints, October 3, 1993, Sunday Morning Session. Published in the Ensign magazine, Volume 23 Number 11, November 1993. An official magazine of the Church of Jesus Christ of Latter-day Saints, published by the Church of Jesus Christ of Latter-day Saints, 50 E. North Temple Street, Salt Lake City, UT, 84150-3220, USA. Also, see Gordon B. Hinckley Churchofjesuschrist.org, retrieved February 14, 2019, from the Churchofjesuschrist.org website: https://www.churchofjesuschrist.org/study/ensign/1993/11/bring-up-a-child-in-the-way-he-should-go?lang=eng.

7 **Sterling W. Sill,** Sterling W Sill. (n.d.). AZQuotes.com. Retrieved August 12, 2019, from AZQuotes.com Web site: https://www.azquotes.com/quote/892287

8 **Henry B. Eyring,** Henry B. Eyring Quotes. (n.d.). BrainyQuote.com. Retrieved August 12, 2019, from BrainyQuote.com Web site: https://www.brainyquote.com/quotes/henry_b_eyring_590543

9 **Jules Renard,** Jules Renard. (n.d.). AZQuotes.com. Retrieved August 12, 2019, from AZQuotes.com Web site: https://www.azquotes.com/quote/242900

10 **Carl B. Cook, 2011 October General Conference, "It Is Better to Look Up,"** The 181st Semiannual General Conference of the Church of Jesus Christ of Latter-day Saints, October 1, 2011, Saturday Afternoon Session. Published in the Ensign magazine, Volume 41 Number 11, page 34 paragraph 01, November 2011. An official magazine of the Church of Jesus Christ of Latter-day Saints, published by the Church of Jesus Christ of Latter-day

Rule #15 'What's Worth Doing is Worth Doing Right'

Saints, 50 E. North Temple Street, Salt Lake City, UT, 84150-3220, USA. Also, see Carl B. Cook, ChurchofJesusChrist.org, retrieved November 24, 2019, from churchofjesuschrist.org website:
https://www.churchofjesuschrist.org/study/ensign/2011/11/saturday-afternoon-session/it-is-better-to-look-up?lang=eng

11 **Spencer W. Kimball, 1979 April General Conference, "Fortify Your Homes Against Evil"** The 149th Annual General Conference of the Church of Jesus Christ of Latter-day Saints, March 31, 1979, Saturday Morning Session. Published in the Ensign magazine, Volume 9 Number 5, May 1979. An official magazine of the Church of Jesus Christ of Latter-day Saints, published by the Church of Jesus Christ of Latter-day Saints, 50 E. North Temple Street, Salt Lake City, UT, 84150-3220, USA. Also, see Spencer W. Kimball, ChurchofJesusChrist.org, retrieved August 21, 2019, from churchofjesuschrist.org website:
https://www.churchofjesuschrist.org/study/ensign/1979/05/fortify-your-homes-against-evil?lang=eng

12 **L. Tom Perry, 1983 April General Conference, "Train Up a Child"** The 153rd Annual General Conference of the Church of Jesus Christ of Latter-day Saints, April 03, 1983, Sunday Afternoon Session. Published in the Ensign magazine, Volume 13 Number 5, May 1983. An official magazine of the Church of Jesus Christ of Latter-day Saints, published by the Church of Jesus Christ of Latter-day Saints, 50 E. North Temple Street, Salt Lake City, UT, 84150-3220, USA. Also, see L. Tom Perry, ChurchofJesusChrist.org, retrieved August 21, 2019, from churchofjesuschrist.org website:
https://www.churchofjesuschrist.org/study/ensign/1983/05/train-up-a-child?lang=eng

13 **Stephen Covey,** Stephen Covey. (n.d.). AZQuotes.com. Retrieved February 14, 2019, from AZQuotes.com Web site:
https://www.azquotes.com/quote/761086.

14 **Philip Stanhope, 4th Earl of Chesterfield,** Philip Stanhope, 4th Earl of Chesterfield Quotes. (n.d.). BrainyQuote.com. Retrieved February 14, 2019, from BrainyQuote.com Web site:
https://www.brainyquote.com/quotes/philip_stanhope_4th_earl_138620.

15 **Hunter S. Thompson.** Hunter S. Thompson. (n.d.). AZQuotes.com. Retrieved February 14, 2019, from AZQuotes.com Web site:
https://www.azquotes.com/quote/1124698. Also see, Hunter S. Thompson, Jann Wenner (2012). "Fear and Loathing at Rolling Stone: The Essential Writing of Hunter S. Thompson," p.312, Simon and Schuster.

16 **Og Mandino.** Og Mandino. (n.d.). AZQuotes.com. Retrieved February 14, 2019, from AZQuotes.com Web site:
https://www.azquotes.com/quote/185477.

17 **Duke Ellington.** Duke Ellington. (n.d.). AZQuotes.com. Retrieved February 14, 2019, from AZQuotes.com Web site:
https://www.azquotes.com/quote/88517.

18 **David Cameron.** David Cameron Quotes. (n.d.). BrainyQuote.com. Retrieved February 14, 2019, from BrainyQuote.com Web site:
https://www.brainyquote.com/quotes/david_cameron_745080.

Rule #15 'What's Worth Doing is Worth Doing Right'

19. **Mike Farrell**. Mike Farrell. (n.d.). AZQuotes.com. Retrieved February 14, 2019, from AZQuotes.com Web site: https://www.azquotes.com/quote/526121.

20. **St. Francis of Assisi**. Francis of Assisi. (n.d.). AZQuotes.com. Retrieved February 14, 2019, from AZQuotes.com Web site: https://www.azquotes.com/quote/11880. Also see President Gellhaus' Speech, annualmeeting.acog.org. 2016.

21. **Laura Ingalls Wilder**. Laura Ingalls Wilder. (n.d.). AZQuotes.com. Retrieved February 14, 2019, from AZQuotes.com Web site: https://www.azquotes.com/quote/314757.

22. **Arthur C. Clarke**. Arthur C. Clarke. (n.d.). AZQuotes.com. Retrieved February 14, 2019, from AZQuotes.com Web site: https://www.azquotes.com/quote/57375.

23. **G.M. Trevelyan**. G. M. Trevelyan. (n.d.). AZQuotes.com. Retrieved February 14, 2019, from AZQuotes.com Web site: https://www.azquotes.com/quote/296725.

Rule #15 'What's Worth Doing is Worth Doing Right'

To Be or Not To Be That is the Question

Rule #16

'Be Honest With Yourself'

Rule #16 'Be Honest With Yourself'

Soapbox Preaching:

The writing for Rule #16 should be (oops I used the word should) the shortest of all the rules that I have written. But since I used the word 'should' as in 'should be' well you can bet by the time I am done with Rule #16, it is going to be one of my longer writings. So, get yourself something to drink, get a little snack, clean your glasses if you need too, and settle into your reading chair. You're going to be here for a bit because this rule gets me standing on my soapbox ready to preach.

How hard do you think it is to really understand what Rule #16 means? The four-word statement is simple, *"Be Honest With Yourself"*. Yet in these latter-days, it seems to me that the people of this world, and I did say world, have changed the meaning of the word 'honest' to mean 'half the truth and not the whole truth.' It seems humankind lately has decided that being honest does not require telling or divulging all of the information and that only half, or something less than the whole truth, will suffice.

You need not read any further if you sincerely believe you understand how easy it is to fail or succeed at this rule. Nor do you need to continue reading if you comprehend how deeply this rule affects your character.

If, on the other hand, there are some doubts about your understanding and the application of Rule #16, then I encourage you to read on. Perhaps you'll find some pearls of knowledge that will open your mind to the disaster that is happening all around us. You may find yourself playing a part in one of these world-changing stories I am about to share with you. Ask yourself, as you read, which side of the story am I on? Do I understand how much Rule #16 affects us all, directly and indirectly?

Stepping On Toes:

I tend to make bold statements. Some people either just can't handle them or don't agree with me. Not agreeing with me, I accept that. Not handling it well when people vocalize differing opinions, that is just plain sad. I believe in a difference of opinion. That is what helps us find that third answer that will support both parties. It is the reason the American Constitution supports freedom of speech. Without differences, we cannot grow. Well, brace yourself, I am about to make one of those statements. So, I will say this first: I am sorry if you take offense with what I am about to say. But I do not apologize for writing it.

Here it goes. Do you think we have perverted the definition of the word "marriage" by included the union of two people of the same-sex in its definition? Well I am one of them that believes we have. Yet there is another less controversial word you may want to look at. Take a long hard look at what people are doing to change the definition of a far more essential word that is destroying our society. That is the word 'honesty.'

Regarding marriage, I want to make my stand very clear, its definition does not include the union of two people of the same-sex. That relationship I would define as a union, companionship, or a partnership, but not a marriage. I agree that marriage is a union, companionship, or a partnership. Those words are part of defining marriage. However, the definition of the word marriage, as constituted by God, also states that it is a union between a male and a female. The additional words "union between a male and female," which completes the definition of marriage, are what same-sex couples want to take out.

The definition of the word "marriage" has been the same for thousands of years and does not have to be changed because a few people do not agree with how it is defined. The definition of what marriage constitutes is very clear in its wording. It was anyway.

Rule #16 'Be Honest With Yourself'

The word "marriage" does not need to be changed. The issue that needs to be addressed is how we treat each other as human beings. I don't agree that a union between two people of the same-sex is a marriage. And I do not believe that being gay is an acceptable lifestyle. But I do believe in having tolerance. I do not have to agree with someone to be a friend to him/her or treat him/her fairly and kindly. God has given us all our free agency, and that includes gay people as well as a lot of other people who chose to live their life differently than me.

God requires kindness, patience, tolerance, and honesty out of all of us when dealing with one another. Redefining the word "marriage" is not going to get people to apply these attributes in their daily lives anymore, then they are already. Just like the redefining of the word "honest" to equal the statement "half honest," will not change the eternal guiding principles that govern the definition of the word "honesty."

We all have issues in our lives, whether it is our lifestyle or just the way we walk and talk that others will not find agreeable. Yet, we all want to be treated just as fairly and honestly as the next guy.

Laws and people's attitudes may need to be changed to better balance how we treat each other, but the word "marriage," which defines another eternal guiding principle, does not.

The definition of words like marriage and honesty are eternal words that have been defined by God since the beginning of time. Man did not define marriage. God did. So, don't go messing with God. We don't need more trouble brought upon us.

If people want a word for man's laws that will give them the same equal rights as married people of different sex, great I am for it. Be honest with yourself, we don't need to change the word "marriage." We need to change the laws that govern the rights that give equality to anyone in any temporally lawfully bonded human-to-human union.

Rule #16 'Be Honest With Yourself'

People do not need to mess with God's words any more than they already have. Make up your own new words and leave God's alone. I make up my own words and definitions when I need a new word that will express what I am saying in a better way. That is how new words are created in our society. So, make up a new word that defines the lawful union of a same-sex couple.

In fact, why don't we legalize plural marriage again? Please stop! I am more than challenged to the max enjoying one wife. Let's not start on the plural marriage discussion. We don't need to go there to cover the subject of Rule #16 *'Be Honest With Yourself'*. We have lots of other fun true stories I have included to raise eyebrows and stir your emotions.

I am also not going to get into a deep discussion about 'Gays' and start quoting scriptures as to whether or not acting upon those sexual feelings is a sin in God's eyes. Nor am I going to start spouting quotes about 'Gays' being a part of the fall and corruption of human society. I am not making either of those statements at all in this rule. Being gay or not is not what this rule is about.

I picked the definition of the word "marriage" not to condemn or justify the right to be gay; I choose the subject of Gays and the word "marriage" to show the half-truths the world is accepting and to stir up your thoughts.

A Few More Soapbox Stories:

I have a few more examples of what I call 'The Accepted Truth' stories I would like to share with you. The next example I call 'The Vanishing 2 by 4.'

Where Did It Go?

In the beginning, there was a piece of lumber that was labeled a 2 by 4 because its width measured 4 inches, and it had a thickness of 2 inches. This piece of lumber could be ordered in many lengths 7 feet, 8 feet, 10 feet, 12 feet, etc. Due to how

Rule #16 'Be Honest With Yourself'

the 2 by 4 was cut during the making, the original 2 by 4 had some unlikable qualities that carpenters found annoying.

The number of processes a piece of lumber has to go through during the milling process adds to the sawmill's cost of the finished product. Also included in the sawmill's profit is the amount of lumber that can be cut from one log; the more lumber, the more profit.

In the early days, the sawmill's cutting blade would leave the 2 by 4's surface bristly. To smooth the 2 by 4, the wood would have to be planed. Planing the 2 by 4 would add another process. And on top of that, the 2 by 4 would have to be cut larger for it to still maintain the measure of 2 by 4, after planing.

While building a house, most 2 by 4s are hidden in the walls and ceilings. So, if the 2 by 4 is a little or a lot rough, it will not distract from the beauty of your home because it's going to be covered up.

The downside of working with a rough-cut 2 by 4 is that the carpenter is apt to get a few splinters in his hands while working with the lumber. This hand full of splinters soon went from being a minor annoyance for the older generation of carpenters to a major annoyance for the younger generation. One sawmill company saw this as an opportunity, and the opportunity was not motivated by saving the poor carpenter's hands from a few splinters either. Instead, the sawmill company saw this as an opportunity to produce a better product called the smooth cut 2 by 4 at a higher price, which would line this company's pockets with a little more cash.

Now, in the end process, the smooth cut 2 by 4 ends up not measuring 2 by 4 as the rough cut did. But the smooth cut 2 by 4 did start out measuring 2 inches by 4 inches. You see, instead of cutting the 2 by 4 larger before planing it smooth, the sawmill would take a rough cut 2 by 4 and run it through a smoothing planer. Because the new, improved smooth cut 2 by 4 started out as a rough cut 2 by 4, carpenters overlooked

Rule #16 'Be Honest With Yourself'

the fact that the new smooth cut piece of lumber only measured only 1 ¾ by 3 ¾, but was still labeled as and called a 2 by 4. The sawmill figured it should be paid for planing the lumber, plus for any wood shavings that were left behind. The sawmill also didn't want the carpenter to feel cheated by the fact that he was getting a smaller piece of lumber at a higher cost, and seeing the smaller dimensions written on the sales tag might irritate the customer. Out of sight, out of mind, right? Besides, the sawmill could justify calling it a 2 by 4 because it started out as a 2 by 4; No dishonesty here is there? I mean, after all, a smooth cut did start out as a rough cut 2 by 4, and that is how they sold the carpenters on accepting a smaller piece of lumber while maintaining the old measurements.

You see, the story of the 'Vanishing 2 by 4' doesn't stop here. Heck no! I've just gotten started.

Now somewhere down the road of time, a Sawmill owner, in his drive to find more profit to line his pockets realized he needed to expand his think power. Out of his inspiration, he came up with the idea of forming a organization of Sawmill owners. He called a meeting with the other Sawmill owners, and they agreed. From which a committee was formed to help each other find ways to increase production and yield, and thereby increase profits.

During one of the Sawmill owner's committee meetings, a struggling Sawmill owner stands up and says, "I have got to increase the yield I get from each log to meet my cost, and I have an idea that will profit us all."

Eager to make more profit, the other Sawmill owners shout out, "Let's hear it."

"It's simple," says the struggling Sawmill owner, "we simply reduce the width and thickness of all the lumber we cut out of the log by a 1/16 of an inch. By doing this, we get more yield from each log we slice up."

"Won't the carpenters complain of this change?" said the other committee members.

"Why?" answers the struggling Sawmill owner, "None of us have made or sold a rough-cut piece of lumber in years, and they were the only boards that measure true. So, the carpenter is already conditioned to accept a piece of lumber that does not measure true. What is one more 1/16 of an inch to bother him? Gentlemen, it is only a 16th of an inch. It is such a small adjustment the carpenter will never miss it. And to get the carpenter to accept the adjustment, we will tell him that with the rising cost of doing business, we are trying to keep his cost down. We can pass the savings on to the carpenter for a year or two to help ease his pain and justify our position. But in the long haul, we help secure our companies' future by increasing our yield and thus our profits. The only 2 hurdles we have are: one, we all have to agree to implement the change together, and two, provide technical engineering specs to the regulators proving that the lumber will still meet the requirements needed to build safe homes."

"Bravo," shout the other Sawmill owners, "what an ingenious plan. We can carry this idea a step further, reduce the dimensions of lumber several times slowly over the years, and make even greater profits. And we won't have to confuse or worry the customer by calling it something different. Thus 2 by 4 will stay a 2 by 4 whether it's true to its measurements or not."

And so, begins another half-truth that the people have accepted. Over the years now, the actual measurement of a 2 by 4 has been greatly reduced. The last time I measured a 2 by 4, it actually measured 1 and 7/16 inches by 3 and 7/16 inches, but it is still labeled a 2 by 4. That is a reduction of size in both thickness and width of over a ½-inch.

The Deception Deepens:

In another example of my own personal experience with the story of the vanishing lumber, I agreed to help a friend with a project putting the finishing touches on the interior of his home by hanging trim and installing baseboards. Though I am not a professional carpenter by trade, my father was a

Rule #16 'Be Honest With Yourself'

skilled carpenter for years, and my brother and I were his workers on weekends and during the summer months when we were not in school.

My friend, who asked me to help him, knows that I am very picky and a perfectionist. My quality of work always goes far beyond the required specifications which is why he asked for my help, but also why I don't make a living as a carpenter. Because of my obsessive attitude and need for perfection, carpentry jobs take way too long.

My friend had finished his basement. He and I were installing trim molding around the windows and doors and baseboards along the flooring. I measured the gaps between the wall and the floating floor to see how wide the base of the baseboard had to be to cover the gap. Because of the imperfections between the basement's walls and floor, some of the gaps were sizeable. So, we decided that we would use the baseboard with the broadest base that measured at a minimum ½-inch. I went to the lumber and hardware store called Lowes. In the baseboard and trim section, in front of each piece of trim, is a label that shows the various dimensions of every size of the trim board. There I found a baseboard that the spec listed a ½-inch base. I pulled out my ruler to be sure I had the correct piece of trim. Sometimes customers don't put things back in the proper place. The base of the piece I picked up only measured 7/16-inch, not a ½ inch. I picked up another and measured and then another. They were all wrong. I then went to the baseboard bin that was marked 7/16th and measured them. But the baseboard trims in the 7/16th bin only measured 5/16th. Well, the 5/16th bin was over there. I figured (assumed, breaking Rule #2) that the 7/16th bin had been improperly filled, and the 5/16th trim had been put into the wrong bin. I decided that I would rearrange all the baseboard trim bins and put things in their proper bins where they belonged, as labeled. You see, the way the ordering system at Lowes works is based on an in-stock count, and with the bins being full, Lowes would never reorder the ½-inch base baseboard.

I still wanted to purchase a baseboard with a ½-inch base width, not 7/16th. So, I found a store associate to assist me. I told him what I needed and what I had done to all their baseboards. I asked him to check my measurements to ensure that my eyes had not gone bad, and I was not crazy. After all, I am an old man these days. The store assistant confirmed my finding, to my delight, and said that he would get an order in right away to replenish the stock. I asked him if he could find out when the new stock would come in. He said, "Sure, give me a moment," and the store assistant went off to make a call to the vendor.

The assistant returned in just a few minutes. As he walked up to me, he had a puzzled look on his face. He then said to me, "Well, the vendor says the 7/16th is the ½-inch and so on."

I asked the store assistant why the store had not changed the signs for the trim to show the proper dimensions? His answer was that it is the vendor's responsibility to ensure the signs show the precise dimensions and not the stores. Where is the honesty here?

I took the baseboard Lowes called ½-inch that only measured 7/16th of an inch to the checkout counter, shaking my head with sadness and disappointment.

Who Owns the Monkey?

Don't think this story is done yet. At this point in the story, we are pointing the finger at the Sawmill companies and the vendors for their deception; and from my point of view of what honesty is and is not, they are guilty. But the facts of this story go deeper than that.

My next remodeling project involved redesigning the stairs leading to our basement. My sweet wife Christine has serious knee issues, and the stair steps leading to the basement were causing her a lot of pain. Christine's daily house chores required her to climb up and down the stairs many times a day. The original steps were too high, narrow, and there was no back kick, making them dangerous for her as well.

Rule #16 'Be Honest With Yourself'

I decided it was time to replace the 50-year old staircase with a new beautiful oak staircase that would match the newly refinished basement. I have to admit that my half of the basement play area (Man Cave) is way cooler and newer than the wife's side. I felt she deserved an upgrade to her half.

Next to the staircase is a 3-inch steel support pipe that supports the basement ceiling, which is also the upstairs floor. The old handrail for the staircase was a 1-inch galvanized pipe, and one end was attached to the support pipe. As cheesy as it looked, the galvanized pipe worked well as a handrail, and without the railing, Christine would have never made it up and down the stairs. As part of the basement staircase upgrade, this handrail had to go, and the ceiling support pipe-jack needed to be trimmed in wood. Only then would this staircase meet my awesome quality standards. I had decided to make the new stairs out of beautiful red oak wood, and galvanized piping just didn't fit with that image.

While I was trimming the support pipe with complementary wood, I got a more in-depth look into "The Vanishing 2 by 4" issue.

I thought I would provide you with during and after pictures to help you visualize the project.

Rule #16 'Be Honest With Yourself'

If you have ever done any woodworking, then you know that red oak is expensive. To keep the cost down a good carpenter knows, you measure twice before you buy or cut. So, here is how it went. Instead of going back to Lowes to get my beautiful oak boards, I decided to go to another similar store called Menards. Now I needed the board to measure at least 7 ½ inches wide and 8 feet tall. So, I figured a 1 inch by 8 inches by 8 feet long should do the trick. Even if the board didn't measure the true measurements as printed on the label, one would think that the board would measure at least 7 9/16th inches wide and meet my needs.

I found the section in the store where the so-called 1-inch thick red oak lumber was located and found the width and length of the board I was looking for. The board was carefully packaged in heat shrink, clear plastic to protect the wood, and show off its beauty. It had a nicely colored picture of perfect looking oak boards on it and marked in big print were the dimensions of the board, 1 inch thick by 8 inches wide by 8 feet long.

Happy to find the board well protected from scratches and dirt stains, I gathered up 4 of the best-looking boards and headed to the cash register to pay $45.00 per board. Ouch, this part of the project was going to cost. I paid the lady and off for home I went.

Eager to get the project going, I unwrapped the first board and measured it for cutting. Wait a minute, what was this my eyes were seeing? This $45.00 red oak board that I had just purchased, which was marked to be 8 inches wide, was only measuring 7 ¼ inches in width. How could this be? I measured again only to get the same measurement. I couldn't believe it. How could anyone reduce a board down to 7 ¼ inches and still call it 8 inches on the label? I was livid. It was looking like my only option to resolve the issue was to purchase a 10-inch wide board at $65.00 per board, and then rip it down to 7 ½ inches. The lumber companies had gone too far this time.

Rule #16 'Be Honest With Yourself'

I had had enough. Just as soon as I got the project done, it was time to try and do something about this, and I did. Although the home I was remodeling is in Iowa, our primary residence is in Florida. So, the first call I made was to the Florida State Consumers Affairs department. My call was transferred to a wonderfully understanding woman. I shared with her my story about the vanishing 2 by 4. She was awestruck. I told her I felt that this was false advertising on the part of the lumber companies and stores part. She agreed 100%. I then took it a step further and boldly asked the woman if she considered herself a Christian, and if not, I would politely keep my other viewpoint on the subject to myself. The woman informed me that she did consider herself very much a Christian, and to continue.

I told the woman, "How about the fact that by overlooking the lumber companies' methods of labeling, that the lumber companies and the stores are teaching my children and grandchildren that it is ok to lie. I mean, think about it. If I send my grandson out to pick-up a couple of 2 by 4s for me, he is going to come back and say, "Grandpa, I measured every board that looked like a 2 by 4 but could not find one." Then I am going to have to tell him that we call it a 2 by 4, but it no longer measures 2 by 4. And he is going to say, "Why? Why don't they put the correct measurement on them?" Then I am going to say, "well, the lumber companies and the stores don't want you to feel cheated because they are giving you something less, and that is just the way it is. Companies tend to tell little white lies these days, and we seem to accept them."

The woman, on the other end of the line, was overwhelmed by my statement and agreed with me on the issue. I was feeling good. I had someone on my side. Then my bubble popped when she said, "however, this is not an issue that this department can help you with. You need to contact your state congressman or senator and tell them your story." She then took my address and looked up my representative's address and phone number.

Rule #16 'Be Honest With Yourself'

My next step was to call my congressman. To which I got one of his assistants. She, too, was a very nice woman to whom I repeated the story and events as I had to the Florida State Consumers Affairs department, and with the addition of the fact that they had agreed with me but felt it was an issue better handled by my state representatives. This polite woman informed me that she agreed with my cause also and thought the congressman would be interested in supporting it. I was back on cloud nine, thinking I am going to get a congressman to help back me, WOW.

Well, no sooner had the feeling of WOW grabbed me when I got the, "however," statement. She stated that the congressman only had two years left on this term in office and was ineligible to run for the next term. She stated that the congressman had more critical bills that he was working on, that he wanted to get through congress before his term ended. She then passed the buck by stating that this would be a great cause to get my senator involved in and that he would be able to do more about it.

Personally, I felt like I was just going to be making another worthless get nowhere call to someone that would agree with me yet do nothing. I wasn't going to push forward. But then after thinking about it, I talked myself into making the call to the senator. Again, a very nice woman answered my call. I repeated the story as I had the last two times. She, too, was shocked and awed by my story and agreed that something should be done to correct the issue.

At this point, I was mentally prepared to receive the 'however' statement. But instead, the woman started telling me what we could do to try and to get a law passed through congress, forcing the companies to label the lumber with their true dimensions.

She told me, "You need to create a petition stating the changes you want to be made and the reasons for the change. Then you need a thousand registered voters to sign a copy of the petition." She says, "Once that's done, send it to us, and we will help you from there." Then she added, "Now if you want to get this change made in other states, you will need the same petition signed and completed for each state, then we can present it to the U.S. Senate."

At first, I was a little overwhelmed by the task she was giving me to do. I thought that was what we paid them to do. I took a moment and thought to myself, 'I started this' and Rule #1 is, *'Failure is Not an Option.'* Besides, I just needed to get a few of my friends from different states to help me out. Right?

As I began this new task, I had high hopes for my cause. I felt it was just. How could I fail? I was pumped. I started talking to my friends, and any person I met that would listen. Not one of them disagreed with my cause, and with their lips, they supported me. But when it came down to requiring them to put some time and effort into that support, well, that was another story.

What is the point? Why am I telling you this part of the story? Now that you have read it, you tell me. With whom do you think the responsibility of the vanishing 2 by 4 lays? Is it with the big companies, or is it with the people that accept and allow it? Who are the ones with the honesty issues, those who create the lie, or those who accept the lie?

Squeeze That Fruit:

If you think the vanishing 2 by 4 is the only story of its kind, you may want to stop a moment and rethink. I could tell you about the 100% pure juice that is not required to be 100% juice to be called 100% juice. However, to tell that story would require me to write another six pages. Instead, I recommend that if you don't know the '100% Juice' story, check out the government standards for classifying juice as 100%.

That's For the Birds:

Then there is the "Ever Changing Bird Feed" story. Have you ever tried to figure out the percentage of which type of seed is in each of the different brands of mixed bird feed? This would be another story of 5 to 6 pages on dishonesty. I'll try to summarize this story to help give you a clue of what bird feed companies are up to. Keep in mind this is another half-truth we allow.

Here is the short of it. We will call this bird feed company 'For the Birds, Bird Feed.' According to this company, they make a mix of bird feed in different packaging and standards. Their mixed bird feed comes in Premium, Supreme, Deluxe, Original, and Budget Mix. All the different 'For the Birds, Bird Feed' mixes contain basically the same type of seeds, but the percentage of the mix is different. Yet the percentage of each seed used in the mix is always changing. Also, note that the percentage of each seed used is not marked on the package.

Why? Because the cost of each seed type changes, and in order to control cost, the company changes the percentages of the seeds used to make the mix. Thus, when you buy the mix called 'Original,' the content varies every time there is a change in seed price. So, I ask you, how can the company name it the 'Original Mix' when the percentage of seed mix is ever-changing? Do you understand my point?

They Are We:

We seem to be a people of finger-pointers, which brings me to the word 'ownership'. We talk about how the government and big companies are dishonest. More and more, it seems that the blame falls on the other guy. Well, as far as the government goes, the last time I read the Constitution of the United States, it still reads "We the People," not "I the President". And as for big corporate businesses and their dishonesty, well without our support they could not be a big company. The truth is, "We the People" need to take ownership. Governments or companies can only get away with the dishonest things that they do if "We the People" let them.

Rule #16 'Be Honest With Yourself'

Since I love quotes, here is a quote you can take from me.

> **(Gerald L. Penhollow)**[6]
> *"When we accept an act of dishonesty, we become a part of it and are therefore as dishonest, at that moment, as the dishonest act itself."*

We say to ourselves, what can I do? I am only one against the big wheels that turn the world.

To start with, we need to act before things become so big that it takes a major act to change it. And as far as being too big to move, well even a mountain can be moved. However, once it becomes a mountain, moving, it can only occur one way. And to answer what that one way is, I believe it was Nelson Mandela that said it best:

> **(Nelson Mandela)**[7]
> *"Change only happens when the many become the power of one."*

A Bigger Soap Box:

Now that I am wound up, I am going to step up on to a much taller soapbox (wait I need to get my ladder) to preach a little louder and try to reach a little deeper into your soul. Then perhaps I can get you to ponder even more deeply the meaning of Rule #16 *'Be Honest With Yourself'*.

On January 29, 1976, the Deseret News report, stated that "seventy percent of all inventory losses are due to employee theft ... [and that] Seventy-six percent of all employees steal from the companies they work for." Today is August 9, 2015, and statistics say the percentages are still well into the seventies.

Think about it. That says that only around ¼ or 25 percent of employees do not steal, period. Stealing from your employer is no different than stealing from your friend. You can try and justify stealing anyway you want, but in the end, when you take anything without consent, it is still stealing.

Rule #16 'Be Honest With Yourself'

The Power of the Pen:

My encounter with the vanishing office supplies is my next story. My employment is considered that of a third-party vendor within the store where I work. This means my work entails selling merchandise the store owns even though I am not employed directly by the store. Instead, I am employed by the manufacturer of the product being sold.

The store's customer service center, and I work together from time to time, helping customers. One day the girls working behind the service counter were complaining about how all their pens go missing every day. And how at the start of each day, it is a struggle to find new pens. The girls told me that the pens they are provided are cheap and don't work worth a hoot anyway. So, why would people want to steal them?

The girls have tried attaching a leash to the pens or decorating them with big flowers attached to the end. Anything to keep them from being stolen or to make them stick out if they do go missing. Yet despite their efforts, the pens continued to disappear, and management was becoming annoyed.

The girls in customer service help me in my job all the time, and I try to return the favor whenever I can. So, I decided I would do something to help them out. I had a personal box of about 25 good quality pens I had bought for my own use. I bought them because of the same issue the girls had, the quality of the pens the store provided were very cheap pens, and I didn't like them.

I took six of my good pens and used my permanent label maker to make labels for each pen. The label read 'For Customer Service Center Use Only' in BIG black lettering on a white background. You couldn't miss the label, and it was almost impossible to remove. I then presented the two girls behind the counter each their own pen and four more as spares. The girls were elated with their gift. A pen that actually worked. It was such a small gift, but I was greatly rewarded with the warm smiles of gratitude on their faces.

Rule #16 'Be Honest With Yourself'

Keep in mind these girls work in customer service where smiles are hard to come by.

The next morning when I had a few moments, I strolled over to customer service to see how things were going. I didn't see any of the pens I had given them just the day before. Concerned, I asked the young ladies if there was an issue with the pens I had given them. As I asked, I was thinking to myself that perhaps the pens didn't write well on the register receipt paper. One of the young ladies turns to me and says, "We only have one left. All the others are gone already." "Really," I said? "In less than 15 hours, 5 of the 6 pens are gone?" The young lady replied, "I know that managers took two of them because they wrote better than the ones they had." "Did you tell them I gave them to Customer Service for your use only?" I asked. "Yep," the girl replied, "And as for the other 3, not sure where they went. We left at 5:30 pm, all the pens were here then, but the store stays open until 8:30 pm, so who knows?"

Now the young ladies in Customer Service had the pens for a whole day, and not one customer had tried to walk off with the new pens. Yet, sometime between 5:30 pm and 8:30 pm (closing), and the following morning when the girls came back into work, 5 of 6 pens went missing. I am not a betting man, but based on the time frame and the 76% employee theft rate, where do you think those pens went? We know where two went for sure. Were the Managers justified in taking two pens? They were not stealing from the company, but they were taking a personal gift given by me from employees who were powerless to defend their property. *"Be Honest With Yourself,"* taking anything without the consent of the owner is stealing. You can make assumptions or try and justify your behavior all you want, but it still boils down to being dishonest and stealing.

I print a lot of things for work using my personal color laser printer. The documents could be printed in black and white, but printing them in color makes it easier to read and simplifies my work, and in other aspects, greatly improves the

Rule #16 'Be Honest With Yourself'

quality of service I provide my customers. Therefore, am I justified in taking other company supplies for my personal use to offset that cost?

Honest Abe:

No hero is perfect, and Abraham Lincoln is one of my heroes. If we look deep enough into any person's life, we will find flaws. But Abe Lincoln's honesty and integrity far out weight any flaws.

Abraham Lincoln earned the nickname 'Honest Abe' and rightfully so. As a young man, Abraham Lincoln worked as a clerk in a general store. One evening he was counting the money in the drawers after closing and found that he was a few cents over what should have been in the drawer. When he realized that he had accidentally short-changed a customer earlier that day, Lincoln walked a long distance to return the money to the customer. On another occasion, Lincoln discovered that he had given a woman too little tea for her money. He put what he owed her in a package and personally delivered it to her. The woman had not realized that she had not been given the proper amount of tea until Lincoln showed up at her doorstep!

One of Abraham Lincoln's closest friends, Leonard Swett said of him:

> **(Leonard Swett)**[8]
> *"Abe Lincoln believed in the great laws of truth, the right discharge of duty, his accountability to God, the ultimate triumph of the right, and the overthrow of wrong."*

Here are a couple of famous quotes regarding honesty from Abraham Lincoln himself that I would like to share with you.

(Abraham Lincoln)9
"If you once forfeit the confidence of your fellow citizens, you can never regain their respect and esteem. It is true that you may fool all of the people some of the time; you can even fool some of the people all of the time; but you can't fool all of the people all of the time. -Speech at Clinton, Illinois, September 8, 1854"

(Mark E. Petersen, 1976 October General Conference, "The Savor of Men", quoting Abraham Lincoln)10
"If we do not do right, God will let us go on our own way to ruin."

Here are several quotes from other American Presidents.

(George Washington)11
"It is better to offer no excuse than a bad one."

(John Quincy Adams)12
"All men profess honesty as long as they can. To believe all men honest would be folly. To believe none so is something worse."

(John Adams, Carved over the fireplace in the White House)13
"May none but honest and wise men ever rule under this roof."

(Thomas Jefferson)14
"Honesty is the first chapter in the book of wisdom."

Benjamin Franklin gave us this famous quote on honesty.

(Benjamin Franklin)15
"Honesty is the best policy."

However, although I am a Yankee at heart, I must agree with Robert E. Lee's famous statement about honesty over that of Ben Franklin's.

(Robert E. Lee)[16]
"The trite saying that honesty is the best policy has met with the just criticism that honesty is not policy. The real honest man is honest from conviction of what is right, not from policy."

As with all my Rules, I love providing great quotes from great people, and on the subject of honesty, there is a plethora of them.

(Gordon B. Hinckley, 1996 October General Conference, "This Thing Was Not Done in a Corner")[17]
"Parents have no greater responsibility in this world than the bringing up of their children in the right way, and they will have no greater satisfaction as the years pass than to see those children grow in integrity and honesty and make something of their lives."

James E. Faust gave a wonderfully inspirational talk on 'Honesty' in 1996. There are three noteworthy moments that touched my heart. I had to include them to inspire you. Read and enjoy.

(James E. Faust, 1996 October General Conference, "Honesty—a Moral Compass")[18]
"Honesty is more than not lying. It is truth telling, truth speaking, truth living, and truth loving."

(James E. Faust, 1996 October General Conference, "Honesty—a Moral Compass")[18]
"Honesty is a principle, and we have our moral agency to determine how we will apply this principle. We have the agency to make choices, but ultimately we will be accountable for each choice we make. We may deceive others, but there is One we will never deceive."

"The keeper of the gate is the Holy One of Israel; and he employeth no servant there; and there is none

other way save it be by the gate; for he cannot be deceived, for the Lord God is his name." 2 Ne. 9:41.

(James E. Faust, 1996 October General Conference, "Honesty—a Moral Compass")[18]
"There are different shades of truth telling. When we tell little white lies, we become progressively color-blind. It is better to remain silent than to mislead."

And the stirring inspiring quotes moments continue.

(Richard C. Edgley, 2006 October General Conference, "Three Towels and a 25-Cent Newspaper")[19]
"There will never be honesty in the business world, in the schools, in the home, or anyplace else until there is honesty in the heart."

(Book of Mormon: 3 Nephi 27:27)[3]
27 Therefore, what manner of men ought ye to be? Verily I say unto you, even as I am.

(Pearl of Great Price: Articles of Faith: Joseph Smith, Articles 13)[5]
13 We believe in being honest, true, chaste, benevolent, virtuous, and in doing good to all men;

(Spencer W. Kimble: 1976 October General Conference, "A Report and a Challenge")[20]
"Today is the day to preach honesty and integrity. Many people have seemingly lost their concept of the God-given law of honesty. Joseph Smith led us in saying, 'We believe in being honest, true, chaste, benevolent, virtuous, and in doing good to all men.' (A of F 1:13)

We find ourselves rationalizing in all forms of dishonesty, including shoplifting, which is a mean, low act indulged in by millions who claim to be honorable, decent people.

Dishonesty comes in many other forms: in hijacking, in playing upon private love and emotions for filthy lucre; in robbing money tills or stealing commodities of employers; in falsifying accounts; in taking advantage of other taxpaying people by misuse of food stamps and false claims; in taking unreal exemptions; in taking out government or private loans without intent to repay; in declaring unjust, improper bankruptcies to avoid repayment of loans; in robbing on the street or in the home money and other precious possessions; in stealing time, giving less than a full day of honest labor for a full day's compensation; in riding public transportation without paying the fare; and all forms of dishonesty in all places and in all conditions.

To all thieveries and dishonest acts, the Lord says, 'Thou shalt not steal.' Four short common words He used.

'Everybody's doing it' is often given as an excuse."

(Mark E. Petersen, 1976 October General Conference, "The Savor of Men")[21]

"Every nation is made up of its individual citizens. When its citizens are evil, the nation is evil. When they are righteous we have an upright nation.

Then righteousness must begin with each person. Each must regard himself as a part of the salt of the earth which is intended to give a sweet savor to his fellowmen. Especially should every follower of Christ be as salt that provides a sweet savor.

But we must remember the Lord's warning: 'If the salt have lost his savor wherewith shall it be salted? it is thenceforth good for nothing, but to be cast out, and to be trodden under foot of men.' (Matt. 5:13.)"

(Joseph B. Wirthlin)[22]
"Honesty is of God and dishonesty of the devil; the devil was a liar from the beginning."

(William Shakespeare)[23]
"No legacy is so rich as honesty."

Rule #16 'Be Honest With Yourself'

(Albert Einstein)[24]
"Whoever is careless with the truth in small matters cannot be trusted with important matters."

(Mahatma Gandhi)[25]
"Truth never damages a cause that is just."

(Kerry Stokes)[26]
"Ethics or simple honesty is the building blocks upon which our whole society is based, and business is a part of our society, and it's integral to the practice of being able to conduct business, that you have a set of honest standards."

(Richard Bach)[27]
"Your conscience is the measure of the honesty of your selfishness. Listen to it carefully."

(Waylon Jennings, Singer)[28]
"Honesty is something you can't wear out."

(Arthur C. Clark, Author)[29]
"The best measure of a man's honesty isn't his income tax return. It's the zero adjust on his bathroom scale."

(Ed McMahon)[30]
"Honesty is the most single most important factor having a direct bearing on the final success of an individual, corporation, or product."

(Mary Kay Ash)[31]
"Honesty is the cornerstone of all success, without which confidence and ability to perform shall cease to exist."

Before Stepping Down:

The subject of honesty covers a wide range of things we could be deceitful about. Of the many deceitful areas, there is one I want to address directly before I step down from my soapbox. I want to talk shortly on lying. A lie in even the smallest form is still a lie. I am not going to dive into this part of honesty with more stories that depict what is or is not a lie. Lying is a moral issue that requires the most profound look into your character or soul. How polished is your character? How bright you shine, not only before the world but also when you are standing before God in Heaven on judgment day, is determined by the stains of lies that darken your character. I believe in repentance; I hope you do as well. We all need it.

On the matter of lying, I am going to provide you with quotes and scriptures to read and let you wrestle with your own individual conscience.

(Bible Old Testament: Proverbs 6:16-19)[1]
16 These six things doth the Lord hate: yea, seven are an abomination unto him:

17 A proud look, a lying tongue, and hands that shed innocent blood,

18 An heart that deviseth wicked imaginations, feet that be swift in running to mischief,

19 A false witness that speaketh lies, and he that soweth discord among brethren.

(Bible Old Testament: Proverbs 17:4)[1]
4 A wicked doer giveth heed to false lips; and a liar giveth ear to a naughty tongue.

(Bible Old Testament: Exodus 20:16)[1]
16 Thou shalt not bear false witness against thy neighbour.

(Bible Old Testament: Proverbs 19:9)[1]
9 A false witness shall not be unpunished, and he that speaketh lies shall perish.

(Bible Old Testament: Proverbs 19:20-22)[1]
20 Hear counsel, and receive instruction, that thou mayest be wise in thy latter end.

21 There are many devices in a man's heart; nevertheless the counsel of the Lord, that shall stand.

22 The desire of a man is his kindness: and a poor man is better than a liar.

(Bible Old Testament: Proverbs 30:5-6)₁

5 Every word of God is pure: he is a shield unto them that put their trust in him.

6 Add thou not unto his words, lest he reprove thee, and thou be found a liar.

(Bible Old Testament: Isaiah 28:15)₁

15 Because ye have said, We have made a covenant with death, and with hell are we at agreement; when the overflowing scourge shall pass through, it shall not come unto us: for we have made lies our refuge, and under falsehood have we hid ourselves:

(Bible Old Testament: Isaiah 59:2-4)₁

2 But your iniquities have separated between you and your God, and your sins have hid his face from you, that he will not hear.

3 For your hands are defiled with blood, and your fingers with iniquity; your lips have spoken lies, your tongue hath muttered perverseness.

4 None calleth for justice, nor any pleadeth for truth: they trust in vanity, and speak lies; they conceive mischief, and bring forth iniquity.

(Bible Old Testament: Ezekiel 13:8)₁

8 Therefore thus saith the Lord God; Because ye have spoken vanity, and seen lies, therefore, behold, I am against you, saith the Lord God.

(Bible New Testament: 1 Timothy 4:2)₂

2 Speaking lies in hypocrisy; having their conscience seared with a hot iron;

(Bible New Testament: 1 John 2:4)₂

4 He that saith, I know him, and keepeth not his commandments, is a liar, and the truth is not in him.

(Book of Mormon: 2 Nephi 9:34)₃

34 Wo unto the liar, for he shall be thrust down to hell.

(Book of Mormon: 2 Nephi 2:18)[3]
18 ... who is the devil, who is the father of all lies, ...

(Doctrine & Covenants: 42:21)[4]
21 Thou shalt not lie; he that lieth and will not repent shall be cast out.

(Pearl of Great Price: Moses 4:3-4)[5]
3 Wherefore, because that Satan rebelled against me, and sought to destroy the agency of man, which I, the Lord God, had given him, and also, that I should give unto him mine own power; by the power of mine Only Begotten, I caused that he should be cast down;

4 And he became Satan, yea, even the devil, the father of all lies, to deceive and to blind men, and to lead them captive at his will, even as many as would not hearken unto my voice.

(Gordon B. Hinckley, 1996 September Ensign, "Four Simple Things to Help Our Families and Our Nations")[32]
President Gordon B. Hinckley has said, "Let the truth be taught by example and precept—that to steal is evil, that to cheat is wrong, that to lie is a reproach to anyone who indulges in it."

(Oliver Wendell Holmes)[33]
"Has many tools, but a lie is the handle which fits them all."

(William Penn)[34]
"Where thou art obliged to speak, be sure to speak the truth: for equivocation is halfway to a lying, as lying the whole way to hell."

(Norman Mailer)[35]
"Each day a few more lies eat into the seed with which we are born, little institutional lies from the print of newspapers, the shock waves of television, and the sentimental cheats of the movie screen."

(Ralph Waldo Emerson)[36]
"Every violation of truth is not only a sort of suicide in the liar, but is a stab at the health of human society."

(Thomas Jefferson)[37]
"He who permits himself to tell a lie once, finds it much easier to do it a second and a third time till at length it becomes habitual."

(Michel de Montaigne)[38]
"I do myself a greater injury in lying that I do him of whom I tell a lie."

(Lyman Beecher)[39]
"Never chase a lie. Let it alone, and it will run itself to death. I can work out a good character much faster than anyone can lie me out of it."

You Talking to Me?

As I stand here still on top of my towering soapbox preaching my rule, you, the reader, are perhaps thinking that all this preaching is directed at you. Well, you're right. Yet, you are not completely right. Remember, this is my book of rules. Thus, I am preaching to myself as much as I am to you. The pressure of temptation with justification is upon all of us. I, as well as you, wrestle with the world and its definition of honesty every waking minute of the day. I do not, however, find making the decision of what is right or wrong all that hard to decipher. All I need to do is to stay in tune with the Spirit of God and the Holy Ghost will guide me. The Lord gave us these two scriptures to help us in our decision making.

> **(Doctrine & Covenants; 9:8)[4]**
> *8 But, behold, I say unto you, that you must study it out in your mind; then you must ask me if it be right, and if it is right I will cause that your bosom shall burn within you; therefore, you shall feel that it is right.*

Rule #16 'Be Honest With Yourself'

(Ezra Taft Benson, 1986 June New Era, page 5, quoted in 1992 April General Conference, "Seeking the Good")[40]
"You cannot do wrong and feel right. It is impossible!"

Vanishing 2 x 4 Conclusion:

It has been several years since I wrote my story of the vanishing 2 x 4. There have been some changes since then. Before closing, I would like to bring you up to date on those changes. They are important.

I went to the lumber store the other day to check out prices for a new project I was about to start. To my surprise, I found new pricing labels on all the lumber. Check out the picture of the price tag for a 2 x 4 Hem-Fir Stud. Can you see it? I don't' believe it! The price tag for all lumber now contains two sets of measurements, the common, and the actual.

My wife says (God love her) that she believes the change is because of all the phone calls and letters I wrote to the government and other organizations protesting the old way. It would be nice to believe that the label change is due to all my hard work. I did make a lot of calls and wrote many different government agencies. It is good to believe our system of government checks and balances works. It feels good to see Heavenly Father's help in answering my prayers.

Rule #16 'Be Honest With Yourself'

My wife gives me all the credit for the change. Isn't she thoughtful? But I hardly believe that is the case. I do believe, however, that there are many people like me out there that are tired of the status quo and are demanding a better world. To those people, I want to thank you for the support in helping to keep honesty alive and real. The picture of the Hem-Fir Standard stud price tag shows that we can make the world a more honest place.

In Closing:

As I step down from my soapbox, I leave you these closing words: You cannot be honest with others without first being totally and truly honest with yourself. I close by leaving you with a few famous words from William Shakespeare's play 'Hamlet'.

> **(William Shakespeare, Hamlet Act I Scene III)**[41]
> *This above all,—to thine own self be true;*
> *And it must follow, as the night the day,*
> *Thou canst not then be false to any man.*

Rule #16 'Be Honest With Yourself'

Endnotes:

1 **King James Version of the Bible, The Old Testament of Our Lord and Saviour Jesus Christ.** Published by The Church of Jesus Christ of Latter-day Saints, Salt Lake City, Utah, USA. Copywrite 2013.

2 **King James Version of the Bible, The New Testament of Our Lord and Saviour Jesus Christ.** Published by The Church of Jesus Christ of Latter-day Saints, Salt Lake City, Utah, USA. Copywrite 2013.

3 **The Book of Mormon Another Testament of Jesus Christ.** Published by The Church of Jesus Christ of Latter-day Saints, Salt Lake City, Utah, USA. First English edition published in Palmyra, New York, USA, in 1830. Copywrite 2013.

4 **The Doctrine and Covenants of The Church of Jesus Christ of Latter-Day Saints.** Containing Revelations Give to Joseph Smith, the Prophet. With some additions by his successors in the Presidency of the Church. Published by The Church of Jesus Christ of Latter-day Saints, Salt Lake City, Utah, USA. Copywrite 2013.

5 **The Pearl of Great Price.** A selection from the revelations, translations, and narrations of Joseph Smith, First Prophet, seer, and revelator to The Church of Jesus Christ of Latter-Day Saints. Published by The Church of Jesus Christ of Latter-day Saints, Salt Lake City, Utah, USA. Copywrite 2013.

6 **Gerald L Penhollow**. Gerald L. Penhollow Quotes, "Jerry's 20 Rules for Managing Life", chapter "Rule 16 Be Honest With Yourself".

7 **Nelson Mandela**. Nelson Mandela Quotes. (n.d.). Unable to find source of quote. I got this quote from a movie I watched about South Africa. When I find the movie, I will give the citation source.

8 **Leonard Swett**. Leonard Swett Quote, Great American History, greatamericanhistory.net. "Lincoln's Honesty" by Gordon Leidner of Great American History. The article this quote came from also appeared in the Washington Times Civil War Page on February 20, 1999. Copyright 1999 by New World Communications, Inc. Reprinted with permission of The Washington Times. Retrieved February 16, 2019, from greatamericanhistory.com website: https://greatamericanhistory.net/honesty.htm.

9 **Abraham Lincoln**. Abraham Lincoln. (n.d.). AZQuotes.com. Retrieved February 16, 2019, from AZQuotes.com Web site: https://www.azquotes.com/quote/345804. Also see Abraham Lincoln (1982). "Abraham Lincoln, wisdom & wit" author Louise Bachelder, Peter Pauper Press, ISBN #: 9780880880664.

10 **Mark E. Petersen, 1976 October General Conference, "The Savor of Men", quoting Abraham Lincoln.** The 146th Semiannual General Conference of the Church of Jesus Christ of Latter-day Saints, October 2, 1976, Saturday Morning Session. Published in the Ensign magazine, Volume 06 Number 11, November 1976. An official magazine of the Church of Jesus Christ of Latter-day Saints, published by the Church of Jesus Christ of Latter-day Saints, 50 E. North Temple Street, Salt Lake City, UT, 84150-3220, USA. Also see, Ensign, Churchofjesuschrist.org. Retrieved February 17, 2019 from

Rule #16 'Be Honest With Yourself'

Churchofjesuschrist.org website:
https://www.churchofjesuschrist.org/study/ensign/1976/11/the-savor-of-men?lang=eng.

11 **George Washington**. George Washington. (n.d.). AZQuotes.com. Retrieved February 16, 2019, from AZQuotes.com Web site: https://www.azquotes.com/quote/307735. Also, see George Washington, Jared Sparks (1839). "The Writings of George Washington: pt. IV. Letters official and private, from the beginning of his presidency to the end of his life: (v. 10) May, 1789-November, 1794. (v. 11) November, 1794-December, 1799", p.201.

12 **John Quincy Adams**. John Quincy Adams. (n.d.). AZQuotes.com. Retrieved February 16, 2019, from AZQuotes.com Web site: https://www.azquotes.com/quote/1977. Also see John Quincy Adams (1968). "Writings of John Quincey Adams."

13 **John Adams (Carved over the fireplace in the White House)**. John Adams. (n.d.). AZQuotes.com. Retrieved February 16, 2019, from AZQuotes.com Web site: https://www.azquotes.com/quote/1308274

14 **Thomas Jefferson**. Thomas Jefferson. (n.d.). AZQuotes.com. Retrieved February 16, 2019, from AZQuotes.com Web site: https://www.azquotes.com/quote/145652. Also see Thomas Jefferson (1854). "The Writings of Thomas Jefferson," p.112.

15 **Benjamin Franklin**. Benjamin Franklin Quotes. (n.d.). BrainyQuote.com. Retrieved February 16, 2019, from BrainyQuote.com Web site: https://www.brainyquote.com/quotes/benjamin_franklin_151625.

16 **Robert E. Lee**. Robert E. Lee. (n.d.). AZQuotes.com. Retrieved February 16, 2019, from AZQuotes.com Web site: https://www.azquotes.com/quote/171534. Also see "Memoirs of Robert E. Lee". Book by A. L. Long, 1886.

17 **Gordon B. Hinckley, 1996 October General Conference, "This Thing Was Not Done in a Corner."** The 166th Semiannual General Conference of the Church of Jesus Christ of Latter-day Saints, October 5, 1996, Saturday Priesthood Session. Published in the Ensign magazine, Volume 26 Number 11, November 1996. An official magazine of the Church of Jesus Christ of Latter-day Saints, published by the Church of Jesus Christ of Latter-day Saints, 50 E. North Temple Street, Salt Lake City, UT, 84150-3220, USA. Also see, Ensign, Churchofjesuschrist.org. Retrieved February 17, 2019 from Churchofjesuschrist.org website: https://www.churchofjesuschrist.org/study/ensign/1996/11/this-thing-was-not-done-in-a-corner?lang=eng.

18 **James E. Faust, 1996 October General Conference, "Honesty—a Moral Compass"**. The 166th Semiannual General Conference of the Church of Jesus Christ of Latter-day Saints, October 5, 1996, Saturday Priesthood Session. Published in the Ensign magazine, Volume 26 Number 11, November 1996. An official magazine of the Church of Jesus Christ of Latter-day Saints, published by the Church of Jesus Christ of Latter-day Saints, 50 E. North Temple Street, Salt Lake City, UT, 84150-3220, USA.

Rule #16 'Be Honest With Yourself'

Also see, Ensign, Churchofjesuschrist.org. Retrieved February 17, 2019 from Churchofjesuschrist.org website: https://www.churchofjesuschrist.org/study/ensign/1996/11/honesty-a-moral-compass?lang=eng.

19. **Richard C. Edgley, 2006 October General Conference, "Three Towels and a 25-Cent Newspaper"**. The 176th Semiannual General Conference of the Church of Jesus Christ of Latter-day Saints, October 7, 2006, Sunday Morning Session. Published in the Ensign magazine, November 2006, Volume 36 Number 11, Page 74 Par 1. An official magazine of the Church of Jesus Christ of Latter-day Saints, published by the Church of Jesus Christ of Latter-day Saints, 50 E. North Temple Street, Salt Lake City, UT, 84150-3220, USA. Also see, Ensign, Churchofjesuschrist.org. Retrieved February 17, 2019 from Churchofjesuschrist.org website: https://www.churchofjesuschrist.org/study/ensign/2006/11/three-towels-and-a-25-cent-newspaper.html?lang=eng#title1.

20. **Spencer W. Kimble: 1976 October General Conference, "A Report and a Challenge."** The 146th Semiannual General Conference of the Church of Jesus Christ of Latter-day Saints, October 2, 1976, Saturday Morning Session. Published in the Ensign magazine, Volume 06 Number 11, November 1976. An official magazine of the Church of Jesus Christ of Latter-day Saints, published by the Church of Jesus Christ of Latter-day Saints, 50 E. North Temple Street, Salt Lake City, UT, 84150-3220, USA. Also see, Ensign, Churchofjesuschrist.org. Retrieved February 17, 2019 from Churchofjesuschrist.org website: https://www.churchofjesuschrist.org/study/ensign/1976/11/a-report-and-a-challenge?lang=eng.

21. **Mark E. Petersen: 1976 October General Conference, 'The Savor of Men**. The 146th Semiannual General Conference of the Church of Jesus Christ of Latter-day Saints, October 2, 1976, Saturday Morning Session. Published in the Ensign magazine, Volume 06 Number 11, November 1976. An official magazine of the Church of Jesus Christ of Latter-day Saints, published by the Church of Jesus Christ of Latter-day Saints, 50 E. North Temple Street, Salt Lake City, UT, 84150-3220, USA. Also see, Ensign, Churchofjesuschrist.org. Retrieved February 17, 2019 from Churchofjesuschrist.org website: https://www.churchofjesuschrist.org/study/ensign/1976/11/the-savor-of-men?lang=eng.

22. **Joseph B. Wirthlin**. Joseph B. Wirthlin. (n.d.). AZQuotes.com. Retrieved February 17, 2019, from AZQuotes.com Web site: https://www.azquotes.com/quote/1202390.

23. **William Shakespeare**. William Shakespeare. (n.d.). AZQuotes.com. Retrieved February 16, 2019, from AZQuotes.com Web site: https://www.azquotes.com/quote/267272. Also see 1604-5 Mariana to Diana. "All's Well That Ends Well," act 3, sc.5, l.12-13.

24. **Albert Einstein**. Albert Einstein. (n.d.). AZQuotes.com. Retrieved February 16, 2019, from AZQuotes.com Web site: https://www.azquotes.com/quote/87347. Also, see Einstein on Politics: His Private Thoughts and Public Stands on Nationalism, Zionism, War, Peace, and the Bomb".

Rule #16 'Be Honest With Yourself'

25. **Mahatma Gandhi**. Mahatma Gandhi. (n.d.). AZQuotes.com. Retrieved February 17, 2019, from AZQuotes.com Web site: https://www.azquotes.com/quote/105932. Also, see Mahatma Gandhi, Thomas Merton (2007). "Gandhi on Non-Violence," p.47, New Directions Publishing.

26. **Kerry Stokes**. Kerry Stokes. (n.d.). AZQuotes.com. Retrieved February 17, 2019, from AZQuotes.com Web site: https://www.azquotes.com/quote/576720.

27. **Richard Bach**. Richard Bach. (n.d.). AZQuotes.com. Retrieved February 17, 2019, from AZQuotes.com Web site: https://www.azquotes.com/quote/14417. Also, see "With a Conscience — 'It's Not You. It's Me.'" by Claudia King, www.huffingtonpost.com. August 20, 2014.

28. **Waylon Jennings**. Waylon Jennings. (n.d.). AZQuotes.com. Retrieved February 17, 2019, from AZQuotes.com Web site: https://www.azquotes.com/quote/146216.

29. **Arthur C. Clark**. Arthur C. Clarke. (n.d.). AZQuotes.com. Retrieved February 17, 2019, from AZQuotes.com Web site: https://www.azquotes.com/quote/57387. Also, see "The Mammoth Book of Zingers, Quips, and One-Liners." Book by Geoff Tibballs (p. 264), 2004.

30. **Ed McMahon**. Ed McMahon. (n.d.). AZQuotes.com. Retrieved February 17, 2019, from AZQuotes.com Web site: https://www.azquotes.com/quote/195336.

31. **Mary Kay Ash**. Mary Kay Ash. (n.d.). AZQuotes.com. Retrieved February 17, 2019, from AZQuotes.com Web site: https://www.azquotes.com/quote/11379.

32. **Gorden B. Hinckley, 1996 September Ensign, "Four Simple Things to Help Our Families and Our Nations"**. Published in the Ensign magazine, Volume 26 Number 09, September 1996. An official magazine of the Church of Jesus Christ of Latter-day Saints, published by the Church of Jesus Christ of Latter-day Saints, 50 E. North Temple Street, Salt Lake City, UT, 84150-3220, USA. Also see, Ensign, Churchofjesuschrist.org. Retrieved February 17, 2019 from Churchofjesuschrist.org website: https://www.churchofjesuschrist.org/study/ensign/1996/09/four-simple-things-to-help-our-families-and-our-nations?lang=eng.

33. **Oliver Wendell Holmes**. Oliver Wendell Holmes, Sr. Quotes. (n.d.). BrainyQuote.com. Retrieved February 17, 2019, from BrainyQuote.com Web site: https://www.brainyquote.com/quotes/oliver_wendell_holmes_sr_118599.

34. **William Penn**. William Penn. (n.d.). AZQuotes.com. Retrieved February 17, 2019, from AZQuotes.com Web site: https://www.azquotes.com/quote/603832. Also, see William Penn (1841). "Fruits of solitude in reflections and maxims relating to the conduct of human life. A new ed," p.35.

Rule #16 'Be Honest With Yourself'

35 **Norman Mailer**. Norman Mailer. (n.d.). AZQuotes.com. Retrieved February 17, 2019, from AZQuotes.com Web site: https://www.azquotes.com/quote/184079. Also see 1959 Advertisements for Myself, "First Advertisement for Myself."

36 **Ralph Waldo Emerson**. Ralph Waldo Emerson. (n.d.). AZQuotes.com. Retrieved February 17, 2019, from AZQuotes.com Web site: https://www.azquotes.com/quote/437497. Also, see Ralph Waldo Emerson (1964). "The Early Lectures of Ralph Waldo Emerson," p.318, Harvard University Press.

37 **Thomas Jefferson**. Thomas Jefferson. (n.d.). AZQuotes.com. Retrieved February 17, 2019, from AZQuotes.com Web site: https://www.azquotes.com/quote/675430. Also, see Thomas Jefferson, John Dewey (2008). "The Essential Jefferson," p.81, Courier Corporation.

38 **Michel de Montaigne**. Michel de Montaigne. (n.d.). AZQuotes.com. Retrieved February 17, 2019, from AZQuotes.com Web site: https://www.azquotes.com/quote/203503. Also see, Michel de Montaigne (2016). "Delphi Complete Works of Michel de Montaigne (Illustrated)," p.901, Delphi Classics.

39 **Lyman Beecher**. Lyman Beecher. (n.d.). AZQuotes.com. Retrieved February 17, 2019, from AZQuotes.com Web site: https://www.azquotes.com/quote/960123.

40 **Ezra Taft Benson, 1986 June New Era, page 5 "To the Rising Generation."** Published in the New Era magazine, Volume 16 Number 06, Page 05, June 1986. An official magazine of the Church of Jesus Christ of Latter-day Saints, published by the Church of Jesus Christ of Latter-day Saints, 50 E. North Temple Street, Salt Lake City, UT, 84150-3220, USA. Also, see New Era, Churchofjesuschrist.org. Retrieved February 17, 2019 from Churchofjesuschrist.org website: https://www.churchofjesuschrist.org/study/new-era/1986/06/to-the-rising-generation?lang=eng.

Also quoted in 1992 April General Conference, "Seeking the Good." The 162nd Annual General Conference of the Church of Jesus Christ of Latter-day Saints, April 5, 1992, Sunday Afternoon Session. Published in the Ensign magazine, Volume 22 Number 05, May 1992. An official magazine of the Church of Jesus Christ of Latter-day Saints, published by the Church of Jesus Christ of Latter-day Saints, 50 E. North Temple Street, Salt Lake City, UT, 84150-3220, USA. Also see, Ensign, Churchofjesuschrist.org. Retrieved February 17, 2019, from Churchofjesuschrist.org website: https://www.churchofjesuschrist.org/study/ensign/1992/05/seeking-the-good?lang=eng.

41 **William Shakespeare**. "Hamlet" (1601) Act 1, Scene 3, 1. 58. Also, see William Shakespeare. (n.d.). AZQuotes.com. Retrieved February 17, 2019, from AZQuotes.com Web site: https://www.azquotes.com/quote/267254.

Are We Done Yet?

Rule #17

'Manage Your Procrastinations, Or They Will Manage You'

Rule #17 'Manage Your Procrastinations, Or They Will Manage You'

A Smack in the Face:

I am going to start out by smacking you right in the face with Rule #1 *'Failure Is Not an Option'*. Why? Because if you are procrastinating, then you are failing at something. Stop procrastinating and just **DO IT NOW.**

Calming It Down:

Now that you are awake, let's calm it down a bit. I'll start over by saying that there is not a person out there in this mortal life that does not have some issue with procrastination. Procrastination is another one of Satan's great tools. I call it, Satan's Vice-Grips. Unlike a regular pair of pliers, Vice-Grips are pliers that can be locked into position and only released by using the lever. When procrastination takes hold of us, we have to press the release lever before it lets us go. I use the Vice-Grip analogy because, for many of us, procrastination has a strong, locked hold on us. Once the Vice-Grip is locked in place, it takes little or no effort to maintain its grip.

It is the same with procrastination; once it locks on to you, it takes very little to no effort to prevent you from completing your tasks, whether they be temporal or spiritual.

As I look at myself in the mirror each morning, I go over the list of the things I could accomplish in the day, and then I start thinking of all the reasons why I don't want to or can't do the task. Isn't that the way with a lot of us?

When we let negativity in, and we start to think of all the reasons not to start a task, that is the moment when Satan clamps down on us using his Vice-Grips of procrastination. Sadly, we are all victims of this in one form or another.

At the end of each day, if we would take an honest accounting of ourselves, we would see just how many times we allowed ourselves to fall into Satan's grip of procrastination. Just think

Rule #17 'Manage Your Procrastinations, Or They Will Manage You'

A Smack in the Face:

I am going to start out by smacking you right in the face with Rule #1 *'Failure Is Not an Option'*. Why? Because if you are procrastinating, then you are failing at something. Stop procrastinating and just **DO IT NOW.**

Calming It Down:

Now that you are awake, let's calm it down a bit. I'll start over by saying that there is not a person out there in this mortal life that does not have some issue with procrastination. Procrastination is another one of Satan's great tools. I call it, Satan's Vice-Grips. Unlike a regular pair of pliers, Vice-Grips are pliers that can be locked into position and only released by using the lever. When procrastination takes hold of us, we have to press the release lever before it lets us go. I use the Vice-Grip analogy because, for many of us, procrastination has a strong, locked hold on us. Once the Vice-Grip is locked in place, it takes little or no effort to maintain its grip.

It is the same with procrastination; once it locks on to you, it takes very little to no effort to prevent you from completing your tasks, whether they be temporal or spiritual.

As I look at myself in the mirror each morning, I go over the list of the things I could accomplish in the day, and then I start thinking of all the reasons why I don't want to or can't do the task. Isn't that the way with a lot of us?

When we let negativity in, and we start to think of all the reasons not to start a task, that is the moment when Satan clamps down on us using his Vice-Grips of procrastination. Sadly, we are all victims of this in one form or another.

At the end of each day, if we would take an honest accounting of ourselves, we would see just how many times we allowed ourselves to fall into Satan's grip of procrastination. Just think

Are We Done Yet?

Rule #17

'Manage Your Procrastinations, Or They Will Manage You'

of the things that could be accomplished and how wise and blessed we would be if we could learn to eliminate procrastination from our daily lives.

What a Waste:

No matter how little we procrastinate, it is still time wasted, and each second of that time keeps adding and growing. We cannot subtract from the amount of time lost in our life; we can only add to it. As I have said and will say again, "Time wasted is time wasted and will forever be gone."

With all of today's high technology at our fingertips, we still cannot travel back in time, nor do we have the means yet to stop time. If we could, it would allow some of us all the time in the world to procrastinate. But I am sorry to tell you that there is only one way to limit the loss of time due to procrastination, and the secret to that I can tell you in two words: don't procrastinate.

Heavenly Father has warned us that the day will come when there will be an account of how we spent our time here in mortality. I can tell you that Heavenly Father is neither a great fan nor a supporter of people wasting time. The scriptures are clear; Heavenly Father gives us many warnings regarding the subject.

> ### (Bible New Testament: 2 Thessalonians 3: 9-12)
> *9 Not because we have not power, but to make ourselves an ensample unto you to follow us.*
>
> *10 For even when we were with you, this we commanded you, that if any would not work, neither should he eat.*
>
> *11 For we hear that there are some which walk among you disorderly, working not at all, but are busybodies.*
>
> *12 Now them that are such we command and exhort by our Lord Jesus Christ, that with quietness they work, and eat their own bread.*

Rule #17 'Manage Your Procrastinations, Or They Will Manage You'

Listen to the Masters:

At the start of this chapter, I hit you with Rule #1 *'Failure Is Not an Option'*, now I would like you to ponder a few writings taken from both scripture and quotes from some wise people that support my testimony of Rule #17. These writings provided a positive motivation to help my mind break free from the vice-like grip of procrastination and kept me moving in a better direction.

Here in order are my 10 top motivating quotes to help deal with procrastination:

1.) **(Mary Ellen Smoot, 2000 April General Conference, "We Are Creators")**[6]
"The time for procrastination is over. Begin! Don't be afraid. Do the best you can. Of course you will make mistakes. Everyone does. Learn from them and move forward."

2.) **(Ian S. Ardern, 2011 October General Conference "A Time to Prepare")**[7]
"Satan will tempt us to misuse our time through disguised distractions. Although temptations will come, Elder Quentin L. Cook taught that "Saints who respond to the Savior's message will not be led astray by distracting and destructive pursuits."

Time marches swiftly forward to the tick of the clock. Today would be a good day, while the clock of mortality ticks, to review what we are doing to prepare to meet God. I testify that there are great rewards for those who take time in mortality to prepare for immortality and eternal life.

The poor use of time is a close cousin of idleness. As we follow the command to "cease to be idle" (D&C 88:124), we must be sure that being busy also equates to being productive."

3.) **(Teachings of Presidents of the Church: Brigham Young [1997], 286)[8]**
"We are all indebted to God for the ability to use time to advantage, and he will require of us a strict account of [its] disposition."

4.) **(Marvin J. Ashton, 1983 April General Conference, "Straightway")[9]**
"If you will that I give unto you a place in the celestial world, you must prepare yourselves by doing the things which I have commanded you and required of you," said the Lord. (D&C 78:7.) To take that first step may require great courage, but somehow possibilities and potential strengths begin to appear once the decision to act positively is made. Unsuspected courage and strength will be given to those who start forward in the right decision."

5.) **(Bible Old Testament: Ecclesiastes 10:18)[1]**
By much slothfulness the building decayeth; and through idleness of the hands the house droppeth through.

6.) **(Bible Old Testament: Ezekiel 16:49)[1]**
Behold, this was the iniquity of thy sister Sodom, pride, fulness of bread, and abundance of idleness was in her and in her daughters, neither did she strengthen the hand of the poor and needy.

7.) **(Book of Mormon: Alma 1:32)[3]**
For those who did not belong to their church did indulge themselves in sorceries, and in idolatry or idleness, and in babblings)

8.) **(Book of Mormon: Alma 34:33)[3]**
And now, as I said unto you before, as ye have had so many witnesses, therefore, I beseech of you that ye do not procrastinate the day of your repentance until the end; for after this day of life, which is given us to prepare for eternity, behold, if we do not improve our time while in this life, then cometh

Rule #17 'Manage Your Procrastinations, Or They Will Manage You'

the night of darkness wherein there can be no labor performed.

9.) (Book of Mormon: Alma 34:35-36)[3]
For behold, if ye have procrastinated the day repentance even until death, behold, ye have become subjected to the spirit of the devil, and he doth seal you his; therefore, the Spirit of the Lord hath withdrawn from you, and hath no place in you, and the devil hath all power over you; and this is the final state of the wicked.

And this I know, because the Lord hath said he dwelleth not in unholy temples, but in the hearts of the righteous doth he dwell;

10.) (Elder Henry B. Eyring, 2007 April General Conference, "This Day")[10]
"All of us will need His help to avoid the tragedy of procrastinating what we must do here and now to have eternal life.

There is a danger in the word someday when what it means is "not this day." "Someday I will repent." "Someday I will forgive him." "Someday I will speak to my friend about the Church." "Someday I will start to pay tithing." "Someday I will return to the temple." "Someday ... "

The scriptures make the danger of delay clear. It is that we may discover that we have run out of time. The God who gives us each day as a treasure will require an accounting. We will weep, and He will weep, if we have intended to repent and to serve Him in tomorrows which never came or have dreamt of yesterdays where the opportunity to act was past. This day is a precious gift of God. The thought "Someday I will" can be a thief of the opportunities of time and the blessings of eternity."

Rule #17 'Manage Your Procrastinations, Or They Will Manage You'

More is too Much More?

I could continue cutting and pasting quotes on the subject of procrastination. There are thousands of them that you can easily find for yourself. There are also thousands of self-help books written on the subject.

If I only included a tenth of all the possible sources, there would be so many pages for me to write that I could possibly procrastinate writing this rule forever. So, since Rule #17 is my rule, and it was intended to help motivate me from procrastinating, I will stick with my top 10 likable quotes.

What's Your Quote?

If you do not find yourself motivated by any of my top 10 picks, do a little research, and you'll be able to find your own inspiration. I can assure you that with very little effort, you can find the positive words of advice and encouragement you need to get to work. After you have found your quotes, take the one you like the best, print it out in nice, big, easy to read characters, and place it where, at the beginning and end of your day, it is clearly staring you in the face.

What Brand Is Yours:

Procrastination would be a lot easier to manage if there was only one type. However, that is not the case. The various forms of procrastination can be compared to the assortment of brands and models of cars on our highways and streets. There is a color, make, and model for every version of procrastination we experience. Yet, at its base, a car is a car no matter the model, and procrastination is procrastination no matter the reason.

On the other hand, having a knowledge and understanding of the model and style of car you own can make you a better driver. Different cars handle differently, for example, how well or how fast you can safely drive on a curvy road depends a lot on the vehicle and its equipment. The same goes for

Rule #17 'Manage Your Procrastinations, Or They Will Manage You'

procrastination; how you handle procrastination depends on your personality and the excuses you make for it.

As I said, there are hundreds of books on how to manage procrastination. The reason there are so many books is that there is no one simple answer. There are just as many different types of personalities as there are reasons to procrastinate. And I am in no way an expert on how to deal with procrastination. I have, however, learned the reasons for my procrastinations and have developed a means of managing them. What I will attempt to do is explain how I learned to understand my personality and its relation to my procrastinations and the method I put in place to deal with and avoid putting off chores and tasks.

Mr. & Mrs. Personality:

'Who am I?' is a big question that people ask themselves every day. Surprisingly, it is easy to answer. There is a core 'you' that makes up your fundamental personality. If you can grasp the fact that there is a core to your being, then you will be able to answer the question of 'Who am I?'

Your core is the fundamental part of your personality that makes you, uniquely you. It is your foundation that supports all your other personality traits, and it rarely changes. It is your core personality that determines how you handle life. It is through life experiences that you learn to manage, or not manage, your core personality. In respect to procrastination, how well you manage yourself is determined by how well you have learned to manage the core you.

Agree or Disagree? That is the Question:

There are those out there in the world that would disagree with me on the philosophy of having a core foundation that makes you who you are. They would also disagree with my statement that this core person rarely changes. If you are one of these people, then **STOP** reading because I can't help you. All of my rules and how I apply them are based on a belief that you have a core person within you, made by God, which makes procrastination; how you handle procrastination depends on your personality and the excuses you make for it.

As I said, there are hundreds of books on how to manage procrastination. The reason there are so many books is that there is no one simple answer. There are just as many different types of personalities as there are reasons to procrastinate. And I am in no way an expert on how to deal with procrastination. I have, however, learned the reasons for my procrastinations and have developed a means of managing them. What I will attempt to do is explain how I learned to understand my personality and its relation to my procrastinations and the method I put in place to deal with and avoid putting off chores and tasks.

Mr. & Mrs. Personality:

'Who am I?' is a big question that people ask themselves every day. Surprisingly, it is easy to answer. There is a core 'you' that makes up your fundamental personality. If you can grasp the fact that there is a core to your being, then you will be able to answer the question of 'Who am I?'

Your core is the fundamental part of your personality that makes you, uniquely you. It is your foundation that supports all your other personality traits, and it rarely changes. It is your core personality that determines how you handle life. It is through life experiences that you learn to manage, or not manage, your core personality. In respect to procrastination, how well you manage yourself is determined by how well you have learned to manage the core you.

Agree or Disagree? That is the Question:

There are those out there in the world that would disagree with me on the philosophy of having a core foundation that makes you who you are. They would also disagree with my statement that this core person rarely changes. If you are one of these people, then **STOP** reading because I can't help you. All of my rules and how I apply them are based on a belief that you have a core person within you, made by God, which makes

Rule #17 'Manage Your Procrastinations, Or They Will Manage You'

More is too Much More?

I could continue cutting and pasting quotes on the subject of procrastination. There are thousands of them that you can easily find for yourself. There are also thousands of self-help books written on the subject.

If I only included a tenth of all the possible sources, there would be so many pages for me to write that I could possibly procrastinate writing this rule forever. So, since Rule #17 is my rule, and it was intended to help motivate me from procrastinating, I will stick with my top 10 likable quotes.

What's Your Quote?

If you do not find yourself motivated by any of my top 10 picks, do a little research, and you'll be able to find your own inspiration. I can assure you that with very little effort, you can find the positive words of advice and encouragement you need to get to work. After you have found your quotes, take the one you like the best, print it out in nice, big, easy to read characters, and place it where, at the beginning and end of your day, it is clearly staring you in the face.

What Brand Is Yours:

Procrastination would be a lot easier to manage if there was only one type. However, that is not the case. The various forms of procrastination can be compared to the assortment of brands and models of cars on our highways and streets. There is a color, make, and model for every version of procrastination we experience. Yet, at its base, a car is a car no matter the model, and procrastination is procrastination no matter the reason.

On the other hand, having a knowledge and understanding of the model and style of car you own can make you a better driver. Different cars handle differently, for example, how well or how fast you can safely drive on a curvy road depends a lot on the vehicle and its equipment. The same goes for you unique and defines the answer to the 'Who I am?' question. Learning to understand who that core person is will help you to manage all aspects of your life. It gives a required understanding, an important piece of knowledge you must have about yourself, to utilize my list of rules effectively.

The Core Me:

I do not have a clue as to who the core you is. I am not you. As I said, we are all unique. The question of who is the core you is a question we each must answer for ourselves. What is the foundation of your personality? That is something only you can answer.

There is a great Disney movie 'Inside Out'[11]. Though it is an animated movie made for children, I think you would really enjoy the concept of it, and it relates directly to what I mean when I talk about the "core you". Watch it!!! Plus, it has some good humor. It's one of my many favorite Disney movies. What a great Sunday night activity!

I will do what I can to help you find the answer to the question, 'who is the core me?'. It would be a lot easier if we were sitting here together having this discussion. My wife says that one of my most cherished gifts from God is the ability to gain a quick understanding of people and situations. Of course, as with any gift, I remind her it can be my curse as well.

My trouble (or curse) with this gift of quickly understanding people is that out of respect for everyone in a conversation or situation, I have to control my impatience while I wait for others to come to the same conclusion that I have come to. But, since you are not here with me, the upside is you don't have to deal with my impatience, the downside is that you are going to have to do all the work and evaluate yourself. I personally don't find the self-evaluation a big downside. I don't believe you can really find the core you if you don't do a large part of the work on your own. Do I need to remind you that the task may be the answer, but it is the journey that got you the answer? Turning to someone else to do an evaluation on you and then giving you a report may help, but it will not provide you the complete solution you need. If you really are sincere about solving your procrastination issue, then you need a comprehensive answer to the question, who is the core me?

Eliminating procrastination from our lives may have a simple answer, but is far from being a simple fix. Knowing the core of who you are is the very heart of understanding why you procrastinate, and the fix requires a profound, honest answer to the question. I know I am repeating myself here, but this message is crucial.

Time to Evaluate:

To find the answer, who is the core you, you will need a serious, heartfelt dose of Rule #16 *'Be Honest With Yourself'*. The better you have Rule #16 down, the easier the evaluation and the better chance of understanding the core you, you will be.

To evaluate yourself, study your reactions to your world around you, ponder them, then study some more. After you think you have a good solid answer ask Heavenly Father his opinion on it. After all, who knows you better?

To help with your self-evaluation, I will share with you the process I went through while seeking to define who my core person is. Perhaps by doing that, you can determine what you need to do to find the core you.

I started by making a list of some questions I would ask someone else as I tried to understand who they are and then answered the question for myself.

One problem I had was that I got so caught up in defining the core me and being honest with myself, I lost track of the fact that I was only supposed to be working on solving my procrastination problem, and not all of my worldly and spiritual issues as well. I needed to apply Rule #6 *'You Cut Down a Forest One Tree at a Time'* to prevent myself from trying to cut down the whole forest of life's imperfections at

Rule #17 'Manage Your Procrastinations, Or They Will Manage You'

the same time. I needed to focus on procrastination, and I needed to remember to keep the questions and answers geared toward helping me understand the how's and why's.

Core Me Q & A:

Here is a list of twenty of the questions I asked myself, with abridged answers:

(Remember Rule #16 *'Be Honest With Yourself'*)

1.) Q: Are You basically an honest person when dealing with others?

    A: Yes

2.) Q: Are You basically an honest person when dealing with yourself?

    A: Yes

3.) Q: To whom do you give more value, yourself, or others?

    A: Others

4.) Q: What is the quantity of your work, meaning, are you a hard worker, or do you only do what is minimal, or somewhere in between?

    A: I work too hard; I am a workaholic.

5.) Q: What is the quality of your work?

    A: I am a detailed perfectionist, rarely am I totally happy with the quality of my work.

6.) Q: Do you avoid work, or do you jump in and help when you see a task that could use your help?

    A: I jump in and help.

7.) Q: Would you prefer to follow or lead when doing a task with others?

    A: Lead

Rule #17 'Manage Your Procrastinations, Or They Will Manage You'

8.) Q: Can you follow directions as stated? (This is a direct statement, and requiring only a Yes or No answer)

   A: Yes

9.) Q: Would you prefer to handle things on a 'To-Do-List' one at a time or multitask them.

   A: Prefer staying focused on one task.

10.) Q: When required to multitask, do you become more stressed?

   A: No, I just prefer not to multi-task, but I can multitask when needed

11.) Q: Do you make lists of things you are working on or need to work on?

   A: Not typically, only if my 'To-Do-List' is longer than 20 things. I get too stressed after 20 if I don't.

12.) Q: Are you easily distracted?

   A: Somewhat and more than I would like.

13.) Q: Do you have a general fear of failure? If yes, does it make you hesitant at starting a task?

   A: Yes, and Yes

14.) Q: Do you generally feel unqualified for the task you are asked to do?

   A: Yes

15.) Q: Do you understand the concept of putting first things first?

   A: Yes, it is one of the seven habits called 'First Things First' from Stephen Covey's 'Seven Habits of Highly Successful People.' It is about understanding how to prioritize based on importance, and the knowledge of what is important. This is my Rule #18.

Rule #17 'Manage Your Procrastinations, Or They Will Manage You'

16.) Q: Do you have any issues at all when it comes to accepting responsibility for things that go wrong?

A: No, I believe strongly in owning up to my responsibilities.

17.) Q: Do you have an issue starting a task?

A: Yes

18.) Q: Do you have an issue with completing a task once you have started it?

A: No, once I start, I don't like to stop until the task is completed. Hard to get me away from the task once I have started.

19.) Q: Give the four most significant reasons you think are the causes for your procrastinating, in order.

A: One-word 'FEAR'.

A: Don't feel I have the knowledge to do a good job; I'm a perfectionist.

A: Don't like the task I have been given to do.

A: Prefer to do other things; therefore, I don't give the task the importance it needs to start it.

20.) Q: Physically, and mentally are you an energetic person with lots of energy or something else?

A: I am an energetic person with a weak starting battery, who could use a few Dr. Peppers to get moving.

These were a few of my questions I asked myself. You will need to come up with your own Q&A list. Both your questions and your answers will help you in two important ways. First, they will help you gain a better knowledge of your strengths and weaknesses towards work/tasks. Second, they will help you learn what it is that motivates you.

Working through this question and answer process will help you to define what things you need to be doing to motivate yourself.

Rule #17 'Manage Your Procrastinations, Or They Will Manage You'

The Discovery:

Answering this list of questions, I didn't discover anything new about myself. The process of analyzing the Q&A helped me to better visualize myself from the inside out. It was like taking a mirror inside my mind and looking at the reflection of my soul. I was better able to see my strengths and use them to overcome my weaknesses. The process also helped me to define actions I could take to motivate myself and overcome the desire to procrastinate.

Here are a few things I put together based on the results of my self-analysis from the Q&A that helped me stop procrastinating. I learned that one of the biggest reasons for my procrastination stemmed from fear. Fear of failure or doubt that I didn't have the knowledge or skills to do a job. I also learned that helping people or not letting them down was one of my biggest motivators. The Q&A reminded me that I am not a lazy person, but I do have a hard time getting started. Recognizing this fact made me feel better about myself. I realized that if the need to complete a task only affects me, I tend not to be as concerned about getting that task done, which in turn feeds my reason to procrastinate.

On the other hand, when I realize that the completion of a task affects others, I don't procrastinate. I also came to understand that the size of a job and/or lack of knowledge concerning a given task, instills in me the most fear. Big jobs or tasks that require expertise beyond my comfort zone incite the procrastinator in me and prevent me from even wanting to start the task. Yet, once I overcome that fear and start a task, I am a hard worker who gets the job done and done right.

So, basically, the Q&A tells me that I don't have trouble doing hard work. My issue is getting started. This, in turn, says that I am the type of person that doesn't need extra motivation once I am working. The Q&A also pointed out that I need to manage distractions. Another fact the Q&A revealed that I prefer to focus on and complete one task at a time. That's too bad for me since life is one big multi-tasking world.

Solution:

Based on my Q&A discoveries, I came up with a solution that works for me. Since my motivation is strong while doing a task, it means I only need to focus on how to get started. Because I care about how the task affects other people more than it might affect me, I use that factor as the main motivator to begin. Another factor that feeds my procrastination and keeps me from starting the task is the knowledge that I will have to stop or pause before the whole task is complete. To overcome this obstacle, either mentally or on paper, I break the job up into mini-tasks. Then I set manageable and achievable goals to complete each mini-task. And I am able to work without focusing on the complete task or feeling anxious about being interrupted before the job is done. This system helps me set breakpoints. Completing each mini-tasks satisfies my need to feel I have accomplished a goal, and in turn, it allows me to work on other tasks without feeling I am neglecting the total task (multi-tasking is now possible).

By breaking the task down into mini-tasks, I don't feel overwhelmed by the whole job. This is why I have Rule #6 *'You Cut down a Forest One Tree at a Time',* and it fits right in with Rule #17.

Wrap-Up:

I hope some of what I have written helps you deal with your procrastination. Procrastination is Satan's favorite tool. It is his Vice-Grip he uses to prevent us from accomplishing so many things. Life is too short, and we do not have time to procrastinate. Satan knows that every time we complete a task, it brings us new knowledge, and that knowledge brings us closer to understanding our Heavenly Father. No matter how big or small the task, God sets every task in our path to help us grow so we may become more like Him. Go forward and **Do It Now**.

Rule #17 'Manage Your Procrastinations, Or They Will Manage You'

(H. L. Hunt, Jr)[12]
Decide what you want, decide what you are willing to exchange for it. Establish your priorities and go to work.

Rule #17 'Manage Your Procrastinations,
Or They Will Manage You'

Endnotes:

1. **King James Version of the Bible, The Old Testament of Our Lord and Saviour Jesus Christ.** Published by The Church of Jesus Christ of Latter-day Saints, Salt Lake City, Utah, USA. Copywrite 2013.

2. **King James Version of the Bible, The New Testament of Our Lord and Saviour Jesus Christ.** Published by The Church of Jesus Christ of Latter-day Saints, Salt Lake City, Utah, USA. Copywrite 2013.

3. **The Book of Mormon Another Testament of Jesus Christ.** Published by The Church of Jesus Christ of Latter-day Saints, Salt Lake City, Utah, USA. The first English edition published in Palmyra, New York, USA, in 1830. Copywrite 2013.

4. **The Doctrine and Covenants of The Church of Jesus Christ of Latter-Day Saints.** Containing Revelations Give to Joseph Smith, the Prophet. With some additions by his successors in the Presidency of the Church. Published by The Church of Jesus Christ of Latter-day Saints, Salt Lake City, Utah, USA. Copywrite 2013.

5. **The Pearl of Great Price.** A selection from the revelations, translations, and narrations of Joseph Smith, First Prophet, seer, and revelator to The Church of Jesus Christ of Latter-Day Saints. Published by The Church of Jesus Christ of Latter-day Saints, Salt Lake City, Utah, USA. Copywrite 2013.

6. **Mary Ellen Smoot, 2000 April General Conference, "We Are Creators".** The 170th Annual General Conference of the Church of Jesus Christ of Latter-day Saints, April 1, 2000, Sunday Morning Session. Published in the Ensign magazine, Volume 30 Number 05, May 2000. An official magazine of the Church of Jesus Christ of Latter-day Saints, published by the Church of Jesus Christ of Latter-day Saints, 50 E. North Temple Street, Salt Lake City, UT, 84150-3220, USA. Also see, Ensign, Churchofjesuschrist.org. Retrieved February 17, 2019, from Churchofjesuschrist.org website: https://www.churchofjesuschrist.org/study/ensign/2000/05/we-are-creators.html?lang=eng#title1.

7. **Ian S. Ardern, 2011 October General Conference "A Time to Prepare".** The 181st Semiannual General Conference of the Church of Jesus Christ of Latter-day Saints, October 1, 2011, Saturday Afternoon Session. Published in the Ensign magazine, Volume 41 Number 11, November 2011. An official magazine of the Church of Jesus Christ of Latter-day Saints, published by the Church of Jesus Christ of Latter-day Saints, 50 E. North Temple Street, Salt Lake City, UT, 84150-3220, USA. Also see, Ensign, Churchofjesuschrist.org. Retrieved February 17, 2019, from Churchofjesuschrist.org website: https://www.churchofjesuschrist.org/study/general-conference/2011/10/a-time-to-prepare?lang=eng.

8. **Brigham Young, "Teachings of Presidents of the Church: Brigham Young"** Published in the Teachings of the Presidents of the Church: Brigham Young, "Eternal Judgment" page-286 paragraph-1. An official manual of the Church of Jesus Christ of Latter-day Saints published 1997 by the Church of Jesus Christ of Latter-day Saints, 50 E. North Temple Street, Salt Lake City, UT, 84150-3220, USA. Also, see Churchofjesuschrist.org. Retrieved February

Rule #17 'Manage Your Procrastinations, Or They Will Manage You'

17, 2019, from Churchofjesuschrist.org website: https://www.churchofjesuschrist.org/study/manual/teachings-brigham-young/chapter-39?lang=eng.

9 **Marvin J. Ashton, 1983 April General Conference, "Straightway"**. The 153rd Annual General Conference of the Church of Jesus Christ of Latter-day Saints, April 2, 1983, Saturday Afternoon Session. Published in the Ensign magazine, Volume 13 Number 05, May 1983. An official magazine of the Church of Jesus Christ of Latter-day Saints, published by the Church of Jesus Christ of Latter-day Saints, 50 E. North Temple Street, Salt Lake City, UT, 84150-3220, USA. Also see, Ensign, Churchofjesuschrist.org. Retrieved February 17, 2019, from Churchofjesuschrist.org website: https://www.churchofjesuschrist.org/study/ensign/1983/05/straightway?lang=eng.

10 **Henry B. Eyring, 2007 April General Conference, "This Day"**. The 153rd Annual General Conference of the Church of Jesus Christ of Latter-day Saints, April 1, 2007, Sunday Afternoon Session. Published in the Ensign magazine, Volume 37 Number 05, page 89 paragraph 5, May 2007. An official magazine of the Church of Jesus Christ of Latter-day Saints, published by the Church of Jesus Christ of Latter-day Saints, 50 E. North Temple Street, Salt Lake City, UT, 84150-3220, USA. Also see, Ensign, Churchofjesuschrist.org. Retrieved February 17, 2019, from Churchofjesuschrist.org website: https://www.churchofjesuschrist.org/study/ensign/2007/05/this-day?lang=eng.

11 **Inside Out**. Inside Out is a 2015 American 3D computer-animated comedy-drama film produced by Pixar Animation Studios and released by Walt Disney Pictures. The film was directed by Pete Doctor and co-directed by Ronnie del Carmen, with a screenplay written by Doctor, Meg LeFauve and Josh Cooley, adapted from a story by Doctor and del Carmen. See Inside out. (n.d.). en.wikipedia.com. Retrieved April 10, 2019, from en.wikipedia.com Web site: https://en.wikipedia.org/wiki/Inside Out_(2015_film)

12 **H. L. Hunt, Jr**. H. L. Hunt. (n.d.). AZQuotes.com. Retrieved February 21, 2019, from AZQuotes.com Web site: https://www.azquotes.com/quote/138947.

And The First Shall Be Last

Rule #18

'First Things First'

Rule #18 'First Things First'

Who's On First?

Some of my rules are power rules. They are for motivating you, like Rule #1 *'Failure is Not an Option'*, Rule #4 *'Always Give a 110 Percent'*, and, Rule #15 *'What is Worth Doing is Worth Doing* Right'.

Other Rules are guiding rules, such as Rule #2 *'Don't Assume'*, Rule #8 *'Don't Catch Idiotitis'*, Rule #16 *'Be Honest With Yourself'*, and Rule #19 *'Preferences Bend, Principles Don't'*.

What's On Second?

Then I have focusing rules such as Rule *#5 'You Always Know Something'*, Rule #6 *'You Cut Down a Forest One Tree at a Time'*, Rule #13 *'Focus on the Journey Not the Task'*, and Rule #17 *'Manage Your Procrastinations'*. These rules are there to teach you how to stay focused, reminding you not to get distracted but to remain attentive to the task at hand and what the real mission is.

I Don't Know is On Third:

Another rule category is what I call the balancing rules, such as Rule #3 *'There are Fluid Goals and There are Solid Goals'*, Rule #11 *'If You Can't Take Care of Yourself, You Can't Take Care of Others'*, and Rule #20 *'If Nothing Changes Nothing Changes, and History Repeats Itself'*. These rules are there to help you get perspective on your priorities and thus keep your life in balance.

Rule #18 *'First Things First'* is one of the rules that fall into the life balance rule category. Although I find all the balancing rules to be vital, Rule #18 carries more weight than the others. At the same time, Rule #18 *'First Things First'* is also the most challenging of the balancing rules for me to manage in my life.

I Am Feeling A Little Overwhelmed:

All of my rules exist to help me deal with the areas of my life where I struggle. So why is Rule #18 so difficult for me to manage? I ask this question to myself regularly as I attempt to adhere to Rule #18. I believe a big part of my issue with this rule stems from the fact that I am a workaholic, and workaholics thrive on work. I have more personal tasks and accomplishments that I want to complete than I feel God has allotted me time. Moreover, my personal task list does not even include the requests made of me by others. I do not believe I will ever complete everything I want to accomplish in this lifetime on Earth.

My big issue in dealing with Rule #18 is getting a good grasp of what is first and what comes second in life. When considering my personal goals, family responsibilities, and contributions to my community, I tend to have lapses in judgment on what task or objective should be my first priority. I allow my mind to become clouded over by work demands and other low priority tasks I want to accomplish. Without proper prioritization, Rule #18 easily becomes a rule of frustration when, in fact, its purpose is to eliminate frustration.

Who Are You?

One of my personal tasks that has caused me great frustration is finding time to write this book. It has taken me years to fit this task into my life. Many times, when I thought I would have a free moment to work on the book, I allowed that time to be stolen away by something else I felt was more important.

I don't cope very well with open-ended tasks, ones with no clear deadline, or never seem to be completed. I am also limited to the number of tasks I can manage. As my brain reaches my task limit saturation point, my attitude is affected negatively. I can tell when I am at my saturation point by my mood, because it becomes grouchy and easily agitated. I get stressed over the task list and start to fear that I am unable to

Rule #18 'First Things First'

do everything on my list. To resolve this disliked mood, I'm forced to evaluate the tasks I don't have time for and ask myself, "how important are these tasks?" Then I have to decide what to do about each item on the list. One way or another I have to deal with a task to be able to remove it from the list and put it out of my mind. I cannot leave jobs unfinished. It will drive me crazy. I either have to complete the job—see it through to the end, decide it is finished as it is, or delete it from my list. If I don't do something with a task to call it finished, I will go crazy, or at the least, be resigned to a very unhappy state of mind.

Most tasks on my list I find hard to delete. After all, they have been put on my list for a reason. People related tasks are almost impossible for me to remove. It is not as if you can just push the 'delete' key on the computer and then poof family, friends, or people in need go away. People related tasks are generally backed by a promise, and breaking promises carries consequences.

In the case of this book, I could easily delete it with the push of a computer key. And there have been a few times I came close to giving up and telling it goodbye. This task certainly has consumed a lot of my time. At one point, I came closer than ever to pushing that delete key. At that moment, I had to decide just how important the completion of this book was to me. Rather than entertaining fantasies, I needed to make a final decision. Do I complete the book? Leave it unfinished? Which I've already mentioned is not in my nature. Or delete years of, thought, care, sacrifice, writing, researching, and rewriting, I have put into this book. Being forced to consider my options was a wake-up call. I had to understand the importance of personal tasks and how I needed to make them a priority. Personal goals need to be considered as a part of my first things first list instead of putting myself in the second or third task category.

This book is an integral part of me. It is my legacy I plan to leave for my posterity. Currently, my posterity consists of 5 children, 18 grandchildren, and 8 great-grandchildren. I have come to the conclusion that this book is very important to me. Periodically I have needed to remind myself just how important this book is, the value I believe it to be worth, and ensure I set aside time to write it. So why do I bring up the writing of this book and my family? Well, it has to do with putting 'First Things First', and family is near the top of my priorities, and this book is for and about family.

The Man of Inspiration:

The inspiration for Rule #18, First Things First, came from reading 'Seven Habits of Highly Successful People' by Stephen Covey. Covey asked the questions, what are the important things in your life? What means the most to you? Then his book challenged me to list them in order of importance. Or, as Stephen says, 'Put first things first, and then second things second and so on.'

I had always felt that I had my list of what was important to me in order. But when Stephen Covey got me to write my list down and really take a hard look at how I was implementing prioritization in my life. Let me tell you, it was more than an eye-opener. I hadn't realized how poorly I was managing the things that meant the most to me. First things were not coming up first nearly as often as they should. Instead, they were coming in third.

I Don't Know On Third:

What is first in your life, then second, and so on? The order in my life is this: God first, family second, work third, and then friends. Putting work before friends may seem a little odd, but without work, you neglect family. Therefore, work and friends have to be balanced. Work will always win over friends if the lack of working will cause undue suffering to the family. Thus, work comes before friends.

Order, Order, We Must Have Order:

I gave you the order in which I prioritize things in my life. Sadly, however, that does not mean I always act on them in that order. The consequences of not adhering to my first things first priority list causes my life to get out of balance. When my life gets out of balance, my life does not flow as smoothly as I would like. When life isn't flowing smoothly, tasks become harder and take longer to complete. When tasks take longer, my list gets longer. When I have too many undone tasks on my list, I become overwhelmed and agitated. When I am in an agitated state, it is neither good for the people around me nor myself. It is hard to feel joy or spread joy to others when you are in an overwhelmed state of mind. There is a law called cause and effect; you can't beat it.

Making a general priority list of what we think should be first, second, and third in life is simple. Sticking to your priority list is not so simple. That is because each area of priority, God, family, work, and friends is a category, and each category has sub-priorities. You see, when we place too much importance on the sub-priorities, we really start to get ourselves in trouble. Those lesser priorities eat up your time, and without realizing it, you're left with no time to handle the higher priorities.

For example, God is at the top of my priorities and my first things first list. Yet not all things God would have me do are of equal importance. The truth is some of those items belong on my second things-to-do list or even my third things-to-do list. Taking care of family is an excellent example of this issue because family also falls under the God category. This is an area where a lot of people get themselves confused and in trouble while trying to manage their priorities and first things first list.

The family is second in the order of priority; however, as I said, taking care of family is also a part of my first priority because it is a commandment of God, and God is first. So, as part of my 'First Thing First' rule, I need to ensure that God's church duties do not overly interfere with God's family duties.

People tend to overload their 'first things first' list with sub-priority obligations, many of which really belong on the 'second things second' or the 'third things third' list. The result is that while you are off doing a less important task, you run yourself out of the time you need to handle your real priorities, those items that should have been on your 'first things first' list. As a result, your real priorities become neglected.

I never said that priority one, in my case, God, was more important than any of the other priority categories. Just because the other lists are of a lower priority does not mark them as any less important. Importance and priority do not equate to the same thing. Yes, there are times when importance and priority will bring you to the same conclusion. Yet, when determining what to place on your 'first things first list', each brings their own unique value to the equation. Take a look at my second, third, and fourth, priorities: family, work, and friends. I find my family, friends, and work very important. My friends are more important to me than work. Yet in my list of priorities, work comes before friends. As I said before, friends and work run neck and neck on my priority list, yet work wins out only because it also affects family, and family comes before friends in priority and in importance. So, what do you think happens when I allow my first priority, God, to overload and I start neglecting the other priority areas of my life?

The two most common areas that tend to overload my first priority list are first, the demands of my professional job, the work category, and second, the unnecessary high priorities that I put on the sub-priorities in the God category.

Work, Work, Work, Work, Work:

You would think that as important as God is to me that the God category would be the one overloading my first things first list. It is not, it is my professional career, the work category that I am allowing to interfere with all my other priorities. Work is in my face every day, pushing and demanding more and more of my time from me. Whereas God quietly and gently tries to remind me of His importance and my priority to Him.

Old McDonald Had A Farm:

My parents taught me the importance of work. But it was the experience of working with my uncle that taught me the real value and necessity of work. During part of my youth, I grew up and worked on my Uncle Johnny's farm. No one I knew worked harder or longer days than Uncle Johnny. By the time my family moved away, the principle of work had been deeply instilled into my soul, and that experience has become a core guiding principle in my life.

I can tell you there is no vacation time from farm work. It is a 365-days-a-year profession, and the demands can quickly become overwhelming. You cannot tell the farm animals that you're taking a two-week vacation, and you'll take care of them when you get back. That would be like locking your pet in the house and leaving for two weeks. Have you ever tried finding a pet sitter for five hundred head of cattle? Even the crop farmer can't just pick up and go. Without constant care and attention, fungus, insects, weeds, or weather could destroy the entire crop. And in the off-season, it takes every bit of time to repair all the equipment for the next planting cycle. No, as a young man on the farm, I didn't see too many vacations or take any trips.

My brother and I were the only two boys working on my Uncle's 1000-acre farm. According to Uncle Johnny, farm work was men's work, and women had other duties. I am not sure I found that fair considering my Uncle had four girls, and my mother was the one providing the only two boys, Dave and I.

I can say that farm life definitely taught me the value and ethics of hard, honest work. In my day, every aspect of farming provided for our necessities and sustained our growth. If you didn't care for the milk cows, there was no milk, if you didn't care for the chickens, there were no eggs or chicken legs, and if you didn't care for the cattle, you would be asking "where is the beef?". When I was a kid, there was no running down to the corner store for milk and eggs. The closest store was 12 miles away. And finding the beef, well,

McDonald's Drive-In was still a dream in some man's head. The best alternative we had to McDonald's was the farm.

The Fabric of Life:

Did you know that at one point not too long ago, in fact, still in my lifetime, that 80% of the United States' job industry was farming? However, nowadays, the life of the small, family, Midwest farmer is almost gone. Farming is now being done on a large, industrial scale. In my father's era, if you grew up living in the Midwest and owned 160 acres of good farmland, you were doing great. My Uncle Johnny's thousand-acre Iowa farm was considered huge. Nowadays, a large, commercial, Midwest farm is easily 5,000 to 15,000 acres and owned by a corporation. Small-time farming is being pushed out and becoming unprofitable. Also being pushed out are the values and work-ethic that farm life teaches young people.

I bring this point up because, as I said, farm living taught me that life requires hard work. A farm provides a unique work environment that requires a particular set of work values. When I was a kid, the farm encompassed all aspects of our life. God, family, work, and friends were all intertwined. We all knew we had to depend on each other to survive. The family worked together from the time the sun came up 'til the sun went down and then some.

As for God, He was in every aspect of our farm life. Living on the farm, it was easy to see that without the blessings of God, you could not make it as a farmer. When it comes to dealing with mother earth and nature, man has only a small part in controlling the outcome.

Priorities on the farm were pretty easy to keep straight. We all knew what chores we had to do as soon as we got out of bed in the morning and we stayed busy, working through our list of daily responsibilities, until the time we went back to bed that night. We all worked together to do what had to be done. On the farm, we understood the fact that we were all a part of the whole.

Environmental Effect:

In the commercial working environment, the word 'work' carries a whole different meaning and value. In the commercial world, it seems to me that it's all about greed and money. Companies are never satisfied with their profits. They always want to increase their profitability. Workers are never happy with their paychecks; they always want to earn more money. Life becomes a collection of things. The philosophy is that of having more material things will make a family happier. In the commercial world, the work you perform is for the betterment of your employer and in accordance with the company's philosophy. The paycheck you bring home is for the betterment of you and your family. It provides the mean for you to buy the things that you need and want. When working for a corporate employer, you have full say over how you spend your paycheck, but little or no influence on how the company does business or when you might receive a raise.

About as close as you can get, work-wise, to understanding what life on a farm is like and the dedication it requires to be successful is if you own and run a family business, where you and your family work together side by side each day to build and sustain a company. On the farm just about everything you do is about family, for family, and with family and friends. In the commercial work field, you spend most of your days and time with co-workers.

In the commercial work field, if you are an hourly employee when the 5 pm whistle blows, it is time to go home whether you are done with your tasks or not. If you are a salaried employee, there is no 5 pm whistle, no definitive end to the workday, the company will try to squeeze every hour of work they can get out of you. Stealing precious hours from the time, you could be spending on your other priorities, like family. I don't want to paint a negative picture of all companies, because there are a few companies that do respect your time away from work. However, most corporate bosses are more concerned about their profit margins and productivity and how much work, time, and talent they can squeeze out of you for the benefit of the company and their stockholders.

On the farm, there is no 5 pm whistle, and you work 'til the day's chores are done. Please note that I didn't say when your chores are done. I said the **day's** chores. If your brother or sister needed help completing their chores, then you pitched in and helped. Why? Because they're family and that is what family is about. And secondly, if a chore does not get done, the consequences affect everyone.

Here is a small example of the cause and effect of the "help thy brother" principle. At the age of five and living on the farm, I had to be out the door, ready for work by 4:30 in the morning. I had two main tasks: one, herd the milk cows from the field and into the barn and get them ready to be milked (hand-milked, not by machines), and two, take care of the chickens, let them out of their pen, check their food and water and gather the eggs.

Milk Does a Body Good:

I had to get the cows into the milk house, so Aunt Pete (Patrina) could start milking. Herding the cows wasn't too bad. Basically, it required a lot of walking. On rainy days, or when the bull was in the pasture, the job was tougher. The rain turned the field into a muddy slip and slide, but it wasn't the slipping, sliding, and falling on my butt in the mud that I hated. The fact that my rubber boots were one size too big for me and as I walked, sometimes my boot would sink a little too deep in the mud and become stuck, then as I stepped forward, my foot would come clean-out of the boot. If I wasn't fast enough to catch myself, the bootless foot got a mud bath. Once I worked the boot free from the mud, I had no alternative than to stick my slimy, muddy foot back in the boot. As bad as that felt, I can tell you that I didn't mind it nearly as much as I did when I accidentally stepped in the occasional cow pie (as in not the kind of pie one would eat). From time to time, Aunt Pete would come along to help. That was a blessing.

That is a Bunch of Bull:

I was particularly grateful for Aunt Pete's help on the days the cows were in the same pasture as the bull. This bull was no small piece of meat. It was a Brahman bull that stood over 7-foot tall at the head, with broad shoulders, a large menacing hump across the back of his neck and shoulders, and weighed in at around sixteen-hundred pounds. Feel free to look up a few pictures of one of these guys on the internet and see how you would size up to it when you were five years old. The cows I had to get from the field are his girls, and you don't mess with the bull's girls, or things can get a little hairy. When you are in a bull's territory, you have to watch what you do. You need to walk at a slow, smooth, quiet pace, and never look at the bull directly in the eye for too long. If he decides he doesn't like what you are up to, and that includes how you are looking at him, you'd better be a good runner and be able to hurtle a barbwire fence with grace, or you might lose one of your God-given blessings of continuing your lineage.

Mom didn't like the fact that Uncle Johnny had me (5-year-old, sixty-pound Jerry) herd the cows all by myself when they were out in the field with the bull. Uncle Johnny would yell at Mom, "Stop treating him like a baby, the boy needs to learn responsibility, or he'll never grow up to be a man." I think the reason my Aunt helped me so often when the bull was around was because of my mom's concerns for my safety. Uncle Johnny negatively shook his head anytime he saw Aunt Pete head out with me to get the cows. At times the job was dangerous, but for the most part, it didn't bother me. I admit, there were a few times when the bull got riled up and came after me, and I didn't think I was going to make it over the fence. And on a couple of occasions, I would not have escaped if it weren't for Aunt Pete's help.

Aunt Pete:

For some reason that I did not understand that bull feared Aunt Pete. She had a power over him that I could only wish to have. My aunt said it was my fear of the bull that got in my way, and the bull could smell it. I can tell you that back then, at my size and age, a little fear was the only thing keeping me alive against that bull.

What Came First the Chicken or the Egg?

The chickens were my second task of the morning before breakfast. Now you would think that dealing with the bull would scare me more than a chicken. Well, you would be wrong. I had to feed the chickens and gather the eggs, which served as part of our morning meal. If you think a hen likes giving her egg up to you after all that hard work to grow and lay it, you'd be wrong again. I can tell you from personal experience that a few of those hens put up a pretty good fight protecting their eggs, and thinking about it today, I don't blame them.

Although the eggs were not fertilized, the hens didn't know that. The chicken thinks the eggs are their children. You see, chickens are not too smart; hence the saying 'You've got bird brains.' Of course, all I cared about was how I, as a boy measuring at just slightly over four-foot-tall, was going to get the egg out from underneath a six-pound vigilant chicken, ready for a fight. The main tactic I deployed was to take some of the morning feed and throw it on the floor as far away from their nest as I could. The strategy behind this was to lure the hen as far away from her nest as possible and thus give me enough time to get the eggs. It was a good strategy, and it worked on most of the bird-brained chickens but not on all of them. A few of the chickens were just a little bit smarter, and could not be tricked into leaving their nest. Then the battle would begin, me versus the chicken.

My Aunt Pete had no issues with the chickens. I mean come on this is a woman the bull feared. Do you think a chicken had a chance against her? When Aunt Pete gathered the eggs and the hen would not leave the nest, she would just push that chicken aside and take the egg. You could see the fear in that chicken as my aunt came to its nest to take its treasure. That hen would crouch down deep into her nest, pull her head against her chest, and start a low squawking as it shivered in fear.

Do you think that chicken did that for me? Not on your life. That chicken would take a long look at this skinny little boy coming at her and start clucking loud as if she were laughing at me. I would go to reach my puny little hand into the hen's nest, and as soon as I came close enough. Bam! Her sharp break would come down on my hand, hard enough to draw blood at times. The response to this was retaliation, a demand to enforce stronger measures on my part. Instead of the slow timid reach into her nest, I would smack that chicken in an attempt to get her to move. Sadly, for me, for every smack I gave her, she gave me three. It was always a fight to the bloody end with a few of those chickens, and it sure wasn't their blood on the ground when it was over.

A few times, I thought I could get away with not collecting all the eggs from those foul hens. However, when I brought the bucket of eggs to the cellar for my Aunt to inspect, she counted them and knew that I had skipped gathering the eggs from those difficult chickens. Let me tell you when you are asked if you did or did not do something you had better not lie. Lying would just get you more chores and no breakfast. And it didn't do me any good to skip the chicken fight either, because my aunt just sent me back out there to finish the job.

Pay It Forward:

As Aunt Pete helped me, I, in turn, was there to help my older brother Dave. Dave had far more work to do than I did, and it had to be done before we could eat breakfast. We couldn't eat breakfast until all the morning chores were done. You see, that was our motivation, we were hungry. Dave fed the pigs, thus the future bacon. Aunt Pete milked the cows, hence good wholesome fresh milk. I got the fresh morning eggs; over easy, please.

I will tell you there were a few days that my older brother acted in a way that did not make it easy to want to help him. But on the whole, my brother always gave me more cause to love him, than to be angry with him. Growing up, I always looked up to, trusted, and respected my older brother, Dave. Working together on the farm was the key factor in bonding our relationship.

I share these stories to help you to understand the dramatic adjustment that has to be made in working in these two totally different environments; farm work versus a commercial job. There is a scripture that I think sums up the difference between the farmer and the hourly employee very well.

> **(Bible New Testament: John 10: 11-13)**[2]
> *11 I am the good shepherd: the good shepherd giveth his life for the sheep.*
>
> *12 But he that is an hireling, and not the shepherd, whose own the sheep are not, seeth the wolf coming, and leaveth the sheep, and fleeth: and the wolf catcheth them, and scattereth the sheep.*
>
> *13 The hireling fleeth, because he is an hireling, and careth not for the sheep.*

Farm living shaped me into the hard worker I am today. It taught me to pour my soul into my work. On the farm, that type of attitude is good because, as I said, farm work generally covered all your priorities. However, in the commercial work environment, this attitude is not so suitable. Therefore, when I changed to a commercial employee, with my farm work ethic as a core principle, my employers loved me, but my relationships with family and friends suffered.

For many years, I couldn't understand how employees could just get up when their shift was over and walk away, leaving their work incomplete with deadlines coming due. I wanted to say, "The sun is still shining people, and there is still plenty of time left in the day. Where are you going?"

Because of this attitude, managing my workload in the commercial world is a challenge for me. Leaving unfinished tasks is like not completing my farm chores, and it is hard for me to deal with it. Working in the commercial environment with my farm boy's work ethic continually gets in the way of handling my personal life and family. It took me many years to understand this issue. Only after I had come to understand my work ethic values and where they stemmed from, was I able to better control this aspect of my personality.

He Just Keeps Going:

I know I have been a bit long-winded in this discussion of how work has ruled my priorities. I believe it has value as we all have experienced and do experience the pressures and demands of work. Giving work too much priority is the number one issue for most people. As I have done with work, you will also need to do the same with the areas of your life that you allow to control you. You will need to determine the reasons why before you'll be able to control it and manage your priority list.

God is in Everything:

The second problem I have in correctly managing my priorities is the God category. I know I said that God is my number one priority, and therefore you would think that it would be the category that gets in my way more than others do, but it is not, as I said work is. The trouble I have with the God category is that pretty much everything I do in life can be placed on the God priority list. This does not mean that everything God asks of us is of high priority. Although God does ask us to go the extra mile, he does not say going an extra 10 miles is better. What God does say is that obedience is better than sacrifice. Just ask King Saul, who thought going an extra 10 miles would please God more. Saul thought that by keeping some of the best spoils, sheep, and oxen, to sacrifice unto the Lord, he was showing God more love and respect. Instead, it showed disobedience.

> **(Bible Old Testament: 1 Samuel 15: 19-22)**[1]
> *19 Wherefore then didst thou not obey the voice of the Lord, but didst fly upon the spoil, and didst evil in the sight of the Lord?*

20 And Saul said unto Samuel, Yea, I have obeyed the voice of the Lord, and have gone the way which the Lord sent me, and have brought Agag the king of Amalek, and have utterly destroyed the Amalekites.

21 But the people took of the spoil, sheep and oxen, the chief of the things which should have been utterly destroyed, to sacrifice unto the Lord thy God in Gilgal.

22 And Samuel said, Hath the Lord as great a delight in burnt offerings and sacrifices, as in obeying the voice of the Lord? Behold, to obey is better than sacrifice, and to hearken than the fat of rams.

In the Book of Mormon, there is a story about Jesus teaching the Nephites. During a sermon where He is teaching some new and old commandments, Jesus also gives them a warning about the law of obedience.

(Book of Mormon: 3 Nephi 18: 12-15)[3]
12 And I give unto you a commandment that ye shall do these things. And if ye shall always do these things blessed are ye, for ye are built upon my rock.

13 But whoso among you shall do more or less than these are not built upon my rock, but are built upon a sandy foundation; and when the rain descends, and the floods come, and the winds blow, and beat upon them, they shall fall, and the gates of hell are ready open to receive them.

14 Therefore blessed are ye if ye shall keep my commandments, which the Father hath commanded me that I should give unto you.

15 Verily, verily, I say unto you, ye must watch and pray always, lest ye be tempted by the devil, and ye be led away captive by him.

Many times, spiritually-minded people will take their duties to God too far. They do this because they think their additional action presents more love and glory to Our Father in Heaven, when, in fact, by doing so, other areas of their life had to be sacrificed. Although, from the person's point of view, they may believe that the sacrificed areas were of less importance; from God's point of view, those other areas were of more value than the additional sacrifice that had been made and was not required by Heavenly Father.

In short, obedience to God is better than sacrificing that which is not required. Believe me, God understands Rule #18 *'First Things First'* much better than we do.

And Then There is You:

When my God and work priorities get out of balance, there is more that suffers than family and friends. I also suffer. As a part of creating your categories of priorities, you need to create a priority category called you. There needs to be time set aside in your life that is just for you if you plan to keep yourself in balance. This is a personal necessity. You are a priority that needs a place on your 'first things first' list. You need, and please note, I said need, which is not the same as a want, a time for you. You need time to eat, a time to relax, a time for personal hygiene, a time for sleeping, which is not the same as relaxing, a time to study for growth, a time for God, and just maybe a little bit of time to breathe. Time for you is a necessity, and in order to make time for you, you must include yourself as a part of your 'first things first' list.

There are governing laws for everything. 'Do this--you get that'; it is called cause and effect. There are laws that determine the reactions of magnetic materials. There is a cause and effect to magnetism as to how it reacts to itself and its cause and effect to things around it.

There are laws that govern you that also have their causes and effects. Those causes and effects will determine the outcome of your life and will also affect the lives of the people you are involved with. Place yourself to high or too low on the priority list, and the cause and effect from the laws that govern your life will not turn out well for you or others around you. As with all things, you must find where the balance is.

Rule #11 *'If You Can't Take Care of Yourself, You Can't Take Care of Others'* can help in understanding your position on the priority list in a relationship with others. We could rehash the issue of self-worth and why you also are a priority, but I feel I have covered the subject well enough in Rule #11. So, if you are having issues including yourself on the 'first things first' list, it is my recommendation that you read or reread Rule #11.

Urgency:

The most significant factor that determines what is first on most people's to-do list is urgency. It is urgency that it is motivating me to move the writing of this book to a higher level on my to-do list. There is not a question in my mind as to how much importance this book holds to me. It is, and was, always my plan to complete this book long before I died. A big part of the plan and hope is to ensure I give myself enough time while I am still alive to share and discuss this book with family and friends.

One day as I was writing, I took a moment to look back and calculate how many years I had spent working on this book thus far. In doing so, I came to the realization of how long it had taken me to reach this point in my writing, and it gave me a wide awakening. It was sort of a shocking moment, you might say. I came to the realization that at my current rate of writing, it was going to take me a very, very long time to finish. That started me wondering how many more years of life, God was going to grant me here on Earth, and if it would be enough to complete this book before I died?

The Fountain of Youth:

There was a time in my young childhood that I had prayed earnestly to God for a blessing to live to the age of 300 years old. At my current rate of writing, I was going to need that blessing. I mean, after all, there are many people mentioned in the Old Testament that lived to be 900 years or better. As for me, I was only praying for a third of that time. Well, I took a good look at my gray head of hair, the wrinkles on my face, and my withered looking hands, and I came to the disappointing conclusion that God was not going to grant my prayer. This left me with the plausible fact that I would be dead and, in my grave, well before this book's completion. The thought of death left me with a feeling of urgency. Hence, I decided it was time to increase my rate of writing. Well, I couldn't physically write this book any faster than I was. My brain and inspiration just don't move too quickly when it comes to writing. I am like a car stuck in second gear where writing is involved. That meant I needed to dedicate more time from my life to the book's completion or give it up. But as Rule #1 states, *'Failure is Not an Option'*.

The thought of being dead and the regrets of not completing something so important to me is what I call the urgency factor at its finest. I cannot think of a better motivator than having thoughts of being dead tomorrow as I look at what I am doing with my time today. That thought becomes a great eye-opener when it comes to managing my priorities.

I Needed It Done Yesterday:

Managing priorities because of urgency alone is where you get yourself in trouble. Using the urgency method to manage the order of your priority list will get you in as much trouble as allowing your other priorities to have dominance. Urgency may have caused me to look at the priority I was giving to the writing of this book, but it did not determine its priority. The book's priority to me had already been established when I started the project. The urgency of time just made me realize that I was neglecting it, and if I continued the neglect, the book would never be completed. This book is just a thing, and things are not as important as people are, however, what this book will leave to my family I feel, and hope will be of great value to them. Thus, I give this book a high priority because it is about people, and it is for people, and the most important people in my life are family.

Rule #18 'First Things First'

How many people do you know that seem to be living in constant stress mode because their lives are mismanaged by urgency? They are always running around, putting out fires. Their lives are busy, busy, busy, running from one fire to another. Yet, are those fires important enough that time should be spent on them? You cannot manage by urgency alone because urgency by itself does not take into account the things that matter most.

Fire, Fire Everywhere:

Ask a firefighter if priority is of any importance when it comes to determining the order in which you put out a fire. Some fires will burn themselves out, and in the process, only causes a small amount of damage. Whereas other fires, if neglected, can destroy everything in its reach. Even in urgent matters, when things are on fire, you cannot forget the order of priority you have placed things in your life.

> **(Johann Wolfgang Von Goethe)**[6]
> *Things that matter most must never be at the mercy of things which matter least.*

Sometimes you have a big fire burning on a lower priority. Its searing flames bellow urgency in its attempt to get your attention. This fire wants your attention now. Yet at the same time, you have a family member who has a small but important fire, which also requires your attention. The question you have to ask yourself is: what is the effect of putting out the bigger fire of the less priority before you attend to the smaller family fire? Neglecting the family member's small fire could end up being catastrophic.

The size of the fire does not determine its priority. No matter the demands of its urgency. Your order of priorities needs to be fixed. It is what is on fire and the damage it could cause that determines the order in which you handle the tasks. The larger screaming fire may have to wait on a smaller fire of a higher priority. If not handled immediately, it could ignite into an urgent fire. You do not want your higher priorities to grow into urgent issues before they are dealt with.

Remember, these are the things that mean the most to you. In my case, God and family. If I waited until family issues became urgent before dealing with them, then over time, my family would have a hard time believing that they were as high a priority as I claimed them to be.

The Rabbit and the Clock (Alice in Wonderland):

You may find this strange, but yet it is true. Time management, although it is needed for handling tasks and priorities, is not the overall answer. It is only a small but essential part. Many people who run around with their clocks and schedulers may disagree with me. But I can tell you that when it comes to the things that matter most, in my case people, using your time efficiently is not a wise move. Try managing time when dealing with an upset son, daughter, wife, girlfriend, or boyfriend. How well do you think that will work? Let us say you have a very distraught wife who's is dealing with a problem (hopefully not you), and she feels she needs some of your time to share this with you. You look at your schedule and say, "Ok." Then in the middle of the conversation, you say to her, "Time is up. That is all I can spare, or it will mess up my schedule?" Hmmm, I know what priority my wife would think I just placed on her if I made that kind of a statement. It would be the doghouse for me. Also, my brownie points bank account would have just been emptied.

Feelings Nothing More Than Feelings:

How about we take it to another level? Let us say you are a guy getting ready to break up with your girlfriend, but you still want to stay good friends. You have concluded that today is the day you need to tell her that you want to change the status of your relationship, but your day is filled with other commitments. You just don't have much time to spare, but at the same time, you feel an urgency to tell her before the relationship goes on another day. You don't feel it would be fair to her if you let the relationship continue any longer. You

Rule #18 'First Things First'

want to avoid a lengthy discussion because your schedule says you don't have the time. Therefore, in the interest of efficiency, you decide to inform her in a text message.

I do not care how delicate and sincere the words of the text message are. Do you think it will substitute for you personally not being there to support and salvage the friendship part of your relationship? How much time do you think you will have to spend now salvaging the friendship and mending hurt feelings?

Tic + Toc = Tic Toc:

There has never been a time calculator invented that can calculate the allotted time you will need to deal with a person that has been through an emotional situation. Dealing with a person's emotional and psychological aspects does not fit nicely into fixed time slices. Thus, you cannot manage people with time slices. Of course, if you don't care about the person's emotional and psychological statuses, well then time slice away.

Sadly, the medical field manages the client/patient relationship in a time-sliced management system. This is their attempt to keep costs down and profits up. In their time-sliced management system, they handle the client/patient more on an efficiency-based relationship method than a one-on-one, personal-based relationship.

In an efficiency-based relationship, you deal with the client/patient in a fixed time based upon their needs. Each need has a set time assigned to it, which is predetermined based upon the bean counters' (upper management) statistical numbers. In my opinion, the ones that use the efficiency-based relationship method believe either they can quantify a person's emotional and psychological needs into a set slice of time, or don't believe it needs to be in the equation.

In a one-on-one personal relationship, you deal with the whole individual, which includes the person's emotional and psychological needs, and that time which is needed is, to some degree, fluid. In this relationship management style, you get to know the person you are dealing with. I mean, genuinely get to know them and share with them. Build trust with them. And if needed, you can help them emotionally and psychologically. The client may only need a simple procedure like the nurse administering medication by an injection to the arm. Now, if we were using the efficiency-based relationship method, the time slice allotted for the nurse to physically give the injection would only be about 20 to 30 seconds. However, you see, I have an emotional and psychological issue with nurses giving shots and the needles required to do so due to an incident from my childhood. I can assure you that it is going to take any nurse a lot longer to give me a shot than her regular patients. First, I have to be convinced of the necessity of the injection, and second, I am going to need time to prepare myself to receive it mentally. Fortunately, I am better adjusted now to receiving injections than I was just after that childhood incident. Back then, it would have taken a good 20 to 30 minutes for that nurse to administer an injection to my arm. So, try time-slicing that.

If you care about a person and your relationship, then you cannot precisely calculate the time needed to manage the emotional and psychological aspect of a given situation, let alone apply that same time value to all people for the same situation.

When you have something that is not calculable, it is unmanageable. Things that are not manageable cannot be controlled, and when things are not controllable, the accurate cost cannot be determined, and in business, the inability to determine cost is not acceptable to the bean counters.

To Care or Not to Care That Is the Question:

At this point in time, as I am writing this chapter, I work in the medical profession as a licensed Hearing Aid Specialist. I deal with the efficiency-based relationship versus the one-on-one personal-based relationship method every day. The bean counters push the efficiency-based relationship because their overall statistics say that the more people I test for hearing loss, the more people will buy hearing aids. Therefore, all day long every working day the bean counters push hearing test count numbers at us trying to get us to compete against each other and to increase the number of people we test.

In the hearing aid company's regional area that I work in, I help more people hear better and have higher profits than any other Hearing Aid Center. Yet the area of my practice is in one of the smallest towns in the region, and I perform the least amount of hearing tests. Why? Because I care about the person's emotional and psychological well-being and do not use the efficiency-based relationship method, and I don't worry about the bean-counting or the Bean Counters. I worry and care about my client. I believe that if you put the best quality into your work and care about the clients' needs, whatever those needs are, the beans needed to run the business will also be taken care of.

Is That the Clock Ticking I Hear?

The company sets the standard for the allotted time for a hearing test and demo to one hour, and then a half-hour more for training and paperwork. Based on what the bean counters say, I should be testing at least four people a day. This is not so on my ship. The company may own the fleet, but I command my ship. The overall hearing test for me to perform can take anywhere from two to five hours. On average, I only test one person a day, and the rest of the time is spent doing service and follow-ups on my clients. Most people do not understand the emotional, psychological, and physical aspects of hearing loss, and the support and the adjustment period needed to deal with new sounds they were not hearing. Each person deals with hearing loss differently, and; each person requires a different amount of assistance, which varies from a little to a lot. That issue is the same when you correct a person's hearing with hearing aids for the first time, or they are currently wearing hearing aids, and they are looking to replace them.

Rule #18 'First Things First'

In many cases, not all the hearing loss can be compensated for. Sometimes speech recognition therapy is recommended as part of the treatment. Putting hearing aids on a person for the first time allowing them to hear at normal standards can be as dramatic a change as taking a person that has been living in a darkened room (based upon the person's hearing loss) and pushing them out into the sunlight for the first time in years. How do you think you would handle that? Do you think any emotional, psychological, or physical adjustment might be needed?

I just want to point out one more time that I use the one-on-one personal relationship method on my ship. The company would prefer I use the efficiency-based relationship method. The size of the regional area I work in for the company is about 60 hearing aid centers. In general, I do the least number of hearing tests per year. Yet I have the highest sales and profits for the region, and I am working in the smallest town. The company operates around 500 hearing aid centers nationwide, with some stores having two hearing aid centers and others operating seven days a week. There is only me in my hearing center, and I am open five days a week. For the last six years, my center has placed in the top 20% against all the hearing aid centers nationwide. Well, I am a small cog in this big company machine, and the bean counters running it don't seem to take notice of my statistics or me because they still believe in the efficiency-based relationship method.

I believe that all people are important, and they are more important than things or money. Sharing and giving service to others is important. Taking the time to care for others is something we all could do more of.

This captain will never give up, and I'll go down with my ship if I have to. For as long as I am with this company and running my ship, I'll keep trying to get them to wear 'hearing aids.' So, perhaps one day the bean counters will hear me, and I can bring them back into the light.

Rule #18 'First Things First'

I Will Have Two Slices of Time Please:

Here is another story of dealing with a person's emotional and psychological needs and fighting against pressing, time-slicing requirements. My little sister Evelyn had cancer and died at the age of 55. She had been fighting it for a few years, and at one point she thought she had it beat. In her last days' due to cancer, she contracted pneumonia and went downhill fast. This happened at an inopportune time in Evelyn's life. Her daughter's wedding was only two months away, and she feared she was not going to be there to see it, and she was right. During Evelyn's last days when she was unsure if she was going to make it, how important do you think spending time with her family was then vs. the other time-stealing tasks that pulled on her?

The last days of Evelyn's life came at a time when the importance of family was a test for me as well. I received a call from my niece, and she stated that they were told her mom, Evelyn, had less than 24 hours to live, and Hospice had been called in to help. It is a two-day drive to my sister's home, and we did not think we would make it in time to say goodbye in person. My other sister, my wife, and I set up a Skype video session with Evelyn to send her our love and support. After the session, I felt inspired that we should make the trip to see her anyway. I called my district manager and was informed that I had three days I could take for a family bereavement. With the additional three days of vacation I had, that gave us four days for travel and two days for the family.

Only that is not how it worked out. God calls people home on his time, and this is a slice of time you cannot manage or control. My sister's health was up, then down. One moment she was given only hours to live, and the next, she was in recovery. This went on for days. Finally, my given time from work was up, and I had to decide whether to return home and work or stay with my sister, who needed me there for support. There was no question that she was going to die. The doctor had almost pronounced her dead three times already. Her

Rule #18 'First Things First'

heart and breathing had diminished to barely detectable, but yet my sister came back.

After her last recovery, the doctor called all the family into a small room for a consultation. The doctor told us that my sister was young and strong, but there was no question that, though she is winning a few small battles, the cancer was going to win the war. The doctor told us she had no idea at this point how much time Evelyn had, it could be weeks. In her medical opinion, Evelyn's' time should have been up the last three times she talked to us.

Time is Up:

Now I had to make a decision, do I stay and support my sister with a chance of losing my job or do I leave for home. I had already spent more days caring for my sister than my job had allotted me. I had a good-paying job, and at the age of 62, it would not be easy to find another one with the same salary. As for me, the decision wasn't that hard to make because I had already made that decision when I had decided what my priorities in life were. I called the district manager and told her I had no idea when I would be back to work, and that the doctor had stated that there was no question as to whether my sister's time on Earth was coming to a close, but she was giving up on determining how long that would be and only God truly knew when He was going to call her back home. I then informed my district manager that I was staying with my sister to the end and if that meant losing my job, I understood. The whole point of this story is that you cannot control the time needed to console a loved one, but you can control the priority of importance you give them.

How Much for Your Time?

Time cannot be the main factor in managing your priority list. It is, however, a valuable asset needed in handling all of life's demands. If asked, which is of more value to me, time, or money? I will always tell you, of course, that it is time, as would most people. To give you a slice of my time is more precious than if I gave you money.

> **(Dallin H. Oaks, 2001 April General Conference "Focus and Priorities")**[7]
> *"Three things never come back—the spent arrow, the spoken word, and the lost opportunity." We cannot recycle or save the time allotted to us each day. With time, we have only one opportunity for choice, and then it is gone forever.*

Time once spent is gone, and not science nor the technology we have to date can reclaim time once it has passed. Money, on the other hand, can be replaced with a little thought and hard work. Well, maybe a lot of thought and hard work. But the point is money can be replaced and currently, time cannot; once gone, it is forever gone. That is why when my wife or children ask for some of my time to do a task or share with them, I feel it is one of the greatest blessings I can give them, and though it may not seem like it sometimes by my actions, I am truly blessed by each second I spend with them. When I spend time with my family, I am blessed far more than anything else I could do or have done with my life.

How do we manage our time in relation to our priority list? The first thing is not to waste your time doing frivolous things. In other words, stop wasting time.

Time is handled by setting proper priorities and sticking to them. In short, focus. The second is not to micromanage time when dealing with a priority. Remember, it is not advantageous when dealing with people. Many tasks have too many variables to set a hard-fixed time for them. Instead of micromanaging time, be organized but flexible with your time. The third is to set well-defined, realistic goals. A short review of Rule #3 *'There Are Fluid Goals and Solid Goals'* can help in this area.

Firm, But Not Solid?

As I stated in Rule #3 *'There Are Fluid Goals and Solid Goals'*, I have very few solid goals and many fluid goals. Life has way too many daily changes to set a firmly fixed path on how you manage your priority list. Let me give you an example of this. God is first on my list. One of the things I do each day to show God that He is first on my priority list is to spend special time with him in prayer and reading the scriptures the first thing in the morning. This allows Him the opportunity to teach me, and it also starts my day heading in the right direction, according to my priority list. When I say I put reading the scriptures first in the morning, I do mean He is first. That means as soon as I am dressed and before I do any other task, which includes feeding my hungry tummy.

My morning goal of reading the scriptures is not solid; it is fluid. It is a rare occasion that I don't read scriptures first. Nevertheless, it does happen. Generally, it is whenever I need to make another priority category first on my list. That being said, I still do not neglect my daily scripture reading with the Lord. I always manage to save some time in my life before the end of each day to read my scriptures. This keeps God a priority in my life every day. There will always be exceptions to managing your priority list, but you must ensure that they are rare exceptions and do not become the general rule.

A Subset of a Subset of a Subset:

To handle the time part in your quest to manage your priorities, you need to learn to balance your task list by weighing the value of the task against all the other priority categories and sub-categories to truly determine where they fall in your to-do list.

Balancing your to-do list is best done weekly and reviewed daily. Making a to-do list from a daily view does not give you a big enough overview of your life to set solid priorities, and essential things in your life will be missed. Likewise making your list on a monthly basis is too large a view because life in a 30-day window changes too much. At least it does in mine.

I cannot make your priority list for you, nor can I manage it for you. Through life's experience, you will learn where your priorities lie. As far as how you manage your priorities, well, there are many self-help options out there, and you'll need to find the one that works for you. If we all had the same priorities in life, training on this subject would be a lot easier.

My whole reason for writing this list of rules was to take and put together what I felt would best benefit me. I will remind you that, as I said in the beginning, I wrote this book for my benefit. When I asked a friend to help proofread my writings, the first thing she asked me was, "I need to know who your audience is. Who are you writing for?" I told her it was myself, and that I hoped that my book of rules would be written well enough to inspire others to write their own book. We all can learn and build by sharing each other's experiences.

For me, putting God first in my life helps determine all my other priorities. When you come to understand what God's will is for you versus your will, it changes things a lot. I know that God knows me better than I know me, and He knows what is best for me far better than I do. Taking God's will into account is a huge advantage in balancing my priority list. That is why scripture study is so important to me. Many times, when I am trying to balance all the things I have and want to do in life, I will find the answer to the help I need for the day in my scripture reading. So, I put prayer and scripture study as the first step.

Did You Hear That?

The second step, which goes hand-and-hand with the first step, is learning to listen to the prompting of the Holy Ghost for guidance. It takes time to learn how to listen when God is inspiring you, and how He inspires is a little different for each of us. This is something we all must work out with God individually. I can tell you that with me, learning to listen and hear God's inspirations is something I have worked at all my life and will need to continue to work at it for the rest of my life.

God talks or inspires me in different ways for different reasons and is not something I can explain to you in a few sentences or pages. There is a book titled 'Seeking the Spirit' by Joseph Fielding McConkie. This book gave a lot of clarity to my understanding of how God communicates with us. I would recommend it to everyone that believes God wants to communicate with him or her as an individual.

Put the Blinders On:

The third step is learning to focus on your priorities. To keep your priorities straight takes lots of focus. Daily life is filled with distractions that try to pull us off course. Keeping yourself focused and not allowing yourself to get overly distracted, some days it seems impossible, but it can be done and is essential if you plan to stay on track. In the end, staying focused on your priority list will allow you to accomplish much, much more in your life, and you will not neglect what is most important to you. For me, it is God, family, and friends. Please note that I said friends before work. People are more important to me than work, but work comes before friends when it affects the family.

God Is in Everything:

Doing service for others is another of God's commandments, and therefore to a degree is covered under the 'God is first priority' list. Wow, think about it, it's no wonder many people seem to have issues prioritizing their life. Everything seems to fall under the 'God is first priority' list. You would be right to think that way if you are not looking at things from the right perspective. Dealing with areas like this make prioritizing our time challenging. Many times, I get overwhelmed by the list of things that I feel creep into my priority one list that should genuinely be in my priority three list. That is where I have to depend on the inspiration of the Lord through the spirit of the Holy Ghost. It is in these moments that God must be number one, and prayer, meditation (listening), and study are the key for me to getting the answers to which task is most important. Everything will scream at once that it is number one, but the fact is they cannot all be number one. I have found that in general, most people are considerate and are willing to wait, as long as they know you will be there to help as soon as you can.

Who Owns the Monkey?

Always remember that someone else's priority list is not necessarily the same as yours. Others' urgency to get something done is not yours unless you make it yours. This is where I ask myself, 'whose monkey is it that's causing the issue?' If they are not my monkeys, then it is not an issue for which I take responsibility. I will help and do what I can, but I do not take ownership of another person's monkey.

Your own priority list comes first. You may think that that statement is a little harsh; however, you will find that the better you take care of your list first, the more time you will have for helping others, and the better you will feel about helping. Not handling your priority list first will leave you always feeling overwhelmed and emotionally and physically drained. Trust me on this one. This rule is one of my most significant issues, and I have learned the hard way that the better I manage my priorities, the less they will manage me.

It is because of my lack of being able to manage all the demands of life, which includes the self-inflicted ones, that Rule #18 *'First Things First'* has become a vital rule for balancing my life. Proper implementation of Rule #18 provides balance and stability in life far greater than any other rule and will bring you greater peace and joy.

God's on First:

I have selected a scripture story from the Bible Old Testament that I feel points out two eternal principles: putting Our Father in Heaven first in your priorities, and the law of obedience. These are the two timeless principles that can be challenging to adhere to. At times, they will push you to your uttermost limits as they serve as a trial of your faith in God,

Rule #18 'First Things First'

faith in you, and your principles themselves. Being committed to your priorities before the trial is the only way you will make it through those times.

> **(Bible Old Testament: Genesis 22; 1-3)**[1]
> *1 And it came to pass after these things, that God did tempt Abraham, and said unto him, Abraham: and he said, Behold, here I am.*
>
> *2 And he said, Take now thy son, thine only son Isaac, whom thou lovest, and get thee into the land of Moriah; and offer him there for a burnt offering upon one of the mountains which I will tell thee of.*
>
> *3 ¶ And Abraham rose up early in the morning, and saddled his ass, and took two of his young men with him, and Isaac his son, and clave the wood for the burnt offering, and rose up, and went unto the place of which God had told him.*

The story of Abraham being asked by God to sacrifice his son is a trial we all go through at some point in life. Though we may not be asked to sacrifice our son, the pattern of being given a commandment from God, and then having our commitment to that commandment tested is the same. That trial is the actual test of one's faith and one's commitment to putting God first.

The difficult challenges we face are not to break us but are to strengthen us. Depending upon your faith at the time and where your priorities are, you may feel otherwise. Do you have enough faith? In whom do you trust? Where are your priorities?

In the end, Abraham did not have to sacrifice his son, but he did not know that. Abraham had the faith that God would not ask so much of him if there were not a better reason for his son's sacrifice than he knew. Abraham had to have his priorities of *'First Things First'* straight, well before receiving this challenge of faith and trust.

God's on First, Family's on Second, & Everything Else is on Third:

Here are a few scriptures and quotes to support why I put God first in 'First Things First'.

(Bible New Testament: Matthew 6:33-34)[2]

33 But seek ye first the kingdom of God, and his righteousness; and all these things shall be added unto you.

34 Take therefore no thought for the morrow: for the morrow shall take thought for the things of itself. Sufficient unto the day is the evil thereof.

(Bible New Testament: Hebrews 10:35-36)[2]

35 Cast not away therefore your confidence, which hath great recompence of reward.

36 For ye have need of patience, that, after ye have done the will of God, ye might receive the promise.

(Book of Mormon: Mosiah 2:23-24)[3]

23 And now, in the first place, he hath created you, and granted unto you your lives, for which ye are indebted unto him.

24 And secondly, he doth require that ye should do as he hath commanded you; for which if ye do, he doth immediately bless you; and therefore he hath paid you. And ye are still indebted unto him, and are, and will be, forever and ever; therefore, of what have ye to boast?

(Book of Mormon: Jacob 2:18-19)[3]

18 But before ye seek for riches, seek ye for the kingdom of God.

19 And after ye have obtained a hope in Christ ye shall obtain riches, if ye seek them; and ye will seek them for the intent to do good—to clothe the naked, and to feed the hungry, and to liberate the captive, and administer relief to the sick and the afflicted.

Rule #18 'First Things First'

Dallin H. Oaks in a General Conference meeting of April 2001 gave several supporting comments on God being first in 'First Things First'.

(Dallin H. Oaks, 2001 April General Conference, "Focus and Priorities")[7]
Our priorities determine what we seek in life.

(Dallin H. Oaks, 2001 April General Conference, "Focus and Priorities")[7]
Seek ... first to build up the kingdom of God" means to assign first priority to God and to His work. Everything else is lower in priority. Think about that reality as we consider some teachings and some examples on priorities. As someone has said, if we do not choose the kingdom of God first, it will make little difference in the long run what we have chosen instead of it.

(Dallin H. Oaks, 2001 April General Conference, "Focus and Priorities")[7]
The ultimate Latter-day Saint priorities are twofold: First, we seek to understand our relationship to God the Eternal Father and His Son, Jesus Christ, and to secure that relationship by obtaining their saving ordinances and by keeping our personal covenants. Second, we seek to understand our relationship to our family members and to secure those relationships by the ordinances of the temple and by keeping the covenants we make in that holy place. These relationships, secured in the way I have explained, provide eternal blessings available in no other way. No combination of science, success, property, pride, prominence, or power can provide these eternal blessings!

Then I'll add this support from Richard Scott.

(Richard G. Scott, 2014 October General Conference, "Make the Exercise of Faith Your First Priority")[8]

Rule #18 'First Things First'

Make the Exercise of Faith Your First Priority

There Must Be Order:

I believe that Rule #18 *'First Things First'* is an eternal principle, which God Himself adheres to. There is an order to all things. And God, our Father in Heaven, is a God of order and has given us the order of priorities for doing all things, in governing His affairs and ours.

> **(Bible Old Testament: Amos 3:7)[1]**
> *7 Surely the Lord God will do nothing, but he revealeth his secret unto his servants the prophets.*
>
> **(Bible New Testament: 2 Thessalonians 2:2-3)[2]**
> *2 That ye be not soon shaken in mind, or be troubled, neither by spirit, nor by word, nor by letter as from us, as that the day of Christ is at hand.*
>
> *3 Let no man deceive you by any means: for that day shall not come, except there come a falling away first, and that man of sin be revealed, the son of perdition;*
>
> **(Bible New Testament: 1 Corinthians 12:27-30)[2]**
> *27 Now ye are the body of Christ, and members in particular.*
>
> *28 And God hath set some in the church, first apostles, secondarily prophets, thirdly teachers, after that miracles, then gifts of healings, helps, governments, diversities of tongues.*
>
> *29 Are all apostles? are all prophets? are all teachers? are all workers of miracles?*
>
> *30 Have all the gifts of healing? do all speak with tongues? do all interpret?*

Rule #18 'First Things First'

(Bible New Testament: 1 Timothy 3:5)[2]
5 (For if a man know not how to rule his own house, how shall he take care of the church of God?)

(Bible New Testament: 1 Timothy 4:13)[2]
13 Till I come, give attendance to reading, to exhortation, to doctrine.

(Book of Mormon: 1 Nephi 15:11)[3]
11 Do ye not remember the things which the Lord hath said?—If ye will not harden your hearts, and ask me in faith, believing that ye shall receive, with diligence in keeping my commandments, surely these things shall be made known unto you.

(Doctrine & Covenants 11:21)[4]
21 Seek not to declare my word, but first seek to obtain my word, and then shall your tongue be loosed; then, if you desire, you shall have my Spirit and my word, yea, the power of God unto the convincing of men.

A Man of Vision:

The author Stephen Covey was a great inspiration to me in writing Rule #18. This rule is my interpretation of how I applied what Stephen Covey calls Habit 3: *'Put First Things First'*. To give respect to Stephen's inspiration and to honor him, I want to share with you a few of his quotes before I bombard you with the pages of Rule #18 supporting quotes. Thanks, Stephen, for your wisdom that helped change a part of my life.

(Stephen Covey)[9]
"It's easy to say "no!" when there's a deeper "yes!" burning inside."

(Stephen Covey)[10]
"How Many People on Their Deathbed Wish They'd Spent More Time at the Office?"

(Stephen Covey)[11]
"If you were to pause and think seriously about the "first things" in your life—the three or four things that matter most—what would they be?"

(Stephen Covey)[12]
Effective leadership is putting first things first. Effective management is discipline, carrying it out.

(Stephen Covey)[13]
The key is not to prioritize what's on your schedule, but to schedule your priorities.

(Stephen Covey)[14]
You have to decide what your highest priorities are and have the courage to pleasantly, smilingly, non-apologetically, say no to other things.

(Stephen Covey)[15]
"The main thing is to keep the main thing the main thing."

(Stephen Covey)[16]
Most of us spend too much time on what is urgent and not enough time on what is important.

More Than Enough, Stop Already:

I found so many good famous quotes by other people that I am afraid I had difficulty in excluding any of them. The quotes that I did keep for this rule are but a small amount compared to how many I started with. I feel sure that the number of quotes I saved in this chapter is far more than you the reader will take the time to read, but my hope is that will not be the case. Almost all the quotes I found I felt were insightful, thought-provoking, or inspiring. Though I thought they were all good, I had to cut the list down; these are the ones that remain. Take the time to read and ponder over the quotes that I've included.

(Dallin H. Oaks, 2015 April General Conference "The Parable of the Sower")[17]
It is up to each of us to set the priorities and to do the things that make our soil good and our harvest plentiful.

(Donald L. Staheli, 1998 April General Conference "Obedience-Life's Great Challenge")[18]
Yet the pressures of everyday living frequently and subtly move us away from that pursuit which we so proudly proclaim. And in the process the priorities that should really matter most to us become captive to those things that, while seemingly important at the moment, have little or no relevance to our long-term goal. And in many cases, the temptations and pressures to pursue the less-important matters lead us down the wrong paths of life.

(Dallin H. Oaks, 2011 April General Conference "Desire")[19]
Desires dictate our priorities, priorities shape our choices, and choices determine our actions.

(J. Richard Clarke, 1985 April General Conference "Hold Up Your Light")[20]
the thought of someone quietly taking mental notes of my actions, attitudes, and values fired my imagination. I realized the weighty responsibility each of us has to demonstrate accurately the principles and priorities to which we are committed. It was like a mini-foretaste of Judgment Day!

(Thomas S. Monson, 1992 March Relief Society Sesquicentennial Satellite Broadcast "The Spirit of Relief Society")[21]
Belle Smith Spafford, when serving as general president of the Relief Society wrote "It is a time rich in rewards if we keep our balance, learn the true values of life, and wisely determine priorities."

Rule #18 'First Things First'

(Ernest Agyemang Yeboah)[22]
"When you climb a fruitless tree, you go hungry!"

(Ernest Agyemang Yeboah)[23]
"Some people exert more energy on less important things; some people exert less energy on less important things."

(Ernest Agyemang Yeboah)[24]
"The great spider never worries itself chasing after its prey with all of its energy and strength. It only exerts its energy each morning to build its web in a magnificent way; relaxes in it and awaits its prey that will miss its path into the web"

(Ernest Agyemang Yeboah)[25]
"The real direction of your vision is as important as your vision. Notwithstanding how large the goal post might be, the power behind your shots least matter as its direction, for it is more of the direction that will determine the goals you shall score and the final score in the end"

(Clive Staples "C. S." Lewis)[26]
When first things are put first, second things are not suppressed but increased.

(Clive Staples "C. S." Lewis)[27]
Put first things first and second things are thrown in. Put second things first and you lose both first and second things.

(James W. Frick)[28]
"Don't tell me where your priorities are. Show me where you spend your money and I'll tell you what they are."

(John Kramer Blythe)[29]
It was no accident that one of the first things God asked of Adam was for him to name the animals he saw around him. Why do you suppose God asked man to do that? Because once you have a name, you have the beginning of understanding, and once you have understanding, you lose fear. God didn't want man to be fearful. He wanted man to be brave."

(Shirley Conran)[30]
First things first, second things never.

(Thomas Watson, Jr)[31]
Put First Things First! These four words cover an entire philosophy which can be applied with profit by every business leader, by every executive and by every employee.

(Kenneth Erwin Hagin)[32]
God wants us to prosper. Our need, however, is to evaluate things as they should be evaluated - to esteem earthly things lightly - to put first things first.

(William Golding)[33]
How can you expect to be rescued if you don't put first things first and act proper?

(Victoria Moran)[34]
A simple life is not seeing how little we can get by with-that's poverty-but how efficiently we can put first things first. . . . When you're clear about your purpose and your priorities, you can painlessly discard whatever does not support these, whether it's clutter in your cabinets or commitments on your calendar. (148)

(Ivy Baker Priest)[35]
We women ought to put first things first. Why should we mind if men have their faces on the money, as long as we get our hands on it?

Rule #18 'First Things First'

(Leo Babauta)[36]
"What tasks are more important? It's hard to know when you're caught up in the flow of things, just doing things left and right, quickly switching between tasks, and so on. Everything seems important. But when we step back and think about what matters most, what will make the most difference in the world and in our lives, we can see what we need to focus on, to make time for. We can't step back unless we're aware that we're getting caught up in less important tasks."

(Dave Willis)[37]
Never be too busy for the people you love. Never allow pursuits or possessions to become bigger than your relationships. Love is what gives meaning to life."

(Leo Christopher)[38]
"There is only one thing more precious than our time and that is who we spend it on.

(Mahatma Gandhi)[39]
"Action expresses priorities."

(Wall Street Journal)[410]
Instead of "I don't have time" try saying "It's not a priority" and see how that feels.

(Steve Maraboli)[41]
Priorities: When someone tells you they are too 'busy'... It's not a reflection of their schedule; it's a reflection of YOUR spot on their schedule.

(Instagram Quote)[42]
You always have time for the things you put first.

(PureHappyLife.com)[43]
Your priorities are your character.

(Myles Munroe)[44]
Our life is the sum total of all the decisions we make every day, and those decisions are determined by our priorities.

Rule #18 'First Things First'

(Phoebe Snow)[45]
Sometimes when you're overwhelmed by a situation - when you're in the darkest of darkness - that's when your priorities are reordered.

(Steven Pressfield)[46]
"The Principle of Priority states (a) you must know the difference between what is urgent and what is important, and (b) you must do what's important first."

(Martin Luther King, Jr.)[47]
What seems so necessary today may not even be desirable tomorrow.

(Brandon Sanderson)[48]
The mark of a great man is one who knows when to set aside the important things in order to accomplish the vital ones.

(Andy Stanley)[49]
We don't drift in good directions. We discipline and prioritize ourselves there.

(Rick Warren)[50]
Living in light of eternity changes your priorities.

(David F. Jakielo)[51]
The most important thing in life is knowing the most important things in life.

(Dwight D. Eisenhower)[52]
The older I get the more wisdom I find in the ancient rule of taking first things first. A process which often reduces the most complex human problem to a manageable proportion.

(Bob Hawke)[53]
The things which are most important don't always scream the loudest.

(Jim Rohn)[54]
Learn how to separate the majors and the minors. A lot of people don't do well simply because they major in minor things.

(Albert Einstein)[55]
Sometimes one pays most for the things one gets for nothing.

(Anthony Robbins)[56]
When you know what's most important to you, making a decision is quite simple.

(Robert J. McKain)[57]
The reason most goals are not achieved is that we spend our time doing second things first.

Summary:

I think the best way I can sum up this rule is to leave you with one last quote from a man of great wisdom and love for others.

(Ezra Taft Benson, 1988 April General Conference "The Great Commandment—Love the Lord")[59]
"When we put God first, all other things fall into their proper place or drop out of our lives. Our love of the Lord will govern the claims for our affection, the demands on our time, the interests we pursue, and the order of our priorities."

And Thanks:

Once again, I want to thank all those that helped by doing research for the quotes in this rule: Elder Anthony Covington, Elder Calvin Cook, Elder Jasmer Boaz, Elder Jonathan Olsen, Elder George Bramall, and Elder Porter Roskelley, to name a few. Thank you, young Elders, for sharing your life, talents, and being a part of our extended family.

Rule #18 'First Things First'

Endnotes:

1 **King James Version of the Bible, The Old Testament of Our Lord and Saviour Jesus Christ**. Published by The Church of Jesus Christ of Latter-day Saints, Salt Lake City, Utah, USA. Copywrite 2013.

2 **King James Version of the Bible, The New Testament of Our Lord and Saviour Jesus Christ**. Published by The Church of Jesus Christ of Latter-day Saints, Salt Lake City, Utah, USA. Copywrite 2013.

3 **The Book of Mormon Another Testament of Jesus Christ.** Published by The Church of Jesus Christ of Latter-day Saints, Salt Lake City, Utah, USA. The first English edition published in Palmyra, New York, USA, in 1830. Copywrite 2013.

4 **The Doctrine and Covenants of The Church of Jesus Christ of Latter-Day Saints.** Containing Revelations Give to Joseph Smith, the Prophet. With some additions by his successors in the Presidency of the Church. Published by The Church of Jesus Christ of Latter-day Saints, Salt Lake City, Utah, USA. Copywrite 2013.

5 **The Pearl of Great Price.** A selection from the revelations, translations, and narrations of Joseph Smith, First Prophet, seer, and revelator to The Church of Jesus Christ of Latter-Day Saints. Published by The Church of Jesus Christ of Latter-day Saints, Salt Lake City, Utah, USA. Copywrite 2013.

6 **Johann Wolfgang Von Goethe**. Johann Wolfgang von Goethe. (n.d.). AZQuotes.com. Retrieved February 18, 2019, from AZQuotes.com Web site: https://www.azquotes.com/quote/344069. Also, see, Attributed to Goethe by Johannes Falk in "Goethe aus näherm persönlichen Umgange dargestellt", 1832.

7 **Dallin H. Oaks, 2001 April General Conference, "Focus and Priorities"**. The 171st Annual General Conference of the Church of Jesus Christ of Latter-day Saints, April 1, 2001, Sunday Afternoon Session. Published in the Ensign magazine, Volume 31 Number 05, May 2001. An official magazine of the Church of Jesus Christ of Latter-day Saints, published by the Church of Jesus Christ of Latter-day Saints, 50 E. North Temple Street, Salt Lake City, UT, 84150-3220, USA. Also see, Ensign, Churchofjesuschrist.org. Retrieved February 17, 2019 from Churchofjesuschrist.org website: https://www.churchofjesuschrist.org/study/ensign/2001/05/focus-and-priorities?lang=eng.

8 **Richard G. Scott, 2014 October General Conference, "Make the Exercise of Faith Your First Priority"**. The 184th Semiannual General Conference of the Church of Jesus Christ of Latter-day Saints, October 5, 2014, Sunday Afternoon Session. Published in the Ensign magazine, Volume 44 Number 11 page-92 Paragraph-1, November 2014. An official magazine of the Church of Jesus Christ of Latter-day Saints, published by the Church of Jesus Christ of Latter-day Saints, 50 E. North Temple Street, Salt Lake City, UT, 84150-3220, USA. Also see, Ensign, Churchofjesuschrist.org. Retrieved February 17, 2019 from Churchofjesuschrist.org website: https://www.churchofjesuschrist.org/study/ensign/2014/11/sunday-afternoon-session/make-the-exercise-of-faith-your-first-priority?lang=eng.

Rule #18 'First Things First'

9. **Stephen Covey, "Put First Things First"**. Stephen Covey. (n.d.). AZQuotes.com. Retrieved February 19, 2019, from AZQuotes.com Web site: https://www.azquotes.com/quote/536588. Also, see Stephen R. Covey, A. Roger Merrill, Rebecca R. Merrill (1997). "First Things First Every Day: Daily Reflections- Because Where You're Headed Is More Important Than How Fast You Get There", Simon and Schuster.

10. **Stephen Covey, "Put First Things First"**. Stephen Covey. (n.d.). AZQuotes.com. Retrieved February 19, 2019, from AZQuotes.com Web site: https://www.azquotes.com/quote/554457. Also, see Stephen R. Covey (2013). "The 7 Habits of Highly Effective People: Powerful Lessons in Personal Change", p.20, Simon and Schuster.

11. **Stephen Covey, "Put First Things First"**. Stephen R. Covey (2013). "The 7 Habits of Highly Effective People: Powerful Lessons in Personal Change", Simon and Schuster. Also see, Stephen Covey. (n.d.). books.google.com. Retrieved February 19, 2019. From books.google.com website: https://books.google.com/books?id-=sqy5CAAAQBAJ&pg=PT467&lpg=PT467&dq=If+you+were+to+pause+and+think+seriously+about+the+%E2%80%9Cfirst+things%E2%80%9D+in+your+life&source=bl&ots=7Z8raxsUF0&sig=ACfU3U1wUqIn8hen-LIkwxz8gnaee6QCPw&hl=en&sa=X&ved=2ahUKE-wjInNOtvsjgAhWM5oMKHc7zDeoQ6AEwDnoECAcQAQ#v=onepage&q=If%20you%20were%20to%20pause%20and%20think%20seriously%20about%20the%20%E2%80%9Cfirst%20things%E2%80%9D%20in%20your%20life&f=false

12. **Stephen Covey**. Stephen Covey. (n.d.). AZQuotes.com. Retrieved February 19, 2019, from AZQuotes.com Web site: https://www.azquotes.com/quote/66164. Also, see Stephen R. Covey (2012). "The Wisdom and Teachings of Stephen R. Covey", p.56, Simon and Schuster.

13. **Stephen Covey**. Stephen Covey. (n.d.). AZQuotes.com. Retrieved February 19, 2019, from AZQuotes.com Web site: https://www.azquotes-.com/quote/66166. Also, see Stephen R. Covey (2016). "The 7 Habits of Highly Effective People: Powerful Lessons in Personal Change Interactive Edition", p.198, Mango Media Inc.

14. **Stephen Covey**. Stephen Covey. (n.d.). AZQuotes.com. Retrieved February 19, 2019, from AZQuotes.com Web site: https://www.azquotes.com/quote/377803. Also, see Stephen R. Covey (2013). "The 7 Habits of Highly Effective People: Powerful Lessons in Personal Change", p.165, Simon and Schuster.

15. **Stephen Covey**. Stephen Covey. (n.d.). AZQuotes.com. Retrieved February 19, 2019, from AZQuotes.com Web site: https://www.azquotes.com/quote/66167. Also, see Stephen R. Covey, A. Roger Merrill, Rebecca R. Merrill (1995). "First Things First", p.75, Simon and Schuster.

16. **Stephen Covey**. Stephen Covey. (n.d.). AZQuotes.com. Retrieved February 19, 2019, from AZQuotes.com Web site: https://www.azquotes.com/quote/364119. Also, see Stephen R. Covey (2012). "The Wisdom and Teachings of Stephen R. Covey", p.25, Simon and Schuster.

Rule #18 'First Things First'

17 **Dallin H. Oaks, 2015 April General Conference "The Parable of the Sower"**. The 185th Annual General Conference of the Church of Jesus Christ of Latter-day Saints, April 4, 2015, Saturday Morning Session. Published in the Ensign magazine, Volume 45 Number 05, May 2015 page-35 Paragraph-8. An official magazine of the Church of Jesus Christ of Latter-day Saints, published by the Church of Jesus Christ of Latter-day Saints, 50 E. North Temple Street, Salt Lake City, UT, 84150-3220, USA. Also see, Ensign, Churchofjesuschrist.org. Retrieved February 17, 2019 from Churchofjesuschrist.org website: https://www.churchofjesuschrist.org/study/ensign/2015/05/saturday-morning-session/the-parable-of-the-sower?lang=eng

18 **Donald L. Staheli, 1998 April General Conference "Obedience-Life's Great Challenge"**. The 168th Annual General Conference of the Church of Jesus Christ of Latter-day Saints, April 5, 1998, Sunday Afternoon Session. Published in the Ensign magazine, Volume 28 Number 05, May 1998. An official magazine of the Church of Jesus Christ of Latter-day Saints, published by the Church of Jesus Christ of Latter-day Saints, 50 E. North Temple Street, Salt Lake City, UT, 84150-3220, USA. Also see, Ensign, Churchofjesuschrist.org. Retrieved February 17, 2019 from Churchofjesuschrist.org Web site: https://www.churchofjesuschrist.org/study/ensign/1998/05/obedience-lifes-great-challenge?lang=eng.

19 **Dallin H. Oaks, 2011 April General Conference "Desire"**. The 181st Annual General Conference of the Church of Jesus Christ of Latter-day Saints, April 2, 2011, Saturday Afternoon Session. Published in the Ensign magazine, Volume 41 Number 05, May 2011. An official magazine of the Church of Jesus Christ of Latter-day Saints, published by the Church of Jesus Christ of Latter-day Saints, 50 E. North Temple Street, Salt Lake City, UT, 84150-3220, USA. Also see, Ensign, Churchofjesuschrist.org. Retrieved February 17, 2019 from Churchofjesuschrist.org website: https://www.churchofjesuschrist.org/study/ensign/2011/05/saturday-afternoon-session/desire?lang=eng.

20 **J. Richard Clarke, 1985 April General Conference "Hold Up Your Light"**. The 155th Annual General Conference of the Church of Jesus Christ of Latter-day Saints, April 7, 1985, Sunday Afternoon Session. Published in the Ensign magazine, Volume 15 Number 05, May 1985 page-35 Paragraph-8. An official magazine of the Church of Jesus Christ of Latter-day Saints, published by the Church of Jesus Christ of Latter-day Saints, 50 E. North Temple Street, Salt Lake City, UT, 84150-3220, USA. Also see, Ensign, Churchofjesuschrist.org. Retrieved February 17, 2019 from Churchofjesuschrist.org website: https://www.churchofjesuschrist-.org/study/ensign/1985/05/hold-up-your-light?lang=eng.

21 **Thomas S. Monson, 1992 March Relief Society Sesquicentennial Satellite Broadcast "The Spirit of Relief Society"**. The 162nd Annual General Conference of the Church of Jesus Christ of Latter-day Saints, March 17, 1992, Relief Society Sesquicentennial Satellite Broadcast. Published in the Ensign magazine, Volume 22 Number 05, May 1992 page-35 Paragraph-8. An official magazine of the Church of Jesus Christ of Latter-day Saints, published by the Church of Jesus Christ of Latter-day Saints, 50 E. North Temple Street, Salt Lake City, UT, 84150-3220, USA. Also see, Ensign,

Rule #18 'First Things First'

Churchofjesuschrist.org. Retrieved February 17, 2019 from Churchofjesuschrist.org website: https://www.churchofjesuschrist.org/study/ensign/1992/05/the-spirit-of-relief-society?lang=eng.

22 **Ernest Agyemang Yeboah**. Ernest Agyemang Yeboah quotes. (n.d.), goodreads, Goodreads.com. Retrieved February 20, 2019, from Goodreads.com website: https://www.goodreads.com/quotes/tag/first-things-first. Also, see the book by: Ernest Agyemang Yeboah, "Distinctive Footprints of Life: Where Are You Heading Towards?".

23 **Ernest Agyemang Yeboah**. Ernest Agyemang Yeboah quotes. (n.d.), goodreads, Goodreads.com. Retrieved February 20, 2019, from Goodreads.com website: https://www.goodreads.com/quotes/tag/first-things-first. Also, see the book by: Ernest Agyemang Yeboah, "Distinctive Footprints of Life: Where Are You Heading Towards?".

24 **Ernest Agyemang Yeboah**. Ernest Agyemang Yeboah quotes. (n.d.), goodreads, Goodreads.com. Retrieved February 20, 2019, from Goodreads.com website: https://www.goodreads.com/quotes/tag/first-things-first.

25 **Ernest Agyemang Yeboah**. Ernest Agyemang Yeboah quotes. (n.d.), goodreads, Goodreads.com. Retrieved February 20, 2019, from Goodreads.com website: https://www.goodreads.com/quotes/tag/first-things-first.

26 **Clive Staples "C. S." Lewis**. C. S. Lewis. (n.d.). AZQuotes.com. Retrieved February 20, 2019, from AZQuotes.com Web site: https://www.azquotes.com/quote/867114. Also see, C. S. Lewis (2003). "A Mind Awake: An Anthology of C. S. Lewis", p.141, Houghton Mifflin Harcourt

27 **Clive Staples "C. S." Lewis**. C. S. Lewis. (n.d.). AZQuotes.com. Retrieved February 20, 2019, from AZQuotes.com Web site: https://www.azquotes.com/quote/799020. Also see, "The Collected Letters of C.S. Lewis, Volume 3: Narnia, Cambridge, and Joy, 1950 - 1963".

28 **James W. Frick**. ThinkExist.com Quotations. James W. Frick quotes. (n.d.). ThinkExist.com Quotations Online 1 Jan. 2019. 20 Feb. 2019 <http://thinkexist.com/quotes/james_w._frick/>.

29 **John Kramer Blythe**. John Kramer Blythe quotes. (n.d.), goodreads, Goodreads.com. Retrieved February 20, 2019, from Goodreads.com website: https://www.goodreads.com/quotes/tag/first-things-first.

30 **Shirley Conran**. Shirley Conran. (n.d.). AZQuotes.com. Retrieved February 20, 2019, from AZQuotes.com Web site: https://www.azquotes.com/quote/777504. Also see, Shirley Conran (1978). "Superwoman", Outlet.

31 **Thomas Watson, Jr**. Thomas Watson, Jr.. (n.d.). AZQuotes.com. Retrieved February 20, 2019, from AZQuotes.com Web site: https://www.azquotes.com/quote/1306643.

32 **Kenneth E. Hagin**. Kenneth E. Hagin. (n.d.). AZQuotes.com. Retrieved February 20, 2019, from AZQuotes.com Web site: https://www.azquotes.com/quote/1403685.

Rule #18 'First Things First'

33 **William Golding.** William Golding. (n.d.). AZQuotes.com. Retrieved February 20, 2019, from AZQuotes.com Web site: https://www.azquotes.com/quote/714499. Also see, William Golding (1954). "Lord of the Flies", p.57, Penguin.

34 **Victoria Moran.** Victoria Moran. (n.d.). AZQuotes.com. Retrieved February 20, 2019, from AZQuotes.com Web site: https://www.azquotes.com/quote/673430.

35 **Ivy Baker Priest.** Ivy Baker Priest. (n.d.). AZQuotes.com. Retrieved February 20, 2019, from AZQuotes.com Web site: https://www.azquotes.com/quote/596315.

36 **Leo Babauta.** Leo Babauta's book, "Zen Habits" published January 11, 2011.

37 **Dave Willis.** Dave Willis. (n.d.). AZQuotes.com. Retrieved February 20, 2019, from AZQuotes.com Web site: https://www.azquotes.com/quote/908470. Also retrieved from FaceBook.com website: https://www.facebook.com/davewillis78/posts/1819365285054201, FaceBook post by Dave Willis from Mar 12, 2017.

38 **Leo Christopher.** Leo Christopher Quotes. (n.d.). pandoraandmax.blogspot.com. Retrieved on February 20, 2019, from pandoraandmax.blogspot.com website: https://pandoraandmax.blogspot.com/2018/05/theres-only-one-thing-more-precious.html, posted May 14, 2018.

39 **Mahatma Gandhi.** Mahatma Gandhi. (n.d.). AZQuotes.com. Retrieved February 20, 2019, from AZQuotes.com Web site: https://www.azquotes.com/quote/880424.

40 **Wall Street Journal.** The Wall Street Journal Quotes. (n.d.). Goodreads.com. Retrieved February 20, 2019, from goodreads.com website: https://www.goodreads.com/quotes/548894-instead-of-saying-i-don-t-have-time-try-saying-it-s.

41 **Steve Maraboli.** Steve Maraboli Quotes. (n.d.). Goodreads.com. Retrieved February 20, 2019, from goodreads.com website: https://www.goodreads.com/quotes/1278942-when-someone-tells-you-they-are-too-busy-it-s-not.

42 **Instagram Quote.** (n.d.). geniusquotes.org. Retrieved February 20, 2019 from geniusquotes.org website: https://geniusquotes.org/you-always-have-time-for-the-things-you-put-first-instagram-2014-sayings/.

43 **PureHappyLife.com.** (n.d.). PureHappylife.com. Retrieved February 20, 2019, from purehappylife.com website: https://purehappylife.com/life_quotes_love_quotes/life-quote-your-priorities-are-your-character.html

44 **Myles Munroe.** Myles Munroe Quotes. (n.d.). BrainyQuote.com. Retrieved February 20, 2019, from BrainyQuote.com Web site: https://www.brainyquote.com/quotes/myles_munroe_699991.

Rule #18 'First Things First'

45 **Phoebe Snow**. Phoebe Snow. (n.d.). AZQuotes.com. Retrieved February 21, 2019, from AZQuotes.com Web site: https://www.azquotes.com/quote/276998. Also, Phoebe Snow Quotes. (n.d.). BrainyQuote.com. Retrieved February 20, 2019, from BrainyQuote.com Web site: https://www.brainyquote.com/quotes/phoebe_snow_537336.

46 **Steven Pressfield**. Steven Pressfield. (n.d.). AZQuotes.com. Retrieved February 21, 2019, from AZQuotes.com Web site: https://www.azquotes.com/quote/458563. Also see, Steven Pressfield (2002). "The War of Art: Break Through the Blocks and Win Your Inner Creative Battles", p.65, Black Irish Entertainment LLC.

47 **Martin Luther King, Jr.**. Martin Luther King, Jr.. (n.d.). AZQuotes.com. Retrieved February 21, 2019, from AZQuotes.com Web site: https://www.azquotes.com/quote/912035.

48 **Brandon Sanderson**. Brandon Sanderson. (n.d.). AZQuotes.com. Retrieved February 21, 2019, from AZQuotes.com Web site: https://www.azquotes.com/quote/463545. Also see, Brandon Sanderson (2011). "The Alloy of Law: A Mistborn Novel", p.69, Macmillan.

49 **Andy Stanley**. Andy Stanley. (n.d.). AZQuotes.com. Retrieved February 21, 2019, from AZQuotes.com Web site: https://www.azquotes.com/quote/1275770.

50 **Rick Warren**. Rick Warren. (n.d.). AZQuotes.com. Retrieved February 21, 2019, from AZQuotes.com Web site: https://www.azquotes.com/quote/1171973.

51 **David F. Jakielo**. David F. Jakielo Quotes. (n.d.). Goodreads.com. Retrieved February 20, 2019, from goodreads.com website: https://www.goodreads.com/quotes/489387-the-most-important-thing-in-life-is-knowing-the-most.

52 **Dwight D. Eisenhower**. Dwight D. Eisenhower. (n.d.). AZQuotes.com. Retrieved February 21, 2019, from AZQuotes.com Web site: https://www.azquotes.com/quote/87662.

53 **Bob Hawke**. Bob Hawke. (n.d.). AZQuotes.com. Retrieved February 21, 2019, from AZQuotes.com Web site: https://www.azquotes.com/quote/728030. Also, see Biography/Personal Quotes, www.imdb.com.

54 **Jim Rohn**. Jim Rohn. (n.d.). AZQuotes.com. Retrieved February 21, 2019, from AZQuotes.com Web site: https://www.azquotes.com/quote/519837. Also, see FaceBook post by Jim Rohn from May 28, 2015 (https://www.facebook.com/OfficialJimRohn/posts/10155547089915635).

55 **Albert Einstein**. Albert Einstein. (n.d.). AZQuotes.com. Retrieved February 21, 2019, from AZQuotes.com Web site: https://www.azquotes.com/quote/87404. Also, see Albert Einstein (2015). "Bite-Size Einstein: Quotations on Just About Everything from the Greatest Mind of the Twentieth Century", p.24, St. Martin's Press.

Rule #18 'First Things First'

56 **Anthony Robbins.** Tony Robbins. (n.d.). AZQuotes.com. Retrieved February 21, 2019, from AZQuotes.com Web site: https://www.azquotes.com/quote/1062138. Also, see Tony Robbins (2012). "Awaken The Giant Within", p.400, Simon, and Schuster.

57 **Robert J. McKain, Author.** Robert J. McKain Quotes. (n.d.). braintrainingtools.org. Retrieved February 21, 2019 from braintrainingtools.org website: http://www.braintrainingtools.org/skills/the-reason-most-goals-are-not-achieved-is-that-we-spend-our-time-doing-second/. Also see, quotation reference retrieved February 21, 2019 from books.google.co.in website: https://books.google.co.in/books?id=bUEtymPqZ-EC&pg=PA153&lpg=PA153&dq.

58 **Ezra Taft Benson, 1988 April General Conference "The Great Commandment—Love the Lord.** The 158th Annual General Conference of the Church of Jesus Christ of Latter-day Saints, April 2, 1988, Saturday Morning Session. Published in the Ensign magazine, Volume 18 Number 05, May 1988. An official magazine of the Church of Jesus Christ of Latter-day Saints, published by the Church of Jesus Christ of Latter-day Saints, 50 E. North Temple Street, Salt Lake City, UT, 84150-3220, USA. Also see, Ensign, Churchofjesuschrist.org. Retrieved February 17, 2019 from Churchofjesuschrist.org website: https://www.churchofjesuschrist.org/study/ensign/1988/05/the-great-commandment-love-the-lord?lang=eng.

Bend But Don't Break

Rule #19

'Preferences Bend, Principles Don't'

Rule #19 'Preferences Bend, Principles Don't'

Short But Sweet:

Preferences are the choices we make in life, and principles are the guiding rules which help determine the boundaries in which our choices are made. Thus, Rule #19 *'Preferences Bend, Principles Don't'*.

A Defining Moment:

Have you ever had one of those moments in life where you are trying to find a simple phrase to explain your thoughts or feelings, and you can't? Instead, your mouth keeps spewing out word after word in its attempt to explain what is in your head. Yet no matter how long you talk it out or think it through, words fail to express the meaning you wish to convey. That is how it was as I tried to find a pure and simple phrase that would define the body of this rule. No matter how hard I tried, I couldn't come up with it.

That is until I attended a combined Priesthood meeting at our church Ward Conference. A few years ago, our Stake President, Douglas Cropper, was giving a lesson and the minute I heard him say the words *"Preferences bend, and principles don't"*, in my mind's eye I could see a sign appear above the door to a room containing all my thoughts on Rule #19. This sign *'preferences bend, and principles don't'* encompassed and explained all those thoughts I had stored within the room in a simple statement.

Moment of Thanks:

I want to take a moment to thank my Stake President, Douglas Cropper, for his inspired lesson. A few weeks after Ward Conference, I attended a meeting with President Cropper at his church office. It was an opportunity to compliment him on his lesson of principles and preferences. I told him; the lesson had greatly helped me solidify Rule #19. It was like

Rule #19 'Preferences Bend, Principles Don't'

putting together a complex puzzle and finding the last key piece to complete the picture. Without that key piece, the true beauty of the art portrayed in the puzzle picture is hollow. But once that final key piece is found and pressed into the empty space, harmony emerges, and completeness is seen and felt.

I told him how the young Elder missionaries had challenged me to write a book about my list of rules with supporting scriptures and quotes for each rule. I asked President Cropper if he had any inspired comments, quotes, or scriptures he would like to share for Rule #19. He replied that he would be more interested in what I had to say about the lesson than what he might add. He then challenged me to write his lesson in my own words.

President Cropper must have gotten hold of a copy of Rule #13 *'Focus on the Journey Not the Task'* and decided that I needed the journey to receive the necessary enlightenment to accomplish the task. It has been at least five years since I had that conversation with President Cropper. So, I believe it is time I end this journey and complete the task. I pray that I will find the inspiring words that will do justice to President Cropper's inspirational lesson on 'Principles & Preferences' and how it applies to me. It is my prayer also that my words will then, in turn, inspire you, the reader, to write your own Rule #19.

Define It For Me:

Principle:

- A fundamental truth or proposition that serves as the foundation for a system of belief or behavior or for a chain of reasoning.
- A fundamental source or basis of something.

Preference:

- A greater liking for one alternative over another.

Who We Are:

A principle is a fundamental core element, foundation, or law that defines a thing. And all principles carry their own unique laws. Take away anything from the core element that formulates a principle, and a major change occurs. For you cannot alter the state of a principle without losing its original meaning. Since it no longer carries its unique meaning, it is transformed into a different principle.

Example: Scientists have determined that water is the principle (basic fundamental core element) of all life here on Earth. Without water, all forms of life as we know them would cease to exist. That includes you and me.

The same holds true when the term principle is applied to human behavior. When a person's fundamental core principle changes, the person's personality or behavior changes, and who they were ceases to exist. Going forward, they will now act and behave differently. They are the same on the outside, but not the same on the inside. This is something I would suggest you spend some time to ponder.

What Principles Are We Talking About?

Principles fall into different categories. Some govern the laws of physics, others the laws of nature, then there are spiritual laws, temporal laws, and so on. These laws that govern these principles are eternal and unchanging. The only principles that change are those made by man.

> **(Elder Russel M. Nelson, 1993 October General Conference, "Constancy amid Change")**[6]
> *"Unchanging principles are so because they come from our unchanging Heavenly Father. Try as they might, no parliament or congress could ever repeal the law of earth's gravity or amend the Ten Commandments. Those laws are constant. All laws of nature and of God are part of the everlasting gospel. Thus, there are many unchanging principles."*

Rule #19 'Preferences Bend, Principles Don't'

On rare occasions, a new principle is discovered. Note, I said, discovered not created. Generally, when this happens, a Nobel Prize is awarded to the discoverer. That is how important principles are to us.

The only principles I am concerned with here are God's eternal governing principles, not the ever-changing man-made principles. In particular, for Rule #19 'Preferences Bend, Principles Don't' I will address how God's principles apply to us. Specifically, those guiding principles that shape and create our human character, that determine how we humans act in a given situation, the choices we make, the examples we set, and the principles, that in the end, determine the outcome of our life.

How Firm a Foundation:

Our principles define who we are and must be solid. That is not to say that they are to be totally inflexible. There are times as we grow and learn that we realize the necessity to change a core principle for the better. On the other hand, that is not to say our principles can flutter like a leaf in the wind either. A person whose principles are not solid will have an unstable personality. That type of person is a double-minded person, and a double-mind person is unpredictable. They are forever changing, tossed to and fro by the whims of the world.

> **(Bible New Testament: James 1:8)**[2]
> *8 A double minded man is unstable in all his ways.*
>
> **(Stephen Covey)**[7]
> *"You can't live principals you can't understand."*
>
> **(Samuel Smiles)**[8]
> *"A man without principles and will is like a ship without compass; it changes direction with every change of wind."*

Chiseled in Stone:

Once a principle is carved in stone, it becomes a part of the fundamental core of who you are and is not easily changed.

Rule #19 'Preferences Bend, Principles Don't'

That is why people who have chosen to develop unrighteous or immoral principles have a hard time changing their ways. This is not to say that a person with unrighteous principles cannot change. Fortunately, steel is harder than stone, and with a hammer and chisel, little by little, a principle can be chiseled away and a new one carved in its place.

For most people, it takes time to erase old habits and replace them with new ones. It is not easy to change a habit or a belief when you have behaved or thought a certain way for an extended period of time. The longer you exist in a state of being, the harder it becomes to make changes. That is why when you are trying to change a core principle, it takes a lot of commitment. For the path, you'll have to take to make that newfound principle a part of your life is not always easy. Generally, there are many pitfalls and setbacks you'll have to work through. Instilling a new principle into your life is not as easy as throwing a railroad track switch to guide your train in a new direction. You may also find that changing some principles is far easier than others.

I can tell you that from my life experiences, any personal changes I made took dedicated effort. Setback was always trying to tackle me. For some principles, change took a lot of dodging as I ran down the field towards the goal. I figured setback would hit me a few times, and I would get taken down. So, I had to keep my determination strong in my mind and heart, and just hope to make ten more yards to that next first and ten that would keep me in the game and moving forward.

To those of you that are out there as mentors and teachers, always remember charity, patience, love, & kindness as you guide others to apply new principles in their life. Remember, the person you are helping is changing a core principle. This is no easy task on their part. For when a person changes a core principle, a part of their personality changes and they must redefine who they are. That is why for most people, something has to happen in their lives before a core principle changes, often a drastic, life-altering event.

Rule #19 'Preferences Bend, Principles Don't'

Bring the Hammer Down:

While humans flail about, it is God who has the ability to bring about change in a person quickly. God has the largest hammer and the sharpest chisel that exists, and when He decides to drop the hammer and chisel on you, you can bet you will feel His power.

For example, take Saul (Paul), in the New Testament. God was not happy with Saul for persecuting the saints.

> **(Bible New Testament: Acts 8:3)[2]**
> *3 As for Saul, he made havoc of the church, entering into every house, and haling men and women committed them to prison.*

The Lord had work for Saul to do, and that work could not be done unless Saul changed his principle way of thinking. In an attempt to bring about this change in Saul's attitude, the Lord gently applied the hammer and chisel, also known as a light from heaven. I have included an abridged version of Saul's conversion story.

> **(Bible New Testament: Acts 9: 1- 9)[2]**
> *1 And Saul, yet breathing out threatenings and slaughter against the disciples of the Lord, went unto the high priest,*
>
> *2 And desired of him letters to Damascus to the synagogues, that if he found any of this way, whether they were men or women, he might bring them bound unto Jerusalem.*
>
> *3 And as he journeyed, he came near Damascus: and suddenly there shined round about him a light from heaven:*
>
> *4 And he fell to the earth, and heard a voice saying unto him, Saul, Saul, why persecutest thou me?*
>
> *5 And he said, Who art thou, Lord? And the Lord said, I am Jesus whom thou persecutest: it is hard for thee to kick against the pricks.*

6 And he trembling and astonished said, Lord, what wilt thou have me to do? And the Lord said unto him, Arise, and go into the city, and it shall be told thee what thou must do.

7 And the men which journeyed with him stood speechless, hearing a voice, but seeing no man.

8 And Saul arose from the earth; and when his eyes were opened, he saw no man: but they led him by the hand, and brought him into Damascus.

9 And he was three days without sight, and neither did eat nor drink.

(Bible New Testament: Acts 9: 17 - 20)[2]
17 And Ananias went his way, and entered into the house; and putting his hands on him said, Brother Saul, the Lord, even Jesus, that appeared unto thee in the way as thou camest, hath sent me, that thou mightest receive thy sight, and be filled with the Holy Ghost.

18 And immediately there fell from his eyes as it had been scales: and he received sight forthwith, and arose, and was baptized.

19 And when he had received meat, he was strengthened. Then was Saul certain days with the disciples which were at Damascus.

20 And straightway he preached Christ in the synagogues, that he is the Son of God.

Saul (Paul) is not the only person God has taken His hammer and chisel to. You see, when God decides a person needs to change their principles in order to live a more righteous life, God has a hammer powerful enough to reshape even the hardest headed person. That is not to say that God takes away your free agency. He will leave you the option to choose. But He can be a strong persuader. We can read an example of this in the Book of Mormon in the conversion story of the sons of Mosiah and the son of Alma.

Rule #19 'Preferences Bend, Principles Don't'

(Book of Mormon: Mosiah 27: 8 - 24)[3]

8 Now the sons of Mosiah were numbered among the unbelievers; and also one of the sons of Alma was numbered among them, he being called Alma, after his father; nevertheless, he became a very wicked and an idolatrous man. And he was a man of many words, and did speak much flattery to the people; therefore he led many of the people to do after the manner of his iniquities.

9 And he became a great hinderment to the prosperity of the church of God; stealing away the hearts of the people; causing much dissension among the people; giving a chance for the enemy of God to exercise his power over them.

10 And now it came to pass that while he was going about to destroy the church of God, for he did go about secretly with the sons of Mosiah seeking to destroy the church, and to lead astray the people of the Lord, contrary to the commandments of God, or even the king—

11 And as I said unto you, as they were going about rebelling against God, behold, the angel of the Lord appeared unto them; and he descended as it were in a cloud; and he spake as it were with a voice of thunder, which caused the earth to shake upon which they stood;

12 And so great was their astonishment, that they fell to the earth, and understood not the words which he spake unto them.

13 Nevertheless he cried again, saying: Alma, arise and stand forth, for why persecutest thou the church of God? For the Lord hath said: This is my church, and I will establish it; and nothing shall overthrow it, save it is the transgression of my people.

14 And again, the angel said: Behold, the Lord hath heard the prayers of his people, and also the prayers of his servant, Alma, who is thy father; for he has

Rule #19 'Preferences Bend, Principles Don't'

prayed with much faith concerning thee that thou mightest be brought to the knowledge of the truth; therefore, for this purpose have I come to convince thee of the power and authority of God, that the prayers of his servants might be answered according to their faith.

15 And now behold, can ye dispute the power of God? For behold, doth not my voice shake the earth? And can ye not also behold me before you? And I am sent from God.

16 Now I say unto thee: Go, and remember the captivity of thy fathers in the land of Helam, and in the land of Nephi; and remember how great things he has done for them; for they were in bondage, and he has delivered them. And now I say unto thee, Alma, go thy way, and seek to destroy the church no more, that their prayers may be answered, and this even if thou wilt of thyself be cast off.

17 And now it came to pass that these were the last words which the angel spake unto Alma, and he departed.

18 And now Alma and those that were with him fell again to the earth, for great was their astonishment; for with their own eyes they had beheld an angel of the Lord; and his voice was as thunder, which shook the earth; and they knew that there was nothing save the power of God that could shake the earth and cause it to tremble as though it would part asunder.

19 And now the astonishment of Alma was so great that he became dumb, that he could not open his mouth; yea, and he became weak, even that he could not move his hands; therefore he was taken by those that were with him, and carried helpless, even until he was laid before his father.

20 And they rehearsed unto his father all that had happened unto them; and his father rejoiced, for he knew that it was the power of God.

Rule #19 'Preferences Bend, Principles Don't'

21 And he caused that a multitude should be gathered together that they might witness what the Lord had done for his son, and also for those that were with him.

22 And he caused that the priests should assemble themselves together; and they began to fast, and to pray to the Lord their God that he would open the mouth of Alma, that he might speak, and also that his limbs might receive their strength—that the eyes of the people might be opened to see and know of the goodness and glory of God.

23 And it came to pass after they had fasted and prayed for the space of two days and two nights, the limbs of Alma received their strength, and he stood up and began to speak unto them, bidding them to be of good comfort:

24 For, said he, I have repented of my sins, and have been redeemed of the Lord; behold I am born of the Spirit.

You Can't Make Me:

Even when God tries his best to influence us to righteousness, not all heed His hammer and chisel. In the Book of Mormon, there is a tale of two unrighteous brothers who just can't seem to change their ways permanently. As they are beating up their younger brothers, an angel appears to them.

> **(Book of Mormon: 1 Nephi 3:28-30)**[3]
> *28 And it came to pass that Laman was angry with me, and also with my father; and also was Lemuel, for he hearkened unto the words of Laman. Wherefore Laman and Lemuel did speak many hard words unto us, their younger brothers, and they did smite us even with a rod.*
>
> *29 And it came to pass as they smote us with a rod, behold, an angel of the Lord came and stood before them, and he spake unto them, saying: Why do ye smite your younger brother with a rod? Know ye not*

Rule #19 'Preferences Bend, Principles Don't'

that the Lord hath chosen him to be a ruler over you, and this because of your iniquities? Behold ye shall go up to Jerusalem again, and the Lord will deliver Laban into your hands.

30 And after the angel had spoken unto us, he departed.

Now you would think that after seeing an Angel, a heavenly messenger from God, that would be enough for a person to straighten out their life permanently. It would be enough for me; but no, not for Lemuel and Laman. Later in the book, the brothers are still causing trouble, and once again, the Lord gives them a warning.

(Book of Mormon: 1 Nephi 17:45-47)[3]
45 Ye are swift to do iniquity but slow to remember the Lord your God. Ye have seen an angel, and he spake unto you; yea, ye have heard his voice from time to time; and he hath spoken unto you in a still small voice, but ye were past feeling, that ye could not feel his words; wherefore, he has spoken unto you like unto the voice of thunder, which did cause the earth to shake as if it were to divide asunder.

46 And ye also know that by the power of his almighty word he can cause the earth that it shall pass away; yea, and ye know that by his word he can cause the rough places to be made smooth, and smooth places shall be broken up. O, then, why is it, that ye can be so hard in your hearts?

47 Behold, my soul is rent with anguish because of you, and my heart is pained; I fear lest ye shall be cast off forever. Behold, I am full of the Spirit of God, insomuch that my frame has no strength.

After being chastened by the love of God, Lemuel and Laman once again humble themselves. However, not long thereafter, they return to their complaining ways.

It is hard for me to believe that the brothers only ever change their principles for a short time, despite the fact that not only had they seen angels, but they had also been repeatedly chastened by the Lord.

God tries His best with all of us. However, in the end, we have been given our free agency to make our choices, and God will not break that principle law. In the case of Laman and Lemuel, that is somewhat unfortunate. Laman and Lemuel continue the cycle of returning to their rebellious ways all their days on Earth.

Help I Need Somebody, Help Me:

Have you known someone that gets in trouble due to their own foolishness? Then they say, "Help show me a better way, and I will change." So, you give them the help and guidance they need, and they do change. But it doesn't take long, and then they are back to their foolish ways again, and they are usually in as much trouble as before, if not more. Once again, they are asking for help, and then again and again and again, the cycle repeats.

Why does the cycle repeat? It is because the person did not truly change. They just took a break from their normal routine.

Let's add into the mix that this is one of your children and you love them very much, so of course, you want to help them and help them and help them. Until finally, a day comes where you, as a parent, feel that you need to protect the child from its own foolishness. The pain of watching your child make these mistakes over and over again drives you to want to stop the cycle for the child's own good. As a parent, the only option left to help them is to take control and forcefully prevent them from making the same foolish decision. Is that the right solution, and if so, why doesn't God force us to change after so many tries?

> **(Quentin L. Cook, 2017 October General Conference, "The Eternal Everyday")**[9]
> *"The eternal principle of agency requires that we respect many choices with which we do not agree."*

Freedom of Choice:

Although God has the power to force us to change, He does not use it. Yet at the same time, God will try to influence us in the right direction. Why? Because of His love for us as our Parent. Though God tries his best to influence us to make wise choices, He does draw a line as to how far He will use His influence before He allows us to suffer the consequences of our actions. So why doesn't God forcibly change us? He has the power. I mean, after all, He is God. So, what stops God from forcibly changing us? It's simple: it is one of His own principle laws that prevent Him, and that is the principle of free agency.

Along with free agency, there is another of God's principles that comes into play as well, and that is equality; meaning temporal and spiritual laws apply to God the same as they apply to us. If God did not enforce equality, He would be breaking one of His own principles and become an unjust God, and thereby cease being God as we know Him.

> **(Bible New Testament: Colossians 3:25)**[2]
> 25 But he that doeth wrong shall receive for the wrong which he hath done: and there is no respect of persons.

I Want to Be Treated Equal:

Since I mentioned equality, I am going to talk lightly on the subject for a moment to clarify how I define the word. Some think that to have equality means if I give an apple to one person, I have to give an apple to the others as well; if we were all clones, that could be true. But we are not clones, we are all different and for a good reason (which is another subject I could write a book on). Therefore, since we are all different, to achieve equality, each person must be dealt with on an individual basis. What is good for one is not always good for the other. One of my four sisters is highly allergic to strawberries. So, should I give them all strawberries to treat them all equally? Or do I give the sister that is allergic, an equal portion of a different fruit? By making a fair adjustment

Rule #19 'Preferences Bend, Principles Don't'

based on individual needs, am I not treating all my sisters equally?

Whom Do the Rules Apply to:

As I stated earlier, change a person's principles, and you change the person. This rule, similar to all other rules, applies to God as equally as they apply to us. I call it the equality principle. The scriptures support this principle very clearly. They state that if God changed even one guiding principle, He would cease to be God.

> **(Book of Mormon: Mormon 9: 19)** [3]
> *19 And if there were miracles wrought then, why has God ceased to be a God of miracles and yet be an unchangeable Being? And behold, I say unto you He changeth not; if so He would cease to be God; and he ceaseth not to be God, and is a God of miracles.*
>
> **(Book of Mormon: Alma 42:25)**[3]
> *25 What, do ye suppose that mercy can rob justice? I say unto you, Nay; not one whit. If so, God would cease to be God.*
>
> **(Book of Mormon: Alma 42:13)**[3]
> *13 Therefore, according to justice, the plan of redemption could not be brought about, only on conditions of repentance of men in this probationary state, yea, this preparatory state; for except it were for these conditions, mercy could not take effect except it should destroy the work of justice. Now the work of justice could not be destroyed; if so, God would cease to be God.*

Cause and Effect:

Whenever we choose to make the wrong choice, God does all He can to help open our minds to a better way of thinking. Part of that help is found in consequence of our actions. Consequences co-exist with principles. Good or bad, there is

Rule #19 'Preferences Bend, Principles Don't'

a consequence associated with every principle; for every action, there is a reaction.

God has a great love for us; in fact, He has more love than we can comprehend, which is why He tries His best to guide us in the direction of developing sound principles.

Because of His love for us, He is always trying to nudge us in the right direction. When I say always, I mean always. Why? Because it saddens Him as much as it does us when we see our children suffer from the consequences of living unrighteous principles.

As I said before, we have our free agency, which allows us to choose what principles we wish to follow. The Apostle Paul, the sons of Mosiah, and the son of Alma could have continued persecuting the followers of Jesus Christ even after God had dropped the hammer and chisel on them.

There is a point where unrighteousness gets its reward, just as righteousness receives its reward; however, that is not to say that both behaviors enjoy the same rewards. All things, laws included, must balance, and that includes injustice to others. There always comes the point where God steps back and no longer uses his hammer and chisel to help remold us, but instead, He balances the books, so to speak.

> **(Book of Mormon: 3 Nephi 20:20)**[3]
> *20 And it shall come to pass, saith the Father, that the sword of my justice shall hang over them at that day; and except they repent it shall fall upon them, saith the Father, yea, even upon all the nations of the Gentiles.*

In the Bible and Book of Mormon, we find many stories that demonstrate God's patience and compassion for us, His children. And many times, we see God's patience and compassion pushed beyond even His limits. At that point, justice must be dealt with to balance the books. In the Book of Mormon, God allows the Nephites and the Jaredites to be completely wiped out in the end, because of their unrighteous principles. From the Bible Old Testament, we have the stories of the Tower of Babel, Noah and the flood, Sodom and Gomorrah.

(Book of Mormon: The Book of Ether 15:19)[3]

19 But behold, the Spirit of the Lord had ceased striving with them, and Satan had full power over the hearts of the people; for they were given up unto the hardness of their hearts, and the blindness of their minds that they (Jaredites) might be destroyed;

(Book of Mormon: The Book of Moroni 9:20 - 23)[3]

20 And now, my son, I dwell no longer upon this horrible scene. Behold, thou knowest the wickedness of this people (the Nephites); thou knowest that they are without principle, and past feeling; and their wickedness doth exceed that of the Lamanites.

21 Behold, my son, I cannot recommend them unto God lest he should smite me.

22 But behold, my son, I recommend thee unto God, and I trust in Christ that thou wilt be saved; and I pray unto God that he will spare thy life, to witness the return of his people unto him, or their utter destruction; for I know that they must perish except they repent and return unto him.

23 And if they (the Nephites) perish it will be like unto the Jaredites, because of the willfulness of their hearts, seeking for blood and revenge.

(Bible Old Testament: Genesis 19:24-25)[1]

24 Then the Lord rained upon Sodom and upon Gomorrah brimstone and fire from the Lord out of heaven;

25 And he overthrew those cities, and all the plain, and all the inhabitants of the cities, and that which grew upon the ground.

(Bible Old Testament: Genesis 6:17)[1]
17 And, behold, I, even I, do bring a flood of waters upon the earth, to destroy all flesh, wherein is the breath of life, from under heaven; and every thing that is in the earth shall die.

(Bible Old Testament: Genesis 11:6-8)[1]
6 And the Lord said, Behold, the people is one, and they have all one language; and this they begin to do: and now nothing will be restrained from them, which they have imagined to do.

7 Go to, let us go down, and there confound their language, that they may not understand one another's speech.

8 So the Lord scattered them abroad from thence upon the face of all the earth: and they left off to build the city.

Stop Complaining:

Are there defining moments in your life where you felt God had laid His hammer and chisel to you? Do you complain when trials come into your life to test and stretch your principles? Should we complain? Though we are deep in the swamp with gators all around us, at that moment, it may not be easy to see the reasons or the whys for our troubles. What I can tell you is that your principles are always being tested, and whether you succeed or fail the test, you can still win. Why do I say we can always come out winning? Well, if you succeed, your principles are strengthened. If you fail, you learn what areas of your principles need reinforcing. Thus, if you look at it from a positive perspective, it is a win-win, and there is no reason to complain. Easy to say, hard to do.

What Do You Prefer?

Preference - a greater liking for one alternative over another or others.

Rule #19 'Preferences Bend, Principles Don't'

Our choices strengthen or weaken our principles, and the choices we make in life are generally determined by our preferences. Unlike principles, preferences can bend; meaning that what a person prefers today is not necessarily what they might prefer tomorrow. And because you prefer something different does not mean you have to break or bend a principle. The whole beauty of preferences is the fact that they are so flexible. The flexibility of our preferences allows us to make so many wonderful choices in life, which in turn enables us to enjoy so many different experiences.

Allowing our preferences to be flexible is ok to a point. Go beyond that point, and you start to bend or break a principle. We all require boundaries, and it is the principles in our life that give our preferences boundaries. It works like this: preferences help guide and direct our choices, and our principles set invisible limits on our choices.

Principles set the boundaries for all of our decisions and thus help to establish harmony in our lives. Like it or not, this is the order of things. All governing laws or principles, both temporal and spiritual, have existed since the beginning of time. They are perfect and as old as God Himself and cannot be changed. That fact has not stopped humankind from trying to defy them and escape their consequences. Since the beginning of man's existence, man has sought to challenge the governing laws and principles, but he can't. Why? Because even the consequences of defying God's principles are a part of the laws or principles.

One of my favorite principle laws is 'for every action there is a reaction.' I think we all have to remind ourselves of that principle from time to time. You cannot escape consequences, whether they are good or bad, they are the natural outcome of the law. You may perhaps delay them, but sooner or later, consequences catch up to you, and the price must be paid and the books balanced. There is a perfectly good reason that there are consequences for everything. It is God's incentive to help guide our preferences, which in turn shapes our principles.

Consequences give principles meaning. If principles had no consequences, then principles would cease to exist. Why follow a rule if there is no benefit or punishment? And if principles are done away with, then our preferences would have no boundaries, and without boundaries, there is no order. Without order, there is no harmony, only chaos, and chaos is not the way of the universe. All things exist because there is order in the universe and that includes God. Order means to exist within the given limits governed by principles and maintained by preferences. Without order, there is no existence.

The Shackles to Freedom?

Some people have a hard time living within limits and feel it means a loss of freedom and happiness. Well, those people would be correct on the loss of freedom. There cannot be unlimited freedom, or we are back to chaos. As a matter of fact, I will go as far as to say without limits, nothing can exist; non-existence, void, empty, not a thing.

This brings me back to the universe again. Matter cannot exist without order, and order cannot exist without limits, and the only way to apply limits is by taking away freedoms. What some people out there in this universe don't understand is that the only way to find true freedom is to find true happiness, and the only path to true happiness is by living within the governing principles that define life and living. To find that path requires us to gain knowledge on what life's governing principles are and then ensure that our preferences are within those limits.

You see, there is the word 'limits' again and the implied loss of freedom. So, to find true happiness requires a loss of freedom, yet once true happiness is found you have true freedom. Think about that for a while.

Rule #19 'Preferences Bend, Principles Don't'

In the Beginning:

In the beginning, God created man, male and female, and He created a beautiful garden for Adam and Eve to live in, called the Garden of Eden.

> **(Bible Old Testament: Genesis 2:4-9)**[1]
>
> *4 ¶ These are the generations of the heavens and of the earth when they were created, in the day that the Lord God made the earth and the heavens,*
>
> *5 And every plant of the field before it was in the earth, and every herb of the field before it grew: for the Lord God had not caused it to rain upon the earth, and there was not a man to till the ground.*
>
> *6 But there went up a mist from the earth, and watered the whole face of the ground.*
>
> *7 And the Lord God formed man of the dust of the ground, and breathed into his nostrils the breath of life; and man became a living soul.*
>
> *8 ¶ And the Lord God planted a garden eastward in Eden; and there he put the man whom he had formed.*
>
> *9 And out of the ground made the Lord God to grow every tree that is pleasant to the sight, and good for food; the tree of life also in the midst of the garden, and the tree of knowledge of good and evil.*

What're My Limits?

God also gave Adam and Eve a set of rules for teaching them righteous principles to guide their preferences and ultimately manage their choices. This, of course, did put limits on Adam and Eve. Since God is Adam and Eve's parent, I like to call these limits, parental limits.

I bet you thought that it was your parents that came up with this 'parental limits' thing which they used on you to help you manage your choices. Well, your parents did not; it was God long ago who was the architect of parental limits and the consequences of following or not following them. It was He who set the example for our parents to follow, and I hope that we, as parents, are following God's example righteously.

One example of God's parental limits on Adam and Eve is spelled out very clearly in the Bible Old Testament.

> **(Bible Old Testament: Genesis 2:16-17)**[1]
> *16 And the Lord God commanded the man, saying, Of every tree of the garden thou mayest freely eat:*
>
> *17 But of the tree of the knowledge of good and evil, thou shalt not eat of it: for in the day that thou eatest thereof thou shalt surely die.*

I Am Hungry:

Adam's and Eve's choice of what food they ate from the trees God had provided for them was almost without limits. Of all the trees in the Garden of Eden, there was only one they had to stay away from, the tree of knowledge of good and evil. Think of it, this left the boundaries of their meal preference open to a wide variety of choices. They could eat from any tree they wanted without suffering a negative consequence except for one. (I wonder if Adam and Eve had to watch their calorie intake.)

Of all the choices Adam and Eve had to choose from, at some point, they chose to eat from the only tree they were commanded not to. In the Bible, it says that the serpent beguiled Eve, yet Eve herself saw the tree to be desirous, and her preference changed that day, and she did partake.

> **(Bible Old Testament: Genesis 3:1-6)**[1]
> *1 Now the serpent was more subtil than any beast of the field which the Lord God had made. And he said unto the woman, Yea, hath God said, Ye shall not eat of every tree of the garden?*
>
> *2 And the woman said unto the serpent, We may eat of the fruit of the trees of the garden:*

3 But of the fruit of the tree which is in the midst of the garden, God hath said, Ye shall not eat of it, neither shall ye touch it, lest ye die.

4 And the serpent said unto the woman, Ye shall not surely die:

5 For God doth know that in the day ye eat thereof, then your eyes shall be opened, and ye shall be as gods, knowing good and evil.

6 And when the woman saw that the tree was good for food, and that it was pleasant to the eyes, and a tree to be desired to make one wise, she took of the fruit thereof, and did eat, and gave also unto her husband with her; and he did eat.

My Opinion or Yours:

There are a lot of theological books written on Adam and Eve's eating of the fruit of that tree, with a lot of different interpretations of the story. I use this story to bring out one small point of many, and that is God was teaching them what the principle of obedience was about. It was God's way of helping Adam and Eve to understand the consequences of following the law and the principle behind it. All Adam and Eve had to do were to keep their preference for what they ate within the boundaries; a preference that had minimal limitations.

I am not going to discuss my opinion on whether or not Adam and Eve had to partake of the tree of knowledge of good and evil. I am, however, going to point out a few of the consequences of allowing your preference to bend a principle. In some cases, you cannot go back to the way it was before you let your preference swing too far, and you bent a principle. In Adam and Eve's case, eating of the forbidden fruit is one of those times. Adam and Eve's bodies had changed, and they were now subjected to physical death. Prior to eating the forbidden fruit, there was no sickness or pain; all was in harmony. There were other consequences of Adam and Eve's action as well that could not be undone.

Defining Moments?

Not all of our preferences and choices we make matter greatly in the big scheme of life. But in situations where they do matter, where our choices, based on our preferences, change, violate, or no longer reflect our current principles; those become defining moments that shape us and the world we live in. The story of Adam and Eve partaking of the forbidden fruit is one of the top ten defining moments where a preference was allowed to bend a principle which changed all our lives. Think about that, your choice to allow a preference to bend a principle does not only affect you, but might also affect those around you, and sometimes those defining moments are not insignificant.

The God Factor:

Like God, righteous earthly parents, from the time their child is born, set up parental limits to teach their child righteous principles and to keep the child's preferences within those boundaries, while still allowing the child freedom to grow as an individual. A child needs space to be allowed to define who they want to be. As I read the stories in the Holy Scriptures, it sure doesn't look as if it was an easy job for God to parent us. So how can we expect the task of raising righteous children to be any easier for us? The mission of parenting was not meant to be easy or hard, it was meant to teach parents how to impart principles.

To the children of the parents that are trying their best to instill righteous principles in you, I say this: if you think God has a hard time with this task, then remember this, your parents are not Gods (yet). Like God, all the things that your parents do for you, such as setting limits, is done out of their love for you, and their desire to protect you from the world, and yourself. Remember, the day will come when you'll develop into an adult and then become a parent yourself.

Even when you are well into your adult years, like God, your parents, if you let them, will be there to help pick you up and guide you down the path you'll need to take to return to your

Heavenly Father. We are all working on returning home to Him, where there will be once again, peace, harmony, and true freedom.

The Sum of All Things:

At the time I wrote Rule #19 *'Preferences Bend Principles Don't,'* I had only two rules left to write. Note, I don't write the rules in order. I wrote Rule #21 five years ago. I share this with you to let you know how difficult it has been to write Rule #19. It was one of the most challenging for me to put my thoughts into words and onto paper. It has taken me over seven months of praying and deep thought as I compiled the writing of this rule. Yet even after all I have put into it, I don't feel my writing does it the honor and the respect it deserves. I am well pleased with what I have written, it makes total sense to me. But I have the perspective of knowing and understanding Rule #19. I wrote the rule. It comes down to more of a question as to whether or not I have conveyed to you, the reader, that understanding.

Rule #19 is a very powerful rule and takes some intense study and pondering to really grasp its power and responsibility. All the rules I have written are equally important, but Rule #19 *'Preferences Bend Principles Don't'* is the keystone that balances and manages all the other rules. It is the rule that keeps all the other rules within their boundaries and governs how they are applied.

Thanking Others:

I have a lot of people to thank for their support in putting this rule on paper: first and foremost, President Cropper from my church Stake, who I mentioned at the beginning of this rule. Without his inspiring lesson on this subject, this rule may have never been written.

Then there are all the wonderful missionaries that took time from their personal day to find quotes and scriptures to support this rule and bring more enlightenment to you. There is Elder Aaron Capell, Elder Blake Garrett, Elder Trent

Walker, Elder Eckes Anitok, Elder Taylor Youngstrom, Elder Marston, and Elder Daniel Welch.

There is one other person I always need to include in my thanks, and that is my wife, who graciously allowed me to read this rule to her over and over and over again as I wrote it. She is my inspiration, as well as my listener. Reading to her helps me bring clarity of understanding to each sentence I write. I have the best wife, and you can't have her.

Good Night:

In closing, I have an inspiring selection of quotes and scripture to share with you, as I do in every rule I write. I hope that you will find one or two that spark a thought in your mind, and perhaps a couple that will bring a smile to your face.

> **(Thomas Jefferson)**[10]
> *"On matters of style, swim with the current, on matters of principle, stand like a rock."*
>
> **(Charles Haddon Spurgeon)**[11]
> *"When you see no present advantage, walk by faith and not by sight. Do God the honor to trust Him when it comes to matters of loss for the sake of principle."*
>
> **(Mahatma Gandhi, "Seven Deadly Sins")**[12]
> *1) Wealth without work.*
> *2) Pleasure without conscience.*
> *3) Knowledge without character.*
> *4) Commerce without morality.*
> *5) Science without humanity.*
> *6) Worship without sacrifice.*
> *7) Politics without principle*
>
> **(Martin Luther, Jr.)**[13]
> *"People must have righteous principles in the first, and then they will not fail to perform virtuous actions."*

Rule #19 'Preferences Bend, Principles Don't'

(Howard W. Hunter, 1976 October General Conference, "The Temptations of Christ")[14]
"Is it just for an individual, or can a body of people withstand the temptations of Satan? Surely the Lord would be pleased with the Saints if they stood before the world as a light that cannot be hidden because they are willing to live the principles of the gospel and keep the commandments of the Lord."

(Mark E Petersen, 1976 October General Conference, "The Savor of Men")[15]
"Lincoln was a devout believer in the Bible and read it often. At one time he said:

'I decided a long time ago that it was less difficult to believe that the Bible was what it claimed to be than to disbelieve it. It is a good book for us to obey.' (John Wesley Hill, Abraham Lincoln—Man of God, New York: G. P. Putnam's Sons, 1927, 4th ed., p. 126.)

Lincoln guided the destinies of the United States during the Civil War period by using the Bible and applying its principles. He exercised faith, and prayer, and deep humility, and out of it all he learned this great fact, as he himself expressed it:

"I have had so many evidences of His [God's] direction, so many instances when I have been controlled by some other power than my own will, that I cannot doubt that this power comes from above. ... I am satisfied that, when the Almighty wants me to do, or not to do, a particular thing, he finds a way of letting me know it.' (Ibid., p. 124.)"

(Paul H. Dunn, 1976 October General Conference, "Follow It")[16]
"And now, years later, I thank God for a great coach who taught me that principles are more important than winning baseball games."

Rule #19 'Preferences Bend, Principles Don't'

(Unknown)[17]
"If you are willing to abandon your principles for social acceptability, they are not your principles, they are your costume."

Rule #19 'Preferences Bend, Principles Don't'

Endnotes:

1. **King James Version of the Bible, The Old Testament of Our Lord and Saviour Jesus Christ.** Published by The Church of Jesus Christ of Latter-day Saints, Salt Lake City, Utah, USA. Copywrite 2013.

2. **King James Version of the Bible, The New Testament of Our Lord and Saviour Jesus Christ.** Published by The Church of Jesus Christ of Latter-day Saints, Salt Lake City, Utah, USA. Copywrite 2013.

3. **The Book of Mormon Another Testament of Jesus Christ.** Published by The Church of Jesus Christ of Latter-day Saints, Salt Lake City, Utah, USA. First English edition published in Palmyra, New York, USA, in 1830. Copywrite 2013.

4. **The Doctrine and Covenants of The Church of Jesus Christ of Latter-Day Saints.** Containing Revelations Give to Joseph Smith, the Prophet. With some additions by his successors in the Presidency of the Church. Published by The Church of Jesus Christ of Latter-day Saints, Salt Lake City, Utah, USA. Copywrite 2013.

5. **The Pearl of Great Price.** A selection from the revelations, translations, and narrations of Joseph Smith, First Prophet, seer, and revelator to The Church of Jesus Christ of Latter-Day Saints. Published by The Church of Jesus Christ of Latter-day Saints, Salt Lake City, Utah, USA. Copywrite 2013.

6. **Russel M. Nelson, 1993 October General Conference, "Constancy amid Change."** The 163rd Semiannual General Conference of the Church of Jesus Christ of Latter-day Saints, October 2, 1993, Saturday Afternoon Session. Published in the Ensign magazine, Volume 23 Number 11, November 1993. An official magazine of the Church of Jesus Christ of Latter-day Saints, published by the Church of Jesus Christ of Latter-day Saints, 50 E. North Temple Street, Salt Lake City, UT, 84150-3220, USA. Also see, Ensign, Churchofjesuschrist.org. Retrieved February 23, 2019, from Churchofjesuschrist.org Web site: https://www.churchofjesuschrist.org/study/ensign/1993/11/constancy-amid-change?lang=eng

7. **Stephen Covey**. Stephen Covey. (n.d.). AZQuotes.com. Retrieved February 23, 2019, from AZQuotes.com Web site: https://www.azquotes.com/quote/898534.

8. **Samuel Smiles**. Samuel Smiles. (n.d.). www.StatusMind.com. Retrieved February 23, 2019, from statusmind.com Web site: http://statusmind.com/men-facebook-status-81/.

Rule #19 'Preferences Bend, Principles Don't'

9. **Quentin L. Cook, 2017 October General Conference, "The Eternal Everyday"**. The 187th Semiannual General Conference of the Church of Jesus Christ of Latter-day Saints, September 30, 2017, Saturday Afternoon Session. Published in the Ensign magazine, Volume 47 Number 11, page-53 Paragraph-10, November 2017. An official magazine of the Church of Jesus Christ of Latter-day Saints, published by the Church of Jesus Christ of Latter-day Saints, 50 E. North Temple Street, Salt Lake City, UT, 84150-3220, USA. Also see, Ensign, Churchofjesuschrist.org. Retrieved February 23, 2019, from Churchofjesuschrist.org Web site: https://www.churchofjesuschrist.org/study/ensign/2017/11/saturday-afternoon-session/the-eternal-everyday?lang=eng.

10. **Thomas Jefferson**. Thomas Jefferson. (n.d.). AZQuotes.com. Retrieved February 23, 2019, from AZQuotes.com Web site: https://www.azquotes.com/quote/145670. Also, see Thomas Jefferson (2013). "The Jefferson Bible [annotated]: Original Old English Version and Modern Updates to The Jefferson Bible", p.139, BookBaby.

11. **Charles Haddon Spurgeon**. Charles Spurgeon. (n.d.). AZQuotes.com. Retrieved February 23, 2019, from AZQuotes.com Web site: https://www.azquotes.com/quote/392739. Also see, Charles H. Spurgeon (2016). "Morning & Evening", p.325, Bible Study Steps.

12. **Mahatma Gandhi, "Seven Deadly Sins"**. Mahatma Gandhi. (n.d.). AZQuotes.com. Retrieved February 23, 2019, from AZQuotes.com Web site: https://www.azquotes.com/quote/352508.

13. **Martin Luther, Jr.**. Martin Luther, Jr.. (n.d.). AZQuotes.com. Retrieved February 23, 2019, from AZQuotes.com Web site: https://www.azquotes.com/quote/180822.

14. **Howard W. Hunter, 1976 October General Conference, "The Temptations of Christ"**. The 146th Semiannual General Conference of the Church of Jesus Christ of Latter-day Saints, October 1, 1976, Friday Morning Session. Published in the Ensign magazine, Volume 06 Number 11, November 1976. An official magazine of the Church of Jesus Christ of Latter-day Saints, published by the Church of Jesus Christ of Latter-day Saints, 50 E. North Temple Street, Salt Lake City, UT, 84150-3220, USA. Also see, Ensign, Churchofjesuschrist.org. Retrieved February 17, 2019 from Churchofjesuschrist.org Web site: https://www.churchofjesuschrist.org/study/ensign/1976/11/the-temptations-of-christ?lang=eng.

15. **Mark E Petersen, 1976 October General Conference, "The Savor of Men"**. The 146th Semiannual General Conference of the Church of Jesus Christ of Latter-day Saints, October 2, 1976, Saturday Morning Session. Published in the Ensign magazine, Volume 06 Number 11, November 1976. An official magazine of the Church of Jesus Christ of Latter-day Saints, published by the Church of Jesus Christ of Latter-day Saints, 50 E. North Temple Street, Salt Lake City, UT, 84150-3220, USA. Also see, Ensign, Churchofjesuschrist.org. Retrieved February 17, 2019 from Churchofjesuschrist.org Web site: https://www.churchofjesuschrist.org/study/ensign/1976/11/the-savor-of-men?lang=eng.

Rule #19 'Preferences Bend, Principles Don't'

16 **Paul H. Dunn, 1976 October General Conference, "Follow It"**. The 146th Semiannual General Conference of the Church of Jesus Christ of Latter-day Saints, October 2, 1976, Saturday Afternoon Session. Published in the Ensign magazine, Volume 06 Number 11, November 1976. An official magazine of the Church of Jesus Christ of Latter-day Saints, published by the Church of Jesus Christ of Latter-day Saints, 50 E. North Temple Street, Salt Lake City, UT, 84150-3220, USA. Also see, Ensign, Churchofjesuschrist.org. Retrieved February 17, 2019 from Churchofjesuschrist.org Web site: https://www.churchofjesuschrist.org/study/ensign/1976/11/follow-it?lang=eng.

17 **Unknown**. Unknown. (n.d.) Pinterest.com. Retrieved February 23, 2019, from Pinterest.com Web site: https://www.pinterest.com/pin/503206958340410507.

Rule #19 'Preferences Bend, Principles Don't'

Wait For It

Rule #20

'If Nothing Changes, Then Nothing Changes, and History Repeats Itself'

Rule #20 'If Nothing Changes, Then Nothing Changes, and History Repeats Itself'

Tic Toc, Tic Toc Goes The Clock:

Any life change must be viewed from a long-term perspective. When you view change over a short period of time, everything may look like it is going well when it is not. The only way to evaluate whether you have made an actual change in your life is determined through the test of time. When you are able to maintain the desired change, life improvement, or simply maintain better habits over the long-term, then and only then will you have succeeded. Only when change endures the test of time can you claim victory.

Define Failure:

There are basically two types of failure when attempting to make a life change. One is what I call 'Short-Term Success' or 'Taking a Break'. The other I call the 'Change/No Change Effect.' Allow me to explain.

Short-Term Success (STS) or Taking a Break (TaB):

Let us say a person succeeds in changing his or her life for the better. They found a way to conquer their demon. Nevertheless, over time, the change does not endure, and before long, the person reverts back to their old ways. The person experiences short-term success but is unable to make a permanent change.

In many cases, this type of change becomes a cycle of successes and failures. Many people continue this loop throughout their life. This repeated cycle is where I draw my two titles: 'Short Term Success' or 'Taking a Break'.

Rule #20 'If Nothing Changes, Then Nothing Changes, and History Repeats Itself'

Change No Change Effect:

Have you ever committed to a new routine or habit thinking and hoping it would help you make a change in your life, except it didn't? Or tried mixing things up with the idea that different equals change? Yet, when you stop mixing and take a closer look, guess what? No change.

There are some cases where you mix things up so well the alteration actually masks the fact that no real change has taken place. On the surface, it looks like a change. But the issue you were trying to improve or the habit you were trying to change is still there. Now the problem is just hidden in the mix. All you have accomplished is that your dilemma is harder to see. Despite what alteration you make, if the issue you are trying to change doesn't really improve, then you haven't made a change at all, have you?

I Got My Eye on You:

I have watched a lot of people try to make changes in their lives, but under close scrutiny, the outcome of their attempt was that there was no change at all. I have an excellent true-life story of the change/no change effect I will share with you later on in this chapter.

All Roads Lead to Town:

A lot of proposed changes that people attempt, appear to make a difference but often really duplicate the same outcome of their old habits and behavior, the only difference is the way they go about achieving the same old results. Thus, they are not truly changed at all. It is like taking a different road but ending up in the same dead-end town.

The Thinking Process:

The wording of Rule #20 is an excellent example of difference being the same. Do you have any idea how many ways other people and I have written the quote for this rule? In fact, a lot

Rule #20 'If Nothing Changes, Then Nothing Changes, and History Repeats Itself'

of the variations of the quote use pretty much the same wording without changing the meaning.

As I was trying to express the meaning of this rule in terms that would be short but memorable to me, I came up with over a page of different titles using the same word variations. I then read that list to my wife. She didn't like any of them. She said that she felt that there was just a little something missing in them all. I knew she was right because I had the same feeling as I read them. So, to find that little extra inspiration I was looking for, I had to put my thinking cap back on and think harder and pray a little longer.

I want to share with you a little of how my thinking process went as I worked toward finding the wording that best suited me. I found it surprising that the deleting or adding of one simple word changed the flow of how the quote read or the ease with which it could be remembered and recalled.

Let's Vary It Up a Little:

Here are a few variations of Rule #20 I found on the internet in which the words change, but the meaning stays the same.

> 'If nothing changes, nothing changes.'
>
> 'Nothing changes if nothing changes.'
>
> 'There is no change without change.'
>
> "Without change, there is no change.'
>
> 'If you change nothing, nothing changes.'
>
> 'If you change nothing, then nothing changes.'
>
> 'If you change nothing, nothing will change.'
>
> 'By changing nothing, nothing changes.'
>
> 'Change nothing, and nothing changes.'

Rule #20 'If Nothing Changes, Then Nothing Changes, and History Repeats Itself'

Let's Put Some Muscle Into It:

Then I found variations of Rule #20 that are worded quite differently but still don't change the meaning of the quote.

(George Bernard Shaw)[6]
"Progress is impossible without change, & those who cannot change their minds cannot change anything."

(Wendy Mass)[7]
"If nothing ever changed, there would be no butterflies."

(Albert Einstein)[8]
"Insanity is doing the same thing over and over again and expecting different results."

(Lao Tzu)[9]
"If you do not change direction, you may end up where you are heading."

(Unknown)[10]
"If the plan doesn't work, change the plan, not the goal."

(Max De Pree)[11]
"We cannot become what we need to be by remaining what we are."

(Bill Phillips)[12]
"The difference between who you are and who you want to be is what you do."

(Movie Quote, "The Samaritan", May 18, 2012)[13]
"If you keep on doing what you've always done you'll keep on being what you've always been."

(Henry Ford)[14]
"If you always do what you've always done, you will always get what you've always got."

(Marcus Garvey)[15]
"A people without knowledge of their past history, origin, and culture is like a tree without roots."

Rule #20 'If Nothing Changes, Then Nothing Changes, and History Repeats Itself'

(Martin Luther King, Jr.)[16]
"We are not makers of history. We are made by history."

Just One Word:

The moment I found the version that suited me, I felt its inspiration. I didn't feel inspired by any of the other variations, because one word was missing. Just one word and that word was 'history.'

Life is all about history. Our history determines our course of action at any given moment. Whatever course of action we take in the present will determine our future. Therefore, our history ultimately determines our future.

In the blink of an eye, the work we do today and decisions we make tomorrow become the life experiences that make up our yesterday, and our yesterdays become our history. In that precious, tiny minuscule moment, when a second passes, it becomes a part of our past and adds to our history. In those precious, tiny minuscule moments as time passes, we have the chance to change our history. Every second that ticks by, we are faced with decisions and opportunities to improve ourselves.

Wasn't I Just Here?

Because our history determines our current course of action, we must keep an extra pair of eyes in the back of our heads to review our past. By keeping an eye on our yesterday, we can ensure that we are growing and moving forward to a better tomorrow. Only by carefully studying our history, we can ensure our forward movement actually leads us to make progress and not merely back to where we started. Without considering our past, there is no assurance that we will learn from our experiences and not repeat our failures.

Rule #20 'If Nothing Changes, Then Nothing Changes, and History Repeats Itself'

Pass the View-Master:

History can be reviewed and studied from many different perspectives, from that of an individual, a culture, a nation, a region, or from a worldly perspective. The principles of Rule #20 apply to history, experience, and the potential for change regardless of perspective. It doesn't matter if the rule is applied to a single person, a nation, or the world as a whole. The only difference is the scale. The broader the perspective, the greater the impact when an actual change is made. Everything I am writing about in Rule #20, it's principles, and the application is the same whether applied locally or globally.

Looking back at history, I find that we, as a people, tend to repeat our ways; whether as an individual or as a global community. For most of us, our lives flow like the seasons. While seasons change through the year, the cycle of our seasons stays the same. Sadly, life's cycle tends to repeat itself from the warmth of summer back to the cold of winter.

Look Your Life Fits Right In:

While I was writing this chapter, I shared Rule #20 and its message with my very good friend, Ann. During our discussion, she offered to share her story and her personal struggle with true change. I hope that as you read her story, you will be amazed at how easily you can see yourself reflected in her story. Your issue may not be the same as her's, but it's one to which we can all easily relate to. Here is Ann's story. She calls it 'Change but the Same.'

Change but the Same:

Ann has trouble getting her days started. She just doesn't seem to have the drive or energy she needs to get moving. This is due to many issues, one of them being that she is plagued with constant body pains that vary in intensity from day to day. On the days that her pain level is low, Ann manages to block it out pretty well on her own. But on those mornings that her pain level is high, it's difficult for her to motivate

Rule #20 'If Nothing Changes, Then Nothing Changes, and History Repeats Itself'

herself to move her body and start her day. On days when her pain level is very high, sitting still is torture, but being physically active is even worse.

However, work doesn't stop. Chores need to be done, or they just pile up and add to the next day's work. For Ann, there is never any guarantee that tomorrow will be any better than today, so waiting for the pain to pass is not an option.

To add to Ann's issues, she also has trouble sleeping. Partly due to her pain and partly due to other health-related complications. Her sleep deprivation, combined with her constant physical pain, contribute to her lack of energy and motivation in the morning.

If you met Ann, you would never realize that she was dealing with so much pain in her life. For Ann, constant pain is normal, and she has learned to live life as normally as anyone else. Her sweet charm, her smile, and warmth on her face rarely reveal the pain that plagues her.

In the beginning, Ann learned that she could gain some relief from the bite of her pain and low energy by drinking coffee with sugar. This seemed like a great solution because Ann loved coffee. It didn't get rid of all her pain or completely restore her energy, but it did give her enough relief that she was able to keep up with her daily tasks.

A little further down the road of life, Ann joined a religion that promotes the religious belief that the human body is a temple where the human soul, a spiritual gift from God, lives. Thus, the human body is to be cared for as if it is a temple of God. In a book called 'The Doctrine and Covenants' (D&C) in section 89, it advises against certain foods or drinks for the betterment of a person's temporal body and spiritual well-being. If you abstain from these things, you are promised a blessing of better health from God. It is called 'The Word of Wisdom.' You'd have to read all of section 89 to understand its message. I'm not including the whole section in this chapter, as it is far too long. I have, however, included the scripture promising good health and more below.

Rule #20 'If Nothing Changes, Then Nothing Changes, and History Repeats Itself'

(Doctrine and Covenants: 89:18-21)[4]

18 And all saints who remember to keep and do these sayings, walking in obedience to the commandments, shall receive health in their navel and marrow to their bones;

19 And shall find wisdom and great treasures of knowledge, even hidden treasures;

20 And shall run and not be weary, and shall walk and not faint.

21 And I, the Lord, give unto them a promise, that the destroying angel shall pass by them, as the children of Israel, and not slay them. Amen.

I have quoted from the D&C often in my book of rules. I find it to be a tremendous spiritual source.

The Lack of Understanding:

Now Ann had thought that drinking coffee wasn't a bad solution to her problem. After all, Ann loved the taste of coffee. She even loved the smell of its fresh roasted granules so much she could hardly walk past an open container or freshly brewed pot without deeply inhaling the coffee's aroma. Ann was drawn to the smell of coffee like the opposite poles of a magnet attracting each other.

Sadly, for Ann, coffee is on the Word of Wisdom no-drink list. So, if she wished to gain the Lord's promises of better health, as stated in D&C section 89, she was going to have to make a change. Without a doubt, Ann not only wanted but needed better health. So, Ann, being the strong woman that she is, and seeing wisdom in the blessings of not drinking coffee, decided to give it up.

Now, what Ann didn't get from reading D&C section 89 was the full intent of the message in the Word of Wisdom. Not drinking coffee is an example that is meant to be applied to anything we drink. The section is called the 'Word of Wisdom' because you are to use wisdom when applying its principles.

Rule #20 'If Nothing Changes, Then Nothing Changes, and History Repeats Itself'

Ann took what knowledge she had gained from D&C section 89 and decided to stop drinking coffee and try a soft drink called 'Tab.' Ann was now consuming more caffeine by drinking Tab than she did from drinking coffee. On the plus side, there is no sugar in Tab. However, it contains an artificial sweetener.

Ann was satisfied with her Tab soft drink as a substitute for coffee. Sadly, what Ann didn't realize was that her body would turn the artificial sweeter into a dangerous chemical. After drinking Tab for a while, she started having issues with partial temporary blindness. So, Ann changes from Tab to 'Pepsi Cola.' Drinking 'Pepsi' keeps her on the caffeine kick, but it also puts her back on the sugar kick. But neither soft drinks are coffee, right? So, Ann is ok, right?

After drinking Pepsi Cola for a while, she starts having digestive issues and is advised by her doctor to abstain from any Cola drinks.

And the Beat Goes On:

Ann was frustrated, in pain, and struggling with low energy. She decided that it was time to do some serious research. Keep in mind that Ann was only looking for a drink that would help boost her energy and ease her pain. What Ann had not yet realized was that the drinks she had picked to help her start her day and ease her pain all contained substances that in the long haul were going to worsen her condition.

Ann's research led her to Green Tea as a suitable morning drink. Ann was still sucking down the caffeine, but, on the other hand, there is no sugar or artificial sweeter in Green Tea. That is a plus in the right direction.

Time goes on, and then one day, while talking with her church Bishop, Ann learned that Green Tea is also on the Word of Wisdom do not drink list. Therefore, Ann and her Green Tea had to part ways.

Rule #20 'If Nothing Changes, Then Nothing Changes, and History Repeats Itself'

Ann evaluated her history (right choice) and decided that merely changing her morning beverage was not the solution to boosting her energy or relieving her pain.

Throw the Switch:

Ann concluded that she needed to stop switching her drinks and instead focus on modifying her breakfast. Still studying her history, she recalled that eating extra dark chocolate seemed to help her feel better. This leads her to pick extra dark chocolate as her new breakfast choice. Now there are useful compounds in extra dark chocolate called antioxidants, which do help the human body. In addition, extra dark chocolate is not on the 'Words of Wisdom' do not eat list per se. But extra dark chocolate also contains a very high amount of caffeine and sugar, which is not healthy for Ann to consume. But Ann has not figured this out yet.

Ann is doing her best to care for herself and receive the Lord's blessings by studying her history to solve her issue; however, Ann has not focused on the fact that she has become addicted to caffeine and sugar. I use the word focused and not learned because Ann knows the cause and effects of caffeine and sugar. She just hasn't applied them to herself. It is a lot easier to see 'the bigger picture' when you are looking at another person's problems than it is looking at your own. This is particularly true in regards to caffeine and sugar because the addiction to these substances, in most cases, is slow and subtle. Also, the amounts needed to become addicted vary. Over time the body requires more substantial quantities of caffeine or sugar to believe it is in a balanced state and for the person to feel the perceived positive effects.

At this point in her story, Ann has attempted to solve her pain and lack of energy at least four times. In her attempts, Ann varied her substance intake, which in its self is the right move. But in her endeavors, she never changed her caffeine and sugar intake. This is where Ann got the title of her story 'Change but the Same'.

Ann's lack of energy and pain was not caused by caffeine and sugar. But in her attempts to solve the underlying issue, the quick fix of the caffeine and sugar, not only magnified her trouble but also caused new health problems.

And She Lives Happily Ever After:

Ann's story doesn't end here. I did tell you that Ann is a smart woman, didn't I? You see, Ann continued to study her history and finally recognized that using caffeine and sugar to solve her problem didn't work. At this time, there is no known way to permanently remove Ann's pain and or improve the quality of her sleep. But both can be managed with proper medical care and training. It was a long road for Ann. But she is now working on a better way. The path she must take is not an easy one, but it is far better and is the most permanent solution at this time. Ann is now on her way to breaking the cycle and on to a better life.

I want to add my prayer of support for Ann, as her battle with pain is a daily struggle. It is one for her that may never end until she passes from this temporal state, it is not easy to live with and extremely difficult to find the right permanent change.

This for That:

Using substitution to solve a bad habit is a good idea. Most people cannot quit a habit without replacing it with something else. Most of us apply this method in our lives. The challenge is how you implement it.

Many people get caught in this substitution solution, where the replacement contains the same issues but comes in a different form or looks and feels different than the original habit. It is an easy trap to fall into considering substitution is a type of change, although in these cases, not the right change.

Ann's story is an excellent example of this type of wrongful substitution. We all do this in our lives to some degree or another. I do it. That is why I have this rule to always remind

Rule #20 'If Nothing Changes, Then Nothing Changes, and History Repeats Itself'

me of it. My issue is work. I am a workaholic. I am always substituting one type of work for another. Being a hard worker is a good habit. But too much is too much, no matter what it is.

The challenge with substitution is having the ability to recognize what to substitute and then finding the right replacement. In Ann's story, she was substituting but not eliminating the right factors. In Ann's case, she needed to eliminate caffeine and sugar from her diet.

In my case of being a workaholic, eliminating work altogether is not an option. Although, I am sure there are a lot of people out there that would love to remove work from their lives. Good, hard work is needed to balance life. So, eliminating work altogether is not a good change. What is required here is a partial substitution of some work time for playtime.

It is through the knowledge we gain from studying our history and learning from our past that we gain the ability to recognize and apply the proper substitutions to better our lives.

STS or TaB:

Short term success (STS) or taking a break (TaB), let us talk about it. In this type of change/no change scenario, a person quits a bad habit only to pick it back up again. They may quit several times, in several different ways, over and over again. Gaining the resolution needed to break this type of bad habit and circular cycle is not easy. And the longer you are caught in this circular cycle habit, the more willpower it will take to break it.

A person converting back to their old habits starts with a small loss of willpower and the denial of that loss. The person will tell themselves, "If I do it only once, that doesn't mean I didn't quit the bad habit. It is only one time." How wrong are they? It is that small loss of willpower that gave you permission to do it just once, is where the failure started and the beginning of a new circular cycle started.

Rule #20 'If Nothing Changes, Then Nothing Changes, and History Repeats Itself'

We see examples of this type of failure to change every day: the smoker who quits only to start smoking again, the alcoholic who cannot stop drinking, the drug addict, or the sex offender who can't stop their behavior regardless of the consequences. These are some of the worst habits that, in the short term, people succeed at quitting, but cannot endure a positive change in the long haul. These bad habits are easy to see and point out.

Many other bad habits are not easily seen but can be just as devastating. They, too, can be just as hard to conquer.

It doesn't matter what the bad habit is. It doesn't matter how long a person has stopped, if they convert back to that bad habit, even one time, then they never really quit. That is why I call it 'Taking a Break' TaB.

I didn't choose the examples above to condemn any person who might be trying to kick a bad habit. That is not my intent at all. I do know and understand the challenges involved in identifying and overcoming bad habits. There can be many obstacles, and in some cases, seem impossible to conquer. Rule #20, however, still applies if you hope to kick a bad habit permanently out of your life.

Rewind Please:

I want to point out that reverting back to one's old ways is a conscious choice one makes and is not a condition that was imposed upon one's self. So, what is it that causes a person to revert back to their old ways? I believe the number one cause is the lack of knowledge to understand why their actions are leading them in circles. I believe and have faith that the majority of humanity would stop a bad habit if they could see the long-term cause and effect of their actions, and had the knowledge needed to stop it.

Getting the Engine Started:

That being said, there is another smaller group of people who have motivation issues that prevent them from stopping their

Rule #20 'If Nothing Changes, Then Nothing Changes, and History Repeats Itself'

We see examples of this type of failure to change every day: the smoker who quits only to start smoking again, the alcoholic who cannot stop drinking, the drug addict, or the sex offender who can't stop their behavior regardless of the consequences. These are some of the worst habits that, in the short term, people succeed at quitting, but cannot endure a positive change in the long haul. These bad habits are easy to see and point out.

Many other bad habits are not easily seen but can be just as devastating. They, too, can be just as hard to conquer.

It doesn't matter what the bad habit is. It doesn't matter how long a person has stopped, if they convert back to that bad habit, even one time, then they never really quit. That is why I call it 'Taking a Break' TaB.

I didn't choose the examples above to condemn any person who might be trying to kick a bad habit. That is not my intent at all. I do know and understand the challenges involved in identifying and overcoming bad habits. There can be many obstacles, and in some cases, seem impossible to conquer. Rule #20, however, still applies if you hope to kick a bad habit permanently out of your life.

Rewind Please:

I want to point out that reverting back to one's old ways is a conscious choice one makes and is not a condition that was imposed upon one's self. So, what is it that causes a person to revert back to their old ways? I believe the number one cause is the lack of knowledge to understand why their actions are leading them in circles. I believe and have faith that the majority of humanity would stop a bad habit if they could see the long-term cause and effect of their actions, and had the knowledge needed to stop it.

Getting the Engine Started:

That being said, there is another smaller group of people who have motivation issues that prevent them from stopping their

Rule #20 'If Nothing Changes, Then Nothing Changes, and History Repeats Itself'

me of it. My issue is work. I am a workaholic. I am always substituting one type of work for another. Being a hard worker is a good habit. But too much is too much, no matter what it is.

The challenge with substitution is having the ability to recognize what to substitute and then finding the right replacement. In Ann's story, she was substituting but not eliminating the right factors. In Ann's case, she needed to eliminate caffeine and sugar from her diet.

In my case of being a workaholic, eliminating work altogether is not an option. Although, I am sure there are a lot of people out there that would love to remove work from their lives. Good, hard work is needed to balance life. So, eliminating work altogether is not a good change. What is required here is a partial substitution of some work time for playtime.

It is through the knowledge we gain from studying our history and learning from our past that we gain the ability to recognize and apply the proper substitutions to better our lives.

STS or TaB:

Short term success (STS) or taking a break (TaB), let us talk about it. In this type of change/no change scenario, a person quits a bad habit only to pick it back up again. They may quit several times, in several different ways, over and over again. Gaining the resolution needed to break this type of bad habit and circular cycle is not easy. And the longer you are caught in this circular cycle habit, the more willpower it will take to break it.

A person converting back to their old habits starts with a small loss of willpower and the denial of that loss. The person will tell themselves, "If I do it only once, that doesn't mean I didn't quit the bad habit. It is only one time." How wrong are they? It is that small loss of willpower that gave you permission to do it just once, is where the failure started and the beginning of a new circular cycle started.

Rule #20 'If Nothing Changes, Then Nothing Changes, and History Repeats Itself'

bad habits. They already have the knowledge they need for change or improvement but fail to put it to use due to a lack of motivation. They have the attitude of, 'What we are doing is good enough. So why should we change?' They do not have the desire or motivation to apply the knowledge needed for change. The worst case of this is those individuals that are lost in the darkness of their world and feel that changing does not matter anymore. It is too late for them.

In my opinion, the lack of knowledge part is the simplest piece to solve. In today's world, we don't lack sources for finding information, and information is knowledge. We have libraries, books stores, the internet, television, good friends, good parents, and grandparents, as some of the sources we can tap. Notice I said 'good' in front of friends and parents? Not all friends can be classified as good. And if you don't have good friends, then it is time to replace them with ones that are. Remember Rule #14 'If You Want to Be an 'A' Student, Hang Out With the 'A' Students'? Your friends should be a part of your 'A' team support. You will more than likely go to your friends first for information and support before going to any other source.

It would be nice if we all went first to our parents and grandparents for answers. They have a wealth of experience and knowledge that, for the most part, is left untapped. To those that do go to their parents first, I say, "Good for you, for seeing the value in our older generations."

The problems we face today may have a different face but are still the same as generations past. We, meaning parents and grandparents, may talk a slightly different talk, and draw a slightly different picture, but the wisdom and truth contained within are priceless. In my book of rules for managing life, parents are the second-best source to go to for trusted knowledge. And they are only second because God is always first.

Rule #20 'If Nothing Changes, Then Nothing Changes, and History Repeats Itself'

I Choose You:

I know for some of us, our biological parents are not the parents we would like them to be. My parents, in many ways, were not good examples to follow. It is not to say that they had no good qualities, for they did. Just not as many as I needed. But to make up for what my parents lacked, there were other 'A' student parents ready to step up and help as long as I was willing to listen.

For those of you who do not have 'A' quality parents to go to, then find one. There is an abundant source of parents out there willing and wanting to help mentor other children that are not their own biological child. Don't be afraid to tap that source. It helped save me from making wrong choices many a time.

Where Did I Put The Key:

The bigger issue is finding the proper motivation; now, that is where the challenge lies. You cannot succeed until you find the key to your personal motivation.

One would think that once one has been given the knowledge required to make a positive change that one would simply start applying it to their life. No, not true. Even though we are armed with the knowledge, we humans seem to still have the need to find our own personal motivating reason for using that information to improve our lives and our relationship with God. This appears to be the way it is with us, humans. This is how I have observed it in action; knowledge without motivation goes nowhere, knowledge with motivation goes anywhere.

What do you need to motivate you? That is a question you will have to find yourself. It is going to require a lot of personal soul searching on your part. As you search, be truthful with yourself, and you will find the answer much easier. I mean some real deep down being honest with yourself searching. There are hundreds of motivational videos, audiotapes, and books out there you can use to help you. They can be of good

Rule #20 'If Nothing Changes, Then Nothing Changes, and History Repeats Itself'

help. But in the end, the answer you need as to what will motivate you will be found within you. You will feel that it is right and therefore you will know it is the correct answer.

Be Strong:

Strength is another element we need to include when we talk about change and motivation. Strength in our motivation fortifies our willpower and helps us succeed in making an enduring change. It is the weaknesses in our motivation that leads us back to our old, bad habits. A person may achieve success without a strong motivator, but you will usually find that it is a short-term success, STS.

From Good Books:

The Old and New Testament Bible and Book of Mormon are filled with stories of STS. The person/people receive the education they need along with what I think would be a good motivator, yet they only succeed in the short-term, and then it is back to failure. God then tries to motivate them in a different way. They succeed briefly only to fail again. And this cycle goes on and on until God says enough is enough.

To give you all of my supporting evidence from the Bible and Book of Mormon, I would pretty much have to include the whole of both books. Instead, I want to share a couple of my favorite instances.

Honor Thy Father:

As you read about the brothers, Laman, Lemuel, Nephi, and Sam, the founding fathers to the Laminates and the Nephites in the Book of Mormon, you can see from the very start that Laman and Lemuel murmur against their father, Lehi, and brother, Nephi. Their father sits in counsel with them several times, and each time the sons claim to see the errors of their ways. But then a very short time later they are back to murmuring again.

Rule #20 'If Nothing Changes, Then Nothing Changes, and History Repeats Itself'

The part of their story I want to share with you is when their father, Lehi, asks his sons to go back to Jerusalem and get possession of the brass plates from Captain Laban, a cruel and powerful man. Reluctantly, Laman and Lemuel accompany Nephi and Sam back to get the plates. After a second failed attempt to obtain the plates, in which Captain Laban steals all their gold and silver, and also attempts to take their lives, Laman and Lemuel want to give up and return to their father without the plates. But Nephi and Sam refuse to return without the plates and plead with their older brothers Laman and Lemuel. Here is what happens to Nephi and Sam next.

> **(Book of Mormon: 1 Nephi 3:29-31)**[3]
>
> *29 And it came to pass as they smote us with a rod, behold, an angel of the Lord came and stood before them, and he spake unto them, saying: Why do ye smite your younger brother with a rod? Know ye not that the Lord hath chosen him to be a ruler over you, and this because of your iniquities? Behold ye shall go up to Jerusalem again, and the Lord will deliver Laban into your hands.*
>
> *30 And after the angel had spoken unto us, he departed.*
>
> *31 And after the angel had departed, Laman and Lemuel again began to murmur, saying: How is it possible that the Lord will deliver Laban into our hands? Behold, he is a mighty man, and he can command fifty, yea, even he can slay fifty; then why not us?*

You would think that seeing a messenger of the Lord face to face would straighten out Laman and Lemuel and fix their defiant attitude. It would mine, I hope. No, it wasn't enough of a motivator for them because as soon as the angel departed, they were back to whining and complaining.

This up and down attitude of Laman and Lemuel goes on for years. Sadly, they never do break the cycle. In fact, after their father dies, they only get worse.

Rule #20 'If Nothing Changes, Then Nothing Changes, and History Repeats Itself'

You may wish to spend some time studying Laman's and Lemuel's history in the Book of Mormon. There are a lot of good life lessons you can learn from them. The study of their past may prevent you from repeating the same mistakes of murmuring and rebelling against God's will.

Pride:

My favorite Old Testament story of an individual caught in the 'Short Term Success' cycle is Saul. I picked Saul's life because it reminds me of what pride can do to a person. Saul's pride shows us how it affects our ability to be obedient to God's will.

God chose and blessed Saul to rule over Israel because of his righteousness. But then Saul's success goes to his head. God then tries to humble Saul several times, but with only short-term success. In the end, God leaves Saul to his own demise. Here is one instance where God deals with Saul's pride.

> **(Bible Old Testament: 1 Samuel 13:10–14)**[1]
> *10 And it came to pass, that as soon as he had made an end of offering the burnt offering, behold, Samuel came; and Saul went out to meet him, that he might a salute him.*
>
> *11 And Samuel said, What hast thou done? And Saul said, Because I saw that the people were scattered from me, and that thou camest not within the days appointed, and that the Philistines gathered themselves together at Michmash;*
>
> *12 Therefore said I, The Philistines will come down now upon me to Gilgal, and I have not made supplication unto the Lord: I forced myself therefore, and offered a burnt offering.*
>
> *13 And Samuel said to Saul, Thou hast done foolishly: thou hast not kept the commandment of the Lord thy God, which he commanded thee: for now would the Lord have established thy kingdom upon Israel forever.*

Rule #20 'If Nothing Changes, Then Nothing Changes, and History Repeats Itself'

> *14 But now thy a kingdom shall not continue: the Lord hath sought him a man after his own heart, and the Lord hath commanded him to be captain over his people, because thou hast not kept that which the Lord commanded thee.*

Book of Mormon Stories That Were Written Long Ago:

I have given you examples of Rule #20 from an individual perspective. Yet the principle behind *'If Nothing Changes, Nothing Changes, and History Repeats Its Self'* applies far beyond that of the individual. It grows to the size of communities, nations, continents, the world, and infinity. Rule #20 is an eternal law that applies to all things. But I'll keep it focused on just us Earthlings for this book.

One Nation Under God:

Let's expand our perspective from the view of an individual to that of a nation or two.

Earlier, we talked about Lehi's sons, Laman, Lemuel, Nephi, and Sam. In the 'Book of Mormon,' the Lamanite nations are mainly the offspring of Laman and Lemuel. The Nephite nation comes primarily from the lineage of Nephi and Sam. Throughout the history of the two nations, the Lamanites are chiefly the bad guys, and the Nephites are primarily the good guys.

The Nephite nation starts out with a solid, righteous understanding of God. Yet, they are continually ping-ponging between being a God-fearing nation to one that allows their good fortune and pride to bring them down. In the Book of Mormon, 3 Nephi chapter 6 tells about one of those moments where the Nephites are righteous, and life is good, but then the people let pride set in.

> **(Book of Mormon: 3 Nephi 6:4–18)**[3]
> *4 And they began again to prosper and to wax great; and the twenty and sixth and seventh years*

Rule #20 'If Nothing Changes, Then Nothing Changes, and History Repeats Itself'

passed away, and there was great order in the land; and they had formed their laws according to equity and justice.

5 And now there was nothing in all the land to hinder the people from prospering continually, except they should fall into transgression.

6 And now it was Gidgiddoni, and the judge, Lachoneus, and those who had been appointed leaders, who had established this great peace in the land.

7 And it came to pass that there were many cities built anew, and there were many old cities repaired.

8 And there were many highways cast up, and many roads made, which led from city to city, and from land to land, and from place to place.

9 And thus passed away the twenty and eighth year, and the people had continual peace.

10 But it came to pass in the twenty and ninth year there began to be some disputing's among the people; and some were lifted up unto pride and boastings because of their exceedingly great riches, yea, even unto great persecutions;

11 For there were many merchants in the land, and also many lawyers, and many officers.

12 And the people began to be distinguished by ranks, according to their riches and their chances for learning; yea, some were ignorant because of their poverty, and others did receive great learning because of their riches.

13 Some were lifted up in pride, and others were exceedingly humble; some did return railing for railing, while others would receive railing and persecution and all manner of afflictions, and would not turn and revile again, but were humble and penitent before God.

Rule #20 'If Nothing Changes, Then Nothing Changes, and History Repeats Itself'

14 And thus there became a great inequality in all the land, insomuch that the church began to be broken up; yea, insomuch that in the thirtieth year the church was broken up in all the land save it were among a few of the Lamanites who were converted unto the true faith; and they would not depart from it, for they were firm, and steadfast, and immovable, willing with all diligence to keep the commandments of the Lord.

15 Now the cause of this iniquity of the people was this—Satan had great power, unto the stirring up of the people to do all manner of iniquity, and to the puffing them up with pride, tempting them to seek for power, and authority, and riches, and the vain things of the world.

16 And thus Satan did lead away the hearts of the people to do all manner of iniquity; therefore they had enjoyed peace but a few years.

17 And thus, in the commencement of the thirtieth year—the people having been delivered up for the space of a long time to be carried about by the temptations of the devil whithersoever he desired to carry them, and to do whatsoever iniquity he desired they should—and thus in the commencement of this, the thirtieth year, they were in a state of awful wickedness.

18 Now they did not sin ignorantly, for they knew the will of God concerning them, for it had been taught unto them; therefore they did wilfully rebel against God.

Because the Nephites had a full understanding of God, He warns the Nephites that if they fall into as wicked a state as their brothers, the Lamanites, and do not repent that He will destroy them off the face of the Earth. In the end, God cannot get the Nephites to stop repeating this cycle between poor behavior and reformation. In fact, in the end, the Nephites do not repent at all and conduct themselves worse than the

Rule #20 'If Nothing Changes, Then Nothing Changes, and History Repeats Itself'

Lamanites. Because they reject God's instruction, He keeps His promise to the Nephites and allows the Lamanites to wipe them out.

On the other hand, the Lamanites may be the wicked ones, yet the Book of Mormon shows that when a Lamanite is taught the word of God and accepts it, they never turn back. The Lamanite has no repeating cycle of failure. Why do you think that is? A history worth studying, don't you think?

The Hand of God:

As with the Book of Mormon, the Old Testament Bible is also filled with instances of nations repeating the same cycle of failure.

My favorite Bible 'Short Term Success' story of a nation comes from the Old Testament. The story is about Moses and his people. Talk about a guy who had to deal with a hard group of people. These people's complaints went far beyond whining and murmuring. My hat is off to Moses. He had to be a Prophet of God to deal with those foolish, hardheaded people. Here you have a nation of people that have personally witnessed God's saving hand. Yet, repeatedly, the nation of Israel must be chastened to mend their wicked ways. Here is my favorite excerpt from Moses's story.

> **(Bible Old Testament: Exodus 32: 7-9)**[1]
> 7 ¶ And the Lord said unto Moses, Go, get thee down; for thy people, which thou broughtest out of the land of Egypt, have corrupted themselves:
>
> 8 They have turned aside quickly out of the way which I commanded them: they have made them a molten calf, and have worshipped it, and have sacrificed thereunto, and said, These be thy gods, O Israel, which have brought thee up out of the land of Egypt.
>
> 9 And the Lord said unto Moses, I have seen this people, and, behold, it is a stiffnecked people:

Rule #20 'If Nothing Changes, Then Nothing Changes, and History Repeats Itself'

The Israelites are forever repeating a cycle of failure. Unlike the Nephites whom God allowed to be wiped out, the Israelites are still with us. God made a promise to Abraham to preserve them. So, despite all their wrongdoings, God has kept that promise. Do you think God is teaching us, by example, the meaning of the statement 'your word is your bond, and a promise is meant to be kept, not broken,' period?

> **(Bible Old Testament: Genesis 26:3-5)**[1]
> *3 Sojourn in this land, and I will be with thee, and will bless thee; for unto thee, and unto thy seed, I will give all these countries, and I will perform the oath which I sware unto Abraham thy father;*
>
> *4 And I will make thy seed to multiply as the stars of heaven, and will give unto thy seed all these countries; and in thy seed shall all the nations of the earth be blessed;*
>
> *5 Because that Abraham obeyed my voice, and kept my charge, my commandments, my statutes, and my laws.*

The Chemist and Cause & Effect:

Back in high school chemistry, I gained insight into understanding how 'change' works. By studying the history of chemistry, I learned about the phenomenon of cause and effect. I learned about having a 'change with no change', in that changing the ingredients in an experiment does not always create a change in the finished product. Or the fact that even when a change is made, and the outcome is different, it does not necessarily produce the desired result. I also learned that some changes are temporary and unsustainable.

For example, when combining different chemicals or compounds, the proper electron bond is required for them to mix. Oil and water will mix if the correct bonding agent is added. Or by adding the incorrect bonding agent, the mix changes, but the oil and water molecules do not bond. Thus, the result is no change. Mix the wrong chemicals, and the

Rule #20 'If Nothing Changes, Then Nothing Changes, and History Repeats Itself'

solution may change permanently, but not necessarily in the way you want.

You Get What You Gain, and Gain What You Get:

To master chemistry requires knowledge, hard work, and dedication, but once you have gained the wisdom and knowledge, predicting and producing the desired chemical outcome is much easier. So, it is in life.

Can We Make It a Little Simpler?

Some people have difficulty understanding the fundamentals of chemistry. They find the information too complex. Other people oversimplify the principles of chemistry and fail to understand the basic rules making it difficult to predict or produce the desired outcome. Sometimes the person gets lucky, and the experiment is successful. I will agree that luck does happen but only on the rarest occasions. But I am not a man that believes in relying on luck to determine my fate.

I believe most failures in chemistry are caused because the person did not put forth enough time and/or effort to comprehend the basic concepts before attempting to understand the more complicated laws. Without a solid foundation, it is close to impossible to get to the next step, leaving luck to determine the outcome. I have already told you how I feel about luck.

Chemistry also taught me to view failure in a positive light. During the process of making new discoveries, the chemist may experience hundreds or thousands of failures. A positive approach to each failure is to review the process, study the history of the experiment, and understand what led to the failure. Through the study of the history of his failures, the chemist finds success.

Rule #20 'If Nothing Changes, Then Nothing Changes, and History Repeats Itself'

Masters of the Universe, Life & Chemistry:

Why the chemistry lesson? Because changes in life can be compared to the lessons learned in a chemistry class. To make changes in your life for the better, you must first gain an understanding of life's basic concepts. In life as in chemistry, each step we take brings us a more in-depth knowledge and its consequential understanding. As we move forward, life, like chemistry, becomes a little more complex to comprehend, and the lessons we learn become more challenging to apply.

Please don't take the words 'knowledge with its appended understanding' lightly. I can assure you that you can have the knowledge and not understand how to use it. I know people that have master's & doctorate degrees. Their book knowledge far outweighs mine. Yet they don't know how to apply their knowledge in order to succeed.

There are laws that govern chemistry, as there are laws that govern life. The outcomes in chemistry are as real and fixed as the outcomes in life. In the case of life, we are governed by both temporal and spiritual laws. But I'll leave that discussion for another time.

In both chemistry and life, we must first start by building a solid foundation of the fundamental knowledge of the laws and principles that govern us. That knowledge will allow us to handle and manage the most complex aspects of our life.

As with chemistry, in life, it is in the study of our history of failures and successes that will lead us to reach our goals.

Liken to chemistry, it is only when we can maintain a constant and stable change in the proper direction that we will be able to predict outcomes better and prevent history from repeating itself.

As with chemistry, we must learn before we can teach. We must master our own life first. Then, and only then, can we apply those needed changes effectively to other areas around us, such as our family, our community, our nation, and the world. I back this statement up by quoting Rule #11 *'If You*

Rule #20 'If Nothing Changes, Then Nothing Changes, and History Repeats Itself'

Can't Take Care of Yourself You Can't Take Care of Others', and support it with a quote I used in Rule #11.

> **(Ezra Taft Benson)**[17]
> *"Only the wholesome have the capacity to lift and encourage one another to greater service, to greater achievement, to greater strength."*

And We Go Around in Circles:

You may become stuck in a cycle as you are working on freeing yourself from a debilitating habit. It happens to us all. That is how we learn. But, if you study your history and the history of others, it will be much easier to prevent a bad habit from forming in the first place. You will also find it much easier to get out of a bad cycle if you are in one.

You will significantly handicap yourself and increase your chance of failure if you do not study your life history and gain the wisdom and knowledge contained within it. You will be leaving your life to the whimsical chance of luck for your success. Leaving your destiny to the whims of life may seem the easier road in the short term, but in the long term, it will wind up being a harder and much longer road to take.

By taking the time to put in the required effort and doing your homework, you can remove chance from life's equation. Thus, your road to success will be straighter and shorter. It may seem the harder road to travel. Most times, it is. Yet I can assure you that it will be the much shorter road to ending your debilitating habit and a quicker road to a much happier life.

It's All About That Shiny Apple:

I am going to take a moment to repeat myself on the topics of knowledge and motivation. Knowledge and motivation are so crucial to this rule; the message is worthy of repeating. I apologize to those of you who understood my message the first time. This is for anyone that may need an extra boost.

Rule #20 'If Nothing Changes, Then Nothing Changes, and History Repeats Itself'

It seems to me that the only way to break a bad habit is by finding the right motivation. You may ask yourself why the need for motivation? Isn't the knowledge of right and wrong good enough?

Well, it is in the opinion of this writer that we humans are naturally a lazy bunch. It is encoded into each of us to act lazy for different reasons and based on various circumstances. Laziness is an essential trait in the make-up of humanity. It is the reason we all do not wish to excel in the same type of work. It is a part of us that allows humanity to be so diverse. Of course, there are always a few extreme cases, those who are overly motivated, and those who can't be motivated at all.

The whys, ways, and reasons for motivating one person to do the same task as another person are as diverse as there are colors from which you can choose to paint the walls of your home. We all must find our own whys, ways, and reasons to be motivated. By studying your successes and failures, which is your history, you will discover what factors do and do not motivate you.

Once you have found what motivates you, that is only the beginning. Even with the right motivation, most people can't change on the first try. It takes work, hard work, and lots of hard work, to strengthen your motivation and find sufficient energy and willpower to succeed.

Usually, a bad habit does not start overnight. So, don't expect it to go away just like that. Over-night success does not generally happen. The odds are you're going to fail a few times. But when you do, don't focus on the failure, but rather look at how much you have accomplished and build on that success. Only by applying what you have learned over and over again will you find the permanent success you seek.

Scriptural Positive Examples:

When is change not a good thing? When you are doing things the right way. What's that old adage? 'If it is not broken, don't fix it.'

Rule #20 'If Nothing Changes, Then Nothing Changes, and History Repeats Itself'

There are positive examples in the scriptures that show us we can make the right permanent changes. In the Old Testament, there is Saul, who becomes Paul, and Aaron, Moses's brother, and the whole city of Enoch. In the Book of Mormon, we have Alma, King Mosiah's sons, and a whole tribe of Lamanites.

Here is the conversion story of Saul, who becomes Paul.

> **(Bible New Testament: Acts 9:3-9, 17-18)[2]**
>
> *3 And as he journeyed, he came near Damascus: and suddenly there shined round about him a light from heaven:*
>
> *4 And he fell to the earth, and heard a voice saying unto him, Saul, Saul, why persecutest thou me?*
>
> *5 And he said, Who art thou, Lord? And the Lord said, I am Jesus whom thou persecutest: it is hard for thee to kick against the pricks.*
>
> *6 And he trembling and astonished said, Lord, what wilt thou have me to do? And the Lord said unto him, Arise, and go into the city, and it shall be told thee what thou must do.*
>
> *7 And the men which journeyed with him stood speechless, hearing a voice, but seeing no man.*
>
> *8 And Saul arose from the earth; and when his eyes were opened, he saw no man: but they led him by the hand, and brought him into Damascus.*
>
> *9 And he was three days without sight, and neither did eat nor drink.*
>
> *17 And Ananias went his way, and entered into the house; and putting his hands on him said, Brother Saul, the Lord, even Jesus, that appeared unto thee in the way as thou camest, hath sent me, that thou mightest receive thy sight, and be filled with the Holy Ghost.*
>
> *18 And immediately there fell from his eyes as it had been scales: and he received sight forthwith, and arose, and was baptized.*

Rule #20 'If Nothing Changes, Then Nothing Changes, and History Repeats Itself'

Here is the conversion story of Alma and the Sons of Mosiah.

> **(Book of Mormon: Mosiah 27:11–12, 18-22)**[3]
>
> *11 And as I said unto you, as they were going about rebelling against God, behold, the angel of the Lord appeared unto them; and he descended as it were in a cloud; and he spake as it were with a voice of thunder, which caused the earth to shake upon which they stood;*
>
> *12 And so great was their astonishment, that they fell to the earth, and understood not the words which he spake unto them.*
>
> *18 And now Alma and those that were with him fell again to the earth, for great was their astonishment; for with their own eyes they had beheld an angel of the Lord; and his voice was as thunder, which shook the earth; and they knew that there was nothing save the power of God that could shake the earth and cause it to tremble as though it would part asunder.*
>
> *19 And now the astonishment of Alma was so great that he became dumb, that he could not open his mouth; yea, and he became weak, even that he could not move his hands; therefore he was taken by those that were with him, and carried helpless, even until he was laid before his father.*
>
> *20 And they rehearsed unto his father all that had happened unto them; and his father rejoiced, for he knew that it was the power of God.*
>
> *21 And he caused that a multitude should be gathered together that they might witness what the Lord had done for his son, and also for those that were with him.*
>
> *22 And he caused that the priests should assemble themselves together; and they began to fast, and to pray to the Lord their God that he would open the mouth of Alma, that he might speak, and also that his limbs might receive their strength—that the eyes of*

Rule #20 'If Nothing Changes, Then Nothing Changes, and History Repeats Itself'

the people might be opened to see and know of the goodness and glory of God.

At one point in the history of both nations, the Nephites and the Lamanites were able to maintain peace. All were treated equally, and there were no poor among them for over 300 years.

(Book of Mormon: 4 Nephi 1: 15-18)[3]

15 And it came to pass that there was no contention in the land, because of the love of God which did dwell in the hearts of the people.

16 And there were no envyings, nor strifes, nor tumults, nor whoredoms, nor lyings, nor murders, nor any manner of lasciviousness; and surely there could not be a happier people among all the people who had been created by the hand of God.

17 There were no robbers, nor murderers, neither were there Lamanites, nor any manner of -ites; but they were in one, the children of Christ, and heirs to the kingdom of God.

18 And how blessed were they! For the Lord did bless them in all their doings; yea, even they were blessed and prospered until an hundred and ten years had passed away; and the first generation from Christ had passed away, and there was no contention in all the land.

Also, in the book, The Pearl of Great Price, which expands on the Old Testament Bible story of Enoch, the people of the City of Enoch became so righteous they reached the state of permanent righteousness (they required no change), and God takes the city of Enoch and its people home to Him.

(The Pearl of Great Price: Moses 7: 69)[5]

69 And Enoch and all his people walked with God, and he dwelt in the midst of Zion; and it came to pass that Zion was not, for God received it up into his own bosom; and from thence went forth the saying, Zion is Fled.

Rule #20 'If Nothing Changes, Then Nothing Changes, and History Repeats Itself'

Can Change Happen?

In our struggles to change, at various times in our life, we ask ourselves the questions: Will things change? Can they change? Can we make things better? I believe the answer is yes and no. Yes, there are some things we can change and need to change. Yet there are other repeated cycles in life that should not or cannot be altered, like birth and death. We all have to go through the cycle of life to learn what we were born here on Earth to learn before we move on. Though what lessons we are put on Earth to learn may be slightly different for each of us, we all are subject to the process of the life cycle.

On the subject of how we interact with each other, I believe there are a lot of areas in our lives that we need to implement a more permanent change. I believe that we humans have the ability within us to improve how charitable we choose to be, and showing love and respect for each other. These are changes I believe humankind can make. By mastering these changes, humanity has a chance at making a permanent change that will lead us to a better world. I believe we humans can become like the people of the City of Enoch.

Things can change. We can change things for the better in our personal life and the world. We just have to put forth the required effects needed to make the correct changes. If it was done once, it can be done again. God did not say it would be easy, but he did say it is possible, and that He would not lay any challenge upon us that we cannot handle.

> **(Bible New Testament: 1 Corinthians 10:13)2**
> *13 There hath no temptation taken you but such as is common to man: but God is faithful, who will not suffer you to be tempted above that ye are able; but will with the temptation also make a way to escape, that ye may be able to bear it.*

Rule #20 'If Nothing Changes, Then Nothing Changes, and History Repeats Itself'

To All My Helpers:

As I do at the end of most of the chapters I write, I take a moment to thank a few people who helped in doing part of the research for the scriptures and quotes. I had two great helpers, not counting my wife, Elder Jenson Haug, and Elder Cody Merrell. I want to thank them for giving their time to complete this final chapter.

I thought this would be one of the most straightforward rules to write, but it has been a lot more work for me to put into words than I thought it would. I believe I have written 18 versions of this chapter. Even though I am going with this version as my final edition, I still feel it could use a little more work.

If we can master the characteristics of being charitable, showing love, and giving each other respect, humanity has a chance at making a permanent change that will lead us to a better world. I believe humankind needs a lot of improvement in these areas. I also believe humanity can make the necessary changes. I believe we humans can become like the people of the City of Enoch.

My love and blessings are with all of you that are reading my writings. I pray you can gain the wisdom I am trying to share with you and that it will inspire you to write your own rules.

I leave you with two of my favorite quotes for this rule from two people I admire.

> **(Tom Hanks)**[18]
> *"If you're concerned about what's going on today, read history and figure out what to do because it's all right there."*
>
> **(Melvin Russell Ballard, 2009 April General Conference, "Learning the Lessons of the Past")**[19]
> *"There is a famous saying attributed to George Santayana. You've probably heard it: 'Those who cannot remember the past are condemned to repeat*

Rule #20 'If Nothing Changes, Then Nothing Changes, and History Repeats Itself'

it' (in John Bartlett, comp., Familiar Quotations, *15th ed. [1980], 703). There are, in fact, several different variations of this quote, including 'Those who do not remember the past are doomed to repeat it.' Regardless of the exact language, the sentiment is profound.*"

Rule #20 'If Nothing Changes, Then Nothing Changes, and History Repeats Itself'

Endnotes:

1 **King James Version of the Bible, The Old Testament of Our Lord and Saviour Jesus Christ.** Published by The Church of Jesus Christ of Latter-day Saints, Salt Lake City, Utah, USA. Copywrite 2013.

2 **King James Version of the Bible, The New Testament of Our Lord and Saviour Jesus Christ.** Published by The Church of Jesus Christ of Latter-day Saints, Salt Lake City, Utah, USA. Copywrite 2013.

3 **The Book of Mormon Another Testament of Jesus Christ.** Published by The Church of Jesus Christ of Latter-day Saints, Salt Lake City, Utah, USA. The first English edition published in Palmyra, New York, USA, in 1830. Copywrite 2013.

4 **The Doctrine and Covenants of The Church of Jesus Christ of Latter-Day Saints.** Containing Revelations Give to Joseph Smith, the Prophet. With some additions by his successors in the Presidency of the Church. Published by The Church of Jesus Christ of Latter-day Saints, Salt Lake City, Utah, USA. Copywrite 2013.

5 **The Pearl of Great Price.** A selection from the revelations, translations, and narrations of Joseph Smith, First Prophet, seer, and revelator to The Church of Jesus Christ of Latter-Day Saints. Published by The Church of Jesus Christ of Latter-day Saints, Salt Lake City, Utah, USA. Copywrite 2013.

6 **George Bernard Shaw.** George Bernard Shaw. (n.d.). AZQuotes.com. Retrieved February 23, 2019, from AZQuotes.com Web site: https://www.azquotes.com/quote/268354. Also see, "Everybody's political what's what?" by George Bernard Shaw, Chapter XXXVII, (p. 330), 1944.

7 **Wendy Mass.** Wendy Mass. (n.d.). AZQuotes.com. Retrieved February 23, 2019, from AZQuotes.com Web site: https://www.azquotes.com/quote/453541.

8 **Albert Einstein.** Albert Einstein. (n.d.). AZQuotes.com. Retrieved February 23, 2019, from AZQuotes.com Web site: https://www.azquotes.com/quote/87281. Also, see Albert Einstein (2010). "The Ultimate Quotable Einstein", p.474, Princeton University Press.

9 **Lao Tzu.** Laozi. (n.d.). AZQuotes.com. Retrieved February 23, 2019, from AZQuotes.com Web site: https://www.azquotes.com/quote/521409.

10 **Unknown.** Unknown. (n.d.). emilysquotes.com. Retrieved February 23, 2019, from emilysquotes.com Web site: http://emilysquotes.com/if-the-plan-doesnt-work-change-the-plan-but-never-the-goal/.

11 **Max De Pree.** Max de Pree Quotes. (n.d.). BrainyQuote.com. Retrieved February 23, 2019, from BrainyQuote.com Web site: https://www.brainyquote.com/quotes/max_de_pree_377124.

12 **Bill Phillips.** Bill Phillips. (n.d.). AZQuotes.com. Retrieved February 23, 2019, from AZQuotes.com Web site: https://www.azquotes.com/quote/748034.

Rule #20 'If Nothing Changes, Then Nothing Changes, and History Repeats Itself'

13 **Movie Quote, "The Samaritan", May 18, 2012.** "The Samaritan". (n.d.) rottentomatoes.com. Retrieved February 23, 2019, from rottentomatoes.com Web site: https://www.rottentomatoes.com/m/the_samaritan/quotes/

14 **Henry Ford**. Henry Ford. (n.d.). goodreas.com. Retrieved February 23, 2019, from goodreads.com Web site: https://www.goodreads.com/quotes/904186-if-you-always-do-what-you-ve-always-done-you-ll-always.

15 **Marcus Garvey**. Marcus Garvey. (n.d.). AZQuotes.com. Retrieved February 23, 2019, from AZQuotes.com Web site: https://www.azquotes.com/quote/107152.

16 **Martin Luther King, Jr.** Martin Luther King, Jr.. (n.d.). AZQuotes.com. Retrieved February 23, 2019, from AZQuotes.com Web site: https://www.azquotes.com/quote/159042. Also see, Martin Luther King, Jr. (2012). "A Gift of Love: Sermons from Strength to Love and Other Preachings", p.13, Beacon Press.

17 **Ezra Taft Benson.** Published in the Teachings of the Presidents of the Church: Ezra Taft Benson, "Leadership" Chapter-19 page-244 paragraph-5. An official manual of the Church of Jesus Christ of Latter-day Saints published 2014 by the Church of Jesus Christ of Latter-day Saints, 50 E. North Temple Street, Salt Lake City, UT, 84150-3220, USA. Also, see Churchofjesuschrist.org. Retrieved February 17, 2019, from Churchofjesuschrist.org Web site: https://www.churchofjesuschrist.org/study/manual/teachings-of-presidents-of-the-church-ezra-taft-benson/chapter-19-leadership?lang=eng

18 **Tom Hanks**. Tom Hanks. (n.d.) cnn.com. Retrieved February 23, 2019, from cnn.com Web site: https://www.cnn.com/2017/10/21/politics/tom-hanks-national-archives/index.html.

19 **Melvin Russell Ballard, 2009 April General Conference, "Learning the Lessons of the Past".** The 179th Annual General Conference of the Church of Jesus Christ of Latter-day Saints, April 4, 2009, Saturday Afternoon Session. Published in the Ensign magazine, Volume 06 Number 39 page-31 paragraph-, May 2009. An official magazine of the Church of Jesus Christ of Latter-day Saints, published by the Church of Jesus Christ of Latter-day Saints, 50 E. North Temple Street, Salt Lake City, UT, 84150-3220, USA. Also see, Ensign, Churchofjesuschrist.org. Retrieved February 23, 2019, from Churchofjesuschrist.org Web site: https://www.churchofjesuschrist.org/study/ensign/2009/05/learning-the-lessons-of-the-past?lang=eng.

What's That Rumbling Noise?

Rule #21
'Yesterday's Meal is Not Enough to Sustain Today's Needs'

Rule #21 'Yesterday's Meal is Not Enough to Sustain Today's Needs'

Intro, a Little Music Please:

Surprise! Yes, I know the title of this book seems to imply that there are only 20 rules. So, where does Rule #21 come from then? If you are a quick thinker, Rule #21 *'Yesterday's Meal is Not Enough to Sustain Today's Needs'* conveys the reason for its existence.

To Infinity and Beyond:

The truth is, there is no end to the rules, nor should there be. Gaining knowledge is a never-ending process, and new truths are forever coming forth into the light. We should never stop seeking, learning, or growing along all avenues of life. As we move beyond yesterday, to today, and then on to tomorrow, our lives change and with it our capacity to govern ourselves. Therefore, as we sand ourselves to a better brilliance with an ever-finer grit of polishing powder, more control must be applied to the polishing wheel. Thus, each day, we hone ourselves closer to perfection.

To put it simply, we do not change our core rules, but as our knowledge and understanding increase, we add rules throughout life to fine-tune our path to perfection. This philosophy highlights the need to put Rule #21 in writing. Rule #21 reminds us that we cannot sustain ourselves, nor will growth come, without constant nourishment.

The Einstein Theory:

All living things need care and nourishment in one form or another, whether we are talking about physical care, intellectual stimulation, or spiritual fulfillment. Without constant nourishment, all living things wither away. Even chemical elements require some form of regeneration to maintain their current form and/or evolve into something new. A piece of wood requires the proper moisture and oil, or it dries, splits, and decays. Yet, then again, give the wood too much water at one time, and the wood swells splits and decays. Let's take a solid stone: the opal. With this stone, the lack of nourishment can easily be seen in time. The opal, without the proper nourishment of moisture, will lose its fiery brilliance and fade.

The human mind is like an opal; without the proper nourishment, it loses its fiery brilliance otherwise known as intelligence. Without a constant input of knowledge, the mind will become dull and unable to maintain that which it has already learned.

Professionals that work in a variety of fields understand the necessity of constant intellectual nourishment. In order to maintain their licenses, most professionals are required to take a certain number of accredited courses a year. This is particularly true of those people who work in the medical field. Medical professionals are required to take a certain number of classes for educational credit associated with their field each year. These are called CEUs and must be turned into the state when renewing their license. Why? Because the industry has learned that without constant re-education, providers may lose part, if not all, of their knowledge. In the field of medicine, harm, or even death to a patient or client could result if skills and knowledge are allowed to diminish.

Nowadays, this same principle of continued education is being applied to lesser-skilled jobs. Companies have discovered that it is cheaper to educate their employees and offer continued training and classes than it is to pay for mistakes when skills diminish. With a couple of refresher classes provided on a regular basis, employees make less costly mistakes. Companies have seen the benefits of continued education and have found it necessary at all job levels. From the Walmart cashier to the person unloading the delivery trucks on the dock, online education courses are a requirement. Even the McDonalds fast-food hamburger maker must take online classes and successfully pass tests to maintain his job. Again, why do companies continue to educate their employees? Because the brain does not stay sharp and retain knowledge unless it is fed with constant nourishment.

From an intellectual point, I can personally testify of the requirement for constant education and review of previously learned information. I have worked as an electronics engineer, a computer system's engineer, a licensed Hearing Aid Practitioner, and I also ran a successful computer company for 30 years. In each of those fields of service, I had to continually nourish my knowledge to stay successful, and that included refreshing myself on subjects I had already studied and learned.

If You Don't Use It You Lose It:

Just yesterday, I was sitting at my dining room table with a young missionary, Elder Courtenay Ackley, from the Marshall Islands. Elder Ackley's mission service was coming to an end, and as we sat at the table, we talked about what he planned to do when he returned home. He said he planned to spend a few months reconnecting with his friends and family and then head to school and study to become a dentist. I told Elder Ackley that I thought studying to be a Doctor of Dentistry would be a lot harder than my studies had been to earn a degree in electronic engineering. During our conversation, Elder Ackley asked me to share with him some of my computer design knowledge involving hardware and peripheral devices. I pulled out a pen and paper and started drawing several different computer chip components, such as And Gates, Or Gates, Nand Gates, Nor Gates, Flip Flops, Drivers, Buffers, Clocks, and Delay Lines. As I drew each component, I explained its function. Then using the components I had drawn, I grouped them together into simple design circuits to show how, when used together, the chips could perform a useful function. The example I drew was just a simple circuit, any first-year electronic engineering student should be able to replicate. Yet, my mind struggled to remember how to put the chips together correctly so that the circuit would perform the task it had been created to accomplish. Thirty-five years ago, I could have whipped that drawing out in a snap without even thinking about it. Yet on this day, 35 years later, because I had not kept the information fresh in my mind by consistent study or some type of continued education, my mind barely recalled what components to use and in what order to use them to create the circuit I wanted.

Are You Quoting Me Again?

Here are some inspiring quotes to enlighten your mind and inspire your heart, and I'll throw in a little humor as well. Enjoy the feast.

(Mahatma Gandhi)[6]
"Live as if you were to die tomorrow. Learn as if you were to live forever."

(Nelson Mandela)[7]
"Education is the most powerful weapon which you can use to change the world."

(Walter Cronkite)[8]
"Whatever the cost of our libraries, the price is cheap compared to that of an ignorant nation."

(Confucius)[9]
"Man who stand on hill with mouth open will wait long time for roast duck to drop in."

(Henry Ford)[10]
"Anyone who stops learning is old, whether at twenty or eighty. Anyone who keeps learning stays young."

(Christopher Paolini)[11]
"Eragon looked back at him, confused. 'I don't understand.'

'Of course you don't,' said Brom impatiently. 'That's why I'm teaching you and not the other way around.'"

(Neil deGrasse Tyson)[12]
"We spend the first year of a child's life teaching it to walk and talk and the rest of its life to shut up and sit down. There's something wrong there."

(Anton Chekhov)[13]
"Wisdom.... comes not from age, but from education and learning."

(Abigail Adams)[14]
"Learning is not attained by chance, it must be sought for with ardor and diligence."

(Mark Twain) [15]
"When I am king they shall not have bread and shelter only, but also teachings out of books, for a full belly is little worth where the mind is starved."

(Eleanor Roosevelt)[16]
"All of life is a constant education."

(Russell M. Nelson, 2015 January Ensign, "What Will You Choose?")[17]
"The glory of God is intelligence. Indeed, our education is for the eternities."

(Gordon B. Hinckley, 1998 April General Conference, "Living Worthy of the Girl You Will Someday Marry")[18]
"Work for an education. Get all the training that you can. The world will largely pay you what it thinks you are worth."

(Gordon B. Hinckley, "Words of the Prophet: Seek Learning," *New Era*, Sept. 2007, 2–4)[19]
"You will be expected to put forth great effort and to use your best talents to make your way to the most wonderful future of which you are capable."

"You have the potential to become anything to which you set your mind. You have a mind and a body and a spirit. With these three working together, you can walk the high road that leads to achievement and

happiness. But this will require effort and sacrifice and faith."

(Doctrine & Covenants 93:36)[4]
"The glory of God is intelligence, or, in other words, light and truth"

If I Only Had the Time:

In the hustle and bustle of daily life, with all of its needs that demand our time, it's no wonder we frequently ask ourselves, 'How will I find the time to do all the things requested of me'? Sometimes we skip eating a meal or two or don't stop to drink the proper fluids our body needs to sustain itself and maintain good health. Why? Because we allow the demands on our lives to keep us so busy, we don't feel we can take the time to eat. However, eventually, we feel the repercussions of skipping too many meals, and our body's built-in protections remind us of this neglect. At that point, we stop to either eat or drop dead. At least the physical body has built-in systems, like the pain of hunger, to remind us when we need to make better choices. Other aspects of our lives that require attention or 'need to be fed' don't always have automatic alarms or warning signals.

Many people seem to handle the feeding of their intellectual mind, much like their stomachs. They do not seem to have enough time to take their education or re-education seriously. When the body is hungry or thirsty, it will remind us daily of its needs with pain until they are met.

Not so for intellectual hunger. It is not until it comes to a point in life that a person may lose their job and the emotional hunger sets in or they are not able to provide food for the body and a physical hunger sets in that a person is then motivated to obtain the education needed.

The person must choose to better himself intellectually or choose to neglect the need for intellectual nourishment and becomes a burden to society. On the other hand, he can choose to starve to death. Either of the choices will solve his troubles. However, only one choice is a better choice.

Soul Food:

The one area that requires some of our time that people seem to sacrifice the most in their attempt to gain more time is the time that is needed for spiritual nourishment. As a quick example, how many people do not attend their church? I am talking about the people that do believe in God, not the ones that do not. Many omit going to church because they feel they do not have the time to spare in their life for this type of spiritual nourishment.

The need for spiritual nourishment is real and as real a need as food is for sustaining our physical body. I will take it a step further and say that spiritual nourishment is a greater need than physical and intellectual food. Intellectual and physical food will sustain the mind and body. But only spiritual nourishment can sustain the soul, and the soul is the essence of who we are. A perfectly healthy body can die from a starved soul.

Just take a look at the world's suicide and depression rates and the number of unhappy people mindlessly floating through their lives. There are those people who care very little for their fellow human beings, they lie, steal, or murder for their own selfish gains. It is common to hear news of mass shootings in our shopping stores, our schools, and even in our churches. But there is a cure for all of these problems; the daily practice of proper spiritual nourishment.

By reviewing history, we find proof that spiritual nourishment is the cure for sadness, evil, and despair in the world. Both the Bible and the Book of Mormon give evidence and testify to this fact. These books show that when people followed the word of God, their life was good and prosperous.

Here is one account from the Book of Mormon that shows what can happen when we are all properly spiritually fed.

Rule #21 'Yesterday's Meal is Not Enough to Sustain Today's Needs'

(Book of Mormon: 4 Nephi 1:2-7)[3]

2 And it came to pass in the thirty and sixth year, the people were all converted unto the Lord, upon all the face of the land, both Nephites and Lamanites, and there were no contentions and disputations among them, and every man did deal justly one with another.

3 And they had all things common among them; therefore there were not rich and poor, bond and free, but they were all made free, and partakers of the heavenly gift.

4 And it came to pass that the thirty and seventh year passed away also, and there still continued to be peace in the land.

5 And there were great and marvelous works wrought by the disciples of Jesus, insomuch that they did heal the sick, and raise the dead, and cause the lame to walk, and the blind to receive their sight, and the deaf to hear; and all manner of miracles did they work among the children of men; and in nothing did they work miracles save it were in the name of Jesus.

6 And thus did the thirty and eighth year pass away, and also the thirty and ninth, and forty and first, and the forty and second, yea, even until forty and nine years had passed away, and also the fifty and first, and the fifty and second; yea, and even until fifty and nine years had passed away.

7 And the Lord did prosper them exceedingly in the land; yea, insomuch that they did build cities again where there had been cities burned.

With the proper spiritual food, you can and will be helped to overcome obstacles and excel in all areas of your life. Your spiritual being forms a bond to your physical and intellectual being. The spiritual allows you to surpass your current physical and intellectual limitations. My life is a living testimony. It is only through the belief in God and His spirit that I was able to overcome my physical hunger as a child growing up in a poor family. It is only through the inspiration of God that I have found ways to overcome many of my mental handicaps.

Moreover, it is only through living the commandments of God with daily scripture study and prayer that I have prospered to the point that not only are all of my physical needs met, but also many of my material wants. I testify to you that I am truly grateful for the abundant blessings the Lord has bestowed upon me. I also testify to you that there is a direct correlation between a successful life and following the Lord's commandments, reading the scriptures and pondering them, and praying for guidance.

In Matthew 4:2-4, we read the words of Christ as he tells us, 'Man shall not live by bread alone'.

> **(Bible New Testament: Matthew 4:2-4)[2]**
> *2 And when he had fasted forty days and forty nights, he was afterward an hungred.*
>
> *3 And when the tempter came to him, he said, If thou be the Son of God, command that these stones be made bread.*
>
> *4 But he answered and said, It is written, Man shall not live by bread alone, but by every word that proceedeth out of the mouth of God.*

And Now A Few Words From the Greats:

As always, I like to give you a surplus of scriptures and quotes to emphasize my point. I do this to provide you, the reader, a variety of examples from which to study and learn.

> **(Bible Old Testament: Deuteronomy 17:19)[1]**
> *19 And it shall be with him, and he shall read therein all the days of his life: that he may learn to fear the Lord his God, to keep all the words of this law and these statutes, to do them:*

(Bible Old Testament: Proverbs 1:5)[1]
5 A wise man will hear, and will increase learning; and a man of understanding shall attain unto wise counsels:

(Bible Old Testament; Proverbs 1:7)[1]
7 The fear of the Lord is the beginning of knowledge: but fools despise wisdom and instruction.

(Bible Old Testament: Proverbs 3:13)[1]
13 Happy is the man that findeth wisdom, and the man that getteth understanding.

(Bible Old Testament: Proverbs 9:9)[1]
9 Give instruction to a wise man, and he will be yet wiser: teach a just man, and he will increase in learning.

(Bible Old Testament: Proverbs 15:14)[1]
14 The heart of him that hath understanding seeketh knowledge: but the mouth of fools feedeth on foolishness.

(Bible Old Testament: Proverbs 16:16)[1]
16 How much better is it to get wisdom than gold! and to get understanding rather to be chosen than silver!

(Bible Old Testament: Proverbs 24:3-4)[1]
3 Through wisdom is an house builded; and by understanding it is established:

4 And by knowledge shall the chambers be filled with all precious and pleasant riches.

(Bible Old Testament: Isaiah 28:9-10)[1]
9 Whom shall he teach knowledge? and whom shall he make to understand doctrine? them that are weaned from the milk, and drawn from the breasts.

10 For precept must be upon precept, precept upon precept; line upon line, line upon line; here a little, and there a little:

(Bible New Testament: 2 Timothy 2:15)[2]
15 Study to shew thyself approved unto God,

(Bible New Testament: 1 Corinthians 14:20)[2]
20 Brethren, be not children in understanding: howbeit in malice be ye children, but in understanding be men.

(Book of Mormon: 2 Nephi 32:7)[3]
7 And now I, Nephi, cannot say more; the Spirit stoppeth mine utterance, and I am left to mourn because of the unbelief, and the wickedness, and the ignorance, and the stiffneckedness of men; for they will not search knowledge, nor understand great knowledge, when it is given unto them in plainness, even as plain as word can be.

(Book of Mormon: Alma 1:26)[3]
26 And when the priests left their labor to impart the word of God unto the people, the people also left their labors to hear the word of God. And when the priest had imparted unto them the word of God they all returned again diligently unto their labors; and the priest, not esteeming himself above his hearers, for the preacher was no better than the hearer, neither was the teacher any better than the learner; and thus they were all equal, and they did all labor, every man according to his strength.

(Book of Mormon: Alma 10:15)[3]
15 Now these lawyers were learned in all the arts and cunning of the people; and this was to enable them that they might be skilful in their profession.

(Book of Mormon: Alma 37:35)[3]
35 O, remember, my son, and learn wisdom in thy youth; yea, learn in thy youth to keep the commandments of God.

(Book of Mormon: Helaman 14:30)[3]
30 And now remember, remember, my brethren, that whosoever perisheth, perisheth unto himself; and whosoever doeth iniquity, doeth it unto himself; for behold, ye are free; ye are permitted to act for yourselves; for behold, God hath given unto you a knowledge and he hath made you free.

(Doctrine & Covenants 6:7)[4]
7 Seek not for riches but for wisdom, and behold, the mysteries of God shall be unfolded unto you, and then shall you be made rich. Behold, he that hath eternal life is rich.

(Doctrine & Covenants 11:22)[4]
22 But now hold your peace; study my word which hath gone forth among the children of men, and also study my word which shall come forth among the children of men, or that which is now translating, yea, until you have obtained all which I shall grant unto the children of men in this generation, and then shall all things be added thereto.

(Doctrine & Covenants 88:77-80)[4]
77 And I give unto you a commandment that you shall teach one another the doctrine of the kingdom.

78 Teach ye diligently and my grace shall attend you, that you may be instructed more perfectly in theory, in principle, in doctrine, in the law of the gospel, in all things that pertain unto the kingdom of God, that are expedient for you to understand;

79 Of things both in heaven and in the earth, and under the earth; things which have been, things which are, things which must shortly come to pass; things which are at home, things which are abroad; the wars and the perplexities of the nations, and the judgments which are on the land; and a knowledge also of countries and of kingdoms—

80 That ye may be prepared in all things when I shall send you again to magnify the calling whereunto I have called you, and the mission with which I have commissioned you.

(Doctrine & Covenants 88:118)[4]
118 And as all have not faith, seek ye diligently and teach one another words of wisdom; yea, seek ye out of the best books words of wisdom; seek learning, even by study and also by faith.

(Doctrine & Covenants 90:15)[4]
15 And set in order the churches, and study and learn, and become acquainted with all good books, and with languages, tongues, and people.

(Doctrine & Covenants 130:18-19)[4]
18 Whatever principle of intelligence we attain unto in this life, it will rise with us in the resurrection.

19 And if a person gains more knowledge and intelligence in this life through his diligence and obedience than another, he will have so much the advantage in the world to come.

(Doctrine & Covenants 131:6)[4]
6 It is impossible for a man to be saved in ignorance.

(Doctrine & Covenants 136:32)[4]
32 Let him that is ignorant learn wisdom by humbling himself and calling upon the Lord his God, that his eyes may be opened that he may see, and his ears opened that he may hear;

(Pearl of Great Price: Abraham 1:2)[5]
2 And, finding there was greater happiness and peace and rest for me, I sought for the blessings of the fathers, and the right whereunto I should be ordained to administer the same; having been myself a follower of righteousness, desiring also to be one who possessed great knowledge, and to be a greater follower of righteousness, and to possess a greater knowledge, and to be a father of many nations, a

prince of peace, and desiring to receive instructions, and to keep the commandments of God, I became a rightful heir, a High Priest, holding the right belonging to the fathers.

(Bonnie L. Oscarson, 09 May 2013 LDS Church News, "Young Women Leaders Ask Women to Set Good Examples")[20]

"I can't overemphasize enough the power of our examples as mothers and grandmothers and youth leaders in influencing the testimonies and belief of our young women. We cannot expect them to dress modestly and attend their Church meetings, to pray daily, study the scriptures, and make wise choices if we are not doing those things ourselves."

(Henry B. Eyring, 1997 October General Conference, "Feed My Lambs")[21]

"Every word we speak can strengthen or weaken faith. We need help from the Spirit to speak the words which will nourish and which will strengthen."

"There are two great keys to inviting the Spirit to guide what words we speak as we feed others. They are the daily study of the scriptures and the prayer of faith."

"The Holy Ghost will guide what we say if we study and ponder the scriptures every day. The words of the scriptures invite the Holy Spirit. The Lord said it this way: 'Seek not to declare my word, but first seek to obtain my word, and then shall your tongue be loosed; then, if you desire, you shall have my Spirit and my word, yea, the power of God unto the convincing of men' (D&C 11:21). With daily study of the scriptures, we can count on this blessing even in casual conversations or in a class when we may be asked by a teacher to respond to a question. We will experience the power the Lord promised: 'Neither take ye thought beforehand what ye shall say; but treasure up in your minds continually the words of

life, and it shall be given you in the very hour that portion that shall be meted unto every man' (D&C 84:85)."

(Henry B. Eyring, 2010 October General Conference, "Serve with the Spirit")[22]

"Our humility and our faith that invite spiritual gifts are increased by our reading, studying, and pondering the scriptures. We have all heard those words. Yet we may read a few lines or pages of scripture every day and hope that will be enough."

"But reading, studying, and pondering are not the same. We read words and we may get ideas. We study and we may discover patterns and connections in scripture. But when we ponder, we invite revelation by the Spirit. Pondering, to me, is the thinking and the praying I do after reading and studying in the scriptures carefully."

(Howard W Hunter, 1979 October General Conference, "Reading the Scriptures")[23]

"When we follow the counsel of our leaders to read and study the scriptures, benefits and blessings of many kinds come to us. This is the most profitable of all study in which we could engage. The portion of scripture known as the Old and New Testaments is often referred to as the great literature of the world."

"There is nothing more helpful than prayer to open our understanding of the scriptures. Through prayer we can attune our minds to seek the answers to our searchings. The Lord said: 'Ask, and it shall be given you; seek, and ye shall find; knock, and it shall be opened unto you' (Luke 11:9). Herein is Christ's reassurance that if we will ask, seek, and knock, the Holy Spirit will guide our understanding if we are ready and eager to receive."

(Dieter F. Uchtdorf, "Seeing Beyond the Leaf")[24]
"The truth will continue to flourish and spread throughout the earth. Sometimes all it takes is a little faith and a little patience. Things which may appear impossible now may become matter-of-fact in years to come."

(Martin Luther, Jr.)[25]
"I am afraid that the schools will prove the very gates of hell, unless they diligently labor in explaining the Holy Scriptures and engraving them in the heart of the youth."

(Henry D. Taylor, 1971 April General Conference, "Man Cannot Endure on Borrowed Light")[26]
"Testimonies need to be nourished and fed. President Lee wisely counseled: 'If we are not reading the scriptures daily, our testimonies are growing thinner, our spirituality isn't increasing in depth.' (Seminar for Regional Representatives of the Twelve, December 12, 1970.)"

The Final Story:

I will end with this final parable from the Bible New Testament. In this parable, Jesus Christ is teaching the lesson of use it or lose it.

(Bible New Testament: Matthew 25: 14-30)[2]
14 ¶ For the kingdom of heaven is as a man travelling into a far country, who called his own servants, and delivered unto them his goods.

15 And unto one he gave five talents, to another two, and to another one; to every man according to his several ability; and straightway took his journey.

16 Then he that had received the five talents went and traded with the same, and made them other five talents.

17 And likewise he that had received two, he also gained other two.

18 But he that had received one went and digged in the earth, and hid his lord's money.

19 After a long time the lord of those servants cometh, and reckoneth with them.

20 And so he that had received five talents came and brought other five talents, saying, Lord, thou deliveredst unto me five talents: behold, I have gained beside them five talents more.

21 His lord said unto him, Well done, thou good and faithful servant: thou hast been faithful over a few things, I will make thee ruler over many things: enter thou into the joy of thy lord.

22 He also that had received two talents came and said, Lord, thou deliveredst unto me two talents: behold, I have gained two other talents beside them.

23 His lord said unto him, Well done, good and faithful servant; thou hast been faithful over a few things, I will make thee ruler over many things: enter thou into the joy of thy lord.

24 Then he which had received the one talent came and said, Lord, I knew thee that thou art an hard man, reaping where thou hast not sown, and gathering where thou hast not strawed:

25 And I was afraid, and went and hid thy talent in the earth: lo, there thou hast that is thine.

26 His lord answered and said unto him, Thou wicked and slothful servant, thou knewest that I reap where I sowed not, and gather where I have not strawed:

> *27 Thou oughtest therefore to have put my money to the exchangers, and then at my coming I should have received mine own with usury.*
>
> *28 Take therefore the talent from him, and give it unto him which hath ten talents.*
>
> *29 For unto every one that hath shall be given, and he shall have abundance: but from him that hath not shall be taken away even that which he hath.*
>
> *30 And cast ye the unprofitable servant into outer darkness: there shall be weeping and gnashing of teeth.*

There are many lessons to be learned from this Bible parable about talent. I would like to point out three noteworthy lessons that apply directly to Rule #21.

The first lesson starts in **Matthew 25:15,** "*And unto one he gave five talents, to another two, and to another one; to every man according to his several abilities,*". What is being taught here is that the Lord will not give us more than we can handle, nor does he expect more than we are able to do. Please note the word 'ability' in this verse is the key to the first of the three lessons. We must all learn what abilities (talents) the Lord has blessed us with, and for each of us, that gift is different. Many people are given abilities and opportunities to accomplish wondrous feats. Yet, through their free agency, they choose not to and instead waste their talents. They bury their talents as did the man with one talent in **Matthew 25:18**.

The second lesson concerns whether you should bury your talent or use it. The Lord gives us talents so that we might cultivate them. To cultivate your talents, you must use them, nourish them, and learn to master them.

I know a young man that the Lord gifted with many talents. School was easy for him, and he was a very talented athlete. He was brilliant in art and could draw a flower that appeared as vivid and alive on paper as it did in real life. He was graceful in social settings and made new friends easily. Yet this young man failed to excel at anything.

Had he put effort into his training, he could have broken the school track records and perhaps even gone on to be on the USA Olympic Track and Field team. When improving his art skills required a little hard work and sacrifice, he quit. In neither case, it wasn't a lack of talent that prevented his success.

This young man was called and accepted the calling to serve as a missionary; a two-year commitment. Serving as a missionary, he would have the opportunity to use, hone, and maximize his social talents, yet he chose not to complete his obligation. Sadly, he was sent home after only serving one year. Why did he not use the talents that he was given?

So many things in life came too easily for him, and he had not learned the value of hard work or the delayed gratification of making a short-term sacrifice. Thus, when life wasn't fun, he quit. Fortunately, as a young man, he still has time to gain some of the blessings his talents offer, hopefully before it's too late and he loses both the talents and the opportunities they offer. On the other hand, you can never regain what is lost. Those past opportunities and blessings are gone forever. At the time, had he used his talents more wisely, I know he could have built on his successes and blessings, and his life would be far better today.

The third lesson from the parable in **Matthew** is that the Lord treats us all equally, even though we are not all given the same talents. In the end, we all are rewarded not by how many talents we have, but by how we use the talents we are given. This is pointed out in **Matthew 25:20-23,** where the man that had five talents and the man that was given two talents both multiplied their talents by two and were rewarded the same. **Matthew 25:27-30** shows us that the man who was given only one talent and did nothing with it received no reward and, in the end, not only was the talent taken back, but the man was additionally punished for his slothfulness.

There are many reasons why people do not nourish their talents. In the example of the young man, he chose worldly pleasure and immediate gratification over the required hard work and self-discipline needed to multiply his talents. **Matthew 25:25** tells us the man with one talent did not use his talent out of fear.

> **(Bible New Testament: Matthew 25: 25)**[2]
> *25 And I was afraid, and went and hid thy talent in the earth: lo, there thou hast that is thine.*

Using our talents each day is a form of re-educating ourselves. Not only does it help us retain our talents, it also opens the doors to new knowledge and wisdom to a talent called life experience.

Each day of my life, as I use my talents, I become more knowledgeable and learn new skills. Old ways of doing things become new ways as I learn and improve. This principle applies equally to my spiritual learning, as well. Each day as I reread the scriptures, the same scriptures that I have read many times before, I reinforce what I have already learned, and I am inspired and enlightened to new understandings. Studying a subject from different sources often gives me a different perspective and opens doors I have not yet walked through even though I may have studied that very same subject a hundred times.

In Summary:

I hope that I have impressed upon you the importance of Rule #21 *'Yesterday's Meal Is Not Enough to Sustain Today's Needs'*. Continue to nourish your body, mind, and spirit each day for as long as you live. Never stop.

Eat & drink, educate & re-educate, read & ponder, and pray over the scriptures daily. Do this, and you will nourish the whole of your being. Do this, and you will boldly go where few have gone, to infinity and beyond.

Rule #21 'Yesterday's Meal is Not Enough to Sustain Today's Needs'

Endnotes:

1 **King James Version of the Bible, The Old Testament of Our Lord and Saviour Jesus Christ.** Published by The Church of Jesus Christ of Latter-day Saints, Salt Lake City, Utah, USA. Copywrite 2013.

2 **King James Version of the Bible, The New Testament of Our Lord and Saviour Jesus Christ.** Published by The Church of Jesus Christ of Latter-day Saints, Salt Lake City, Utah, USA. Copywrite 2013.

3 **The Book of Mormon Another Testament of Jesus Christ.** Published by The Church of Jesus Christ of Latter-day Saints, Salt Lake City, Utah, USA. The first English edition published in Palmyra, New York, USA, in 1830. Copywrite 2013.

4 **The Doctrine and Covenants of The Church of Jesus Christ of Latter-Day Saints.** Containing Revelations Give to Joseph Smith, the Prophet. With some additions by his successors in the Presidency of the Church. Published by The Church of Jesus Christ of Latter-day Saints, Salt Lake City, Utah, USA. Copywrite 2013.

5 **The Pearl of Great Price.** A selection from the revelations, translations, and narrations of Joseph Smith, First Prophet, seer, and revelator to The Church of Jesus Christ of Latter-Day Saints. Published by The Church of Jesus Christ of Latter-day Saints, Salt Lake City, Utah, USA. Copywrite 2013.

6 **Mahatma Gandhi.** Mahatma Gandhi. (n.d.). AZQuotes.com. Retrieved February 24, 2019, from AZQuotes.com Web site: https://www.azquotes.com/quote/105831.

7 **Nelson Mandela**. Nelson Mandela. (n.d.). AZQuotes.com. Retrieved February 24, 2019, from AZQuotes.com Web site: https://www.azquotes.com/quote/185308.

8 **Walter Cronkite.** Walter Cronkite. (n.d.). goodreads.com, Retrieved February 25, 2019, from goodreads.com Web site: https://www.goodreads.com/quotes/220528-whatever-the-cost-of-our-libraries-the-price-is-cheap.

9 **Confucius.** Confucius. (n.d.). AZQuotes.com. Retrieved February 24, 2019, from AZQuotes.com Web site: https://www.azquotes.com/quote/567066.

10 **Henry Ford.** Henry Ford. (n.d.). AZQuotes.com. Retrieved February 24, 2019, from AZQuotes.com Web site: https://www.azquotes.com/quote/99151.

11 **Christopher Paolini.** Christopher Paolini. (n.d.). AZQuotes.com. Retrieved February 24, 2019, from AZQuotes.com Web site: https://www.azquotes.com/quote/369651. Also see, Christopher Paolini (2014). "The Inheritance Cycle Complete Collection: Eragon, Eldest, Brisingr, Inheritance", p.187, Knopf Books for Young Readers

12 **Neil deGrasse Tyson**. Neil deGrasse Tyson. (n.d.). AZQuotes.com. Retrieved February 24, 2019, from AZQuotes.com Web site: https://www.azquotes.com/quote/482280.

Rule #21 'Yesterday's Meal is Not Enough to Sustain Today's Needs'

13. **Anton Chekhov**. Anton Chekhov. (n.d.). AZQuotes.com. Retrieved February 24, 2019, from AZQuotes.com Web site: https://www.azquotes.com/quote/425297. Also see, Anton Pavlovich Chekhov (1929). "The Works of Anton Chekhov"

14. **Abigail Adams**. Abigail Adams. (n.d.). AZQuotes.com. Retrieved February 24, 2019, from AZQuotes.com Web site: https://www.azquotes.com/quote/1556.

15. **Mark Twain**. Mark Twain. (n.d.). AZQuotes.com. Retrieved February 24, 2019, from AZQuotes.com Web site: https://www.azquotes.com/quote/384273. Also, see Mark Twain (2015). "The Prince and the Pauper", p.19, Xist Publishing

16. **Eleanor Roosevelt**. Eleanor Roosevelt. (n.d.). AZQuotes.com. Retrieved February 24, 2019, from AZQuotes.com Web site: https://www.azquotes.com/quote/399835. Also, see Eleanor Roosevelt, David Emblidge (2009). "My Day: The Best of Eleanor Roosevelt's Acclaimed Newspaper Columns, 1936-1962", p.107, Da Capo Press.

17. **Russell M. Nelson, 2015 January Ensign, "What Will You Choose?"**. From a Church Educational System devotional address, "Youth of the Noble Birthright: What Will You Choose?" delivered at Brigham Young University–Hawaii on September 6, 2013. For the full address, go to cesdevotionals.churchofjesuschrist.org. Published in the Ensign magazine, Volume 45 Number 1, January 2015. An official magazine of the Church of Jesus Christ of Latter-day Saints, published by the Church of Jesus Christ of Latter-day Saints, 50 E. North Temple Street, Salt Lake City, UT, 84150-3220, USA. Also see, Ensign, Churchofjesuschrist.org. Retrieved February 25, 2019, from Churchofjesuschrist.org Web site: https://www.churchofjesuschrist.org/study/ensign/2015/01/what-will-you-choose?lang=eng.

18. **Gordon B. Hinckley, 1998 April General Conference, "Living Worthy of the Girl You Will Someday Marry"**. The 168th Annual General Conference of the Church of Jesus Christ of Latter-day Saints, April 4, 1998, Priesthood Session. Published in the Ensign magazine, Volume 28 Number 05, May 1998. An official magazine of the Church of Jesus Christ of Latter-day Saints, published by the Church of Jesus Christ of Latter-day Saints, 50 E. North Temple Street, Salt Lake City, UT, 84150-3220, USA. Also see, Ensign, Churchofjesuschrist.org. Retrieved February 25, 2019, from Churchofjesuschrist.org Web site: https://www.churchofjesuschrist.org/study/ensign/1998/05/living-worthy-of-the-girl-you-will-someday-marry?lang=eng.

19. **Gordon B. Hinckley,** "Words of the Prophet: Seek Learning," *New Era*, Sept. 2007, 2–4. 'New Era' magazine, Volume 37, Number 9 Page-2 Paragraph-5, September 2007. An official magazine of the Church of Jesus Christ of Latter-day Saints, published by the Church of Jesus Christ of Latter-day Saints, 50 E. North Temple Street, Salt Lake City, UT, 84150-3220, USA. Also, see New Era, Churchofjesuschrist.org. Retrieved February 25, 2019, from Churchofjesuschrist.org website: https://www.churchofjesuschrist.org/study/new-era/2007/09/words-of-the-prophet-seek-learning?lang=eng.

Rule #21 'Yesterday's Meal is Not Enough to Sustain Today's Needs'

20 **Bonnie L. Oscarson**. Bonnie L. Oscarson. (n.d.). Churchofjesuschrist.org. Retrieved February 25, 2019, from Churchofjesuschrist.org Web site: https://www.churchofjesuschrist.org/church/news/leaders-say-young-women-need-good-examples?lang=eng&_r=1. Taken from the Church of Jesus Christ of Latter-day Saints (LDS Church) church news article "Young Women Leaders Ask Women to Set Good Examples" Contributed by: Marianne Holman, LDS Church News staff writer on May 9, 2013

21 **Henry B. Eyring, 1997 October General Conference, "Feed My Lambs"**. The 167th Semiannual General Conference of the Church of Jesus Christ of Latter-day Saints, October 5, 1997, Sunday Afternoon Session. Published in the Ensign magazine, Volume 27 Number 11, November 1997. An official magazine of the Church of Jesus Christ of Latter-day Saints, published by the Church of Jesus Christ of Latter-day Saints, 50 E. North Temple Street, Salt Lake City, UT, 84150-3220, USA. Also see, Ensign, Churchofjesuschrist.org. Retrieved February 25, 2019, from Churchofjesuschrist.org Web site: https://www.churchofjesuschrist.org/study/ensign/1997/11/feed-my-lambs?lang=eng.

22 **Henry B. Eyring, 2010 October General Conference, "Serve with the Spirit"**. ". The 180th Semiannual General Conference of the Church of Jesus Christ of Latter-day Saints, October 2, 2010, Priesthood Session. Published in the Ensign magazine, Volume 40 Number 11 page-60 paragraph-4, November 2010. An official magazine of the Church of Jesus Christ of Latter-day Saints, published by the Church of Jesus Christ of Latter-day Saints, 50 E. North Temple Street, Salt Lake City, UT, 84150-3220, USA. Also, see Ensign, Churchofjesuschrist.org. Retrieved February 25, 2019, from Churchofjesuschrist.org Web site: https://www.churchofjesuschrist.org/study/ensign/2010/11/priesthood-session/serve-with-the-spirit?lang=eng.

23 **Howard W Hunter, 1979 October General Conference, "Reading the Scriptures"**. The 149th Semiannual General Conference of the Church of Jesus Christ of Latter-day Saints, October 7, 1979, Sunday Morning Session. Published in the Ensign magazine, Volume 09 Number 11, November 1979. An official magazine of the Church of Jesus Christ of Latter-day Saints, published by the Church of Jesus Christ of Latter-day Saints, 50 E. North Temple Street, Salt Lake City, UT, 84150-3220, USA. Also, see Ensign, Churchofjesuschrist.org. Retrieved February 25, 2019, from Churchofjesuschrist.org Web site: https://www.churchofjesuschrist.org/study/ensign/1979/11/reading-the-scriptures?lang=eng.

24 **Dieter F. Uchtdorf, "Seeing Beyond the Leaf"**. Taken from Dieter F. Uchtdorf, a member of the First Presidency of The Church of Jesus Christ of Latter-day Saints, who delivered the following address at the BYU Church History Symposium at the Conference Center in Salt Lake City on March 7, 2014. Also see, Churchofjesuschrist.org. Retrieved February 25, 2019, from Churchofjesuschrist.org Web site: https://www.churchofjesuschrist.org/prophets-and-apostles/unto-all-the-world/seeing-beyond-the-leaf?lang=eng.

25 **Martin Luther, Jr.**. Martin Luther, Jr. (n.d.). AZQuotes.com. Retrieved February 24, 2019, from AZQuotes.com Web site: https://www.azquotes.com/quote/686632

26 **Henry D. Taylor, 1971 April General Conference, "Man Cannot Endure on Borrowed Light"**. The 141st Annual General Conference of the Church of Jesus Christ of Latter-day Saints, April 6, 1971, Tuesday Afternoon Session. Published in the Ensign magazine, Volume 01 Number 06, June 1971. An official magazine of the Church of Jesus Christ of Latter-day Saints, published by the Church of Jesus Christ of Latter-day Saints, 50 E. North Temple Street, Salt Lake City, UT, 84150-3220, USA. Also see, Ensign, Churchofjesuschrist.org. Retrieved February 17, 2019, from Churchofjesuschrist.org Web site: https://www.churchofjesuschrist.org/study/ensign/1971/06/man-cannot-endure-on-borrowed-light?lang=eng.

Rule #21 'Yesterday's Meal is Not Enough to Sustain Today's Needs'

Who Are You?
The Greats Past & Present

The Greats Past & Present

A Biography of Those Quoted:

This section of the book gives a short biography of the people I have quoted in my book. I do this to ensure that those I have quoted are better recognized for the contributions they bring, and also to bring the reader a little closer to those I quoted. Please take the time to read this section. It is my hope that you will gain a closer understanding of those people who have left us a little something of themselves.

Most of the biography information for these people came from Wikipedia at https://en.wikipedia.org/. Some people question the accuracy of all the information on Wikipedia's Web site. Yet, to date, I have found no source equal to it. What we believe we know about history and its people is forever changing. I want to give thanks to all that support Wikipedia in their efforts to provide the public clear and precise information.

There are other sources I have used to obtain the information on the people listed in this chapter, but they are few, and I am not going to take the time to cite them. I will, however, apologize for any errors contained in this chapter. We are all imperfect, and I am a part of the word 'all.'

Who Am I?

Abigail Adams - Abigail Adams (Born Abigail Smith; in Weymouth, Massachusetts Bay, British America, November 22, [O.S. November 11] 1744 – October 28, 1818) was the wife and closest advisor of John Adams, as well as the mother of John Quincy Adams. She is sometimes considered to have been a Founder of the United States, and is now designated as the first Second Lady and second First Lady of the United States, although these titles were not used at the time.

Abraham Lincoln - Abraham Lincoln (born Sinking Spring Farm, Kentucky, U.S., February 12, 1809 – April 15, 1865) was an American lawyer and politician. He served as the 16th president of the United States from 1861 until his assassination in April 1865. Lincoln led the nation through the Civil War, its bloodiest war, and its greatest moral, constitutional, and political crisis. He preserved the Union, abolished slavery, strengthened the federal government, and modernized the U.S. economy. Lincoln is remembered as America's martyr hero. He is consistently ranked both by scholars and the public as among the greatest U.S. presidents.

Albert Einstein - Albert Einstein (March 14, 1879 – April 18, 1955) was a German-born theoretical physicist who developed the theory of relativity, one of the two pillars of modern physics (alongside quantum mechanics). His work is also known for its influence on the philosophy of science. He is best known to the general public for his mass-energy equivalence formula $E = mc^2$, which has been dubbed "the world's most famous equation." He received the 1921 Nobel Prize in Physics "for his services to theoretical physics, and especially for his discovery of the law of the photoelectric effect", a pivotal step in the development of quantum theory.

Albert Guinon - Albert Guinon (1863-1923) was a French playwright.

Alistair MacLeod – Alistair MacLeod (Born in North Battleford, Saskatchewan, Canada ,July 20, 1936, Died in Windsor, Ontario, Canada, April 20, 2014) was a Canadian novelist, short story writer and academic. MacLeod's 1999 novel No Great Mischief was voted Atlantic Canada's greatest book of all time.[4] The novel also won several literary prizes including the 2001 International Dublin Literary Award. He has been praised for his verbal precision, his lyric intensity and his use of simple, direct language that seems rooted in an oral tradition.

Andre Gide - André Paul Guillaume Gide (born in Paris, French Empire, November 22, 1869 – February 19, 1951) was a French author and winner of the Nobel Prize in Literature (in 1947). Gide's career ranged from its beginnings in the symbolist movement, to the advent of anticolonialism between the two World Wars. He was the author of more than fifty books.

Andy Stanley - Charles Andrew Stanley (born in Atlanta, Georgia, U.S., on May 16, 1958), known as Andy Stanley, is the senior pastor of North Point Community Church, Buckhead Church, Browns Bridge Church, Gwinnett Church, Woodstock City Church, and Decatur City Church. He also founded North Point Ministries, which is a worldwide Christian organization. Stanley received a bachelor's degree in journalism from Georgia State University and later earned a master's degree from Dallas Theological Seminary.

Anthony Robbins - Anthony Jay Robbins (born as Anthony J. Mahavoric in North Hollywood, California, U.S.A., February 29, 1960) is an American author, entrepreneur, philanthropist, and life coach. Robbins is known for his infomercials, seminars, and self-help books, including "Unlimited Power" and "Awaken the Giant Within."

Anton Chekhov - Anton Pavlovich Chekhov (born in Taganrog, Ekaterinoslav Governorate, Russian Empire, January 29, 1860 – July 15, 1904) was a Russian playwright and short-story writer, who is considered to be among the greatest writers of short fiction in history. His career as a playwright produced four classics, and his best short stories are held in high esteem by writers and critics. Along with Henrik Ibsen and August Strindberg, Chekhov is often referred to as one of the three seminal figures in the birth of early modernism in the theatre. Chekhov practiced as a medical doctor throughout most of his literary career: "Medicine is my lawful wife", he once said, "and literature is my mistress."

The Greats Past & Present

Antonio Porchia - Antonio Porchia (born in Conflenti, Italy, November 13, 1885 – November 9, 1968) was an Italian-born Argentine writer. His sole book Voces ("Voices") is a collection of aphorisms.

Aristotle – Aristotle (lived 384–322 BC) was an ancient Greek philosopher and scientist born in the city of Stagira, Chalkidiki, Greece. Along with Plato, he is considered the "Father of Western Philosophy."

Arnold H. Glasgow - Arnold H. Glasgow (born as Arnold Henry Glasow in Fond du Lac, Wisconsin, U.S., died in Freeport, Illinois) was a famous Businessman from the USA, who lived between 1905 and 1998. His business was a humor magazine that he marketed to firms nationally, which firms would turn it into their "house organ" to send to their customers. He carried on this business for over 60 years, publishing his first book at age 92.

Arthur C. Clarke - Sir Arthur Charles Clarke CBE FRAS (born in Minehead, Somerset, England, United Kingdom December 19, 1917 – March 19, 2008) was a British science fiction writer, science writer and futurist, inventor, undersea explorer, and television series host. In 1961 he was awarded the Kalinga Prize, an award which is given by UNESCO for popularizing science. His other science fiction writings earned him several Hugo and Nebula awards.

Arvind Devalia - Arvind Devalia was living in London at the time I wrote this book. He is an author, blogger, coach, and social entrepreneur. He was born and raised in Kenya – and came to the UK at the age of 13 with all of his family.

Babe Ruth - George Herman "Babe" Ruth, Jr. (born in Baltimore, Maryland, U.S.A., February 6, 1895 – August 16, 1948) was an American professional baseball player whose career in Major League Baseball (MLB) spanned 22 seasons, from 1914 through 1935. Nicknamed "The Bambino" and "The Sultan of Swat", he began his MLB career as a stellar left-handed pitcher for the Boston Red Sox but achieved his greatest fame as a slugging outfielder for the New York Yankees. Ruth established many MLB batting (and some pitching) records, including career home runs (714), runs batted in (RBIs) (2,213), bases on balls (2,062), slugging percentage (.690), and on-base plus slugging (OPS) (1.164); the latter two still stand as of 2018. Ruth is regarded as one of the greatest sports heroes in American culture and is considered by many to be the greatest baseball player of all time. In 1936, Ruth was elected into the Baseball Hall of Fame as one of its "first five" inaugural members.

Barack Obama - Barack Hussein Obama II (born August 4, 1961) is an American attorney and politician who served as the 44th president of the United States from 2009 to 2017. President Barack Obama was awarded the 2009 Nobel Peace Prize for his "extraordinary efforts to strengthen international diplomacy and cooperation between people."

Benjamin Franklin - Benjamin Franklin FRS FRSE (born on Milk Street, in Boston, Massachusetts, January 17, 1706 – April 17, 1790) was an American polymath and one of the Founding Fathers of the United States. Franklin was a leading author, printer, political theorist, politician, freemason, postmaster, scientist, inventor, humorist, civic activist, statesman, and diplomat.

Betty Bender - The author is unknown, and there is no other information than that given at this time.

The Greats Past & Present

Bill Phillips - William Nathaniel Phillips (born in Golden, Colorado, U.S.A., September 23, 1964) is an American entrepreneur and author. He wrote "Body for Life: 12 Weeks to Mental and Physical Strength" with Mike D'Orso. He is also the author of "Eating for Life", and is the founder and former editor in chief of "Muscle Media" magazine and the former CEO of EAS, a performance nutritional supplement company.

Billy Connolly - Sir William Connolly, CBE (born in Glasgow, Scotland, United Kingdom, November 24, 1942) is a Scottish stand-up comedian, musician, presenter, actor, and artist. He is sometimes known, especially in his homeland, by the Scots nickname "The Big Yin" ("The Big One").

Bob Hawke - Robert James Lee Hawke, AC, GCL (born in Bordertown, South Australia, December 9, 1929) is an Australian former politician who was the 23rd Prime Minister of Australia and the Leader of the Labor Party from 1983 to 1991. He is the longest-serving Labor Party Prime Minister. Hawke remains Labor's longest-serving Prime Minister, Australia's third-longest-serving Prime Minister, and at the age of 89 years, 74 days, Hawke is the oldest living former Australian Prime Minister. Hawke is the only Australian Prime Minister to be born in South Australia, and the only one raised and educated in Western Australia.

Bonnie L. Oscarson - Bonnie Lee Oscarson (born Bonnie Lee Green in Salt Lake City, Utah, U.S.A., on October 23, 1950) was the fourteenth president of the Young Women organization of The Church of Jesus Christ of Latter-day Saints (LDS Church) from 2013 to 2018. Bonnie was called to serve by Thomas S. Monson, and at the church's April 2013 general conference, she was sustained as the new general president of the Young Women organization. Oscarson earned a bachelor's degree, with an emphasis in British and American Literature, from Brigham Young University.

Brandon Sanderson - Brandon Sanderson (born in Lincoln, Nebraska, on December 19, 1975) is an American fantasy and science fiction writer. He is best known for the Cosmere universe, in which most of his fantasy novels (most notably the "Mistborn" series and "The Stormlight Archive") are set. He is also known for finishing Robert Jordan's epic fantasy series, "The Wheel of Time."

Brian Tracy - Brian Tracy (born in Charlottetown, Prince Edward Island, Canada, January 5, 1944) is a Canadian-American motivational public speaker and self-development author.

Brigham Young - Brigham Young (born in Whitingham, Vermont, U.S.A., June 1, 1801 – August 29, 1877) was an American religious leader, politician, and settler. He was the second president of The Church of Jesus Christ of Latter-day Saints (LDS Church) from 1847 until his death in 1877. He founded Salt Lake City, and he served as the first governor of the Utah Territory. Young also led the foundings of the precursors to the University of Utah and Brigham Young University. He was called to the Quorum of the Twelve Apostles on February 14, 1835, by Oliver Cowdery, David Whitmer, and Martin Harris, known as the Three Witnesses to the Book of Mormon.

The Greats Past & Present

C. S. Lewis - Clive Staples Lewis (born in Belfast, Ireland, November 29, 1898 – November 22, 1963) was a British writer and lay theologian. He held academic positions in English literature at both Oxford University (Magdalen College, 1925–1954) and Cambridge University (Magdalene College, 1954–1963). He is best known for his works of fiction, especially *The Screwtape Letters*, and *The Chronicles of Narnia*.

Cammi Pham - Cammi Pham is a geek in stilettos. She loves building a community and pushing boundaries to optimize every aspect of life. Cammi accidentally fell into digital marketing when she founded and ran an environmental nonprofit at the age of 17. She later helped many technology startups gain traction and grow their communities online. Cammi is a Medium Top Contributor and Quora Top Writer. Her work has reached millions of views and has been translated into many different languages. Cammi has been featured in the BBC, Business Insider, Adweek, Yahoo, Lifehacker, and more. Cammi lives by her personal motto, "Learn, Unlearn, Relearn." Helping people when you don't have the skills or time will do more harm than good. You can follow her at https://www.facebook.com/cmipham

Carl B. Cook - Carl Bert Cook (born in Ogden, Utah, U.S.A. October 15, 1957) Elder Carl B. Cook was sustained as a General Authority Seventy of The Church of Jesus Christ of Latter-day Saints on April 2, 2011. He was called to serve by Thomas S. Monson. Carl was named a member of the Presidency of the Seventy on March 31, 2018. At the time of his call to the Presidency of the Seventy, he was assigned to Church headquarters.

Carlos H. Amado-. Elder Carlos Humberto Amado was born on September 25, 1944, in Guatemala City, Guatemala. He was sustained a member of the Second Quorum of the Seventy of The Church of Jesus Christ of Latter-day Saints on April 1, 1989. In June 1992, Elder Amado was called to serve in the First Quorum of the Seventy.

Catherine Pulsifer - Catherine Pulsifer worked for a large corporation for 26 years, living in Saint John, NB, in Dartmouth, NS, and in Mississauga, Ontario. In 2003 we relocated to New Brunswick, Canada. She is an author and co-author of motivational books.

Charles Haddon Spurgeon - Charles Haddon Spurgeon (born in Kelvedon, Essex, England, June 19, 1834 – January 31, 1892) was an English Particular Baptist preacher and author. His oratory skills held his listeners spellbound in the Metropolitan Tabernacle, and many Christians hold his writings in exceptionally high regard among devotional literature.

Chinese Proverb – The author is unknown, and there is no other information than that given at this time.

Christopher Paolini - Christopher James Paolini (born in Los Angeles, California, U.S.A., on November 17, 1983) is an American author. He is the author of the "Inheritance Cycle", which consists of the books "Eragon", "Eldest", "Brisingr", and "Inheritance." He lives in Paradise Valley, Montana, U.S.A., where he wrote his first book.

The Greats Past & Present

Confucius - Confucius (551–479 BC) was a Chinese teacher, editor, politician, and philosopher of the Spring and Autumn period of Chinese history. The philosophy of Confucius, also known as Confucianism, emphasized personal and governmental morality, correctness of social relationships, justice and sincerity.

Dallin H. Oaks - Dallin Harris Oaks (born in Provo, Utah, U.S.A., August 12, 1932) is an American jurist, educator, and religious leader who since 2018 has been the First Counselor in the First Presidency of The Church of Jesus Christ of Latter-day Saints (LDS Church). He was called as a member of the church's Quorum of the Twelve Apostles in 1984. After graduating from high school in 1950, he attended Brigham Young University (BYU) and graduated in 1954 with a B.S. in accounting. He then studied at the University of Chicago Law School, where he was the editor-in-chief of the *University of Chicago Law Review* and graduated in 1957 with a J.D. *cum laude*. Oaks was BYU's president from 1971 until 1980 and was then appointed to the Utah Supreme Court, on which he served until his selection to the LDS Church's Quorum of the Twelve Apostles in 1984. During his professional career, Oaks was twice considered by the U.S. president for nomination to the U.S. Supreme Court: first in 1975 by Gerald Ford, who ultimately nominated John Paul Stevens, and again in 1981 by Ronald Reagan, who ultimately nominated Sandra Day O'Connor.

David B. Haight - David Bruce Haight (born in Oakley, Idaho, September 2, 1906 – July 31, 2004) At the time of this conference Elder David B. Haight was a member of the Quorum of the Twelve Apostles in The Church of Jesus Christ of Latter-day Saints. He received a degree from Utah State University, served as a commander in the Navy during World War II, served as mayor of Palo Alto, California from 1959 to 1963, and was the owner of the Palo Alto Hardware store.

David Cameron - David William Donald Cameron (born in Marylebone, London, England October 9, 1966) is a British politician who served as Prime Minister of the United Kingdom from 2010 to 2016. He was the Member of Parliament (MP) for Witney from 2001 to 2016 and Leader of the Conservative Party from 2005 to 2016.

David F. Jakielo - Dave Jakielo, CHBME, (born on January 1, 1953) is an international speaker, consultant, executive coach, author, and is president of Seminars & Consulting (www.davespeaks.com).

David Joseph Schwartz - David Joseph Schwartz, Jr. (born in U.S.A., March 23, 1927 – December 6, 1987) was an American motivational writer and coach, best known for authoring *The Magic of Thinking Big* in 1959. He was a professor of marketing, chairman of the department, and Chair of Consumer Finance at Georgia State University.

David M. McConkie - David Merrill McConkie (born in Salt Lake City, Utah, U.S.A., October 13, 1948) is an American lawyer and has been a member of the general presidency of the Sunday School of The Church of Jesus Christ of Latter-day Saints (LDS Church) from 2009 to 2014.

Dave Willis – Author, pastor, Encourager. See Dave Wills on Facebook.com Web site: https://www.facebook.com/davewillis78 or DaveWillis.org.

The Greats Past & Present

Denis Waitley - Denis E. Waitley (born in San Diego, California, U.S.A., 1933), is an American motivational speaker, writer, and consultant. He has been recognized as the best-selling author of the audio series, The Psychology of Winning and books such as "Seeds of Greatness" and "The Winner's Edge." Waitley has been inducted into the International Speakers' Hall of Fame.

Denis M. Wagner III. He is the grandson of Gerald L. Penhollow. Denis contributed his personal quotes to support this book and helped in the editing.

Dieter F. Uchtdorf - Dieter Friedrich Uchtdorf (born in Mährisch-Ostrau, Protectorate of Bohemia and Moravia (now Ostrava, Czech Republic) November 6, 1940) is a German aviator, airline executive, and religious leader. At the time of this conference, he was serving as Second Counselor in the First Presidency of the Church of Jesus Christ of Latter-day Saints. He served as Second Counselor in the First Presidency to Thomas S. Monson from February 3, 2008 – January 2, 2018. Dieter F. Uchtdorf was ordained an apostle on 7 October 2004 by church president Gordon B. Hinckley.

Don Zimmer - Donald William Zimmer (born in Cincinnati, Ohio, U.S.A., January 17, 1931 – June 4, 2014) was an American infielder, manager, and coach in Major League Baseball (MLB). Zimmer was involved in professional baseball from 1949 until his death, a span of 65 years.

Donald L. Staheli - Donald Lafayette Staheli (born in St. George, Utah, U.S.A., October 19, 1931 – May 29, 2010) was an American business executive and was a general authority of The Church of Jesus Christ of Latter-day Saints (LDS Church) from 1997 to 2006. He served in the LDS Church as the first president of the Draper Utah Temple from its dedication in March 2009 until his death on May 29, 2010. He received a B.S. degree from Utah State University, followed by M.S. and Ph.D. degrees from the University of Illinois. He also served for two years in the United States Air Force. Staheli was the CEO of Allied Mills and then CEO of Continental Grain. He was the CEO of Continental Grain and the chair of the U.S.–China Business Council at the time of his call as a general authority. He was also an advisor to the mayor of Shanghai, Zhu Rongji.

Donny Osmond - Donald Clark Osmond was born on December 9, 1957, in Ogden, Utah is an American singer, dancer, actor, and former teen idol. Osmond has also been a talk and game show host, record producer, and author.

Dr. Norman Vincent Peale - Norman Vincent Peale (born in Bowersville, Ohio, U.S.A., May 31, 1898 – December 24, 1993) was an American minister and author known for his work in popularizing the concept of positive thinking.

Dudley Nichols - Dudley Nichols (born in Los Angeles, California, U.S.A., April 6, 1895 – January 4, 1960) was an American screenwriter and director.

Duke Ellington - Edward Kennedy "Duke" Ellington (born in Washington, D.C., U.S.A., April 29, 1899 – May 24, 1974) was an American composer, pianist, and leader of a jazz orchestra, which he led from 1923 until his death over a career spanning more than fifty years. He was awarded a posthumous Pulitzer Prize Special Award for music in 1999.

The Greats Past & Present

Dwight D. Eisenhower - Dwight David Eisenhower, nicknamed "Ike", was born David Dwight Eisenhower (born in Denison, Texas, U.S.A., October 14, 1890 – March 28, 1969). He was an American army general and statesman who served as the 34th president of the United States from 1953 to 1961. During World War II, he was a five-star general in the United States Army and served as supreme commander of the Allied Expeditionary Forces in Europe. He was responsible for planning and supervising the invasion of North Africa in Operation Torch in 1942–43 and the successful invasion of France and Germany in 1944–45 from the Western Front.

Earl Nightingale - Earl Nightingale (Born in Los Angeles, California, U.S.A., March 12, 1921 – March 25, 1989) was an American radio speaker and author, dealing mostly with the subjects of human character development, motivation, and meaningful existence.

Ed McMahon - Edward Leo Peter McMahon, Jr. (Born in Detroit, Michigan, U.S.A., March 6, 1923 – June 23, 2009) was an American announcer, game show host, comedian, actor, and singer. McMahon and Johnny Carson began their association in their first TV series, the ABC game show "Who Do You Trust?", running from 1957 to 1962. Then afterwards, McMahon would make his famous thirty-year mark as Carson's sidekick, announcer, and second banana on NBC's "The Tonight Show Starring Johnny Carson" from 1962 to 1992.

Edmund Hilary - Sir Edmund Percival Hillary KG ONZ KBE (born in Auckland City Hospital, Auckland, New Zealand, July 20, 1919 – January 11, 2008) was a New Zealand mountaineer, explorer, and philanthropist. On 29 May 1953, Hillary and Nepalese Sherpa mountaineer Tenzing Norgay became the first climbers confirmed to have reached the summit of Mount Everest. They were part of the ninth British expedition to Everest, led by John Hunt. Hillary had numerous honors conferred upon him, including the Order of the Garter in 1995. Upon his death in 2008, he was given a state funeral in New Zealand.

Elbert Hubbard - Elbert Green Hubbard (born in Bloomington, Illinois, U.S.A., June 19, 1856 – May 7, 1915) was an American writer, publisher, artist, and philosopher. He and his second wife, Alice Moore Hubbard, died aboard the RMS *Lusitania* when it was sunk by a German submarine off the coast of Ireland on May 7, 1915.

Eleanor Roosevelt - Anna Eleanor Roosevelt (born in Manhattan, New York City, New York, U.S.A., October 11, 1884 – November 7, 1962) was an American political figure, diplomat, and activist. She served as the First Lady of the United States from March 4, 1933, to April 12, 1945, during her husband President Franklin D. Roosevelt's four terms in office, making her the longest-serving First Lady of the United States.

Ernest Agyemang Yeboah - Ernest Agyemang Yeboah is a Ghanaian born writer. His books depict the essence, reasons, and realities of life. He is currently a teacher in Accra - Ghana, Writer, and a CA student. He attended the Presbyterian College of Education, Akropong -Akuapim-Ghana, and the University of Education, Winneba- Ghana.

The Greats Past & Present

Ernest Hemingway - Ernest Miller Hemingway (born in Oak Park, Illinois, U.S.A., July 21, 1899 – July 2, 1961) was an American journalist, novelist, and short-story writer. His economical and understated style—which he termed the iceberg theory—had a strong influence on 20th-century fiction, while his adventurous lifestyle and his public image brought him admiration from later generations. Hemingway produced most of his work between the mid-1920s and the mid-1950s, and he won the Nobel Prize in Literature in 1954. He published seven novels, six short-story collections, and two non-fiction works.

Ezra Taft Benson - Ezra Taft Benson (born on a farm in Whitney, Idaho, U.S.A., August 4, 1899 – May 30, 1994) was an American farmer, government official, and religious leader who served as the 15th United States Secretary of Agriculture during both presidential terms of Dwight D. Eisenhower and as the 13th president of The Church of Jesus Christ of Latter-day Saints (LDS Church) from 1985 until his death in 1994. He received his priesthood calling to the Quorum of the Twelve Apostles in the LDS Church from Heber Grant. Ezra received his bachelor's degree from Brigham Young University in 1926, received a master of science degree in agricultural economics in 1927 from Iowa State University, and did preliminary work on a doctorate at the University of California at Berkeley, but never completed it.

Franklin Roosevelt - Franklin Delano Roosevelt (born in Hyde Park, New York, U.S.A., January 30, 1882 – April 12, 1945), often referred to by his initials FDR, was an American statesman and political leader who served as the 32nd president of the United States from 1933 until his death in 1945.

G.M. Trevelyan - George Macaulay Trevelyan OM CBE FRS FBA (born in Stratford-upon-Avon, Warwickshire, England February 16, 1876 – July 21, 1962), was a British historian and academic. He was a Fellow of Trinity College, Cambridge, from 1898 to 1903. He then spent more than twenty years as a full-time author. He returned to the University of Cambridge and was Regius Professor of History from 1927 to 1943. He served as Master of Trinity College from 1940 to 1951. In retirement, he was Chancellor of Durham University.

Geoffrey F. Abert - Geoffrey F. Abert was an author. He wrote the book "After the Crash," which was published in 1980.

Gerald L. Penhollow – Gerald Leon Penhollow is also known by the name Jerry Penhollow, (born in Prairie du Chien, Wisconsin, U.S.A., on March 21, 1955) is the author of this book. He has written other unpublished works such as "Stories From the Heart: Of a Child."

George Bernard Shaw - George Bernard Shaw (born at 3 Upper Synge Street in Portobello, a lower-middle-class part of Dublin, Ireland, July 26, 1856 – November 2, 1950), was known at his insistence simply as Bernard Shaw, was an Irish playwright, critic, polemicist, and political activist. Shaw became the leading dramatist of his generation, and in 1925 was awarded the Nobel Prize in Literature.

The Greats Past & Present

George Krueger - George Krueger is Co-Founder, BIGG Success, Home of The Financial Freedom Tool | Helping good people have more money to do more good. As of March 2019, he lived in Champaign, Illinois, U.S.A. Krueger is teaching at Adjunct Lecturer - Entrepreneurial Finance, University of Illinois at Urbana-Champaign, since January 1995. He teaches seniors in Finance and Entrepreneurship, along with Accounting graduate students. Krueger received his education from Gies College of Business - University of Illinois Urbana-Champaign, and University of Illinois at Urbana-Champaign, Degree Name BS Business Field Of Study Entrepreneurship, Corporate Finance, Investments, Real Estate, Accounting.

George P. Lee - George Patrick Lee (Born in Towaoc, Colorado, U.S.A. March 23, 1943 – July 28, 2010) was the first Native American to become a general authority of The Church of Jesus Christ of Latter-day Saints (LDS Church). He was a member of the church's First Quorum of Seventy from 1975 to 1989, when he was excommunicated from the church.

George Washington - George Washington (born in Popes Creek, Colony of Virginia, British America, February 22, 1732, December 14, 1799) was an American political leader, military general, statesman, and Founding Father of the United States, who also served as the first president of the United States (1789–1797). Washington commanded Patriot forces in the new nation's vital American Revolutionary War and led them to victory over the British. Washington also presided at the Constitutional Convention of 1787, which established the new federal government. For his manifold leadership during the American Revolution, he has been called the "Father of His Country."

Gordon B. Hinckley - Gordon Bitner Hinckley (born in Salt Lake City, Utah, U.S.A., June 23, 1910 – January 27, 2008) was an American religious leader and author. President Gordon B. Hinckley served as the 15th President of the Church of Jesus Christ of Latter-day Saints (LDS Church) and server as president from March 12, 1995, thru January 27, 2008. He was sustained to the Quorum of the Twelve in the LDS Church on October 4, 1986, and ordained an apostle on October 5, 1951, by David O. McKay. He is considered a Prophet, Seer, and Revelator by the church members.

H. Jackson Brown, Jr. - Harriett Jackson Brown, Jr. (born in Middle, Tennessee, U.S.A., in 1940) is an American author best known for his inspirational book, "Life's Little Instruction Book", which was a *New York Times* bestseller (1991–1994). Its sequel "Life's Little Instruction Book: Volume 2" also made it to the same bestseller list in 1993.

H. L. Hunt - Haroldson Lafayette Hunt, Jr. (born in Ramsey, Illinois, U.S.A., February 17, 1889 – November 29, 1974), known throughout his life as H. L. Hunt, was a Texas oil tycoon and conservative Republican political activist.

The Greats Past & Present

Harold B Lee - Harold Bingham Lee (born in Clifton, Idaho, U.S.A., March 28, 1899 – December 26, 1973) was an American religious leader and educator who served as the 11th president of The Church of Jesus Christ of Latter-day Saints (LDS Church) from July 1972 until his death on December 1973. Lee was called by Heber J. Grant as a member of the LDS Church's Quorum of the Twelve Apostles on April 10, 1941, and served in that position for nearly 32 years, and was the quorum president from January 23, 1970, to July 7, 1972. Harold B. Lee became the LDS Church's president on January 23, 1972. He is accepted by the church as a prophet, seer, and revelator.

Helen Keller - Helen Adams Keller (born in Tuscumbia, Alabama, U.S.A., June 27, 1880 – June 1, 1968) was an American author, political activist, and lecturer. She was the first deaf-blind person to earn a bachelor of arts degree.

Henry B. Eyring - Henry Bennion Eyring (born in Princeton, New Jersey, U.S.A., May 31, 1933) is an American educational administrator, author, and religious leader. Eyring was called by Gordon B. Hinckley to the Quorum of the Twelve Apostles of The Church of Jesus Christ of Latter-day Saints (LDS Church) on April 1, 1995, and ordained an apostle later that week. President Eyring was president of Ricks College in Rexburg, Idaho, from 1971 to 1977. He was on the faculty at the Graduate School of Business at Stanford University from 1962 to 1971. He holds a B.S. degree in physics from the University of Utah and a master of business administration and doctor of business administration degrees from Harvard University.

Henry D. Taylor - Henry Dixon Taylor (born in Provo, Utah, U.S.A., November 22, 1903 – February 24, 1987) was a general authority of The Church of Jesus Christ of Latter-day Saints (LDS Church) from 1958 until his death. Taylor received a bachelor's degree from Brigham Young University (BYU) and a master's degree from New York University. For most of his life, he was employed by his family's mercantile business, Dixon–Taylor–Russell Home Furnishers in Utah County. Taylor died in Salt Lake City, Utah, and was buried in Provo.

Henry Ford - Henry Ford (born in Greenfield Township, Michigan, U.S., July 30, 1863 – April 7, 1947) was an American captain of industry and a business magnate, the founder of the Ford Motor Company, and the sponsor of the development of the assembly line technique of mass production.

Henry Louis Mencken - Henry Louis Mencken (born in Baltimore, Maryland, U.S.A., September 12, 1880 – January 29, 1956) was an American journalist, essayist, satirist, cultural critic, and scholar of American English.

Henry Wadsworth Longfellow - Henry Wadsworth Longfellow (born in Portland, Maine, U.S.A., February 27, 1807 – March 24, 1882) was an American poet and educator.

Herbert G. Lingren - There is no other information on the author than that given at this time.

The Greats Past & Present

Howard W. Hunter - Howard William Hunter (born in Boise, Idaho, U.S.A., November 14, 1907 – March 3, 1995) was an American lawyer and was the 14th president of The Church of Jesus Christ of Latter-day Saints (LDS Church) from 1994 to 1995. His nine-month presidential tenure is the shortest in the church's history. Hunter was the first president of the LDS Church born in the 20th century and the last to die in it. He was sustained as an LDS apostle at the age of 51 and served as a general authority for over 35 years. He was called as an Apostle for the LDS Church by David O. McKay on October 10, 1985.

Hunter S. Thompson - Hunter Stockton Thompson (born in Louisville, Kentucky, U.S. July 18, 1937 – February 20, 2005) was an American journalist and author, and the founder of the gonzo journalism movement. He first rose to prominence with the publication of "Hell's Angels" (1967), a book about the Hells Angels motorcycle gang for which he spent a year living and riding with in order to write a first-hand account of its members.

Ian S. Ardern - Ian Sidney Ardern (born in Te Aroha, New Zealand, February 28, 1954) received a bachelor's degree in education in 1982 and a master's degree in education from the University of Waikato in New Zealand in 1994. Ian S. Ardern was sustained as a General Authority Seventy of The Church of Jesus Christ of Latter-day Saints on April 2, 2011.

Indian Proverb - The author is unknown, and there is no other information than that given at this time.

Inside Out – Inside Out is a 2015 American 3D computer-animated comedy-drama film produced by Pixar Animation Studios and released by Walt Disney Pictures. The film was directed by Pete Docter and co-directed by Ronnie del Carmen, with a screenplay written by Docter, Meg LeFauve and Josh Cooley, adapted from a story by Docter and del Carmen. The film is set in the mind of a young girl named Riley Andersen (Kaitlyn Dias), where five personified emotions—Joy (Amy Poehler), Sadness (Phyllis Smith), Anger (Lewis Black), Fear (Bill Hader) and Disgust (Mindy Kaling)—try to lead her through life as she and her parents (Diane Lane and Kyle MacLachlan) adjust to their new surroundings after moving from Minnesota to San Francisco.

Ivy Baker Priest - Ivy Baker Priest (born in Kimberly, Utah, U.S.A., September 7, 1905 – June 23, 1975) was Treasurer of the United States from 1953 to 1961 and California State Treasurer from 1967 to 1975.

J. K. Rowling - Joanne Rowling CH, OBE, FRSL, FRCPE, FRSE, (born in Yate, Gloucestershire, England, July 31, 1965), writing under the pen names J. K. Rowling and Robert Galbraith, is a British novelist, philanthropist, film producer, television producer and screenwriter, best known for writing the *Harry Potter* fantasy series.

J. Richard Clarke - John Richard Clarke (born in Rexburg, Idaho, U.S.A., April 4, 1927) has been a general authority of The Church of Jesus Christ of Latter-day Saints (LDS Church) since 1976. He has been a member of the church's presiding bishopric and a member of the Presidency of the Seventy.

James Allen - James Allen (born in Leicester, England, United Kingdom, November 28, 1864 – January 24, 1912) was a British philosophical writer known for his inspirational books and poetry and as a pioneer of the self-help movement. His best-known work is, "As a Man Thinketh."

The Greats Past & Present

James E. Faust - James Esdras Faust (born in Delta, Utah, U.S.A., July 31, 1920 – August 10, 2007) was an American religious leader, lawyer, and politician. Faust was Second Counselor in the First Presidency of The Church of Jesus Christ of Latter-day Saints (LDS Church) from 1995 until his death, an LDS Church apostle for 29 years, and a general authority of the church for 35 years.

James W. Frick - James W. Frick (born in New Bern, North Carolina, U.S.A., August 5, 1924 – April 9, 2014) was the former vice president for public relations, alumni affairs, and development at the University of Notre Dame. He served in the U.S. Navy during World War II before enrolling in Notre Dame as a 23-year-old freshman, working part-time in the University's development office — then called the Notre Dame Foundation — before his graduation in 1951. He became the first administrator in Notre Dame's history to engage exclusively in development work. He was appointed Notre Dame's director of development in 1961 and four years later elected vice president for public relations and development, the first lay officer in the University's history.

Jay Leno - James Douglas Muir "Jay" Leno (born in New Rochelle, New York, U.S.A. on April 28, 1950) is an American comedian, actor, writer, producer, and television host. After doing stand-up comedy for years, he became the host of NBC's *"The Tonight Show with Jay Leno"* from 1992–2009.

Jean-Jacques Rousseau - Jean-Jacques Rousseau (born in Geneva, Republic of Geneva, June 28, 1712 – July 2, 1778) was a Genevan philosopher, writer, and composer. His political philosophy influenced the progress of the Enlightenment throughout Europe, as well as aspects of the French Revolution and the development of modern political and educational thought.

Jerry Bridges – Jerry Bridges (born in Tyler, Texas, U.S.A., December 4, 1929 – March 6, 2016) was an evangelical Christian author, speaker, and staff member of The Navigators. Born in Tyler, Texas, United States, he was the author of more than a dozen books, including "The Pursuit of Holiness," which has sold more than one million copies. His devotional "Holiness Day By Day" garnered the 2009 ECPA Christian Book Award for the inspiration and gift category.

Jesse Jackson - Jesse Louis Jackson Sr. (born in Greenville, South Carolina, U.S.A., October 8, 1941) is an American civil rights activist, Baptist minister, and politician. He was a candidate for the Democratic presidential nomination in 1984 and 1988 and served as a shadow U.S. Senator for the District of Columbia from 1991 to 1997.

Jim Rohn - Emanuel James "Jim" Rohn (born in Yakima, Washington, U.S.A., September 17, 1930 – December 5, 2009) was an American entrepreneur, author, and motivational speaker. Rohn was the recipient of the 1985 National Speakers Association CPAE Award for excellence in speaking. He is also the author of 17 different written, audio, and video media, including "The Power of Ambition", "Take Charge of Your Life", and "The Day That Turns Your Life Around."

The Greats Past & Present

Joan D. Vinge - Joan D. Vinge (born Joan Carol Dennison in Baltimore, Maryland, U.S.A., April 2, 1948) is an American science fiction author. She is known for such works as her Hugo Award-winning novel "The Snow Queen" and its sequels.

Joe Lo Truglio - Joseph Lo Truglio (born in Queens, New York City, New York, U.S.A., December 2, 1970) is an American actor, comedian, and writer best known for his role as Charles Boyle on the NBC sitcom "Brooklyn Nine-Nine."

Johann Wolfgang Von Goethe - Johann Wolfgang von Goethe (born in Free Imperial City of Frankfurt, Holy Roman Empire (a free state within Germany), August 28, 1749 – March 22, 1832) was a German writer and statesman. His works include four novels; epic and lyric poetry; prose and verse dramas; memoirs; an autobiography; literary and aesthetic criticism; and treatises on botany, anatomy, and colour. In addition, there are numerous literary and scientific fragments, more than 10,000 letters, and nearly 3,000 drawings by him extant.

John A. Green - John Alden Green (born in Cardston, Alberta, Canada, November 4, 1925 – February 4, 2001) was a professor of French at Brigham Young University and father of nine children, lived in Orem, Utah. Green studied the writings of the French author, Marcel Schwob, related to the Dreyfus Affair (French military scandal, 1894-1906.) In 1980, Green suffered a stroke and never permanently recovered.

John Adams - John Adams (born in Braintree, Massachusetts Bay, British America, October 30, 1735[a] – July 4, 1826) was an American statesman, attorney, diplomat, writer, and Founding Father who served as the second president of the United States from 1797 to 1801. Before his presidency, he served as the first vice president of the United States from 1789 to 1797. He was a leader of American independence from Great Britain. Adams was a dedicated diarist, and correspondent with his wife and adviser Abigail, recording important historical information on the era.

John Bartlett - John Bartlett (also John Barlet was born in Norwalk, Connecticut Colony, October 5, 1677 – August 5, 1761) was a member of the Connecticut House of Representatives from Norwalk, Connecticut Colony in the May 1718 session.

John F. Kennedy - John Fitzgerald "Jack" Kennedy (born in Brookline, Massachusetts, U.S.A., May 29, 1917 – November 22, 1963), commonly referred to by his initials JFK, was an American politician and journalist who served as the 35th president of the United States from January 1961 until his assassination in November 1963.

John Kramer Blythe - John Kramer Blythe (born in Las Cruces, New Mexico, U.S.A. in 1965). He is a religious author for the books "Blythe" and "The Jesus Boy" both can be found on Goodreads.com.

John Quincy Adams - John Quincy Adams (born in Braintree, Massachusetts Bay, British America (now Quincy, Massachusetts, U.S.) July 11, 1767 – February 23, 1848) was an American statesman who served as the sixth president of the United States from 1825 to 1829. He served as the eighth United States secretary of state immediately before becoming president. During his long diplomatic and political career, Adams also served as an ambassador and represented Massachusetts

The Greats Past & Present

John Wooden - John Robert Wooden (born in Hall, Indiana, U.S.A., October 14, 1910 – June 4, 2010) was an American basketball player and head coach at the University of California, Los Angeles. Nicknamed the "Wizard of Westwood," he won ten NCAA national championships in a 12-year period as head coach at UCLA, including a record seven in a row. No other team has won more than four in a row in Division 1 college men's or women's basketball. Wooden won the prestigious Henry Iba Award as national coach of the year a record seven times and won the AP award five times. He also won a Helms national championship (which was decided by a poll) at Purdue as a player 1931–1932 for a total of 10 NCAA Titles and 1 Helms Championships (which doesn't count as an NCAA title). He is considered one of the most revered coaches in the history of sports.

Joseph B. Wirthlin - Joseph B. Wirthlin (born in Salt Lake City, Utah, U.S.A., June 11, 1917 – December 1, 2008) was an American businessman, and at the time of this conference was serving as a member of the Quorum of the Twelve Apostles Church of Jesus Christ of Latter-day Saints. He was sustained to the Twelve on October 4, 1986, and ordained an apostle on October 9, 1986, by Thomas S. Monson.

Joseph de Maistre - Joseph-Marie, Comte de Maistre (born in Chambéry, Kingdom of Sardinia, Duchy of Savoy, April 1, 1753 – February 26, 1821) was a French-speaking Savoyard philosopher, writer, lawyer, and diplomat, who advocated social hierarchy and monarchy in the period immediately following the French Revolution.

Joseph Smith - Joseph Smith, Jr. (born in Sharon, Vermont, U.S.A., December 23, 1805 – June 27, 1844) was an American religious leader and founder of the Church of Jesus Christ of Latter-day Saints. Joseph served as the 1st President of the Church of Jesus Christ of Latter-day Saints. He is considered a Prophet, Seer, and Revelator by the church members.

Julus Renard - Pierre-Jules Renard or Jules Renard (born in Châlons-du-Maine, Mayenne, France on February 22, 1864 – May 22, 1910) was a French author and member of the Académie Goncourt, most famous for the works Poil de carotte (Carrot Top, 1894) and Les Histoires Naturelles (Nature Stories, 1896). Among his other works are Le Plaisir de rompre (The Pleasure of Breaking, 1898) and the posthumously published Huit Jours à la campagne (A Week in the Country, 1912).

Kathy Seligman - Kathy A. Seligman was born on June 29, 1949. She died on April 27, 2011, at 61 years of age.

Kenneth A. Wells - The author is unknown, and there is no other information than that given at this time.

Kenneth E. Hagin - Kenneth Erwin Hagin (born in Tulsa, Oklahoma, U.S., August 20, 1917 – September 19, 2003) was an American preacher. Hagin founded 'RHEMA Bible Training College' (RBTC) in 1974. On May 20, 1994, Hagin received an Honorary Doctor of Divinity Degree from Faith Theological Seminary in Tampa, Florida.

The Greats Past & Present

Kerry Stokes - Kerry Matthew Stokes, AC (born John Patrick Alford in Melbourne, Victoria, Australia on September 13, 1940) is an Australian businessman. He holds business interests in a diverse range of industries, including electronic and print media, property, mining, and construction equipment. He is most widely known as the chairman of the Seven Network, one of the largest broadcast repeating corporations in Australia. He was invested as a Companion in the General Division of the Order of Australia (AC) in recognition of his contributions to Australian business.

Kevin W. Pearson - Kevin Wayne Pearson (born in Salt Lake City, Utah, on April 10, 1957) was sustained as a General Authority Seventy of The Church of Jesus Christ of Latter-day Saints (LDS Church) on April 5, 2008. He was previously CEO of Ingenix, Inc. (1998-2005) and Mission President of the LDS Church Washington Tacoma Mission. As a young man, Pearson was an LDS Church full-time missionary in the Finland Helsinki Mission. He received a bachelor's degree in finance from the University of Utah and an MBA from Harvard Business School.

Khwāja Shams-ud-Dīn Muḥammad Ḥāfeẓ-e Shīrāzī, or "Hafiz" - Khwāja Shams-ud-Dīn Muḥammad Ḥāfeẓ-e Shīrāzī known by his pen name Hafez (*Ḥāfeẓ* 'the memorizer; the (safe) keeper'; born 1315 in Shiraz, Fars and died 1390) and as "Hafiz", was a Persian poet who "lauded the joys of love and wine but also targeted religious hypocrisy." His collected works are regarded as a pinnacle of Persian literature.

L. Tom Perry - Lowell Tom Perry (Born in Logan, Utah, United States on August 5, 1922 – May 30, 2015) was an American businessman and religious leader who was a member of the Quorum of the Twelve Apostles of The Church of Jesus Christ of Latter-day Saints (LDS Church) from 1974 until his death. Perry graduated from the Utah State Agricultural College (now Utah State University (USU)) in 1949 with a bachelor's degree in finance.

Lao Tzu - Laozi (born 604 BC and died 531 BC (age 67) (literally "Old Master"; also rendered as Lao Tzu)) was an ancient Chinese philosopher and writer. He is the reputed author of the *Tao Te Ching*, the founder of philosophical Taoism, and a deity in religious Taoism and traditional Chinese religions.

Larry K. Langlois, Ph.D. - Larry Kent Langlois, Ph.D. – NPI #1972720506, was born June 20, 1940, and is a healthcare provider in Salt Lake City, Utah. The provider is a marriage and family therapist is a person with a master's degree in marriage and family therapy, or a master's or doctoral degree in a related mental health field with substantially equivalent coursework in marriage and family therapy, who receives supervised clinical experience, or a person who meets the state requirements to practice as a marriage and family therapist—retrieved February 10, 2019, from 'Health Providers Data' Web site: https://healthprovidersdata.com/hipaa/codes/NPI-1972720506-dr-larry-kent-langlois-phd.

Laura Ingalls Wilder - Laura Elizabeth Ingalls Wilder (born in Pepin County, Wisconsin, U.S. February 7, 1867 – February 10, 1957) was an American writer known for the "Little House on the Prairie" series of children's books, published between 1932 and 1943, which were based on her childhood in a settler and pioneer family.

The Greats Past & Present

Leo Babauta - Leo Babauta (born April 30, 1973), a blogger, journalist, and author from the United States territory of Guam, who currently lives in Davis, California, U.S. Leo Babauta is the creator of the Blog Site Zen Habits that was launched February 2007.

Leo Christopher – Leo Christopher is a writer and poet, and is the author of the book "Sleeping in Chairs" Published October 16th, 2015 by Underwater Mountains, ISBN - 1682410056.

Leo Tolstoy - Count Lev Nikolayevich Tolstoy (born in Yasnaya Polyana, Tula Governorate, Russian Empire, September 9, 1828 – November 20, 1910), usually referred to in English as Leo Tolstoy was born Lev Nikolaevich Tolstoy, was a Russian writer who is regarded as one of the greatest authors of all time. He is best known for the novels *War and Peace* (1869) and *Anna Karenina* (1877).

Leonard Swett - Leonard Swett (born in Turner, Maine, U.S.A. August 11, 1825 – June 8, 1889) was a civil and criminal lawyer who advised and assisted Abraham Lincoln throughout the president's political career.

Lillian Russell - Lillian Russell (born in Clinton, Iowa, U.S.A., December 4, 1860/1861 – June 6, 1922), born Helen Louise Leonard, was an American actress and singer. She became one of the most famous actresses and singers of the late 19th and early 20th centuries, known for her beauty and style, as well as for her voice and stage presence.

Lori Deschene - Lori Deschene is the author of Tiny Buddha: Simple Wisdom for Life's Hard Questions and Tiny Buddha's Guide to Loving Yourself. She has presented at the Wisdom 2.0 Conference, and her writing has been featured in Good Housekeeping, Cosmopolitan, Shambhala Sun, Tricycle: The Buddhist Review, and Chicken Soup for the Soul. Lori lives in San Mateo, California.

Lyman Beecher - Lyman Beecher (Born in New Haven, Connecticut Colony (now Connecticut, U.S.A.), October 12, 1775 – January 10, 1863) was a Presbyterian minister, American Temperance Society co-founder and leader.

Madonna Louise Ciccone - (born in Bay City, Michigan, U.S.A., on August 16, 1958) is an American singer-songwriter, actress, and businesswoman. Referred to as the "Queen of Pop" since the 1980s, Madonna is known for pushing the boundaries of songwriting in mainstream popular music and for the imagery she uses onstage and in music videos. Madonna is often cited as an influence by other artists.

Mahatma Gandhi - Mohandas Karamchand Gandhi (October 2, 1869 – January 30, 1948), commonly known as Mahatma Gandhi, was the preeminent leader of Indian nationalism in British-ruled India. Employing non-violent civil disobedience, Gandhi led India to independence and inspired movements for non-violence, civil rights, and freedom across the world. Gandhi was a prolific writer. He was born in Porbandar (also known as *Sudamapuri*), a coastal town on the Kathiawar Peninsula, and then part of the small princely state of Porbandar in the Kathiawar Agency of the Indian Empire, present-day is called Gujarat, India.

Matthew Henry - Matthew Henry (Born in Flintshire, Wales, October 18, 1662 , Died June 22 1714 in Cheshire, England) was a nonconformist minister

The Greats Past & Present

and author, born in Wales but spending much of his life in England. He is best known for the six-volume biblical commentary Exposition of the Old and New Testaments.

Marcus Geduld - Marcus Geduld is a Shakespearean director, computer programmer, teacher, writer, likes dinosaurs. Studied at School of Theatre at Ohio University. He was born in 1970 and was living in Atlanta, Georgia, U.S.A., at the time this book was written.

Marcus Garvey - Marcus Mosiah Garvey, Jr. ONH (born in Saint Ann's Bay, Jamaica, August 17, 1887 – June 10, 1940) was a Jamaican-born political leader, publisher, journalist, entrepreneur, and orator. He was President-General of the Universal Negro Improvement Association and African Communities League (UNIA-ACL). He also was President and one of the directors of the Black Star Line, a shipping and passenger line incorporated in Delaware. The Black Star Line went bankrupt, and Garvey was imprisoned for mail fraud in the selling of its stock. His movement then rapidly collapsed.

Marion G. Romney - Marion George Romney (born in Colonia Juárez, Chihuahua, Mexico, September 19, 1897 – May 20, 1988) was an apostle and a member of the First Presidency of The Church of Jesus Christ of Latter-day Saints (LDS Church). Romney received his bachelor's degree at the University of Utah, in political science and history in 1926.

Mark E Petersen - Mark Edward Petersen (born in Salt Lake City, Utah, U.S.A., November 7, 1900 – January 11, 1984) was an American news editor and religious leader who served as a member of the Quorum of the Twelve Apostles of The Church of Jesus Christ of Latter-day Saints (LDS Church) from 1944 until his death.

Mark Twain - Samuel Langhorne Clemens (born in Florida, Missouri, U.S.A., November 30, 1835 – April 21, 1910). Born in Florida, Missouri He is better known by his pen name Mark Twain, was an American writer, humorist, entrepreneur, publisher, and lecturer. Among his novels are "The Adventures of Tom Sawyer" (1876) and its sequel, the "Adventures of Huckleberry Finn" (1885), the latter often called "The Great American Novel."

Martin Luther King, Jr. - Martin Luther King, Jr. (born in Atlanta, Georgia, U.S.A., January 15, 1929 – April 4, 1968) was an American Baptist minister and activist who became the most visible spokesperson and leader in the civil rights movement from 1954 until his assassination in 1968. King is best known for advancing civil rights through nonviolence, and civil disobedience, tactics his Christian beliefs, and the nonviolent activism of Mahatma Gandhi helped inspire. King was posthumously awarded the Presidential Medal of Freedom and the Congressional Gold Medal.

Marvin J. Ashton - Marvin Jeremy Ashton (born in Salt Lake City, Utah, U.S.A., May 6, 1915 – February 25, 1994) was a member of the Quorum of the Twelve Apostles of The Church of Jesus Christ of Latter-day Saints and was ordained an apostle on December 2, 1971,, he served in that church position until his death.

The Greats Past & Present

Mary Ellen Smoot - Mary Ellen Wood Smoot (born in Ogden, Utah, U.S.A., August 19, 1933) was the thirteenth Relief Society General President of The Church of Jesus Christ of Latter-day Saints (LDS Church) from 1997 to 2002. Mary Ellen Smoot holds a Juris Doctorate from Brigham Young University, a master's degree in Management Science from Stanford University, a bachelor's degree in Political Science from Utah State University, and an associate degree in Arts and Sciences from Ricks College.

Mary-Lynn Foster - Mary-Lynn Foster is Co-Founder, BIGG Success, Home of The Financial Freedom Tool | Helping good people have more money to do more good. She received her education from Illinois Wesleyan University from 1989 - 1991. As of March 2019, she lived in Champaign, Illinois, U.S.A..

Mary Kay Ash - Mary Kay Ash, birth name was Mary Kathlyn Wagner (born in Hot Wells, Harris County, Texas, May 12, 1918 - November 22, 2001) was the founder of Mary Kay Cosmetics. Both during her life and posthumously, Ash received numerous honors from business groups, including the Horatio Alger Award. Ash was inducted into the Junior Achievement U.S. Business Hall of Fame in 1996. Her most recent acknowledgments were the "Equal Justice Award" from Legal Services of North Texas in 2001, and "Most Outstanding Woman in Business in the 20th Century" from Lifetime Television in 1999.

Max De Pree - Max De Pree (Born in Zeeland, Michigan, U.S.A., October 28, 1924 – August 8, 2017) was an American businessman and writer.

Melvin Russell Ballard - M. Russell Ballard, Jr. (born in Salt Lake City, Utah, U.S.A., October 8, 1928) is an American businessman and religious leader who is currently the Acting President of the Quorum of the Twelve Apostles of The Church of Jesus Christ of Latter-day Saints (LDS Church). He has been a member of the church's Quorum of the Twelve Apostles since 1985. As a member of the Quorum of the Twelve, Ballard is accepted by church members as a prophet, seer, and revelator. Currently, he is the third most senior apostle in the church.

Michel de Montaigne - Michel Eyquem de Montaigne, Lord of Montaigne (born in Château de Montaigne, Guyenne, Kingdom of France, February 28, 1533 – September 13, 1592), was one of the most significant philosophers of the French Renaissance, known for popularizing the essay as a literary genre. His work is noted for its merging of casual anecdotes and autobiography with intellectual insight. His massive volume "Essais" contains some of the most influential essays ever written. He is most famously known for his skeptical remark, "*Que sçay-je?*" ("What do I know?", in Middle French; now rendered as "*Que sais-je?*" in modern French). During his lifetime, Montaigne was admired more as a statesman than as an author.

Michael Pritchard - The author is unknown, and there is no other information than that given at this time.

Mike Farrell - Michael Joseph Farrell, Jr. (born in Saint Paul, Minnesota, U.S. February 6, 1939) is an American actor, best known for his role as Captain B.J. Hunnicutt on the television series *M*A*S*H* (1975–83). He is also an activist and public speaker for various political causes.

The Greats Past & Present

Morgan Freeman - Morgan Freeman (born in Memphis, Tennessee, U.S.A. on June 1, 1937) is an American actor, producer, and narrator. Freeman won an Academy Award in 2005 for Best Supporting Actor with "Million Dollar Baby" (2004), and he has received several Oscar nominations for his performances.

Morgan Scott Peck - Morgan Scott Peck (born in New York City, New York, U.S.A., May 22, 1936 – September 25, 2005) was an American psychiatrist, and best-selling author who wrote the book *The Road Less Traveled*, published in 1978.

Mother Teresa - Mary Teresa Bojaxhiu, commonly called Mother Teresa, and known in the Roman Catholic Church as Saint Teresa of Calcutta (born as Anjezë Gonxhe Bojaxhiu, August 26, 1910 – September 5, 1997), was an Albanian-Indian Roman Catholic nun and missionary. She was born in Skopje (now the capital of Macedonia), then part of the Kosovo Vilayet of the Ottoman Empire. Teresa received a number of honours, including the 1962 Ramon Magsaysay Peace Prize and 1979 Nobel Peace Prize. She was canonized (recognized by the church as a saint) on September 4, 2016, and the anniversary of her death (September 5th) is her feast day.

Myles Munroe - Myles Munroe, OBE (born in Grand Bahama, Bahamas, April 20, 1954 – November 9, 2014) was a Bahamian evangelist and ordained minister avid professor of the Kingdom of God, author, speaker and leadership consultant who founded and led the Bahamas Faith Ministries International (BFMI) and Myles Munroe International (MMI).

Neil deGrasse Tyson - Neil deGrasse Tyson (born in Manhattan, New York City, U.S., on October 5, 1958) is an American astrophysicist, author, and science communicator. He was awarded the NASA Distinguished Public Service Medal in the same year. The U.S. National Academy of Sciences awarded Tyson the Public Welfare Medal in 2015 for his "extraordinary role in exciting the public about the wonders of science."

Nelson Mandela - Nelson Rolihlahla Mandela (born in Mvezo, Cape Province, South Africa July 18, 1918 – December 5, 2013) was a South African anti-apartheid revolutionary, political leader, and philanthropist who served as President of South Africa from 1994 to 1999. He was the country's first black head of state and the first elected in a fully representative democratic election.

Norman Mailer - Norman Kingsley Mailer (born in Long Branch, New Jersey, U.S. January 31, 1923 – November 10, 2007) was an American novelist, journalist, essayist, playwright, film-maker, actor, and liberal political activist. His novel "The Naked and the Dead" was published in 1948 and brought him renown. His 1968 nonfiction novel "Armies of the Night" won the Pulitzer Prize for non-fiction as well as the National Book Award. His best-known work is widely considered to be "The Executioner's Song", the 1979 winner of the Pulitzer Prize for fiction.

Nozomi Morgan- Nozomi Morgan, MBA, is a certified Executive Coach and the Founder and President of Michiki Morgan Worldwide LLC. In addition to coaching, she speaks and trains on leadership, career, professional development, and cross-cultural business communication.

The Greats Past & Present

Og Mandino - Augustine "Og" Mandino II (born in Framingham, Massachusetts, U.S.A. December 12, 1923 – September 3, 1996) was an American author. He wrote the bestselling book, "The Greatest Salesman in the World," and is an inductee of the National Speakers Association's Hall of Fame.

Oliver Wendell Holmes, Sr. - Oliver Wendell Holmes Sr. (born in Cambridge, Massachusetts, U.S.A., August 29, 1809 – October 7, 1894) was an American physician, poet, and polymath based in Boston. A member of the Fireside Poets, he was acclaimed by his peers as one of the best writers of the day. His most famous prose works are the "Breakfast-Table" series, which began with *The Autocrat of the Breakfast-Table* (1858). He was also an important medical reformer. In addition to his work as an author and poet, Holmes also served as a physician, professor, lecturer and inventor and, although he never practiced it, he received formal training in law.

Pablo Picasso - Pablo Ruiz Picasso (born in Málaga, Spain, October 25, 1881 – April 8, 1973). He was born Pablo Diego José Francisco de Paula Juan Nepomuceno María de los Remedios Cipriano de la Santísima Trinidad Ruiz y Picasso, a series of names honouring various saints and relatives. He was a Spanish painter, sculptor, printmaker, ceramicist, stage designer, poet, and playwright who spent most of his adult life in France. Exceptionally prolific throughout the course of his long life, Picasso achieved universal renown and immense fortune for his revolutionary artistic accomplishments and became one of the best-known figures in 20th-century art.

Paul H. Dunn - Paul Harold Dunn (born in Provo, Utah, U.S.A., April 24, 1924 – January 9, 1998) was a general authority of The Church of Jesus Christ of Latter-day Saints (LDS Church). Dunn was widely considered one of the most dynamic speakers among the general authorities in the 1970s and 1980s. Dunn earned a bachelor's degree from Chapman College in 1953 and master's and doctorate degrees in educational administration from the University of Southern California. In 1952, Dunn began his professional career as a seminary teacher for the Church Educational System in Los Angeles. He was called to the First Quorum of the Seventy of the LDS Church April 6, 1964, by David O, McKay, and called as a General Authority in the LDS Church September 330, 1989 by Ezra Taft Benson.

Paul Valéry - Ambroise Paul Toussaint Jules Valéry (October 30, 1871 – July 20, 1945) was a French poet, essayist, and philosopher. He was born in Sète, a town on the Mediterranean coast of the Hérault, but he was raised in Montpellier, a larger urban center close by. In addition to his poetry and fiction (drama and dialogues), his interests included aphorisms on art, history, letters, music, and current events. Valéry was nominated for the Nobel Prize in Literature in 12 different years.

Paulo Coelho - Paulo Coelho de Souza (born in Rio de Janeiro, Brazil August 24, 1947) is a Brazilian lyricist and novelist. He is best known for his novel "The Alchemist."

The Greats Past & Present

Peter Ferdinand Drunker - Peter Ferdinand Drucker (born in Kaasgraben, Vienna, Austria-Hungary, November 19, 1909 – November 11, 2005) was an Austrian-born American management consultant, educator, and author, whose writings contributed to the philosophical and practical foundations of the modern business corporation. He was also a leader in the development of management education, he invented the concept known as management by objectives and self-control, and he has been described as "the founder of modern management."

Peter Senge - Peter Michael Senge (born in Stanford, California, U.S.A., 1947) is an American systems scientist who is a senior lecturer at the MIT Sloan School of Management, co-faculty at the New England Complex Systems Institute, and the founder of the Society for Organizational Learning. He is known as the author of the book *The Fifth Discipline: The Art and Practice of the Learning Organization* (1990, rev. 2006).

Philip Stanhope, 4th Earl of Chesterfield - Philip Dormer Stanhope, 4th Earl of Chesterfield, KG, PC (born in London, England, September 22, 1694 – March 24, 1773) was a British statesman, diplomat, man of letters, and an acclaimed wit of his time. He was born in London.

Phoebe Snow - Phoebe Snow (born as Phoebe Ann Laub; in New York City, New York, U.S.A., July 17, 1950 – April 26, 2011) was an American singer, songwriter, and guitarist, best known for her 1975 song "Poetry Man." She was described by *The New York Times* as a "contralto" grounded in a bluesy growl and capable of sweeping over four octaves

Publilius Syrus - Publilius Syrus (85–43 BC), was a Latin writer, best known for his sententiae. He was a Syrian who was brought as a slave to Italy, but by his wit and talent, he won the favour of his master, who freed and educated him.

Quentin L. Cook - Quentin LaMar Cook (born in Logan, Utah, U.S.A., September 8, 1940) is an American lawyer, business executive, and religious leader who is currently a member of the Quorum of the Twelve Apostles in The Church of Jesus Christ of Latter-day Saints. He was called as a General Authority in April 1996, he served in the Second Quorum, the First Quorum, and the Presidency of the Seventy until he was called to the Quorum of the Twelve Apostles by Gordon B. Hinckley on October 6, 2007.

Rabindranath Tagore - Rabindranath Tagore FRAS (born in Calcutta, British India, May 7, 1861 – August 7, 1941) was a Bengali polymath, a poet, musician and artist from the Indian subcontinent. He reshaped Bengali literature and music, as well as Indian art with Contextual Modernism in the late 19th and early 20th centuries.

Ralph Waldo Emerson - Ralph Waldo Emerson (born in Boston, Massachusetts, U.S.A., May 25, 1803 – April 27, 1882) was an American essayist, lecturer, philosopher, and poet who led the transcendentalist movement of the mid-19th century. He was seen as a champion of individualism and a prescient critic of the countervailing pressures of society, and he disseminated his thoughts through dozens of published essays and more than 1,500 public lectures across the United States.

The Greats Past & Present

Raymond Lindquist- Raymond Irving Lindquist (born in Nebraska, U.S.A., April 14, 1907 – October 5, 2001) was an American Presbyterian Pastor in California, Awarded The Frederick Neumann Award for Excellence in Greek and Hebrew. Raymond died in Irvine, Orange County, California, U.S.A.

Reba McEntire - Reba Nell McEntire (born in McAlester, Oklahoma, U.S.A. March 28, 1955) is an American singer, songwriter, actress, and record producer.

Richard Bach - Richard David Bach (born in Oak Park, Illinois. U.S. on June 23, 1936) is an American writer. Bach is widely known as the author of some of the 1970s biggest-sellers, including "Jonathan Livingston Seagull" (1970) and "Illusions: The Adventures of a Reluctant Messiah" (1977).

Richard Cecil - (born in London, England, November 8, 1748 – August 15, 1810) was a leading Evangelical Anglican priest of the 18th and 19th centuries.

Richard C. Edgley - Richard Crockett Edgley (born in Preston, Idaho, U.S.A., February 6, 1936) has been a general authority of The Church of Jesus Christ of Latter-day Saints (LDS Church) since October 1992. He was the first counselor in the church's presiding bishopric from 1995 to 2012 and as the second counselor from 1992 to 1995. He was designated as an emeritus general authority in March 2012. Edgley was a vice president of General Mills and the managing director of the church's Finance and Records Department. He has a bachelor's degree in political science from Brigham Young University and a master's degree in business administration from Indiana University.

Richard G. Scott - Richard Gordon Scott (born in Pocatello, Idaho, U.S, November 7, 1928 – September 22, 2015) was an American scientist and religious leader who served as a member of the Quorum of the Twelve Apostles of The Church of Jesus Christ of Latter-day Saints (LDS Church). Elder Richard G. Scott was sustained an Apostle of The Church of Jesus Christ of Latter-day Saints on October 1, 1988, by Ezra Taft Benson.

Rick Warren - Richard Duane Warren (born in San Jose, California, U.S., on January 28, 1954) is an American evangelical Christian pastor and author. He is the founder and senior pastor of Saddleback Church, an evangelical megachurch in Lake Forest, California, that is the sixth-largest megachurch in the United States (including multi-site churches). He is also a bestselling author of many Christian books, including his guide to church ministry and evangelism, "The Purpose Driven Church."

Robert A. Heinlein - Robert Anson Heinlein (born in Butler, Missouri, U.S.A., July 7, 1907 – May 8, 1988) was an American science-fiction writer and aeronautical engineer. Often called the "dean of science fiction writers." Heinlein was named the first Science Fiction Writers Grand Master in 1974. Four of his novels won Hugo Awards. In addition, fifty years after publication, seven of his works were awarded "Retro Hugos"—awards given retrospectively for works that were published before the Hugo Awards came into existence.

The Greats Past & Present

Robert D. Hales - Robert Dean Hales (born in New York City, New York, U.S.A, August 24, 1932 – October 1, 2017) was an American businessman and member of the Quorum of the Twelve Apostles of The Church of Jesus Christ of Latter-day Saints (LDS Church) from 1994 until his death. As a member of the Quorum of the Twelve, Hales was accepted by the church as a prophet, seer, and revelator. At the time of his passing, he was the fifth most senior apostle in the church. He obtained a bachelor's degree at the University of Utah, he was a fighter pilot for four years in the U.S. Air Force. Hales later also received a degree from the Harvard Business School (HBS).

Robert E. Lee - Robert Edward Lee (born in Stratford Hall Plantation in Westmoreland County, Virginia, January 19, 1807 – October 12, 1870) was an American and Confederate soldier, best known as a commander of the Confederate States Army. His nicknames were Bobby Lee, Uncle Robert, Marse Robert, Granny Lee, King of Spades, Old Man, and Marble Man.

Robert J. McKain - Robert James McKain (born in Ohio, U.S., April 3, 1933 – April 16, 2002). He was an Estate Planner with Connecticut General, author of "Realize Your Potential" and "How to get to the top and stay there," AMA 1970's. His work noted for its depth of understanding of "balance" as the goal of success was used by the famous Stephen Covey in his successful work. Quoted extensively, McKain remains an inspirational thinking leader today. A graduate of The Wharton School, University of Pennsylvania, McKain achieved Cigna Corporations' top honor for excellence. His legacy continues through his daughter's work, Carol McKain Gregor, in film and writing, which promotes the thinking behind creating balance in home design and construction.

Russell M. Nelson - Russell Marion Nelson Sr. (born in Salt Lake City, Utah, U.S.A. on September 9, 1924) is an American religious leader and former surgeon who is the 17th president of The Church of Jesus Christ of Latter-day Saints (LDS Church). Nelson was called by Spencer W. Kimball as a member of the LDS Church's Quorum of the Twelve Apostles on April 7, 1984, and served in that position for nearly 34 years, and was the quorum president from 2015 to 2018. Nelson became the LDS Church's president on January 14, 2018. Russell M. Nelson is accepted by the church as a prophet, seer, and revelator.

Russell Simmons - Russell Wendell Simmons (born in Queens, New York City, New York, U.S.A. October 4, 1957) is an American entrepreneur, record producer, and author. Simmons's net worth was estimated at $340m in 2011.

Samuel Butler - Samuel Butler (born in Langar, Nottinghamshire, England, December 4, 1835 – June 18, 1902) was the iconoclastic English author of the Utopian satirical novel *Erewhon* (1872) and the semi-autobiographical Bildungsroman *The Way of All Flesh*, published posthumously in 1903. Both have remained in print ever since.

Samuel Smiles - Samuel Smiles (born in Haddington, East Lothian, Scotland, December 23, 1812 – April 16, 1904) was a Scottish author and government reformer. Although he campaigned on a Chartist platform, he concluded that more progress would come from new attitudes than from new laws. His masterpiece book, "Self-Help" (1859), has been called "the bible of mid-Victorian liberalism" and raised Smiles to celebrity status almost overnight.

The Greats Past & Present

Sarah Dessen - Sarah Dessen (born in Evanston, Illinois, U.S.A. on June 6, 1970) is an American novelist who, at the time this book was written lived in Chapel Hill, North Carolina.

Shannon L. Alder - Shannon L. Alder is an inspirational author that writes on the topic of relationships. Her biography states that she has been quoted in over 100 books by relationship authors and in online magazine articles. Her philosophy is known as Shannonisms.

Shirley Conran - Shirley Conran (born as Shirley Pearce, in the United Kingdom, September 21, 1932) is a British novelist and journalist. Conran has written for "Vanity Fair", women's editor of "The Daily Mail" and "The Observer." Published in 1982, her book "Lace" spent 13 weeks on the "New York Times" Best Seller list, reaching as high as No. 6, and was adapted into a 1980s US miniseries. Her book, *Lace*, was published by Simon & Schuster.

Spencer W. Kimball - Spencer Woolley Kimball (born in Salt Lake City, Utah Territory, United States, March 28, 1895 – November 5, 1985) was an American business, civic, and religious leader, and was the 12th president of The Church of Jesus Christ of Latter-day Saints (LDS Church), from 1973 to 1985. Grandson of the LDS apostle Heber C. Kimball, Spencer, was born in Salt Lake City, Utah Territory. He served as a stake president in his hometown from 1938-1943, when he was called to serve as a member of the Quorum of the Twelve Apostles by Heber J. Grant. Spencer W. Kimball is accepted by the church as a prophet, seer, and revelator.

St. Francis of Assisi - Saint Francis of Assisi, born as Giovanni di Pietro di Bernardone, informally named as Francesco (born in Assisi, Italy, (was Assisi, Duchy of Spoleto, Holy Roman Empire) 1181/1182 – October 3, 1226), was an Italian Catholic friar, deacon and preacher. He founded the men's Order of Friars Minor, the women's Order of Saint Clare, the Third Order of Saint Francis, and the Custody of the Holy Land. Francis is one of the most venerated religious figures in history.

Stephen R. Covey – Stephen Richards Covey (born in Salt Lake City, Utah, U.S.A., October 24, 1932 – July 16, 2012) was an American educator, author, businessman, and keynote speaker. His most popular book is *"The 7 Habits of Highly Effective People."* He was a professor at the Jon M. Huntsman School of Business at Utah State University at the time of his death.

Stephen Richards - Stephen Richards (born in England) is an author writing in the self-help genre. The first book he wrote in 1998 was in the true crime genre for Mirage Publishing. He has co-written a number of books with others but now concentrates on writing in the mind, body, spirit subjects of Cosmic Ordering, and mind power.

Sterling W. Sill – Sterling Willing Sill (born in Layton, Utah, United States, on March 31, 1903 – May 25, 1994) He was a general authority in The Church of Jesus Christ of Latter-day Saints (LDS Church). He was an Assistant to the Quorum of the Twelve Apostles from 1954 to 1976 and was a member of the First Quorum of the Seventy from 1976 to 1978. In 1978, he received general authority emeritus status.

Steve Maraboli - Steve A. Maraboli (born in Port Washington, New York, U.S.A., April 18, 1975) He is an internet radio commentator, motivational speaker, and author.

The Greats Past & Present

Steven Pressfield - Steven Pressfield (born in Port of Spain, Trinidad on September 1943) is an American author of historical fiction, non-fiction, and screenplays. Pressfield's first book, "The Legend of Bagger Vance", was published in 1995, and was made into a 2000 film of the same name directed by Robert Redford and starring Will Smith, Charlize Theron, and Matt Damon.

Sophie Tunnell - Sophie Letitia Tunnell (born in Edwardsville, Madison County, Illinois, U.S.A., February 14, 1884 – September 14, 1936) was an author and poet.

Sydney J. Harris - Sydney Justin Harris (born in London, England, September 14, 1917 – December 7, 1986) was an American journalist for the *Chicago Daily News* and, later, the *Chicago Sun-Times*. He wrote 11 books, and his weekday column, "Strictly Personal," was syndicated in approximately 200 newspapers throughout the United States and Canada.

Swami Sivananda - Sivananda Saraswati or Swami Sivananda (born as Kuppuswamy, in Pattamadai, Tamil Nadu, India, September 18, 1887 – July 14, 1963) was an author, a Hindu spiritual teacher, and a proponent of Yoga and Vedanta.

Thomas Fuller - Thomas Fuller (born in Aldwinkle St Peter's, Northamptonshire, England, was baptized June 19, 1608 – August 16, 1661) was an English churchman and historian. He is now remembered for his writings, particularly his Worthies of England, published in 1662 after his death. He was a prolific author, and one of the first English writers able to live by his pen.

Thomas Jefferson - Thomas Jefferson (born in Shadwell, Virginia, British America, April 13, 1743 – July 4, 1826) was a statesman, diplomat, architect, and Founding Fathers of the United States who served as the third president of the United States from 1801 to 1809. Previously, he had been elected the second vice president of the United States, serving under John Adams from 1797 to 1801. Jefferson is considered the principal author of the Declaration of Independence.

Thomas S. Monson - Thomas Spencer Monson (born in Salt Lake City, Utah, U.S.A., August 21, 1927 – January 2, 2018) was an American religious leader, author, and the 16th President of The Church of Jesus Christ of Latter-day Saints (LDS Church). As president, he was considered by adherents of the religion to be a "prophet, seer, and revelator." Monson's early career was as a manager at the *Deseret News*, a Utah newspaper owned by the LDS Church. He spent most of his life engaged in various church leadership positions and public service. Monson was ordained an apostle on October 10, 1963, by the LDS Church by David O. McKay.

The Greats Past & Present

Thomas Watson, Jr. - Thomas John Watson, Jr. (born in Dayton, Ohio U.S., January 14, 1914 – December 31, 1993) was an American businessman, political figure, and philanthropist. He was the 2nd president of IBM (1952–1971), the 11th national president of the Boy Scouts of America (1964–1968), and the 16th United States Ambassador to the Soviet Union (1979–1981). He received many honors during his lifetime, including being awarded the Presidential Medal of Freedom by Lyndon B. Johnson in 1964. *FORTUNE* called him "the greatest capitalist in history," and *TIME* listed him as one of "100 most influential people of the 20th century."

Tom Hanks - Thomas Jeffrey Hanks (born in Concord, California, U.S.A., July 9, 1956) is an American actor and filmmaker. Hanks is known for his comedic and dramatic roles in such films as "Splash" (1984), "Big" (1988), "Turner & Hooch" (1989), "A League of Their Own" (1992), "Sleepless in Seattle" (1993), "Apollo 13" (1995), "You've Got Mail" (1998), "The Green Mile" (1999), "Cast Away" (2000), "Road to Perdition" (2002), "Cloud Atlas" (2012), "Captain Phillips" (2013), "Saving Mr. Banks" (2013), and "Sully" (2016). He has also starred in the "Robert Langdon" film series and voices "Sheriff Woody" in the "Toy Story" film series. He won a Golden Globe Award and an Academy Award for Best Actor for his role in "Sleepless in Seattle" (1993), as well as a Golden Globe, an Academy Award, a Screen Actors Guild Award, and a People's Choice Award for Best Actor for "Forrest Gump" (1994). In 1995, Hanks became one of only two actors who won the Academy Award for Best Actor in consecutive years. In 2004, he received the Stanley Kubrick Britannia Award for Excellence in Film from the British Academy of Film and Television Arts (BAFTA). In 2014, he received a Kennedy Center Honor, and in 2016, he received a Presidential Medal of Freedom from President Barack Obama, as well as the French Legion of Honor.

Tony Robbins - Anthony Jai Robbins (born as Anthony J. Mahavoric in North Hollywood, California, U.S.A., on February 29, 1960) is an American author, entrepreneur, philanthropist, and life coach. Robbins is known for his infomercials, seminars, and self-help books.

Unknown - The author is unknown, or we are unsure who the original author is. There is no other information than that given at this time.

Victoria Moran – Victoria M. Moran (born in Kansas City, Missouri, March 21, 1950) is an American author and speaker. She has written a number of books specializing in both spirituality and veganism. Moran hosts the "Main Street Vegan" radio show and podcast on *Unity Online Radio*. Her work in the field of veganism led her to win the 'Vegan of The Year' award in 2012; her podcast won a Vegan Media Outlet Award in 2015.

Viktor E. Frankl - Viktor Emil Frankl (born in Vienna, Austria-Hungary, March 26, 1905 – 2 September 1997) was an Austrian neurologist, psychiatrist, and author, as well as a Holocaust survivor. His best-selling book "Man's Search for Meaning" is a 1946 book chronicling his experiences as a prisoner in Nazi concentration camps during World War II, and describing his psychotherapeutic method, which involved identifying a purpose in life to feel positively about, and then immersivity imagining that outcome.

The Greats Past & Present

W. Clement Stone - William Clement Stone (born in Chicago, Illinois, U.S.A., May 4, 1902 – September 3, 2002) was a businessman, philanthropist, and New Thought self-help book author.

Wall Street Journal – "The Wall Street Journal" is a U.S. business-focused, English-language international daily newspaper based in New York City. The *Journal*, along with its Asian and European editions, is published six days a week by Dow Jones & Company, a division of News Corp. The newspaper is published in the broadsheet format and online. The *Journal* has been printed continuously since its inception on July 8, 1889, by Charles Dow, Edward Jones, and Charles Bergstresser. *The Wall Street Journal* is one of the largest newspapers in the United States by circulation. According to News Corp, in its June 2018.

Walter Cronkite - Walter Leland Cronkite, Jr. (born in St. Joseph, Missouri, U.S.A., November 4, 1916 – July 17, 2009) was an American broadcast journalist who served as anchorman for the "CBS Evening News" for 19 years (1962–1981). During the heyday of CBS News in the 1960s and 1970s, he was often cited as "the most trusted man in America" after being so named in an opinion poll. He was also known for his extensive coverage of the U.S. space program, from Project Mercury to the Moon landings to the Space Shuttle. He was the only non-NASA recipient of an Ambassador of Exploration award. Cronkite is well known for his departing catchphrase, "And that's the way it is," followed by the date of the broadcast.

Walter F. Gonzalez - Walter Fermin González was born in Montevideo, Uruguay, on November 18, 1952. At the time of this conference, Elder Walter F. Gonzalez was serving in the Presidency of the Seventy of the Church of Jesus Christ of Latter-day Saints. On March 31, 2001, he became a general authority and a member of the First Quorum of Seventy, and on October 6, 2007, González became a member of the Presidency of the Seventy, and then was released January 6, 2013, to become president of the South America South Area. He earned a bachelor's degree in general studies at Indiana University and a technician's certificate in business administration at CEMLAD Institute.

Warren Edward Buffett - Warren Edward Buffett (born in Omaha, Nebraska, U.S.A. on August 30, 1930) is an American business magnate, investor, speaker, and philanthropist who serves as the chairman and CEO of Berkshire Hathaway. He is considered one of the most successful investors in the world and has a net worth of US$84.9 billion as of February 12, 2019, making him the third-wealthiest person in the world.

Waylon Jennings - Waylon Arnold Jennings (born in Littlefield, Texas, U.S. June 15, 1937 – February 13, 2002) was an American singer, songwriter, and musician. In 1958, Buddy Holly arranged Jennings's first recording session and hired him to play bass.

Wayne Dyer - Wayne Walter Dyer (born in Detroit, Michigan, U.S.A., May 10, 1940 – August 29, 2015) was an American self-help author and a motivational speaker. His first book, *Your Erroneous Zones* (1976), is one of the best-selling books of all time, with an estimated 35 million copies sold.

The Greats Past & Present

Wendy Mass - Wendy Mass (born in Livingston, New Jersey, U.S.A., April 22, 1967) is an author of young adult novels and children's books. Her 2003 novel, "A Mango-Shaped Space" which won the American Library Association (ALA) Schneider Family Book Award for Middle School in 2004. Her other notable works include: "11 Birthdays", "A Mango-Shaped Space" and "Every Soul a Star." Mass's novel "Jeremy Fink and the Meaning of Life" was adapted into a feature film in 2011.

Wilford Woodruff, Sr. - Wilford Woodruff, Sr. (born in Farmington, Connecticut, U.S.A., March 1, 1807 – September 2, 1898) was an American religious leader who served as the fourth president of The Church of Jesus Christ of Latter-day Saints (LDS Church) from 1889 until his death. Woodruff's large collection of diaries provides an important record of Latter-day Saints history, and his decision to formally end the practice of plural marriage among the members of the LDS Church in 1890 brought to a close one of the most controversial periods of church history. As an adult, Woodruff was a farmer, horticulturist, and stockman by trade and wrote extensively for church periodicals.

Will Rogers - William Penn Adair Rogers (November 4, 1879 – August 15, 1935) was an American stage and motion picture actor, vaudeville performer, American cowboy, humorist, newspaper columnist, and social commentator from Oklahoma. He was a Cherokee citizen born in the Cherokee Nation, Indian Territory which is now Oklahoma, U.S.A.

Willard Richards - Willard Richards (born in Hopkinton, Massachusetts, U.S.A., June 24, 1804 – March 11, 1854) was a physician and midwife/nurse trainer and an early leader in the Latter Day Saint movement. He served as Second Counselor to church president Brigham Young in the First Presidency of The Church of Jesus Christ of Latter-day Saints (LDS Church) from 1847 until his death.

William Faulkner - William Cuthbert Faulkner (born in New Albany, Mississippi, U.S.A., September 25, 1897 – July 6, 1962) was an American writer and Nobel Prize laureate from Oxford, Mississippi. Faulkner wrote novels, short stories, screenplays, poetry, essays, and a play. He is primarily known for his novels and short stories set in the fictional Yoknapatawpha County, based on Lafayette County, Mississippi, where he spent most of his life.

William Golding - Sir William Gerald Golding, CBE (born in Newquay, Cornwall, England, September 19, 1911 – June 19, 1993) was a British novelist, playwright, and poet. Best known for his novel "Lord of the Flies", he won a Nobel Prize in Literature and was awarded the Booker Prize for fiction in 1980 for his novel "Rites of Passage", the first book in what became his sea trilogy, "To the Ends of the Earth." Golding was knighted in 1988.

William Penn - William Penn (born in Ruscombe, Berkshire, England, Great Britain, October 14, 1644 – July 30, 1718) was an English nobleman, writer, early Quaker, and founder of the English North American colony the Province of Pennsylvania.

The Greats Past & Present

William Shakespeare - William Shakespeare (born in Stratford-upon-Avon, Warwickshire, England, baptized April 26, 1564 – April 23, 1616) was an English poet, playwright, and actor, widely regarded as the greatest writer in the English language and the world's greatest dramatist. He is often called England's national poet and the "Bard of Avon."

Woodrow M. Kroll - Woodrow Michael Kroll (born in Ellwood City, Pennsylvania, A. on October 21, 1944) is an evangelical preacher and radio host. He was the president and Bible teacher for the international "Back to the Bible" radio and television ministry. He was president of Davis College (formerly Practical Bible College) in Johnson City, New York, United States. In addition to preaching and teaching, Kroll is a prolific writer, having authored more than 50 books expounding on the Bible and Christian living.

Yogi Berra - Lawrence Peter "Yogi" Berra (born in St. Louis, Missouri, U.S.A., May 12, 1925 – September 22, 2015) was an American professional baseball catcher, who later took on the roles of manager and coach. In 1972, Berra was elected to the Baseball Hall of Fame. On November 24, 2015, Berra was awarded the Presidential Medal of Freedom posthumously by President Barack Obama.

Zig Ziglar - Hilary Hinton "Zig" Ziglar (born in Coffee County, Alabama, U.S.A., November 6, 1926 – November 28, 2012) was an American author, salesman, and motivational speaker.

The Greats Past & Present

Where Can I Find It?
Index

Index

A

Abigail Adams · 572, 589, 594
Abraham Lincoln · 105, 412, 413, 424, 525, 594, 610
Albert Einstein · ix, 178, 210, 214, 330, 338, 417, 426, 491, 497, 535, 565, 595
Albert Guinon · 117, 131, 595
Alistair MacLeod · 252, 261, 595
Andre Gide · 110, 131, 595
Andy Stanley · 490, 497, 595
Anthony Robbins · 491, 498, 595
Anton Chekhov · 572, 589, 595
Antonio Porchia · 68, 72, 596
Aristotle · 37, 52, 596
Arnold H. Glasgow · 36, 52, 596
Arthur C. Clarke · 388, 391, 427, 596
Arvind Devalia · 245, 596

B

Babe Ruth · 83, 90, 596
Barack Obama · 211, 215, 596, 620, 623
Benjamin Franklin · 127, 133, 413, 425, 596
Betty Bender · 80, 89, 596
Bill Phillips · 535, 565, 597
Billy Connolly · 154, 165, 597
Bob Hawke · 490, 497, 597
Bonnie L. Oscarson · 581, 590, 597
Brandon Sanderson · 490, 497, 597
Brian Tracy · 35, 51, 327, 337, 597
Brigham Young · 21, 126, 133, 433, 445, 589, 597, 599, 602, 604, 607, 612, 616, 622

C

C. S. Lewis · 214, 495, 598
Cammi Pham · 230, 244, 598
Carl B. Cook · 377, 389, 598
Carlos H. Amado · 149, 164, 598
Catherine Pulsifer · 37, 52, 598
Charles Haddon Spurgeon · 524, 528, 598
Chinese Proverb · 91, 105, 107, 598
Christopher Paolini · 571, 588, 598
Confucius · 211, 215, 571, 588, 599

D

Dallin H. Oaks · 475, 482, 486, 492, 494, 599
Dave Willis · 489, 496, 599
David B. Haight · 10, 599
David Cameron · 387, 390, 599
David F. Jakielo · 490, 497, 599
David Joseph Schwartz · 83, 90, 599
David M. McConkie · 126, 132, 599
David O. McKay · 603, 605, 619
Denis M. Wagner III · 68, 72, 600
Denis Waitley · 53, 600
Dieter F. Uchtdorf · 20, 31, 600
Don Zimmer · 69, 72, 600
Donald L. Staheli · 600
Donny Osmond · 327, 337, 600
Dr. Norman Vincent Peale · 35, 51, 600
Dudley Nichols · 81, 90, 600
Duke Ellington · 387, 390, 600
Dwight D. Eisenhower · 490, 497, 601, 602

E

Earl Nightingale · 35, 51, 153, 165, 601
Ed McMahon · 417, 427, 601
Edmund Hilary · 37, 53, 601
Elbert Hubbard · 35, 51, 601
Eleanor Roosevelt · 83, 84, 91, 572, 589, 601
Ernest Agyemang Yeboah · 487, 495, 601
Ernest Miller Hemingway · 602
Ezra Taft Benson · 213, 215, 237, 244, 422, 428, 491, 498, 557, 566, 602, 614, 616

F

Franklin Roosevelt · 51, 602

G

G.M. Trevelyan · 388, 391, 602
Geoffrey F. Abert · 37, 52, 602
George Bernard Shaw · 68, 72, 210, 214, 535, 565, 602
George Krueger · 57, 58, 63, 64, 65, 71, 603
George P. Lee · 241, 244, 603
George Washington · 413, 425, 603
Gerald L. Penhollow · 36, 52, 72, 375, 409, 424, 600, 602
Gordon B. Hinckley · 9, 11, 68, 72, 362, 363, 389, 414, 420, 425, 486, 572, 589, 600, 603, 604, 615

H

H. Jackson Brown, Jr. · 153, 165, 603
H. L. Hunt · 444, 446, 603
Harold B Lee · 127, 133, 604
Helen Keller · 36, 52, 294, 604
Henry B. Eyring · 365, 389, 434, 446, 581, 582, 590, 604
Henry D. Taylor · 583, 591, 604
Henry Ford · 331, 338, 535, 566, 571, 588, 604
Henry Louis Mencken · 80, 89, 604
Henry Wadsworth Longfellow · 67, 71, 155, 166, 604
Herbert G. Lingren · 130, 134, 604
Howard W. Hunter · 525, 528, 605
Hunter S. Thompson · 387, 390, 605

I

Ian S. Ardern · 432, 445, 605
Indian Proverb · 105, 107, 605
Inside Out · 437, 446, 605
Ivy Baker Priest · 488, 496, 605

J

J. K. Rowling · 84, 91, 605
J. Richard Clarke · 486, 494, 605
James Allen · 36, 52, 605
James E. Faust · 85, 86, 91, 414, 415, 425, 606
James W. Frick · 487, 495, 606
Jay Leno · 330, 337, 606
Jean-Jacques Rousseau · 154, 166, 606
Jerry Bridges · 154, 166, 606
Jesse Jackson · 152, 165, 606
Jim Rohn · 35, 36, 51, 52, 211, 214, 215, 491, 497, 606
Joan D. Vinge · 80, 89, 607
Joe Lo Truglio · 331, 338, 607

Johann Wolfgang Von Goethe · 467, 492, 607
John A. Green · 124, 125, 132, 607
John Adams · 254, 261, 413, 425, 594, 607, 619
John Bartlett · 127, 133, 564, 607
John F. Kennedy · 211, 215, 607
John Kramer Blythe · 488, 495, 607
John Quincy Adams · 413, 425, 594, 607
John Wooden · 84, 91, 330, 338, 608
Joseph B. Wirthlin · 67, 71, 281, 295, 416, 426, 608
Joseph de Maistre · 68, 72, 608
Joseph Smith · 10, 21, 31, 32, 51, 71, 89, 107, 131, 141, 164, 189, 214, 244, 250, 261, 282, 288, 294, 337, 389, 415, 424, 445, 492, 527, 565, 588, 608
Julus Renard · 608

K

Kathy Seligman · 37, 52, 608
Kenneth A. Wells · 118, 132, 608
Kenneth E. Hagin · 495, 608
Kerry Stokes · 417, 427, 609
Kevin W. Pearson · 5, 10, 82, 90, 609
Khwāja Shams-ud-Dīn Muḥammad Ḥāfeẓ-e Shīrāzī, or "Hafiz" · 81, 609

L

L. Tom Perry · 381, 390, 609
Lao Tzu · 105, 107, 535, 565, 609
Larry K. Langlois, Ph.D. · 609
Laura Ingalls Wilder · 387, 391, 609
Leo Babauta · 489, 496, 610
Leo Christopher · 489, 496, 610
Leo Tolstoy · 211, 215, 610
Leonard Swett · 412, 424, 610
Lillian Russell · 81, 90, 610
Lori Deschene · 242, 245, 610
Lyman Beecher · 421, 428, 610

M

Madonna Louise Ciccone · 210, 214, 610
Mahatma Gandhi · 91, 105, 152, 165, 211, 215, 417, 427, 489, 496, 524, 528, 571, 588, 610, 611
Marcus Garvey · 535, 566, 611
Marcus Geduld · 329, 337
Marion G. Romney · 243, 245, 611
Mark E Petersen · 525, 528, 611
Mark Twain · 329, 337, 572, 589, 611
Martin Luther King Jr · 68, 71, 105, 107, 490, 497, 611
Martin Luther King, Jr. · 71, 105, 107, 490, 497, 536, 566, 611
Marvin J. Ashton · 80, 89, 241, 245, 433, 446, 611
Mary Ellen Smoot · 432, 445, 612
Mary Kay Ash · 417, 427, 612
Mary-Lynn Foster · 57, 58, 63, 64, 65, 71, 612
Matthew Henry · 254, 261, 610
Max De Pree · 535, 565, 612
Melvin Russell Ballard · 563, 566, 612
Michael Pritchard · 81, 90, 612
Michel de Montaigne · 421, 428, 612
Mike Farrell · 387, 391, 612
Morgan Freeman · 142, 164, 613
Morgan Scott Peck · 114, 131, 613
Mother Teresa · 153, 165, 613
Myles Munroe · 489, 496, 613

N

Neil deGrasse Tyson · 572, 588, 613
Nelson Mandela · 105, 409, 424, 571, 588, 613
Norman Mailer · 420, 428, 613
Nozomi Morgan · 240, 244, 613

O

Og Mandino · 387, 390, 614
Oliver Wendell Holmes, Sr. · 132, 427, 614

P

Pablo Picasso · 38, 53, 614
Paul H. Dunn · 127, 133, 525, 529, 614
Paul Valéry · 152, 165, 614
Paulo Coelho · 153, 165, 614
Peter Ferdinand Drunker · 276, 281, 294, 615
Peter Senge · 111, 131, 615
Philip Stanhope, 4th Earl of Chesterfield · 387, 390, 615
Phoebe Snow · 490, 497, 615
Publilius Syrus · 84, 92, 615

Q

Quentin L. Cook · 85, 92, 432, 511, 528, 615

R

Rabindranath Tagore · 83, 91, 615
Ralph Waldo Emerson · 37, 52, 81, 90, 210, 214, 421, 428, 615
Raymond Lindquist · 84, 91, 616
Reba McEntire · 330, 338, 616
Richard Bach · 417, 427, 616
Richard C. Edgley · 616
Richard Cecil · 154, 166, 616
Richard G. Scott · 482, 492, 616
Rick Warren · 490, 497, 616
Robert A. Heinlein · 36, 52, 616
Robert D. Hales · 19, 31, 617
Robert E. Lee · 413, 414, 425, 617
Robert J. McKain · 491, 498, 617
Rule #0 · i, ii
Rule #¼ · v, vi, xx
Rule #½ · xix, xx
Rule #1 · viii, ix, 1, 2, 3, 7, 14, 45, 67, 69, 88, 118, 342, 343, 350, 371, 407, 430, 432, 448, 466
Rule #2 · x, 13, 14, 16, 30, 69, 111, 118, 343, 401, 448
Rule #3 · 7, 8, 33, 34, 69, 366, 448, 475, 476
Rule #4 · 21, 22, 55, 56, 65, 66, 67, 69, 326, 448
Rule #5 · 73, 74, 75, 79, 81, 87, 94, 96, 106, 448
Rule #6 · 79, 88, 93, 94, 95, 96, 438, 443, 448
Rule #7 · 109, 110, 111, 220
Rule #8 · xxviii, 135, 136, 168, 170, 172, 220, 342, 352, 358, 359, 448
Rule #9 · 167, 168, 170, 171, 172, 178, 188
Rule #10 · 191, 192, 209, 213
Rule #11 · 217, 218, 219, 220, 221, 225, 231, 234, 240, 242, 243, 448, 465, 556
Rule #12 · 88, 247, 248
Rule #13 · 96, 236, 263, 264, 266, 276, 281, 292, 448, 501
Rule #14 · 297, 298, 299, 303, 316, 317, 318, 325, 327, 350, 545
Rule #15 · 339, 340, 341, 342, 345, 346, 347, 348, 349, 352, 353, 358,

359, 362, 364, 372, 375, 376, 377, 380, 381, 382, 383, 448
Rule #16 · 393, 394, 397, 409, 438, 439, 448
Rule #17 · 96, 106, 429, 435, 443, 448
Rule #18 · 447, 448, 449, 451, 479, 483, 484
Rule #19 · 448, 499, 500, 501, 503, 523
Rule #20 · 448, 531, 532, 533, 534, 537, 544, 550
Rule #21 · 523, 567, 568, 585, 587
Russell M. Nelson · 124, 132, 572, 589, 617
Russell Simmons · 330, 338, 617

S

Samuel Butler · 81, 90, 617
Samuel Smiles · 84, 91, 503, 527, 617
Sarah Dessen · 330, 338, 618
Shannon L. Alder · 152, 165, 618
Shirley Conran · 488, 495, 618
Sophie Tunnell · 81, 90, 619
Spencer W. Kimball · 126, 127, 133, 380, 390, 617, 618
St. Francis of Assisi · 387, 391, 618
Stephen R. Covey · 131, 294, 493, 618
Stephen Richards · 211, 215, 618
Sterling W. Sill · 365, 389, 618
Steve Maraboli · 153, 165, 489, 496, 618
Steven Pressfield · 490, 497, 619
Swami Sivananda · 68, 72, 619
Sydney J. Harris · 154, 166, 619

T

The Greats Past & Present · 593, 625
The Samaritan · 535, 566
Thomas Fuller · 36, 52, 619
Thomas Jefferson · 413, 421, 425, 428, 524, 528, 619
Thomas S. Monson · 43, 53, 486, 494, 597, 598, 600, 608, 619
Thomas Watson Jr · 488, 495
Thomas Watson, Jr. · 495, 620
Tom Hanks · 563, 566, 620
Tony Robbins · 36, 52, 498, 620

U

Unknown · 68, 72, 81, 84, 90, 91, 105, 107, 153, 155, 165, 166, 526, 529, 535, 565, 620

V

Victoria Moran · 488, 496, 620
Viktor E. Frankl · 211, 215, 620

W

W. Clement Stone · 83, 91, 621
Wall Street Journal · 489, 496, 621
Walter Cronkite · 571, 588, 621
Walter F. Gonzalez · 29, 621
Warren Edward Buffett · 621
Waylon Jennings · 417, 427, 621
Wayne Dyer · 154, 166, 621
Wendy Mass · 535, 565, 622
Wilford Woodruff Sr. · 622
Will Rogers · 37, 53, 622
Willard Richards · 141, 164, 622
William Faulkner · 210, 214, 622

William Golding · 488, 496, 622
William Penn · 420, 427, 622
William Shakespeare · 416, 423, 426, 428, 623
Woodrow M. Kroll · 154, 166, 623

Y

Yogi Berra · 69, 72, 623

Z

Zig Ziglar · 7, 36, 44, 51, 53, 623

About the Author

Born in Prairie du Chien, Wisconsin, in 1955, Jerry Penhollow has spent his life employing the values and work ethic he learned growing up on a farm and in farming communities. From the time he was old enough to help with chores, Jerry learned the true value of tough, honest work and the importance of contributing to the welfare of his family. Jerry has spent his life employing the values he learned as a kid. He served his country by enlisting in the Air Force, and was active-duty during the Vietnam War. His military service honed his values to commitment, duty, honor, and trust. Jerry graduated from college, built a successful computer business of 30 years and retired. Bored of retirement he returned to school, and currently works in the medical field as a Hearing-aid Instrument Specialist. While material success is an important component of well-being, Jerry constantly works to prioritize caring for family, helping friends, and stepping in to assist when those in his community call for help.

As a young man, Jerry's search for spiritual direction and fulfillment led him to the Church of Jesus Christ of Latter-day Saints. Based on his faith, the teaching of his church, and his life experience, Jerry formulated these 21 concrete rules to guide him on his temporal journey. He has worked tirelessly on this book. Here, Jerry puts his rules in order, with real-life stories, scriptures and spiritual teachings to illustrate how these rules have helped guide him through tough times and blessings. In sharing his rules, Jerry hopes to encourage and inspire you, dear reader, as you make your way on your own temporal path.

Jerry splits his time between Florida and the town he calls home, Dubuque, Iowa. He lives with his beautiful, saintly wife, Christine. Together they have five children, 17 grandchildren and 7 great-grandchildren. Jerry and Christine host young missionaries and are active in their local church.